KT-442-767

CONTENTS

ACTIONLISTS

Planning

Refining and Protecting Your Idea

Setting Up or Acquiring a Business

Finding Premises

Figuring It Out

A Note to the User

The Good Small Business Guide is aimed at anyone thinking of starting or growing a business in the United Kingdom. Designed for readers to dip into as and when they need practical help on a range of issues, the *Guide* contains advice on:

- planning
- setting up or acquiring a business
- getting to grips with the figures
- finding premises
- marketing your idea
- working with customers
- communicating with customers
- growing your business
- working and selling online
- managing yourself and others
- dignified retreats

All of the above topics are covered in over 130 easy-to-read actionlists, which feature:

GETTING STARTED—an overview of the main points addressed in the actionlist
FAQS—a series of frequently asked questions on the topic
MAKING IT HAPPEN—fuss-free advice on how to achieve your goal
WHAT TO AVOID—tips on how to avoid common mistakes
RECOMMENDED LINKS—a selection of the very best websites to help you investigate the topic further
SEE ALSO—cross-references (listed in alphabetical order) to other actionlists and information sources to help you get the most from all the topics on offer

Not everyone who wants to set up their own company will necessarily have business experience already, so this book explains all you need to know in jargon-free language. Its contents take you from the beginnings of developing your idea right the way through to steps to help you expand your business successfully. For more in-depth comment and advice on some key topics, look at the 'Focus On' series of actionlists, for example, pp. 47–49. These articles have been written by some of the world's leading business writers, including Meredith Belbin, Adrian Cadbury, and Al Ries, and bring together their considerable experience.

This book also contains the **Essential Information Directory** (pp. 477 onwards). This section covers over 30 key topics of interest to anyone in business, and offers carefully chosen information on the most helpful books, organisations, and a wider selection of Internet sites.

The **Essential Information Directory** is also available free online to all subscribers to www.ultimatebusinessresource.com. All links are live, so you can click straight through to the site you're interested in. To subscribe, please go to:

www.ultimatebusinessresource.com/register, type in your e-mail address and key in your password: **smallbiz**

Finally, turn to our 'Viewpoints' section between pp. 270–71 to read about the experiences of other people running and growing small businesses.

Contributors

Meredith Belbin is consultant to the European Commission and the OECD, and is senior associate professor at Cambridge University. He is a partner in Belbin Associates, a company known principally as the producer of Interplace—a company-based, team-role advice system, used internationally. Belbin has written several successful business books, including the European bestseller, *Management Teams: Why They Succeed or Fail* (reissue, Butterworth-Heinemann, 2003) and *Team Roles at Work* (Butterworth-Heinemann, 1995).

Robert Buttrick is the author of the best-selling book, *The Project Workout* (Prentice Hall/Financial Times, 2000), which has been adopted by companies and business schools in both the United Kingdom and around the world.

Sir Adrian Cadbury joined the Cadbury business in 1952, becoming chairman of Cadbury Limited in 1965 and retiring as chairman of Cadbury Schweppes in 1989. He is a European expert on corporate governance, and was chairman of the UK Committee on Corporate Governance from 1991 to June 1995 and member of the OECD Corporate Governance Business Advisory Group. He has also served as director of the Bank of England, director of IBM (UK), chancellor of Aston University, and was a member of the Panel of Conciliators for the International Centre for Settlement of Investment Disputes.

Liam Fahey is adjunct professor of strategic management at Babson College, Massachusetts, and visiting professor of strategic management at the Cranfield School of Management. He is the author or editor of eight books and over 40 articles or book chapters. His most recent books, all published by John Wiley, include *Learning from the Future* (1997), *Competitors: Outwitting, Outmaneuvering and Outperforming* (1998), and *The Portable MBA in Strategy* (2nd ed, 2001).

Patrick Forsyth runs Touchstone Training & Consultancy, an independent firm specialising in marketing, sales, and communications skills. He conducts courses for individual clients, public seminars for a number of management institutes, and has worked in a range of industries in many parts of the world. He writes extensively on matters of marketing and management for management journals and is the author of a number of successful books, including *Communicating with Your Staff* (Texere, Orion Toolkit Series, 1999).

Tim Hindle is business features editor of *The Economist*. He is the author and editor of many books including *Guide to Management Ideas* (Profile Books, 2002) and *Essential Manager's Manual* (Dorling Kindersley, 1998; co-edited with Robert Heller).

Max Landsberg is a partner in the leadership practice of Heidrick & Struggles, a leading international executive search firm. Previously he was a partner at McKinsey, a business author, and executive coach. His books include *The Tao of Coaching* (HarperCollins, 1996), *The Tao of Motivation* (HarperCollins, 1999), and *The Tools of Leadership* (HarperCollins, 2000).

Malcolm McDonald is professor of marketing and deputy director at Cranfield School of Management, with special responsibility for e-business. He has extensive industrial experience, including a number of years as marketing director of Canada Dry. He is now chairman of six companies and has written or co-written 30 books, including the best-selling title, *Marketing Plans: How to Prepare Them, How to Use Them* (5th ed, Butterworth-Heinemann, 2002), and many of his papers have been published.

Michael de Kare-Silver is the managing director, Europe, for Modern Media. He is the author of several books, including *E-Shock 2000: The Electronic Shopping Revolution* (Palgrave Macmillan, 1999).

Al Ries and Laura Ries are a father and daughter team. Al is chairman and Laura is president of Ries & Ries, a marketing strategy firm located in Roswell, Georgia, which they founded in 1994. They are the best-selling authors of *The 22 Immutable Laws of Branding* (HarperCollins, 1998), and *The 11 Immutable Laws of Internet Branding* (HarperCollins, 2000).

Philip Sadler is former chief executive of Ashridge Management College, where for many years he led the team which built the college's reputation as one of the world's leading business schools. He has also written several books, including *Building Tomorrow's Company* (Kogan Page, 2002).

Introduction by Martha Lane Fox

'A headless chicken on amphetamines' is how Mike Lynch, founder of the software company, Autonomy, described being an entrepreneur in the technology sector. Nothing I have experienced in my life so far has brought with it so many incredible highs, so many challenges and ultimately so many rewards as building your own business. Creating something from scratch, picking and motivating a team and delivering your vision for customers is hard, requires tenacity, and involves taking risks. It is also part of a long culture of entrepreneurship that I believe fosters innovation, development, and economic progress in a society.

Interestingly, there are as many women entrepreneurs as men and they do not conform to any stereotype or fall into any particular age group. There is no textbook training and there is no ideal background—this means anyone with an idea, drive, and enthusiasm should be able to have their shot at launching a company. As a young woman with no formal training this fact was a comfort to me at some of the more difficult moments.

I think one of the defining characteristics of great entrepreneurs, and I count my co-founder of lastminute.com, Brent Hoberman, as one of these, is an unstinting belief in their idea and in their ability to make it happen. Certainly what I have learnt from working with Brent and having had the privilege to meet a number of other people running their own business are three things: think big, act fast, and hire the best people as quickly as you can.

At the beginning of 2001, I stood up in front of the UK team at lastminute.com and told them that by the middle of 2003 we would have a turnover of over $1billion and we would be used by customers every day. Everyone's faces fell in shock, but it set an ambition that meant people thought in a different way and this is how to get the most done; set a big scary goal and you are more likely to get near it.

The great American entrepreneur, Dale Carnegie, highlighted the importance of dynamism and self-confidence when he wrote: 'Take a chance! All life is a chance. The man who goes the furthest is generally the one who is willing to do and dare.' From day one at lastminute.com people said to us 'this idea will never work. It will take five years to build the technology and it will cost £5 million'. We did not listen to the naysayers and in fact had the website live in three months and on a budget of £600,000. An ability to break down walls and not put them up, and an enthusiasm to make the impossible happen is essential in the early stages of any business life.

Moving at breakneck speed is also critical in any new environment. We are paranoid, even now, that our competition may eclipse us and that keeps a team on its toes. A lot of what we have worked on over the last five years has been based on gut instinct and allowed us to move quickly. If you are constantly thinking about your customers, testing your product, and asking for feedback you can make decisions fast and you can change direction in seconds.

If this sounds daunting, don't worry, it can be but it can also be stimulating—we make multiple mistakes every day at lastminute.com but we try not to be scared of them and we try not to make them twice. What will help you to set up and run your own business is a good mentor and good people around you that you can work with; this often makes the difference between success and failure. I am extremely fortunate at lastminute.com to work with talented, intelligent, motivated people whose expertise I value and whose company I enjoy. You will need to find your own source of wise counsel, practical help, and personal support. The *Good Small Business Guide* provides a great start, as the book has assembled a ready-made team of mentors and features an extensive series of informative and practical articles bringing their knowledge and experience to bear for your benefit. You'll turn to it time and again.

Finally, the great pleasure of entrepreneurship, and one that is rarely mentioned, is that it is means building something valuable, overcoming difficulties, realising opportunities, and accomplishing something unique: your business, established and developed *your* way. If you are unsure, wondering whether to take the plunge, then you need to consider the advantages and disadvantages, what you will gain and what you will lose. Read this book to help you make that decision. However, while starting a small business is not for everyone, it is suited to many more people than actually make the move. Starting and building a business offers a great deal, so don't decide against it for the wrong reasons.

I will never forget the pleasure I have had from hearing about great experiences our customers have had using our site, from the woman who took a trip to propose to a long-term pen pal to the man who booked his honeymoon 45 minutes before the wedding. These customer testimonials make you want to jump out of bed and make your product even better.

Making last minute decisions is rarely wise for an entrepreneur, but if you do feel a need to be impulsive and take a break...you know where to look!

Martha Lane Fox
www.lastminute.com

Foreword
Ten Myths About Small Businesses
by Tim Hindle

Few things are more exciting than starting a new business, and few things are more satisfying than making one work. So it is not surprising that so many people give it a go. There are more than two and a half million small businesses in Britain today. Lots of them are corner shops with no great ambitions to expand. But at least as many are run by people with seemingly impossible dreams.

Small businesses account for a big chunk of the economy. By number, 99% of all registered companies in the United Kingdom are small (ie, firms with fewer than 50 employees). These same companies account for 44% of all industrial jobs in the country, and 36% of all industrial turnover. They may be small individually, but they are quite large collectively.

Sadly, this huge body of businesses does not stay the same from one year to the next. There is a steady turnover: approximately 400,000 new companies open every year in Britain, and about the same number close down. In times of recession this balance changes. At the worst time in 1992, for instance, almost twice as many companies were closing down as were opening up. Even in the best of times, only about 50% of new businesses survive for more than four years; 10% disappear within 12 months, and very few make their owners seriously wealthy.

Making lots of money, however, is only part of the dream. There are many other reasons why people start new businesses.

High on the list is the idea of being your own boss, of pleasing yourself as to where and how you spend your working day. But here we come across one of the many myths that there are about small businesses. The truth is that anyone starting their own company is unlikely to be able to dictate how they spend their working day. The founders of most small businesses are in a constant whirl of activity. Naturally busy when there is lots of business, they are even busier when there is none. For then they are eagerly looking around for new markets and for new customers. They can rarely relax, in good times as well as bad.

Let's look at a few more of these myths. The rest of this book contains a wealth of sound advice on how to do what and when. But, on the principle that to be forewarned is to be forearmed, before you get stuck into the hows, whats, and whens, consider the rest of my top ten myths about running a small business:

Myth number two. You can make your fortune by the time you are 40 and then move on to what you really want to do – play golf or ride horses. For the vast majority of us, enough is never enough. Bill Gates founded Microsoft and made it into the biggest company in the world. But he has not yet let go of the reins.

The drive to get bigger and bigger in business is hard to resist. For a start, growth is an in-built assumption in 99.9% of all business plans. 'Small is beautiful', they say. But most small businessmen behave as if they think the famous title of E. F. Schumacher's book is propaganda put out by their bigger rivals to keep them in their place. If golf and horses are your true passions, then open a stables or a golf club. That way you can indulge in your passion both before and after your 40th birthday.

Myth number three. Everyone loves a small business entrepreneur and is out to help them. At best, this is a short-lived phenomenon; hot-blooded competition soon comes into play. Competitors will want to make life as hard as possible for you from the very beginning. As the animal kingdom shows us, the young and inexperienced are the most vulnerable. Moreover, every unemployable youth with the slightest trace of your DNA will claim the right to a job in your organisation, while Uncle Henry, 20 years on the board of MegaCorp PLC, will continue to exchange no more than a dozen words with you every Christmas.

Banks are much more helpful than they used to be. In the early 1980s, one budding entrepreneur was crisply told by his bank manager, 'We are not a charity'. Today the problem is finding a bank manager who has the time to talk to small businesses at all. Banks will try to encourage you to do business with them impersonally—over the Internet or the phone.

Myth number four. It takes a certain type to be a successful entrepreneur. This is, of course, not true. Successful entrepreneurs range from the Alexander the Great 'type' to the Jane Austen 'type'. There is no one type of personality best suited to starting a small business. I defy anyone to find a common trait in the people described in our case studies.

The only thing that can be said about successful entrepreneurs is that they rarely emerge from among the most academically brilliant pupils at school; very few successful small businesses have been started by people who got a first-class degree from Oxford or Cambridge. You don't need a Harvard MBA (or even a degree) to start a business. Richard Branson is an outstanding example of a successful entrepreneur who never went to a university.

Myth number five. I only need one big, well-known customer and I'm made. This is known as the Marks & Spencer myth. But it is very dangerous to become too dependent on one customer—just imagine what happens when you lose them. What's more, someone the size of Marks & Spencer is likely to be so demanding on your limited resources that you are going to find it hard to cultivate other significant customers at the same time.

Moreover, as a general rule, the bigger the firm, the slower they pay. Big firms have systems that grind exceedingly slow. Despite recent legislation that gives businesses a statutory right to claim interest and compensation on overdue commercial debts, big firms well know that you are unlikely to sue if they are a bit late in their payment.

Myth number six. There is nothing more valuable than a satisfied customer. This needs some modification. Customers come in all shapes and sizes, and they can be a real pain in the neck. Horror stories abound. The travel industry, for example, has an unusually high number of small businesses, and small tour operators almost invariably receive demands from returning holidaymakers for a free holiday next year, 'because the spaghetti was cold/the bed was too narrow/the buses were late'. Some seem to have spent half their time on the beach composing their letters of complaint. There are customers who can never be satisfied. Identify them as fast as you can, then let them go.

Myth number seven. I can leave all the figures to my accountant. Be warned: if you're no good at maths, you need to find someone who is vaguely numerate to join you at an early stage. Small businesses need to be on top of their numbers all the time. The cash flow, the sales figures, the prices of competitors' products–they're changing all the time, and their latest lurch could presage disaster for your business. You need to turn your brain into a sort of living Excel spreadsheet. In any case, if things go wrong and the taxman starts getting excessively curious about your returns, it is no excuse to say that you left it all to your accountant because sums were never your strong point.

Myth number eight. You are going to share responsibilities across the board with a partner. If you think you are going to be Hewlett and Packard, forget it. For every one of them there's 50 partnerships that fall out before they're 12 months old. Don't assume your small business can manage with more than one boss. Do climbers reach the summit of Everest as members of an egalitarian co-operative? No, they don't. Be sure in yourself that you can carry on alone if you need to.

Myth number nine. Export or die. For a lot of businesses, it has been a case of 'export *and* die'. Exporting can be very difficult. The paperwork involved is often daunting, even within the EU. But, more importantly, if you're having difficulty getting domestic customers to pay on time, imagine what it's like trying to extract payment from a small customer in, say, Sicily. The average payment period for an Italian customer is 80 days—in the United Kingdom it's 43 days. (Incidentally, the best payers, statistically, are the Russians, where the average is 24 days. But before you catch the next plane to Moscow, remember this is only because there is very little trust among businessmen there—much of the Russian economy is run on a cash basis.)

Myth number ten. To start a successful new business you need cutting-edge technology or a big new idea. Not true. Look at the 2002 winner of the UK's small business of the year award. It's called Historic Newspapers and it's in the business of finding original papers going back 150 years. And another point to note: Historic Newspapers is not in the throbbing south-east of England nor in Britain's version of Silicon Valley along the banks of the M4. It's in Wigtown, in Dumfries, south-west Scotland. Successes can turn up in the most unlikely places.

This is not to say that the best small businesses hang around in the backwoods and ignore new technology altogether. There are plenty of software tools that can help make a one-man band seem like an orchestra. And the Internet is an encyclopedia and a DIY manual all at the same time. More than a third of UK small businesses say that they use the Internet daily as a source of business advice.

This book is similarly designed for dipping into daily, and one section, the Essential Information Directory, is available online at www.ultimatebusinessresource.com. Go to the sections that cover issues you are having to face today or in the near future, and we hope that you will find there some help and some comfort.

The very best of luck to everyone who is trying to build a small business. It is not easy, as these myths have probably demonstrated, but it is extraordinarily invigorating—far more so than playing golf!

Tim Hindle

Assess Yourself

The fact that you're reading this now means that you must be pretty serious about setting up your own business. You've got an idea, you've done some research, and you've picked up this book in search of some sound advice about how to take it to the next level and beyond. Or perhaps you're already on your way and are looking to hone your entrepreneurial skills, plug any gaps in your knowledge, and shore up your business acumen with some expert guidance. Either way, you have already shown that you have one of the key attributes belonging to the entrepreneurial mindset: you are willing to question yourself, to take stock of what you do know and then deal with what you don't. You are here because you want to know the answer to two big questions: 'can I do it?' and then, 'how do I do it?'.

Here are some more questions to guide you towards those answers. This quick quiz is designed to help you assess your strengths and weaknesses, and in so doing, point you to the pages within this book that will be most useful to you.

YOU

Would you describe yourself as an 'ideas person'?
a) Yes—I always have a list of ideas that I am thinking about.
b) I have the odd flash of inspiration, but don't tend to dwell on it.
c) Not really—I don't like to be distracted from the job in hand.

How often do you talk to friends and family about your new ideas?
a) Regularly.
b) From time to time, when something particularly interests me.
c) Never.

How do you think your friends and family would react if you were to start your own business?
a) Positively—from the evidence of my past successes they will feel confident in my business abilities.
b) Apprehensively—I've talked about setting up on my own a lot but haven't ever done anything about it.
c) Negatively—I've never mentioned it before, so it will come as a complete surprise.

How persistent are you?
a) I'm ready to try many new approaches until I have a successful outcome.

b) I keep trying, but I do get discouraged.
c) I'm easily discouraged, and don't like to feel I'm 'pestering' people.

How do you enjoy working with people?
a) Very much—I like to get to know as many people as possible.
b) I enjoy spending time with certain people, but don't make an effort with everyone.
c) I prefer to work alone and concentrate on doing my job.

How do you feel about taking risks?
a) I thrive on risk-taking—I find it exciting and stimulating.
b) I will take the odd risk, but on the whole prefer to be confident about the outcome of my actions.
c) I dislike not knowing what will come of the choices I make—I don't take risks.

How many of the following attributes do you consider yourself to have: dedication, persistence, drive, stamina, intuition, courage, positive outlook, good communication skills, good 'people' skills, ambition, pragmatism, adaptability, financial savvy, energy, self-awareness?
a) 11-15
b) 6-10
c) 1-5

If you answered mostly **a**, you're already in an entrepreneurial mindset. The next stage is to take time working on your business idea and researching your target market. This book's **Refining and Protecting Your Idea** (pp. 20–41) section will help you do that.

If you answered mostly **b**, you're part of the way there. If you answered mostly **c**, you may not be sure that being your own boss is really for you. The **Planning** section (pp. 2–18) will give you some key pointers on evaluating your idea, yourself, and your current circumstances.

Whether you answered **a**, **b**, or **c**, read the **Viewpoints** between pp. 270–71 to find out how other entrepreneurs started their own businesses.

YOUR IDEA

Can you explain your business idea succinctly?
a) Yes, I can get the basics across in a sentence.
b) Yes. A paragraph should do it.
c) Not really. I need a five-page document to explain it.

How clear are you about your target market?
a) I've done a lot of research and I know exactly the group I am aiming at.
b) I have a fair idea of who will use my product/service.
c) Not very, but it's such a good idea I just know it will appeal to a lot of people.

How do you rate research?
a) Essential.
b) Useful.
c) An unnecessary extra cost.

Are you ready to take on board other people's comments?
a) Absolutely. It will be good to get some feedback and I'll adjust my plans accordingly.
b) I'll bear in mind any feedback, but I'd be reluctant to change to change my plans.
a) No. I don't want to compromise my idea.

Whatever your area of interest of area or expertise, thorough market research is essential when you're thinking about starting your own business. If you answered mostly **a**, you're aware of this already. The **Marketing Your Idea** (pp. 206–20) section will help you take your idea further.

If you answered mostly **b**, this section will be helpful to you too, but also look at pp. 13–15 in the **Planning** section (Coming Up with a Business Idea) to reinforce the importance of research. Read this too if you answered mostly **c**. Research in the early stages of your business is well worth the time and money you'll spend on it.

YOUR FINANCES

How do you handle your personal finances?
a) Well. I'm rarely in debt.
b) I take some risks, but I'm not often out of my depth.
c) I'm often in debt for prolonged periods.

How do you view your business or your business idea?
a) As a long-term source of income.
b) As an investment, to sell as soon as possible for a profit.
c) As a way of escaping my current job.

How well can you cope with financial matters?
a) I have quite a lot of experience and am confident when working with figures.
b) I have some experience, but some terms confuse me.
c) I don't know where to start.

Have you considered how you will cover yourself financially if things go wrong?
a) I have set aside a financial 'bumper' to allow for unforeseen expenses.
b) I have planned my expenditure and income very carefully and do not

envisage any problems.
c) I'm banking on things not going wrong.

If you answered mostly **a**, you are already financially aware and have realised that you'll need some funds for a 'rainy day'. The **Figuring It Out** section (pp. 104–204) offers advice on a wide range of funding issues, from understanding budgets to applying for funding from various sources.

The **financial ratios** (pp. 159–204) will be particularly helpful if you are going to be doing the book-keeping for your business.

If you answered mostly **b** or **c**, you have some financial knowledge but need a bit more support. **Figuring It Out** will also be helpful to you as it explains many key issues without using jargon. **The Essential Information Directory** (pp. 478–555) also contains the best sources of help for you if you want to research further.

YOU AND OTHERS

How do you react to advice or complaints?
a) I see negative feedback as an opportunity to change plans and ideas for the better. I believe in being proactive.
b) I do listen to and remember complaints and advice, but don't tend to act
c) I prefer to follow my own plans, and don't like others to interfere—no-one knows my business like I do.

How do you rate your people-management skills?
a) I think they're good. I can usually sense how people are feeling and react appropriately.
b) They're not too bad. I generally get on well with most people, but I feel I lose touch from time to time
c) They could be better. I often find it hard to connect with others.

You'll have many demands on your time when you're setting up or growing your business. How do organise what you need to do?
a) I'm prioritise tasks and build in extra time if I can.
b) I get through everything in the end, but I tend to underestimate how long things will take.
c) I work all night if I have to.

Pressure affects everyone who works, whatever their job, but you're the boss it can seem overwhelming at times. Can you deal with pressure?
a) Yes, I can recognise the signs and try to keep things in perspective.
b) I thrive on stress, but my partner doesn't so that can lead to extra tension.
c) Sometimes, but I find it hard to say 'no'.

Once you're company is up and running, you'll need to develop or gain management skills to get the best from yourself and your team if you employ others. Stress can also put a strain on personal and business relationships, which can make challenges harder to deal with.

If you answered mostly **a**, you have a good appreciation of what makes yourself and others tick. **The Focus On...** articles on pp.446–453 of the **Managing Yourself and Others** section will help you develop the skills you have already.

If you answered mostly **b** or **c**, the **Managing Your Time** (pp.404–406), **Managing Pressure** (pp.407–409), and **Delegating** (pp.412–14) actionlists in this section will help you manage your day better.

If you answered **c** more than **b**, the **Essential Information Directory** (pp. 478–555) will offer you further support.

Acknowledgments

We would like to thank the following people for their help during the compilation of this book:
Cobweb Information Ltd
Kate Gaylor
Tim Hindle
Philip Holden
Martha Lane Fox and lastminute.com
Ian Linton
Hughie Naughton
Richard Scriven

The following articles are © Cobweb Information Ltd 2003 (www.cobwebinfo.com):

A Guide to Business Regulations When
  Starting Up
A Guide to Health and Safety at Work
A Guide to UK Trade & Investment
An Introduction to Intellectual Property
Applying for a Patent
Buying a Business Property
Choosing and Using an Architect
Complying with Fire Safety Regulations
Complying with the Copyright of Others
Delegating
Developing and Protecting an Invention
Employing People with Disabilities
Ergonomics at Work
Export Documentation
Exporting for the First Time
Exporting—Methods of Market Entry
Financing a New Business
Implementing Job Share Arrangements
Importing for the First Time

Insuring a Business
Modern Apprenticeships
Obtaining Planning Permission
Planning Staff Needs
Registering a Trademark
Renting a Business Property
Selling by Mail Order
Setting Up a Business As a Non-profit
  Organisation
Setting Up a Business As a Private Limited
  Company
Setting Up a Payroll
Starting a Business Under the Age of 18
Telemarketing
Understanding Building Regulations
Understanding the Minimum Wage
Using Copyright to Protect Your Work
Working Time Regulations 1998
Writing a Sales letter

Business Information Sources © Chartered Management Institute 2003
Index prepared by Indexing Specialists (UK) Ltd.

ACTIONLISTS: PLANNING

Deciding Whether to Start a Business

GETTING STARTED

Setting up your own business can be very rewarding, but there are pressures involved. It's not enough just to have a good, viable idea: you also need to have the right skills and temperament to make the opportunity succeed. Starting your own business is also a risky thing to do, so you need to be aware of what problems to look out for as early as possible. This will help you decide if you are willing and able to take those risks, and will also help you to apply strategies that will reduce them.

Before you go any further, it's important to find out as much as you can about what sort of person you are. Be honest and objective, and discuss the project with friends, colleagues, and relatives. Think about how you have dealt with past challenges, as an indication of your response to difficult new situations. This actionlist will help you to decide whether starting a business is the right thing for you to do.

FAQS

Do I have the right personality to start a business?

While the technical aspects of your business will require specific qualifications, skills, or experience, there are broader demands that are as important. These could include the ability to negotiate with suppliers, mediate between staff, be sociable with customers, be convincing with prospects, think clearly under pressure, take criticism, portray confidence, and use your time effectively.

There is no single type of self-employed person, but experience has shown that there are some characteristics which successful self-employed people often have in common. They tend to be logical, perceptive, organised, and responsible. They are usually extrovert and confident, and able to communicate and get their point across. They are also often sociable, with the ability to lead. Self-employed people are generally single-minded, but able to take advice. They are flexible and adaptable, quick to take opportunities, and ready to take risks. They tend to be tough-skinned, and able to handle failure. They are usually creative and imaginative, always coming up with new ideas for the business, and also hard working, committed, and determined. Finally, they are often individualists, who are not afraid to stand out from the crowd.

Are older people more successful at running a business?

There is no doubt that it helps to have some experience in the workplace, and particularly in the sector in which you want to start a business. Surveys reveal that many successful businesses have been started by people in their 30s who have some management experience. People over the age of 50 (sometimes called 'third-age entrepreneurs') are also responsible for many business start-ups and many think about a change of direction after taking early retirement. Having said that, a wide range of people have established their own businesses successfully and have much to offer. For example, young people have fewer domestic commitments, plenty of energy, new ideas, and the potential to develop and adapt to the challenges of self-employment.

What kinds of skills will I need?

You will almost certainly need technical skills. If you have qualifications relevant to your business activity this will obviously be helpful. Customers, and anyone lending your business money, will be more comfortable if you have the right qualifications. Additionally, certain businesses require exceptional ability, for example design skills, artistic skills, or technical skills.

Business skills are also essential. It is important to understand the principles of business and management, including marketing, strategic planning, accounts, personnel management, and so on. Ideally, you should aim to get some basic training in business administration before you start. If this is not possible (and many people do not have the time or money initially), then read as much as you can to fill the gaps in your knowledge. Leadership skills are important, too. If you expect the business to grow, you will inevitably have to employ people, and the ability to show leadership and to manage people will be critical.

All businesses require an element of selling, and you will need to develop skills in this area if you do not already possess them. Initially it is important to persuade people to support you and your idea, and crucial to be able to win over potential customers. It is possible to learn basic selling techniques, but being outgoing and articulate are equally important.

Your organisational skills will also be essential to the success of your business. To generate sufficient income, small businesses must be well organised and efficient. It is important that you can organise yourself and others, plan ahead, and manage your time. You also need to have the discipline to set and meet deadlines.

Try to think laterally about how many of these skills you have, and don't be put off too easily. Starting a business is challenging, yes, but think about the skills you use in everyday life and how you could apply them to a different context. For example, if you are a woman with a family, or one who has juggled full- or part-time work with family life, think about how you have developed your time management skills, probably without even noticing what you have achieved.

MAKING IT HAPPEN
Assess your abilities and resources
Starting your own business is a risky thing to do, so you should get to grips with the various risks as early as possible. Set aside plenty of time to think about them. This will help you decide if you are willing and able to

take those risks. It will also help you to apply strategies that will reduce the risk.

You need to ask yourself several questions. Do you have the financial resources to start your own business, and can you afford to risk these? For example, you might take a secured loan based on the value of your home; what are your plans if the business fails and you are forced to sell your house? Do you have sufficient experience and technical skills to perform the core functions of your new business? Are you familiar enough with the market you want to enter to be able to assess its needs and adapt to its changes? Do you have the tenacity and discipline to see through hard times when cash will be short and demands will be heavy (from customers, bankers, staff, and, crucially, your family)?

While you might not be able to answer all these questions completely, it really is important to find out as much as you can about what sort of person you are, and to do that you must be honest and objective. Discuss the project with a wide range of people, including friends, colleagues, and relations. Think about how you have dealt with past challenges, as an indication of what your response to difficult new situations might be.

Look at your motives
Why *do* you want to start your own business? There are many good reasons, but there is often the danger of having unrealistic expectations. Here are some reasons that people often give, and some related notes of caution:

- **independence.** Yes, it can be irksome working for someone else, but you still need to be disciplined, motivated, and able to get on with others when you work for yourself.
- **greater job satisfaction.** Self-employment allows you to do the job in your own way, and it is very satisfying when your way is shown to work. You do, of course, also have to take responsibility for your way when it *doesn't* work.
- **achievement and success.** For many people, there can be some cachet attached to the idea of running their own business,

but make sure that you are not trying to prove that you're something you're not. If the venture failed, would you be able to deal with it?

- **more money.** While the thought of being better off financially is naturally attractive, doing it for the money is not usually a good enough motive in itself, and greater wealth is by no means guaranteed. In particular, beware of starting a business when you have no other choice. If you do find yourself in this position, remember the importance of maintaining a positive but pragmatic vision of what you can achieve.

Assess your skills

Assessing your skills is a useful process, as it will help you identify your strengths as well as areas in which you need training. These in turn will contribute towards your chances of being successful in business. There are many sources of training available to small businesses, and several courses are run by local colleges and universities. The addresses of specialist training providers can be found in the *Yellow Pages* under 'Training Services'. Also bear in mind Trade Associations and Sector Skills Councils— they may run industry-specific courses.

Advice on, and assistance with, training is available from local Learning and Skills Councils (LSCs) in England, Education and Learning Wales (ELWa), Local Enterprise Companies (LECs) in Scotland, and the Department for Employment and Learning (DEL) in Northern Ireland. Many of these organisations will also be able to provide details of any loans and financial assistance available to help with training for small businesses, such as the Small Firms Training Loan run by the Department for Education and Skills.

Business Links (Business Gateways in Scotland, Business Eye in Wales, Invest Northern Ireland), Chambers of Commerce, and Enterprise Agencies will often run business courses and provide information on training providers.

Be prepared for the pressures

The pressures of being self-employed are inescapable. You may have to work long hours, and there will be times when things get on top of you. You may well get into debt in order to finance the enterprise. You will need to maintain your faith in your business, often in the face of other people's doubts.

There will be times when you feel lonely and isolated. If you employ people, you will need to be positive and show leadership all the time, even when you least feel like it. There will be times when you need to be tough and you will have to discipline difficult employees, or make difficult demands of your suppliers. Similarly you will have to be polite and helpful, even when an awkward customer is giving you a hard time.

Many of those who successfully start their own business have the backing of their family. You will be under pressure, working long hours. Your family must be prepared for the impact this can have on family life. Also, you must be sure that your family can accommodate the risks that self-employment can bring, especially in terms of lower income in the initial stages, and maybe even the implications of the business failing. Take time to talk to all members of your family who might be affected by your choice to be your own boss.

WHAT TO AVOID
Assuming that being your own boss is easy

Everyone at some point has come across a boss who makes his or her life difficult, but don't assume that working for yourself will be all plain sailing. There are many benefits, to be sure, but you have to get used to the idea that the buck stops with you and you alone. Make sure you're ready take on that responsibility.

Doing it for the wrong reasons

As noted above, don't do it for the money alone. Weigh up the pros and cons of your idea and the impact that starting a business will have on all areas of your life. It will take a lot of effort, but you *can* do it—read on to find out how.

RECOMMENDED LINKS

Business Eye (Wales):
www.businesseye.org.uk
Business Gateway (Scotland):
www.bgateway.com
Business Link (England):
www.businesslink.org
Department for Education and Skills:
www.dfes.gov.uk
Invest Northern Ireland:
www.investni.com
Learndirect:
www.learndirect.co.uk

Sector Skills Development Agency:
www.ssda.org.uk

SEE ALSO

**Assessing Your Entrepreneurial Profile:
Do You Have What It Takes? (p. 6)
Coming Up with a Business Idea
(p. 13)
Entrepreneurs (p. 510)
Small and Growing Businesses
(p. 478)
Understanding Business Models
(p. 44)**

Assessing Your Entrepreneurial Profile: Do You Have What It Takes?

GETTING STARTED

Once you've started thinking about starting a business, you need to start thinking about your own role in it. Are you the right type of person to make a success of a new venture? There's a great deal of romance surrounding the notion of being an entrepreneur, but not everyone has the aptitude. And it's important to understand that there's nothing wrong with *not* being an entrepreneur. The world wouldn't function half as well if it were peopled solely with them.

Nevertheless, there are some general personality traits that are key for being an entrepreneur. If the following list seems to fit your personality, you may have what it takes:

- I am persistent, with a great deal of drive and stamina. I see problems as opportunities. I have a good intuitive sense and thrive on new ideas.
- I tend to rebel against authority. I want to be my own boss.
- I am positive, communicate well, and enjoy working with people.
- I have a strong need to succeed, financially and otherwise.
- I'm not afraid to make mistakes, and I learn from them.

FAQS

How can I be sure I've got what it takes?
Before leaving your job and using your savings to start a business, you owe it to yourself to approach your entrepreneurial venture with some practicality. Take a more in-depth personality test and talk to small business advisers, who are often available at no cost through business associations.

How much money will I need?
Whether you want to buy an existing business, purchase a franchise, start your own company, or merely offer services to others from a home office, starting a business depends on first knowing the numbers. People in the same or similar businesses are a good source of information—use your ingenuity to find out what it cost them to get started, and where they got the funds to do so. Other sources include trade associations, franchise organisations, business articles in magazines and newspapers, Internet research, or business consultants.

Besides being an ideas person, what else do I need to be good at?
Success in a new enterprise depends on dedication and the consistent application of good business principles. Some of these principles include: being good with money; being good with people (investors, suppliers, employees, and so on); being a good promoter (marketing, sales, PR); and being good to yourself. Many entrepreneurs burn out before their businesses take hold. In this game, pacing yourself and your business is important.

MAKING IT HAPPEN
Check that you have the right idea
If you've got a great new idea and no competition in sight, you must be sure that the product or service will be of value to customers—at a price at which you can afford to sell it. If your aim is to enter a field with established competitors, you have to know your own strengths and weaknesses, as well as those of your competition. You have to be certain that you can provide a better product or service for a competitive price. Finding out all these things is called 'market research', and you'll have to do a thorough job of it to succeed.

Develop a detailed, professional business plan
This is the key to building a successful business. Having a well-considered and systematic plan allows you to recognise problems

as they arise in time to be able to take corrective action. The plan should be a living document, flexible over time to adapt to changes in the marketplace and your industry. It should include sections on every facet of your business—whether you're a sole proprietor or the executive director of a new manufacturing venture.

Get financial backing for your idea

Take your ideas and business plan to a variety of people, starting with friends and close supporters. Be prepared for critical feedback, and be flexible. Take the inevitable first few comments of 'no thanks' as opportunities to fine-tune the next presentation. One of the hallmarks of an entrepreneur is the ability to regroup, rethink, and reach a goal in another way.

Seeking publicity for your business is a way not only to notify potential customers but also to get the attention of possible investors. The more people who know about your idea, the better the chances that you'll attract the right investor.

Be willing to share a portion of the company with the right partners, but be wary of finance companies and investors who want full control, or the lion's share of the proceeds.

Consider entering a joint venture with another company, or position your company to attract start-up funds from government sources.

Practise your networking

Being entrepreneurial doesn't mean being a lone ranger. Being successful often depends on your ability to network with potential customers, suppliers, new investors, and even those in government who control certain aspects of the business environment.

Plan your marketing and PR

An integral part of your business plan involves a marketing plan—how you intend to create the demand for your product or service. While market research tells you the 'what' and 'where' of your opportunities, the marketing plan outlines the steps by which you will find potential customers and convince them to buy from you. Networking, advertising, and PR are all forms of marketing and promotion.

Make sure you have the right financial and management support

Most entrepreneurs are better at ideas than at managing budgets, business operations, and employees. Anticipate that you'll need more capital than you reckoned on at the start, and don't be lavish with spending beyond the company's means. If you find yourself in a questionable position, make sure you have a network of trusted and experienced advisers to help you see the proper perspective and cover the things you are not naturally good at.

WHAT TO AVOID
Setting up equal partnerships

Entrepreneurs often share the start-up responsibilities with a partner or partners. However, sharing 50–50 or by thirds or quarters is a big mistake, because conflicts will inevitably arise and need someone in a controlling position to make a final decision. Choose (or employ) a CEO—someone with the experience and skills needed for success—and give that person a greater decision-making authority and a bigger salary, even if it is only bigger by a small margin.

Having inadequate people and planning

Entrepreneurs must become strong managers when the company gets going. Many businesses fail because the people in charge don't have the managerial qualities or strength to cope with the challenges. In addition, stress can put a strain on personal relationships and this can make the challenges harder to deal with. Personality assessments can determine if you're cut out for a managerial position, and managerial training can prepare you for your new role as an executive.

Without proper market research and a solid business plan, a business is more likely to fail. The more advanced preparation that is done, the better the chances for success.

Relying too heavily on one or two customers

Having too few customers makes your business vulnerable, because it ties your future to the decisions of other organisations. If their business falters, it puts your hard work and dedication at risk, through no fault of your own. The advice of personal financial consultants is appropriate here. Having lots of customers, even though none of them are gigantic, is healthier in the long run.

Causing cash-flow troubles through insufficient financing

While some people are successful at jump-starting their own enterprise with little or no outside investment, they do so by being fortunate, being modest in their spending, and by ploughing profits back into the business.

The majority of businesses, however, don't deliver the projected first-year sales volume. It's better to overestimate your need for capital resources at the beginning and to underestimate your projected sales figures. It's better to be pleasantly surprised at your success than to lose the business and your house because the money isn't there when it's needed.

When contemplating an expansion of your business, be wary of spiralling costs. If you're in a cyclical business, or one vulnerable to recession, be sure to be very calculating about your expenses—and develop 'Plan B' well before you need to implement it.

Failing to admit mistakes

Entrepreneurs are sometimes the last to admit that their idea hasn't the sparkle it once had. Having advisers that you trust is important—either as staff members or contract workers. Be willing to cut your losses and move on if your advisers all agree that you should. Doing so may save the company, if you can move quickly enough to capitalise on your mistakes, or shift the product or service to take advantage of other opportunities.

Underestimating the competition

Your competition won't stand still for long, once you've demonstrated their weakness in the marketplace with your product or service. Expect them to plug the hole quickly and even try to outflank you in the process. Your business and marketing plans should anticipate how to deal with new initiatives from your competition. If you conduct ongoing research, product and service evaluations, and marketing campaigns, you should always be one step ahead of the competition.

RECOMMENDED LINKS

The Entrepreneurship Programme:
www.entrepreneur.co.uk
iVillage.co.uk:
www.ivillage.co.uk/workcareer/ experts/divaex
UK Business Incubation:
www.ukbi.co.uk/news

SEE ALSO

Coming Up with a Business Idea (p. 13)
Deciding Whether to Start a Business (p. 2)
Entrepreneurs (p. 510)
Small and Growing Businesses (p. 478)

Making the Decision to Take a Risky Career Move

GETTING STARTED

Everything in business today is risky. There is no such thing as a safe bet. It is certainly risky to leave a familiar job with routines, expectations, and objectives that you're comfortable with to test the limits of your courage and skills in a strange environment, but, as thousands of redundant employees in global companies can attest, it's not exactly safe holding onto a job that is as dependable as a leaky lifeboat.

Whether you should decide to make that risky career move is entirely up to the nature of the risk and your ability to absorb the possible negative consequences. The risk itself may be made up of any number of factors, such as your ability to move into an unfamiliar job or your ability to move into an unfamiliar organisation. Are you jumping from an Old Economy position to a New Economy one? Or are you leaping back into the Old Economy world after trying your luck in a high-tech, high-pressure, go-go New Economy environment? Are you considering leaving a stable, secure position that's limited in its prospects in favour of the white-knuckle environment of a bootstrap start-up? Are you about to move from a solid public organisation into a family-owned business? Is the family that owns the business your own?

For some people, the notion of going into a shaky entrepreneurial environment after drawing a steady salary for years would be intolerable. For others, depending on only one income source, as opposed to the multiple sources of revenue available to an entrepreneur, may make them feel vulnerable.

The decision you make is entirely yours. The risk you take is entirely yours.

The following points are key questions to ask yourself while considering whether you should take the risk or not:

- Does the benefit outweigh the potential cost of the risk?
- How many people depend utterly on the regular income your current job provides?
- Is there a back-up plan in case your gamble fails?
- Is it possible to return to your original position should you decide that your experiment was not as rewarding as you hoped?

FAQS

How can I be sure that I don't regret my ultimate decision?

Give yourself all the time you need to make your choice wisely and calmly. Think it through methodically, and then make the decision. Whatever the outcome, be sure to learn from it in some way.

I'm not comfortable in risky situations. Is there any way I can avoid this problem?

Not if you intend to grow in your career. Indeed, there are no guarantees in today's marketplace, so taking steps to avoid taking a risk might actually be the worst thing you could do.

MAKING IT HAPPEN
Identify what 'acceptable risk' means to you

If you are young and single (with no obligations other than to yourself), you can probably afford to take on a few risky career moves. These high-profile actions can give you early boosts that could position you for more momentum-driven rewards later in your career.

If you are older, perhaps with a family, you may not be quite as willing to try your luck with a high-risk/high-reward venture, such as a start-up enterprise.

Your capacity to accept risk is entirely a personal one.

Know your goals

Make a list of your short- and long-term objectives. Is your current position more or less likely to help you achieve them? If your position is less likely to help you achieve these goals, can you make slight adjustments to your present job in order to position yourself better for achieving your dreams? Or is it necessary to depart from your position entirely, regardless of what you are heading for?

Know what you value

List your less tangible values. Which opportunity is most likely to help you manifest those values? Your current job or your new possibility? Does one opportunity actually position you to behave in ways that are contrary to those values?

Conduct a risk/benefit analysis

This is the process that will help you determine whether the potential reward outweighs the potential pain. There are several methods for analysing your potential costs, but the easiest is simply to create two columns. List the potential pain in one column and the potential reward in the other. The column that has the longer list is the one that should receive serious consideration. A variation of this method is to assign points or anticipating pound values to each item. You can then either compare the grand totals or assess each pain/reward item on its own merit.

Consider the people you would be working with

Who do you have the most in common with? This is not a question of who you would be most comfortable spending an afternoon watching television or playing tennis with. Rather, whose visions and ideals are most compatible with your own?

WHAT TO AVOID

Making the wrong choice

As there are no guarantees, there is always a chance that you will make the wrong choice—or at least the choice that feels wrong to you as you begin to experience 'buyer's remorse'. Have faith in your risk-assessment strategy, and carefully watch how that risk plays itself out. There is always something positive to be gained from every adventure.

Not making any choice at all

Making no choice is still making a choice. And this is the one that is almost guaranteed to net you no gain at all.

Modern business is full of risky moves. Those who relish that aspect will be the ones who will ultimately benefit from the growth and added self-awareness that comes from the adventure of being engaged in contemporary commerce.

RECOMMENDED LINKS
Monster:
www.monster.co.uk
Executive Action International:
www.executive-action.co.uk

Identifying the Purpose of a Business

GETTING STARTED

Whether you're starting up or in business already, it's crucial to be clear about what your business does or will do, so that you can stay focused on the appropriate target market. Prospective lenders or investors in your business will look closely at this purpose when they assess whether you have the strategic direction for future success. You also need to be clear about why you are going into this business in the first place, and what you want out of it. Investors need to understand your motivation and your intentions, so that they can judge whether these match the plans that you set out for the development of the business. This actionlist aims to help you define both your own inspiration and the purpose of your business in order to bring clarity to your direction.

FAQS

Why am I in business and what do I want out of it?

Ask yourself this crucial question first of all, and then consider the other questions that arise in consequence. Will the business supplement your main income or replace it? Are you starting it as an investment, to sell as soon as you can? Is it to provide jobs for family members?

The answers to questions like these will have an impact on the business's aims, development, and strategies. For example, if you are starting a business as an investment opportunity, the focus of your planning will be leading up to your exit—the sale of the business. Your strategies must focus on building the business quickly and maximising its value to get the best selling price possible. On the other hand, if you are building up a business for a less experienced family member, your plan will focus on a succession strategy. This might mean keeping the business small and easily manageable.

What exactly should my business do?

Be as specific as possible about the kind of business that you are starting. If you are going to open a restaurant, for example, will it be a family restaurant serving good quality, local food at competitive prices in a family-friendly environment? Or will it be more up-market, serving gourmet dishes to discerning customers?

Describe your business in terms of a mission statement that clearly summarises its purpose and is easily understood by you, your staff, your customers, and your potential investors. If you cannot describe your business in these terms, rethink your business idea; focus on your business's core activities and direction.

What is a business's vision?

A vision reflects what you care about most and represents what your business is trying to achieve. Defining purpose expresses what the business does, while the vision drives the business forward to its long-term aims. Vision is about having challenging but achievable goals within defined time scales. It is simply a statement of your desired competitive position within your best guess of the future environment. Realistic visions can be achieved and will improve staff morale, and once a vision is reached you can further expand your business aims.

A vision is created from the fundamental values of the employees and an awareness of the business's purpose and the current economic climate.

MAKING IT HAPPEN
Identify your customer

Product-driven businesses focus on making a product, then trying to get customers to buy it. A better starting point is to define the purpose of your business in response to customer needs—making your business market-driven. Define your business purpose in terms of your customer, and what you perceive their needs to be. For example, a fast food take-away selling healthy food might see its purpose as: 'Providing health-conscious eaters with quick, convenient, and tasty take-away meals and snacks all day'.

Make your purpose different

To succeed against competitors, your business needs to offer something different. Build this differentiation into your purpose, so that everything you do can be judged in terms of whether it supports the purpose or not. Potential investors want to see your business's unique selling proposition (USP), as this is the basis on which you will compete and on which customers will be attracted.

Write a mission statement

At its simplest, your business's mission is a statement of purpose that guides your activities. It is a summary of 'what you do'. The mission provides the guiding direction for developing strategy, searching out opportunities, and making resource allocation choices. It is built on your core values, so should be easily understood by staff, customers, and financial backers. You can often establish your mission in terms of the question: 'What business are we in?'

For example, the company Blooming Marvellous describes its mission as follows: 'We design, make, and market clothes for the fashion-conscious mother-to-be'. As can be seen from this statement, it has carefully defined what it does, its specific product, and its market niche.

Decide what you want your business to be after two years

Start by considering what the working environment is going to be like in, say, two years' time. Ask yourself what opportunities and threats there might be, and summarise your vision in a single statement. For example: 'Octo aims to be respected as a leading design group working throughout Europe'. This business has chosen not to disclose publicly the timescale to which it is working, but it makes it clear it has a vision.

Try to envisage this so that you can start to move your business towards that point. For instance, you might work towards becoming a market leader, an innovator, specialist, a good employer, a large concern, or a supplier of superior quality.

WHAT TO AVOID

Working without a clearly defined purpose

If you don't know exactly what the purpose of your business is, it is going to be very difficult to plan for the future, formulate objectives and goals, and design a strategy to achieve them. One of the good reasons for writing a business plan is that it will force you to clarify your purpose; without that clarity, it is difficult to define your markets and your marketing plans.

Taking on work outside your core business

It is always a temptation for service-based businesses to take on jobs that are not in their usual line of work. These can often end up taking longer and costing more than anticipated, with poor results for the customer and little likelihood of any repeat business for you. A well-worded business purpose, however, can help keep your mind focused on what your business aims to do and what it is best at doing. One useful book that may help you keep your mind on the job is *The On-Purpose Business: Doing More of What You Do Best More Profitably* by Kevin McCarthy, published in 2002 by Navpress Publishing Group.

RECOMMENDED LINKS

Business Eye (Wales):
www.businesseye.org.uk
Business Gateway (Scotland):
www.bgateway.com
Business Link (England):
www.businesslink.org
Invest Northern Ireland:
www.investni.com

SEE ALSO
Entrepreneurs (p. 510)

Coming Up with a Business Idea

GETTING STARTED

You've decided that you want to go into business, but you don't know what that business is going to be. You're looking for a great idea. The best advice is to begin by breaking down the bigger picture into more manageable pieces. First, look at your own skills and knowledge. Consider your present occupation, and whether you could you do your present job working for yourself rather than being employed by someone else. Successful businesses are frequently started by people with practical experience in the type of work that the new venture is entering. They go into business because they decide that they want more independence in their working lives.

It may be that you feel that the skills you have are already over-supplied. If this is the case, it's possible that there is no room in the marketplace for yet another joiner, furniture restorer, or undertaker. Or it may be that you simply do not want to carry on doing the same thing for yourself that you've done for others in the past. You perhaps then need to think of ways in which you could modify the skills and experience that you've acquired while working for somebody else.

Take a careful look at yourself; it could be that your personality or physique suggests a business idea. If you've persistence, charm, and good communication skills, for example, you might be a good salesperson. There are frequent openings for self-employed sales agents to sell other people's products. If you're good at dealing with people, you might be just the person to take up a retail franchise.

FAQS

How do I identify new ideas?

Try brainstorming with friends or relations to see if you can identify any totally new ideas. There are opportunities for entirely new products or services, such as energy conservation, providing better insulation in homes and factories. You may have an idea for a simple device which you think people might use. It might be worth commissioning a search at your local patent office to see if anyone has thought of the idea already.

Can I look at an existing idea in a new way?

Contrary to popular belief, there are few original ideas. Most successful businesses come from modifying, refining, or re-thinking an existing business idea. Post-it notes resulted from a glue product that went wrong. Perhaps more important is the fact that it might not have happened if the company had not deliberately set aside time when staff could think about innovative product ideas. Try thinking laterally about existing products or materials you know about.

What goods or services could I provide locally?

Think of the problems and difficulties you've experienced in getting things for your home, garden, or at work, or in your leisure activities. Analyse what the problems were which caused you most inconvenience, or cost you the most to put right. Think about times when you've urgently required a service, and then found that it was not available. Alternatively, you might be able to think of parts or products that were hard or impossible to obtain locally. Think about the things that you and your neighbours and friends most frequently complain about. Listen to people talking in the pub, at the gym, or in the supermarket checkout queue. Then ask yourself whether there is any way of providing a local service or product for any of these markets, and whether people would actually pay for it.

What goods or services could I provide to local companies?

Do some research among local companies. Find out whether there are any goods or services that they have difficulty in obtaining. A new industrial estate for example, may contain a number of small and medium-sized firms, none of which have their own staff canteen, but all of which need some kind of catering service. Perhaps a sandwich bar could be set up on the estate. There may be room in the market for a despatch service linking the estate with other industrial centres.

How do I find out about opportunities for tourism or leisure businesses in my area?

The type of tourism business you consider will depend on whether the area is urban or rural, whether it's a popular tourist region, and the demographics of the local population. For example, a business such as a teashop may thrive in an area with a high population of pensioners and a high influx of tourists. You may want to consider opening an outdoor activity centre in a rural area. Try talking to people working in the local sports centre or Tourist Board. They may have suggestions for market opportunities in the area.

How could I find out about selling goods made by other people?

Many new firms start off by selling goods that somebody else makes. A number of opportunities exist to distribute foreign goods in Britain. For example, the United States Department of Commerce publishes a regular magazine listing businesses looking for facilities and distributors (this is available from all US embassies and consulates). Chambers of Commerce have regular listings of businesses seeking partners willing to manufacture under licence, or to act as sole distributors.

What do large companies, local authorities, and other public bodies buy in from outside the area?

In many cases they will be buying goods from outside the region because there is no one to supply them locally. Similarly, local councils and organisations like the Area Health Authority and the Police Force are purchasers of equipment and services. Try contacting the purchasing officer of your local council to find out what large and frequent purchases they make. In order to help new suppliers, some companies produce briefing documents for small businesses explaining what they buy and their purchasing procedure.

Is there potential for import substitution in the area?

One stage further is to look at things which are currently being bought from abroad. Look around in shops and factories to see where the goods on sale, or being used, were made. Customs and Excise keep lists of imported products. The single European market has opened up new opportunities abroad too. Do you have language skills? Have you worked abroad before? You could have enough useful knowledge of another country to enable you to act as an export agent.

MAKING IT HAPPEN
Turn your hobby into a business

You may have skills that you acquired as a hobby, but which could form the basis for a business. For example, if you like gardening, you might consider starting a garden design business. If you're good at cooking, you could think about starting a catering service for people entertaining at home.

Work from home

If you're a parent, and consequently at home a lot of the time, you could think about working from home (if space allows). It might be possible for you to set aside space to sew, knit, or perhaps make soft toys. Another option is to sell products for other people over the phone. There are also an increasing number of opportunities for people to do office work using a computer and modem. This can include anything from word processing letters and keeping accounts up to date, right through to freelance writing and consultancy.

Buy an existing business

Another option is to consider buying an existing business. However, if you do, make sure you find out why the owner is selling. Even if the seller is retiring, make sure you find out why it wasn't worth his or her while to continue with the business. Make sure you've looked at the business's accounts, and that you understand them. Businesses for sale are usually advertised in the local paper, and could also be advertised in relevant trade magazines.

WHAT TO AVOID

Not giving it enough time

Don't expect an idea to come to you in a flash; sometimes ideas take time to develop. Also remember that the time you spend on planning will be time well spent when you finally do come up with a great idea.

Not doing enough research

If you fail to do any market research, you'll have far less chance of success. Research will save you time and money in the long run.

RECOMMENDED LINKS

Business Eye (Wales):
www.businesseye.org.uk
Business Gateway (Scotland):
www.bgateway.com
Business Link (England):
www.businesslink.org
Invest Northern Ireland:
www.investni.com

SEE ALSO

Assessing Your Entrepreneurial Profile: Do You Have What It Takes? (p. 6)
Deciding Whether to Start a Business (p. 2)
Developing and Protecting an Invention (p. 23)
Entrepreneurs (p. 510)
New Product Development (p. 530)

Networking and Marketing Yourself

GETTING STARTED

Everyone can always benefit from networking and marketing themselves, but those setting up or running a small business can certainly benefit from getting themselves and their company known. Business is driven by relationships and marketing yourself requires you to build strong and meaningful relationships—many that will be long term. The following are questions to consider as you prepare to network and to market yourself:

- Why are you networking? What is your personal or professional goal?
- What are your strengths that will help you to market yourself?
- What organisations or events will be valuable places for networking?
- How much time do you want to spend on networking, and when will you do it?
- How will you know when you've been successful?

FAQS

Why should I bother to network and to market myself?

Research has shown that people who have a vast network of contacts, who are involved in professional and community activities outside their business, and who look for opportunities to be visible are more successful in their careers.

Isn't networking blatant self-promotion, and won't it look bad?

No. Networking is done for the good of your business, rather than for personal gain. If you are a successful networker, people are drawn to you because they know you are well connected and that you have good resources.

When is the best time to network?

Networking should become a way of life, a way of being. You should be networking all the time. As you build professional relationships, be constantly thinking: 'What can I offer this person?' 'How can I be of help?' The more you try to be of service to others, the more people will want to do things for you, and in the initial stages of a new business this will be a huge help.

MAKING IT HAPPEN

Clarify the purpose of your networking and why you are marketing yourself

There are many reasons for networking and for marketing oneself. When you are start-ing up or trying to grow a small business, these reasons may include gaining support for a major project, finding funding, or setting up a partnership with other local businesses. Although it is important to continually build relationships, it is much more effective to know why you are building these relationships and what you hope to accomplish. Everyone has limited time, and this will help you to decide how to prioritise your networking activities.

Make a list of your strong points

It is important to have a sense of who you are and what your strengths are when you are networking and marketing yourself. What are your special skills and abilities? What unique knowledge do you have? What experiences will other people find valuable? What characteristics and beliefs define who you are? Once you have made this list, make copies for your bathroom mirror, for your car dashboard, and for your wallet. Knowing your strengths helps you to remember that other people will value what you have to offer.

Never network from a position of weakness. Always network from a position of strength. Have something of value to offer; otherwise people will see you as an annoyance. And remember to begin networking before you need anything from other people. Join or create a network to build relationships, and do what you can to help others or the organisation.

Make a list of organisations and events for networking

Identify professional organisations and events that may be helpful to you in your career or with your project. Look for special interest groups like those for 'entrepreneurial women' for example. Get involved. When you are at professional events, make sure that you attend social functions, that you join people for dinner, and that you seek out volunteer opportunities.

Create a contact list

Keeping in mind your reasons for networking, brainstorm all the people you know who might be of help to you. Prioritise the list according to who is most likely to be helpful. Think about people you have done favours for in the past who might not be of direct help, but who may know someone who can be. After you have spoken to each one, ask him or her, 'Who else do you know that can be of help to me?'

Create an action plan with a schedule

Take your list of organisations and events and your contact list, and put together an action plan for making connections. Schedule networking events in your diary, along with organisational meetings, conferences and so on. Using your contact list, set up a schedule for making a certain number of calls per day or per week.

Meet with people and attend events

Before you meet with someone or attend an event, review your list of strengths, and focus on your purpose for networking and marketing yourself. It helps to visualise or picture a successful outcome. Be friendly and professional, but most of all, be yourself. Spend time connecting with people on a personal level before asking for help or sharing your reason for networking. If you are meeting in person with someone on your contact list, always bring a gift— something they can remember you by.

Network on the Net

The Internet is a valuable place to make connections and to learn fruitful information from colleagues. If you have a special interest or a special field, there is sure to be a newsgroup or threaded bulletin board on your topic. If not, start one by setting up a listserv at **www.egroups.com**: **www.topica.com**, or at similar sites.

Market yourself

The actions you take depend on why you are marketing yourself, but think of yourself as a brand; 'Brand You'. When marketers are marketing a product, they look for the 'Unique Selling Proposition' (USP). A USP is something relevant and original that can be claimed for a particular product or service. The USP should be able to communicate: 'Buy our brand and get this unique benefit'. When marketing yourself, you need to define who your 'customers' are and what your Unique Selling Proposition is. Your list of strengths above should give you some clues, but the USP needs to be stated in a short phrase. People who are closest to you can often give you suggestions. It might be something like: 'I help people to realise their dreams', or 'My leadership brings out the best in others', or 'I solve problems quickly and simply'.

Once you know your USP, brainstorm ways that you can market yourself and your uniqueness. The key is to let people know what you have to offer. Write an article for the company newsletter or a professional newsletter related to your USP. Volunteer to give a talk. Design a project that uses your unique talents and propose it to the right people. Be visible.

Assess your progress towards networking goals

You may wish to keep a notebook of your action plans and your progress. It also helps to have someone as a sounding board. That person can be a friend, a partner, or a professional adviser. When we feel accountable for our actions to someone we trust, we are much more likely to follow through. It also helps to have someone who is willing to celebrate your successes and accomplishments with you.

Always say 'thank you'

As you network, many people will offer you information, opportunities, and valuable contacts. In your notebook, keep track of the favours that people have done for you and make sure that you write each one a short and simple thank-you letter. People are always more willing to help someone who has been appreciative in the past.

Be patient

Networking is a long-term activity. Steven Ginsburg of the *Washington Post* describes networking as 'building social capital'. You may not see results overnight, and at first should expect to give more than you get. But over time, your network will become one of your most valued assets.

WHAT TO AVOID
Not wanting to bother anyone

Remember that people love to help others. Don't take up too much of their time, and come well prepared. When you ask for someone's time, be specific. Say, 'I'd like 30 minutes of your time', and then stick to it. Don't outstay your welcome. Whenever you meet with someone, always be thinking, 'Is there something I can do to help this person?' Create a win-win situation.

Coming on too strong

Networking is not about selling something to someone who doesn't want it. You are looking for opportunities to create a mutual relationship, where there is give and take. In order for networking to be successful, you have to be interested in developing a long-term relationship. Remind yourself that your focus is on relationship building, not on immediate results.

Not coming on strongly enough

You put yourself in networking situations, but never talk about your needs or interests. This may be because you are not clear enough about why you are networking, or you are networking for reasons that are not particularly important to you. Go back to step one and think about what you are doing and why.

RECOMMENDED LINKS

City Women's Network:
www.networking-cwn.co.uk
Networking People UK:
www.npuk.com

SEE ALSO

Assessing Your Entrepreneurial Profile: Do You Have What It Takes? (p. 6)

REFINING AND PROTECTING YOUR IDEA

Profiling Your Target Market

GETTING STARTED

Before your business can realistically or effectively begin a marketing campaign, you'll need to be able to answer two vital questions: who is your target market, and what does your target market want or need that your business can provide?

Without detailed and precise answers to these questions you won't be able to define your marketing strategy, or implement an effective sales and marketing plan.

It's worth recalling the classic tale of two shoe sales representatives out exploring opportunities in a country in which their company had yet to establish a market. The first sales representative sent back an initial report saying, 'everyone goes barefoot in this country, no market here at all'. The second sales representative's report, however, was somewhat different: 'everyone goes barefoot, massive opportunity for us'. Who was right?

This illustrates the necessity for any business to understand accurately the needs of its target customers, in terms of knowing enough about them and gathering sufficient information about what they really want. Without this precise understanding your efforts to market your goods and services won't be effective.

FAQS

How do I identify my target customers?

Your first job when profiling a target market is to be able to identify precisely who your audience is. Can you accurately describe the characteristics of your ideal customers? Which clients currently spend the most with you? Why do they do this? If you don't know the answers, you need to find out.

You'll probably already have a good idea about the groups of people or types of businesses that you think you can sell your service to. For individual customers this might be people of a certain age, gender, socio-economic status, occupation, or a group with common or special interests such as sports or hobbies. For business customers these might be located in a specific area, or in a particular sector, or could have similarities in terms of the customer groups they sell to.

Your aim should be to concentrate your marketing on these groups of people, businesses, or existing customers who are most likely to buy your product or service. Doing this in the most profitable way takes experience, but you may find useful advice in the book *Targeting Profitable Customers: How to Do It, How to Profit from It* by Malcolm McDonald and Ian Dunbar, published by Palgrave Macmillan.

Once you have identified this target group of people or businesses, you'll have completed the first step in profiling your market and now have your list of target prospects—your ideal customers.

Is it about quality or quantity of prospects?

A precision-driven marketing approach—where you have a high-quality list of prospective clients or leads—will, pound-for-pound of marketing spend, prove far more productive and profitable than an untargeted blanket approach to generate sales.

Quality of leads, based on your understanding, knowledge, and careful profiling of your customers and their needs, will massively increase your ability to convert them into sales.

MAKING IT HAPPEN

Pinpoint what your customers and prospects need or want

Having selected your ideal customer groups you'll now need to be absolutely clear about what they want and need, and exactly what it is that you are going to offer them. This understanding will enable you to develop the specific marketing message and proposition that will most effectively sell the benefits of your product or service to them.

If you get these messages wrong then it's almost certain that your marketing efforts will fail, as your customers will buy from your competitors instead. Your product, service, or business proposition will have missed the target completely.

Speak to target customers before developing your marketing strategy

Before you start to develop or choose your marketing strategy it's always worthwhile to speak first to a sample from your target audience. By doing this you'll be able to check that your profile of your intended market has been the right one, and test your assumptions about what you think they want and why they could buy from you.

You could do this by speaking directly to a group of people or you could undertake a survey in the form of a questionnaire which can be posted to a sample of target customers. Alternatively, you could talk to passers-by in a location that is frequented by your ideal customers.

Don't forget that you could also speak to your existing clients or, even better, clients of your competitors if that is possible.

Double check that your marketing message is right for your target market

Once you have spoken to a sample of your target market and you are satisfied that you have confirmed your assumptions about their needs, you'll be in a position to create or adapt a marketing proposition to sell the benefits of your product or service to that audience. After you have established the basic proposition, consider carefully whether there is anything further that will make your marketing message even more appealing. Will these communications convince them that your service can provide the benefits that meet their exact needs?

Check that your list of prospects is as precise as possible

Your prospects list will only be of real use in your marketing campaign if it accurately reflects the profile of the audiences you are targeting. Have the consumers of your product or service been identified in terms of their geographic and demographic profile, their employment status, profession, special interests, membership of clubs, and so on? Have you compiled a list of your business targets in terms of where they are located, their size, names of the main buyer, repeat purchase rate? Have you identified the best sales channels to enable you to reach these target customers?

Your sales efforts can only be as good as the list of prospects you have selected in your target markets, and that list must reflect the profile of the audience you are developing your marketing proposition to reach.

Be sure that you are giving them what they want

With a thorough understanding of the needs of your ideal customers, you should then strive to create an offering and proposition based on four criteria that will give them a product or service that is:

- exactly what they want from you
- precisely when they need it
- in a way that is convenient for them
- at a price they can afford and are prepared to pay

If you are not convinced that your sales proposition meets all of these criteria, then you'll need to study the profile of your customers again and revise your offering.

WHAT TO AVOID
Failing to test

The most common mistakes made when targeting products and services towards specific users or customer groups are caused by not testing the assumptions you have made about your audience. You'll waste valuable time and marketing budget if you launch a campaign towards an audience when you have not accurately identified who those customers are, and cannot precisely define what they want, and why they could buy from you instead of your competitors.

Lack of focus

Do not buy into a list of unknown prospects, no matter how attractive it seems to get names of thousands of people you can blanket sell to in the short term.

Find out who they are, where they are located, and test your assumptions about what you believe they want. By testing, you can either confirm that your profiling was right, or you can adjust your offering until you get it right. Being precise will lead to more sales more quickly, and more profit over the longer term. One book you might find helpful when learning to sharpen your focus is *The Discipline of Market Leaders: Choose Your Customers, Narrow your Focus, Dominate Your Market* by Michael Treacy and Fred Wiersma, published by Perseus Books.

RECOMMENDED LINKS
Business Link:
www.businesslink.org
Chartered Institute of Marketing:
www.cim.co.uk
Internet marketing:
www.it-advice.org

SEE ALSO
Coming Up with a Business Idea (p. 13)
Deciding Whether to Start a Business (p. 2)
Market Research and Competitor Intelligence (p. 526)

Developing and Protecting an Invention

GETTING STARTED

A new invention is often the starting point for a successful business, but the journey from an idea or prototype to a product on a store shelf can be long and difficult. This actionlist looks at the steps involved in this journey, from the protection of the idea, to the financing and marketing of the final product.

FAQS

How can I tell if my invention will sell?

If your invention exists only as a sketch, simple model, or even just an idea, your first step is to express this in concrete form. This could be a proper set of manufacturing drawings or a scale model that can be shown and demonstrated to others while you fully research your idea and evaluate its commercial potential.

To succeed in the market, your product must solve a problem for the purchaser in an original and cost-effective way. Your research and evaluation phase has to achieve four main aims, each of which has spin-off benefits. You must prove that your product is original and demonstrably better than competing products, so that it can be protected with a patent. You must also show that it is marketable, in order to attract venture capital and interest retailers. You must demonstrate that your product can be made, and that the cost and quality of the component parts allow the product to be produced economically. Finally, you must ensure that your product offers a unique selling proposition, and that the scope and cost of reaching the target market is affordable.

How do I prove that my product is original?

You have ownership rights to your original creation that allow you to exploit it commercially but, unlike copyright on a book, song, or work of art, these rights are not automatic and must be secured by registration. This means filing a patent claim for your new product. (Remember that it is the actual product that is protected, not the original idea.) You may need the services of a patent lawyer to assist with a search of previous patents and help you register your patent.

How do I show that my product is marketable?

Appropriate market research is essential. You will probably need to carry out qualitative and quantitative research to get an idea of the value and potential of your product in the market. You could try this on your own. Alternatively, if you can afford it, get a market research agency to draw up survey questions from your input.

Qualitative research should show you what people think of your idea or product— its visual appeal, its practicality, and its perceived acceptability. It should also show what people perceive your product as lacking, and what improvements they think need to be made. Other questions can be directed at finding suitable names, colours, shape, pack sizes, and an acceptable price range for the product. Remember that the comments and answers you get do not necessarily indicate how well your product will sell; this may depend upon other factors, such as competitive activity or unexpected fashion trends.

Quantitative research evaluates the sales potential of your product: how many people would buy it; how different pricing levels would affect projected sales; whether there would be demand for different versions of the product, and so on.

How do I demonstrate that my product can be made?

This may require the services of a professional designer or engineer to perform a component analysis, and to set optimum specifications and quality levels for every part of the product. Other aspects to be determined are the availability and price stability of raw materials, the labour costs and skill required, and the factory or workshop location.

Do I have a unique selling proposition?

The unique selling proposition (USP) is what puts your product ahead of a competitive field, and is a key aspect of your marketing plan. The truly unique feature of your idea can make your product the most desirable in the marketplace, and become the lynchpin of a successful advertising campaign.

Having decided on your product's USP, you should draw up your marketing plan. The plan should include your thoughts on distribution. You need to decide whether the product is a consumer product, or for businesses. Think about whether it will be sold regionally, nationally, or internationally, through direct, retail, or wholesale methods. Also consider whether you will use your own transport to deliver it or use outside carriers.

Packaging is an important part of your marketing plan. Decide what you will call the product. Consider whether the packaging needs to be suitable for display purposes, whether the produce will be disposable or returnable, and whether packaging regulations might affect your product.

Two other important factors are advertising and promotion. Think about which media will be the most appropriate for advertising: newspapers, magazines, pamphlets, direct mail, the Internet, posters, radio, television, or point-of-sale material. Consider whether you could use exhibitions and trade fairs, and whether you have your own sales force or use agents.

Price is an important consideration, and you need to consider what sales volumes you can expect at different price levels, and how different volumes and prices would affect cash flow. You might need to think about making promotional offers.

Where can I go to for more information?

The Institute of Inventors is an inventors' club run by professional engineers. It helps private inventors to evaluate new ideas, gadgets, and inventions, as well as assisting with prototype drawings and development, patent specification, drawings and applications, and licensing of intellectual property.

The Institute of Patentees and Inventors campaigns on behalf of its members and inventors in general, and is recognised as an advocate for the invention process and the fair treatment of inventors. The Innovation Relay Centre Gateway is a European source for innovative technologies or new technology solutions run for people wanting to market your innovation, looking for new technologies to exploit, or searching for an innovative solution to a technology need.

The Innovators' Club is a programme providing practical assistance to business people with the task of driving innovative practices in their organisation or using innovation to take an idea to the market place. The programme is managed by Potential Development Ltd and supported by the Department of Trade and Industry, the Confederation of Business and Industry, the Chartered Institute of Marketing, the Chartered Institute of Management Accountants, the Design Council, the Patent Office, and the SBS/Business Link network.

The websites for all these organisations are given below.

MAKING IT HAPPEN
Choose the next step

Once the research has shown a potential market for your product, you have several options available: you could choose to manufacture and market your invention yourself; you could outsource production, but distribute and market the product yourself; you could merge your production, sales, and marketing with an established partner; or you could license the rights to the invention for others to make and market it.

If you go for any of the first three options, the deciding factor will be your own level of management expertise. If your planned business is small, you will need to decide if you have sufficient skills in manufacture, marketing, and distribution, and the time to give each area the attention it needs. The last option of licensing to others may well be the preferable one if your real interest is in developing new ideas and innovations.

Develop your business plan

Your invention may have too much scope for you fully to exploit its potential on your own. Or you may feel you do not have the depth of specialised knowledge and skills to develop all the individual aspects of a successful business plan—management, finance, manufacture, marketing, sales, and distribution—without professional aid, but do not wish to consider a partnership or merger at this stage. Additionally, your potential investors will more easily be persuaded to fund a well-structured business venture that presents an attractive and totally developed plan to them.

There are agencies that will help you develop your investment proposition to its full potential before presenting it to their investors. They can also provide management support for the start up of your operation from their pool of proven specialist managers; skilled management is often a requirement imposed by investors to ensure the success of the business. Government business support agencies provide specialist help and advice for individuals and businesses with a good product idea, or who are seeking technical advice and financial support for product design and development. Initial consultations are usually free and other services may be offered at a subsidised cost. The four national business support networks are Business Link (England), Business Gateway (Scotland), Business Eye (Wales), and Invest Northern Ireland. Website addresses are given below.

Raise capital

The three main options open to you are private equity, a business loan from a bank, and venture capital. In some cases, there may be the further possibility of a government grant.

WHAT TO AVOID ✘
Talking too early about your invention

Do not describe your invention to anyone before filing a patent application. If you really need to discuss your invention with others before filing, always get them to sign a confidentiality agreement.

Not considering the options

Remember the objective is to maximise the revenue from your invention. Consider the option of simply licensing your design to others; this could save you a lot of expense.

RECOMMENDED LINKS

Innovation Relay Centres (Innovation in Practice link):
www.cordis.lu
Innovators' Club:
www.theinnovatorsclub.co.uk
Institute of Inventors:
www.newgadgets.freeserve.co.uk
Institute of Patentees and Inventors:
www.invent.org.uk
Patent Office:
www.patent.gov.uk
World Intellectual Property Organization (WIPO):
www.wipo.org

SEE ALSO
Applying for a Patent (p. 29)
Coming Up with a Business Idea (p. 13)
Intellectual Property (p. 518)
Registering a Trade Mark (p. 39)

An Introduction to Intellectual Property

GETTING STARTED

Intellectual property (IP) enables people to own their creativity and innovation in the same way that they can own physical property. The owner of IP can control, and be rewarded for, its use. The four main types of IP are patents for inventions, trade marks for brand identity, designs for product appearance, and copyright for written material and artistic works. This actionlist gives an overview of each of these rights and briefly describes how to obtain them.

FAQS

What do I need to know?

Owners of intellectual property (IP) have the right to benefit from it, sell it, hire it, or license it out. IP is quite easy for other people to steal or use without permission, so IP law has been developed to define the rights of IP owners and provide them with the ability to protect their rights and defend them through legal action. Some of these rights apply automatically, while others require a registration process to become legally enforceable. It is almost always necessary to register before disclosing your IP concept to others, or your rights will not exist. The Patent Office is the government agency responsible for administering the UK IP rights system.

MAKING IT HAPPEN

Patents

A patent gives an inventor the right, for a limited period, to stop others from making, using, or selling an invention without his or her permission. Patent rights are specific to the country they are granted in. Patent rights last for up to 20 years in the United Kingdom.

See the actionlist 'Applying for a Patent' for full information on how to do what, and when.

Copyright

Copyright is an automatic right that protects the way an original idea is expressed in a piece of work, and is relevant to any business that produces original literature, drama, music, publications, films, videos, or broadcasts.

Copyright for artistic, dramatic, literary, and musical works originating within the European Union lasts for 70 years after the author's death. The owner can control how the work is exploited, including copying, adaptation, public performance, broadcasting, and public distribution, and can transfer ownership of copyright to someone else. Some unlicensed use of a copyright work is allowed under a concept known as Fair Dealing. This includes limited photocopying and quotation of extracts for teaching or review purposes.

Copyright comes into effect immediately, as soon as something is created and recorded in some way. Marking your work with the copyright symbol © followed by your name and the date is not legally required in the United Kingdom and most other countries but may help should there be any infringement proceedings. Providing evidence that you created the work at a particular time is also a useful precaution. A number of private companies operate unofficial registers, but you should check carefully what you will be paying for before engaging their services.

Design

There are two levels of design right, unregistered and registered. Unregistered design right is automatically owned by the designer (unless the design was commissioned). It provides protection for purely functional, three-dimensional designs, and only protects their shape and configuration. (Two-dimensional designs are covered by copyright.) Unregistered design right protects for a maximum period of 15 years, depending on when the product comes to market. It must be an original design to qualify; one that has not been used or sold before in its specific design sector. Recorded evidence may be required to prove the commencement date of the design right.

You can give your design increased legal protection by registering it through the Design Registry within the Patent Office. Design registration enables you to stop others from making, using, importing, or selling articles to which the design has been applied, for a period of five years. This can be extended at five-year intervals up to 25 years maximum from the date of filing. A renewal fee is required each time. To qualify for registration, your design must be novel, that is, materially different from any other previously published design. Registering a design is usually done through a patent agent, and involves submitting your design along with an application form and filing fee.

Design registration protects the appearance of all, or part of an industrially produced product, in particular its outward shape, colours, texture, construction materials, and its ornamentation. A design must be registered under a particular category of manufactured product, for example, a clock or a coffee pot. A design does not need to have aesthetic qualities to be registered. Some designs can't be registered. Generally, these will be designs where copyright protection applies instead, such as sculptures or calendars.

European Community design regulation provides two additional rights: registered Community design right, similar to a UK registered design, which applies across the whole Community from a single application to the Office for Harmonization in the Internal Market (OHIM); and unregistered Community design right, which protects the same type of designs from copying for three years from first disclosure, without the need for registration.

Trade marks

A trade mark is a distinctive symbol that makes a business's goods and services immediately recognisable. The Trade Marks Act 1994 defines a trade mark as 'any sign that is capable of being represented graphically, capable of distinguishing goods or services of one undertaking from those of another undertaking'. Signs that can be represented graphically include a marking such as words, letters, and numerals, the shape of the goods or their packaging, and musical jingles (or even smells).

Registration of a mark is not compulsory, but by registering a trade mark, your business gets the right to prevent others from using an identical or confusingly similar mark on goods and services that are the same (or similar) to your own. Before making your application, search the Trade Mark Register at the Patent Office (also available on the Patent Office's website) for existing marks that might prevent your mark from being registered. Alternatively, on application, the Search and Advisory Service will ensure that a new mark fulfils the correct criteria. To make an application, a form must be completed and sent with the fee to the Trade Marks Registry. Applications can be made by an individual or by a trade mark agent.

Protection lasts for 10 years from the date of registration, and can be renewed every 10 years, for a fee. Once a mark has been registered, no changes can be made to the mark itself (except in a few circumstances), so it is important that the description submitted is clear and correct. A third party can request a mark's removal from the register if it has not been used for five years. The Madrid Protocol provides for international registration of trade marks through the World Intellectual Property Organization (WIPO). An application for registration can be made to the Office for Harmonization in the Internal Market. Registration prevents the use of identical or similar marks by other firms anywhere in the European Union.

Moral rights

The Copyright, Designs, and Patents Act 1988 gives additional protection to creative people through the introduction of moral rights. These include: the right of an author/director to be identified as such whenever a work is used by someone else;

the right of authors not to have their works altered in a way that may prejudice their reputation or honour; preventing false statements being made about the true authorship or directorship of works; and the right to privacy (a person who has commissioned photographs or film of themselves can control the number of copies made public).

 WHAT TO AVOID

Not keeping records
Mark your products as protected, and keep records of the design and (if applicable) the registration process. This will strengthen any case should registration be challenged or design rights infringed.

Not taking out insurance
It is a good idea to take out insurance against the cost of bringing legal action for infringement of rights.

RECOMMENDED LINKS
British Copyright Council:
www.britishcopyright.org.uk
Chartered Institute of Patent Agents:
www.cipa.org.uk
Design and Artists Copyright Society:
www.dacs.co.uk
European Patent Office:
www.european-patent-office.org
Institute of Trade Mark Attorneys:
www.itma.org.uk
Office for Harmonization in the Internal Market (Trade Marks and Designs):
www.oami.eu.int
Patent Office:
www.patent.gov.uk
World Intellectual Property Organization (Small and Medium-Sized Enterprises Division):
www.wipo.int/sme/en/index.html

SEE ALSO
Intellectual Property (p. 518)

Applying for a Patent

GETTING STARTED

Patents are granted by the Patent Office to inventors, giving them the right to prevent exploitation of their inventions by others. The full process of patenting a new invention is expensive and requires the services of a professional patent agent. You need to be very sure of the commercial viability of your idea before you go ahead with the full process.

You can obtain a useful period (one year) of protection at minimal cost just by filing an initial application. This has two advantages:

- it allows you to discuss the full details of your invention with others (for example, with possible financial backers or purchasers)
- it allows you time to investigate the marketability of your idea before committing yourself to the expense of the full process

This actionlist explains the steps to follow to lodge both an initial and a full patent application.

FAQS

What can be patented?

Your invention must meet four requirements before you can apply for a patent:

1. It must be new. This means that information about the invention must not have been previously published (even by you). So you are not allowed to make any public disclosure in any way at all before making your application to the Patent Office.

2. It must have an inventive step. It may not simply be an obvious modification of an existing piece of equipment or process.

3. It must be industrially applicable. Your invention must be made or used in some kind of industry, in the form of a new machine, product, or manufacturing process.

4. It must not be on the excluded list. This list includes scientific theories and mathematical methods, animal and plant varieties, and works of art or literature.

What rights do I have as the patent holder?

You own your invention. Like any other form of property you own, you may sell it or rent it out. However, patents are territorial rights only. Protection is limited to the countries to which the patent application extends.

What is an 'initial application' and what protection does it give?

To obtain a patent you must first lodge an application at the Patent Office. They then allocate a patent application number to you. You may now say 'patent pending' or 'patent applied for' in relation to your invention. This gives you precedence over patent applications for similar inventions should they be lodged later by others.

Additionally, you are free to disclose publicly whatever information you have lodged at the Patent Office without affecting the validity of any subsequent patent that is granted to you. If 12 months have elapsed from the date when your documentation was received by the Patent Office and you have taken no further steps, this initial application is terminated. You may still file another new application at this stage to restart the patenting process, should you wish.

What should I do before making an application?

It's a good idea to research past and recent work in your area of technology on the Patent Office website (see below), where you can review more than 30 million patents from all countries. You should also perform a patent search to avoid wasting time and money trying to patent an existing invention. You can attempt this yourself on the Patent Office website, but it will be far more effective to use the services of a professional patent searcher. The Patent Office's Search and Advisory Service can perform a commercial patent search. Try looking through several previous applications as well, to get a good idea of what a well prepared patent application should contain.

MAKING IT HAPPEN
File an initial application
This is a very straightforward procedure and one you can easily complete yourself. Your only cost is the time taken to prepare a suitable description of your invention. Should you not feel confident in taking the do-it-yourself approach (perhaps you have a particularly complex invention to describe), you can use a professional patent agent, who will charge a fee based on the complexity of the application. Your application needs to include just two items:

1. A 'request for grant of a patent', made on Form 1/77. You get this form from the Patent Office and it contains comprehensive instructions. You must provide a brief title for the invention, your name and address, and details of any patent agents you have used. As your application is for an initial filing, you can bypass the sections dealing with earlier applications and declaration of priority.

2. Two copies of a written description ('specification') of your invention. Bear in mind the following when you write the description:

- The description of your invention has to be fully comprehensive.
- Always include all the features that may be incorporated, even if you are not yet sure about them. They can easily be deleted at a later time, whereas you are not allowed to add any additional technical details or improvements to your application after the filing date. Difficulties will occur afterwards if any critical features are not mentioned in the initial application.

- Describe the advantages of your invention versus the disadvantages of previously known products or processes.
- State all the ways you can think of in which your invention can be used or applied.
- Give a more detailed description (as an example only) of one particular way in which your invention can be put into practice.
- Your written description should be able to stand alone in providing a clear summary of all aspects of your invention, but it is always a good idea to supplement it with drawings of any parts and equipment incorporated. Clear freehand pencil sketches are fine for this purpose.
- Working models are neither required nor accepted by the Patent Office.

Steps to complete the full patent application
It normally takes about four years from the initial filing date to obtain a granted United Kingdom patent. During this period, there are procedures to be completed by certain times after the initial filing date. These include extensive legal and technical requirements, so a chartered patent agent normally carries out the procedures on your behalf. Patent agent fees can be high, but by appointing a professional you can be assured that your patent is made as secure as possible.

Within 12 months
You have 12 months from the date of filing to develop your invention and look into its commercial viability. If you decide to pursue your application for a full patent, you will need to file further information by that time. This includes a set of 'claims', an abstract that will give a brief summary of the invention, and a request for a search (with a fee payable). The Patent Office will conduct a search of earlier patents and technical journals in the relevant technology, to determine if the alleged invention is both novel and inventive as claimed.

Within 18 months

The application will be published 18 months after the first filing date (sooner if requested). This makes public notice that you are seeking certain rights in relation to your invention. From this day onwards, if anyone tries to copy your invention, damages can be sought for any infringement of the technology occurring—provided the patent is eventually granted.

Publishing the application before granting it gives third parties the opportunity to read about your invention. Should they feel it is not worthy of being granted a patent, they can write to the Patent Office explaining why they think it is not a 'patentable' invention.

Within two years

You must request a detailed examination of your invention by filling in Form 10/77. This also has to be accompanied by the required fee.

Within about another 12 months, the Patent Office will carry out a detailed examination. The Examiners consider the citations found during the earlier search and any more which have come to light since. They may request you to disclaim any features in your application that are not novel or inventive or otherwise not meeting criteria for a patent. If they then agree that, after these exclusions, what remains of your invention is both novel and inventive, your patent will be granted. Your application will be republished as granted and you will be issued with a certificate.

WHAT TO AVOID
Talking too early about your invention

Don't tell anyone about your invention before filing an application. If you really have to discuss your invention with others before filing, always use confidentiality agreements.

Not seeking the right advice

Basic advice from the Chartered Institute of Patent Agents (CIPA) is freely available at their clinics throughout the United Kingdom. Full details can be found on the CIPA website (see below). The CIPA website also provides a searchable directory of patent agents by geographical area. Before using the services of any agent, you should check their qualifications and reputation. If patents are key to your business, you may wish to make use of a patent watching service. This will report on the patent activities of your competitors, as well as all other activity in your field in foreign countries.

Worrying that the whole process is taking too long

There is a 'fast track' procedure available whereby the whole process from initial filing to grant can be achieved within 18 months. This will require a full patent specification from the outset, so you will have to be prepared to pay patent agent fees up front.

RECOMMENDED LINKS

Chartered Institute of Patent Agents:
www.cipa.org.uk
Copyright Directorate:
www.intellectual-property.gov.uk
European Patent Office:
www.european-patent-office.org
Institute of Inventors:
www.newgadgets.freeserve.co.uk
Patent Office:
www.patent.gov.uk

SEE ALSO
Developing and Protecting an Invention (p. 23)
Intellectual Property (p. 518)

Using Copyright to Protect Your Work

GETTING STARTED

Copyright is an automatic right that protects the way an original idea is expressed in a piece of work. It is relevant to any business that produces original literature, drama, music, publications, films, videos, or broadcasts. There are no forms to fill in and no fees to pay, but copyright gives the creator or first owner of any original work the legal right to control how this material may be used.

This actionlist explains the principle of copyright and how you can use it to protect your original material. It also gives guidelines on what to do if you think your copyright is being infringed.

FAQS

What is the purpose of copyright?

Copyright helps creators to gain economic rewards for their efforts and encourages future creativity. It gives rights to creators of certain kinds of material to control the ways in which their material may be used. The rights broadly cover: copying and adapting the work; issuing, renting, and lending copies to the public; performing the work in public; or broadcasting the work. In many cases, the creator will also have the right to be identified on the work. The creator will decide how to exploit the work and how to enforce his or her copyright. He or she can also benefit by selling or agreeing a transfer of copyright to someone else. Without protection, it could be very easy for others to exploit material without paying the creator.

Who owns copyright?

In the case of a written, dramatic, musical, or other artistic work, the person who created the work is the first owner of the economic rights under copyright. This rule also applies to commissioned works. However, where a work is created during employment, the employer is the first owner of these rights, unless an agreement has been made between the employee and employer indicating otherwise.

Copyright, like physical property, can be bought or sold, inherited, or transferred to another person in another way, for example, as a gift. So some or all of the economic rights may later belong to someone other than the first owner.

What laws enforce copyright?

United Kingdom legislation is based on the Copyright, Designs and Patents Act 1988, which defines copyright as a property right which can be given away, licensed, or sold. There are several other major pieces of legislation that add to the scope and detail of the 1988 Act.

The Copyright (Computer Programs) Regulations 1992 extends the definition of literary work to include design material for programs, allows some back-up copying of licensed software, and provides for limited 'decompiling' of licensed programs to make them work with other programs. The Copyright and Rights in Database Regulations 1997 determines the circumstances for copyright protection to apply to databases.

The Duration of Copyright and Rights in Performances Regulations 1995 harmonises the copyright and related rights across member states of the European Union, and the Copyright and Related Rights Regulations 1996 implements European Union Directives on rental, lending, and other rights in the copyright field, and on copyright and related rights in relation to cable and satellite broadcasting.

An EC directive on Copyright and Related Rights in the Information Society came into force on 9 April 2001. The directive harmonises the rights for the use of copyright material in e-commerce (that is the rights of copying and electronic transmission) and will be transposed into UK law during 2003.

The Broadcasting Acts 1990 and 1996 made certain changes to the 1988 Act, particularly in introducing a statutory licence for broadcasting of sound recordings where copyright owners license this use collectively.

What kind of work does copyright protect?

This includes original literary, dramatic, and artistic works, original music, and published editions of works (that is, the style and layout of a publication). Sound recordings on any medium—which can also include recordings of other copyright works, films, and videos—and broadcasts and cable programmes are also protected.

How does copyright apply to the Internet?

Under UK law, copyright material available over the Internet will generally be protected in the same way as material in other media. Generally, it is a good idea to mark each page you put on a website with the international © mark, followed by the name of the copyright owner and year of publication. You could also include information on your website about allowing others to use your copyright material without permission.

Websites are accessible from all over the world. If material on your website is used without your permission, you would probably need to take action for copyright infringement in the location where the infringement occurs.

MAKING IT HAPPEN
Ensure copyright protection

There is no official register for copyright (unlike patents, registered designs, or trademarks). You don't actually need to take any action for your copyright to be protected. There are no application forms to fill in or fees to pay. Copyright comes into effect immediately, as soon as something is created and recorded in some way, for example, on paper, on film, as a sound recording, or on the Internet.

It is a good idea, however, to mark your work with the copyright symbol ©, followed by your name and the date, to warn others against copying it. While this is not legally required in the United Kingdom and most other countries, marking in this way may help you during infringement proceedings. Take steps to provide evidence that you created the work at a particular time. For example, a copy of your work could be deposited with a bank or solicitor. Alternatively, send yourself a copy by special delivery, leaving the envelope unopened when you receive it.

A number of private companies operate unofficial registers, but check carefully what you will be paying for. Using one of these options does not prove that a work is original or created by you. However, it might be useful to be able to show that the work was in your possession at a particular date, for example if someone else claims that you have copied something of theirs that was actually created after your work.

'Fair dealing'

One of the exceptions to copyright protection is the concept of 'fair dealing'; this allows some unlicensed copying and other use without infringing copyright. Some copyright works may be used (photocopied, for example) to a limited extent, for research and private study, even if for commercial ends (except where work is a database). Making single copies of short extracts of a work or a single article from a journal may count as fair dealing. Copying by someone other than a researcher or student is not allowed if copies will be given to more than one person at the same time for the same purpose, for example, for a training session.

The economic impact of the use on the copyright owner is an important factor that the courts consider when deciding whether use is fair dealing.

License your copyright

As a copyright owner, it is for you to decide whether and how to license use of your work. An exclusive licence could be granted, which enables the licensee to use the copyright work to the exclusion of all others, including you, the copyright owner. A licence can be limited, for example, in duration, or in any other way. It is a contractual agreement between the copyright owner and user.

There are various organisations that can license certain uses of your work on your behalf, for example, the Performing Rights Society. Collective licensing means that a user may be offered a licence covering use of all the works covered by the collecting society.

Enforce your rights

Copyright is essentially a private right, so it is up to you how you decide to enforce it. It is sensible to try to resolve the matter with the party you think has infringed your copyright without resorting to official proceedings. If you are unable do this, you might have to go to court. Courts may grant a range of remedies, such as injunctions (to stop the other person making use of the material), damages for infringement, or orders to produce infringing goods. In some cases it may be necessary to demonstrate to the court that you have tried to solve the matter by mediation or arbitration if you wish the court to consider awarding you the best available remedy, including an award covering your costs. If you decide to go ahead with legal action you must get some professional advice, as this is a particularly complicated area of law. One of the many organisations representing copyright owners may also be able to give you advice, or sometimes act on your behalf if you are a member.

Deliberate infringement of copyright can be considered a criminal offence. If it is on a large scale, for example, pirate or counterfeit copies of compact discs, then you should inform either the police or your local trading standards department. They can decide whether action, including potential prosecution, is justified. If the police or trading standards decide not to take any action, you could still consider a private criminal prosecution if you believe there is a criminal offence, and you can still pursue a civil action against the alleged infringer.

Other ways of protecting your product

Copyright does not protect ideas. Although the work itself may be protected, the idea behind it is not. To protect an original idea, you will need to obtain a patent, which is a fairly complicated procedure. Names, titles, slogans, or phrases are also not protected by copyright; however, these could possibly be registered as a trade mark.

Copyright may protect the drawing from which an article is made, but it can not prevent the manufacture of purely industrial articles. However, articles that are replicated by an industrial process but which are of an aesthetically pleasing appearance may be protected by copyright where the article itself is an artistic work. This includes sculptures as well as works of artistic craftsmanship. Where it is possible to obtain a registered design for such articles, the copyright term will be reduced to match the term of protection for registered designs.

Protect your material overseas

Copyright material is protected in most other countries. The United Kingdom is a member of several international conventions in this field, including the Berne Convention for the Protection of Literary and Artistic Works, and the Universal Copyright Convention (UCC). Copyright material created by UK nationals or residents is protected in each member country of the conventions by the national law of that country. Most countries belong to at least one of the conventions, including all the Western European countries, the United States, and Russia. A full list of the conventions and their member countries may be obtained from the Copyright Directorate at the Patent Office.

In order to benefit from the automatic protection in other countries arising from the UCC you must mark your work with the international © symbol, followed by the name of the copyright owner and year of publication. Protection overseas can also arise from obligations in the agreement on Trade-Related Aspects of Intellectual Property Rights (TRIPS), which forms part of the World Trade Organization (WTO)

Agreement. Once again, this is automatic so you may also find your work is protected in WTO countries.

WHAT TO AVOID
Not keeping records
It is essential to keep records showing the date and author of any work produced in which copyright exists.

Failing to negotiate fair limits for copying needs
Check with trade associations or professional bodies to ensure that fair limits have been negotiated for typical copying needs within the type of business you are dealing with.

Not using the copyright symbol
Marking with a copyright symbol ©, followed by the copyright owner's name and year of publication is not required by UK law, but it can deter infringement. It may also be needed for protection overseas.

RECOMMENDED LINKS
Alliance Against Counterfeiting and
  Piracy:
www.aacp.co.uk
British Copyright Council:
www.editor.net/bcc
Copyright Directorate:
www.intellectual-property.gov.uk
Copyright Licensing Agency:
www.cla.co.uk
Federation Against Software Theft:
www.fast.org.uk
Patent Office:
www.patent.gov.uk

SEE ALSO
**Complying with the Copyright of Others
  (p. 36)**
Intellectual Property (p. 518)

Complying with the Copyright of Others

GETTING STARTED

If your business uses articles, literature, music, or other published work in producing goods or providing services, you may be at risk of contravening the copyright on that work. This actionlist outlines the types of published work that are protected by copyright, and gives guidance on how they may be used in compliance with copyright legislation. All small businesses need to be aware of these issues, as non-compliance can lead to a fine or even imprisonment.

FAQS

What kinds of material do you need permission to use?

Copyright protects various types of works. Any original literary works, for example, books, training materials, computer programs, song lyrics, newspaper articles, and some types of databases, are all protected by copyright. So too are original dramatic works, including dance or mime, and original music. Original artistic works, for example, paintings, engravings, photographs, sculptures, architectural designs, technical drawings, diagrams, maps, and logos are also protected, as are published editions of works (that is, the style and lay-out of a publication). Sound recordings on any medium, for example, tape or compact disc, are protected, and this can also include recordings of other copyright works. Finally, films and videos, and broadcasts and cable programmes also come under the protection of copyright. You will need to get permission from the owner of the copyright to use this material or any part of it unless it is subject to a copyright exception (see below).

When do you need permission?

In the majority of cases where you are intending to copy or use copyright material, you need to obtain permission from the copyright owner. If you are copying large amounts of material and/or making multiple copies, it is likely that you will need permission.

You must remember that buying or owning an original or a copy of a copyright work doesn't grant you permission to use it any way you wish. For example, buying a copy of a book, compact disc, video, or computer program does not necessarily give you the right to make copies (even for private use). Also, you will not necessarily have the right to play or show them in public. Other uses of copyright material, such as photocopying, scanning, or downloading from a CD-ROM or online database, all involve copying the work, so permission is generally needed.

However, there are certain exceptions to copyright. 'Fair dealing' is a concept that allows some unlicensed copying and other use without infringing copyright. Some copyright works may be copied (photo-copied, for example) to a limited extent for research and private study without infringing copyright, even if this is for commercial ends. The exception to this is where the work you are copying is from a database. Making single copies of short extracts of a work or a single article from a journal may count as fair dealing, too.

Other copyright exceptions exist, for example, where a work is accidentally included in an artistic work, sound recording, film broadcast, or cable programme. You can find out more about copyright exceptions by visiting the government's intellectual property website (address given below).

Do I need permission to use material published on the Internet?

If you wish to put copyright material on the Internet, or distribute or download material that others have placed on the Internet, you should ensure that you have the permission of the copyright owners.

MAKING IT HAPPEN
Check that permission is required
Your first step is to approach the copyright owner to find out whether you need his or her permission to use the work. This can either be done directly, by going straight to the owner, or you can also make enquiries via one of the various copyright licensing bodies, if the owner belongs to one of them.

It is more usual to approach the copyright owner directly and ask for a licence to cover the use you require. The licence is a contract between you and the copyright owner and you can negotiate the terms and conditions, including the way the work is to be used and the cost of licence. There are no rules in copyright law governing what are acceptable terms and conditions.

Sometimes copyright owners are members of collective licensing bodies who can be approached for a licence. In particular, collective bodies exist for licensing the use of music and sound recordings, printed material, artistic works and characters, broadcast material, films, and television listings. More information about these licensing bodies is given in the next section.

The main collective licensing bodies
One of the major issuers of copyright licences is the Copyright Licensing Agency (CLA). This is a non-profit making agency that licenses organisations for photocopying and scanning.

It licenses business, education, and government copying of extracts from books, journals, and periodicals. It also pays authors and publishers their share of fees. Licences include, for example, copying one book chapter or one article (under 30 pages) from a periodical, copying up to 5% of a law report, or making up to nine photocopies of extracts from books, journals, or periodicals. There are also licences for copies from published originals (not from faxed or photocopied books, journals, or periodicals) and the supply of copies to colleagues and those outside the organisation working together on related matters.

It is important to remember that copies made under the licence cannot be sold. If you need to exceed the limits of your licence, the CLA Rapid Clearance Service (CLARCS) generally allows you to pay for extra permissions.

The CLA's licensed works include all books, periodicals, and journals published in the United Kingdom and other countries where a reciprocal agreement exists. However, there are exceptions. These include works on the Excluded Works List (this list can be found on the CLA website, the address of which is given below), newspapers, maps, charts or books of tables, printed music (including words), public examination papers, workbooks, work cards or assignment sheets, in-house business publications, and works published overseas where there is no agreement.

There are many other licensing bodies. The Newspaper Licensing Agency (NLA), licenses the photocopying, faxing, and digital copying of all of the United Kingdom's national newspapers and many regional and international newspapers. It offers sole traders, companies, and any other body a one-stop-shop for a licence to copy, for internal management use. The British Library Document Supply Centre enables you to obtain copies of a huge range of published work. Customers pay for standard photocopying costs, as well as a copyright fee, which varies according to the individual publisher. This is then passed on to the CLA for distribution to copyright owners worldwide. The Performing Right Society (PRS) administers the performing right in the musical works of its members, who comprise composers, songwriters, and music publishers. It issues licences and distributes fees on behalf of music copyright holders. You will need a PRS licence if you plan to play or perform music in public (even if it is just a radio in a shop or factory). The Music Publishers' Association (United States) provides contact details of copyright owners if you wish to photocopy printed music, arrange music, or use music in a film or commercial. This will enable you to contact the copyright owner directly.

The Mechanical Copyright Protection Society (MCPS) licenses the recording of copyright music. You will need to contact it if you want to record copyright musical works. The Phonographic Performance Ltd (PPL) issues licenses for the public performance or broadcasting of sound recordings, and collects licence fees from broadcast and public performance users on behalf of the record companies. Generally, any business which plays recorded music should have a PPL licence. Video Performance Ltd is the UK collecting society that licenses music videos for broadcast, and issues licenses for the public performance of video recordings.

If you, as a user or prospective user of copyright works that are licensed collectively, are dissatisfied with the terms or conditions of licences or licensing schemes operated by collective licensing bodies, you can apply to the Copyright Tribunal for independent adjudication on the matter.

WHAT TO AVOID
Not checking with the copyright owner
It is vital to check with the copyright owner before using copyright material. You may be liable for a fine or even imprisonment for infringing copyright work. The name of the copyright owner should be provided somewhere on the piece of work, but if you are unable to find it, contact the relevant licensing body for help.

Not seeking the right advice
The Copyright Directorate is an executive agency of the DTI providing information and advice on all intellectual property issues, and is part of the Patent Office. The government's intellectual property website (address given below) can provide you with detailed information about copyright and whether you will need to get copyright permission.

RECOMMENDED LINKS
Copyright Directorate:
www.intellectual-property.gov.uk
The Copyright Licensing Agency Ltd:
www.cla.co.uk
Newspaper Licensing Agency:
www.nla.co.uk
British Library Document Supply Centre:
bl.uk/services/document/dsc.html
Performing Right Society:
www.prs.co.uk
Music Publishers Association:
www.mpaonline.org.uk
Mechanical Copyright Protection Society Ltd:
www.mcps.co.uk
Patent Office:
www.patent.gov.uk
Phonographic Performance Ltd:
www.ppluk.com
Video Performance Ltd:
www.patent.gov.uk/copy/tribunal/

SEE ALSO
Intellectual Property (p. 518)
Using Copyright to Protect Your Work (p. 32)

Registering a Trade Mark

GETTING STARTED
A trade mark is a distinctive symbol that your business can use to make its goods and services immediately recognisable to consumers. It is a good way of differentiating your products and services from those of your competitors, and it implies a consistent level of quality or service. There are several restrictions on what can be registered and protected as a trade mark. This actionlist looks at what is involved in successfully registering a trade mark, both in the United Kingdom and abroad.

FAQS
What is a trade mark?
The idea of trade marks was developed in the late 1800s to help established businesses stop competitors stealing their sales and possibly damaging their reputation by imitating their products. A trade mark may be a brand name for a specific product or be representative of the business as a whole. Today, a successful brand name or company logo is a valuable asset to its owner.

The Trade Marks Act 1994 defines a registerable trade mark as 'any sign that is capable of being represented graphically, capable of distinguishing goods or services of one undertaking from those of another undertaking'. This Act also makes provision to harmonise UK law with that of the European Union.

A sign that can be represented graphically is a marking such as words, letters, and numerals; the shape of the goods or their packaging; and musical jingles (or even smells). There are other special types of trade marks, for example, Certification Trade Marks, which are used to show that items to which they apply possess specific characteristics (such as materials used, place of origin, or method of manufacture). The owners of Certification Trade Marks can obtain a monopoly on such marks provided that they do not trade in the goods/services themselves. The owners can also authorise others to use the mark in regard to its specific qualities. Collective Marks are marks for use by members of an organisation or association. The Trade Marks Act 1994 also provides for the registration and use of Collective Marks.

When is it important to register a trade mark?
Registration of a mark is not compulsory, but it does protect the use of the reputation that the mark represents. By registering a trade mark, your business gets the right to prevent others from using an identical or confusingly similar mark on goods and services that are the same (or similar) to your own.

If your mark is registered, your business can sue for infringement, with its certificate of registration as evidence of ownership. Without this, you would have to demonstrate that a reputation has been established with regard to that mark and that its use by others will damage this reputation.

When registering a trade mark, you will specify the class of goods and services that your business wants to protect; but the legislation allows you to protect the trade mark against confusion with a wider range of goods, including those that may not be similar to your own.

How can I protect a trade mark overseas?
Registration within the United Kingdom does not give automatic protection overseas, but several schemes allow international registration without having to undertake individual applications in each country. If you think that you may trade overseas, it is worth investigating existing countries' trade marks before investing in packaging and promotional literature that may have to be changed.

When a UK application has been filed, the date can be used to establish a priority date within countries party to the Paris Convention, provided this is taken up within six months. A UK application can also be used as the basis for an international application within the member countries of the Madrid Protocol, through the World Intellectual Property Organization (WIPO). This gives protection in the states that are members of the Madrid Protocol, by designating which states are to be covered.

You can apply for a European Union trade mark from the Office for Harmonization in the Internal Market (OHIM) in Spain. This gives protection in all 15 member states of the European Union, including the United Kingdom. Applications can be submitted directly to the OHIM or through the United Kingdom Patent Office. Applications are usually submitted directly to OHIM. If protection is required in only one or two states, it may be cheaper to make a direct application to the Trade Mark office in each country, as opposed to an European Union application.

What are the requirements for new trade marks?

The definition of what can be registered as a trade mark was widened in the Trade Marks Act 1994, but a number of conditions still apply. Getting it right first time will save you time and money.

A new trade mark must be distinct from all existing marks (including those of overseas registers that can claim protection in the United Kingdom) and from words and symbols that may be in use in the normal course of trade, or are customary in the current language. A mark containing geographical marks, or referring to the quality or character of the goods, can now be registered, but only if it has become distinctive and associated with that product through use.

A mark that arises exclusively from the nature of the goods, gives substantial value to the goods, or is necessary to obtain a technical result, cannot be registered. A mark must not be misleading or contrary to public morality, and marks containing representations such as the crown or heraldic symbols are restricted. Registered trade marks should not consist of words or symbols in common usage, or which will unnecessarily restrict other traders' activities, because of the monopoly granted to the owner. The exception to this is if it can be shown that the mark has become established as distinguishable through use.

If a mark should be refused registration, Hearing Officers can advise on the amendments that will meet the requirements.

MAKING IT HAPPEN
The registration process

Before making your application, you can search the Trade Mark Register at the Patent Office (also available on the Patent Office's website) to see if any existing marks might prevent your mark from being registered. Alternatively, upon application, the Search and Advisory Service will ensure that a new mark fulfils the correct criteria.

To make an application, complete form TM3 and send it, with the fee, to the Trade Marks Registry. Currently the application fee stands at £200, for one class of goods or services, with a further £50 for each additional class under which protection is sought. Applications can be made by an individual or by a trade mark agent; a UK address must be provided for correspondence.

The Patent Office will examine the application within two months. Applicants then have up to six months to overcome any objections or put their application in order. Following this, the new mark will be published in the weekly *Trade Marks Journal*, to allow any objections by others to be raised, before it is entered onto the register.

Protection lasts for 10 years from the date of registration, and can be renewed every 10 years, for a fee. Once a mark has been registered, no changes can be made to the mark itself (except in a few circumstances), so it is important that the description submitted is clear and correct. It is the responsibility of the trade mark owners to uphold the rights afforded by the registration of their trade marks. Any infringements have to be pursued through the courts, inevitably involving specialised legal services and costs; these costs would normally be recoverable by the trade mark owner if the case against the infringement is successful. A third party can request a mark's removal from the register if it has not been used for five years.

If you have already applied to register a trade mark in a country which is party to the Paris Convention or the Madrid Protocol, you may be able to use the date of that application as the priority date of application for registration in the United Kingdom.

Domain names and trade marks

In recent years, use of the Internet as a trading medium has grown, resulting in a conflict between the allocation of domain names and trade marks. The Internet Corporation for Assigned Names and Numbers (ICANN) has partly resolved these issues through an administrative system for resolving domain name disputes involving trade marks. These measures have led to fewer cases of 'cybersquatting' of trade marks in the generic top-level domains. Further consultation is now under way to protect intellectual property at the level of the country code in top-level domains.

WHAT TO AVOID
Not carrying out thorough research

Before investing in registration, think about why you're doing it. This will help you determine how many classes of goods and services you wish to apply for, and whether you will require protection overseas, now or later. When designing product names and promotional literature, check what your competitors (or businesses in similar fields) have already registered; this will avoid possible complaints later.

Not being consistent in the use of your trade mark

Always display your trade mark in the form in which it was registered. The symbol © should be used in conjunction with the trade mark in countries in which it is registered, and ™ where it is not.

Not enforcing your rights

Check what is being registered through the Office for Harmonization in the Internal Market, as those marks have rights throughout the European Union. Also check the *Community Trade Mark Bulletin* for applications. It is possible to subscribe to a professional watching service, so that either the trade mark holder or the client can be notified if a third party tries to register a trade mark, company name, or domain name which is confusingly similar to that of the client.

RECOMMENDED LINKS
Institute of Trade Mark Attorneys (ITMA):
www.itma.org.uk
Patent Office:
www.patent.gov.uk

SEE ALSO
Intellectual Property (p. 518)

SETTING UP OR ACQUIRING A BUSINESS

Understanding Business Models

GETTING STARTED

There are three main types of legal status available to you when starting a business. These are sole trader, partnership, and limited company. You will need to take into account several considerations when deciding which of these will be best for your new business. For example, you will need to think about tax and administration implications, the image of the business, legal requirements, financial issues, and so on. This actionlist shows you how to decide which status is most suitable for your business, and raises some of the issues you may need to consider.

FAQS

When is sole trader status suitable?

The status of sole trader is convenient in situations where just one person will own the business, and will have final responsibility for its management and development. It is possible to employ other people if you are a sole trader, but ultimately the business is the individual, and there is no separate legal status.

There are various advantages to operating as a sole trader. You are not required to register the business with Companies House. This means that you can avoid the costs involved in registration, such as employing accountants or lawyers to carry out the registration process. There is also less paperwork to deal with, regarding legislation and tax, than for a limited company. The National Insurance contribution levels for sole traders are generally lower than those paid by limited companies. Also, the owner is entitled to all the profits made by the business. He or she is also able to keep overall control of the business.

When is partnership status suitable?

A partnership is a good vehicle to use when your business will involve two or more people owning a business together. Like a sole trader, a partnership has no separate legal identity, and does not need to register with Companies House.

There are several advantages to operating as a partnership. The structure of a partnership can be flexible, according to the deed of partnership. As with sole traders, there is less paperwork to deal with, regarding legis-

lation and tax, than for a limited company. However, unlike sole traders, management responsibilities, risks, and losses are shared. Partners can often bring a variety of different skills and experience to the business. Also, involving more people means that more capital can be raised among them. Another advantage is that partnerships cannot be taken over by other businesses.

There are two other kinds of partnership, a limited partnership and a limited liability company. A limited partnership is a partnership which has at least one partner who is a general partner (that is to say, he or she has management rights and unlimited liability), and at least one limited partner. A limited partner, who may be an individual or a company, contributes a fixed amount (as capital or property) to the partnership, but is only liable for partnership debts or liabilities up to the amount they have contributed. A limited partnership must register its details with Companies House.

A limited liability partnership (LLP) has the flexibility and tax status of a partnership, but the benefits of limited liability. The liability of all of the partners is limited to their capital contribution to the LLP, so personal assets cannot be seized to settle debts. Limited liability partnerships are required to register with Companies House.

When is limited company status suitable?

The main advantage of limited company status is that the owners (shareholders) have limited liability for the debts of the business up to the value of their shareholding; they are not personally liable for company debts. This means that the liability of the owners of the business is limited to the initial cost of their shares.

The status of a limited company tends to raise the credibility of the business in the eyes of suppliers and customers, as it suggests that business is large and relatively established. This could be important if your business is competing in a market dominated by large companies, or where customers may feel less comfortable with small or new businesses.

Other advantages include the following:

- finance can be raised by selling shares in the business
- employees are able to own a share in the business
- a limited company has a separate legal identity to that of its owners, and this allows the company to continue trading despite the death or resignation of a member
- the name of the company is protected

What is a franchise?

A franchise is where a licence has been granted by one business (the franchisor) to another (the franchisee), allowing the franchisee to use the trade mark and name of the franchisor, as well as its methods for marketing, managing, administration, and so on, within the business.

There are several advantages to franchising. The franchisee, by investing in a proven business format, can become the owner of a business with a well-known brand name, while at the same time overcoming some of the difficulties associated with a new business. The franchisee also receives help in finding and refurbishing premises. Help will be given in obtaining any planning permission and purchasing stock and equipments, as well as with staff training, marketing, and advertising. The franchisee is therefore able to concentrate on the day-to-day running of the business, without many of the pressures usually associated with self-employment. The franchisor will be able to provide specialist managerial advice and guidance to help overcome any problems that a small

business is likely to encounter, and the franchisee will benefit from the economies of scale of operating as part of a large organisation.

MAKING IT HAPPEN
Set up as a sole trader

As a sole trader, you can simply start trading; there is no requirement to register with Companies House, although there are certain rules about disclosure of ownership. It is important to remember, however, that during the first three months of trading you must contact your local Inland Revenue office to register for income tax and National Insurance. If you don't, you may be liable for a fine.

Set up as a partnership

If you decide to set up a partnership, each partner must tell the Inland Revenue that he or she is starting in business. All letterheads, business cards, and other business stationery must be printed to display both trading names and personal names, if these are different. Partners should draw up a deed of partnership with a solicitor to set out the terms and conditions of the partnership.

Set up as a limited company

A limited company must be registered with Companies House before trading commences. This requires certain documents, available from Companies House, to be completed and submitted with a registration fee of £20. An accountant or solicitor can help you to draw up and submit these documents. A private company must have at least one shareholder, one director, and a company secretary (who must be different from the sole director). If you are setting up a limited company, it is possible to buy existing or 'off-the-shelf' companies via a Company Registration Agent, accountant, or solicitor. All the paperwork will have already been prepared, and the company can begin trading almost immediately.

Set up a franchise

Before you make a decision, contact the British Franchise Association (BFA), and talk to existing franchisees, to find out more information about the franchise you are considering purchasing. If you decide to go ahead, and your application is accepted, you will probably find that a first interview with the franchisor is offered. This is valuable, as it gives both parties the opportunity to appraise one another. Provided both parties wish to continue, there will be a second interview to begin formalising the agreement. It is a good idea to take advice from a specialist professional adviser before signing any documents.

WHAT TO AVOID
Underestimating your liability
A sole trader has unlimited liability for the debts of the business, such as bank loans and amounts owing to creditors. This means that if your business fails, your personal savings and assets could be at risk.

In a partnership there is also unlimited liability, and each partner is personally responsible for the debts of the partnership. As a partner, therefore, your personal assets may be seized to pay off debts.

A limited company must comply with a wide range of complex and detailed legislation which is not applicable to sole traders and partnerships; this can add to the administrative and financial burden.

Underestimating the role of franchisors
Franchisors exert a fairly high degree of control over the franchise operation, so although the franchisee is legally independent, he or she will never be completely independent of the franchisor.

Underestimating the cost of a franchise
Franchises can be expensive investments. After the initial fee, there will be ongoing fees for the continuing support provided by the franchisor. Under the franchise agreement the franchisee may be obliged to buy supplies and equipment from the franchisor, which they may have been able to purchase cheaper elsewhere.

RECOMMENDED LINKS
British Franchise:
www.british-franchise.org.uk
Companies House:
www.companieshouse.gov.uk
Companies Registry:
www.companiesregistry-ni.gov.uk

SEE ALSO
Deciding Whether to Start a Business (p. 2)
Setting Up a Business as a Non-profit Organisation (p. 59)
Setting Up a Business as a Private Limited Company (p. 56)
Small and Growing Businesses (p. 478)

Focus On: Working Effectively As a Board Director
Adrian Cadbury

GETTING STARTED
If you have established a limited company, your business will have directors, often referred to as the 'board'. Boards are in place to direct and not to manage, and they have the task of defining the purpose of their enterprises and of agreeing the strategy for achieving that purpose. In particular, it is important to understand that boards are responsible for:

- appointing chief executives to turn strategic plans that build the long-term value of the business into action
- supporting and counselling CEOs in how to achieve this
- providing leadership above all, and it is in this context that the roles of board members need to be considered

This actionlist explains the workings of a board and how to improve its success.

FAQS
What is the role of the board?
- The role of the board is to direct not to manage.
- Balance of board membership and choice of individuals are key.
- The chairman (this term refers to both men and women in this role) is responsible for the effectiveness of the board.
- Non-executive directors have a particular contribution to make to the work of a board.
- Board committees are important structurally and for the tasks they undertake.
- Executive directors should be appointed solely for the value they can add to the board.
- Board members have different roles; what matters is how they combine to form the board team.

What should be the board's composition?
A single board at the head of a company is the commonest form of board structure and are often called 'unitary boards'. They are made up of executive and non-executive, or outside, directors. ('Two-tier' boards separate these two kinds of director.) Given that both executive and outside directors sit on unitary boards, the first issue is the balance between them. Ten years ago, the ratio for UK boards was around two-thirds executive directors and one-third outside directors. This has now moved closer to parity and in future I would expect outside directors to be in the majority. This is already the position in the United States where the chief executive is often the only executive on the board and is usually its chairman as well.

How big should a board be?
There is a clear move to smaller boards in both the United Kingdom and the United States. Some commentators recommend a maximum board size of ten and favour eight or nine, the argument for smaller boards being that they enable all the directors to get to know each other and to contribute effectively in board discussions, thus arriving at a true consensus. The crucial point is that boards are teams and provide collective leadership, so the balance of membership and choice of individuals are key to forming the team.

MAKING IT HAPPEN
Work as a team

Although board members have different roles, what counts is the way those roles are combined in the board team, and this is why board selection is so fundamental. Directors should only be appointed for the value they can add to the board. All directors should have terms of office to enable renewal to take place, although I am against rigid rules tying retirement to age or length of board service. If you are looking for outside directors, aim to fill gaps in the experience and backgrounds of the existing directors, and involve the board as a whole during the selection process. The chairman, however, has a particular responsibility for the choice of board members since it is his or her responsibility to turn them into an effective team.

Focus on priority issues

This can be accomplished by:

- making sure that the board concentrates on corporate purpose, appropriate strategy, and appointing a chief executive who can turn strategy into action
- appointing a chairman who is *not* the chief executive, and who will put in place effective measures of the board's performance
- keeping the board to an absolute maximum of ten members, with a majority of external, non-executive directors
- making sure that non-executive directors are independent of management and free from connections that may affect (or be seen to affect) their judgment
- using the whole board to pick outsiders who can fill gaps in the experience and backgrounds of existing directors
- training executives in filling their non-managerial boardroom role and letting them learn from non-executive posts elsewhere

Maximise the contribution of outside directors

All directors are equal in that they all carry the same legal responsibilities. Outside or non-executive directors are in that sense no different from their executive colleagues. They do, however, have particular contributions to make to their boards by virtue of standing further back from the business. One is in reviewing the performance of the chief executive and the executive team; clearly the outside directors are the only board members in a position to do this objectively.

Another contribution is in relation to potential conflicts of interest, such as those between the interests of the executives and those of the shareholders. Examples are directors' pay, dividends versus re-investment, and whether top appointments should be made from within or outside the company. Decisions on these matters are ultimately the decision of the whole board, but outside directors are well placed to offer direction on where the best interests of the company—to which all directors owe their duty—lie.

Outside directors bring with them their experience in fields which are different from those of the executive directors, and this external experience is of particular value in strategy formulation.

The role of these directors in helping to resolve conflicts of interest does not imply that they have higher standards than their executive colleagues—the difference is simply that they can judge these matters more objectively because their interests are involved less directly.

Clearly understand the role of executive directors

The duties of executive directors are the same as those of the outside directors. They are as responsible for the monitoring task of the board as the outside directors, who in turn are as responsible for the strategy and leadership of the company as the executives. This means that executive directors have to take their executive hats off upon entering the boardroom and put on their directorial ones. They should only be appointed for the contribution they can make to the board and they are there to further the company's interests—not those of their function or department. It is not an easy transition to make and executive directors can be helped in the adoption of their new non-managerial role through appropriate training or through a non-executive directorship elsewhere.

Manage the role of board committees

As the responsibilities of directors have become more demanding, boards have increasingly formed committees to deal with some of their more detailed work. All quoted companies in the UK must establish audit and remuneration committees and, unless they have a small board, nomination committees. These committees strengthen the position of the outside directors, of whom they are made up, and are important for the work they do. The essential point is that they are committees of the board. The board appoints them, sets their terms of reference and turns their recommendations into decisions.

✘ WHAT TO AVOID
Poor chairmanship

The chairman is responsible for the effectiveness of the board, and this responsibility rests with that person whatever his or her other duties. It leads to the point that all companies are different and the issues they face are constantly changing. Individual boards have to follow accepted board principles, but in ways which meet their particular circumstances. It is the chairman who has the responsibility of making sure that the make-up of the board is appropriate for the challenges ahead. Similarly, it is the chairman who has the task of welding their directors into an effective team. Effective boards are not brought into being simply by seating competent individuals around a board table—creating effective boards requires effort by their members, but above all coaching and leadership by the chairman, which is an argument for the chairman not also being chief executive.

The chairman is responsible for the running of the board. Responsibilities include the agenda, the provision of adequate and timely information to all directors and the actual conduct of board meetings. The chairman is also, provided he or she is not chief executive, responsible for putting in place a means by which the board can evaluate their own performance. Where the chairman is also chief executive, his or her duties in relation to their board remain the same, but a deputy or a senior outside director would be responsible for the appraisal of the chief executive and for the review of the board's performance.

Misunderstanding the role of the board

Many boards fail to function adequately because their members have differing views, not only about the main challenges faced by the business but even about more fundamental issues, such as the role of the board and its priorities in the short, medium and long-term. One of the first priorities must therefore be to develop a consensus about what needs to be achieved, and how the board will work to do this.

Failing to work with the company secretary

The chairman and board members should be able to look to the company secretary for impartial and professional guidance on their responsibilities and all directors should have access to the advice and services of a company secretary, who is responsible for ensuring that board procedures are followed. The company secretary must be informed and supportive, working with the chairman to make sure that the board works effectively.

RECOMMENDED LINKS
Corporate Board Member:
www.boardmember.com
Institute of Directors:
www.iod.com

Evaluating an Existing Business

GETTING STARTED

It's often thought that buying a business is simpler than starting your own, but remember that many businesses are sold because they have inherent problems that prevent them from generating sufficient income. If you're buying a business, it's vital that you carry out comprehensive research and analysis in the same way as if you were setting the business up from scratch.

FAQS

What's my first step towards buying a business?

Your first step is to decide on the type of business you're looking for. Think about what size of business you want. Are you, for example, looking for a small local business, or are you aiming for a large national one? Also think about what business sector you're most drawn to—is it manufacturing, retailing, or perhaps services? Consider location too. Are you prepared to change your location and travel, or would you prefer to stay where you are and travel relatively short distances?

What should I be looking for in a business?

Look first and foremost for skills and experience. The most common reason for business failure is people taking on businesses outside their area of expertise, so think long and hard about the skills and knowledge that already exist in the potential business, and whether you can add to those skills. You also need to consider the products and/or services that the business provides. Again, ideally, you should be looking for a business which deals in a product or service that you have some experience of, especially if the operation is particularly complex or technical.

Remember to investigate the level of competition facing the business, especially locally. Make sure you know your competitors' strengths and weaknesses relative to the business you're considering buying, and what their share is of the market. Look at the size of the business, and find out how fast it has grown in the past, and whether

this rate is likely to continue, increase, or decline.

Another important factor to consider is location. Ensure that the business is located appropriately, for example, close to its target market (if location is relevant), and within reach of appropriately skilled employees. You'll also need to judge whether the business needs any major changes requiring a large investment of management time—you may be able to acquire a business at a lower price if this is the case. If the business is already successful, it can probably continue to operate in the same manner, regardless of a change of ownership.

Capital requirements are another issue. Calculate how much money needs to be invested in the venture. This is a crucial factor in determining whether to buy a particular business. Consider whether you'll be able to secure finance for future investment if it's required. Evaluate too the level of profitability of the business. Does it make the amount of profit you're looking for; does it have the potential to expand and grow?

How do I value the business?

It may be useful to employ a business transfer agent or financial adviser when valuing the business. The three methods often used are asset value, earnings multiple, and return on capital.

Asset value—To obtain the business's net asset value (that is, what it is worth, in basic terms), the value of the liabilities (that is, a business's financial obligations, such as outstanding debts, loan repayments, outstanding invoices, etc), is subtracted from the value of the assets. The value for the entire business will be the net asset value, plus a value for goodwill representing the business's reputation and existing customer base.

Earnings multiple—The earnings multiple method requires you to apply a multiple to the earnings from the business. Earnings should take account of interest charges to be paid after purchasing the business, and any loans needed to make improvements. To come up with an earnings multiple, divide the company's market price by its after-tax earnings over a one year period.

Return on capital—To find the return on capital, you'll need to define a desired rate of return. (Rate of return can be defined as a ratio of the profit made in a financial year as a percentage of the capital employed.) Then the income of the business before interest and tax should be calculated, and this figure should also be given as a percentage of the capital invested. If the figure is less than the desired rate of return, then any purchase should not go ahead.

MAKING IT HAPPEN
Evaluate the business

You'll need to carry out some research properly to evaluate any business you're considering for potential purchase. You should be able to obtain much of the information you require from the present owner; ask for details including the business plan, accounts, details of established customers, and so on.

It's a good idea to carry out a SWOT analysis (Strengths, Weaknesses, Opportunities, and Threats) on any potential business purchase. Consider the present position of the business in the market, its past performance, and its potential for growth. Look at its available resources, for example money, assets, manpower, and so on. Investigate the training, experience, and skills available within the business. Check its sources of supply, costs, reliability of material, stock supply, and relations with suppliers.

Find out who the competition is, where it is, and what its strengths and weaknesses

are. Research your customers, making sure you know who and where they are, and how loyal they are. You'll need to examine external factors like industry trends, regulations, and political and economic developments. Consider how much money you'll need for advertising and marketing. The way the business is promoted may have to change. Look at the business's distribution channels, asking yourself how reliable they are, and whether they can be maintained once the business changes hands. Calculate the profitability of the business after any initial capital outflow for improvements.

Determine a price

Obviously, if you become interested in purchasing a business, you'll need to value it and determine a reasonable price in conjunction with the seller. The price of a business may be derived from some of the factors mentioned in the previous section. It will also depend upon an appraisal of the land and buildings. The fair market value of the property is affected by a number of factors. These include the business's location in relation to its customers and suppliers, employees, and competition. The condition of the premises, for example whether improvements are necessary to bring them up to legally acceptable standards, is also an important consideration.

Financial considerations, such as the costs of property maintenance, transfer of title, licences, leases, property taxes, and so on, need to be taken into account. There may also be problems over the transfer of a lease on premises. Some leases prohibit assignment.

External factors, such as current interest rates and the state of the property market, influence a property's value. So too will the future outlook, for example whether the property will continue to meet the needs of the business as it grows. There will also need to be a valuation of fixtures and fittings. There may be equipment leases that need to be transferred (for example, the photocopier). Check for any contingent liabilities.

Consider other factors

You'll need to negotiate the transfer value of the stock. This should be cost or 'net realisable value' (NRV), whichever is lower. For redundant stock the NRV is zero. A recorded valuation and stock count should be carried out by a third party. You'll also need to engage an accountant to evaluate the business's books, bank statements, and tax records to get an accurate picture of the current financial situation and future profitability.

Valuing the goodwill of the business is especially important. Goodwill reflects the cumulative effect of the reputation of the business; its relationship with customers, suppliers, and competition; its market position, and the skills of the staff. You'll need to consider whether the existing staff are suitable for the business, and how they are likely to react to a new owner/manager. Think about how you'll replace those not keen to stay on. The effects of the Transfer of Undertakings (Protection of Employment) Regulations 1981 (TUPE) must be considered. If long-serving staff are transferred it will be expensive to make them redundant. Decide what benefits will be offered, for example, maternity benefits, holidays, and so on. National Insurance (NI) requirements, pension schemes, and personal liability insurance must also be considered.

Make sure that you evaluate the outstanding loans to the business, its relationship with its creditors, and its repayment history. Be realistic about whether you'll be able to obtain financing for the venture, and to repay the loan. Look at pro-forma income statements, balance sheets, and cash budgets. When you estimate how much income the business is likely to generate, it's important to be conservative, especially in the early stages.

WHAT TO AVOID

Rushing through the research stage

If you don't carry out thorough research, you may find you have made the wrong decision. Without enough information, facts and figures, and forecasts, a view of any business's prospects can be easily distorted and misleading.

Not exercising due diligence

You should always exercise due diligence when purchasing a business. You must make sure that what the vendor is saying is correct. Examine all accounts carefully. Ask yourself whether customers are likely to remain loyal once you have taken over the business, and whether suppliers will maintain the same relationship with you. If you don't exercise due diligence, you'll only have yourself to blame for any problems you could have discovered before the purchase.

Not setting a price before bidding

You should have a price band in mind before bidding, otherwise you'll be at a disadvantage. The seller may state an asking price outright, at which time the buyer must be prepared to negotiate. This way you shouldn't spend more than you can afford.

RECOMMENDED LINKS

Business Eye (Wales):
www.businesseye.org.uk
Business Gateway (Scotland):
www.bgateway.com
Business Link (England):
www.businesslink.org
Invest Northern Ireland:
www.investni.com

SEE ALSO
Small and Growing Businesses (p. 478)

A Guide to Business Regulations When Starting Up

GETTING STARTED
When you start up in business, there are many regulations with which you need to comply. This actionlist will help you to be aware of these regulations. It will also help you to work your way methodically through each of them before you start trading, to avoid penalties.

FAQS
What issues should I be thinking about?
There are several main areas to consider, all of which are explained in more detail in the next section. You will first need to notify the correct authorities of your intention to set up in business, and register your business if necessary. You will also need to consider financial issues, such as income tax, National Insurance, Value Added Tax (VAT), corporation tax, and capital gains tax.

You may need to obtain planning permission, and this can be a lengthy process. You may also need to think about applying for a patent, trade mark, or licence, and again, applying for these can take a long time. If copyright issues are likely to affect your business, you need to find out about these too.

If you are employing staff, you will need to comply with health and safety and fire safety regulations, and you will need to consider taking out insurance. Your business will also need to comply with other regulations to do with employing staff, such as the National Minimum Wage Act and Maternity and Parental Leave Regulations.

MAKING IT HAPPEN
Register your company
The status of your business venture will determine which specific regulations are applicable to it and who should be contacted. Further advice on all of the information given in this section should be sought from a solicitor, an accountant, or a relevant support organisation, for example, Business Link.

If you are a sole trader, or in a partnership, you must inform Inland Revenue

(which governs income tax and National Insurance contributions) within three months of starting to trade. As a sole trader or a partner you are classed as self-employed, and therefore need to make arrangements for self-assessment of income tax and for paying your own National Insurance.

If you are an incorporated company, you are required by the Companies Act to register the name and address of your company with the Registrar of Companies at Companies House. Various other documents must also be lodged at Companies House, including the memoranda and articles of association of the company.

If a business operates as a sole trader or partnership under a name other than that of the owner(s) of the business, there is a legal requirement for the name(s) and address(es) of the owner(s) of the business to be displayed at its premises and on its stationery. For limited companies, the registered name of the company must be displayed outside its office and on all relevant company publications, including e-mail. It is also important to verify the acceptability of the name itself with Companies House.

Understand financial issues
National Insurance and income tax must be paid. Self-employed persons should register for Class 2 National Insurance contributions on form CWF1 from the Inland Revenue. This form is then sent on to the appropriate Tax Office. If net profit is above a certain level, Class 4 contributions may have to be paid. All businesses that employ staff must register with the Inland Revenue as employers, and they must deduct National

Insurance contributions from employees' salaries.

Sole traders pay normal rates of income tax on the business's trading profits. In a partnership, each partner will be liable to pay income tax on their individual share of the business's trading profits. The Inland Revenue's Self Assessment system, which is applicable to all unincorporated businesses, means that self-employed people must assess their own tax liabilities. Any business employing staff must make pay-as-you-earn (PAYE) tax deductions from employees' earnings, and pay these over to the Inland Revenue.

Your business needs to register for Value Added Tax (VAT) if its annual sales turnover exceeds a certain level. Current turnover threshold levels should be checked with the VAT Office. A business may also register voluntarily if its sales are below the threshold. Limited companies must pay corporation tax on any profit made from total sales and income gained from investment excluding certain allowable expenses. Capital gains tax (CGT) is applied to profits over a certain level gained from the sale of items such as land or investments. It may affect businesses run from home if the business owner decides to sell the house.

Be aware of health and safety issues

Employers are required to make sure that staff operate in a safe working environment and must regularly carry out a health and safety risk assessment. Various regulations are in force that cover, for example, working with computers, first aid, and basic conditions of work for employees including heating and lighting. If you are operating a factory or workshop, the Health and Safety Executive (HSE) should usually be contacted to register the business.

Implement fire safety procedures

If there are more than 20 people working in your building, then a fire certificate may be needed. If there are more than 10 people other than on a ground floor (including a basement), then a fire certificate is required.

The Fire Precautions (Workplace) (Amendment) Regulations 1999 require all employers to assess their fire safety arrangements even if they already have their own certificate. The local fire brigade should be contacted to see whether a fire certificate is required.

Obtain planning permission if necessary

If the business is moving into a new building or changing the use of the building, the local authority's planning department may need to be consulted. If existing premises need to be altered structurally, or the business requires the installation of plant or machinery, the local authority planning department or building regulations department should be consulted.

Understand the concept of intellectual property

Legislation exists to protect infringement of other people's intellectual property rights on designs, trade marks and copyright, or inventions that may already be patented. In addition, the business may generate certain intellectual property rights itself that may be of value and require adequate protection or exploitation. It is important to investigate these thoroughly and speak to appropriate sources such as the Patent Office or a solicitor before setting up in business.

Understand licences

If your business holds information about people on a database, the Information Commissioner's Office must be contacted to find out whether the business needs officially to notify the Commissioner of that fact. If it does, there are strict requirements to be met under data protection legislation. If the business is involved in lending/collecting credit, or in the hire of goods, it may need a credit licence, obtainable from the Office of Fair Trading.

Certain types of business require licences before they can operate. Speak to your local authority or business support organisation for advice on which licences would be relevant to your business.

Have insurance cover

Compulsory—Subject to some exemptions, a limited company employing staff (other than the owner/manager's immediate family) is legally required to maintain a minimum of £5 million employers' liability insurance. A copy of the certificate of insurance should be displayed at all business premises. Other compulsory insurance includes third party motor insurance on vehicles used for business. Periodic inspections of certain types of plant and machinery will require an annual inspection policy or contract.

Recommended—Public liability insurance, which covers bodily and property injury to the public, might be important if you have a walk-in retail business that receives many customers every day. Professional indemnity insurance covers legal liability for professional errors or omissions. It might be a good idea to seek advice from an accountant or tax specialist.

Employ staff

If your business intends to employ people, it needs to comply with certain regulations. These include the BIF 091 Maternity and Parental Leave Regulations 1999 (as amended), the National Minimum Wage Act 1998, the Working Time Regulations 1998 (as amended), and the Part-time Workers (Prevention of Less Favourable Treatment) Regulations 2000 (as amended). You are not allowed to discriminate against a person on the grounds of race, gender, disability, or sexual orientation. Employees must be provided with a written statement of their main employment terms.

There are payroll regulations which stipulate that all employees must be given itemised pay slips stating any deductions. You must inform the Inland Revenue when taking on an employee. They will set up a PAYE scheme and send you a new employers starter pack. The Inland Revenue or New Employers Helpline can be contacted for advice.

WHAT TO AVOID
Not doing your homework

It really pays to research every area thoroughly before you go ahead and start trading. This will not only save you time, but also money, as you can be heavily fined for not following regulations. Ignorance is not an excuse!

RECOMMENDED LINKS

Advisory, Conciliation and Arbitration Service (ACAS):
www.acas.org.uk
Business Eye (Wales):
www.businesseye.org.uk
Business Gateway (Scotland):
www.bgateway.com
Business Link (England):
www.businesslink.org
Companies House Enquiry Service:
www.companieshouse.gov.uk
Department for Environment, Food and Rural Affairs (DEFRA):
www.defra.gov.uk
Health and Safety Executive (HSE):
www.hse.gov.uk
Industrial Common Ownership Movement (ICOM):
www.icom.org
Information Commissioner's Office:
www.dataprotection.gov.uk
Inland Revenue:
www.inlandrevenue.gov.uk
Invest Northern Ireland:
www.investni.com
Office of Fair Trading:
www.oft.gov.uk
Patent Office:
www.patent.gov.uk
US Copyright Office:
www.loc.gov/copyright
US Patent and Trademark Office:
www.uspto.gov

SEE ALSO
Small and Growing Businesses (p. 478)

Setting Up a Business As a Private Limited Company

GETTING STARTED

Private limited companies balance the advantages of limited liability and better access to finance against greater administrative burdens and disclosure of the business's financial position. This actionlist looks at the advantages and disadvantages of companies, and describes how to set up a business as a company. It also discusses other relevant issues including administrative and accounting responsibilities, tax, National Insurance, and limited liability.

FAQS

What is a private limited company?

A private limited company has a legal identity separate to that of its owners; this is unlike a sole trader or a partnership, where there is no distinction. Companies have to comply with a wide range of legislation, particularly the Companies Act 1985 (as amended). There are two main types of limited company: public and private. Most small businesses that wish to trade as a company will take the route of a private (rather than public) limited company.

Public limited companies can offer their shares to the public and trade them on the Stock Exchange. The letters 'plc' (or the Welsh equivalent, 'ccc') must appear at the end of the business name. To trade as a public limited company, the business must have issued share capital of £50,000 or more. The owners of a company are its shareholders or 'members'. Public companies must have at least two shareholders.

A private company may be formed with one shareholder (a single member company). It must also have at least one director and a company secretary. Private limited companies cannot publicly trade their shares (these are usually held by employees, other businesses, family members, and acquaintances). There can be no more than 50 shareholders. If there is just one shareholder, he or she can be the sole director but not also the company secretary. In most small companies, the shareholders and directors will be the same people. Directors are often referred to as the 'board'.

What are the advantages of operating as a company?

The owners of a limited company have limited liability for the debts of the business, up to the value of their shareholding. If the business fails, the shareholders will simply lose the amount they have invested in the company. (A company may also be limited by guarantee. This means that members' liability is limited to an amount they have agreed to contribute if the company is wound up.)

Issuing shares in return for capital allows you to raise capital for expansion or other purposes. A limited company has a separate legal identity to that of its owners, so you can continue trading despite the death or resignation of a shareholder. Employees may be more motivated if they are able to own a share in the business. Suppliers and customers may perceive that limited companies have more credibility, which could be a competitive advantage.

What are the disadvantages of operating as a company?

You will have to comply with a wide range of complex and detailed legislation that is not applicable to sole traders and partnerships. There are also additional costs, including costs of incorporation and the recurring costs for statutory requirements such as auditing (compulsory when turnover exceeds £1 million). Public disclosure of the company's accounts can be seen as another disadvantage, and also, directors of new companies often still have to give personal guarantees to banks when seeking loans.

MAKING IT HAPPEN
Set up a private limited company

You must send the documents listed below to the Registrar of Companies before a certificate of incorporation can be issued. The fee for registering a private company is currently £20.

Memorandum of Association. This describes the purpose of the company and its powers.

Articles of Association. This details the rights of the shareholders and the powers of the company's directors. A complete draft of the articles can be found in Table A set out in the Companies Act 1985. Most companies use this table as a basis for their articles and amend it to suit their particular requirements. You can also alter the Articles of Association later, using certain procedures laid down in the legislation.

Form 10. This is the 'Statement of the First Directors, Secretary and Registered Office'. It can be downloaded from the Companies House website.

Form 12. This is the 'Declaration of Compliance with the Requirements of the Companies Act'. It can also be downloaded from the Companies House website.

These documents are subject to certain checks, including confirmation of whether any of the prospective directors are on the disqualified directors' register. When the documentation is satisfactory, the Registrar of Companies will issue a Certificate of Incorporation. The company can then start trading.

Buy an 'off-the-shelf' company

Company registration agents and solicitors can provide ready-made companies. If you choose this option, all the documentation will be prepared for you and the company will be registered, naming the agency's own staff as directors and secretaries, but no business will be transacted. When you buy the company, the agency simply changes the company's details to match your business and notifies the registrar. An 'off-the-shelf' company can cost anything from £150 to £350. Although this method can be a lot quicker than doing it yourself, initial costs can increase considerably if changes to the documentation are needed to suit your needs.

Choose a company name

You cannot register the same name as another company, certain words are restricted, and names that may cause offence are not permitted. Check the index of company names kept by the Registrar of Companies at Companies House to make sure that another company is not already using your chosen name.

You must display the company name outside all your premises so that it can be easily seen and read. It must also appear on all company publications, including business letters, cheques, invoices, and notices. The company's directors and secretary may be fined if the business name is displayed incorrectly. The company's place of registration and registered number must also be displayed on business letters and order forms.

You must also display the letters 'ltd' or the word 'limited' after the company name. Private companies, limited by guarantee, can become exempt from including 'limited' in their name. However, they must still state on business letters and order forms that they are a limited company.

The tax implications of setting up as a company

Income tax and National Insurance. The directors of a company are treated as employees and must pay income tax on their earnings as well as Class 1 National Insurance contributions (NICs). The company must also pay NICs on behalf of its employees.

Corporation tax. Limited companies are eligible to pay corporation tax on the profits they make. The current standard rate of corporation tax is 30%, but rates vary depending upon the amount of profit you make. Companies are required to carry out self-assessment for corporation tax. The company's completed corporation tax return is due 12 months after the company's financial year-end. Corporation tax must be paid within nine months and one day from the end of the financial year. The Inland Revenue will send you reminders about this.

VAT. If the company's annual turnover reaches a certain level (£56,000 for 2003–4), it will also be required to register for VAT. You may, however, register the business voluntarily if its turnover is lower than this threshold. This can have advantages, such as allowing your company to claim back VAT on purchases. More details are available from HM Customs and Excise.

Legal responsibilities following incorporation

Administration. After incorporation you must inform Companies House about the appointment of any new officers, the resignation of any officers, and changes to officers' names and addresses or other details originally registered on Form 10. There are strict time limits for the filing of such information, often as little as 14 days.

Once a year, every company must supply basic information to Companies House known as the 'annual return'. This is a snapshot of general information about a company's directors and secretary, registered office address, shareholders, and share capital.

Accounts. Directors of limited companies must prepare, maintain, and submit accounts to Companies House annually, including a profit and loss account and a balance sheet. The accounts must start on the day of incorporation, and its first financial year (known as the 'accounting reference period') will end on the last day of the month of the anniversary of formation. For example, if your company is formed on 2 November 2004, your first financial year will end on 30 November 2005, and the second financial year will start on 1 December 2005.

Your first set of accounts must be submitted to Companies House within 10 months of the end of the first financial year. There are automatic fines for accounts that are filed late. These accounts will be available to anyone who wishes to inspect them.

Northern Ireland
Company registration in Northern Ireland is dealt with by the Companies Registry, which is responsible to the Department of Enterprise, Trade, and Investment. Registering a company in Northern Ireland follows very similar procedures to the rest of the United Kingdom. It involves the submission of a Memorandum and Articles of Association, Form 21 (Statement of the First Directors, Secretary and Registered Office), and Form 23 (Declaration of Compliance with all the legal requirements relating to incorporation of a company). The standard registration fee is £35. Submission of accounts and annual returns must also be made to Companies Registry and they have similar procedures to the rest of the United Kingdom.

WHAT TO AVOID
Not using a solicitor or accountant
If you decide to set up your business as a company, it is important that you get advice from a solicitor or accountant, as the procedures involved can be quite complex. Company law changes constantly. Your solicitor or accountant should keep you informed of any new developments so that you can ensure that your business complies.

Not taking advantage of technology
Companies can now legally e-mail certain documents, including the Memorandum and Articles of Association, to the Registrar of Companies. This will save you a lot of time and also means that you have a record of when you sent what and when.

RECOMMENDED LINKS
Companies House:
www.companieshouse.gov.uk
Companies Registry:
www.companiesregistry-ni.gov.uk
HM Customs and Excise:
www.hmce.gov.uk
Inland Revenue:
www.inlandrevenue.gov.uk

SEE ALSO
Small and Growing Businesses (p. 478)
Understanding Business Models (p. 44)

Setting Up a Business As a Non-profit Organisation

GETTING STARTED
A not-for-profit business, or non-profit organisation, is an organisation that does not distribute its profit to its owners. All surpluses are put back into the business, or used for other charitable purposes in the community. Sectors including charities, the arts, education, and health care often operate in this way. This actionlist looks at various types of not-for-profit businesses, how they are set up and how they can obtain finance to fund the business.

FAQS
What kinds of not-for-profit businesses are there?

Social entrepreneurs use their business skills to address social problems rather than make a profit. It is common for them to set up a not-for-profit business to achieve this. Their aim is to improve the quality of life of a section of the community, often in some of the most deprived areas of society. Social entrepreneurs can set up all kinds of businesses, from youth clubs to mobile libraries. The School for Social Entrepreneurs works with local organisations around the UK to establish networks of local social entrepreneur programmes. Its website address is given below.

Charities generally aim to improve the welfare of others (people or animals) and often have to raise money to do so. Examples of large charities include Oxfam, Greenpeace, and Save the Children. These secure the majority of their funding through donations. There are many smaller charities, however, that generate their income through a combination of trading and donations, and these can be clearly identified as businesses (for example, performance arts organisations).

A **credit union** is a co-operative that gives members facilities for saving, borrowing, and other financial services, and is set up, owned, and run by its members. Members save together to create a pool of money from which low-cost loans are made. There must be at least 21 members.

MAKING IT HAPPEN
Setting up a not-for-profit business

Usually a not-for-profit business will either be an unincorporated association, or incorporated as a company, limited by guarantee, without share capital. There are also special registration requirements for charities and credit unions. The Registrar of Companies, for companies incorporated in England and Wales, is based at Companies House in Cardiff. For companies incorporated in Scotland, contact Companies House in Edinburgh, and for Northern Ireland, the Companies Registry in Belfast. Website addresses are given below.

Unincorporated associations
An unincorporated association does not have a separate legal identity to its owners. The association normally has a constitution that sets out its aims and objectives. It will also have a committee, normally elected during an Annual General Meeting, where members are nominated to serve as officers and members. Committee members are all personally liable for debts incurred by the business.

An unincorporated association cannot start legal action, borrow money, or enter into contracts in its own name. This is because it has no legal identity of its own, and in legal terms is only a collection of individuals. It also can't hold property without appointing trustees (usually committee members) to do so on its behalf. There are no formal registration requirements for setting up an unincorporated association.

Company limited by guarantee

The more usual route for a not-for-profit business is to incorporate as a company limited by guarantee. This type of company does not have shares or shareholders, instead it has members. Members agree, in the event of liquidation, to guarantee a sum of money that may be required to meet the demands of any creditors. The amount is defined in the Memorandum of Association. Companies, whether limited by guarantee or by shares, have to abide by the requirements of the Companies Acts.

Charities

The majority of charities in England and Wales need to register with the Charity Commission. Charities based in Scotland and Northern Ireland must register with the Inland Revenue. The website addresses are given below. If setting up a charity as a company limited by guarantee, you must submit the Memorandum and Articles of Association to the Charity Commission. The Memorandum and Articles should be agreed with the Charity Commission before incorporation, as this will save any difficulties later.

Credit unions

Credit unions must be authorised by the Financial Services Authority (FSA). In order to register, a credit union must identify that a 'common bond' exists between all members; this is to ensure that all members will abide by credit union principles. All credit unions must operate within the Credit Union Act 1979, which covers registration, members' eligibility, limits on loans and savings, the amount of interest that can be charged on loans, and distribution of profits. All credit unions must have a written set of rules that outline the duties of its officers and committees. The FSA is currently developing proposals for the future regulation of credit unions.

Tax issues for the not-for-profit business

Any new business must register with the Inland Revenue. Charities have the absolute right not to pay tax on any income. Not-for-profit businesses can usually negotiate a tax exemption, but this is not automatic, and will largely depend on their sources of income. Businesses that are largely trading, for example, will have to pay tax like any other business. All businesses (including charities) need to register for VAT if their turnover is going to (or is expected to) exceed the annual threshold. However, some charity fundraising events, and sales of donated goods in charity shops, are exempt from VAT.

Annual accounts and audit

Limited companies may be required to have their end of year accounts audited. Under the Companies Act 1985 (Audit Exemption) (Amendment) Regulations 1997 (amended 2000), small businesses with a turnover of up to £1 million are exempt from the audit requirement. However, they will still have to satisfy their boards of management and supporters that the money is well managed. Charities are only exempt from audits if their gross income does not exceed £90,000. Charities must submit their accounts to the Charity Commission and Companies House.

Sources of help and finance for not-for-profit businesses

Many non-profit organisations look for **grant aid** to cover all their costs. Grant aid might come from large companies, grant-giving charitable foundations, or the government through a range of initiatives, the largest of which is the Single Regeneration Budget. Grant aid may also be secured from the European Union Structural Funds. You should remember that there is far more demand for grant aid than can ever be met. (Website addresses are given below.)

Comic Relief, Scarman Trust, Community Action Network, and several other organisations have set up the partnership unLtd, which has been awarded £100 million of Millennium Heritage Lottery finding. This money is used to make awards to individuals who wish to become social entrepreneurs. Levels of grant are £2,500 for start-ups, and £10,500 for those developing and expanding a project.

The **Local Investment Fund (LIF)** can lend between £25,000 and £250,000 to community, not-for-profit organisations in England which have been denied funding from banks, or which need top-up funding. LIF clients can also access ProHelp free of charge. This is a national network of professionals, for example architects, accountants, solicitors, marketing specialists, and IT consultants, who can provide strategic support, free of charge, to voluntary and community groups in their local area.

The Directory of Social Change provides information on grants as well as details on courses and conferences aimed at the voluntary sector and community organisations. The Charities Aid Foundation also aims to help not-for-profit businesses to make the most of their resources by providing advice and consultancy services. It can also provide small grants.

Further information and advice about sources of finance for not-for-profit businesses can be obtained from Business Links, Business Connects, Small Business Gateways, and Invest Northern Ireland. The Charities Aid Foundation provides specialist financial services to charities and their supporters. FunderFinder is a website that helps individuals and not-for-profit organisations in the UK to identify charitable trusts that might give them money.

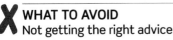

WHAT TO AVOID
Not getting the right advice
If the business wishes to register as a charity, it is advisable in all cases to contact the Charity Commission for advice, as charity law is extremely complex. The Charity Commission is the statutory organisation that regulates charities in England and Wales. The Commission seeks to ensure that charities operate within a framework that

enables them to work effectively for the purposes for which they were set up. Community Action Network (CAN) was launched in 1998 as a learning and support network for social entrepreneurs, with the aim of strengthening communities in the United Kingdom. Using this network, CAN members share information about events, research and grants, as well as any useful contacts or advice to strengthen the network.

Not taking it seriously
It is important to remember that the management of not-for-profit organisations should be taken just as seriously as the management of for-profit organisations.

RECOMMENDED LINKS
Charities Aid Foundation:
www.cafonline.org
The Charity Commission:
www.charity-commission.gov.uk
Community Action Network:
www.can-online.org.uk
Companies House:
www.companieshouse.gov.uk
Companies Registry:
www.companiesregistry-ni.gov.uk
Directory of Social Change:
www.dsc.org.uk
EU Structural Funds, Department of Trade and Industry:
www.dti.gov.uk/europe/structural.html
Financial Services Authority:
www.fsa.gov.uk
FunderFinder:
www.funderfinder.org.uk
Local Investment Fund:
www.lif.org.uk
School for Social Entrepreneurs:
www.sse.org.uk
Single Regeneration Budget:
www.urban.odpm.gov.uk/programmes/ srb/index.html

SEE ALSO
Small and Growing Businesses (p. 478)
Understanding Business Models (p. 44)

Starting a Business While Under 18

GETTING STARTED

The rewards for anyone starting a business can be great, but it's a major decision. It can be particularly difficult for those under 18 because of various legal requirements and other constraints. The success rate of such businesses is hard to comment on as many operate invisibly, either within a 'training for business' scheme or in a form of partnership with a relative. There are, however, many successful young entrepreneurs and good sources of help for them. This actionlist looks at some of the issues.

FAQS

Why might I want to set up a business at this age?

You may have a strong interest or skill in a certain business area; you may want more independence, and greater job satisfaction; the idea that any profits made will belong to you may also be a great incentive; you may look forward to feeling a sense of achievement and pride in the venture.

If you are really serious about starting a business, you will probably be a positive person, enthusiastic, and motivated to work hard and succeed. Also, you will probably have fewer domestic commitments, like family or a mortgage, than many older people.

What problems will I face?

There are drawbacks to starting a business before the age of 18. Greater independence brings greater responsibility. Any business decisions are up to the manager. Any failures or problems faced by the business are also the sole responsibility of the manager, who must be able to cope.

Lack of experience can cause serious problems in establishing credibility with both finance providers, for example, bank managers, and potential customers. They may feel that someone under the age of 18 could not know enough about managing a business. Some under 18s have work experience, but this is unlikely to be enough to convince potential backers or customers that they know what they're doing. You will need to work much harder to prove yourself. Such lack of confidence in the manager's ability to run the business effectively can have an adverse effect on sales and profitability. Lack of qualifications, technical skills, and business training can also hinder anyone starting a business. This could cause problems of credibility, particularly with banks.

There are also legal issues. Persons under the age of 18 are legally described as 'young persons'. Legislative requirements stipulate that they may not work in certain business areas. For example, to sell alcohol a person must be 18 or over. Street trading and driving on public roads are both illegal for under 17s. If the planned business involves the use of certain industrial machinery, there may be age restrictions on its use; at the very least, full training will be required.

A young person may be unable to hire or lease equipment. However, it may be possible to set up a hire/purchase agreement through a trusted friend or relative, who would act as a guarantor for payments to a given company. Alternatively a 'contract' could be established by which to pay them. This brings up another problem, as 'young persons' cannot legally sign contracts. Again, it may be possible to have an arrangement with a relative by which they legally own the business, even though the under 18 is actually the owner. While this could seem an uncomfortable situation, it may be the only way around the legal constraints.

Another potential problem is the lack of business start-up finance for those under 18. A few specialised loan funds exist to help people that most lenders won't assist because of their age. However, many of these, such as the 'Northern Youth Venture

Fund', are aimed at 18 to 30 year olds. It is also very difficult to open a business bank account in your own name at this age. This will make it difficult for the young entrepreneur to sign cheques, make payments, and so on.

MAKING IT HAPPEN
Schemes for under 18s starting a business

The schemes mentioned below are available to those wanting to start a business while under 18. Some do not run all of the time in all areas of the country. A few of the schemes offer financial support. However, many treat the 16 to 17 age range as a time to plan for starting up after 18, so many students are encouraged to attend college instead of entering the world of business.

Shell *Live*WIRE

Sponsored by Shell UK Ltd, Shell *Live*WIRE is the only national organisation providing free, extensive support and advice to 16 to 30 year olds from before start up through to early growth. It was established in 1982 with backing from Strathclyde Regional Council but by 1986 had gone nation-wide. Every person making an enquiry receives an essential business kit which is tailored to their specific business idea. They are also put in touch with a local *Live*WIRE co-ordinator. The annual Young Business Start Up Awards give firms trading for less than 18 months the chance to compete for county, regional, and national prizes, gaining publicity along the way.

Young Enterprise

Young Enterprise is a national charity and a company which aims to educate young people (between 14 and 19 years) about issues relating to starting and managing a business. The company achieves this through four Young Enterprise programmes.

1. Project Business UK (aimed at 14 and 15 year olds) gives students a practical insight into business life through business/ works visits and activity-based sessions.

2. Company Programme (15 to 19 years) involves students setting up and managing their own business for one year, allowing them to learn about the practicalities of running a business in the real world. The scheme can also contribute to achieving business-related qualifications.

3. Team Enterprise is similar to the Company Programme but aimed at disabled students (15 to 19 + years).

4. Entrepreneurship Masterclasses are one-day seminars for those students who have already participated in the Company Programme.

Youth and Business

Youth and Business schemes are run by Teesside Learning and Skills Council (LSC). The schemes are not nationwide and vary according to location. The schemes are aimed at individuals between the ages of 16 and 18 considering starting up their own business. The individual works as a partner with the training company or LSC involved. Students are provided with advice, training, and guidance, and also a period of work experience. They also receive a weekly training allowance based on unemployment benefits, and some schemes train towards recognised qualifications such as the NVQ in Owner Management—Business Planning (level 3). Much of the Youth in Business scheme centres on planning for business. This involves around six months of test marketing and research into the business idea.

The Prince's Trust

The Prince's Trust was established by the Prince of Wales in 1976 to help young people realise their full potential. Aimed at those aged 14–30 (or 14–25 in Scotland), the Trust offers support and financial assistance across a range of core programmes including business start-ups.

Since 1983, the Trust has helped over 50,000 businesses and its business programme currently offers: a low-interest loan of up to £5,000; a marketing grant of up to £250; advice lines and seminars; access to a volunteer business mentor.

Preparing for business

Most schemes, finance, and advice are available to people over 18. This makes it preferable to use the time between 16 and 17 to prepare for starting a business. Advice can be obtained from various organisations such as Jobcentres, Learning and Skills Councils (LSCs) in England, Local Enterprise Councils (LECs) in Scotland, and the National Council for Education and Training in Wales, Business Links in England, Small Business Gateways in Scotland, Business Connects in Wales, the Prince's Trust, the Prince's Scottish Youth Business Trust, and Chambers of Commerce. Trade associations may offer advice specific to a chosen business area. Making good use of the advice available will ensure that your planning is effective.

Gaining further qualifications may be essential to the success of some businesses. Professional qualification can gain credibility for a business. Any courses taken in further or higher education should be geared towards following a business career. Aim to combine specific subject knowledge with business skills, for example combining photography with business National Vocational Qualifications or marketing training. If there isn't a specific course available for the business idea, continue developing your skills as a hobby, while undertaking more conventional business training.

You could negotiate with Jobcentres to ensure that any training for work scheme offered to you is geared towards starting a business. Where possible, your work placements should be with small businesses, with any courses geared towards business start up. Spend the time before you are 18 in gaining relevant skills, experience, or finance. This could be through part-time paid employment or a placement.

While getting practical work experience, draw up a comprehensive business plan, seek advice, and research the market for your idea. Consider the costs of setting up, and think about premises, equipment, and labour requirements. Develop as complete a picture as possible of the way your business should be running in the future.

The moral support and advice of parents, relatives, and friends can be crucial in the early stages of business. You may need to rely on their financial assistance too, not only directly for the business, but also in terms of living expenses. Parental support can also be useful when establishing contacts, signing cheques, and so on. They could take responsibility for this side of the business until you reach 18 and are able to take over.

WHAT TO AVOID

Not being fully committed

Only people who are entirely committed to the idea should attempt to set up in business. It can take time to establish yourself, so you need to be tenacious and be prepared for knockbacks.

Not being fully prepared

Your business approach should be planned as comprehensively as possible prior to start up. A clear plan will be considered more positively by banks/sponsors/relatives. It is also a useful tool for ongoing management of the business. Also, be fully aware of potential legal and financial constraints.

Not getting the right advice and support

The nearest Business Link/Business Gateway/Business Eye or enterprise agency may be able to provide details of training schemes, loans, and grants available in a particular area. The Prince's Trust may be able to help with grants towards training or equipment for 14 to 18 year olds.

Not thinking through the alternatives

As a young entrepreneur, you may wish to consider the alternatives to starting a business straight away. Consider the long-term advantages of continuing in education or gaining work experience before deciding to be your own boss.

RECOMMENDED LINKS
Business Eye (Wales):
www.businesseye.org.uk

Business Gateway (Scotland):
www.bgateway.com
Business Link (England):
www.businesslink.org
Invest Northern Ireland:
www.investni.com
Prince's Scottish Youth Business Trust:
www.psybt.org.uk
Prince's Trust:
www.princes-trust.org.uk
Shell LiveWIRE:
www.shell-livewire.org

Young Enterprise UK:
www.young-enterprise.org.uk
SCORE (Service Corps of Retired
Executives):
www.score.org

SEE ALSO
Coming Up with a Business Idea (p. 13)
**Deciding Whether to Start a Business
   (p. 2)**
Small and Growing Businesses (p. 478)

FINDING PREMISES

Renting a Business Property

GETTING STARTED

Many businesses occupy premises on a rental basis, covered by a lease or tenancy agreement. This actionlist explains what a lease is, and goes over some of the main issues you need to consider before signing a lease.

FAQS

What is a lease?

A lease is a legal document issued by the landlord of the premises covering the terms of the tenancy. It confers the exclusive right to occupy premises for a fixed term in exchange for the payment of rent.

Check with your solicitor that the conditions in the lease serve the purposes of your business and are reasonable.

MAKING IT HAPPEN

The description of premises

The description of the premises must be accurate, in order to avoid disputes. Be particularly wary of undefined boundaries, and ask for an accurate plan to be attached to the lease. Your legal rights should be stated in the lease and should include right of access from the nearest public highway. If you are renting part of a building, the right to use common areas leading to your section of the premises should also be included, as should the provision of essential services, for example, gas, electricity, and drainage. The landlord or tenant of adjoining premises is also expected to keep his or her property in good condition. Landlords have rights and obligations under the lease but must allow tenants to occupy the property without interference.

The term of a tenancy agreement

The term means the length of time the agreement is for. Make sure that the occupancy start date corresponds with the date on the lease. It may be difficult to withdraw if the premises are no longer required before the end of the term. Even if premises cease to be in use, you will be liable for payment until the lease lapses. For a small business, a shorter lease or periodic tenancy (from month to month, or quarter to quarter) may be more appropriate.

Some landlords may be prepared to offer a contract called a 'tenancy at will', or 'licence', which can be ended at short notice by either side. Such contracts don't offer any security of tenure and are excluded from the protection of the Landlord and Tenant Act 1954. If extensive alterations or improvements are intended, a short-term tenancy, tenancy at will, or licence is inadequate.

Your obligations as a tenant

On signing a lease, the tenant agrees to take responsibility for a number of things. These are explained in more detail below.

Rent

Ensure that the rent and its payment dates are clearly stated. Compare the rents of similar property in the area and, if possible, negotiate a rent free period, for example, towards the costs of initial repairs or refurbishment. Consider instructing a General Practice Chartered Surveyor, experienced in commercial property, to negotiate on your behalf.

Repairs

These may be split into three stages. The first stage is before you occupy the property. It should be in a suitable state of repair, but if it is in poor condition, it will be necessary to prepare a schedule of condition with photographs. The second stage is during the lease. Be aware of your business's responsibility regarding repairs before occupying the premises. The third stage is the end of the lease. The property must be left in an acceptable state of repair. Businesses may be served with a schedule of dilapidation, itemising repairs that must be carried out.

Allowances should be made for fair wear and tear.

If the entire premises are leased, the landlord may expect the tenant to take full responsibility for all repairs (including structural). In this case, it is advisable to have a survey done and to have any defects remedied before signing the lease. It may be possible to negotiate an upper limit to the contributions made to the cost of repairs or an inclusive rent. Small businesses should go for an internal repairing lease with no liability for structural repairs.

Insurance

The tenant pays for insurance, although the landlord may initially make the payment, reclaiming pro rata from the tenant. Always ensure that insurance is adequate and that policy terms are reasonable.

Service charge

This applies to a multi-occupied building. The landlord will usually pay for common costs, for example, structural repairs, common areas, heating, and caretaker. This cost is re-charged to the tenants on a pro-portional basis (normally a ratio of floor areas). It is advisable to ensure that the basis of calculation is stated, that you have the right to see and check the landlord's expend-iture, and that you are not paying for any empty areas.

Use

Leases usually contain restrictions on the use of the property. These may relate to a specific type of business, or to a nuisance, for example, noxious fumes and noise. The restrictions normally reflect those imposed by the planning authority. If the use may change in the future, discuss the possibility with both your landlord and the local authority. The lease should contain a clause which permits a change of use, subject to the landlord's approval and stating that he or she must act reasonably.

Assigning and sub-letting

Check that the lease allows you to sub-let to another business, or better still, to assign the lease. Sub-letting means that the business is still liable for the rent, whereas assignment transfers all responsibility to the new ten-ant. With leases made before 1 January 1996, the business can still be liable if the assignee defaults under the original contract with the landlord. For leases dated 1 Janu-ary 1996 or later, complex new provisions exist. These mean that although the busi-ness might be obliged to guarantee the per-formance by the assignee of the lease (including the payment of rent and other monies), it cannot be liable for any default by subsequent assignees.

Alterations

Most standard leases prohibit the tenant from making alterations to the property unless the landlord finds it reasonable to do so. Before signing, consider any potential alterations that may be required, and re-member that tenants are normally required to reinstate the property at the end of their lease.

Rent reviews

Leases normally contain a section stating that regular rent reviews will take place at any interval subject to contractual agree-ment. The section also indicates how new rents are agreed and disputes are resolved. Most standard leases only make a provision for rent to increase, but it is a good idea to try to make the landlord agree that rent can also be decreased. Rent is normally reviewed to open market value at the date of review. If the landlord and tenant cannot agree on a rent, an independent arbitrator can be brought in, providing that this is a term of the lease.

Option to terminate the lease

Leases may contain an option to terminate before the end of the lease term on a specific date or dates. This is known as a break clause. One advantage is that if increased or decreased space is required, it is not neces-sary to wait until the lease ends. If a prop-erty is no longer suitable, but the lease term has not expired, it is possible to approach the landlord to see if he will accept a surrender of the lease. This absolves the tenant from all future liability, but the landlord may not agree, or may require extra payment.

Guarantor

If the landlord insists that the business act as a personal guarantor, the business will be liable for paying the rent and other costs should it fail. A landlord may request that a third party, for example, an associate company, is obtained to act as guarantor. You may find it difficult to find someone to act on behalf of the business in this capacity. A returnable deposit may be an alternative to this. It is important to avoid giving guarantees.

Improvements

Tenants who carry out improvements beyond repairs at their own expense will not obtain any compensation from the landlord, even if the term is cut short, unless they follow a procedure of giving advance notice. A legal representative should be contacted for more information.

The end of a lease

At the end of the lease, businesses are protected against eviction by the Landlord and Tenant Act 1954. This protection cannot be enforced if the business is, or has been, in breach of its contract, or if the landlord wants to regain the premises for his own use. The Act entitles the tenant to request a renewal of the lease at an up-to-date rent. If it is not granted, compensation may be awarded for disturbance (but not for improvement).

Six to twelve months notice by the landlord must be given, if the lease is to be terminated on the expiry date. If this is not given, the tenant can remain on the premises indefinitely, or can personally request a new tenancy. Tenancy laws are complicated, and a solicitor should therefore be consulted.

If the lease is registered as being outside the Landlord and Tenant Act 1954, the rights of the tenant will be reduced. If the landlord and tenant have agreed to contract out of part II of the Act, the tenant is not entitled to compensation upon expiry. A tenancy of less than six months, a tenancy at will, and a licence are all excluded from the protection of the Act.

WHAT TO AVOID
Not doing your homework

Past or nearby tenants could be contacted for information about the landlord and how he performs his duties. You will need to check that the correct planning permission has been obtained to use the premises for your type of business.

Not getting the right advice

Be wary of one-sided lease agreements and seek professional advice if you are unsure. Avoid committing to a Full Repairing lease, particularly if the property is relatively old or is in a state of disrepair, except in circumstances where the tenant commits to such a lease in return for discounted rent or a rent-free period of occupancy.

RECOMMENDED LINK

Royal Institution of Chartered Surveyors: **www.rics.org.uk**

SEE ALSO

Buying a Business Property (p. 71)
Complying with Fire Safety Regulations (p. 87)
Ergonomics at Work (p. 93)
Insuring a Business (p. 83)
Setting Up and Maintaining Your Home Office (p. 96)

Buying a Business Property

GETTING STARTED

Buying a property involves greater risks and financial commitment than renting, but sometimes it's the only way to get the right property for your business. Before making the choice, it's a good idea to list all of the factors affecting your decision, ranking them in order of importance. The main factors will be price, location, available finance, and whether the property meets the operational needs of the business. Everyone's needs are different and as few buildings are perfect, a compromise may be necessary. Once you have found your 'ideal' property, you will need to make an offer, raise the finance, and go through the relevant legal procedures.

FAQS

Where can I find out about available property?

There are plenty of places where you can look for the kind of information you're after. Try contacting local authorities, which keep a register of industrial property, estate agents, or the real estate departments of commercial companies. Check the ads in local and national newspapers, and specialist and trade magazines, and keep an eye out for notices or billboards posted on interesting looking premises. Don't forget also to spread the word among your personal contacts.

How do I evaluate my requirements when buying a property?

When choosing a building, you need to focus on which attributes are essential for your business to operate effectively. You may also need to decide whether it's preferable to convert an existing building or to buy purpose-built premises. The budget available for the actual purchase, and potential renovation/conversion will also need to be taken into account.

MAKING IT HAPPEN

Features to rank when evaluating potential buildings

You've got a list of properties to look at—there may be a large number of buildings to choose from. The easiest way through the selection process is to list all the important features you require, and then score each property you see against each feature. A major constraint will be the price of the building. Costs can vary significantly. Try evaluating buildings on a 'cost per square metre' basis. Check whether the location qualifies for any financial incentives, for example, if it's located in a low-income area.

Location is key. Think about whether the location will be appropriate for your customers, and whether the facilities are appropriate. Does your business need to cater to passing trade? Would it be preferable to be nearer to a key customer or supplier? The location needs to be right for your staff, too. Make sure that the right staff can be recruited locally, and that there is access to reliable public transport. Staff should feel secure in the area, and have access to facilities such as nearby shops and banks.

Look at the surrounding businesses. Are they growing or declining? Are any of them likely to be a nuisance, for example through noise or dust caused by the processes? Also, think about where your competitors are sited. Should the business be located near to competitors?

The size of the building will be an issue. There should be a balance between sufficient space, not more than is needed or can be afforded, and enough space to allow for reasonable expansion. Floor space is allocated in square feet or metres so it's a good idea to keep in mind how large, for example, 500 or 1,000 square metres are, as a frame of reference. If it's too large, will it be possible to sub-let the extra space? An allowance of 11 cubic metres per person is recommended in the Workplace (Health,

Safety and Welfare) Regulations 1992 Approved Code of Practice. New Royal Institute of Chartered Surveyors measuring practice states that building space should be quoted in metres squared primarily, with square feet listed as secondary information only.

Think about the physical nature of the building. The layout of the site itself should meet all of the operational requirements. Issues to consider are building density, the number of stories, and the condition of the building, in relation to the amount of money available for repairs. You also need to consider visitor flow, the availability of services, car parking (especially in residential areas), and accessibility (including stairs, lifts, and so on). Other issues to think about are security, storage, and lighting (natural and artificial).

Make an offer on a property

Once you've identified a suitable property, an offer should be made to the agent. This offer should be conditional upon planning permission, the building survey, and the Fire Officer's report. It should also be conditional upon raising the finances, the valuation, and whether or not the building is vacant possession, as well as upon certain contract conditions. For example, some new developments have maintenance charges with unregulated annual rises.

After your conditional offer is accepted, a surveyor should be employed to undertake a full detailed structural survey. It's advisable to shop around for quotes from surveyors and to check which details the surveyor will evaluate. The survey will usually include a valuation for mortgage purposes.

Obtain advice on buying a property

You will need to consult a number of officials in order to ensure that the building can be used for the intended purposes.

Planning permission

This is the most important approval required (and the one which the business is most likely to need assistance with). It's required when building development or change of use occurs. Development is defined in Town and Country Planning legislation, and some situations do not require permission. The local authority planning department can be contacted for more information. It will also be necessary to carry out a business search to find out more about the property. You will need to research the planning authority's zoning area proposals, to ensure that the building will not be affected. You will also need to find out about any restrictions due to preservation orders which could hinder development, and additional restrictions on the property because of local by-laws. Finally, make sure you identify the exact use of the building.

Building regulations

These regulations are administered by the Building Control Department of the local authority. Building regulations apply to the erection, re-erection, or extension of a building, the material alteration of a building, the material change of use of a building, and the provision, extension, or material change of use of a controlled service or fitting, in or in connection with a building.

Environmental health officers

Fire officers grant fire certificates and are responsible for confirming that fire precautions are up to standard.

The HSE makes sure employees have a safe environment in which to work. Local authorities are responsible for ensuring health and safety guidelines are enforced in shops, offices, and some other service industries, while the HSE concentrates on larger-scale concerns, such as factories. Visit its useful website (**www.hse.gov.uk**) or contact its information line on 08701 545500 if you are unsure about any health and safety matters in relation to your business.

Legal aspects when buying a property

Before you buy, it's advisable to consult a solicitor or licensed conveyancer experienced in commercial property transactions. They can advise on contracts, planning regulations, financial research, history of building searches, and completion. They should also ensure that statutory regulations are met and that there are no outstanding notices on the property.

Stamp duty is payable by the purchaser on a property costing more than a certain amount. This is subject to alteration in the government's budgets. Since the Finance Act 1989, the freehold sale of a commercial building under three years old has attracted VAT at the standard rate (currently 17.5%). When VAT is paid on a building, stamp duty is due on the total price paid, not the price before VAT.

Financing the purchase of a property

Once you have decided on a building, the purchase will need financing. Property is usually financed over 20 or 25 years with the amount advanced as a loan being 60–70% of the property valuation. Lenders will expect a legal charge on the property for security. Once you have decided on a building, the purchase will need financing.

There are several sources of funding. If using high street banks, call around for the best rates of interest. Merchant banks may provide a large portion of money, but prefer proven businesses. Many will lend on an equity basis, meaning they take stock in the company in return for the capital loaned. You could also look at building societies, which may give mortgages for industrial and commercial purchases, and at local authority schemes, which are designed to help promote economic development (availability varies between different authorities).

 WHAT TO AVOID

Not considering all the financial implications of buying freehold
Purchasing a building is a major move, as it ties up a lot of capital in the building rather than in the business. It's essential to ensure that this will not damage the business. Most small businesses do grow, so they should consider carefully before buying a freehold. Remember that even when house prices are rising, commercial property values tend to rise at a lower rate. There is often no real financial advantage in buying instead of renting. Businesses should make sure that any advantages that do accrue are worth the cost. Also bear in mind that owning a property commits the business to additional expenditure, through obligations to undertake regular checks on electrical supplies and wiring for safety reasons. It's very important to ascertain the rateable value and rates payable on a property, as these can make a huge difference to the overall cost.

Not seeking the right advice

It's advisable to seek advice from estate agents, local businesses, small business advisers, local authority development officers, and enterprise agencies when making decisions about properties. It's also a good idea to talk to firms in the surrounding area about the property. It may be worthwhile asking why the previous tenant left. It's important to consult your solicitor once a property has been found, and to avoid signing anything straight away.

RECOMMENDED LINKS

European Society of Chartered Surveyors: **www.escs.org**
Royal Institution of Chartered Surveyors: **www.rics.org.uk**
Royal Institution of Chartered Surveyors in Northern Ireland:
www.rics-northernireland.org.uk
Royal Institution of Chartered Surveyors in Scotland:
www.rics-scotland.org.uk

SEE ALSO
A Guide to Health and Safety at Work (p. 90)
Complying with Fire Safety Regulations (p. 87)
Insuring a Business (p. 83)
Renting a Business Property (p. 68)
Setting Up and Maintaining Your Home Office (p. 96)

Choosing and Using an Architect

GETTING STARTED

If you are considering doing work of any sort to a building—whether new or existing—you should consult an architect. He or she will not only listen to your ideas, but will also be able to suggest alternative options. It is also part of the architect's service to help with planning permission and building regulations, and to ensure that the plan that is decided upon is strictly followed by the builders. You will also need an architect when planning works to a listed building or a building in a conservation area, or when you are considering a change of use of a building or site. An architect will also be required when you have site or building development proposals, or planning or enforcement notice appeals (these often become necessary because an architect was not appointed in the first instance).

FAQS

How do I choose an architect?

An obvious but potentially risky way of finding an architect is to select one from the Yellow Pages. Another is to base the choice upon a personal recommendation, or find out who designed projects that are similar to yours that you like. A recommended alternative to these methods is to contact client services at the Royal Institute of British Architects (RIBA), who act as a broker between clients and architects; they will provide a list of practices suitable for the potential project. The local public library should hold a RIBA Directory of Members in which the particular architect's expertise is mentioned. RIBA also has an on-line bookshop, and you may find the 'Engaging an Architect' series useful. (The RIBA website address is given below.)

It's not advisable to rely on 'fee-bidding' to locate appropriate services: it's important to choose an architect based on the quality of service and product, not solely on the fee. Ask to see a portfolio of the architect's work and visit completed buildings. It's also a good idea to check that your architect has worked on similar projects and has the appropriate design skills.

What is the architect's role?

The architect will discuss your requirements and help you to prepare a brief and an agreed action plan. He or she will then identify appropriate sites, carry out an evaluation and visit the proposed site before undertaking a feasibility study and investigating any statutory regulations applicable, as well as giving advice regarding other services the project requires. The architect will then prepare a timetable and details for planning permission/building regulation applications, as well as developing designs, working drawings, and models; determining the cost of the exercise and the deadline; and preparing production details.

He or she will also advise on appropriate procurement methods and prepare tender documentation, obtaining tenders and advising on them. They will negotiate with potential builders and draw up a building contract. Once the work has begun they will inspect the site and the progress made. The architect's role includes administering the building contract, submitting financial reports, giving advice on maintenance regimes, and finally providing drawings of the building as built. The full range of services is set out in the RIBA Standard Appointment documents.

MAKING IT HAPPEN

Find out about the conditions of appointment of an architect

When appointing an architect, a Conditions of Appointment document should be completed, checked and agreed upon. The points covered should include: the architect's authority and duty of care, use of consultants, site inspection, client's instructions, copyright assignment, suspension and termination, settlement of deposits, and governing law. There are standard forms for this purpose.

Investigate architects' fees and expenses

The Royal Institute of British Architects (RIBA) has a scale of indicative percentage fees based upon construction costs, building type, and nature of the work. Fees are usually charged by negotiation on an hourly basis for small jobs, or as a percentage of the building works for larger contracts. Any agreement should also include stage payments, suspension, resumption and termination, expenses and disbursements, variations, and VAT. Detailed guidance on these matters can be obtained by contacting RIBA.

Prepare for discussions

Once you've appointed your architect, the first stage of the work involves a discussion of the requirements, budget, timetables, and fees. After this discussion and the preparation of a full brief, the architect will draw up a plan of action which should be agreed. In preparation for this discussion, it is a good idea for you to become familiar with ownership rights of the property, for example, rights of way or boundary fences. It is important for you to keep focused on what is to be achieved.

Plan the construction project

The second stage is for the architect to visit the site in order to evaluate what might be done. If a site has not been identified, the architect may be able to advise on appropriate locations and accommodation. A sketch proposal may be prepared at this stage as an initial point of discussion and agreement with you.

A feasibility study can then be undertaken by the architect, giving possible alternative options of spatial arrangements and elevational treatment. Restrictions may be imposed on the design by statutory items such as Town and Country Planning, building regulations, and fire and means of escape regulations. Health and safety legis-lation will have to be taken into account, as well as the Disability Discrimination Act 1995.

During this design process the architect will advise whether other consultant disciplines will need to be appointed, such as a quantity surveyor, structural engineer, landscape architect, mechanical and electrical engineering consultant, and a planning supervisor to deal with health and safety. The Construction (Design and Management) Regulations 1994 (as amended in 2000) affect work on all types of commercial and public buildings.

On smaller projects the architect may carry out their own survey of the land or building in question. The cost of this is usually based on an hourly rate, and is not included in the percentage fee quoted by the architect.

Preparation of the architect's designs

Once the plan of action has been agreed, the architect will organise meetings and surveys with all the other bodies involved in the project, which will enable cost estimates and outline proposals to be prepared. It's important to be aware that changes to the plans may be necessary as part of this planning process. Decisions on quality of workmanship, materials, and so on are made at this stage, to enable the quantity surveyor to monitor the costs. A planning application may be submitted, for which a statutory fee will be paid by you to the local authority. As planning approval cannot be guaranteed, it may be prudent to await consent before instructing the architect to prepare building regulations documentation. Again, you—as the client—will be responsible for statutory fees, one at the time of formal application, and further fees for site inspections.

Once planning and building regulation approvals have been obtained, the architect will be in a position to prepare detailed design drawings. The number of drawings will be dependent on the size and complexity of the project and may be used initially by the quantity surveyor to prepare a Bill of Quantities, and by the contractors at tender stage, and then on site during construction.

Architects and building contractors

The architect can now prepare production information and tender documents. These are then sent to contractors tendering for the work. The architect will provide advice regarding the suitability of tenders submitted. Once a contractor is selected, you can ask the architect to draw up a building contract between the business and the contractor.

Once the project is underway, the architect can visit the site at regular intervals to inspect the work being carried out. He or she will convene site meetings, to which you may be invited (or will otherwise be given the minutes), and will generally administer the terms of the building contract, give advice on maintenance, and arrange for drawings of the building pinpointing drainage lines, services, and so on, to be provided.

At various stages during construction, the architect will issue interim certificates for payment to the contractor. During the defects liability period (or retention period)—usually six or twelve months after practical completion of the project—an amount will be retained by the business until any defective work is satisfactorily completed.

Architects' services

In addition to construction projects, many practising architects can provide a range of additional services. These may include: surveying and inspection, furniture and interior design, cost estimating and financial advice, and undertaking negotiations.

WHAT TO AVOID
Choosing your architect on a 'fee basis'

The Royal Institute of British Architects (RIBA) fee scale is a guide to architects and clients based on historic data. Fees should be negotiated, and for larger contracts, it is important to meet the architect who will be dealing with the project, as dealings with them could last for a couple of years. This can help in avoiding personality clashes or misunderstandings over requirements. This can be a more important issue than the fee. Decisions should not be made on the basis of fee alone but on the overall value of service.

Not choosing the right architect for the job

An architect should be selected who can demonstrate an ability to do a job within a specified budget. It is important to ask to see evidence of professional indemnity insurance and to ensure that the sum covered for each and every claim is adequate. If required, architects will be happy to discuss undertaking some or all of the services with a commensurate variation in fees. The most useful advice is usually provided when still considering a project. It is a good idea to discuss ideas with an architect before being constrained by leases, loans, and so on. He or she may be able to identify suitable sites/premises for your business to consider.

RECOMMENDED LINKS
Architects Registration Board:
www.arb.org.uk
Architecture and Surveying Institute:
www.asi.org.uk
Association of Consultant Architects (ACA):
www.acarchitects.co.uk
Client Services, Royal Institute of British Architects (RIBA):
www.architecture.com
RIBA Bookshop:
www.ribabookshop.com
RIBA Directory of Members:
www.ribafind.org
Royal Incorporation of Architects in Scotland (RIAS):
www.rias.org.uk
Royal Society for Ulster Architects:
www.rsua.org.uk

SEE ALSO
A Guide to Building Regulations (p. 77)

A Guide to Building Regulations

GETTING STARTED

The Building Regulations 2000 form the main United Kingdom legislation for the construction of, and changes to, all types of buildings. The regulations exist to protect anyone in or near a building. They also deal with energy conservation and issues concerning access and facilities for disabled people. For anyone involved in running a small business, it's therefore important to have a working knowledge of what the regulations involve. This actionlist provides a basic guide, but much more detailed information can be found on the websites listed at the end.

FAQS

In what instances are businesses affected by building regulations?

There are four main situations where building regulations apply:

1. the construction or extension of a building
2. a change of use of a building (even if the building itself is not changing, a change of use may require new ventilation or access arrangements that will need approval)
3. addition of extra fittings such as air conditioning and kitchen equipment
4. building changes such as underpinning or major structural modifications

Where can I find out exactly what is involved in and required by building regulations?

The building regulations and all associated approved documents, along with other guidance, can be downloaded from the Department for Transport, Local Government and the Regions website. An up-to-date list of approved inspectors is available from the Association of Corporate Approved Inspectors website. Both website addresses are given below.

✔ MAKING IT HAPPEN

Comply with building regulations

Before you go ahead with making any changes to a building, you need first to have your plans checked and approved. You can do this in two ways—either through the local authority's Building Control department, or through an approved inspector. If you decide to use the local authority, there are two ways of obtaining approval:

1. **Deposit of full plans**
   Your application should contain all relevant structural details and be submitted well in advance of starting on site. The local authority has to pass or reject plans within five weeks, but it can request an extension of up to eight weeks from the date of application. It will consult with all the necessary bodies such as fire, water, and highways before issuing a notice of approval. It can also request modifications to the plans or lay down conditions. If the plans are rejected, full reasons will be given in the notice.

2. **A building notice**
   This is suitable for minor works, as the application needs only outline details. The notice allows for building works to start without the need for drawing up full plans, which can be costly.

Once a set of full plans or a building notice have been lodged with the local authority, two clear days' notice (so not weekends or bank holidays) must be given to the local authority before work starts. If work is started before approval is given on a full-plans submission, it may prejudice any future appeal against the local authority's decisions about the work.

If an approved inspector is used, he or she will discuss, check, and issue a plans certificate. An initial notice will be sent to the local authority and, once this has been accepted, the inspector will monitor the work as it progresses. You may start the work as soon as the notice is accepted by the local authority, as long as there are no further requests from the local authority within five days of lodging the notice. Work must not start if the notice is rejected. The inspector will issue a final certificate on completion.

If plans are rejected by the local authority, they may be altered and resubmitted, or an appeal may be lodged. For details of how to lodge an appeal, refer to the guidelines issued by the local authority.

Before you go ahead with making any changes to a building, you need first to have your plans checked and approved. You can do this by filing an application for a building permit with your local building inspector's office or building commission. In addition to the application, you may need to submit a proposal for the work that is to be done as well as evidence of liability insurance and a copy of your building contractor's license.

Costs and fees

A fee is payable to the local authority for administering applications. However, each local authority sets its own charges depending on the type of work. Details of charges should be obtained direct from the local authority, who publish their fees and costs which are based on the Building (Local Authority Charges) Regulations 1998. If the work is solely for disabled people, Regulation 9 provides for an exemption from certain charges.

A full-plans application may involve a two-stage payment: the first stage is when the plans are submitted (plan charge), and the second follows a site inspection (inspection charge) if the local authority feels it is necessary to visit the site. The cost for submitting a building notice (building notice charge) will cost the same as the total of a plan charge and an inspection charge together, and is payable when the building notice is submitted to the local authority.

If the services of an approved inspector are employed, then the fee is negotiable but is usually based on a percentage of construction costs.

Enforcement of the building regulations

Before starting and during any work, the local authority may request additional information such as structural calculations. A building control surveyor monitoring the work will issue notification of any work contravening building regulations.

The approved inspector may make recommendations as work progresses. If the recommended amendments are not made within three months, a final certificate will not be issued and the inspector is obliged to notify the local authority, which in turn may use its powers of enforcement. The local authority can issue a notice insisting on alterations to the work or its complete removal within 28 days.

If the local authority is not informed of any relevant building works, it is entitled to prosecute. Currently the fine is a maximum of £5,000 plus £50 a day until the work is rectified. The local authority also has the power to undertake the work itself, even including demolition, and is entitled to start legal proceedings to recover its costs.

Other regulations relating to building

The list of related legislation is extensive and depends on the type of building work. Some of the most important are:

- the Construction (Design and Management) Regulations 1994, and 2000 amendment—these concern all owners of commercial property. Under these regulations, owners must appoint an individual as planning supervisor to co-ordinate the health and safety plan for the project. The regulations apply to all construction, maintenance, and demolition work
- the Construction (Health, Safety, and Welfare) Regulations 1996 (as amended)
- the Building Regulations (Approved Inspectors etc) Regulations 2000
- the Building (Disabled People) Regulations 1987 and the Building Standards (Scotland) Regulations 1990, as revised by the Building Standards and Procedure Amendment (Scotland) Regulations 1999
- The Fire Precautions Act 1971, as modified by the Fire Precautions (Workplace) Regulations 1997 and 1999 amendments
- The Party Wall Act 1996

Definitions relating to the building regulations

There are various terms which come up regularly in connection with building regulations, and it's useful to know exactly what is meant by each of them. Here is a list of the most common:

- *Local authority*: administrative office of local government
- *Building regulations*: legislation concerning building works
- *Planning permission*: permission by the local authority to carry out building works
- *Approved inspector*: a qualified and registered surveyor who can oversee building works
- *Site inspection*: visit to building works by the building control surveyor
- *Full plans*: complete details of building works, including structural details
- *Plan charge*: fee payable on submission of full plans
- *Inspection charge*: fee payable if a site inspection is required
- *Building notice*: outline details of minor building works
- *Notice of approval*: confirmation that plans or details of building works conform to the regulations

WHAT TO AVOID
Not obtaining planning permission first

Before getting building regulations approval, it may be necessary to obtain planning permission. Normally, planning permission is applied for first; once approval has been granted, building regulations are then set in motion. If permission is not sought or granted beforehand, the penalties can be severe.

Not seeking professional advice

Building regulations can be complicated, so get professional advice if you feel out of your depth. The local authority's Building Control department can be contacted for guidance, free information booklets, and advice even before an application is made. The following three publications may also be useful: *Manual to the Building Regulations*, by Michael Billington, published by Stationery Office Books, 1999; *The Building Regulations Explained and Illustrated*, by Vincent Powell-Smith, published by Blackwell Science, 1999; and *The Guide to Construction Adjudication*, published by Construction Industry Council Publications, 1998.

RECOMMENDED LINKS

Association of Corporate Approved Inspectors:
www.acai.org.uk
Construction Industry Council:
www.cic.org.uk
Department for Transport, Local Government and the Regions:
www.construction.dtlr.gov.uk/bregs/building.htm
National House-Building Council:
www.nhbc.co.uk
Northern Ireland Office, Department of Finance and Personnel, Building Regulations Section:
www.ni-assembly.gov.uk
Royal Institution of Chartered Surveyors (RICS):
www.rics.org.uk
Scottish Executive, Building Standards:
www.scotland.gov.uk
The Stationery Office:
www.legislation.hmso.gov.uk
Welsh Assembly Government, Housing Division:
www.wales.gov.uk

SEE ALSO
A Guide to Health and Safety at Work (p. 90)
Choosing and Using an Architect (p. 74)
Complying with Fire Safety Regulations (p. 87)
Insuring a Business (p. 83)
Obtaining Planning Permission (p. 80)

Obtaining Planning Permission

GETTING STARTED

The aim of the planning system is to balance the need for development with the need to protect the environment. To obtain planning permission, your business will need to apply to its local city, borough, or district council, or the development corporation if there is one in the area. Councils should grant permission unless there is a sound and clear-cut planning reason not to do so.

The Planning Inspectorate publishes two guides which you may find useful: *Making Your Planning Appeal* and *A Guide to Taking Part in Planning Appeals*.

The Stationery Office publishes four guides on the subject, *PPG1 General Policy and Principles*, *PPG4 Industrial and Commercial Development and Small Firms*, *PPG6 Town Centres and Retail Development*, and *PPG18 Enforcing Planning Control*.

FAQS

Is planning permission necessary?

Your business will need to check with its local council to find out if proposed developments will need planning permission. A fee will be payable for a formal decision, known as a lawful development certificate. In areas such as Conservation Areas, National Parks, and areas of outstanding natural beauty, tighter controls do apply.

Certain work is considered to be 'permitted development'. This includes internal alterations, unless the project will affect the exterior. However, internal alterations to a listed building may need listed building consent. Planning permission is not required for repairs to outside building works. Neither is it required for factory expansions, although this depends upon the size and volume of the extension. The expansion must also be related to the current use of the building, or the provision of staff facilities.

No planning permission is needed for demolition, although if it is a listed building or a building in a conservation area, other controls may apply. No planning permission is required for the exhibition of a sign if the sign displays the name of the firm or business, and the goods or services supplied. The sign must also not exceed the sizes and heights specified by the local authority. The exception to this is, however, when it is on a listed building, or a building in a conservation area. In general, no planning permission will be required for using a domestic residence for business, unless the home will no longer be used mainly as a private residence. You will need to consider other factors too. For example, will the change in use result in a rise in traffic in the immediate area; and will it disturb the neighbours, or cause a nuisance, for example, in terms of noise or smells?

You will need to consult the local planning officer if you are planning to erect a fence with a height of over one metre. Building new premises nearly always requires planning permission, and the development plan of the area should be checked with the council to see if proposals are acceptable. Office and shop extensions require planning permission, and so will change of use, unless both the present and the proposed business fall within the same 'use class'. However, it is also possible to change use between certain classes. Use classes are set out by the Town and Country Planning (Use Classes) Order 1987, and changes of use are set by the Town and Country Planning (General Permitted Development) Order 1995. The classes include shops, financial and professional services, food and drink, business, assembly, and leisure. If a property does not fall within any category listed, it is termed 'sui generis', a use on its own.

What does the council look out for?

In considering a planning application, the council will take into account the character of the area, road safety and traffic congestion, the need to reserve land for other purposes, and the adequacy of water disposal and sewerage. It will also consider the suitability of the site, any development plan policies relevant to the application, archaeological implications, and environmental impacts. The council will also be concerned with building regulations, listed building and conservation area consents, fire regulations, and even crime prevention and security.

MAKING IT HAPPEN
Apply for planning permission
Anyone can apply for planning permission. You may, however, prefer to appoint an agent to carry out the application on your behalf. The agent could be a solicitor or an architect, for example. If you, as the applicant, are not the true owner, or only have part ownership, of the property mentioned in the proposal, then you must inform those who do own or part own it. Planning permission decisions can take up to eight weeks, although large and complex applications can take longer.

Your first step is to inform the council of your plans. If necessary, your next step will be to ask to see the Development Plan, in order to assess any possible problems. You should then obtain the application form and find out how many copies to submit. You must then decide on the type of permission you want to apply for, and consult neighbours and people who may be affected by the proposal. Finally, you should submit your application, together with a certificate of ownership or notification, and the fee. (A list of fees can be obtained from the planning department of the local authority.)

Understand the different types of planning permission
There are several different types of planning permission.

Outline planning permission simply looks to see whether the development is acceptable in principle. It can only be applied for where the development involves the erection of a building. Detailed drawings are not normally needed for outline planning permission. Permission, if granted, will be subject to certain conditions. It will be necessary to obtain approval for details, for example of appearance, landscaping, and design.

Full planning permission is required if the business intends to change the use of the property, or to legalise existing works which were built without the necessary permission. To obtain full planning permission, all of the details of the proposal should be submitted. Application for Renewal of Temporary Permission or Relief from Conditional Permission applies if the business intends to extend the time by which work must be started, continue a time limited use, or retain planning permission without conditions.

After the application for planning permission
After you have applied, the application will be acknowledged. At this point, a discrete reference number will be issued. Your application will also be made available to anyone who wishes to see it. A report will be prepared for the planning committee. Applicants should hear within eight weeks unless there is a problem. Delays may occur if a site visit or further information is required. If the application is granted, the planned changes must be commenced within five years. After this time it will probably be necessary to reapply. When an application is rejected, the applicant must be told why.

Appeal against planning permission rejection
It is possible to appeal within six months of a planning permission proposal being rejected. Before appealing, applicants should make every effort to sort out the council's objections, either by negotiation or amendment. It is usual to opt for written representation. This is a relatively inexpensive option. However, it will require a lot of effort and time, and you should expect to

wait for anything up to 18 weeks for a written appeal, and up to 24 weeks for an informal hearing.

WHAT TO AVOID
Not getting the right advice
This can be a complex area, and it is essential that you get the right advice. It is a good idea, if you are at all unsure, to use an architect or surveyor to assist with the proposal. If in doubt, applicants should consult an expert, or the local planning officer. If a business proceeds without planning permission, the consequences can be serious.

Not being prepared
The more prepared you are, the less likely it will be that delays will occur. It will be important to find out when the Planning Committee dates are, and to ensure that the information submitted meets the Committee timetable. It is advisable not only to consult the neighbours about a planning proposal, but also to contact other affected parties, such as the water and sewerage company, highway authority, and the Health and Safety Executive. It is also important to make sure that the information submitted with the application is complete and easily understood. It will be helpful to ask what additional information, such as photographs, may be required.

Worrying that it is taking too long
Planning permission is a fraught business and it's easy to lose your sense of proportion when the process seems to be dragging on for weeks. Remember that planning officers have a difficult job to do, and that it pays to be patient and respectful in any dealings with them. It is worth noting that planning applications are determined by elected members, not planning officers, who simply make recommendations. However, new council structures have led to the greater use of delegated powers for non-contentious applications.

Not abiding by the rules
Once the planning permission is obtained, it is essential that you make sure that any work carried out is as described in the approved plans.

Giving false information
It is a serious offence to give false information, or to withhold information, in order successfully to obtain a lawful development certificate. Penalties include a fine of up to £5,000 and two years' imprisonment.

RECOMMENDED LINKS
Office of the Deputy Prime Minister:
www.odpm.gov.uk
Planning Division, Welsh Assembly Government:
www.wales.gov.uk/subiplanning
Planning Inspectorate:
www.planning-inspectorate.gov.uk
Royal Town Planning Institute:
www.rtpi.org.uk

SEE ALSO
A Guide to Building Regulations (p. 77)

Insuring a Business

GETTING STARTED

Your business needs insurance against risks that might threaten its profitability, such as the theft of equipment, or a work-related injury to staff. Small businesses are more vulnerable to the impact of these incidents, as they often do not have the resources for unexpected expenditure.

This actionlist tells you what insurance your business is legally required to have and describes some optional types of insurance that you could use to protect your business.

FAQS

What insurance is compulsory for businesses?

As soon as your business employs someone (outside of your direct family), you are obliged to take out employers' liability insurance to cover all your employees' injuries or illness, whether they are caused on or off site. Employees include trainees and contract staff. By law you must have cover of £5 million, although most policies now automatically provide £10 million cover. You must exhibit a certificate of employers' liability insurance at each place of business and keep it for 40 years (see the 40-year rule below). You can be fined if you do not hold a current employers' liability insurance policy.

Any injuries or illness relating to motor accidents that occur while your employees are working for you may be covered separately by your motor insurance. All vehicles, whether cars, commercial vehicles, or motorcycles that are used on the road must be insured for minimum third party liability. Insurers normally need to know who will be using the vehicle for business purposes (especially any drivers whose age is lower than 25), what the business use entails, who owns the vehicle, and how it will be used. Make sure you check the licences of all your drivers. Any serious motor convictions must be advised to your insurer.

What is the 40-year rule?

Employers must keep employer's liability insurance certificates, the ones you are required to display at each workplace, for

not less than 40 years, starting with certificates issued in 1999. This is because claims for diseases can be made many years after the disease is contracted.

Health and safety inspectors have the right to see any certificates issued since 1999. These certificates can be kept electronically. You can be fined up to £2,500 for any day that you are without suitable insurance. If you do not display the certificate of insurance, or refuse to make it available to HSE inspectors when they ask, you can be fined up to £1,000.

Where can I go for more information?

The Health Insurance Annual Report, the Employers' Liability (Compulsory Insurance) Act 1969 and the Employers' Liability (Compulsory Insurance) Regulations 1998 are all published by The Stationery Office. *Employers' Liability (Compulsory Insurance) Act 1969: A guide for employers* is published by the Health and Safety Executive (HSE).

The Association of British Insurers (ABI) produces advice files specifically for smaller businesses. The National Enterprise Insurance Scheme is run by Local Enterprise Agencies and offers a range of independent professional advice to new and established businesses. The scheme helps businesses to identify basic insurance needs and can also help you get advice from an insurance broker.

All available website addresses for the above organisations are given below.

MAKING IT HAPPEN
Choosing an insurer

Any insurance company you use should be

authorised by the Insurance and Friendly Societies Division of the Financial Services Authority (FSA). Most are members of the Association of British Insurers. Check an insurer is authorised by calling the FSA's enquiry line (0845 606 1234) or visiting the website (address given below). It is always a good idea to shop around for advice and quotes.

Using the services of a reputable insurance broker will help you find the best product to suit your requirements, at the best value. A broker's services are usually free and they will search the market to obtain the best deal for you. Ideally, talk to insurance brokers or consultants who have experience of small businesses.

Different types of business insurance

There are a number of areas of risk for which insurance cover is prudent. Some of the main ones are given under the headings below.

Building and contents

Building and contents insurance can be important if you manufacture, repair, install, or even retail goods. Property cover can be provided for specific risks (such as fire or flood), or for a wide range of risks in one package. You should cover all your property, including buildings (if you own them), contents, stock, and fixtures. Most policies automatically insure you for up to £100,000 against terrorist attack. You will need to arrange extra insurance if your property and possessions exceed this replacement cost. If you rent, ask to see the landlord's insurance policy and check the range of protection that is in place.

Computer insurance

Computer insurance policies cover you for breakdowns and for loss of information. Check that your insurance covers the computer environment, including the e-mail and Internet access system. Different types of engineering insurance policies are available for machinery. This can cover breakdown and statutory inspection cover.

Business interruption

Business interruption insurance (also known as consequential loss insurance) protects your company's income and overheads. This insurance compensates you for extra costs incurred and trading profits lost if your business suffers serious disruption, for example, after a fire. You are usually covered for an interruption period of up to 12 months from the date of any loss or damage. If damage to your office would increase the cost of working, you can claim added expense such as the cost of fitting temporary offices, removal costs and expenses, and increased rent and rates.

Legal insurance

The increasing volume of legislation affecting small businesses, and the financial and other penalties that may result in the event of non-compliance, has created an upsurge in demand for both helplines and commercial legal expenses if things go wrong. You can now get insurance for commercial legal expenses. A wide range of cover is available, ranging from employment matters, contractual disputes with customers, or accountants' fees following tax or VAT investigations.

Personal and public liability insurance

A director or officer of a company can be sued personally over an increasingly wide range of matters relating to the business. The personal liability of a director is unlimited. Legally, the directors of a company and the company itself are separate entities, and so both may be defendants, separately or jointly, in any legal action or prosecution. To protect the personal assets of individuals and, crucially, to cover the costs of their defence, directors and officers insurance is widely used. Modern insurance policies insure directors and senior managers, and extend to protect all other employees too. Directors and officers insurance extends to protect the company, rather than leaving it to fund its own defence, acting as a mechanism that also protects the value of a director's personal holding in the company.

Public liability covers you against accidents to members of the public, or damage to property that occurs as a result of your business activities. It also covers any related legal costs. This type of insurance is compulsory for certain types of business, for example health and fitness instructors.

Professional indemnity and product liability

Professional indemnity insurance covers you against being sued for giving poor advice or having been in some way negligent. This insurance is obligatory in certain professions such as medicine, law, accountancy, and financial services. It is now common in areas such as management and computer consultancy, engineering, and design. Cover usually includes breach of professional duty, breach of copyright, breach of confidentiality, libel and slander, and loss of documents.

Product liability insurance is the same principle as the professional indemnity, protecting you against claims arising from faulty products that you have sold, manufactured, or installed.

Key man

Key man cover pays a benefit to the business if a key employee, for example, a business partner, is lost through death or incapacity that would otherwise result in financial hardship for the business.

Income protection

Income protection insurance schemes cover employees in the event of long-term sickness, paying their salaries during the period of incapacity. This relieves your business of the burden of paying for a sick employee. The benefit is paid tax-free after a deferred period that is selected by the policyholder and is paid until retirement, recovery, or death.

Critical illness

Critical illness insurance provides a benefit in the event of diagnosis of any one of a list of serious illnesses, incapacities, or conditions. Benefits can be lump sum or income based, and for any term. Premiums can vary dramatically, so independent advice and quotations are important and it's worth taking the time to find the best deal.

Credit insurance

Credit insurance covers you against debtors who are unable to pay money owed to you because they have gone bankrupt.

Employee litigation

Employee litigation insurance covers you against claims brought by your employees on the basis of disability, race, and gender status.

Home workers

A growing number of start-up businesses begin in a person's home. Home workers' insurance may be needed as ordinary household insurance policies will not usually cover business risks such as employers', public, or product liability. If you work from home or use your car for business, your household and motor insurance may be invalidated so do investigate your situation with your insurer.

WHAT TO AVOID
Not taking time to think clearly

Take time to think clearly about the amount of insurance cover you need. Insure stock for its replacement cost price, without any addition for profit. Plant and machinery should normally be insured on a 'replacement as new' basis.

Not taking out sufficient cover

This is a common mistake. If you have too little cover, an insurance company can reduce any claim by the percentage to which you are under-insured.

Having inappropriate excess on your insurance policy

Most insurance policies require you to pay an excess or deductible, covering the first part of any loss. Make sure the excess on your policy is appropriate. You can often negotiate a reduction in premiums by agreeing to a higher excess. If most of your claims fall beneath the excess threshold, you should consider switching to a policy with lower excess, but remember, it will cost you more. On the other hand, you may want to avoid making claims just above the excess, if they would mean increased premiums in subsequent years.

RECOMMENDED LINKS
Association of British Insurers (ABI):
www.abl.org.uk
Financial Services Authority:
www.fsa.gov.uk
Health and Safety Executive (HSE):
www.hse.gov.uk

National Federation of Enterprise Agencies (NFEA—through which you can find out about the Enterprise Insurance Scheme):
www.nfea.com
The Stationery Office:
www.legislation.hsmo.gov.uk

SEE ALSO
A Guide to Building Regulations (p. 77)
A Guide to Health and Safety at Work (p. 90)
Buying a Business Property (p. 71)
Drawing Up a Budget (p. 122)
Renting a Business Property (p. 68)
Setting Up and Maintaining Your Home Office (p. 96)

Complying with Fire Safety Regulations

GETTING STARTED

As well as endangering life, a fire can be a serious blow to any business. This actionlist will give suggestions on how you can prevent fires breaking out and measures you can take to minimise damage and danger should one occur. Businesses also have legal obligations to protect people in the workplace, and this is also explained.

FAQS

What are my legal obligations?

Three pieces of legislation lay down the general responsibilities of employers. The Fire Precautions Act 1971 applies to hotels (most of which require a fire certificate), also to factories, offices, shops, and railway premises where people are employed to work. A fire certificate must be applied for where more than 20 people are employed at any one time (or more than 10 employed at any one time elsewhere than on the ground floor), and in the case of factories where explosives or highly flammable materials are stored or used. A Fire Officer will inspect the premises and either grant an exemption, issue a certificate if the premises are satisfactory, or notify the business of the action required to bring things up to standard.

The Fire Precautions (Workplace) Regulations 1997 provide the main legislation on duties and responsibilities for fire safety in the workplace. They are more far reaching than the Act, and emphasise the employer's responsibilities. They also require you to carry out a fire risk assessment. The Regulations apply to most workplaces (with very few exceptions), including those that also require a fire certificate under the Fire Precautions Act 1971.

The Fire Precautions (Workplace) (Amendments) Regulations 1999 amend the 1997 legislation. The main change to the 1997 legislation is to increase the number of workplaces to which the regulations apply by removing many of the excepted workplaces. As an employer, you have to prove that you have taken all reasonable steps to comply with the regulations: to identify the hazards in the workplace and those people at risk; to provide appropriate fire fighting equipment and fire alarms as necessary, and to have clear routes to emergency exits. The risk can be significantly reduced by removing the hazards and therefore preventing an incident. The fire authorities and the courts also have more power in the implementation and enforcement of legislation.

How do I carry out a risk assessment?

You can do this within a general health and safety risk assessment, or as a separate exercise. The risk assessment must consider features of the workplace, such as dimensions and layout, substances used or stored on site, the maximum number of occupants, the activities carried out there, and any other relevant circumstances.

Look for hazards such as combustibles, flammables, and sources of ignition, and consider who will be at risk because of them. Look for places where fire will spread rapidly, or where people might be trapped or injured trying to escape. If your business has five or more employees, you must write your findings down. Use your findings to try to reduce the chances of a fire occurring and to take steps to reduce death, injury, or damage to property should a fire occur. Draw up an emergency plan, detailing what to do in the event of a fire.

Inform employees of the assessment findings. If the workplace is shared with other employers, inform them of the risks that are found and the action taken (or required) to address them. Co-operation is the key, especially where shared escape routes, fire alarm systems, and so on, are involved.

MAKING IT HAPPEN
Reduce risks

It is often possible to reduce risks quite cheaply, for example, by removing or reducing the amount of combustible/flammable materials, moving stored materials to a safer location, and removing or reducing the sources of ignition. Materials should not be stored in corridors, stairways or gangways, or obstruct an exit. Waste should not be allowed to build up and should be stored away from the premises until disposed of. Waste and rubbish are major fire hazards. If structural features of the workplace add to the risk, the cost of remedial work may be too high to justify. In such cases, the funds may be better spent on equipment for early detection and/or automatic fire fighting.

Detect and warn of fire

Detection of a fire may be rapid and straightforward in an open plan office or rooms that are always occupied. Fires in storage areas and places that are often unoccupied could become serious before they are detected, and you may need to fit fire detection equipment in such areas.

You must have a way of giving warning in case of fire. This need not be a fire alarm system; a shouted warning, handbell, or whistle may be sufficient, as long as it is appropriate to the premises. Any warning method should provide an audible alarm throughout the workplace. The warning method should be tested, and a record kept that this has been done.

Identify escape routes

Make sure there are safe means of escape from the premises. The normal ways in and out will often be sufficient. A building with relatively recent Building Regulation approval (and which has not since been modified), or which has been inspected recently by the fire service and found satisfactory, will normally have acceptable means of escape. The distance people have to travel to an escape route should be limited so they reach safety quickly. A reasonable evacuation time is two and a half minutes. When timing this, consideration should be given to what people must do before leaving, for example, shutting down machines, taking security measures, and checking that areas are clear. If employees know exactly what to do, they will be able to clear the workplace more quickly. If times are too long, rearranging the workplace may cost less than providing extra escape routes.

Doors should ideally open in the direction of escape. They must open in the direction of escape when at the foot of a staircase, or if used by more than 50 people. Fire exits and escape routes must be useable at all times. Doors should be quick and easy to open without the use of a key. Lighting should be adequate: readily available torches may be sufficient in a small workplace, but emergency lighting units may be necessary in larger premises.

Exit signs may be required to mark the route. These should have graphic symbols and directional arrows on a green background. Text may also be used. Locate signs where necessary to indicate the route.

Have means of fighting fire

Fire-fighting equipment, such as fire extinguishers, should be available as appropriate and staff should be aware of its location and how to use it. There are several different types of extinguisher—water, foam, dry powder, and carbon dioxide—for different types of fire. They are usually colour coded by type for easy identification. A modern extinguisher will be predominantly red with a small area coloured to denote the contents, with pictograms to indicate the type of fire it is suited for. Sprinkler systems are becoming increasingly popular within the United Kingdom, despite their high cost. They are triggered off in the event of a fire, and tackle the blaze early on. For certain new buildings under construction, fitting of sprinkler systems is compulsory. Fire blankets can be effective in putting out a fire but require the right technique in use. The equipment should be visually checked at least monthly, and the check should be recorded. It should be tested annually, usually by outside contractors, and the test recorded.

Train staff on fire safety

An employer may nominate someone to help with fire safety measures but still has overall responsibility. Staff must know who the nominee is. That person may need training, including using fire extinguishers. It is increasingly common within the workplace to appoint a Fire Safety Officer. All employees should be familiar with escape routes, how to give the alarm, where the fire extinguishers are, and how to use them. Written instructions should be displayed in the workplace and should also be given to every employee. New employees and anyone else spending some time on site should be taken through the procedure verbally by the person responsible for fire safety. Staff should also be made aware of any particular hazards and how they can ensure their own and other people's safety.

Act in the event of fire

A person discovering a fire must raise the alarm at once. Call the fire brigade; a person may be designated to do this upon hearing the alarm. Attempt to extinguish the fire if practicable, but it must be stressed to everyone that they must not put themselves at risk. Ensure that certain parts of the building have been cleared (a previously designated person may be responsible for this). Implement a system of checking that everyone has left the building, possibly by a designated person taking a roll call at the established fire assembly point. Don't take risks, use lifts, or return to the building after it has been evacuated.

WHAT TO AVOID

Not reviewing risk assessments

Risk assessments should be reviewed regularly, especially after changes in the workplace, activity, or staffing have occurred.

Not getting the right advice

The Health and Safety Executive can give advice related to specific manufacturing processes.

Not spreading the word

Draw up a fire precautions document, including responsibilities and fire instructions, and ensure that all employees receive a copy.

RECOMMENDED LINKS

British Safety Council:
www.britishsafetycouncil.org
FireNet:
www.fire.org.uk
Fire Protection Association (FPA):
www.thefpa.co.uk
Health and Safety Executive (HSE):
www.hse.gov.uk
Institute of Fire Prevention Officers:
www.fire.org.uk/IFPO

SEE ALSO

A Guide to Building Regulations (p. 77)
Buying a Business Property (p. 71)
Renting a Business Property (p. 68)

A Guide to Health and Safety at Work

GETTING STARTED

Businesses have a legal responsibility to protect the health and safety of their staff and others on their premises, and there is a range of laws to ensure that they do this. This actionlist explains the main steps you must take to ensure your business complies with health and safety regulations. It contains guidance on policy, obtaining a fire certificate, carrying out a risk assessment, reporting accidents, providing personal protective equipment, establishing a first aid procedure, and setting up a safety committee.

FAQS

What are my legal obligations with regard to health and safety?

The Health and Safety at Work Act 1974 requires every employer with five or more employees to produce a written policy on health and safety. The policy should contain a general statement acknowledging your legal responsibilities, an outline of the staff appointed to specific roles and their duties, and an outline of your procedures for ensuring appropriate standards are maintained. This might cover personal protective equipment, manual handling of loads, the use of display screens, safe handling of substances, maintenance records for plant and equipment, evacuation procedures in the event of fire, arrangements for first aid, the reporting of accidents, and staff training.

An appendix can also be helpful to record the legislation relevant to your business, your policies on specific issues such as smoking, drugs, alcohol, and HIV/AIDS, and how your staff will be informed about the policy and subsequent changes.

Under the Health and Safety at Work Act 1974, you must appoint a person to be responsible for putting the policy into practice. Make a formal list of duties, and ensure that everyone knows who the responsible person is. Their role will be to ensure that the safety standards and procedures outlined in the policy are adhered to on a day-to-day basis.

Where can I go for more information?

There are several organisations that provide advice about health and safety, including The British Safety Council, The Royal Society for the Prevention of Accidents (RoSPA), and the Health and Safety Executive (HSE). The website addresses for these three are given below.

The British Safety Council publishes a couple of useful guides, *Occupational Health* and *Update on Health and Safety Law*. RoSPA publishes a guide called *Essentials of Health and Safety at Work*, and the HSE also offers three useful publications, *Essentials of Health and Safety at Work*, *Introduction to Health and Safety for Small Firms*, and *5 Steps to Risk Assessment*. Two other useful publications are *An A-Z of Health and Safety Law*, by Peter Chandler, and *Manager's Guide to Health and Safety at Work*, by Jeremy Stranks, both published by Kogan Page.

MAKING IT HAPPEN

Understand fire regulations

The Fire Precautions (Workplace) Regulations 1997 (amended 1999) apply to all workplaces. You must obtain a fire certificate from the fire officer if the premises are used for sleeping, treatment or care, leisure or entertainment, teaching, training, worship, or access to the general public. You will also need one if the premises are classed as a factory, shop, office, or railway, and at least one of the following conditions apply: 20 or more people are on the premises at any one time; 10 or more people work on floors above ground-level; or explosives or highly flammable materials are used or stored on the premises.

Assess risk

Under the Management of Health and Safety at Work Regulations 1999, all employers (regardless of how many employees they have) and the self-employed are required to carry out a risk assessment. Businesses with five employees or more must record any significant risks discovered. The purpose of the risk assessment is to help you identify the measures that your business needs to take to comply with health and safety law.

You should examine whether employees are exposed to risk either because of the work they are doing, or by the condition of the premises, plant, equipment, or vehicles. You are also responsible for any risk posed to others, such as contractors and members of the public, which might arise out of the nature of your work, or the state of your premises.

Report accidents

Your responsibilities here are two-fold, involving an internal and an external procedure. To comply with the Health and Safety at Work Act 1974, you must establish an internal system for reporting and recording accidents. You also have to report work-related deaths, major injuries, diseases, and dangerous incidents to the Health and Safety Executive (HSE) and/or your local authority. This is stipulated in the Reporting of Injuries, Diseases and Dangerous Occurrences Regulations 1995 (RIDDOR).

Deaths, major injuries, and dangerous occurrences must be reported immediately, and followed up with a report submitted to the enforcing authority within 10 days. An accident which leaves a worker unable to do the full range of their normal duties for more than three days must be reported within 10 days. Records must be kept for three years from the date of the incident. The enforcing authority may request to see them.

Details of what must be reported, together with an accident report form, are set out in the free leaflet 'RIDDOR explained—Reporting of Injuries, Diseases and Dangerous Occurrences Regulations' (HSE31, rev 1). It is available from the HSE (website address given below).

Provide protective equipment

Under the Personal Protective Equipment at Work Regulations 1992, employers must provide suitable safety equipment (such as hard hats, reinforced footwear, and reflective jackets) for use at work wherever there are risks that cannot be adequately controlled in other ways. You will have to assess what type of equipment is suitable to offer protection against the hazards of the job, and to ensure compatibility where more than one item of equipment is needed.

You must ensure that the personal protective equipment is kept clean and in good repair, stored correctly, and replaced when necessary. Your employees must be given adequate information about the equipment, and be properly trained to use it.

Offer first aid

Employers must have facilities to offer first aid to employees if they are injured or become ill at work. The Health and Safety (First Aid) Regulations 1981 and Code of Practice and Guidance outline the requirements.

Your first task is to assess the level of first aid likely to be needed. To do this, consider the nature and degree of risk, the number of employees involved, and the location of the business. Extra consideration should be given to employees working in isolated locations, travelling through remote areas, or using potentially dangerous tools and machinery. The HSE has guidelines on the number of first aid personnel a business should have, depending on the number of employees and the assessment of risk.

The procedures for first aid should be detailed in your health and safety policy, and all staff should be made aware of them. You should also set up a first aid post. At least one notice should be posted in each premises indicating the location of the first aid kit, and the names and locations of the trained first aiders and appointed persons. A first aider is someone who has passed a training course in administering first aid at work, and holds a current first aid at work certificate. The training has to be approved by HSE. The certificates are currently valid for three years, and employers need to arrange refresher training before they expire.

An appointed person is an employee who is selected to take charge in the event of illness or an accident. Their responsibilities will include calling an ambulance if needed, and restocking the first aid box. An appointed person is not a certified first aider, so they should not attempt to administer first aid.

Think about a safety committee

Under the Safety Representatives and Safety Committees Regulations 1977 (SRSCR), recognised trade unions have the right to consult with employers about workplace safety. If requested, the employer must set up a safety committee to supervise the implementation of health and safety policy. If it is not a recognised trade union, then the Health and Safety (Consultation with Employees) Regulations 1996 apply. These require employers to consult their employees either directly or via elected safety representatives. However, unlike the SRSCR, the regulations do not make any formal provision for safety committees.

Train employees

Employers have an obligation to provide training for new employees as part of the induction process. This needs to cover safety systems used in the workplace, fire safety and evacuation procedures, the health and safety policy, and the identity of employees responsible for first aid, fire safety, and the reporting of accidents.

Secure premises

Contractors and visitors to your premises are entitled to the same considerations of health and safety as your employees, and they should follow the same safety procedures. The premises should also be secured against unauthorised entry.

WHAT TO AVOID
Not getting the right advice

For more detailed information, as well as practical advice, the Health and Safety Executive website is very useful (address given below).

Not keeping employees informed

A health and safety law poster must be displayed in your premises. Entitled 'What You Should Know', it is available from HSE Books (see website below).

Not keeping the HSE informed

If you plan to use premises as a factory, make sure that you inform the HSE (in writing) at least a month before you start (this is required in terms of the Factories Act 1961).

RECOMMENDED LINKS

British Safety Council:
www.britishsafetycouncil.co.uk
Health and Safety Executive (HSE):
www.hse.gov.uk
HSE Books:
www.hsebooks.co.uk
Institution of Occupational Safety and
    Health (IOSH):
www.iosh.co.uk
International Institute of Risk and Safety
    Management:
www.iirsm.org
Royal Society for the Prevention of
    Accidents (RoSPA):
www.rospa.co.uk

SEE ALSO
A Guide to Building Regulations (p. 77)
Buying a Business Property (p. 71)
Ergonomics at Work (p. 93)
Insuring a Business (p. 83)

Ergonomics at Work

GETTING STARTED

Ergonomics concerns the adaptation of equipment, procedures, and surroundings to the people who use them. Its aims involve creating a safe, comfortable, and stress-reduced environment by selecting the right products and systems to customise a workspace for an individual. Ergonomics is normally associated with computer seating and work stations, though it can apply equally to assembly-line work and production, construction, and maintenance.

You may find the following publications useful. All are published by the Health and Safety Executive (website address given below): *A pain in your workplace? Ergonomic problems and solutions* (HSG 121); *Ergonomics at Work* (INDG 90); *Work-related upper limb disorders: A guide to prevention* (HSG 60).

This actionlist looks at the concept of ergonomics, particularly within the office environment. It then suggests how you might apply the concept to your working surroundings, creating and maintaining a workplace that increases comfort and reduces stress for everyone working in that space.

FAQS

What are the benefits of ergonomics?

Business managers have only recently recognised the benefits ergonomics can bring to their companies. It can improve production and efficiency levels, quality of service, and reduce staff turnover and insurance premiums. Benefits for employees include increased motivation and job satisfaction, less pain and fewer injuries, reduced absenteeism, and general well-being in the workplace.

What can happen if ergonomics are ignored?

If ergonomic practices are not adhered to in the workplace, there may be a number of consequences, ranging from the relatively minor to serious injury. These include general symptoms, such as stress and fatigue, which can build up slowly over a period of time. In some cases, in particular those involving prolonged and repetitive activity, the worker may suffer physical injuries caused by poor posture, applying excessive force, making repetitive movements, and taking too few recovery breaks. Computer-based injuries are commonly known as Repetitive Strain Injury (RSI), Work Related Upper Limb Disorder (WRULD), and Cumulative Trauma Disorder (CTD). RSI includes work-related injuries to the muscles, tendons, and nerves of the limbs; back and wrist injuries are the most common ailments. Workers in construction and maintenance, who regularly use vibrating hand tools, may suffer hand-arm vibration syndrome (HAVS), the most common of which is 'white finger'. Employees working with VDUs and computers, or workers doing precise assembly tasks, are prone to blurred vision or unusual eye irritability.

MAKING IT HAPPEN
Ergonomic awareness

Carry out a diagnostic test of working areas to identify any potential risk factors that may cause discomfort or stress. It is essential to involve all employees in this process, as far as possible, to make them feel they have some control over their working environment. You could start by asking which tasks involve prolonged activity that may lead to physical discomfort, and whether any aspects of the job cause stress. Find out whether particular tasks cause stress or discomfort and which equipment or furniture could improve the working environment.

On the basis of the diagnostic test of the workspace and an awareness of potential problem areas, make the changes necessary. They will help reduce the risk of strain or injury and enhance the working environment. To optimise any ergonomic practices put in place, it is advisable to train employees on the best ways of using the equipment or furniture, as well as on the principles behind it.

Ergonomic problems in the workplace

Workplace seating is a common problem and the position and height of chairs and desks are not always suitable. The chair should fit the user, be comfortable, and support the back. No chair is suitable for every worker for every task, therefore adjusting a chair may be essential. Chair backrests and armrests can both help to reduce strain on the back.

Computers and VDUs are another problem area. The glare and/or reflections on monitor screens may make it difficult to read information clearly on the screen. Desks should be positioned perpendicular, rather than parallel, to windows in order to help minimise reflections. Using anti-glare filters or screens can also be a useful remedy. Some office lighting, such as unshielded fluorescent strip lighting, is not suitable for use with VDUs. Indirect lighting should be used, such as uplighters or lights with suitable diffusers, which provide glare-free lighting for personal computers. Individual task lighting could be provided for hard-copy work.

The temperature in the office needs to be regulated, as the indoor climate can sometimes be too warm, too cool, or draughty. Furthermore, electrical equipment dries the air, and static build up around a computer screen attracts dust. A comfortable temperature for office work is between 20 and 24 degrees Celsius.

Selecting ergonomic equipment

Once risks have been identified, consideration can be given to the design of the workspace. People vary in height and weight, in physical strength, sensory abilities (vision, hearing, and so on), their ability to handle information and make decisions, and general health. It is therefore essential to take account of these attributes when providing a comfortable and safe workspace and equipment.

Choosing ergonomic office furniture is essential if the working environment is to be improved for employees. The manager should be aware of the performance criteria and standards of various office products, know what they are looking for, and buy from a reputable, knowledgeable manufacturer. Going for the cheapest option may not always result in obtaining the right piece of equipment.

Devising a product check list, like the one below, is a good idea before selecting office furniture. For example:

- Is the item convenient and easy to use?
- Is the item easy to adjust, and does it come with clear instructions?
- Are the materials of the product durable and of good quality?
- Does it offer good fit and comfort?
- Does the item cause any discomfort if used for a prolonged period of time?
- Is the item made by a reputable manufacturer?
- Does the item conform to British/European/International Standards?

A number of manufacturers sell ergonomic office equipment in the United Kingdom. Using ergonomic office equipment may prevent injury in the first place, avoid an injury recurring, or be useful for workers with disabilities. Examples are an ergonomic mouse to reduce strain on the wrist and lower arm muscles; a keyboard to reduce RSI by using palm rests; and anti-glare computer screens to reduce eyestrain.

Best practice

No amount of ergonomic furniture and equipment in the workplace can compensate for bad practice. It should be ensured that every employee takes a number of preventative measures to reduce the risks of fatigue, stress, and work-related injuries in the workplace. This can be achieved by distributing best practice leaflets throughout the organisation, and holding ergonomic awareness training sessions.

Highlight the important areas for improvement and point out the benefits, for example, improving posture can result in reduced risk of back and wrist injuries. Suggest other simple measures, such as taking frequent short breaks throughout the working day (which is far better than taking one or two long breaks). This can be combined with doing frequent stretching exercises and breathing exercises to loosen up the muscles and reduce tension.

There are a few ergonomic tips which, if followed by you and your employees, should help reduce the risks of injury and stress. When you lift heavy loads, keep your knees bent and your back straight. Avoid extremes in reaching, twisting, or lifting, and keep any items you use frequently within arm's reach.

Adjust the backrest and armrests of the chair you use to allow you to sit in an upright position without slouching. The backrest should follow the natural 'S' curve of your spine. The height of the chair should be adjusted so that your wrists, hands, and forearms are horizontal with the desk. Your feet should be placed flat on the floor; use a footrest if you need to. Keep your head up and your shoulders relaxed. Your legs and feet should fit comfortably under the desk, so remove any obstacles that prevent this.

Your computer monitor should be at a comfortable distance from the eyes. Make sure there is space on the desk to rest hands and wrists, so that you can keep movement of the wrists to a minimum. Adjust the brightness and colour contrast of your computer screen and make sure that all screens are reflection-free and clean. Avoid long periods of repetitive activity; for example, alternate computer-based work with other tasks, such as filing, telephoning, or photocopying.

Relevant legislation
Although applying ergonomic practices to the workplace is a matter of common sense, it is the business's responsibility to be aware of health and safety legislation in order to create and maintain a safe working environment. A large number of Acts and Regulations outline how this can be done, and some are listed here:

- Health and Safety at Work Act 1974
- Management of Health and Safety at Work Regulations 1999
- Workplace (Health, Safety, and Welfare) Regulations 1992
- Health and Safety (Display Screen Equipment) Regulations 1992
- Provision and Use of Work Equipment Regulations 1998

WHAT TO AVOID
Doing too little too late
Ergonomics awareness should not just be introduced after a problem becomes apparent, although this is often a common reason for introducing ergonomic practices.

Insufficient training
Running staff training programmes is crucial to raising awareness and gaining commitment to ergonomic practices. Employees should be trained on the best ways to use ergonomic furniture and equipment in their workspace. The reasons for adjusting the equipment to suit their needs should be highlighted.

Not selecting the right equipment
Make sure that the ergonomic equipment you select is suitable for your business and your staff. Carry out a diagnostic test of the workplace before making any decision. An ergonomic consultant could be employed if it is not clear what the best ergonomic practices for the workplace are, or if complicated changes need to be made.

RECOMMENDED LINKS
HSE Books:
www.hsebooks.co.uk
Health and Safety Executive (HSE) Information Centre:
www.hse.gov.uk
Ergonomics Society:
www.ergonomics.org.uk

SEE ALSO
A Guide to Health and Safety at Work (p. 90)

Setting Up and Maintaining Your Home Office

GETTING STARTED

Many people choose to work from home these days, and most new businesses start off in the home of their owner-managers. If you are thinking about basing your company in your house to begin with, you may need to get used to a new way of working, especially if you've previously been working in a more formal, structured setting. To start, ask yourself the following questions:

- Can I handle the social isolation of a home office on a full time basis?
- Am I a self-starter?
- How do I rate as a decision-maker, organiser, book-keeper, and secretary?
- Could I separate business and personal life if both were under the same roof?
- Am I a workaholic and would an office at home worsen that problem?

FAQS

Is working from home as wonderful as it sounds?

Yes and no. For convenience, cost, and comfort, there's nothing quite like a home office. Low overheads, no commuting hassles, no office politics, and setting your own hours are a few of the pluses. On the minus side, there's only you—and if you're not disciplined, you'll be spending more time with the children, the pets, or in front of the fridge than working where you belong. It can be a simple formula for failure.

How can I make a home-based business seem professional to customers?

It depends on the type of business, but start with a professional attitude and then buy some good-looking business cards and stationery. Think about adding an attractive logo and using a two-colour design on business cards, letterheads, and envelopes. Having a well-produced flier or brochure that describes your business is also a plus. Quality customer service will do the rest.

E-commerce is relatively easy to conduct from a home office, especially with a website that attracts customers. Clients need not know whether you work at home or in a sophisticated office building, so long as you get the job done for them. As with your other materials, the website should reflect the personality and professionalism of your business.

What sort of investment is necessary to equip a home office?

This, too, depends on the type of activity you will be doing—whether it be business or teleworking , or a personal or family office. But generally, spending between £1,000 and £3,000 should make you well equipped and comfortable. Make a list and a budget beforehand. You don't want to blow your entire savings on setting up the office, then have nothing to spend on attracting business.

MAKING IT HAPPEN

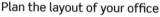

Plan the layout of your office

Planning a home office involves decisions about where to locate the office, how to decorate it, and how to furnish it. You should give lots of thought to this, as it will be the hub of a small business. Some people even make a scale drawing of the room they intend to use, then place to-scale furniture in there to decide on the best layout.

Take account of tax considerations

As you're planning to use the office for a small business, the Inland Revenue will allow you to deduct certain expenses connected to the business. For that reason, the office must be completely dedicated to the business and not merely a spare bedroom with a fold-up desk and your cordless phone. Good record keeping is very important if you plan to deduct expenses and part of the mortgage interest, utilities, and phone bills for business activity.

Make sure you're comfortable and have the right equipment

Office décor is important. Besides getting the right atmosphere (lighting, paint/wallpaper, floor covering), you may need to run more phone lines and electrical sockets into the room to support the office equipment. Beyond that, having comfortable, functional furniture will allow you to work productively.

Your package of office equipment will depend on your level of activity, but will probably include computer(s) and peripherals, software, phones and phone service for voice, fax, and computer, and perhaps even a separate copier and/or scanner. Add a digital camera if you plan to put photos of yourself or your products on your website. Consider upgrading connections to the Internet, rather than relying on a computer modem to your Internet provider, especially if you are engaged in e-commerce.

Finally, there are the necessary office supplies and extra storage space for files and records to consider.

Impose proper discipline on yourself

One of the most difficult aspects of the home office is the home itself. How easy it is to be distracted by jobs round the house, watch TV, weed the garden, get involved with family things, have a snack in the kitchen, and otherwise avoid the work that awaits you in your office. Two factors will help avoid the home trap: being excited about your office space and the work—and discipline. Set regular office hours, have a separate business phone, organise your time, and stick to your deadlines.

Don't let yourself get isolated

Being isolated in your home office, you may develop a tendency to cocoon yourself in there or to avoid keeping in touch with the outside world, both of which can be unhealthy.

Having a business gives you plenty of opportunity to break away from the office to meet other people socially and professionally. Even if much of your business is conducted over the phone and by computer, it's still important to network. Invite customers and prospective customers to lunch, if they happen to do business nearby. Join a civic group or professional organisation to stay connected and also to generate local interest in your business. Get physical exercise away from the home. Join an evening class. All these things will help keep you connected, bring in new ideas, and generate lots of personal energy—things you'll value when working alone.

WHAT TO AVOID
Going halfway with the office arrangement

Starting a home office on the dining-room table is not a good idea, nor is committing only half-heartedly to making a guestroom into a real office. If you don't treat the office seriously, there's a better than even chance you won't take your work seriously either.

Carve out a separate space and dedicate it as the office. You'll feel better and your work will benefit from that decision.

Succumbing to workaholic syndrome

If, while working in an office setting, you've had a tendency to stay there until the work is done, operating from home is a workaholic's dream come true. With the office only a few rooms away, there's a temptation to 'get one last thing done' after dinner or at weekends.

It's important to be professional about your business, but it's also important that you don't let the office become your new home. Set hours, try to manage your workflow into those hours, then shut the door and leave it all behind.

Family issues

Lots of women see working at home as the answer to two issues—making a living and raising a family. If it were easy to mix children and work, parents would have been doing it at their offices long ago.

That said, it isn't entirely impossible either. The trick is balance. You can't afford to be at the beck and call of your children while you're working, but you certainly don't want them to feel totally ignored. Racing from the office to untangle toys and do the washing every hour will soon turn your work world upside-down. Closing the door and ignoring the family will have an equally unfortunate effect.

Obviously, child care is an option. Consider it for the days that you might need to concentrate on your most important work. On days you set aside for more mundane tasks, such as paying bills, book-keeping, research on the Internet, and so forth, you might find it easier to have the family there.

Lacking certain office job skills

When working for other companies, you probably relied on others with jobs that complemented your own. When you are your own boss, working from your home office, you have a lot more duties besides the specific ones that 'bring home the bacon'. You will be responsible for executive and marketing decisions, financial and administrative details and deadlines, as well as clerical and reception work. Until your business becomes profitable enough to employ other people, it's all down to you.

This is where a business plan makes sense. You need to work out the details of how you'll charge for your products or services. Be careful to account for the 'cost of doing business', which includes the clerical and administrative things, too. Add in a 'fudge factor' and some profit. Assuming that you'll work a 40-hour week, set your sights on making a living in 30 hours, then use the other 10 hours to take care of the other parts of the business—marketing, promotion, invoicing, book-keeping, and business errands.

If you feel you lack the skills to juggle all of these things, or don't have the interest in becoming your own secretary, perhaps you're not cut out for a home business. But if you want to give it a try, you can certainly learn what you need to know about the care and feeding of a small business from books, the Internet, or your local small-business advisory service.

RECOMMENDED LINKS

Entrepreneur:
www.entrepreneur.com
Go Home:
www.gohome.com
Inland Revenue:
**www.inlandrevenue.gov.uk/menus/
b_taxpayers.htm**
Setting up a home office:
**www.money.guardian.co.uk/
advicebank/planyourworkinglife/**

SEE ALSO
Buying a Business Property (p. 71)
**Computers, Information Technology, and
E-commerce (p. 499)**
**Drawing Boundaries: How to Manage
Working at Home (p. 99)**
Renting a Business Property (p. 68)

Drawing Boundaries: How to Manage Working at Home

GETTING STARTED

Many small businesses are run from the home of the owner-manager. Working from home has become much easier over recent years, especially as technology has become more sophisticated, but for some people (especially those who have been used to working in larger companies) it can take a while to get used to working in a less-structured setting. This actionlist offers some advice on how to get the best from working at home.

FAQS

Will I be able to concentrate on my work when at home? There are so many distractions.

Setting up a suitable work environment and creating boundaries is of vital importance when working from home. It is hopeless trying to balance your laptop on your knee in the kitchen whilst you attempt to avoid intrusions from family or friends; you need to set rules for yourself and others so that everyone can support your efforts rather than sabotage them.

I'm really looking forward to being my own boss, but also enjoy very much the buzz of being in the office. How can I find this level of stimulation?

If you are an extrovert and enjoy the energy of having other people around, it's important to recognise and cater for this. You could try planning a certain number of days in the office and balance these with quieter, more productive days at home. If you are self-employed, you may need to schedule visits and meetings sufficiently regularly for you to feel involved with and energised by others.

MAKING IT HAPPEN

Plan, plan, plan

Once people get used to working from home, they often find they prefer it to working in an office. However, to be successful, you need to plan ahead. You will need all the elements of a 'real' office: furniture, computer, software, telephone, fax, an e-mail account, and so on. Spend some time setting up your office as you will probably spend much more time in it than you envisage. Make sure you have a dedicated telephone line so that calls related to work and home don't get confused. Experiment with different office layouts until you feel comfortable with your arrangements.

Create boundaries

If you have other people at home, make sure you create boundaries around the time you set aside for working. Non-work interruptions can be frustrating when you're trying to complete a task. Set up boundaries by establishing in advance how you are going to manage your time at home, including things like the beginning and ending of your working day. It also helps to have a separate room to call your office, with a door you can close so you won't be disturbed. Stick to your guns and people will soon get the message.

If your work requires you to receive visitors, try to find an area where they won't be distracted by your domestic arrangements. Having to ignore the pile of washing on the kitchen floor can be very off-putting when the point of the meeting is anything but domestic. If you are unable to avoid these situations, find a local hotel or restaurant where you can meet for an hour or two. Again, this is about creating boundaries that will enable you to maintain focus and create an impression of professionalism.

Establish a routine

It is important to differentiate your day between being 'at work' and 'at home'. If your working and resting time becomes confused, it can feel as if you are always on duty, and when you do take a break you can feel guilty that you are not finishing a project. This differentiation comes naturally when you have to travel to and from work. In the absence of this, you will need to provide the means of making this shift. It could be signalled by a routine; making a cup of coffee, taking it to your desk, closing your door, and switching on the computer. Once you've done this a few times, this routine creates the boundary within which you can work effectively.

Plan your day so that you don't find yourself wasting time. The advantage of working from home is that you have greater control over interruptions. People will no longer be able to wander past your desk at will and ask you for some information or, worse, to do something for them. A great deal of time is wasted in these 'Oh, by the way...' moments that happen mostly because you are accessible or visible.

Take a break

Make sure you take breaks throughout the day. It's commonly understood that powers of concentration diminish after about twenty minutes, and continuing to work after this time can lead to a point where thinking becomes a struggle. Taking a break, perhaps a short walk, can re-energise your thinking capability. Of course, breaks need to be balanced by the need to be productive. Try not to get distracted by picking up something else that needs doing. You will only end up wasting time and lowering your efficiency by spreading your energies too thinly.

Maintain your work/life balance

Make sure you plan for the end of the day also. It is far too easy to remain sitting in your workspace well into the evening and ignore the private side of your life. Keeping a work/life balance is just as important in the home as it is in the organisational setting.

Find out about your tax status

If you are self-employed, you will find that having an office in the home may qualify you for tax concessions. Tax relief is available on your mortgage interest, heating and telephone bills, and the cost of capital equipment and services needed to support your business. The Inland Revenue or your accountant will guide you on what tax benefits you may receive. Anyone starting a new business must register with the Inland Revenue within a strict time period. Visit their website (details below) for full information. If your income is going to reach £54,000 in a 12 month period you must register for VAT beforehand. Contact your local VAT registration office or find more information at **www.hmce.gov.uk**. (HM Customs and Excise has responsibility for collecting revenue in VAT, rather than the Inland Revenue.)

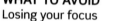

WHAT TO AVOID
Losing your focus

For those who enjoy dynamic environments and the cut and thrust of being in a busy office, working from home may not be enjoyable. It is tempting for this type of person to create dynamism for themselves by finding activities that distract them from their own company.

Flitting around from task to task can create a feeling of being in the flow but may not be very productive. Time spent at the beginning of the day creating a 'to do' list can focus your energy and ensure that there is a valuable output to the day's activities.

Not switching off

It is very easy for people to work beyond the call of duty when the office is located in the home, especially during the hectic first stages of a new business when very long hours are often unavoidable. 'I'll just go and answer a few e-mails...' can become a lengthy session in front of the computer that eats into private time. Try to discipline yourself to keep to the 'rules' that you have set, with only occasional exceptions for real emergencies or key deadlines.

Losing track of the time

If you derive energy from being with people and are not used to working on your own, you may naturally turn to the telephone as a substitute for their presence around you. It's easy to pass much of the day on the telephone and find that the concrete tasks you have to do are pushed into the evening. Again, this is a question of discipline. Give yourself time when you can interact with others, but keep control of it. A large clock on the wall in front of you can be a good reminder of how long you are spending on each activity.

RECOMMENDED LINKS

Homeworking.com:
www.homeworking.com
Inland Revenue:
www.inlandrevenue.gov.uk

SEE ALSO

Assessing Your Entrepreneurial Profile: Do You Have What It Takes? (p. 6)
Setting Up and Maintaining Your Home Office (p. 96)

FIGURING IT OUT

Financing a New Business

GETTING STARTED

New businesses need finance to cover the cost of equipment and expenses before sales generate enough cash to make the operation self-supporting. This actionlist describes the main ways of financing your business (equity finance, loan finance, and grants). It explains how to work out the amount of finance you need, and what proportion of debt to equity is advisable.

FAQS

What is a business angel?

A business angel is an individual who is willing to invest money in a business. The amount available from angels is usually much less than from venture capitalists, but they are often willing to take bigger risks.

What is equity finance?

Equity, or shareholder capital, is the money introduced into a business by the owners. If it is a company, then the equity is introduced in exchange for shares. Investors expect a share of the business's profit. In the case of limited companies, this takes the form of dividends. The person starting a business will normally introduce equity capital, but it can also be raised from external investors, including business angels and venture capitalists. Investors will be looking for an annual dividend, which often can be quite small, and a good return when they sell their shares. Equity is best suited, therefore, to businesses that expect to grow quickly.

What is loan finance?

Loan finance is money that is borrowed from a finance company, such as a bank. Loans are repaid over a period of time, at either fixed or variable rates of interest. The lender will usually require security against a business or personal asset. Terms can vary in length from one year to 25 years, and will usually be determined by the asset that is being financed. The interest rate will reflect the lender's perception of the risk in providing the loan. Loan finance can be provided in different ways.

An overdraft is money that a business can borrow from a bank up to an agreed limit. It provides a business with short-term finance, effectively by running a negative balance on the bank account. This is a particularly good way of funding short-term requirements, such as providing working capital during the course of each month.

Term loans are funds borrowed for a fixed term. Usually, such loans are repayable in equal instalments over the term of the loan, although sometimes they can be repaid in a lump sum at the end of the term. Term loans are more attractive than overdrafts for long-term borrowing because repayments are fixed and the cost is usually less. However, lenders are increasingly writing into the small print that term loans are repayable on demand. If the loan has been used to finance capital assets, this could cause problems.

Creditor finance is an excellent way of 'borrowing' money, effectively at no cost. Typically, suppliers may give 30 to 60 days' credit for their goods or services before payment is due. If you can sell your product or service and get paid before paying your creditors, then it will generate cash into the business. Your business may have to establish a trading record before credit is given, and it can be withdrawn at any time.

Debtor finance is particularly useful if your business is growing rapidly and is providing credit accounts to its customers. Instead of waiting for your own customers to pay your invoices within a 30- or 60-day period, you can use the services of a third party invoice discounting or factoring firm. Factoring can be an expensive way of speeding up cash flow, but it may reduce administration costs since the factor normally takes on the role of invoice clerk.

Grants are usually 'one off' payments providing a percentage of the costs towards a specific purpose, usually for capital expenditure, but sometimes for a specific activity such as taking part in an exhibition or trade fair. Amounts vary depending on the scheme. A grant may be available from the government, the European Union, the local authority, or a related organisation. Grants are usually treated as income to the business and, as such, are shown on the profit and loss account. There are several sources of grant aid worth investigating when starting in business, and whenever you are buying equipment.

Capital asset finance can often be done through 'off-balance-sheet' finance. There are different ways of doing this. Financial leasing allows you to finance the use of an asset rather than owning it. The equipment remains the property of the leasing company; the business has the legal right to use the equipment for the period of the lease, provided that the lease payments are up to date. In a lease purchase arrangement, you have an option to purchase the equipment at the end of the lease period. Through hire purchase, you pay regular instalments to a third party, normally a finance house, to purchase ownership of plant and machinery from a supplier. The finance house will own the equipment throughout the period of the agreement, until the last instalment has been paid.

MAKING IT HAPPEN
Work out how much capital you need

The working capital of a business is its current assets (typically stock, cash at the bank, and debtors) minus its current liabilities (typically trade creditors, other creditors such as PAYE and VAT, and your bank overdraft). This information is summarised on the balance sheet, although this only gives a snapshot of the working capital requirements at a specific moment in time. Generally, this is the finance required for the short-term running of the business.

The amount of working capital needed will vary during the course of the year and even during the course of a month. You need to allow for the maximum likely working capital requirement. Consideration needs to be given to the variation that can occur within each month. As a rule of thumb, it makes sense to aim for minimum working capital of a month's average sales multiplied by the number of months it takes to collect payment. If you want to be more accurate, then use the following procedure:

1. Determine the average number of weeks that the raw material is in stock.
2. Deduct from this figure the credit period from suppliers, in weeks.
3. Then add the average number of weeks to produce goods or service, the average number of weeks finished goods are in stock, and the average time customers take to pay.
4. Take the total, and divide it by 52 (the number of weeks in the year). Multiply the result by your estimated sales for the year. The answer will give you a figure for the maximum working capital required.

It would be more accurate to use the cost of sales (direct and fixed), rather than the full selling price, but the above calculation is close enough. If your business is growing, then you need to use the budgeted sales figures, and it is advisable to calculate your working capital needs on a regular basis.

Understand gearing and interest cover

Gearing is the proportion of debt to total capital in the business. The more debt there is relative to equity, the higher the gearing. Introducing more equity, or retaining more of the profits, can reduce the gearing ratio. Most banks look for a gearing of no more than 50%; in other words, your debt should be no more than half of the total capital.

Once you have built up a track record with your bank, you should be able to attract medium-term loans (three- to seven-year loans) to cover the cost of plant and equipment. Established companies may be able to raise long-term debt as a debenture or convertible loan stock, which normally receives a fixed rate of interest and is repayable in full at the end of the term. Long-term debt is usually included with the capital on the balance sheet. The banks will also be more comfortable with a higher gearing, though they still do not like to see it too high. Lease and hire purchase companies will not have as great a concern about gearing as the banks. They will, however, be interested in your cash flow and whether you can afford the repayments.

If you expect to grow quickly and do not have enough of your own money to provide the necessary finance, then you may need to look for equity early on. Banks will be reluctant to keep on providing additional working capital as that simply increases the gearing and increases their risk. Growing too quickly is often known as 'over-trading' and is a major cause of business failure. The banks will also want to reassure themselves that you can afford the interest on the loan. So they will look for profits that are at least three or four times the expected interest charge.

WHAT TO AVOID
Not thinking ahead
Regularly calculate the total level of funding required for the next year, and split the funding into fixed asset requirements and working capital requirements. Think carefully about the term, the cost, the suitability, the timescale, and any security required. Remember that cost should not be the sole criterion. Keep your lenders informed of your financial position, giving ample warning if you are likely to need to increase your overdraft, for example.

Not changing with the times
In times of recession, keep as much of your debt as possible as fixed medium-term loans, and keep your overdraft requirement to the minimum. In times of expansion, when finance is more readily available, it may be more cost effective to use an overdraft.

RECOMMENDED LINKS
British Venture Capital Association:
www.bvca.co.uk
Factors and Discounters Association:
www.factors.org.uk
The Prince's Trust:
www.princes-trust.org.uk

SEE ALSO
Addressing Cash-flow Problems (p. 145)
Applying for Grants and Funding (p. 113)
Budgeting (p. 494)
Controlling Costs (p. 119)
Drawing Up a Budget (p. 122)
Preparing a Successful Business Plan (p. 110)
Understanding the Role of the Bank (p. 107)
Venture Capital (p. 554)

Understanding the Role of the Bank

GETTING STARTED

Every entrepreneur understands you need a bank account to facilitate payments and receipts, but banks can help your business in other ways too. They provide a range of banking services such as overdrafts, term loans, and equity, as well as financial services like insurance and pensions. This actionlist explains how to choose the best bank for you, and looks at some of the services banks can offer.

FAQS

What is the best way to choose a bank?

Banking is intensely competitive nowadays, so it pays to gather as much information as possible on the services offered. All the major banks have customer charters, or codes of practice, with full details of their charges and tariffs, so you should be able to estimate the likely cost to your business. All the banks offer incentives for new customers, for example free banking for the first 12 months; these incentives should only come into play for you as a factor if the decision between banks is marginal. However, most businesses require a loan or overdraft at some point in their development, so ask different banks about this before deciding where to open your business account.

Relationships are critical. You should seek advice and recommendations from professionals and small businesses in the same area, for example your local enterprise counsellors or your solicitor, to help find a bank with a good track record. This is probably the most important factor. The relationship between a business and the local enterprise agency is a crucial factor for most banks when they consider financing a business. The chosen bank should, in turn, also have good relations with the local enterprise networks. Finally, talk to the bank manager to help you decide whether this is someone with whom you can work.

How do I open a business bank account?

Opening a business bank account is, like opening any other bank account, pretty straightforward, although it does involve some red tape caused by the Government's drive to crack down on money laundering so be prepared to provide appropriate identification. If you are seeking a loan, banks can often give very fast answers, especially if you need less than £10,000, but expect them to make enquiries about your credit history.

MAKING IT HAPPEN

Borrow from the bank

Banks offer a number of different arrangements, each tailored to suit various business needs. The most flexible and simple form of borrowing is the **overdraft**. This provides a business with short-term finance, so do not use it for anything that will take a long time to repay (such as fixed assets). The interest rate charged is usually linked to the Bank Base Rate, and should be agreed at the outset. In addition, an arrangement fee (a percentage of the amount borrowed, normally around 1.5%) may be payable. Overdrafts also often attract annual renewal fees.

It is important to be aware of the charges connected with exceeding the agreed overdraft level. Charges may be levied at a set amount every time you exceed the agreed level, or per day when the agreed overdraft limit is exceeded. Additional interest will be charged, and banks usually charge for informing the account holder (by telephone, letter, or additional statement). There are also charges for returned cheques. Monies provided by an overdraft are repayable on demand.

A **loan** is the ideal form of finance to purchase fixed assets. (A fixed asset is a long-term asset of a business, such as a piece of machinery or a building.) The loan term will be geared to the expected working life of the asset being bought. The interest rate may be fixed, which helps accurate budgeting and protects the business's cash flow in times of rising interest rates. Loans with variable rates are also available. Depending on your circumstances, you may be able to negotiate a capital repayment holiday. The banks can offer insurance to cover disruption to repayments, and loans can be linked to an endowment or pension policy with life and disability cover also available.

Ask the bank to confirm the loan terms and conditions in writing, and analyse them carefully before proceeding. When considering loans, banks normally require a business plan and references from a small business adviser. An arrangement fee is usually charged, often in the region of 2%.

Few banks will provide an unsecured loan to a business. The bank will normally expect the business to have something to act as security against the loan (property, for example). Alternatively, the bank may ask the directors of your business to provide personal guarantees on the loan. If the only impediment to you being given a loan is lack of suitable collateral, then you may qualify for the Small Firms Loan Guarantee Scheme; in this case, the Government will guarantee 75% of the loan (for an additional premium on the interest rate), which should enable the loan to proceed.

Banks provide other services, which may be charged for separately on an 'as used' basis, and will be in addition to normal bank charges. Such services can make your banking much more flexible. For example:

- open credit arrangements enable the business to withdraw cash regularly from a branch of the bank other than the branch holding the account
- your credit cards or payment cards can have facilities for multiple use, and statements can be broken down to show clearly areas of expenditure
- electronic funds transfer enables funds to be transferred from a business account to another account at another branch or bank on the same day

Banks can also help with payment issues. For example:

- banker's references are enquiries carried out on behalf of a business into the creditworthiness of its suppliers and customers
- night safes enable cash or cheques to be deposited outside normal banking hours. There is usually a set quarterly charge plus a charge per usage
- stopped cheques are where the bank is instructed not to pay a cheque that has been issued
- special presentations allow you to request express payment of a cheque that has been paid into your business account
- sterling drafts are similar to cheques but are drawn on the head office of the business's bank, thus ensuring payment

Use additional bank services

Many banks offer a range of international trade services for businesses trading in overseas markets whose suppliers or customers are based abroad. All the banks have systems and services in place to offer current, deposit, and loan accounts in euros and other major currencies. You may be able to ask for cross-border payment services, and your bank may be able to offer its clients a factoring service for customers in the United Kingdom or overseas.

Online banking services are increasingly available, allowing users to deal with the bank via the Internet. This allows instant access to information about their account, saving time and paperwork. It also means users can integrate their internal computerised account system more efficiently with that of the bank. Telephone banking is offered by many banks. As with online banking, this can be used to check accounts, transfer money, pay bills, and so on.

To meet legal requirements and to ensure that the business is covered for unforeseen events, businesses require insurance cover. The banks all have arrangements or partnerships to provide appropriate cover. They can also help with life cover, pensions, and personal savings if required. Linked savings accounts with competitive interest rates can help your business make the most of surplus funds. Reserve accounts allow money to be put aside for tax, VAT, and working capital.

Many banks offer free business counselling to new businesses to identify potential difficulties and suggest new facilities and services that may be helpful. Most major banks publish literature on business start-up and offer comprehensive information services.

WHAT TO AVOID
Not giving the bank enough appropriate information

You expect an efficient and helpful service from your bank; the bank also has expectations of you. Banks do not like surprises, so keep them informed about your business, particularly if you have a loan. If you think that your requirements may change, give the bank good warning. As far as possible, run your accounts and loans in accordance with your agreement with the bank. The bank will then be far more likely to respond positively if you need, for example, to borrow more money. Once your business is up and running, send the bank a copy of your annual accounts each year. If you have a loan, this may be a condition; but even if you haven't, it may help if you think you may need a loan at some point.

Exceeding an overdraft limit without permission

If you overdraw your account without prior arrangement, or exceed your overdraft, you will be charged interest on the unauthorised borrowing, as well as being charged for the letter the bank sends you informing you of the interest charge.

Using an overdraft instead of a loan

Beware of 'easy' overdrafts. A bank may offer an overdraft facility rather than a loan. Overdrafts are usually more expensive than a loan and are repayable on demand, so only use an overdraft for working capital requirements.

Being unaware of the bank's charges

Watch out for hidden charges. People new to business are often surprised by the range of charges imposed on them by the bank in contrast to the free banking personal customers receive, though recently the banks have begun to reduce some of the charges imposed on business customers.

RECOMMENDED LINKS

Banking Code Standards Board:
www.bankingcode.org.uk
British Bankers Association:
www.bba.org.uk/public/smallbusiness/
Financial Ombudsman Service:
www.financial-ombudsman.org.uk

SEE ALSO

Budgeting (p. 494)
Financing a New Business (p. 104)

Preparing a Successful Business Plan

GETTING STARTED

Many new owner-managers write business plans with the sole purpose of convincing a financier to lend them money for starting up. However, a good business plan can help build a stronger foundation for your business. It can help you to clarify your business purpose to yourself and communicate it to your partners and staff; predict future scenarios and address them before they threaten the success of the business; and set targets and objectives so that you can monitor your business performance.

Your plan must be a coherent description of how your business will move from where it is now to where you want it to be. Obviously each business will be different, but the headings below are useful stepping stones to include in your business plan and will make sure that you cover the most important aspects.

FAQS

What should I say about my business?

Be as specific as possible about the kind of business that you are starting. Describe your business in terms of a mission statement or 'executive summary' that clearly summarises its purpose and is easily understood by you, your staff, customers, and potential investors. If you cannot describe your business in these terms, rethink your business idea; focus on the core activities and direction.

What should I use as my starting point?

Try to envisage where you might want your business to be in five years' time, so that you can start to move towards that point. For instance, you might work towards becoming a market leader, an innovator, a specialist, a good employer, a large concern, or a supplier of superior quality.

MAKING IT HAPPEN

Make sure you cover all the important issues in your business plan

As well as being very specific about the type of business you are starting and thinking ahead to where you want to be in five years, there are a number of important elements that you will need to include in your business plan.

Current market situation

To earn enough revenue, your business must be able to achieve a share of the markets available. To do this, you'll need to have a thorough understanding of your market environment to do this, including its size and the share that you can realistically achieve. The size of your share will depend on:

- market trends—find out what influences your target market now, and how your product can take advantage of this
- target customers—describe who your target customers are and how many there are; also justify your estimate of the market share you aim to get
- competition—list your competitors and describe their products; also describe how your product will be different.

Current target customers

Define the characteristics of the target groups of customers that could buy from your business. Make a list of the features that your products have, and the associated benefits that these features can provide to your customers, then build up a picture of your target customers. For individuals, describe them in terms of characteristics like age, income, location, lifestyle, and marital status. For businesses, consider location, numbers of employees, public or private sector, industry type, and turnover. Carry out some research into how many customers there are in your target group, and how much they spend, and also try to identify trends that tell you whether this group is growing or shrinking.

Competitor analysis

Competitors may be in the same (direct competition) or similar (indirect competition) business to you. The level and strength of competition in a market indicates how difficult it will be to gain a share of the market. However, it is not simply the number of competitors that you should be concerned about; analyse the following aspects of each competitor's business:

- their products: are their products and services the same as yours? Do your competitors provide something that you don't?
- their customers: are your competitors targeting the same customer segments as your business?
- their share of the market: how large is it, and could you take some of it?
- their strategies: how they grow, market themselves, and price their products. Can you learn from how they conduct business, or do it better?
- their operations and facilities: what levels of service are customers demanding?

Marketing strategy

With a clear understanding of your market, you can define your overall strategy. Break this down into objectives and targets relating to the volume and share of the market (or market segments) you hope to achieve, and when you intend to achieve them by. Ask yourself, for example:

- who are your initial marketing targets?
- what products, services or particular deals will you be offering?
- is there a specific volume, value, or share of these markets that you hope to achieve?
- when do you hope to achieve these targets by?
- why are you choosing these markets first?
- who will you target next, in the next 6 or 12 months?

Marketing plan

Now that you have a coherent marketing strategy, you need to be clear about how you are going to make it happen. A detailed marketing plan must explain how you go about achieving each of your marketing targets and objectives, either by particular target segment, by type of marketing activity, or both. Such a plan will include some, or all of the following:

- the marketing methods you will use for each segment of the target market
- the specific action you are going to undertake
- a timescale or timetable for each marketing activity
- the people or organisations that are going to carry it out
- the estimated costs to undertake particular marketing activities
- how you will monitor and review progress
- how you will handle the response to your marketing

It will also be important to identify how you will manage the overall marketing plan, in other words ensuring that the entire budget is not spent in the first couple of months, monitoring results, adjusting the plan, and introducing new tactics as you go along.

Sales targets and objectives

Your marketing plan, when implemented, needs to be converted into perhaps the most important business goal of all: sales revenues. Set out your forecasts in terms of sales of different product types by volume and value; sales from different customer groups; and sales from different distribution channels.

Operational requirements

Information about your operational requirements will be required for your financial forecasts, while other information will be needed for your basic operational planning. Outline your plans for premises, equipment, staff, suppliers, and compliance and licensing, and estimate the respective costs involved.

Current financial requirements and financial forecasts

Your business plan should include a breakdown of your financial requirements, the sources of finance you have available to you, and any additional amount that you may need. This breakdown should include: the cost of starting your business; your personal budget; details of your own personal finance that you intend to invest, as well as of additional finance; a detailed cash flow forecast that will help estimate how much available cash you will have in any particular month; a profit and loss forecast to help estimate when your business will start to make a profit (which will be essential to your medium-term success); and a balance sheet forecast to provide you with a snapshot of the trading position of your business, to identify what your business will owe, what it will own, and how financially strong it will be at a particular point in the future.

Management processes

Even if you are the only person involved in your business, it is still important to consider your key skills, responsibilities, and management processes. Think about all the following in your plan:

- management team—outline skills and experience
- key staff and responsibilities—summarise roles and contribution to the business. Be sure to cover these tasks: marketing and sales, finance, recruitment, product development, general management, and administration
- monitoring and co-ordination—set out how you plan to monitor performance (against objectives and targets), and to co-ordinate the key roles in the business.

Business risks

Your plan should include an honest awareness of the risks involved, as well as how you plan to minimise them. Consider which of the following risks are relevant to your businesses: lack of management experience; no trading history; economic uncertainties; reliance on key staff; reliance on a few suppliers; reliance on a small customer base; bad customer debts; partnership difficulties; increased competition; security and insurance against burglary and loss; and failure to meet your sales targets. Show that you have thought about all of these issues

and that you have contingency plans for coping with them should they occur.

Present your plan in a professional manner

Once you have researched and drafted all the necessary information, you can compile the plan. Produce a simple but stylish cover for it, not forgetting to include the business name, your address, your phone numbers, e-mail address, and the date. Put an edited, proofed, and double-checked final draft together. Use a transparent plastic cover with a binder, and letter-quality printer and paper. The order should be cover, title page, executive summary, contents page, contents, and appendices.

WHAT TO AVOID
Producing unrealistic sales forecasts

It is a good idea to produce more than one sales forecast, including one for the worst-case scenario, and how you intend to deal with this. If you are over-optimistic you may not be able to make the necessary repayments. You must also make sure that any market research is comprehensive enough to give you realistic sales targets.

Not proof-reading the plan

You must check that the plan is accurate and contains no mistakes. Ensure that at least two people read it thoroughly to look out for errors.

RECOMMENDED LINKS
Business Eye (Wales):
www.businesseye.org.uk
Business Gateway (Scotland):
www.bgateway.com
Business Link (England):
www.businesslink.org
Invest Northern Ireland:
www.investni.com

SEE ALSO
Applying for Grants and Funding (p. 113)
Budgeting (p. 494)
Financing a New Business (p. 104)

Applying for Grants and Funding

GETTING STARTED

A grant is financial assistance, usually for a specific project, given to a business by an awarding body. The grant might help you to develop a new product, buy equipment, or run a training scheme. A grant is usually a one-off payment and will provide funding that covers a percentage of the costs of the project. Unlike loans and venture capital, a grant does not have to be repaid, unless you fail to adhere to the specific terms and conditions of the scheme. This actionlist gives information about what grants are available, where to apply for them, and how to make the application.

FAQS

What can I get a grant for?

Grants are available for a variety of projects, but each individual scheme will offer funding for a specific purpose. Whether or not you qualify for a grant can also depend on other factors such as the kind of business you run, the size of the business, whether the project will create jobs, and where your business is located. The sorts of areas which a grant might cover include consultancy, design, advertising, marketing, and promotion. Grants are also obtainable for business expansion and relocation, improving business premises, and security, and also for businesses going into exporting. They can be awarded for starting up a business, market testing, and capital equipment. Grants are also available for co-operatives and community enterprises, and for environmental improvements. There are grants for information technology (IT) and e-commerce, new technology and innovation, and research and development (R&D), as well as recruitment and training.

Where can I get a grant?

At local or regional levels, you may be able to get a grant from organisations such as Business Link (England), Business Gateway (Scotland), Business Eye (Wales), and Invest Northern Ireland. Grants are also provided by local authorities, enterprise agencies, the Government Office for the Region (GOR), and Regional Development Agencies (RDA). The Chambers of Commerce and the Learning and Skills Councils (LSC) also provide grants.

Nationally, grants are available from various government departments and agencies, such as The Department of Trade and Industry (DTI), The Countryside Agency, UKTrade&Investment,andTheDepartmentfor Environment, Food and Rural Affairs (DEFRA). Grants are also available from organisations such as The Prince's Trust, the Crafts Council, and the English Arts Board.

At a European level, grants are usually not available directly to businesses. Instead, the European Commission provides finance to local or regional grant administering bodies via its four Structural Funds. These are the European Regional Development Fund (ERDF), the European Social Fund (ESF), the European Agricultural Guidance and Guarantee Fund (EAGGF), and the Financial Instrument for Fisheries Guidance (FIFG). These grants can usually be accessed through local and regional organisations such as those listed above.

How long does a grant application take?

The application process for some grants can take several months (see below), so if your project needs funding immediately it'd be a good idea for you to investigate alternative sources of finance, such as loans. Also bear in mind that businesses are usually required to meet some of the costs of the project (usually at least 50 percent of overall expenditure), so you'll have to be prepared to raise some finance as well.

It's always worth finding out whether your business could attract grant funding, but it may be risky to base any business idea *solely* on the presumption that you'll get it.

Most grant funding is conditional and your business will need to meet the specific criteria of the grant program.

✔ MAKING IT HAPPEN
Before applying
Your first step is to contact your local Business Link, Small Business Gateway, Business Connect, or Invest Northern Ireland office. Most will have a directory of assistance available locally, nationally, and at a European level. Their advisers will be able to put you in touch with the relevant grant-awarding bodies, and will also be able to help you through the application process.

You will then need to contact the awarding body and check that your project meets the specified criteria of the scheme. It's important at this stage to find out whether it is actually worth applying, as grant application forms can take a lot of time and effort to complete. If you do decide to proceed, ask them to send you an application form and more detailed information about the grant.

Many schemes will require you to supply a project plan or proposal. Within this you will need to include a project description. This should detail the aim of the project, and also how the project will benefit your business. You will also need to give information about the people who will run the project, and what experience, knowledge, and skills they have. Don't forget to include the cost of the project, as well as its length and key deadlines, and make sure you explain where the project is located. You will also need to make a convincing case as to why your project needs the support of the grant. Outline what would happen if the support wasn't provided, and state clearly how much money is required. Give details of how you intend to fund your share of the project's costs. You will need to work out how the project complies with the criteria set by the grant provider. Give details about your business, when it was set up, its activities, and so on, as well as financial information about the business. This might require the submission of accounts and forecasts.

Make the application
Read any guidance notes that are supplied with the application. These will give you information on how to complete the form. Application forms will differ widely. The proposal should follow the format required, be clear and concise, and should be tailored to the grant you are applying for.

For national and European grants, you may have to submit two forms. These will be a short initial form to assess your eligibility for the grant, and then a second form providing detailed information about your business and the project you intend to undertake. It is a good idea to speak to someone involved with administering the grant. They will be able to help you with completing the form. Alternatively, seek the assistance of a Business Link adviser or accountant to help you with your application.

Your business plan will provide a lot of the detail for your grant application. You should make sure that your business plan is up to date and includes information about your experience, future plans, and financial requirements.

After the application
When you have completed the application, make sure that you check it over thoroughly and that you've supplied all the information required. After you've sent your application, the awarding body may contact you to get more information to help with the assessment. They may also ask you to come to an interview or visit your business themselves.

If your application is successful, you'll probably receive a formal letter offering the grant. This will probably include the agreed programme of work, eligible costs, start date, and the timescale. You'll probably have to accept the conditions that apply to the offer within a given period of time. Read the letter carefully, as you will be signing up to a legally binding agreement.

It's likely that you'll have to wait some time before getting a decision on your grant application. This could range from a few weeks (for local grants) to a year (for national and European grants). Again, bear this in mind and make sure you have some alternative sources to pursue, especially if you need finance quickly.

✘ WHAT TO AVOID
Not completing the application form properly
If your application is incomplete, it will take longer to process and is more likely to be rejected. Also, if you provide incorrect information the grant may be reclaimed.

RECOMMENDED LINKS
Business Eye (Wales):
www.businesseye.org.uk

Business Gateway (Scotland):
www.bgateway.com
Business Link (England):
www.businesslink.org
Invest Northern Ireland:
www.investni.com

SEE ALSO
Budgeting (p. 494)
Financing a New Business (p. 104)
**Preparing a Successful Business Plan
 (p. 110)**

Controlling a Budget

GETTING STARTED

Controlling budgets is a headache for businesses of all sizes. Many smaller businesses start off on the right foot by putting in place a good book-keeping system, but then fail to exercise proper financial control and end up in trouble. The only way to make sure that you make a profit is to control the budget efficiently. To do this, you need to estimate your sales income reasonably accurately, estimate your costs precisely, and keep both under control. You also need to charge the right price for your end product in your chosen market(s). It is important systematically to collect all financial documents in a methodical way, and keep all your figures up to date on a daily basis. This actionlist will look at some of the most common problems in controlling a budget, and suggest ways to tackle them.

A book which you might find useful on this subject is *Cash Flows and Budgeting Made Easy*, written by Peter Taylor and published in 2002 by How To Books.

FAQS

What is budgeting?

Each year you should prepare a business plan for the business, including your best forecast of sales. A budget is simply that forecast turned into figures. In other words, it is an estimate of sales income together with the costs required to produce those sales.

What is financial control?

Financial control is different to book-keeping. Book-keeping is about recording the figures—in other words income and expenditure, receipts and payments, and assets and liabilities. Accurate book-keeping, of course, is a pre-requisite for effective financial control, and computerised accounting packages make accurate book-keeping far easier.

You then, however, need to use the figures as a basis for effective financial control. It can be difficult to keep the complete picture in your head all the time, so calculating a few simple ratios or using a graph are both good techniques to help you keep up to date.

MAKING IT HAPPEN

Set targets

Each year, set objectives and prepare a business plan. Define your objectives in financial terms, as well as in terms of marketing, quality, and people. If a venture capitalist or business angel has invested in your business, his or her primary concern will often be the rate of return on investment (often referred to in financial documents as 'ROI'). If you've invested your own money into the business, you may be expecting smaller returns initially, planning for your business to provide higher returns over a longer period.

Keep the books

A reliable, easy-to-use accounting system is essential for straightforward effective financial control. Make sure that you keep proper records. The information to record includes: any sales orders received; invoices issued by the business for sales; purchase orders placed by the business; invoices received by the business for purchases; cash receipts, and cash expenditure. Turning this information into graphs, tables, and charts can help to reveal trends, which in turn will help you to revise your forecasts and future planning. A range of accessible computer software, such as Microsoft Excel, will help you to do this.

Carry out a monthly check

Bring the cash book up to date and carry out a bank reconciliation every month. The cash book balance represents the business's liquidity; it is the cash immediately available to the business.

Prepare an operating statement by combining the revenue, direct costs, and overhead costs. This records income and expenditure (as does the profit and loss account), not receipts and payments. It ignores some items such as depreciation or bad debts. Each month, you should compare your actual performance with your forecast both for the month and, ideally, for the year to date. You can then look at some simple ratios and the variances.

Analyse the available information

Carry out a ratio analysis. Do this by defining your costs as a percentage of the sales income. This gives you a very quick method of determining whether or not you are on target. If your costs are rising as a percentage of your sales income, then you know that you have a problem to address. Consider your gross profit margin. If the margin is falling, it could be a sign of trouble. Ask yourself the following questions. Has wastage increased? Have costs increased? Monitoring changes closely will help you to react to any problems, preventing them from escalating any further.

Then carry out a variance analysis. A variance is the difference between your target and your actual performance. Variance analysis looks at the differences themselves, rather than comparing different figures, as happens in ratio analysis. Review figures for: sales, inquiry and order position; material and labour usage; overheads; cash position/cash forecast; stock; and capital expenditure. As you work through the analysis, remember that analysing variances means thinking about more than just differences in cash; there may be major variances even though the overall cash position remains more or less as forecast. Make sure you understand why the figures are changing. There are various possible reasons; for example, is it possible for a reduction in raw material cost to be cancelled by increased wastage?

Manage cash

The operating statement shows the net trading profit but does not show the liquidity (that is, the cash position of your business, and the ability to meet payments). It is important, therefore, that you also prepare a monthly cash-flow statement. This reflects when money is received or paid out and includes items such as drawings, VAT, or tax, which are not regarded as trading expenses. All the figures should be readily available from the cash book.

Remember the importance of actively controlling the budget. Generating the figures is only the first part of the process; you must then take some action. Keep a tight grip on anyone that owes the business money (your debtors). If the level of debtors rises, this could be because your sales are increasing or because your debtors are taking longer to pay. Make sure you define in your terms of trade how quickly you expect debtors to pay, and then ensure that they stick to these guidelines. Put processes in place to deal with late payments or debtors who continually delay their payments.

Similarly, try not to get on the wrong side of your suppliers by taking too long to pay *them*, as they may withdraw your credit facilities. To gain the most benefit, you need to take the maximum amount of credit possible without abusing your agreed terms. Take care to ensure your PAYE and VAT payments are made on time, otherwise you could incur substantial penalties.

Controlling your debtors and creditors carefully will ensure that you're controlling your working capital carefully. If you're building up large sums of cash, do something worthwhile with them, even if only to move it to an account that pays you a better rate of interest. If you expect to need additional working capital, for example because debtors are rising as your sales increase, then talking to the bank—or your investors—early will reassure them that you really are in control of your business, and they will be more likely to help.

Watch your stock levels carefully. Consider how much stock you have tied up in raw materials, work in progress, and finished goods. If you have too much stock, you may be using excessive storage space and tying up money that could be used in other ways.

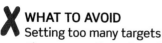

WHAT TO AVOID
Setting too many targets

Choose a small number of appropriate targets and focus on a handful of key issues, such as revenue growth, profit, and cash flow. Compiling and analysing huge amounts of information can be time-consuming and not always of great use if the major points are buried underneath too much detail.

Letting your books get out of date

You need up-to-date financial records before you can control your budget properly, so record transactions accurately and promptly.

Losing track of cash

The key to making a profit is through the careful control of cash, so that you can pay your debts as they fall due.

RECOMMENDED LINKS

Institute of Credit Management:
www.icm.org.uk
Small Business—Information and Cash Flow;
www.credit-to-cash.com

SEE ALSO
Budgeting (p. 494)

Controlling Costs

GETTING STARTED
The basis of any successful business is that income should exceed expenses. One way to improve profitability is to increase the sales of your business, but you can also enhance profitability through the reduction of costs. A business that keeps its costs under control will be able to release more resources for growth in the good times, and will be in a better position to survive in recession. This actionlist gives some suggestions on ways to control (and in some cases reduce) the costs of your business.

FAQS
Which costs do I need to control?
In order to be able to control costs, you first need to know about them. Start by identifying each cost clearly, and make sure that you keep records of all bills, receipts, and so on. You will need to review your costs on a regular basis. This will depend on when your accounts are normally completed. It is not enough to calculate whether the business is in profit or loss; you also need to be aware of what normal costs are, so that you can spot anomalies and take action to address them. Some costs will be more important to control than others. It will be important to know what the business's critical costs are, and to concentrate on reducing them.

Who is responsible for controlling costs?
Cost control is the responsibility of everyone working in the business. If you have a team of people working for you, all your employees have countless opportunities to affect costs throughout each day. It is important to be aware that if employees are unhappy at work, they are in a position to do a lot of damage, if only through what they *don't* do. If they are motivated and feel part of the business, they will work economically without supervision. Rising to the challenge of providing this kind of environment for your employees is a test of good management; one approach is to involve employees by asking them to come up with ideas to reduce costs. If you do decide on this approach, though, be careful with the way you phrase this request. Unless the company is in dire straits and you are thinking of making redundancies, don't give them the impression that their jobs are on the line as part of this cost-cutting measure!

Many people assume that because the volume of expenditure is so much larger than they are used to in home life, any savings they might make are insignificant. Every little does help, though, so let your team know that cutting back on what look like insignificant costs will help the business overall.

MAKING IT HAPPEN
Use cost control measures

One effective cost control measure is to carry out a cost benefit analysis. Cost awareness should be part of the planning process. In meetings, planning sessions, or in personal planning, the overall impact of any decision should be understood in terms of business profitability. In other words, the benefits of a particular course of action should be set against the cost. For example, a person may be assigned to carry out a piece of research that could, in fact, be done quicker by a consultant, or bought off the shelf. Additionally, the work may in fact have an insignificant impact on profitability, and you need to ask whether it is worth doing at all. In such cases, you will need to be quite pragmatic and ruthless.

Another method of cost control is value analysis (VA), which involves a detailed examination of each part of a product, service, or system to determine if there is any way in which its costs could be reduced without affecting quality. Value analysis is usually done in a group and it is therefore a good way to involve employees and increase general awareness of cost control. Each aspect of the product should be brought under the spotlight. The group has to decide, for example, whether the product is necessary; whether it can be made with cheaper materials; whether it is actually cheaper to buy than to make; whether it can be made more quickly; or whether it can be simplified to reduce potential faults. Other aspects to look at might be reducing the material that is used to make it, or reducing wastage. Economising on the use of raw materials can be a very effective cost-saving measure.

Your company could also examine its purchasing methods. It is a good idea to look for discounts for buying in bulk. You should also be prepared to haggle, and it is important to review the cost of supplies and suppliers on a regular basis. In fact, no bill or invoice that your business receives should be taken for granted. For example, your landlord could be persuaded to reduce rent payments if you think they are unfair. If you feel that rates are too high, you can appeal to have the rateable value reduced. In this case, the local Inland Revenue valuation office should be contacted for the relevant forms. Stock control is another potential area for savings. Accurate control will reduce storage and working capital costs. Providing effective security should reduce the cost of stock lost through theft.

Look at potential areas for cost savings

Staff costs often contain the greatest scope for savings. Aspects that you might consider include employing fewer people to do the same task. Also ask yourself whether your employees are motivated and monitored appropriately, to ensure that they deliver value for money. Look at their remuneration to check that it is appropriate; too much is costly, too little may lead to a high staff turnover (which is also costly) and may damage performance. Effective management techniques will increase the value you get from staff.

Energy costs could be reduced if your employees are encouraged to use energy responsibly, in the same way as they do at home. Most people today care about the environment and this can motivate them to save energy. It is often overlooked that some of the biggest savings available to businesses lie within some of their most basic costs, for example gas and electricity. It is worth having meters double checked, especially if the business uses a lot of energy. Thermostats should be set correctly. You shouldn't underestimate the impact of proper insulation measures, which can produce long-term savings. Your business may also be eligible for grants to insulate the property. The Energy Efficiency Office provides free advice and information on ways of saving energy. Another area for you to consider is changing long-standing suppliers of telecommunications, gas, and electricity. You will need to compare the prices and contract terms offered by the numerous companies now supplying basic utilities and telecommunications.

Telephone calls are another basic company cost offering potential savings. It is necessary for some private calls to be made from work, but you may find that some of your staff are taking advantage. Make sure that you outline a policy for the use of phones for personal calls. This should be agreed and circulated. Staff should also be made aware of any possible disciplinary action that could be taken against them for breach of the policy. It is possible to get itemised bills for each extension, which should discourage misuse of phones. Staff should also be trained in the efficient use of the telephone, to reduce the length of calls.

Photocopiers are easy to use and the expense can soon get out of control if usage is not monitored. Make sure that all copies are logged, allocated to a cost centre, and that the initials of the person taking the copy are recorded. Staff should be charged for personal copies, and discouraged from making unnecessary copies. Someone should be made responsible for monitoring copying, and usage should be reviewed regularly. Make sure that all staff know exactly how to use all the facilities on the copier. This in itself can reduce costs, for example printing double-sided copies can save time and money.

Some staff may be tempted to take office stationery home for their own use. You could consider keeping the stationery cupboard locked and making someone responsible for issuing materials. Scrap paper can be recycled as stapled writing pads. Used laser printer cartridges can be sent off to be refilled at a discount price. Recycling is good for the environment, and can save a business money. All waste should be considered for potential recycling or resale to recycling companies. For example, there are companies who will buy industrial plastic waste for recycling.

Finally, It is a good idea to have a clear expenses policy. It is possible to reduce misuse of expenses by drawing up guidelines so that everyone understands what is, and is not, acceptable. Expense claims should be cleared by a manager before being paid. Make sure that expenses for individuals are reviewed periodically, and anomalies investigated.

X WHAT TO AVOID
Making false economies
Don't cut back on the wrong things. If you reduce the level of service your customers are used to, you'll probably end up losing the business money. Similarly, if you make working conditions too harsh, for example, by cutting back on pay, benefits, and training, your staff will become demoralized and will not perform—indeed, you run the risk of them leaving.

Ignoring rising costs
Confront cost problems immediately rather than put them off and hope they'll go away. It's much better to act sooner and to stop the problem from escalating.

RECOMMENDED LINKS
Building Research Energy Conservation Support Unit:
www.bre.co.uk
Energy Efficiency Hotline:
www.saveenergy.co.uk
Energy Watch:
www.energywatch.org.uk

SEE ALSO
Budgeting (p. 494)
Drawing Up a Budget (p. 122)
Financing a New Business (p. 104)

Drawing Up a Budget

GETTING STARTED

Every business needs to plan its spending on the basis of what it expects from sales income; without this tool, you can't be sure that your business will survive. Budgeting is simply the name given to the process of working out what you expect your business to earn and spend in a given period. It also gives you the ability to check how the business is doing from week to week, or month to month; without this check, you can easily overspend. This actionlist explains how you can make use of your budget, and how to draw one up.

FAQS

What can I use a budget for?

It's important that you use your budget as a control mechanism. At the end of each month, you should enter the actual figures for sales and expenses next to the figures that were forecast. If there are substantial differences between the budgeted figures and the actual figures, then you need to do something about it.

For instance, if your sales are too low, you may need to reconsider your marketing strategies. If sales, on the other hand, are higher than planned, then you may need to reconsider your staffing levels or raw material supplies, in order to cope with the rising demand. Also, if you find your expenditure is too high, you'll need to look for ways to bring costs down.

How do I estimate sales and expenditure?

The starting point for drawing up a budget is for you to estimate future sales and expenditure. The sales budget can be split into the number of different products your business plans to sell; the number of units of each product that you plan to sell; the price that you plan to sell each unit for; and the place or area where you plan to sell them.

You'll need to split your expenditure budget into production costs or variable costs (such as materials, power, and subcontractors); overhead costs or fixed costs (such as rent and salaries); and capital costs (such as equipment and the purchase of property).

MAKING IT HAPPEN

Budgeting for sales

If your business is a new one, forecasting sales will be particularly tricky for you, because you don't have actual sales from the past on which you can base your expectations. Instead, you'll have to make sure that your budget is based on good research. It must also be closely tied to a realistic marketing plan that will generate the sales you expect. It's important not just to guess your sales figures. Also, don't start by looking at your planned expenditure and then just deriving a sales forecast to cover the cost.

Make the sales budget as detailed as you can. You need to make it very clear what you plan to sell, and at what price. Set out your expected sales on a monthly or quarterly basis. If your business sells a range of products, make sure that you prepare sales budgets for each of them. If your products are sold in more than one area, then you may find it helpful to have a sales budget for each area.

Budgeting for expenditure

Now that you have prepared the sales budget, you have the basic foundations for working out what your expenditure will be. For your purposes, the expenditure budget can be split into a production budget and an overheads budget. If you know how many products you'll sell, you can work out the direct costs of producing them. These direct costs will then make up the production budget, and will vary with the level of production. The overhead costs will stay more or less constant.

The production budget

The production budget is made up of items like the materials and components that go into the product.

If you have a sales team, you also need to include commission paid to them. (If sales people earn a regular retainer as well, this retainer would normally be regarded as a fixed cost.) Make sure that you include the cost of subcontractors, where people are being paid as independent contractors to perform a certain, defined job.

Discounts are usually shown in the budget as a direct cost.

There are some expenses, such as depreciation, that are usually treated as fixed overheads. However, if you want to be particularly accurate with your production budget, you could include these, especially if you can clearly associate them with specific products.

The overheads budget

Once you have prepared the production budget, you'll need to consider the other costs that the business will incur. These will include the salaries for you and your staff, National Insurance contributions, and pension contributions. You'll also need to include rent and company insurance, and telephone, Internet, and e-mail account costs. Any interest on money that you have borrowed will also need to be included in your overheads.

If your business is in manufacturing, it's likely that the above will represent a relatively small proportion of the total costs. On the other hand, if you have a service sector business, it's likely that overheads will represent a very high proportion of the cost. Include all overhead costs, including interest payments and drawings (how much money you plan to take out of the business). Remember that you are taxed on the total profit (if you are self-employed), so allow for this too. If your business is registered as a company, and you expect to take high dividends, make sure that you budget for this as well.

Your business may aim to allocate the overheads to each product, or may prefer to retain overheads as a single budget. Whichever path you choose, it's important that you ensure that the price for each product makes a reasonable contribution to the overheads.

Budgeting for the full cost of production

You're now in a position to pull together the production budget and the overheads budget into a single production cost budget. If there is more than one product or service, then there will be a production budget for each. There will also be variable overheads for you to add for each product. There is no need for you to split fixed overheads across products at this point, since the object of this exercise is for you to be able to determine the total costs.

Capital expenditure budget

If you expect to buy capital equipment, you'll need to decide how you'll pay for it (whether in cash or through a loan), and make sure that you budget for these payments in the relevant months. This is essential information if an accurate forecast is to be prepared, particularly where the business may have to take out a loan to finance the purchase and will have to meet a repayment schedule that includes interest.

If the business decides to lease equipment, it's important to make sure that you read all the small print. While the selling is carried out by a supplier, the leasing is done by a finance company. Usually the conditions are more favourable for them than for your business. On the other hand, the organisation leasing the equipment to you usually has a responsibility to ensure the equipment keeps working, even if the supplier can no longer support it.

Cash flow

If you operate your business on a cash basis, in other words taking in cash for your sales and paying cash for your purchases, then it's fairly easy to see if you are living within your means because you'll have cash left over at the end of the month if you're making a profit. Very few businesses, however, operate like this. It's far more likely that you'll be selling goods or services in one month, and not receiving payment until the following month, or the month after that. Similarly, you may be buying raw materials one month, but not paying for them for at least another four weeks. A budget will help you keep track of your cash flow in and out of the business, and keep control.

Once the budgets have been prepared, you can use the data that has been accumulated in order to prepare financial forecasts. This will include a cash flow forecast, but you should also include a forecast of the profit and loss statement, and the balance sheet. The cash flow forecast should set out, on a month-by-month basis, all cash inflows and outflows from the business for the following 12 months; this will help you to determine your working capital needs. The profit and loss forecast will help you to check that your business remains profitable.

WHAT TO AVOID
Not setting realistic targets
If you set realistic targets, you'll be able to tell whether sales and expenditure have gone to plan, and you'll also be able to foresee problems and opportunities in time to take action.

Not bothering to prepare a cash-flow forecast
It's important to remember that a cash-flow forecast is as important as the budget itself. While the budget can tell you if your business is generally profitable, it might not alert you to cash-flow problems.

RECOMMENDED LINKS
Institute of Credit Management:
www.icm.org.uk
Small Business—Information and Cash Flow:
www.credit-to-cash.com

SEE ALSO
Budgeting (p. 494)
Controlling Costs (p. 119)
Financing a New Business (p. 104)

Getting to Grips with Income Tax

GETTING STARTED

Income tax is payable on an individual's income in any particular tax year if it exceeds an annual threshold. The government writes and re-writes tax law and the courts have the job of interpreting exactly what it means, in any particular circumstance. The Inland Revenue inspectors are responsible for the collection of tax and National Insurance in the United Kingdom.

Income tax can be collected from a whole range of sources. These include: employment salary and benefits; the net profit from a sole business; the partnership profit share in the case of partnerships; dividends paid on shareholdings; investments; pensions; foreign income; income from property; and trust income.

It is particularly important, if you are self-employed or run a small business, that you maintain a good grip on your tax liability and plan ahead so that you can meet your tax bills. This actionlist aims to act as a guide and a reminder to help you run your tax affairs smoothly.

FAQS

What is income?

Tax is charged on income arising from an enterprise. It can be described as the fruits of an endeavour, rather than just a receipt of money. This means that in most circumstances, gifts or transfers of capital are not counted towards your income in a tax year—although they might have to be taken into account for capital gains tax purposes instead. Any occupation or profession that produces an annual sum in terms of money can be a source of 'income'. Even a one-off job producing income is included.

Who has to pay income tax?

As has often been said, nothing is certain in life except death and taxes. So if you are resident in the United Kingdom, or working for a UK employer, the income tax rules apply. The Pay As You Earn (PAYE) system means that most employees have the correct tax deducted at source by their employers. If you are self-employed, you need to fill in a self-assessment form each year and, depending on when you submit this to the Inland Revenue, either calculate the tax you need to pay yourself, or have it calculated for you by the Revenue.

How much is it?

Tax is only payable if your total income for a tax year exceeds certain limits. In the United Kingdom, personal allowances for individuals start at £4,615 per annum as a tax-free allowance. Tax on any income above that level is then paid at the following rates:

- a starting rate of 10% on the first £1,920 of income above the personal allowance
- the standard rate of 22% on the next £27,980
- the higher rate of 40% on the remainder of your income (there is no upper limit)

Personal allowances are due to everyone from 0 years to 64 years, and the basic allowance is due whatever your total income. This basic allowance can be augmented with an additional amount for those over 65, and again at 75, if the individual has a moderate income.

MAKING IT HAPPEN

Recognise that tax is a cost of running a successful business

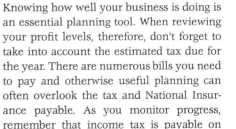

Knowing how well your business is doing is an essential planning tool. When reviewing your profit levels, therefore, don't forget to take into account the estimated tax due for the year. There are numerous bills you need to pay and otherwise useful planning can often overlook the tax and National Insurance payable. As you monitor progress, remember that income tax is payable on your net profits, but it is not a deductible expense so it has to be funded from those profits.

Plan for your tax bills

It is important to know when your tax is payable and how much it is likely to be—and then to set aside sufficient funds to pay it. The date of payment for the self employed, whether sole traders or in partnership, is dependent on your accounting year end. Businesses can make up annual accounts to any date to suit their particular trade, and that date falls within a particular tax year. The tax on those profits and a payment on account of the next year is payable on the 31 January and 31 July following the 5 April of that tax year.

Take advantage of all the allowances available

Under self-assessment, it is up to you to make sure that you claim any and all allowances that you are eligible for. The Inland Revenue adopts a file-now/check-later process which means that it is unable to consider whether you have filled the form in to your best advantage. Take time to ensure everything you can claim is included in your accounts and tax return. It is a good idea to get proper advice from an accountant, as there are usually ways of organising things to ensure that you make optimum use of your allowances.

Check as you go

Deductions in computing profits have to be made in accordance with recognised accountancy principles. Items like wages come off your gross income, but capital expenses are not deductible in the same way; there is a delay in receiving tax relief for most of these items. This may mean you have to plan carefully to fund your tax bills if capital investment has been high in particular years.

Get good advice

Tax law is continuously being modified. If in doubt, seek help—and always check with a professional adviser before relying on being able to deduct expenses or claim allowances.

WHAT TO AVOID
Spending your tax fund

When starting in business there is a delay before you have to pay your first tax bill. It can come as a nasty surprise if, when payment time does eventually come, you find that you did in fact make a healthy profit but have spent all the money. Even if every penny went back into the business, the Revenue will have little sympathy with you if you get behind with tax payments. Interest, penalties, and court action will swiftly follow if you are unable to pay.

Comparing one year with another

The annual nature of tax means that every tax year will involve a different set of figures. Annual changes to allowances and rates are proposed by the chancellor in the budget each November, and finalised by the Queen's speech. In some years, an incoming government makes amendments. From your own point of view profits may fluctuate; after a bad year it may take a while to increase your profits, but when you do, the tax will have to be paid.

Not preparing accounts soon enough

Individuals are now responsible for providing the Revenue with enough information to be able to calculate the tax bill themselves. Since the self-assessment system came into effect, tax has to be paid in January and July following the 5 April. This can mean that if your accounting date is 5 April you have less than ten months to work out and fund the tax bill. If the return is filed later than 30 September after the tax year ends, you also have to work out the tax due yourself rather than having it done by the tax office.

RECOMMENDED LINK
Inland Revenue:
www.inlandrevenue.gov.uk

SEE ALSO
Budgeting (p. 494)
Taxation (p. 549)

Getting to Grips with National Insurance

GETTING STARTED

National Insurance (NI) is a contribution towards state benefits such as pensions and unemployment and incapacity benefits. Contributions are paid by everyone who works, whether as an employee or on a self-employed basis, and by all employers. Businesses that employ staff are required to collect and pay the employers' and employees' contributions each month. The self-employed have a separate arrangement. This actionlist explains how National Insurance works.

FAQS

How are contributions assessed?

Contributions are assessed according to the National Insurance (NI) class into which a person fits. Some people may fall into more than one class. **Class 1** is for individuals in employment. There is no liability for employee or employer National Insurance contributions (NICs) on wages at, or below, the current earnings threshold (£89 per week for 2003/04). Both employee and employer have to pay contributions on all earnings above the threshold. There is an Upper Earnings Limit for employees' contributions, but not for employers' contributions.

Employers providing benefits in kind such as company cars for employees have a further National Insurance liability under **Class 1A**. Contributions are payable on the amount charged to income tax as a taxable benefit. Childcare benefits provided by an employer are exempt from these contributions.

Everyone who is self-employed pays **Class 2** contributions. There is a Small Earnings Exception, below which National Insurance Contributions are not payable. **Class 3** contributions are voluntary. This allows people to protect their right to contributory benefits, even if they're not liable to National Insurance Contributions under Class 1 or 2. The self-employed are liable to pay **Class 4** contributions as well as Class 2. Class 4 is set as a percentage rate of profit between lower and upper thresholds (between £4,615 and £30,940 in 2003/04).

Is anyone exempt from paying National Insurance Contributions?

Some employees will not be liable for any National Insurance contributions. These include those who are under 16 years old, and also those who have reached pensionable age (currently 60 years old for women, and 65 for men). If an employee has more than one job and will pay the maximum amount from one of the jobs, he or she doesn't need to pay contributions on his or her employment with the second employer. However, the employer must still pay employer's contributions for them. The self-employed who reach pensionable age are exempt from Class 2 and Class 4 contributions.

What forms do I need?

When you first tell the Inland Revenue that you are employing people, they will send you their employers' pack, which includes a number of forms to be used if you intend to maintain a manual payroll system.

The **Deductions Working Sheet P11** is for keeping weekly or monthly records. Each of your employees will have a P11, on which are recorded their personal details, National Insurance number, and details of National Insurance and tax contributions each time they are paid.

The **End of Year Summary P14/P60** form must be returned at the end of the year to the Inspector of Taxes. There should be one for each employee, containing the employee's details, and total National Insurance contributions and tax paid. The P60 must be given to employees by 31 May each year.

The **Payslip Booklet P30BC** contains bank credit slips that are completed monthly. Every month, or every quarter if the business is a PAYE small employer, your business must fill in and send a P30BC payslip to the Inland Revenue Accounts Office, together with any payment of National Insurance Contributions and tax deducted in the previous month or quarter.

The **Employer's Payment Record P32** is used to record tax details, and National Insurance payment details, as well as Statutory Sick Pay (SSP) and Statutory Maternity Pay (SMP) recovered in the year. There are also columns covering tax credits and student loan deductions.

The **Employer's Annual Return P35** must be returned at the end of the tax year to the Inspector of Taxes. You must submit this form by 19 May.

MAKING IT HAPPEN
Assess how much National Insurance is payable

National Insurance contributions are assessed on gross pay. There are many payments that might be made to employees. Some are included in National Insurance liability, while others are exempt. These payments include income tax deduction, arrears of pay (such as a back-dated pay rise), and commission. They also include Christmas, productivity, and completion bonuses, as well as holiday pay (subject to certain exemptions), Statutory Sick Pay, and Statutory Maternity Pay. Payments made to company directors in anticipation of future earnings are also included. You will find that although this list is not exhaustive, it does include most elements of gross pay for National Insurance liability purposes.

Not included in gross pay are board and lodging provided free, uniforms purchased for staff, personal, unexpected gifts made to an employee, redundancy, termination or pay in lieu of notice payments (though this may be chargeable if it is in the contract or if it is the norm to pay it), and compensation awarded by an employment tribunal.

Collect National Insurance contributions (NICs)

National Insurance contributions on wages are deducted at source under the PAYE scheme. If you use a manual payroll system, the Inland Revenue will provide you with tables to calculate the amounts due, and forms on which to record your calculations. If you run a computerised payroll system, the software will do all the calculations for you, and will also provide the summaries that you need to complete the Inland Revenue return.

Class 1A contributions are generally calculated at the end of the tax year and then paid direct to the Inland Revenue. The self-employed can pay Class 2 contributions by monthly direct debit. Class 4 contributions are collected with income tax each year in January and July. Voluntary contributions can be paid by quarterly bill or direct debit.

Claim back National Insurance contributions

In certain circumstances, some or even all National Insurance contributions can be claimed back. There are also provisions for over-payment or under-payment on the business's part, or by deductions made from employees' pay.

Statutory Maternity Pay (SMP)

Your business may be entitled to Small Employers' Relief if Class 1 contributions of £40,000 or less have been paid in the qualifying tax year. (The qualifying tax year is the last complete tax year before the employee's qualifying week. The qualifying week is the 15th week before expected childbirth.) All the employer's NICs paid on SMP can be recovered, plus 4.5% compensation. If the business is not entitled to relief, it can recover 92% of the NI paid on SMP. This is reclaimed by deduction from the monthly NI and tax payments. The amount due to be recovered should be recorded on the employee's form P11.

Statutory Sick Pay (SSP)

The business may qualify for the Percentage Threshold Scheme, designed to reimburse employers who have a high percentage of workers off sick at any one time. It is not restricted to small businesses. You can perform the following calculation to assess whether the business qualifies. Add together the employer and employee NI Class 1 contributions for the tax month, then multiply by 13%. If the total SSP payments for the month come to more than this calculation, the business can recover the difference through its NICs.

WHAT TO AVOID
Deducting too much from employees' pay
If you accidentally deduct too much from employees' pay, you can refund them and amend your pay records if the error is from the current tax year.

Underpaying Class 1 Contributions
If you underpay an employee's Class 1 contributions you have no right to recover the underpayment from the employee after the tax year the mistake was made in. You as an employer have to pay the underpayment to the Inland Revenue. If you discover the mistake within the relevant tax year you can make further deductions from the employee's pay during that year to recover the underpayment.

RECOMMENDED LINK
Inland Revenue Business Support Team for your area:
www.inlandrevenue.gov.uk/bst/index.htm

SEE ALSO
Budgeting (p. 494)
Taxation (p. 549)

Getting to Grips with Corporation Tax

GETTING STARTED

If your business is set up as a company, then the company will have to pay corporation tax on its profits. If you are a partner in either a traditional partnership or limited liability partnership, or a sole trader, you will not pay corporation tax, but you will pay income tax instead. This actionlist aims to give you some advice on the most common problems. You may also find the Inland Revenue's Helpline for the Newly Self-Employed useful—the telephone number is 0845 915 4515.

FAQS

Which profits get taxed?

Trading profits are liable to tax. These profits are the money from your business trading activities, minus expenses. That means, if you make products to sell, you will pay tax on the profits of selling your products, once you have deducted the cost of making the product. The same applies if you sell a service; once you have calculated how much it costs to provide the service, and deducted the cost from the price of selling the service, the amount of profit left will be subject to corporation tax.

Capital gains are also taxed. This is the money earned by selling company assets. If you sell, for example, property belonging to the company, the difference between the original price paid and the price it is sold for (that is to say, the profit from the sale) is subject to corporation tax. The only way to avoid this is by reinvesting the profit back into the company, for example, by buying another property.

What are the different rates of corporation tax?

The main rate of corporation tax is 30% for the financial year ending 31 March 2004. However, there are lower rates for companies with taxable profits of less than £1.5 million. You should note that all your profit is taxed at the same rate once you reach a specified threshold, though there is some marginal relief for profit levels below £1.5 million.

There is also the small companies' rate. For the purposes of corporation tax, 'small' is defined by the company's profits. For companies with profits below £300,000, the small companies' rate of 19% applies. For companies with profits below £10,000 the rate is zero. In addition, there is marginal relief between £10,000 and £50,000, and between £300,000 and £1.5 million. This means that you are not hit with the full charge if you exceed the threshold.

The rates are summarised in the table below:

Profit	Percentage tax rate
Up to £10,000	0.00
£10,001 – £50,000 (effective rate)	23.75
£50,001 – £300,000 (small companies' rate)	19.00
£300,001 – £1.5m (effective rate)	32.75
Greater than £1.5m	30.00

What relief and allowances apply to corporation tax?

Relief and allowances must be claimed on the company's tax return, or an amended return. Depreciation cannot be deducted. Instead, allowances are given for acquisitions of industrial buildings, fixtures, plant, equipment, and motor vehicles. Expenditure for the purposes of the trade can be set off against profit—for example, wages, salaries, energy, rent, rates, stationery, telephone, cleaning, and advertising expenditure.

You can claim relief on charges on income, such as patent royalties or covenants to charities. You can also claim relief for trading losses. These can be set against income or gains of the current or previous accounting period. If the loss is not claimed for some other relief, it will automatically be carried over and set against future profits. If the company ceases to trade, the previous 12 months' losses can be set against trading profits of the previous three years.

MAKING IT HAPPEN
Understand the collection of corporation tax

Companies are expected to work out their own tax liability and to pay their tax without prior assessment by the Inland Revenue. You are liable to penalties if you do not make a tax return by the statutory filing date.

File a corporation tax return

The company's completed corporation tax return will be due 12 months from the company's accounting date or three months from the Inland Revenue notice, whichever is later. It must be on an official form or an accepted substitute. Incorrect or fraudulent returns incur interest and penalties.

Three months after the end of the accounting period, the Inland Revenue will send the company a notice to send in a return form, plus the form itself. If your company is liable for corporation tax but does not receive this notice, contact Inland Revenue before the due date to avoid penalties.

Inland Revenue may carry out an enquiry into the tax return; they will let you know when this is to take place. At the end of the enquiry, Inland Revenue will tell you of any necessary adjustments and the company will have 30 days to amend the self assessment.

Understand the payment of corporation tax

Corporation tax must be paid within nine months and one day from the end of the accounting period (the due date). Large firms (those with taxable profits of £1,500,000 or more) must pay their tax quarterly. The Inland Revenue will send a pay-slip and pre-paid envelope three months after the end of the accounting period, and then a further two reminders just before and just after the due date. The company's payment should go to the Inland Revenue Accounts Office. Interest (linked to commercial rates) is payable on under/over payments from the due date.

WHAT TO AVOID
Underpaying corporation tax

If your company has underpaid corporation tax, the additional tax should be paid as soon as it is discovered. If the company has paid too much, it will not be reimbursed until after the company corporation tax return has been filed.

Not filing on time

The Inspector should be informed as soon as figures are finalised, to avoid incurring penalties. If circumstances out of the company's control prevent filing on time, make sure you tell the Inspector in advance; the Inland Revenue may extend the deadline. Late returns incur fixed penalties that increase substantially if this happens repeatedly.

If your figures are not finalised by the time corporation tax is due, and an exact assessment cannot be made, then corporation tax should be estimated and that amount paid by the due date. If it is not paid, the Inland Revenue will collect any outstanding tax (together with any interest which has accrued), once it has received the company's corporation tax return.

RECOMMENDED LINKS
Inland Revenue Business Support Team
     for your area:
www.inlandrevenue.gov.uk/bst/index.htm
Inland Revenue's Corporation Tax Self
     Assessment Orderline:
www.inlandrevenue.gov.uk/ctsa

SEE ALSO
Budgeting (p. 494)
Taxation (p. 549)

Getting to Grips with VAT (Value Added Tax)

GETTING STARTED

If your business turnover is more than £56,000 a year, you will have to register with HM Customs and Excise as a Value Added Tax (VAT) vendor and charge VAT on all goods and services that you provide. The disadvantage to this is that it involves some administrative effort on your part. However, the advantage is that it lets you claim back the VAT that you pay to suppliers.

At the end of each VAT accounting period (usually each month or quarter), you complete a one page form for Customs and Excise known as the VAT return. This must be returned, and the money paid, within a month of the end of the VAT accounting period. This actionlist explains who is liable for VAT, and how to register. The telephone number of the VAT National Advice Service is 0845 010 9000, and the HM Customs and Excise website address is given below.

FAQS

What are the different rates of VAT?

There are currently three rates of VAT. The standard rate of 17.5% covers all those goods and services that are not exempt, zero, or reduced rated. The reduced rate (5%) is charged on domestic fuel and power, as well as other domestic energy-saving products. The renovation and conversion of certain buildings is also subject to the reduced rate. The zero rate (0%) applies to specified categories of goods including children's clothes, exports (outside the European Union), food (excluding fast food, restaurant meals, and catering supplies), books, and newspapers. Exempt goods include insurance, finance, some education and training, lotteries, and transactions involving land or existing buildings.

If your product consists of both zero-rated and standard-rated goods (for example, food in a decorative container), there may be occasions when VAT will be charged at a proportional rate. Customs and Excise have special retail schemes to assist retailers selling a mix of standard and zero-rated products.

Do I need to register for VAT?

You need to register for VAT as soon as your annual turnover exceeds £56,000 a year. You can determine this simply by totalling the past 12 months' sales (taxable supplies). You can also register for VAT if it looks likely that you will exceed the limit of £56,000 in the next month's trading. If your business acquires goods with an annual value in excess of £56,000 from other European Union countries, or supplies goods with an annual value of £70,000 under the United Kingdom's distance selling arrangements, then it must register for VAT.

Registration is straightforward. All you need to do is complete and submit form VAT 1 to Customs and Excise within 30 days from the end of the month when taxable supplies reached £56,000, or within 30 days from the date when it became clear that taxable supplies would exceed the annual limit.

A business cannot register for VAT if it only makes exempt supplies. If the business's taxable supplies are zero-rated, you can apply for exemption from registration. If a business makes taxable and exempt supplies, you may be 'partly exempt'.

MAKING IT HAPPEN

Charge VAT

VAT must be charged from the date your business became liable for registration, not from the actual date of registration. Before you are issued with a VAT number, VAT should not be shown separately on invoices; rather, a tax invoice should be issued as soon as the number is received. Any customers who are VAT registered should be informed that they will be sent a tax invoice within 30 days. Retailers do not have to provide a VAT invoice for every transaction. However, if a taxable person requires it, the retailer must issue a tax invoice.

Keep account of VAT

Once your business is VAT registered, you must ensure that you keep a VAT account. This record will usually be made up of tax invoices. It must be kept up to date, show all supplies made and received, and show a VAT summary for every tax period the tax return covers. Records must be kept for six years.

Businesses collecting more VAT from their sales of goods and services than they pay out in business purchases, make up the bulk of VAT-registered businesses.

VAT accounting schemes

Customs and Excise have different schemes for businesses to choose from, depending on their trading circumstances. The standard accounting scheme is an arrangement whereby your output VAT is levied as soon as you issue a sales invoice, and your input VAT is reclaimable as soon as a purchase invoice is received. The cash accounting scheme applies to businesses with a taxable turnover of less than £600,000. Instead of accounting for VAT using issued and received tax invoices, you account for receipts and payments as they are made.

After a year's registration for VAT, businesses with a turnover of less than £600,000 can join the annual accounting scheme, in which you only make one annual VAT return. Businesses with a taxable turnover of less than £150,000 can join this scheme as soon as they register for VAT. If your business has a taxable turnover of less than £150,000 you may be able to join the flat-rate scheme. Under this scheme, businesses calculate their VAT payment by using a fixed percentage of their VAT-inclusive turnover. Different percentages have been assigned to different trade sectors. You still have to issue tax invoices, but you will not need to keep full records of invoices issued and received.

WHAT TO AVOID
Not sending back your return on time

If a business has not made its return or sent the full payment due on time, it is regarded as being in default. Customs and Excise will inform the business that if it defaults again within a 12-month 'surcharge period', a penalty will be applied.

Not sending back your return at all

If Customs and Excise do not receive a return from you, they will send a computer-generated assessment that demands payment of tax. Customs and Excise is now taking a harder line in relation to businesses that do not submit returns or pay on assessment. In some circumstances Customs and Excise will treat underpayments as either civil or criminal fraud, with much heavier penalties including, for the latter, a possible term of imprisonment.

It may be that you have a genuine problem completing your VAT return, for example because of an IT systems failure. If this is the case, Customs and Excise can be approached to approve an estimate of the tax. This must be done as soon as the problem is discovered and before the due date for the return. If your business takes this action, it may be able to avoid incurring a default that might otherwise apply if the return or payment were delayed.

RECOMMENDED LINK
HM Customs and Excise:
www.hmce.gov.uk

SEE ALSO
Budgeting (p. 494)
Taxation (p. 549)

Getting to Grips with Benefits in Kind

GETTING STARTED

The taxation of benefits can affect anyone paid under Pay As You Earn (PAYE). Employers can also be subject to taxation on the 'perks' they provide. You can be affected whether you are a sole trader, paid by a limited company, or in a partnership. It is important to be aware that providing employees or directors with the use of anything free of charge could be affected by tax legislation. This actionlist aims to raise your awareness of what constitutes a benefit in kind, and suggests alternative ways of rewarding your employees.

The Government's own website provides very useful information, and the address is given below. There are specialist books on the subject produced by the accountancy profession, and up to-date copies of these are essential. A good example, which is updated quarterly, is *Employer's Pay and Benefits Manual*, by W.J.B. Chiltern, published by LexisNexis

FAQS

What is a benefit in kind?

Anything paid for, or given to, an employee to use can be classed as a benefit. If the cost to you is not included in the salary figures subject to PAYE it could be a benefit in kind for tax purposes. You may think that this is confined to the more glamorous items, such as chauffeur-driven luxury cars. It may surprise you to learn that even things that an employee might consider an inconvenience, such as a brightly liveried company van parked at home overnight, are considered by the Inland Revenue to be benefits in kind.

Who has to pay the tax?

Employees have to pay tax and National Insurance on benefits as if they were earnings. As an employer, you are obliged to notify the Inland Revenue of any benefits you provide so that they can be included in the code number. The company also has to pay Employers' National Insurance on the value of the benefits.

Why can't we just sort it out at the end of the financial year?

Some benefits need to be notified to the Inland Revenue quarterly, and financial penalties will be imposed if you fail to inform Inland Revenue of any benefits' details. For this reason alone, management and payroll staff need to be right up to date.

MAKING IT HAPPEN

Identify the benefits you provide

The best way to avoid problems later on is to be absolutely aware of the tax implications of offering remuneration packages that include 'perks' to your employees. It is important that you take early responsibility, by researching the most cost effective way to reward your employees. Benefits in kind can be powerful recruitment and retention tools, but they also bring compliance responsibilities.

Cost the whole benefits package

If you can source the items (for example, vehicles) that your employees need to use more effectively and cheaply than they can, it makes sense to pass that saving on. However, you need to consider carefully if the end use is wholly for business. If it is not, you must decide whether to provide this benefit free of charge, at cost, or at retail price. Providing key staff with company cars has traditionally proved popular, but the related tax cost has increased significantly in recent years. It is worth reviewing the current cost of all benefits, as in some cases the tax cost may exceed the true value to the employee. Make sure that you cost the alternatives, as well. For example, you might consider paying a tax-free mileage allowance to the employee to use their own vehicle on business trips.

Know your benefits

To be a benefit in kind, an item must have been provided by the employer for the employee to have, or to use. You, as the employer, will not have recouped the cost of the item from the employee. Also, the item will not be used for wholly business purposes, and the employee does not refund the cost of private use. If all these criteria do apply, then you have given your employee a benefit in kind which would otherwise be taxed as pay if you gave them the money rather than the goods.

The main classes of benefit in kind often provided include vehicles, for example cars, motorcycles, and vans. They also include fuel for private journeys, including travel between home and work, and parking costs. Expenses for travel, subsistence, and telephone calls are also considered to be a benefit in kind, as are health care and insurance, and incentive schemes. Any discounts, or goods provided for the employee's own use are considered benefits in kind, and so is any entertainment provided by the company, such as office parties.

Be aware of tax-free 'benefits'

There are situations where you provide facilities or refund business expenses incurred out of the employee's own pocket. The Inland Revenue will allow you to claim a dispensation in limited cases, and letting the Inland Revenue know what you intend to pay for, and in what circumstances, should allow you to take advantage of this valuable relaxation of the rules. If it is clear that no benefit accrues to the employee, it is accepted that a dispensation saves everyone considerable paperwork. Some things that can be covered by this include certain travel and overnight subsistence, canteen meals, and workplace parking. Childcare, relocation costs, and re-employment counselling are also included, as are sports and training, pooled vehicles, and mobile phones.

Know the consequences

When you give someone a benefit, you must remember that it is not only a business expense; it is costing the employee tax on the benefit. Careful planning is also essential to prevent exposure to hidden costs in Employers' National Insurance. Getting the compliance paperwork wrong can result in an adverse tax enquiry, or financial penalties.

WHAT TO AVOID ✗
Not realising tax is a factor

When you are planning remuneration packages, make sure everyone is aware of the tax implications. Try not to leave this to the payroll department to sort out later. Employees are not going to be happy to receive surprise tax bills, or an unexpectedly low code number because of the otherwise attractive benefits package you provided. Make sure that you consider the alternatives, such as increasing basic pay or paying a tax-free expense allowance.

Not keeping good records

It is vitally important to be able to support your remuneration strategy with complete paperwork. It is no good trying to convince the Inland Revenue that no private use was made of an asset, if you didn't actually record what happened during the year. The tax year runs to 5 April each year so it may well not tie in with your accounting year end. You need to notify the Inland Revenue and your employees of any benefits by 6 July each year, so records need to be accurate and up to date. It is not only the financial information that is important here. Especially with cars, it is essential to have detailed records of business and private mileage. You also need to know who the vehicles have been made available to and (in the case of pool vehicles) where they were kept overnight. The quality and accuracy of your records will help to avoid fines for poor record keeping. If you find it difficult to calculate the value of benefits provided, you can negotiate a PAYE Settlement Agreement with the Revenue to pay over the agreed tax due.

Thinking the Inland Revenue won't bother to check

The Inland Revenue have dedicated staff which spends its time looking for errors on the part of employers. Its job is to collect the correct amount of tax, and if you get it wrong you will have to pay back the tax and National Insurance, plus interest and penalties. Make sure you carry out a comprehensive review now, in order to save time and money later.

Not keeping up to date

The Chancellor of the Exchequer's annual budget statement usually changes various rates and allowances, as well as revising benefits in kind legislation. This is a good place to start looking out for upcoming changes in the rules so that you can plan ahead to deal with any costs and paperwork.

RECOMMENDED LINK
Inland Revenue:
www.inlandrevenue.gov.uk

SEE ALSO
Budgeting (p. 494)

Getting to Grips with the Tax Credit System

GETTING STARTED

There is a new tax credit system that came into effect on 6 April 2003, designed to ease the tax burden for people on lower incomes. Under the new system, employees and the self-employed can claim, as can people caring for children—and there is also an element of help for employees with disabilities, and employees over 50 years old.

There are two main elements to tax credits: working tax credit (WTC) and child tax credit (CTC). From October 2003 there will also be a state pension credit, which introduces a guaranteed minimum income to anyone aged over 60. This will replace the minimum income guarantee. It will also set a level of savings income that can be taken into account in deciding if pension credits are due.

This actionlist explains what is involved in the credits, who is eligible to claim them, and who is responsible for ensuring that anyone eligible receives the benefits.

FAQS

What exactly in involved in tax credits?

Working tax credit (WTC) can apply to working people on relatively low incomes, where they work an average of at least 16 hours per week. The effect of the WTC is to reduce the amount of tax deducted, or to pay a credit where necessary. If the claimant is employed, the responsibility for paying WTC falls on the employer. Employers need to be aware that they have to pay it, in addition to wages, on behalf of the government. The amounts are funded from the money you would normally send to the Inland Revenue for PAYE deductions.

Child tax credit (CTC) is for children, and is paid directly into the main carer's bank account. This replaces the tax allowance which previously reduced the amount of tax paid by the main earner of a family.

Who can claim?

Individuals or couples can claim. In the case of a couple, a joint claim has to be made. For both types of credit, you must be UK resident or a European Economic Area (EEA) citizen working in the United Kingdom.

WTC—this is paid to the person working more than 16 hours per week. If both people in a couple both work, one person must be nominated to receive the whole amount, and it cannot be divided between them both.

It can, however, be requested that the amount due is paid into a joint account. The main classes of claim are:

- individuals over 16 years of age in low-income households with children
- the working disabled
- workers paid for at least 16 hours
- workers paid for over 30 hours
- people over 50 and returning to work after receiving certain benefits

Approved childcare costs can be an added element of WTC, which is always paid directly to the person with main responsibility for childcare.

CTC—this is paid directly to the person who is mainly responsible for caring for the child or children. Employers are not involved with any payment processes, as the payment goes straight into the claimant's bank account. It is paid to qualifying people on the following basis:

- to the carer responsible for at least one child
- in respect of children until the September following their 16th birthday, or to 19 if continuing in full time education
- you do not need to be in paid employment to receive CTC.

How are the credits made up?

The amount paid to an individual is initially based on income to 5 April 2002. Claimants will be notified of the range by which family income can rise or fall before needing to notify a change in financial circumstances.

WTC is made up of the following elements: basic; lone parent; couples; over 25 and 30 hours work; disability; severe disability; 50 plus (if you have returned to work at age 50 after 6 April 2003); and childcare.

CTC is made up of the following elements: family basic; a child element for each child; disability; severe disability; and extra payment for babies under one year old. If family earnings rise above a relatively high amount, the CTC will be reduced in line with the rise in income.

When do claims need to be made?

The new system came into effect on 6 April 2003. Claim forms were sent out to all known claimants who were already in receipt of the children's tax credit. Claims must be lodged within three months of becoming eligible for the credit, otherwise entitlement will lapse.

Can credits be backdated?

Tax credits can only be backdated for three-month periods, making it essential to put forward claims in good time. Changes in eligibility criteria should be notified to the Inland Revenue as quickly as possible, because the credits can be recovered from the date of a past change in circumstances.

MAKING IT HAPPEN
Remember practical considerations

Employers are required by law to make WTC payments to their eligible employees after receiving an official notice to pay from the Inland Revenue. The WTC payments are funded by diverting the PAYE and National Insurance contributions, together with any student loan deductions that would normally be sent off to the Inland Revenue on behalf of staff.

Careful planning is required to budget for the payments. In practice, it is an additional payment on top of wages, made initially by you (the employer) on behalf of the government, with payroll staff needing to be able to show it separately on the payslip.

There may be very little warning that an amount is due to be added to staff wages each week or month, and if there is little cash leeway, you may find it difficult to fund the extra payments—even though ultimately you will be able to recover them from the Inland Revenue.

Make timely applications to the tax office if you need funding

Small businesses have the opportunity to request funding from the Inland Revenue to cover the payments due, so review your projected cash flow as soon as you receive notification that you'll have to pay the credits to any of your staff. You should apply as soon as possible so that the money goes into your bank before you need to pass it on to the employee.

Keep employees informed

If you receive a notification for payment, let the employee know that you will be making the payments on time. Reassure him or her that it will be dealt with confidentially. The general advice about claiming can be shared with staff, so that everyone is aware of the changes they need to tell the Inland Revenue about, and how to claim.

WHAT TO AVOID
Getting your timing wrong

Employees are told when to expect payments, and that their employer has been authorised to make payment with their wages. A small business, with low deductions to make each week or month, may have chosen to pay the PAYE amounts over quarterly. A previous cash-flow advantage from this can disappear because employees have to receive their WTC with weekly or monthly pay. Remember to keep all your bank details up to date so that you receive the amounts into the right accounts.

Getting involved in disputes about eligibility

Like all means-tested benefits, the application and verification process can be time consuming and difficult for claimants to sort out. Your staff need to be aware of the system and that you are obliged to pay whatever the tax office authorises you to. The information backing up a claim is confidential between the Inland Revenue and taxpayers; you should not be expected to get involved with sorting out claimant's eligibility.

RECOMMENDED LINK
Inland Revenue:
www.inlandrevenue.gov.uk

SEE ALSO
Budgeting (p. 494)

Repaying Employees' Student Loans

GETTING STARTED

The Student Loan Scheme (SLS) was set up by the UK government to allow students to borrow money to help them meet their costs and expenses while studying in higher education. The SLS is administered by the Student Loans Company (SLC), but repayments are the responsibility of the Inland Revenue and collected through the Pay As You Earn (PAYE) or self-assessment tax systems. All companies employing new or recent graduates will have to manage the repayment of their employees' student loans by making deductions from their salary and paying the deductions to the Inland Revenue through the PAYE system. This actionlist is a guide to your duties and responsibilities as an employer.

FAQS

As an employer, when do I start making student loan repayments?

An employer should only start to make deductions from an employee's salary when formally advised to do so by the Inland Revenue or through the employee's P45.

Student Loan Repayments (SLRs) usually start in the April following completion of studies. The Inland Revenue will send you a Start Notice, form SL1, which will identify the employee and instruct you to start making deductions. The notice will give a start date, which is usually at least six weeks from the date of issue. You should only start to make deductions on the first payday after that start date.

If an employee starts work with you having had a previous job, then he or she should have a P45 from their previous employer. The P45 has a box that is marked 'Y' if student loan deductions (SLDs) should continue to be made. If this box is completed then you should set up your payroll system for deductions to be made for the employee from the next payday. If the employee does not have a P45 then you should complete a P46, which is a form you use to tell the Inland Revenue about the employee in this situation. You then need to do nothing more until the Inland Revenue issues a Start Notice to you.

How do I calculate how much to deduct?

How much employees repay on loans is directly related to their income. If the employee began his or her higher education course on or after 1 September 1998, repayments are set to start once the student is earning £833 per month (£192 per week), which equates to £10,000 per annum. Once the employee is earning above this level he or she pays 9% on any earnings above the threshold. The Inland Revenue provides student loan deduction tables for employers using manual payroll systems, to help calculate the amounts to deduct at different income levels. Most computerised payroll systems will automatically run the repayment calculations.

Who do I contact if I have a query?

If your employee has any queries over the process for repaying their student loan or the deductions that you are making then they should contact the SLC directly.

If you, as the employer, have any queries about the process of student loan deductions then you should contact the Inland Revenue helpline. You should not contact the SLC, as they will not give information to a third party.

When do I stop making deductions?

If an employee's salary falls below the threshold level then payments will automatically be temporarily suspended. The only other time that you will stop making deductions is when the Inland Revenue advises you to do so. This will usually be through the issuing of a Stop Notice, form SL2. This notice will tell you when to stop making the deductions and normally gives you at least six weeks to do so.

You cannot stop making deductions because your employee requests you to do so.

MAKING IT HAPPEN
Set up your payroll system
The repayment of student loans through the PAYE system means that the process can be tied in with the regular payroll system. Most businesses now use computerised payroll systems that greatly simplify the process, and make the administration of these additional requirements fairly straightforward. If you do not run a computerised system, it may be worth looking at using the services of a payroll bureau.

Check that you are meeting your responsibilities
Employers have the following responsibilities regarding student loan repayments:
- making student loan deductions when asked to do so by the Inland Revenue
- providing employees with a wage slip which records the amount of deductions
- keeping records of the deductions made for each employee
- paying the deductions to the Inland Revenue
- providing the Inland Revenue with details of the SLRs that have been deducted
- when an employee leaves, identifying on his or her P45 that the individual is liable to make SLRs

Payments of the deductions should be sent to the Inland Revenue accounts centre with your income tax and National Insurance contributions. This payment should be made by the 19th of the month following the month of pay, and the SLR should be included with your income tax figures.

Ensure you complete the right tax forms
SLRs must be recorded on several key Inland Revenue end of year tax forms:
- P35 summary of tax
- P14 end of year summary
- P60 certificate of pay

The Inland Revenue processes the end of year tax forms and passes details of the specific deductions made from each employee to the SLC, so that the correct repayment amounts can be applied to outstanding loans.

WHAT TO AVOID
Miscalculating earnings
SLRs are non-cumulative, and so you should not take into account earnings from an earlier pay period when calculating the deduction in the current pay period. If you find that you have deducted too much then you should repay to your employee the amount wrongly deducted and make a similar adjustment to your next PAYE payment.

Thinking employers alone are responsible for repayments
It is not the employer's responsibility to identify which of their employees are liable to make SLRs, and when to stop making these payments. It is up to the Inland Revenue to keep you informed.

RECOMMENDED LINKS
Inland Revenue:
www.inlandrevenue.gov.uk
Student Loans Company:
www.slc.co.uk

SEE ALSO
Budgeting (p. 494)

Managing Creditors and Debtors

GETTING STARTED

All businesses have trading relationships with both suppliers and customers. At any point in time, those suppliers who are extending credit to your business by letting you pay for goods or services after you have received them, are known as your creditors. Customers who owe you money for goods or services that you have supplied are known as your debtors.

The balance between when you need to pay your creditors and when you receive payment from your debtors has a major effect on the cash flow of your business. Getting the balance right is important in determining what cash will be available to your business in the short term, and for identifying the cash needs (often referred to as 'working capital') of your business as it grows.

FAQS

Why do I need to manage creditors and debtors?

Knowing how much you owe, how much you are owed, and when payments are due to be made or received, allows you to forecast your cash flow over several months and ensures that you will have enough money in the bank for other regular business payments, such as salaries and rent. This can be particularly important for businesses that are seasonal, or that have a high spend with their suppliers several months before their customers pay them.

How does this affect the working capital required by a business?

When the value of your creditors equals the value of your debtors, there is no effect on the working capital needs of your business, assuming payment terms are the same. However if the value of your debtors increases relative to the value of your creditors, then the working capital used by your business rises. This is a typical situation faced by businesses as they grow. If you are able to increase the value of your creditors while maintaining the value of your debtors then you can reduce the working capital needed by your business.

What are standard payment terms?

There are no firm rules for credit terms, but there are accepted practices that are widely adopted. Normally the credit period is either based on the date of the invoice, or on the month of the invoice. The most standard credit term based on the date of invoice is 30 days—that is, the invoice is due for payment 30 days after the date on the invoice. If you are providing several invoices to a customer in any one month, it is normal to use 'net monthly terms'. This means that all invoices for a particular month are grouped and paid together at the end of the following month. Using net monthly terms greatly simplifies the process for both supplier and customer, reducing the payment process to only once a month, irrespective of the number of invoices issued.

What is debtor finance?

For many businesses the amount owed by their debtors is the largest single element of their balance sheet. If your business is trading in a business-to-business environment, there is the potential to use the services of a third-party finance company who will make money available to you, based on the security of your debtor balances. This service is called 'factoring' and can range from the provision of just finance against your debtor list to a full sales ledger and credit-control service. The initial advance payment is usually up to 80% of the value of the invoice, with the remaining balance being due either at an agreed maturity date, or when your customer pays the factor. This type of service is especially useful for fast-growing businesses who can suffer from a shortage of working capital.

What is creditor finance?

This is the term used for 'borrowing' money from your creditors to fund your working capital. It is typically used by retail businesses, where you sell your products or services for cash, and yet obtain credit from your suppliers.

Are trade suppliers my only short-term creditors?

Although trade suppliers are usually viewed as being the creditors of your business, you should actually include all of the organisations that you owe money to in the short term. This means that the term 'creditors' is more formally split between trade creditors—which will include your trade suppliers to your business—and other creditors, which will include organisations such as the Inland Revenue, if you are an employer and Customs and Excise if you are VAT registered.

MAKING IT HAPPEN

Managing your creditors and debtors is vitally important to the smooth and effective operation of your business. Doing this effectively will save you money, and may even make the difference between your business surviving or failing.

Manage the relationship with your creditors

Suppliers are vital to the operation of your business and the role that they play is often undervalued. For many suppliers, how you manage the payment of their account is a key to a successful long-term relationship. The main issues for a good working relationship with your suppliers are for you to be:

- professional in your handling of their account, by conforming to the agreed credit terms, and not wasting their time through poor administration
- honest with them if you have cash-flow problems and are unable to meet their normal payment terms
- straightforward in your commercial negotiations—look to negotiate better terms from your suppliers, but base this on the

volume of business and how this has grown over a period of time, and the fact that you manage your account well

Use a credit card to obtain credit

In situations where it is difficult to obtain credit from your suppliers, then you should consider using a credit card to make payment for goods. This has the effect of giving the supplier immediate payment, but also giving you 30–50 days credit. However, there can be an additional charge added to the invoice of 1–3%, and it is essential that you pay it off promptly or you will incur further cost.

Manage the relationship with your debtors

If providing credit to your customers is important to your business, then it is vital to set up effective credit-control procedures.

Get your customers to complete an account application form, giving details about their business and its legal structure, and details of references. Supply them with a copy of your standard terms and conditions of sale, and make sure they are aware of (and acknowledge) your payment terms, and what their credit limit is. Keep records of quotations and delivery notes to ensure that disputes can be quickly resolved by you providing the missing information, if needed, and ensure that you have efficient accounts administration systems that allow you to send invoices promptly, and follow up with regular statements and reminders.

Monitor your customers' payments. If you are unhappy with them then speak to the person who places the order as well as the finance department. If they still do not pay, be prepared to halt supplies and to take further action to collect the debt if necessary. You may even decide to withdraw credit facilities if a customer is a persistently poor payer.

You should produce a regular debtors list, preferably in balance order, so that you can easily review how much each business owes to you, and how old their debt is. You need to concentrate your efforts on those customers that have the oldest and largest debts to ensure that your time is used most cost effectively.

 WHAT TO AVOID

Taking a narrow focus

Do not focus all of your efforts on getting better payment terms from your creditors at the expense of not managing your debtors more effectively. If your business regularly struggles to pay its creditors because of slow payment from your debtors, this will be an indication that your business does not have sufficient working capital. You will then need to decide if you can manage your debtors better, and reduce the average credit period given, or whether you will need to get additional finance into the business to increase your available working capital.

RECOMMENDED LINKS

Better Payment Practice Campaign:
www.payontime.co.uk
Factors and Discounters Association:
www.factors.org.uk

SEE ALSO

Addressing Cash-flow Problems (p. 145)
Budgeting (p. 494)
Issuing Invoices and Collecting Debts (p. 148)

Addressing Cash-flow Problems

GETTING STARTED

Running out of cash is probably the biggest cause of small businesses failing. There are many reasons behind a cash crisis, so it is crucial that you understand them and know how to prevent a short-term problem leading to business failure. No matter how good your balance sheet may look in terms of physical assets and outstanding debtors, your ability to convert these to actual cash at critical times can make the difference between survival and failure. This actionlist looks at some of the main causes of cash-flow problems, and suggests some ways of overcoming such problems.

For more information on cash-flow issues, you might like to read *Positive Cash Flow: Powerful Tools and Techniques to Collect Your Receivables, Manage Your Payables and Fuel Your Growth*, written by Robert A. Cooke, and published by the Career Press in June 2003. 'Small Business—Information and Cash Flow' is a website offering resources and links for small businesses on credit management, cash flow, debt collection, and related topics. The website address is given below.

FAQS

How does the behaviour of my customers affect my cash flow?

Slow payment by your customers is a main cause of cash-flow problems. Remember that a sale is only completed when your invoice has been paid in full. Many businesses concentrate on generating new sales, but fail to set up credit-control procedures until they actually experience cash-flow problems. These procedures should be in place from the start.

If a key customer becomes insolvent this can also cause cash-flow problems. If your business is very dependent on a few major customers, you are always exposed to the risk of one of them having their own financial problems, which could result in you not getting paid. This could be disastrous if the income from that client makes up a big chunk of your overall revenue and you are relying on that money to pay your creditors or employees.

How does poor planning affect cash flow?

Poor financial planning can cause huge problems. Your business must plan for certain payments, such as Value Added Tax, Pay As You Earn tax, and personal or business tax bills. You need to build these payments into your cash-flow forecasts and

then ensure that sufficient funds will be available at those key times. Also make sure that any purchase of equipment is scheduled for payment when your cash position is stronger, or is structured over a longer period to reduce its impact on your cash flow.

If your business plan focuses on turnover, and neglects profit, this can also lead to a cash-flow crisis. A business is only able to generate a positive cash flow by generating profits from its trading activities. If you prioritise the turnover of your business, then you may improve sales but this might lead to spending more than you earn (a problem known as negative cash flow). This can be a particular problem if the business has to invest in new equipment and staff as it grows, as these costs are often incurred well in advance of you receiving your additional sales revenue.

Another common reason for cash-flow problems is inappropriate planning for stock purchases. It is very tempting to over-commit, especially as many suppliers will offer you discount incentives to purchase larger quantities of their goods; on the face of it, this could look very attractive because it holds the promise of making you a larger profit. However, you need to think carefully before committing to large orders of stock, particularly while you are establishing your business. If you order bulk purchases and then the items quickly go out of fashion or have a short shelf life, you can be left with stock that you cannot sell but that you still have to pay for.

How does the rate of growth of my business affect cash flow?

Another common reason for problems with cash flow is insufficient working capital. This means that there is not enough money initially invested in the business to allow it to operate effectively on a day-to-day basis. It can also be a problem when a business grows rapidly and needs to produce more than normal without having the income to fund that growth; this is called over-trading.

MAKING IT HAPPEN
Plan effectively

Preparing a cash-flow forecast and then putting it to good use is the basis for avoiding many cash-flow problems. The forecast allows you to anticipate most cash-flow problems that could occur during the normal course of running your business. It also allows you to do a sensitivity analysis, in which you can test the effect of lower sales or slower payment on your cash flow.

Develop good relationships with suppliers and customers

You must adopt tight credit-control procedures. Set up procedures for managing the whole process of giving your customers credit. Start with only giving credit to approved customers, check when their accounts are due for payment, and ensure that they pay according to your agreed terms. Also make sure that you have efficient administration procedures for raising your invoices promptly and sending statements to your customers. In this way, you will not add to payment delays.

Offering incentives for early payment is another good way to encourage your customers to pay more quickly. You could do this by offering a discount if they either pay on delivery, or within a certain number of days (typically between 7 and 14 days) from the invoice date. Typical levels of discount

are between 2% and 5%, but the exact level will depend on your profit margins and on how important early payment is to you.

As your business grows, you can look to negotiate better credit terms with your suppliers. Initially, this may be achieved by progressing from paying at the time of purchase, to having a 30-day credit account. If the majority of your customers expect to have 60-day credit accounts, then you should aim to agree 60-day payment terms with your suppliers.

Get help

Debtor finance is an option for businesses that are growing rapidly. In this case, it is possible to use the services of an invoice discounter or factoring company. These companies enter into an arrangement where they will provide your business with an advance (usually 80%) on the value of your invoices, as soon as these invoices are raised. Interest is then charged on the balance drawn, and there is a service charge. Factoring companies can also take control of collecting payments from your customer directly, which can save you the costs of using your own staff to manage this process.

An agreed overdraft facility with your bank allows you to borrow money as and when required, up to an agreed limit. It is a relatively cheap way to finance working capital if you have large variations in cash flow during the course of a month (or if your business is very seasonal), because you only pay interest on the amount actually borrowed. However, if you are continually relying on your overdraft, it can be expensive; more importantly, it may also highlight that your business needs additional working capital, or a longer-term form of finance. With an overdraft, you are also exposed to 'repayment on demand', which means that your lender can ask for full repayment at any time; a 'term loan' with fixed monthly instalments is safer from your point of view, as the lender can usually only demand full repayment if you default on your instalments.

If your business needs to invest in new equipment, but does not have the cash, then you can look to fund this with asset financing, in the form of a term loan, a hire purchase loan, or a leasing deal. This avoids the large cash outflow on the full price of the equipment, and gives you a fixed level of repayment over a set period (usually between two and five years). In situations where the asset is being used as security for the finance, it is likely that you will still need to provide at least a 10% deposit.

WHAT TO AVOID

Not thinking ahead

Don't be taken by surprise. Keep a close eye on your bank balance and your debtors' book and look ahead a few weeks at what expenditure you will have to make. Cash-flow problems are best caught early, and the more time you can give yourself to respond, the better.

Procrastinating

Don't be fooled into thinking that cash-flow problems will resolve themselves; they won't go away! Talk to your bank and your suppliers as soon as you think there might be a problem. This way, you assure them that you are at least doing your homework, even if there are difficult times ahead. If you don't act, you run the risk of affecting your relationship with your bank, suppliers, and customers. Your bank will be far more receptive to dealing with your cash-flow problems if you approach it before the problem occurs.

RECOMMENDED LINKS

Institute of Credit Management:
www.icm.org.uk
Small Business—Information and Cash Flow:
www.credit-to-cash.com

SEE ALSO

Budgeting (p. 494)
Financing a New Business (p. 104)
Managing Creditors and Debtors (p. 142)

Issuing Invoices and Collecting Debts

GETTING STARTED

When your business supplies goods or services to its customers, you need to record these transactions formally with a document called an invoice. This document becomes particularly important when you let your customers defer payment for the transaction, by offering them credit. From the date that the invoice is issued, until it is paid, the value of the invoice is regarded as a debt to the business. This actionlist explains the invoicing procedure and offers advice on how to deal with customers who won't pay up on time.

FAQS

Why do you need to issue invoices?

An invoice is a formal record of trading between two parties. It confirms details of the goods or services supplied, and the prices charged. It is used as the basis for all financial management and accounting processes in a business, and is a key document in business tax records. An invoice that is issued by your business to confirm a sale is then a crucial document for customer, as it acts as proof of purchase.

Are there different types of invoices?

Yes. There are three types of invoice documents that can be issued.

1. Pro-forma invoice—this is issued by a business when it does not have credit facilities set up with its customer, and acts as a request for payment for goods prior to despatch. This ensures that payment is received, and is often used when two businesses have not traded before.

2. Standard invoice—a standard document issued to confirm a trading transaction. It is normally classed as a sales invoice by the business that has sold the goods, and as a purchase invoice by the buyer. When an invoice is issued by a VAT-registered business, it is known as a VAT invoice. This must provide specific information about the rate and amount of VAT charged.

3. Credit note—this is issued to cancel an original invoice or part of an invoice when goods are returned or a pricing error has been made. If the original invoice has been settled prior to the credit note being issued, then the buyer will be entitled to alternative goods up to the value of the credit note.

What details should be included on an invoice?

All invoices need to convey certain key pieces of information as supporting evidence for tax and VAT purposes, and to avoid queries from customers which may lead to delays in payment. These are:

- a unique identifying number
- your business name, address, its legal status, and VAT number (if relevant)
- a date of issue, which becomes the tax point
- your customer's name (or trading name) and address
- a description of the quantity and type of goods or services supplied, along with the price charged, and, where appropriate, the VAT charged
- the payment terms for the invoice

Must an invoice always be issued?

You do not always need to issue an invoice to your customer, but you will need to keep a record of the transaction. Many retail businesses issue till receipts to their customers rather than fully-detailed invoices. This is acceptable for small one-off transactions that are paid for at the time of purchase. Most business-to-business transactions require an invoice to be issued, and this is especially important if you and your customer are VAT registered.

Is there anything that can be done if the customer will not pay the invoice?

You need to establish as soon as possible why your customer will not pay the invoice. If it is a simple issue, such as a genuine pricing or quantity error, then it should be simple to resolve. However, if the reason given is not acceptable and a compromise cannot be reached, you will need to take action to recover the money owed. This can be done in several ways:

- using the County Courts and the small-claims procedure for debts of less than £5,000
- instructing a solicitor to pursue the debt for you. This may just involve him or her sending a letter on your behalf, or managing the whole process of pursuing your claim through the court process
- engaging the services of a debt collection agency, who will either manage the process for a fixed fee, or work on a commission of the debt that is collected

You need to balance the time that it will take for you to pursue your customer for payment against the costs involved with using the services of a solicitor or debt collection agency.

MAKING IT HAPPEN

If your business only issues a small number of invoices then you can use a computer and word-processing package, or even manually write out the invoices. You will need to produce two copies, one for your customer and one for your own records. This simple approach can work well, but once you start to offer credit or have the complication of being VAT registered, it makes more sense to use an integrated accounts system that manages both invoicing and credit control.

Set up procedures for credit control

If you offer credit to your customers, then the issuing of a sales invoice is just part of the sales process, and the transaction is not completed until the invoice has been fully settled. Many businesses are very successful at selling their goods or services and yet still fail because they are unable to collect the money owed to them. Therefore, it is vital to set up processes that minimise the risk of your customers failing to pay you.

Make sure that credit is only offered to credit-worthy customers, and that you agree payment terms with them in advance. Check the accuracy of invoices before you send them out, and provide customers with monthly statements showing their account balance. When credit terms are exceeded, send reminder letters and follow up with telephone calls, and be prepared to put a customer's account on hold if there is no good reason for non-payment. Finally, don't be afraid to charge interest under the Late Payment of Commercial Debts (Interest) Act 1998.

Investigate reasons for non-payment

Even when you adopt these procedures there are going to be situations that lead to an invoice not being paid on time. You will then have to decide on the best approach to recover your debt, and a lot will depend on the approach of your customer, their size and importance to your business, and the size of the debt. There are several reasons for non-payment.

Habitual slow payer—Sometimes new customers are won suddenly, and it is only after you've supplied them for a while that you find out why: their previous supplier had closed their account because of continuing problems with late payment. These types of customers will go through long delaying tactics as a matter of course, and can waste a huge amount of your (or your finance department's) time in chasing them. Undertaking credit checks can help to minimise this risk, but often it is only by adopting very tight credit control and setting low credit limits initially that you can limit the problem. If the problems continue you may then have to decide between charging higher prices to reflect your extra costs, or refusing to give your customer credit.

Disputed invoices—Misunderstandings about the terms of a transaction are quite common, and the easiest way to avoid them is to make sure that each stage of the sales process has been documented. If this information is not complete, you may have to face negotiating a compromise with your customer, which should mean that you get paid for at least part of the invoice. If there is no room for compromise and you believe that your case is strong, then you should look at formal recovery of your debt as the best way forward—although the process can be time consuming and expensive. If the dispute does end up in court, you will need to be able to demonstrate that you have explored all avenues to resolve it, so you should document the process carefully.

Financial difficulty—This is probably the most common reason for non-payment of an invoice, and is often masked by your customer behind lots of other reasons. You need to identify whether this is a short term cash-flow glitch or a major financial problem that is likely to result in your customer becoming insolvent. In situations where a customer faces a short-term difficulty, it may be possible to agree to payments by instalment over a specific period. If you do agree to this approach, make sure you confirm it in writing and then monitor the situation carefully to ensure that your customer maintains these special payments.

If a customer's business faces long-term or extreme cash-flow problems it is likely to be unable to pay your debt. Knowing the legal status of your customer's business is important under these circumstances, because this will determine how you can pursue the recovery of your debt. Often the best that you can hope for is that you can claim title to the goods that you have supplied, which may still have some value to you. For this reason, you should ensure that a retention-of-title clause is used in all of your terms of sale and all invoices which involve the sale of goods.

WHAT TO AVOID
Delaying sending out invoices

Issue invoices promptly after a sale. Taking too much time will lead to delays in you getting paid because payment terms will be based on the invoice date and not the date that you supplied the goods or services.

Being overly sympathetic to customers' financial problems

If there's no valid reason for non-payment, don't delay the process of debt collection because you're worried about upsetting your customer. This may just lead to your business being owed more, and possibly not getting paid at all if the customer's business ceases trading.

RECOMMENDED LINKS

Court process and forms (tel:
020 7210 2266):
www.courtservice.gov.uk
Credit Services Association (information about Debt Recovery Agencies):
www.csa-uk.com
Users guide to the Late Payment Act 1998:
www.payontime.co.uk

SEE ALSO
Budgeting (p. 494)
Managing Creditors and Debtors (p. 142)

Understanding the Role of Price

GETTING STARTED

The price that you charge for your product or service needs to reflect your costs on the one hand and the strength of the market on the other. Setting a price too high can result in lost sales, while undercharging can eat into your profits and possibly lead to you being unable to deliver on your contracts. This actionlist contains advice on how to go about calculating prices, in a way that will suit both your business and the market. One book on the subject that you might also find useful is *Power Pricing: How Managing Price Transforms the Bottom Line* by Robert J. Dolan and Hermann Simon, published in 1996 by Simon & Schuster.

FAQS

What is the difference between price and cost?

The *cost* of producing your product or service is the total costs for the business, both direct and fixed, divided by the number of products that you sell. The *price* that you charge depends on what the market will stand, that is, on what the customer will pay. The difference between price and cost is profit—or loss!

How do I work out how much I can charge?

You need to research the market carefully in order to determine the price that you can charge. This is most difficult when you are starting up, since you have little information on which to base your pricing decisions, other than reviewing the prices charged by your competitors and your own market research with potential customers. Once you are in business it becomes easier, since you can adjust your prices and review the effects they have on demand.

Will charging less than my competitors win customers?

Many people have difficulty calculating the cost of their products or services and, as a result, let their competitors effectively set the price, thinking that as long as they undercut that price, then they will succeed. However, cost leadership is a strategy that often fails for small businesses since they lack the economies of scale necessary to make the price really competitive, and end up losing money as a result.

What is gross profit?

The gross profit is the selling price less the direct costs involved in making the product or delivering the service. Direct costs (sometimes known as variable costs, because they vary with the output) include such items as raw materials, bought in components, and sub-contracting. Fixed costs (sometimes known as overheads—items such as rent, utilities, depreciation, and insurance) are then deducted from the gross profit, resulting in the net profit. So you need to sell enough at your chosen price to cover all the direct and fixed costs, and make a profit as well.

What is the breakeven point?

The breakeven point is the point where the income from sales exactly equals all the costs incurred by the business. More sales will result in a profit; fewer sales will result in a loss.

Can I change the price once it is set?

The price can always be changed, but there is often customer resistance to the raising of price if the rise is too great, or if you change it too frequently.

MAKING IT HAPPEN

Remember the two-step process

There are two steps in setting price: the first step is to determine the costs of delivering a product or service; the second step is to set a price that is high enough to cover the costs, but low enough to be competitive.

Research the market

You need to start with an idea of what you may be able to sell and the price at which you might be able to sell it. This information comes from your market research. It is necessary to have a sensible estimate of likely sales volumes, otherwise you will not be able to calculate the direct costs. This is less important if you are selling a service where there are very low, if any, direct costs. But it is very important if you are in manufacturing, particularly if the direct costs (like raw materials) are of a high value. Prepare an income and expenditure forecast using different prices. Estimate what effect a price increase will have on your sales. Consider the prices offered by your competitors. If your prices are much higher, are you offering sufficient extra benefit to entice customers to buy from you?

Calculate the costs

There are a number of different ways of allocating costs to products and services, but the key requirement is to know all the costs—direct and fixed—for an expected level of sales. Don't forget to include depreciation and your deductions if you are self-employed. Once you have the cost, then you have the bare minimum price for a given level of sales.

Provided the costs are less than the price that you set when you did your market research, you will make a profit—assuming, of course, that you also sell the volumes that you predicted.

Carry out a breakeven analysis

Once you know your costs and estimated selling price, you are in a position to calculate how many products, or hours of your time, you need to sell to break even (that is, to cover all your costs).

One way to calculate the breakeven point is to draw a graph that shows sales volume on the horizontal axis and money on the vertical axis. First show the overhead costs. This will be a horizontal line since these costs are, generally, fixed for all volumes of production.

The direct costs can then be added to the overhead costs to give total costs for a given volume of output. A line representing total costs can be plotted. The sales income can then be plotted to show how much income will be generated for a given volume of sales. Remember that sales income starts at zero for zero sales.

The point where the sales income equals the total cost shows the breakeven point. A higher price will achieve breakeven with fewer sales. A lower price may attract more customers, but will require higher sales to break even. The further above breakeven that a business can operate, the greater its margin of safety.

Set targets

Once you have determined your price and defined the breakeven volume that you need to sell, set an annual target, broken down into monthly targets, designed to generate you a reasonable profit.

It can often be helpful to plot the targets for sales and actual sales on a graph to monitor progress regularly. If the business does not achieve its targets you will need to take remedial action.

Review

Review your sales volumes and income regularly. Ensure that you are making a profit; if you are not, you will need to take corrective action, perhaps involving changing the price.

WHAT TO AVOID
Setting the price too low

The greatest danger when setting a price for the first time is to pitch it too low. Raising a price is always more difficult than lowering one, yet there are great temptations to undercut the competition. It is clearly important to compare your prices to your competitors', but it is essential that your price covers all your costs and contributes towards your profit.

Failing to cost accurately

Many businesses run into difficulties, and some fail, because they do not cost their work accurately. They fail to check the actual costs of a job against the estimated costs. While they cannot turn back history and re-price, they can at least amend their prices for future sales. Not doing this is likely to result in failing to achieve targets for profit and profitability.

Under-utilising assets

Many businesses buy expensive equipment and fail to include all the depreciation when they are costing. If you are buying expensive equipment, you need to think carefully about how you will recover the cost.

RECOMMENDED LINK

Bizpeponline (offers business software and tools that help with pricing, budgeting, forecasting, and other business issues):
www.bizpeponline.com

SEE ALSO
Budgeting (p. 494)
Determining Price Positioning and Flexibility (p. 154)
Pricing (p. 537)

Determining Price Positioning and Flexibility

GETTING STARTED

Setting the price of a product or service is often regarded as a financial issue, but in reality it's also a marketing issue. Of course, the price has to cover all the costs and generate a profit, otherwise the business will not survive, but equally, you won't necessarily want to charge the most that you can manage, because you want customers to think that you offer good value for money, and you want repeat business. This actionlist looks at some of the main issues for you to consider when setting your prices.

FAQS

How do I set the price?

Setting a price is a two-part exercise. First, you need to calculate all of your costs, and then divide this figure by the number of products, or days of service, that you expect to sell. This gives a minimum price, at which your business can break even but not make a profit. Second, you need to research the market to determine the maximum price that could be achievable for your product or service. You can then set your actual price somewhere between the two.

If my price is lower than my competitors', will I sell more?

Many businesses believe that if they set their price lower than their competitors, then they will win greater market share. This is known as 'cost leadership'. Small businesses, however, are usually too small to achieve the economies of scale necessary to enable them to fix a really competitive price. If you are in this position, you need to 'differentiate' your product or service in order to secure a competitive edge. This could be done on the basis of better quality, better service, or quicker delivery for example. You may find that quicker delivery is an extra benefit for which your customers might be willing to pay.

What happens if I increase my prices?

Fixing a price is a juggling act between strategy, pricing, and cash flow. If your price is too low, the income may not cover all your costs. If the price is too high, even with a

well-differentiated product, you may have difficulty attracting enough customers. However, maximising profit does not necessarily mean selling high volumes at low profit. It may be possible to sell low volumes at high profit. The challenge that you face is to find the right balance.

In general, changing the price will cause a change in demand. Small businesses often find that they can put up the price without losing too many customers, thus increasing profitability. But you also need to understand the potential effect that a price change will have on your customers. It's a good idea to warn them that prices are going to rise, and to explain why. A good relationship with your customers can improve their perception of the value you are offering.

How much flexibility do I have?

The amount of flexibility that you have largely depends on the way that your product or service is perceived in the marketplace. A cost leadership strategy gives you almost no flexibility, because you have to respond to the price set by your competitors. A differentiated strategy is based on demonstrating how your product or service is quite different to your competitors; the particular benefits of what you offer give you more flexibility in setting your price.

MAKING IT HAPPEN
The marketing mix

The marketing mix, often referred to as the four Ps (product, position, price, and promotion), covers the different aspects of marketing. It's the marketing mix that conveys your message to your customers.

Your price needs to reflect the position that you want to adopt in the market place. If you adopt a position of quality, you will want (and will probably need) to charge a premium price. If your product or service is regarded as mass-produced, and therefore of lower quality, then the price should be at the bottom end of the spectrum.

Pricing strategies

There are a number of possible pricing strategies that you could adopt:

- **Cost-based pricing** is when total costs are calculated and a mark-up is added to give the required profit. The mark-up is usually expressed as a percentage of the cost. Different types of businesses will apply varying mark-ups, for example, the mark-up on jewellery is enormous compared to the mark-up on food products.
- **'Skimming'** is where you initially charge a relatively high price to recover investment costs quickly if the product is new. As your competitors follow your lead and launch their own products to compete and enter the market, you lower the price.
- **Negotiating prices individually** with customers, based on the quantities they are prepared to buy. If you wish to sell to a particular market, then you might sell one product or service more cheaply (as a **loss leader**) to gain market entry. You balance this by selling other products or services at a higher price. This can be risky, as the danger is that everything becomes a loss leader.
- **Expected price** involves finding out what the customer expects to pay. If you are selling a high-quality product, do not underprice. Often the customer expects to pay more (for instance, if the product or service has a certain 'snob' value), and you could diminish the premium value of your product or service if you under-price, making it less attractive to the customer.
- **Differential pricing** is where you charge different segments of your market different prices for the same service; for example, you may decide to offer discounts to certain people, such as pensioners or the unemployed, or charge lower rates for quiet periods.
- **Lifetime pricing** is a technique you can adopt if your product price is higher than your competitors' and you want to encourage customers to look at the cost of ownership over the *lifetime* of the product. This might work well if, for example, your product is likely to last longer, thus reducing depreciation. Also, the cost of maintenance may be lower, consequently reducing the annual cost.

WHAT TO AVOID

Relying on cost leadership

Do not simply aim to undercut your competitors; cost leadership is a difficult strategy for small businesses to pursue. Instead, aim to differentiate your product or service.

Not selling enough

Ensure that you are selling enough products at your chosen price to cover all of your costs and to generate a profit. Keep a careful eye on your sales and if you are not selling enough at your chosen price, then you need to take remedial action.

Treating price as a simple calculation

It's best to regard price as part of the marketing mix, rather than a straight financial calculation. You need to consider all the parts of the equation carefully. Make sure that you research the market thoroughly, and that you are familiar with your competitors' pricing strategies and your customers' needs.

RECOMMENDED LINKS

Professional Pricing Society:
www.pricingsociety.com

SEE ALSO
Budgeting (p. 494)
Pricing (p. 537)
Understanding the Role of Price (p. 151)

Focus On: Pricing
Michael de Kare-Silver

GETTING STARTED

In recent years, many companies of all sizes have not found it easy to increase profits. Economic conditions, government policies against inflation, increased competition on pricing (including producers from the less-developed countries), and more sophisticated customers around the world have all put pressure on volume and price in many industries. Not surprisingly, companies have turned to levers more directly in their control—such as reducing costs and better process management—as sources of profit growth. This has led to a focus on what is known as re-engineering (a method of changing the processes within a business in order to improve the quality of the products and thereby gain competitive advantage), downsizing, and outsourcing.

However, re-engineering can only go so far in boosting profits and there is a growing realisation that more opportunity and potential may lie on the top line. Pricing, especially, is an undiscovered weapon. There is significant profit potential for companies in challenging this area, and in 're-engineering' their price position.

How can a company check whether it making full use of its pricing opportunities? Consider the following questions, all of which focus internally on the business:

- What percentage of senior management time is spent on pricing?
- How much senior management time is spent with customers?
- Is competitor pricing tracked in similar detail?
- How frequently is pricing specifically and rigorously reviewed?
- Is the company organised in a way that makes sure that a 'balanced' pricing decision is made?

Also, consider the external issues, that is, those facing the market:

- Do you understand your competitors' future pricing strategies and plans?
- Is there a clear understanding of what the company sees as added value, compared to what the customer sees? Do the two match up?
- Does your company have a clear pricing strategy? Is it differentiated for the differing circumstances and market position of each product group and each customer?

This actionlist explains how to use pricing to improve profitability.

FAQS

What are the main issues affecting pricing?

- **Economic forces**, including monopoly and the extent of competition. There is an increasing amount of anti-trust legislation designed to ensure that prices are fair and do not abuse a market dominant position at consumers' expense. Supply and demand affects pricing, as generally when supply exceeds demand, prices will fall. The converse is also true: when demand exceeds supply, prices will rise.
- **Market issues** such as customer perceptions and behaviour. Successful pricing is based on a clear understanding of the specific needs and nature of the target market. The culture and maturity of the market also affects pricing decisions, so if there is an acceptance of a particular type of pricing structure or approach then strategies will often follow this. Finally, if the market is in decline then prices may need to be cut simply to compete for a dwindling number of available customers.
- **Market competitiveness** clearly affects pricing decisions. If there are a large number of direct competitors, pricing can be a valuable tool—or at times it can be a complete irrelevance, as the market knows the

price and will accept no deviation from it. Where few direct competitors exist then there may often be a greater degree of latitude for pricing decisions.

- **Product issues** such as cost are fundamentally significant when setting prices. It may be desirable for products to be sold at a loss to establish market-share or drive out competitors. Frequently of greatest significance are the product's benefits and the value it provides customers, although this needs to be closely related to other factors such as costs and competition.

MAKING IT HAPPEN
Understand the routes to effective pricing

The more you know about which products make money and which lose, the more you can adopt a better strategic and selective pricing policy. Three main routes can be identified that lead to more effective pricing:

- exploiting market advantages
- changing the decision-making process on pricing
- testing whether all the different pricing options are being proactively pursued

Of course, some companies enjoy market or structural circumstances that make pricing management easier. Have they just fallen by luck into those situations, or have their advantages been 'engineered' more deliberately? Some companies have used strategic alliances to create market and structural barriers deliberately—by locking up a vital supply of raw materials, say, and making it hard for others to function.

Select the best pricing strategy

Not only can companies make structural moves that are more easily within their control, there are also as many as 12 different pricing strategies available. They often appear to be underexploited. The challenge is frequently not lack of familiarity with the particular pricing option. It is more about:

- having enough management time to check whether the particular pricing options have been fully considered

- understanding the significance of pricing for competitiveness (the market's price sensitivity)
- examining price opportunities and developing insights on an individual product line basis, rather than across a range
- management's ability to challenge sales-led pricing decisions
- the effectiveness and rigour with which the pricing strategies are implemented
- the information systems needed to support, monitor, and refine these activities.

Use customer information management

There are four approaches to consider, the first of which are based on 'segmentation'. In simple terms, this means dividing up data relevant to your research into appropriate sections.

- **Category segmentation**. You can gain insight into each of your product lines by looking at each one's profitability and pricing.
- **Customer segmentation.** This approach identifies pricing opportunities by using detailed customer information.
- **'Bundling'**. As core product/service prices come under pressure, companies add related products and services where pricing is more robust (and which equally reinforce the value proposition of the core product/service).
- **Managing trade terms.** This means managing the level of discounts given to customers to improve overall returns.

Exploit structural advantages

Four options are highlighted here:

- **lowest cost/lowest price**: cost advantages allow market invaders to price lower their products or services and thereby grow share rapidly.
- **supply and demand management**: as an illustration, better hotel occupancy systems have enabled leaders to quote more aggressive room tariffs.
- **supplier-customer 'balance of power'**: this can be exploited to make sure that suppliers 'contribute' to gross margin success. Tough management of the supply price means that you will have greater flexibility

when you come to fix the price for your end-consumer.

- **'open-book' and partnership-pricing**: the open-book approach was pioneered in the automotive industry. Sharing information about costs has enabled better suppliers to justify and push through selective price increases.

Develop an innovative pricing strategy and lead the market

Pricing can be used to innovate and establish a leadership position in the market. This is accomplished first with branding. It means developing consistently high levels of branding and advertising, enabling the company to maintain a price premium. Next, consider the total value proposition of your product or service, and which of the following five strategies are most appropriate:

- **technology-driven**: continuously developing a niche. This works best with technically advanced products that can really boost your gross margin.
- **first in**: continually focusing on being first to market gives initial pricing advantages, as well as other benefits.
- **best at**: leadership on all features valued by the customer can give price leadership in both 'value pricing' of certain products and 'premium pricing' for certain others.
- **share leadership**: restructuring the portfolio of products offered so that it focuses only on market share leaders where you have more control over pricing and other levers.
- **innovative consumer value**: providing a clear mixing of quality, value, and service to lead in the eyes of the customer.

 ## WHAT TO AVOID
Not consulting widely on pricing issues

Price decisions are too often made by too few people. Only by sharing the responsibility for pricing can managers begin to understand the importance that pricing can have on the success of any business. Ultimately, decisions on pricing must be measured against other critical factors, such as data on customers. In the final analysis, pricing

can be an exercise in both innovation and leadership.

Avoiding short-term action

Short-termism in pricing is, as in most other areas, something to avoid. There are, however, at least two short-term pricing options to increase profits, without damaging the company's future prospects or room for manoeuvre:

- **price squeeze**: at one company that had recently been brought back from the brink of business failure, the new chief executive insisted that each product line price be 'squeezed' up 1%. Despite initial internal resistance, this was successfully implemented, and had an immediate impact on the company's net profit.
- **price elasticity**: have you looked at the way that price and volume relate to each other? Do they balance? For example, products with a low margin (that is, where there isn't a big difference between their production cost and their selling price) can be priced up relatively aggressively so that even if you sell fewer of them (less volume), the impact won't be that bad.

Failing to understand the potential value of changes in pricing

How can you tap into significant pricing potential exists? By removing the roadblocks that typically operate within the organisation—such as:

- leaving responsibility for pricing to your sales team (Who has ever seen a salesman who wanted to increase prices?)
- allowing little or no finance team involvement to make sure that decision making is balanced
- if you're not the owner-manager, accepting senior management's remoteness from the reality of your market—this makes it difficult to challenge sales views
- a lack of data on the true net profitability of individual services/products to either your company or your customers

RECOMMENDED LINK
Pricing Advisor:
www.pricingadvisor.com

Creating a Balance Sheet

WHAT IT MEASURES
The financial standing, or even the net worth or owners' equity, of a company at a given point in time, typically at the end of a calendar or fiscal year.

WHY IT IS IMPORTANT
The balance sheet shows what is owned (assets), what is owed (liabilities), and what is left (owners' equity). It provides a concise snapshot of a company's financial position.

HOW IT WORKS IN PRACTICE
The format of a company's balance sheet is strictly defined by the 1985 Companies Act. Essentially, assets must be in balance with liabilities and shareholders' equity. In other words, assets must equal liabilities and owners' equity.

Assets include cash in hand and cash anticipated (receivables), inventories of supplies and materials, properties, facilities, equipment, and whatever else the company uses to conduct business. Assets also need to reflect depreciation in the value of equipment such as machinery that has a limited expected useful life.

Liabilities include pending payments to suppliers and creditors, outstanding current and long-term debts, taxes, interest payments, and other unpaid expenses that the company has incurred.

Subtracting the value of aggregate liabilities from the value of aggregate assets reveals the value of owners' equity. Ideally, it should be positive. Owners' equity consists of capital invested by owners over the years and profits (net income) or internally generated capital, which is referred to as 'retained earnings'; these are funds to be used in future operations.

As an example:

LIABILITIES	£
Payables	7,000
Taxes	4,000
Misc.	3,000
Bonds & notes	25,000
TOTAL LIABILITIES	39,000
SHAREHOLDERS' EQUITY (stock, par value shares outstanding)	80,000
RETAINED EARNINGS	10,000
TOTAL LIABILITIES AND SHAREHOLDERS' EQUITY	129,000

ASSETS	£
Current:	
Cash	8,200
Securities	5,000
Receivables	4,500
Inventory & supplies	6,300
Fixed:	
Land	10,000
Structures	90,000
Equipment (less depreciation)	5,000
Intangibles/other	
TOTAL ASSETS	129,000

TRICKS OF THE TRADE

- The balance sheet does not show a company's market worth, nor important intangibles such as the knowledge and talents of individual people, nor other vital business factors such as customers or market share.
- The balance sheet does not express the true value of some fixed assets. A six year-old manufacturing plant, for example, is listed at its original cost, even though the price of replacing it could be much higher or substantially lower (because of new technology that might be less expensive or vastly more efficient).

- The balance sheet is not an indicator of past or future performance or trends that affect performance. It needs to be studied along with two other key reports: the income statement and the cash-flow statement. A published balance sheet needs to include prior period comparatives.

RECOMMENDED LINKS

Conetic.com:
www.conetic.com

SEE ALSO

Accounting (p. 487)

Reading a Balance Sheet

GETTING STARTED
A balance sheet will tell us something about the financial strength of a business on the day that the balance sheet is drawn up. That situation changes constantly, so you could say it is more like a snapshot than a film. Although the method of producing a balance sheet is standardised, there can be a certain element of subjectivity in interpreting it. Different elements of the balance sheet can tell you different things about the how the business is doing.

This actionlist gives an overview of a balance sheet and looks at a brief selection of the more interesting figures that help with interpretation. It's important to remember that a lot of these figures do not tell you that much in isolation; it is in trend analysis or comparisons between businesses that they talk more lucidly.

FAQS

What is a balance sheet?
A balance sheet is an accountant's view of the book value of the assets and liabilities of a business at a specific date and on that date alone.

The term 'balance' means exactly what it says—that those assets and liabilities will be equal. In showing how the balance lies, the balance sheet gives us an idea of the financial health of the business.

What does a balance sheet not do?
A balance sheet is not designed to represent market value of the business. For example, property in the balance sheet may be worth a lot more than its book value. Plant and machinery is shown at cost less depreciation, but that may well be different from market value. Stock may turn out to be worth less than its balance-sheet value, and so on.

Also there may be hidden assets, such as goodwill or valuable brands, that do not appear on the balance sheet at all. These would all enhance the value of the business in a sale situation, yet are invisible on a normal balance sheet.

MAKING IT HAPPEN
Here is a very simple company balance sheet:

		£
Fixed assets		1,000
Current assets	700	
Less current liabilities	400	
Net current assets		300
		1,300
Less long-term loans		200
Net assets		1,100
Profit and loss account		500
Share capital		600
Shareholders' funds		1,100

Define the individual elements
- *Fixed assets*—items that are not traded as part of a company's normal activities but enable it to function, such as property, machinery or vehicles. These are tangible assets (meaning you can kick them). This heading can also include intangible assets (you cannot kick them). A common example is 'goodwill', which can arise upon the acquisition of one business by another.
- *Current assets*—items that form the trading cycle of the business. The most common examples are stock, debtors, and positive bank balances.
- *Current liabilities*—also items that form the trading cycle of the business but represent short-term amounts owed to others. Examples will be trade creditors, taxes, and bank overdrafts—broadly, any amount due for payment within the next 12 months from the date of the balance sheet.

- *Net current assets*—not a new figure, but simply the difference between current assets and current liabilities, often shown because it may be a useful piece of information.
- *Long-term loans*—debt that is repayable more than one year from the date of the balance sheet.
- *Net assets*—also not a new figure, but the sum of fixed assets plus net current assets less long-term loans. In other words, all of the company assets shown in its books, minus all of its liabilities.
- *Profit and loss account*—the total of all the accumulated profits and losses from all the accounting periods since the business started. It increases or decreases each year by the net profit or loss in that period, calculated after providing for all costs including tax and dividends to shareholders.
- *Share capital*—the number of shares issued, multiplied by their nominal value. The latter is the theoretical figure at which the shares were originally issued and has nothing to do with their market value.
- *Shareholders' funds*—not a new figure, but the sum of the profit and loss account plus the share capital. It represents the total interest of the shareholders in the company.

Learn to interpret them

Note that balance sheets differ between one industry and another in the sense of the range and type of assets and liabilities that exist. For example, a retailer will have little in the way of trade debtors because it sells for cash, or a manufacturer is likely to have a far larger investment in plant than a service business like an advertising agency. So the interpretation must be seen in the light of the actual trade of the business.

Reading a balance sheet can be quite subjective—accountancy is an art, not a science and, although the method of producing a balance sheet is standardised, there may be some items in it that are subjective rather than factual. The way people interpret some of the figures will also vary, depending on what they wish to achieve and how they see certain things as being good or bad.

Look first at the net assets/shareholders' funds

Positive or negative? Our example, being a healthy business, has net assets of a positive £1,100. Positive is good. If there were 600 shares in issue, it would mean that the net assets per share were £1.83.

If it had negative assets (same thing as net liabilities), this might mean that the business is heading for difficulty unless it is being supported by some party such as a parent company, bank, or other investor. When reading a balance sheet with negative assets, consider where the support will be coming from.

Then examine net current assets

Positive or negative? Again, our example has net current assets of a positive £300. This means that, theoretically, it should not have any trouble settling short-term liabilities because it has more than enough current assets to do so. Negative net current assets suggest that there possibly could be a problem in settling short-term liabilities.

You can also look at NCA as a ratio of current assets/current liabilities. Here, a figure over one is equivalent to the NCA having a positive absolute figure. The ratio version is more useful in analysing trends of balance sheets over successive periods or comparing two businesses.

A cut-down version of looking at NCA considers only (debtors + cash)/(creditors), thus excluding stock. The reasoning here is that this looks at the most liquid of the net current asset constituents and again a figure over one is the most desirable. This is also a ratio that is more meaningful in trends or comparisons.

Understand the significance of trade debtor payments . . .

Within current assets, we have trade debtors. It can be useful to consider how many days worth of sales are tied up in debtors—given by (debtors × 365)/annual sales. This provides an idea of how long the company is waiting to get paid. Too long, and it might be something requiring investigation. However, this figure can be misleading where sales do not take place evenly throughout the year. A construction company might be an example of such a business: one big debtor incurred near the year end would skew the ratio.

. . . and trade creditor payments

Similar to the above, this looks at (trade creditors × 365)/annual purchases, indicating how long the company is taking in general to pay its suppliers. This is not so easy to calculate because the purchases for this purpose include not only goods for resale but all the overheads as well.

Recognise what debt means

Important to most businesses, this figure is the total of long and short-term loans. Too much debt might indicate that the company would have trouble, in a downturn, in paying the interest. It's difficult to give an optimum level of debt because there are so many different situations, depending on a huge range of circumstances.

Often, instead of an absolute figure, debt is expressed as a percentage of shareholders' funds and known as 'gearing' or 'leverage'. In a public company, gearing of 100% might be considered pretty high, whereas debt of under 30% may be seen as on the low side.

WHAT TO AVOID
Believing that balance sheet figures represent market value

Don't assume that a balance sheet is a valuation of the business. Its primary purpose is that it forms part of the range of accounting reports used for measuring business performance—along with the other common financial reports like profit and loss accounts and cash-flow statements. Management, shareholders, and others such as banks will use the entire range to assess the health of the business.

Forgetting that the balance sheet is valid only for the date at which it is produced

A short while after a balance sheet is produced, things could be quite different. In practice there frequently may not be any radical changes between the date of the balance sheet and the date when it is being read, but it is entirely possible that something could have happened to the business that would not show. For example, a major debtor could have defaulted unexpectedly. So remember that balance sheet figures are valid only as at the date shown, and are not a permanent picture of the business.

Confusion over whether in fact all assets and liabilities are shown in the balance sheet

Some businesses may have hidden assets, as suggested above. This could be the value of certain brands or trademarks, for example, for which money may not have ever been paid. Yet these could be worth a great deal. Conversely, there may be some substantial legal action pending which could cost the company a lot, yet is not shown fully in the balance sheet.

SEE ALSO
Accounting (p. 487)
Reading a Cash-flow Statement (p. 169)

Creating a Profit and Loss Account

WHAT IT MEASURES

A company's sales revenues and expenses over a period, providing a calculation of profits or losses during that time.

WHY IT IS IMPORTANT

Reading a P&L is the easiest way to tell if a business has made a profit or a loss during a given month or year. The most important figure it contains is net profit: what is left over after revenues are used to pay expenses and taxes.

Companies typically issue P&L reports monthly. It is customary for the reports to include year-to-date figures, as well as corresponding year-earlier figures to allow for comparisons and analysis.

HOW IT WORKS IN PRACTICE

A P&L adheres to a simple rule of thumb: 'revenue minus cost equals profit'.

There are two P&L formats, multiple-step and single-step. Both follow a standard set of rules known as Generally Accepted Accounting Principles (GAAP). These rules generally adhere to requirements established by governments to track receipts, expenses, and profits for tax purposes. They also allow the financial reports of two different companies to be compared.

The multiple-step format is much more common, because it includes a larger number of details and is thus more useful. It deducts costs from revenues in a series of steps, allowing for closer analysis. Revenues appear first, then expenses, each in as much detail as management desires. Sales may be broken down by product line or location, while expenses such as salaries may be broken down into base salaries and commissions.

Expenses are then subtracted from revenues to show profit (or loss). See the next page for a basic multiple-step P&L layout.

P&Ls of public companies may also report income on the basis of earnings per share. For example, if the company issuing this statement had 12,000 shares outstanding, earnings per share would be £5.12, that is, £61,440 divided by 12,000 shares.

TRICKS OF THE TRADE

- A P&L does not show how a business earned or spent its money.
- One month's P&L can be misleading, especially if a business generates a majority of its receipts in particular months. A retail establishment, for example, usually generates a large percentage of its sales in the final three months of the year, while a consulting service might generate the lion's share of its revenues in as few as two months, and no revenues at all in some other months.
- Invariably, figures for both revenues and expenses reflect the judgements of the companies reporting them. Accounting methods can be quite arbitrary when it comes to such factors as depreciation expenses.

RECOMMENDED LINKS

Biz/ed:
www.bized.ac.uk

SEE ALSO

Accounting (p. 487)

MULTIPLE-STEP PROFIT & LOSS ACCOUNT (£)

NET SALES			750,000
Less: cost of goods sold			450,000
Gross profit			300,000
LESS: OPERATING EXPENSES			
Selling expenses			
Salaries & commissions	54,000		
Advertising	37,500		
Delivery/transportation	12,000		
Depreciation/store equipment	7,500		
Other selling expenses	5,000		
Total selling expenses		116,000	
General & administrative expenses			
Administrative/office salaries	74,000		
Utilities	2,500		
Depreciation/structure	2,400		
Misc. other expenses	3,100		
Total general & admin expenses		82,000	
Total operating expenses			198,000
OPERATING INCOME			102,000
LESS (ADD): NON-OPERATING ITEMS			
Interest expenses	11,000		
Interest income earned	(2,800)		8,200
Income before taxes			93,800
Income taxes			32,360
Net Income			**61,440**

Reading a Profit and Loss Account

GETTING STARTED

A profit and loss account is a statement of the income and expenditure of a business over the period stated, drawn up in order to ascertain how much profit the business made. Put simply, the difference between the income from sales and the associated expenditure is the profit or loss for the period. 'Income' and 'expenditure' here mean only those amounts directly attributable to earning the profit and thus would exclude capital expenditure, for example.

Importantly, the figures are adjusted to match the income and expenses to the time period in which they were incurred—not necessarily the same as that in which the cash changed hands.

FAQS

What is a profit and loss account?

A profit and loss account is an accountant's view of the figures that show how much profit or loss a business has made over a period. To do this, it is necessary to allocate the various elements of income and expenditure to the time period concerned, not on the basis of when cash was received or spent, but on when the income was earned or the liability to pay a supplier and employees was incurred. While capital expenditures are excluded, depreciation of property and equipment is included as a non-cash expense.

Thus if you sell goods on credit, you will be paid later but the sale takes place upon the contract to sell them. Equally if you buy goods and services on credit, the purchase takes place when you contract to buy them, not when you when you actually settle the invoice.

What does a profit and loss account not show?

Most importantly, a P&L account is not an explanation of the cash coming into and going out of a business.

MAKING IT HAPPEN

Below is a simple example of a profit and loss account for a particular year.

Sales		1,000
Opening stock	100	
Purchases	520	
	620	
Closing stock	80	
Cost of sales		540
Gross profit		460
Wages	120	
Other overheads	230	
		350
Net profit before tax		110
Tax		22
Net profit after tax		88
Dividends		40
Retained profit		48
Retained profit brought forward		150
Retained profit carried forward		198

Note that the presence of stock and purchases indicates that the business is trading or manufacturing goods of some kind, rather than selling services.

Define the individual elements

- *Sales*—the invoiced value of the sales in the period.
- *Stock*—the value of the actual physical stock held by the business at the opening and closing of the period. It is always valued at cost, or realisable value if that is lower, never at selling price.
- *Purchases and other direct costs*—the goods or raw materials purchased by the business for resale—not capital items used in the business, only items used as part of the direct cost of its sales. In other words, those costs which vary directly with sales, as distinct from overheads (like rent) which do not.

Where a business holds stock, the purchases figure has to be adjusted for the opening and closing values in order to reach the right income and expenditure amounts for that period only. Goods for resale bought in the period may not have been used purely for that period but may be lying in stock at the end of it, ready for sale in the next. Similarly, goods used for resale in this period will consist partly of items already held in stock at the beginning of it. So take the amounts purchased, add the opening stock and deduct the closing stock. The resulting adjusted purchase figure is known as 'cost of sales'.

In some businesses there may be other direct costs apart from purchases included in cost of sales. For example, a manufacturer may include some wages if they are of a direct nature (wages of employees directly involved in the manufacturing process, as distinct from office staff say). Or a building contractor would include plant hire in direct costs, as well as purchases of materials.

- *Gross profit*—the difference between sales and cost of sales. This is an important figure as it measures how much was actually made directly from whatever the business is selling, before it starts to pay for overheads.

The figure is often expressed as a percentage ratio, when it is known as the 'gross profit margin'. In our example the GPM is 460:1,000—or 46%. Ratios are really only useful as comparison tools, either with different periods of the same business or with other businesses.

- *Overheads*—the expenses of the business which do not vary directly with sales. They include a wide range of items such as rent, most wages, advertising, phones, interest paid on loans, audit fees, and so on.
- *Net profit before tax*—the result of deducting total overheads from gross profit. This is what the business has made before tax is paid on that profit.
- *Tax (or corporation tax)*—This will not actually have been paid in the year concerned, but is shown because it is due on the profit for that period. Even then the figure shown may not be the actual amount due, for various reasons such as possible overpayments from previous years. Tax can be a very complex matter, being based upon a set of changeable rules.
- *Net profit after tax*—the result after deducting the tax liability—the so-called bottom line. This is the amount that the company can do with as it wishes, possibly paying a dividend out of part of it and retaining the rest. It is the company's reward for actually being in business in the first place.
- *Dividends*—a payment to the shareholders as a reward for their investment in the company. Most publicly listed companies of any size pay dividends to shareholders. Private companies may also do so, but this may be more for tax reasons. The dividend in the example shown is paid out of the net profit after tax, but legally it is not permitted to exceed the total available profit. That total available profit is comprised of both the current year's net profit after tax and the retained profit brought forward from previous years.
- *Retained profit*—the amount kept by the company after paying dividends to shareholders. If there is no dividend, then it is equal to the net profit after tax.
- *Retained profit brought forward*—the total accumulated retained profits for all earlier years of the company's existence.

- *Retained profit carried forward*—the above figure brought forward, plus the current year's retained profit. This new total will form the profit brought forward in the next accounting period.

Learn to interpret the figures

A lot of accounting analysis is valid only when comparing the figures, usually with similar figures for earlier periods, projected future figures, or other companies in the same business.

On its own a P&L account tells you only a limited story, though there are some stand-alone facts that can be derived from it. What our example does show, even in isolation, is that this business was successful in the period concerned. It made a profit, not a loss, and was able to pay dividends to shareholders out of that profit. Clearly a pretty crucial piece of information.

However, it is in comparisons that such figures start to have real meaning.

The example figures reveal that the gross profit margin was 46%, an important statistic in measuring business performance. The net profit margin before tax was 110:1,000, or 11%. You could take the margin idea further and calculate the net profit after tax ratio to sales as 88:1,000, being 8.8%. Or you could calculate the ratio of any expense to sales. In our example, the wages:sales ratio is 120:1,000 or 12%.

If you then looked at similar margin figures for the preceding accounting period, you would learn something about this business. Say the gross margin was 45% last year compared with 46% this year—there has been some improvement in the profit made before deducting overheads. But then suppose that the net profit margin of 8.8% this year was 9.8% last year. This would tell you that, despite improvement in profit at the gross level, the overheads have increased disproportionately. You could then check on the ratio of each of the overheads to sales to see where this arose and find out why.

Advertising spending could have shot up, for example, or perhaps the company moved to new premises incurring a higher rent. Maybe something could be tightened up.

Another commonly used ratio

Another ratio often used in business analysis is return on capital employed. Here we combine the profit and loss account with the balance sheet by dividing the net profit (either before or after tax as required) by shareholders' funds. This tells you how much the company is making proportionate to money invested in it by the shareholders—a similar idea to how much you might get in interest on a bank deposit account. It's a useful way of comparing different companies in a particular industry, where the more efficient ones are likely to derive a higher return on capital employed.

WHAT TO AVOID ✗
Assuming that the bottom line represents cash profit from trading

It does not! There are a few examples where this is the case: a simple cash trader might buy something for one price, then sell it for more; his profit then equals the increase in cash. But a business that buys and sells on credit, spends money on items that are held for the longer term, such as property or machinery, has tax to pay at a later date, and so on, will make a profit that is not represented by a mere increase in cash balances held. Indeed, the cash balance could quite easily decrease during a period when a profit was made.

RECOMMENDED LINK
The Motley Fool UK:
www.fool.co.uk

SEE ALSO
Accounting (p. 487)
Reading a Cash-flow Statement (p. 169)

Reading a Cash-flow Statement

GETTING STARTED

In their annual report, most public companies must publish a cash-flow statement—together with the profit and loss account and a balance sheet. As the name suggests, the purpose of a cash-flow statement is to explain the movement in cash balances or bank overdrafts held by the business from one accounting period to the next.

The balance sheet shows the assets and liabilities at the end of the period, with comparative figures for the start of it. The profit and loss account shows how much profit was generated by the business in the period. The cash-flow statement is the third part of the financial picture of the business over the period.

FAQS

What is a cash-flow statement?

Over an accounting period, the money held by a business at the bank (or its overdrafts) will have changed. The purpose of the cash-flow statement is to show the reasons for this change. If you look at the actionlist on profit and loss (**Reading a Profit and Loss Account (p. 166)**), one of the common mistakes illustrated was the erroneous belief that the profit was equal to the cash generated by a business. It is not, but the cash-flow statement is the link between profit and cash balance movements. It takes you down the path from profit to cash. The figures are derived from those published in the annual accounts, and notes will explain how this derivation is arrived at.

What does a cash-flow statement not show?

In the same way that a profit and loss account does not show the cash made by the business, a cash-flow statement does not show the profit. It is entirely possible for a loss-making business to show an increase in cash, and the other way round too.

MAKING IT HAPPEN

Here is a simple example of a cash-flow statement for a particular year:

		£
Net cash inflow from operating activities		7,020
Returns on investments and finance costs		
Interest paid	820	
Less interest received	90	
Net cash outflow from finance costs		(730)
Taxation		(1,060)
Capital expenditure		
Sale of fixed assets	760	
Less purchase of fixed assets	4,420	
Net cash outflow from capital expenditure		(3,660)
Dividends paid		(1,530)
Net cash inflow before financing		40
Financing		
New loans	1,000	
Loan repayments	(300)	
Finance lease repayments	(100)	
Net cash inflow from financing		600
Increase in cash		640

Define the individual elements

- *Net cash inflow from operating activities*—broadly this is the profit of the business, before depreciation plus the change in debtor and creditor balances. There may also be other items included here. In the statutory annual accounts of companies, there will be an explanation to show how this net cash inflow figure is derived from the profit and loss account and balance sheet. Depreciation is excluded because it does not represent a cash cost.

Debtor and creditor balance changes are included here because they represent an inflow or outflow of cash to the business. Thus if customers owe you less or more at the end of a period than at the beginning of it, it follows that there must have been cash flowing in or out of the business as a result. A reduction in debtors means that cash has come in to the business, and the reverse for an increase in debtors. The same applies to the creditor balances of suppliers. An increase here means a cash inflow, with a decrease denoting an outflow.

- *Returns on investments and finance costs*—these figures comprise interest received on cash balances, less interest paid on debt. There could be other forms of investment income here, such as dividends on shares owned.
- *Net cash outflow from finance costs*—this is not a new figure but the net result of the above items, identified as returns on investments. In our example the result is an outflow of cash. That is, the interest paid on debt exceeded the interest received on cash. It could in some circumstances be the other way round, where for example a business has substantial cash balances earning interest.
- *Taxation*: self explanatory; this is the outflow of cash arising from corporation tax paid by the business. It can on occasion be an inflow, where the company has obtained a repayment of corporation tax for some reason.
- *Capital expenditure*—this is cash expended on fixed assets bought for the business, less cash received from the sale of assets no longer required by the business.

- *Net cash outflow from capital expenditure*—this is not a new figure but the net result of the above items, identified as expenditure on new fixed assets less receipts from the sale or disposal of such items. In our example there is a large outflow, which generally would be the norm. It can happen sometimes though that a business realises more from the sale of fixed assets in a particular period than it expends on items acquired.
- *Dividends paid*—self-explanatory; this is the outflow of cash arising from paying dividends to shareholders.
- *Net cash inflow before financing*—this is not a new figure but a subtotal of the items above. In our example, the figure of £40 shown happens to be an inflow but it could just as easily have been an outflow. There is no typical figure here; it is just as common to see net inflows as outflows.

It is important to understand what this figure represents. It is the net cash result of running the business in the period concerned, after paying tax to the government and dividends to the shareholders. However, as its label indicates, it doesn't include any financing.

- *Financing*—this term includes the raising of new loans, the repayment of old ones, and other methods of financing such as issuing new shares. In the example the company borrowed £1,000 in new loans, which created a cash inflow of that sum, and repaid £300 on old debt plus a further £100 on equipment leases (which are another form of finance), making a net inflow on finance of £400.
- *Increase in cash* (the bottom line)—adding the net inflow of £600 from finance to the £40 generated by business operations gives us an overall net cash inflow of £640. This is the bottom line. It means that we have £640 more in the bank at the end of the accounting period than at the beginning of it.

Learn to interpret the figures

As suggested above, the cash-flow statement is the third section of the primary set of accounting documents used to explain and analyse businesses. It is a 'derived schedule', meaning that the figures are pulled from the profit and loss account and balance sheet statements, linking the two.

Its purpose is to analyse the reasons why the company's cash position changed over an accounting period. For example, a sharp increase in borrowings could have several explanations—such as a high level of capital expenditure, poor trading, an increase in the time taken by debtors to pay, and so on. The cash-flow statement will alert management to the reasons for this, in a way that may not be obvious merely from the profit and loss account and balance sheet alone.

The generally desirable situation is for the net position before financing to be positive. Even the best-run businesses will sometimes have an outflow in a period (for example in a year of high capital expenditure), but positive is usually good. This becomes more apparent when comparing the figures over a period of time. A repeated outflow of funds over several years is usually an indication of trouble. To cover this, the company must raise new finance and/or sell off assets, which will tend to compound the problem, in the worst cases leading to failure.

Cash is critical to every business, so the management must understand where its cash is coming from and going to. The cash-flow statement gives us this information in an abbreviated form. You could argue that the whole purpose of a business is to start with one sum of money and, by applying some sort of process to it, arrive at another and higher sum, continually repeating this cycle.

WHAT TO AVOID
Confusing 'cash' and 'profit'

As mentioned previously, the most common mistake with cash-flow statements is the potential confusion between profit and cash. They are not the same!

Not understanding the terminology

It is clearly fundamental to an understanding of cash-flow statements that the reader is familiar with terms like 'debtors', 'creditors', 'dividends', and so on. But more than appreciating the meaning of the word 'debtors', it is quite easy to misunderstand the concept that, for example, an increase in debtors is a cash outflow, and equally that an increase in creditors represents an inflow of cash to the business.

RECOMMENDED LINK
The Motley Fool UK:
www.fool.co.uk

SEE ALSO
Accounting (p. 487)
Reading a Balance Sheet (p. 161)
**Reading a Profit and Loss Account
   (p. 166)**

Creating a Cash-flow Statement

WHAT IT MEASURES
Cash inflows and cash outflows over a specific period of time, typically a year.

WHY IT IS IMPORTANT
Cash flow is a key indicator of financial health, and it demonstrates to investors, creditors, and other core constituencies a company's ability to meet obligations, finance opportunities, and generally 'come up with the cash' as needs arise. Cash flow that is wildly inconsistent with, say, net income, often indicates operating or managerial problems.

HOW IT WORKS IN PRACTICE
In its basic form, a cash-flow statement will probably be familiar to anyone who has been a member of a club that collected and spent money. It reports funds on hand at the beginning of a given period, funds received, funds spent, and funds remaining at the end of the period.

That formula still applies to a business today, even if creating a cash-flow document is significantly more complex. Cash flows are divided into three categories: cash from operations; cash-investment activities; and cash-financing activities. Companies with holdings in foreign currencies use a fourth classification: effects of changes in currency rates on cash.

A standard direct cash-flow statement looks like this:

CRD Ltd
Statement of Cash flows
For year ended 31 December 20__

CASH FLOWS FROM OPERATIONS	£
Operating Profit	82,000
Adjustments to net earnings	
Depreciation	17,000
Accounts receivable	(20,000)
Accounts payable	12,000
Inventory	(8,000)
Other adjustments to earnings	4,000
Net cash flow from operations	**87,000**

CASH FLOWS FROM INVESTMENT ACTIVITIES	
Purchases of marketable securities	(58,000)
Receipts from sales of marketable securities	45,000
Loans made to borrowers	(16,000)
Collections on loans	11,000
Purchases of plant and land and property assets	(150,000)
Receipts from sales of plant and land and property assets	47,000
Net cash flow from investment activities:	**(-121,000)**

CASH FLOWS FROM FINANCING ACTIVITIES	
Proceeds from short-term borrowings	51,000
Payments to settle short-term debts	(61,000)
Proceeds from issuing bonds payable	100,000
Proceeds from issuing capital stock	80,000
Dividends paid	(64,000)
Net cash flow from financing activities	**106,000**
Net change in cash during period	72,000
Cash and cash equivalents, beginning of year	27,000
Cash and cash equivalents, end of year	**99,000**

TRICKS OF THE TRADE
- A cash-flow statement does *not* measure net income, nor does it measure working capital.
- A cash-flow statement does not include outstanding accounts receivable, but it does include the preceding year's accounts receivable (assuming these were collected during the year for which the statement is prepared).

- Add to a cash inflow any amounts charged off for depreciation, depletion, and amortisation, since cash was actually spent.
- Cash equivalents are short-term, highly liquid investments, although precise definitions may vary slightly by country. These should be included when recalculating the movement of cash in the period.
- There are alternative ways to present cash flow from operations. Some texts, for example, omit earnings and adjustments, and list instead cash and interest received, cash and interest paid, and taxes received.

RECOMMENDED LINK

International Accounting Standards Committee:
www.iasc.org.uk

SEE ALSO

Accounting (p. 487)

Calculating Accounts Receivable Turnover

WHAT IT MEASURES

The number of times in each accounting period, typically a year, that a firm converts credit sales into cash.

WHY IT IS IMPORTANT

A high turnover figure is desirable, because it indicates that a company collects revenues effectively, and that its customers pay bills promptly. A high figure also suggests that a firm's credit and collection policies are sound.

In addition, the measurement is a reasonably good indicator of cash flow, and of overall operating efficiency.

HOW IT WORKS IN PRACTICE

The formula for accounts receivable turnover is straightforward. Simply divide the average amount of receivables into annual credit sales:

$$\text{sales / receivables = receivables turnover}$$

If, for example, a company's sales are £4.5 million and its average receivables are £375,000, its receivables turnover is:

$$4,500,000 / 375,000 = 12$$

TRICKS OF THE TRADE

- It is important to use the average amount of receivables over the period considered. Otherwise, receivables could be misleading for a company whose products are seasonal or are sold at irregular intervals.
- The measurement is also helpful to a company that is designing or revising credit terms.
- Accounts receivable turnover is among the measures that comprise asset utilisation ratios, also called activity ratios.

RECOMMENDED LINK

The Motley Fool UK:
www.fool.co.uk

SEE ALSO

Accounting (p. 487)
Calculating Asset Utilisation (p. 181)

Calculating Acid-test Ratio

WHAT IT MEASURES
How quickly a company's assets can be turned into cash, which is why assessment of a company's liquidity also is known as the quick ratio, or simply the acid ratio.

WHY IT IS IMPORTANT
Regardless of how this ratio is labelled, it is considered a highly reliable indicator of a company's financial strength and its ability to meet its short-term obligations. Because inventory can sometimes be difficult to liquidate, the acid-test ratio deducts inventory from current assets before they are compared with current liabilities—which is what distinguishes it from the current ratio.

Potential creditors like to use the acid-test ratio because it reveals how a company would fare if it had to pay off its bills under the worst possible conditions. Indeed, the assumption behind the acid-test ratio is that creditors are howling at the door demanding immediate payment, and that an enterprise has no time to sell off its inventory, or any of its stock.

HOW IT WORKS IN PRACTICE
The acid-test ratio's formula can be expressed in two ways, but both essentially reach the same conclusion. The most common expression is:

**(current assets – inventory) /
current liabilities = acid-test ratio**

If, for example, current assets total £7,700, inventory amounts to £1,200, and current liabilities total £4,500, then:

(7,700 – 1,200) / 4,500 = 1.44

A variation of this formula ignores inventories altogether, distinguishes assets as cash, receivables, and short-term investments, then divides the sum of the three by the total current liabilities, or:

**cash + accounts receivable +
short-term investments /
current liabilities = acid-test ratio**

If, for example, cash totals £2,000, receivables total £3,000, short-term invest-

ments total £1,000, and liabilities total £4,800, then:

(2,000 + 3,000 + 1,000) / 4,800 = 1.25

There are two other ways to appraise liquidity, although neither is as commonly used: the cash ratio is the sum of cash and marketable securities divided by current liabilities; net quick assets is determined by adding cash, accounts receivable, and marketable securities, then subtracting current liabilities from that sum.

TRICKS OF THE TRADE
- In general, the quick ratio should be 1:1 or better. It means a company has a unit's worth of easily convertible assets for each unit of its current liabilities. A high quick ratio usually reflects a sound, well-managed organisation in no danger of imminent collapse, even in the extreme and unlikely event that its sales ceased immediately. On the other hand, companies with ratios of less than 1 could not pay their current liabilities, and should be looked at with extreme care.
- While a ratio of 1:1 is generally acceptable to most creditors, acceptable quick ratios vary by industry, as do almost all financial ratios. No ratio, in fact, is especially meaningful without knowledge of the business from which it originates. For example, a declining quick ratio with a stable current ratio may indicate that a company has built up too much inventory; but it could also suggest that the company has greatly improved its collection system.
- Some experts regard the acid-test ratio as an extreme version of the working capital ratio because it uses only cash and equivalents, and excludes inventories. An acid-test ratio that is notably lower than the working capital ratio often means that inventories make up a large proportion of current assets. An example would be retail stores.
- Comparing quick ratios over an extended period of time can signal developing trends

in a company. While modest declines in the quick ratio do not automatically spell trouble, uncovering the reasons for changes can help find ways to nip potential problems in the bud.

- Like the current ratio, the quick ratio is a snapshot, and a company can manipulate its figures to make it look robust at a given point in time.
- Investors who suddenly become keenly interested in a firm's quick ratio may signal their anticipation of a downturn in the firm's business or in the general economy.

RECOMMENDED LINK

Business Owner's Toolkit:
www.toolkit.cch.com

SEE ALSO

Accounting (p. 487)

Calculating Amortisation

WHAT IT MEASURES
Amortisation is a method of recovering (deducting or writing off) the capital costs of intangible assets over a fixed period of time. Its calculation is virtually identical to the straight-line method of depreciation.

Amortisation also refers to the establishment of a schedule for repaying the principal and interest on a loan in equal amounts over a period of time. Because computers have made this a simple calculation, business references to amortisation tend to focus more on the term's first definition.

WHY IT IS IMPORTANT
Amortisation enables a company to identify its true costs, and thus its net income, more precisely. In the course of their business, most enterprises acquire intangible assets such as a patent for an invention, or a well-known brand or trademark. Since these assets can contribute to the revenue growth of the business, they can be—and are allowed to be—deducted against those future revenues over a period of years, provided the procedure conforms to accepted accounting practices.

For tax purposes, the distinction is not always made between amortisation and depreciation, yet amortisation remains a viable financial accounting concept in its own right.

HOW IT WORKS IN PRACTICE
Amortisation is computed using the straight-line method of depreciation: divide the initial cost of the intangible asset by the estimated useful life of that asset. For example, if it costs £10,000 to acquire a patent and it has an estimated useful life of 10 years, the amortised amount per year is £1,000.

$$£10,000 / 10 = £1,000 \text{ per year}$$

The amount of amortisation accumulated since the asset was acquired appears on the organisation's balance sheet as a deduction under the amortised asset.

While that formula is straightforward, amortisation can also incorporate a variety of non-cash charges to net earnings and/or asset values, such as depletion, write-offs, prepaid expenses, and deferred charges. Accordingly, there are many rules to regulate how these charges appear on financial statements. The rules are different in each country, and are occasionally changed, so it is necessary to stay abreast of them and rely on expert advice.

For financial reporting purposes, an intangible asset is amortised over a period of years. The amortisable life—'useful life'—of an intangible asset is the period over which it gives economic benefit. Several factors are considered when determining this useful life; for example, demand and competition, effects of obsolescence, legal or contractual limitations, renewal provisions, and service life expectations.

Intangibles that can be amortised can include:

Copyrights, based on the amount paid either to purchase them or to develop them internally, plus the costs incurred in producing the work (wages or materials, for example). At present, a copyright is granted to a corporation for 75 years, and to an individual for the life of the author plus 50 years. However, the estimated useful life of a copyright is usually far less than its legal life, and it is generally amortised over a fairly short period.

Cost of a franchise, including any fees paid to the franchiser, as well legal costs or expenses incurred in the acquisition. A franchise granted for a limited period should be amortised over its life. If the franchise has an indefinite life, it should be amortised over a reasonable period not to exceed 40 years.

Covenants not to compete: an agreement by the seller of a business not to engage in a competing business in a certain area for a specific period of time. The cost of the not-to-compete covenant should be amortised over the period covered by the covenant unless its estimated economic life is expected to be less.

Easement costs that grant a right of way may be amortised if there is a limited and specified life.

Organisation costs incurred when forming a corporation or a partnership, including legal fees, accounting services, incorporation fees, and other related services. Organisation costs are usually amortised over 60 months.

Patents, both those developed internally and those purchased. If developed internally, a patent's 'amortisable basis' includes legal fees incurred during the application process. Normally, a patent is amortised over its legal life, or over its remaining life if purchased. However, it should be amortised over its legal life or its economic life, whichever is the shorter.

Trademarks, brands, and trade names, which should be written off over a period not to exceed 40 years. However, since the value of these assets depends on the changing tastes of consumers, they are frequently amortised over a shorter period.

Other types of property that may be amortised include certain intangible drilling costs, circulation costs, mine development costs, pollution control facilities, and reforestation expenditures. They can even include intangibles such as the value of a market share or a market's composition: an example is the portion of an acquired business that is attributable to the existence of a given customer base.

TRICKS OF THE TRADE

- Certain intangibles cannot be amortised, but may be depreciated using a straight-line approach if they have a 'determinable' useful life. Because the rules are different in each country and are subject to change, it is essential to rely on specialist advice.

- Computer software may be amortised under certain conditions, depending on its purpose. Software that is amortised is generally given a 60-month life, but it may be amortised over a shorter period if it can clearly be established that it will be obsolete or no longer used within a shorter time.

- Under certain conditions, customer lists that were purchased may be amortised if it can be demonstrated that the list has a finite useful life, in that customers on the list are likely to be lost over a period of time.

- While leasehold improvements are depreciated for income tax purposes, they are amortised when it comes to financial reporting—either over the remaining term of the lease or their expected useful life, whichever is shorter.

- Annual payments incurred under a franchise agreement should be expensed when incurred.

- The Internet has many amortisation loan calculators that can automatically determine monthly payments figures and the total cost of a loan.

RECOMMENDED LINK

Best Software:
www.bestsoftware.com

SEE ALSO

Accounting (p. 487)
Calculating Depreciation (p. 189)

Calculating Annual Percentage Rate

WHAT IT MEASURES
Either the rate of interest that invested money earns in one year, or the cost of credit expressed as a yearly rate.

WHY IT IS IMPORTANT
It enables an investor or borrower to compare like with like. When evaluating investment alternatives, naturally it's important to know which one will pay the greatest return. By the same token, borrowers want to know which loan alternative offers the best terms. Determining the annual percentage rate provides a direct comparison.

HOW IT WORKS IN PRACTICE
To calculate the annual percentage rate (APR), apply this formula:

$$APR = [1 + i/m]m - 1.0$$

In the formula, i is the interest rate quoted, expressed as decimal, and m is the number of compounding periods per year. For example:

If a bank offers a 6% interest rate, paid quarterly, the APR would be calculated this way:

$$
\begin{aligned}
APR &= [1 + i/m]m - 1.0 \\
&= [1 + 0.06/4]4 - 1.0
\end{aligned}
$$

$$
\begin{aligned}
&= [1 + 0.015] 4 - 1.0 \\
&= (1.015) 4 - 1.0 \\
&= 1.0614 - 1.0 \\
&= 0.0614 \\
&= 6.14\% \ APR
\end{aligned}
$$

TRICKS OF THE TRADE
- As a rule of thumb, the annual percentage rate is slightly higher than the quoted rate.
- When using the formula, be sure to express the rate as a decimal, that is, 6% becomes 0.06.
- When expressed as the cost of credit, remember to include other costs of obtaining the credit in addition to interest, such as loan closing costs and financial fees.
- APR provides an excellent basis for comparing mortgage or other loan rates; in the United Kingdom, lenders are required to disclose it.
- When used in the context of investment APR also can be called the 'annual percentage yield', or APY.

RECOMMENDED LINK
Investorguide.com:
www.investorguide.com

SEE ALSO
Accounting (p. 487)

Calculating Asset Turnover

WHAT IT MEASURES
The amount of sales generated for every pound's worth of assets over a given period.

WHY IT IS IMPORTANT
Asset turnover measures how well a company is leveraging its assets to produce revenue. A well-managed manufacturer, for example, will make its plant and equipment work hard for the business by minimising idle time for machines.

The higher the number the better—within reason. As a rule of thumb, companies with low profit margins tend to have high asset turnover; those with high profit margins have low asset turnover.

This ratio can also show how capital-intensive a business is. Some businesses, software developers, for example, can generate tremendous sales per pound of assets because their assets are modest. At the other end of the scale, electric utilities, heavy industry manufacturers and even cable TV firms need a huge asset base to generate sales.

Finally, asset turnover serves as a tool to keep managers conscious of the company's balance sheet along with its profit and loss account.

HOW IT WORKS IN PRACTICE
Asset turnover's basic formula is simply sales divided by assets:

sales revenue / total assets

Most experts recommend using average total assets in the formula. To determine this figure, add total assets at the beginning of the year to total assets at the end of the year and divide by two.

If, for instance, annual sales totalled £4.5 million, and total assets were £1.84 million at the beginning of the year and £1.78 million at the year end, the average total assets would be £1.81 million, and the asset turnover ratio would be:

4,500,000 / 1,810,000 = 2.49

A variation of the formula is:

sales revenue / fixed assets

If average fixed assets were £900,000, then asset turnover would be:

4,500,000 / 900,000 = 5

TRICKS OF THE TRADE
- This ratio is especially useful for growth companies to gauge whether or not they are growing revenue, for example, turnover, in healthy proportion to assets.
- Asset turnover numbers are useful for comparing competitors within industries. Like most ratios, they vary from industry to industry. As with most numbers, the most meaningful comparisons are made over extended periods of time.
- Too high a ratio may suggest overtrading: too much sales revenue with too little investment. Conversely, too low a ratio may suggest undertrading and an inefficient management of resources.
- A declining ratio may be indicative of a company that overinvested in plant, equipment, or other fixed assets, or is not using existing assets effectively.

RECOMMENDED LINK
Biz/ed:
www.bized.ac.uk

SEE ALSO
Accounting (p. 487)
Calculating Asset Utilisation (p. 181)

Calculating Asset Utilisation

WHAT IT MEASURES
How efficiently an organisation uses its resources and, in turn, the effectiveness of the organisation's managers.

WHY IT IS IMPORTANT
The success of any enterprise is tied to its ability to manage and leverage its assets. Hefty sales and profits can hide any number of inefficiencies. By examining several relationships between sales and assets, asset utilisation delivers a reasonably detailed picture of how well a company is being managed and led—certainly enough to call attention both to sources of trouble and to role-model operations.

Moreover, since all the figures used in this analysis are taken from a company's balance sheet or profit and loss statement, the ratios that result can be used to compare a company's performance with individual competitors and with industries as a whole.

Many companies also use this measure not only to evaluate their aggregate success but also to determine compensation for managers.

HOW IT WORKS IN PRACTICE
Asset utilisation relies on a family of asset utilisation ratios, also called activity ratios. The individual ratios in the family can vary, depending on the practitioner. They include measures that also stand alone, such as accounts receivable turnover and asset turnover. The most commonly used sets of asset utilisation ratios include these and the following measures.

Average collection period is also known as days sales outstanding. It links accounts receivable with daily sales and is expressed in number of days; the lower the number, the better the performance. Its formula is:

accounts receivable / average daily sales = average collection period

For example, if accounts receivable are £280,000, and average daily sales are 7,000, then:

$$280,000 / 7,000 = 40$$

Inventory turnover compares the cost of goods sold (COGS) with inventory; for this measure, expressed in 'turns', the higher the number the better. Its formula is:

cost of goods sold / inventory

For example, if COGS is £2 million, and inventory at the end of the period is £500,000, then:

$$2,000,000 / 500,000 = 4$$

Some asset utilisation repertoires include ratios like debtor days, while others study the relationships listed below.

Depreciation / Assets measures the percentage of assets being depreciated to gauge how quickly product plants are ageing and assets are being consumed.

Depreciation / Sales measures the percentage of sales that is tied up covering the wear and tear of the physical plant.

In either instance, a high percentage could be cause for concern.

Income / Assets measures how well management uses its assets to generate net income. It is the same formula as return on assets.

Income / Plant measures how effectively a company uses its investment in fixed assets to generate net income.

In these two instances, high numbers are desirable.

Plant / Assets expresses the percentage of total assets that is tied up in land, buildings, and equipment.

By themselves, of course, the individual numbers are meaningless. Their value lies in how they compare with the corresponding numbers of competitors and industry averages. A company with an inventory turnover of 4 in an industry whose average is 7, for example, surely has room for improvement, because the comparison indicates it is generating fewer sales per unit of inventory and is therefore less efficient than its rivals.

TRICKS OF THE TRADE

- Asset utilisation is particularly useful to companies considering expansion or capital investment: if production can be increased by improving the efficiency of existing resources, there is no need to spend the sums expansion would cost.
- Like all families of ratios, no single number or comparison is necessarily cause for alarm or rejoicing. Asset utilisation proves most beneficial over an extended period of time.
- Studying all measures at once can take up a lot of time, although computers have trimmed hours into seconds. Management teams in smaller organisations may conduct asset utilisation on a continuing basis, tracking particular measures on a monthly basis to stay abreast of operating trends.

RECOMMENDED LINK
Powerinvestor.com:
www.powerinvestor.com

SEE ALSO
Accounting (p. 487)
Calculating Accounts Receivable Turnover (p. 174)
Calculating Asset Turnover (p. 180)

Calculating Contribution Margin

WHAT IT MEASURES
The amounts that individual products or services ultimately contribute to net profit.

WHY IT IS IMPORTANT
Contribution margin helps a business decide how it should direct or redirect its resources.

When managers know the contribution margin—or margins, as is more often the case—they can make better decisions about adding or subtracting product lines, investing in existing products, pricing products or services (particularly in response to competitors' actions), structuring sales commissions and bonuses, where to direct marketing and advertising expenditures, and where to apply individual talents and expertise.

In short, contribution margin is a valuable decision-support tool.

HOW IT WORKS IN PRACTICE
Its calculation is straightforward:

sales price – variable cost = contribution margin

Or, for providers of services:

total revenue – total variable cost = contribution margin

For example, if the sales price of an item is £500 and variable cost is £350, the contribution margin is £150, or 30% of sales.

This means that 30 pence of every sales pound remain to contribute to fixed costs and to profit, after the costs directly related to the sales are subtracted.

Contribution margin is especially useful to a company comparing different products or services. See the next column for an example.

Obviously, Product C has the highest contribution percentage, even though Product A generates more total profit. The analysis suggests that the company might do well to aim to achieve a sales mix with a higher proportion of Product C. It further suggests

	Product A	Product B	Product C
	£	£	£
Sales	260	220	140
Variable costs	178	148	65
Contribution margin	82	72	75
Contribution margin (%)	31.5	32.7	53.6

that prices for Products A and B may be too low, or that their cost structures need attention. Notably, none of this information appears on a standard income statement.

Contribution margin also can be tracked over a long period of time, using data from several years of income statements. It can also be invaluable in calculating volume discounts for preferred customers, and break-even sales or volume levels.

TRICKS OF THE TRADE
- Contribution margin depends on accurately accounting for all variable costs, including shipping and delivery, or the indirect costs of services. Activity-based cost accounting systems aid this kind of analysis.
- Variable costs include all direct costs (usually labour and materials).
- Contribution margin analysis is only one tool to use. It will not show so-called loss leaders, for example. And it doesn't consider marketing factors such as existing penetration levels, opportunities, or mature markets being eroded by emerging markets.

RECOMMENDED LINK
Business Owner's Toolkit:
www.toolkit.cch.com

SEE ALSO
Accounting (p. 487)

Calculating Cost of Goods Sold (COGS)

WHAT IT MEASURES
For a retailer, COGS is the cost of buying and acquiring the goods that it sells to its customers. For a service firm, COGS is the cost of the employee services it supplies. For a manufacturer, COGS is the cost of buying the raw materials and manufacturing its finished products.

WHY IT IS IMPORTANT
Cost of goods sold may help a company determine the prices to charge for its products and services, and the volume of business that it needs to maintain in order to operate profitably.

For retailers especially, the cost of the merchandise sold is typically the largest expense, and thus an absolutely critical business factor. However, understanding COGS is an important success factor for any business because it can reveal opportunities to reduce costs and improve operations.

COGS is also a key figure on an income statement (also called the profit and loss account), and an important consideration in computing income taxes because of its close relationship to inventories, which taxation authorities treat as future income.

HOW IT WORKS IN PRACTICE
Essentially, COGS is equal to a company's opening stock of goods and services, plus the cost of goods bought and direct costs incurred during a particular period, minus the closing stock of goods and services.

A critical consideration is the accounting policy that a company adopts to calculate inventory values, especially if raw materials prices change during the year. This may happen often, particularly when inflation is high. The Accounting Standards Board of the Institute of Chartered Accountants in England and Wales publishes Statement of Standards Accounting Practice 9, which deals with stocks and work in progress.

COGS for a manufacturer will include a variety of items, such as raw materials and energy used in production, labour, benefits for production workers, the cost of raw materials in inventory, shipping fees, the cost of storing finished products, depreciation on production machinery used, and factory overhead expenses.

For a retail company such as Marks and Spencer, COGS is generally less complex; the total amount paid to suppliers for the products being sold on its shelves.

COGS is calculated as follows:

Stocks at beginning of period	£20,000
Purchases during period	+ £60,000
Cost of good available for sale	= £80,000
Less inventory at period end	− £15,000
Cost of goods sold (COGS)	= £65,000

Because the counting of inventory is an exhaustive undertaking for retailers, doing it quarterly or monthly would be open to error. Accordingly, taxation authorities allow them to estimate cost of goods sold during the year.

Determining these estimates requires details of the gross profit margin (retailers typically use the preceding year's figure). This figure is then used to calculate the cost ratio.

Begin by assuming that net sales are 100%, then subtract the gross profit margin, say 40%, to produce a cost ratio of 60%: 100% − 40% = 60%. A monthly COGS calculation then looks like this:

Inventory at beginning of month	£10,000
Purchases during month	+ £25,000
Cost of goods available for sale	= £35,000
Less net sales during month	− £28,000
Cost ratio 100% − 40%	= 60%
Estimated cost of goods sold	= £16,800
	(£28,000
	× 60%)

Calculating COGS for manufacturers requires additional factors, such as those shown in the following example:

Inventory at beginning of year	£20,000
Purchases during year	+ £50,000
Cost of direct labour	+ £15,000
Materials and supplies	+ £12,000
Misc. costs	+ £3,000
Total product expenses	= £100,000
Less inventory at year end	− £15,000
Cost of goods sold (COGS)	= £85,000

TRICKS OF THE TRADE

- Anyone who wants to determine COGS must maintain inventories and know their value!
- Because goods returned affect inventory values and, in turn, cost of goods sold, returns of goods must be reflected in COGS calculations.
- Merchandising firms may use different inventory accounting systems, but the choice has no bearing on the actual costs incurred; it only affects allocation of costs.
- COGS should not include indirect costs like administration and marketing costs, or other activities that cannot be directly attributed to producing or acquiring the product.

RECOMMENDED LINK
Biz/ed:
www.bized.ac.uk

SEE ALSO
Accounting (p. 487)

Calculating Creditor and Debtor Days

WHAT THEY MEASURE

Creditor days is a measure of the number of days on average that a company requires to pay its creditors, while debtor days is a measure of the number of days on average that it takes a company to receive payment for what it sells. It is also called accounts receivable days.

WHY THEY ARE IMPORTANT

Creditor days is an indication of a company's creditworthiness in the eyes of its suppliers and creditors, since it shows how long they are willing to wait for payment. Within reason, the higher the number the better, because all companies want to conserve cash. At the same time, a company that is especially slow to pay its bills (100 or more days, for example) may be a company having trouble generating cash, or one trying to finance its operations with its suppliers' funds. Ultimately, companies whose creditor days soar have trouble obtaining supplies.

Debtor days is an indication of a company's efficiency in collecting monies owed. In this case, obviously, the lower the number the better. An especially high number is a telltale sign of inefficiency or worse. It may indicate bad debts, dubious sales figures, or a company being bullied by large customers out to improve their own cash position at another firm's expense. Customers whose credit terms are abused also risk higher borrowing costs and related charges.

Changes in both measures are easy to spot, and easy to understand.

HOW THEY WORK IN PRACTICE

To determine creditor days, divide the cumulative amount of unpaid suppliers' bills (also called trade creditors) by sales, then multiply by 365. So the formula is:

(trade creditors / sales) × 365 = creditor days

For example, if suppliers' bills total £800,000 and sales are £9,000,000, the calculation is:

(800,000 / 9,000,000) × 365 = 32.44 days

The company takes 32.44 days on average to pay its bills.

To determine debtor days, divide the cumulative amount of accounts receivable by sales, then multiply by 365. For example, if accounts receivable total £600,000 and sales are £9,000,000, the calculation is:

(600,000 / 9,000,000) × 365 = 24.33 days

The company takes 24.33 days on average to collect its debts.

TRICKS OF THE TRADE

- Cash businesses, including most retailers, should have a much lower debtor days figure than non-cash businesses, since they receive payment when they sell the goods. A typical target for non-cash businesses is 40–50 days.
- An abnormally high creditor days figure may not only suggest a cash crisis, but also the management's difficulty in maintaining revolving credit agreements.
- An increasing number of debtor days also suggests overly generous credit terms (to bolster sales) or problems with product quality.

RECOMMENDED LINK

Global Investor:
www.finance-glossary.com

SEE ALSO

Accounting (p. 487)

Calculating Current Ratio

WHAT IT MEASURES
A company's liquidity and its ability to meet its short-term debt obligations.

WHY IT IS IMPORTANT
By comparing a company's current assets with its current liabilities, the current ratio reflects its ability to pay its upcoming bills in the unlikely event of all creditors demanding payment at once. It has long been the measurement of choice among financial institutions and lenders.

HOW IT WORKS IN PRACTICE
The current ratio formula is simply:

current assets / current liabilities = current ratio

Current assets are the ones that a company can turn into cash within 12 months during the ordinary course of business. Current liabilities are bills due to be paid within the coming 12 months.

For example, if a company's current assets are £300,000 and its current liabilities are £200,000, its current ratio would be:

300,000 / 200,000 = 1.5

As a rule of thumb, the 1.5 figure means that a company should be able to get hold of £1.50 for every £1.00 it owes.

TRICKS OF THE TRADE
- The higher the ratio, the more liquid the company. Prospective lenders expect a positive current ratio, often of at least 1.5. However, too high a ratio is also cause for alarm, because it indicates declining receivables and/or inventory—signs that portend declining liquidity.

- A current ratio of less than 1 suggests pressing liquidity problems, specifically an inability to generate sufficient cash to meet upcoming demands.

- Managements use current ratio as well as lenders; a low ratio, for example, may indicate the need to refinance a portion of short-term debt with long-term debt to improve a company's liquidity.

- Ratios vary by industry, however, and should be used accordingly. Some sectors, such as supermarket chains and restaurants, perform nicely with low ratios that would keep others awake at night.

- One shortcoming of the current ratio is that it does not differentiate assets, some of which may not be easily converted to cash. As a result, lenders also refer to the quick ratio.

- Another shortcoming of the current ratio is that it reflects conditions at a single point in time, such as when the balance sheet is prepared. It is possible to make this figure look good just for this occasion: lenders should not, therefore, appraise these conditions by the ratio alone.

- A constant current ratio and falling quick ratio signal trouble ahead, because this suggests that a company is amassing assets at the expense of receivables and cash.

RECOMMENDED LINK
Business Owner's Toolkit:
www.toolkit.cch.com

SEE ALSO
Accounting (p. 487)

Calculating Days Sales Outstanding

WHAT IT MEASURES

A company's average collection period, or the average number of days it takes a firm to convert its accounts receivable into cash. It is also called the collection ratio.

WHY IT IS IMPORTANT

Knowing how long it takes a company to turn accounts receivable into cash is an important financial indicator. It indicates the efficiency of the company's internal collection, suggests how well a company's customers are accepting its credit terms (net 30 days, for example), and is a figure that is routinely compared with industry averages.

Ideally, DSOs should be decreasing or constant. A low figure means the company collects its outstanding receivables quickly. Typically, DSO is reviewed quarterly or yearly (91 or 365 days).

DSO also helps to expose companies that try to disguise weak sales. Large increases in DSO suggest that a company is trying to force sales either by accepting poor receivable terms or selling products at discount to book more sales for a particular period. An improving DSO suggests that a company is striving to make its operations more efficient.

Any company with a significant change in its DSO merits examination in greater detail.

HOW IT WORKS IN PRACTICE

Regular DSO requires three figures: total accounts receivable, total credit sales for the period analysed, and the number of days in the period (annual, 365; six months, 182; quarter, 91). The formula is:

accounts receivable / total credit sales for the period × number of days in the period = days sales outstanding

For example: if total receivables are £4,500,000, total credit sales in a quarter are £9,000,000, and number of days is 91, then:

4,500,000 / 9,000,000 × 91 = 45.5

Thus, it takes an average 45.5 days to collect receivables.

TRICKS OF THE TRADE

- Companies use DSO information with an accounts receivable ageing report. This lists four categories of receivables: 0–30 days, 30–60, 60–90, and over 90 days. The report also shows the percentage of total accounts receivable that each group represents, allowing for an analysis of delinquencies and potential bad debts—a figure that appears on a profit and loss account.
- A rarely used related calculation, best possible DSO, shows how long it takes a company to collect current receivables:

  current receivables / total credit sales for the period × the number of days in the period = best possible DSO

  So, current receivables of £3,000,000 and total credit sales of £9,000,000 in a 91-day period would result in a best possible DSO of 30.3 days (3,000,000 / 9,000,000 × 91).
- Only credit sales of merchandise should be used in calculating DSO; cash sales are excluded, as are sales of such items as fixtures, equipment, or land and property.
- Properly evaluating an acceptable DSO requires a standard for comparison. A traditional rule of thumb is that DSO should not exceed a third to a half of selling terms. For instance, if terms are 30 days, acceptable DSO would be 40 to 45 days.
- A single DSO is only a snapshot. A fuller picture requires at least quarterly calculations.
- DSO can vary widely by industry as well as company. For example, clothing wholesalers have to have the goods on retailers' shelves for months before they will be sold and the retailer is able to cover invoices. However, a computer wholesaler with a lengthy DSO suggests trouble, since computers become obsolete quickly.

RECOMMENDED LINK

Dun & Bradstreet:
www.dnbcollections.com/kdso.htm

SEE ALSO

Accounting (p. 487)

Calculating Depreciation

GETTING STARTED

Depreciation is a basic expense of doing business, reducing a company's earnings while increasing its cash flow. It affects three key financial statements: balance sheet; cash flow; and income (or profit and loss). It is based on two key facts: the purchase price of the items or property in question, and their 'useful life'.

Depreciation values and practices are governed by national tax laws, which must be monitored continuously for any changes that are made. Accounting bodies, too, have developed standard practices and procedures for calculating depreciation.

Depreciating a single asset is not difficult: the challenge lies in depreciating the many assets possessed by even small companies, and is intensified by the impact that depreciation has on income and cash-flow statements, and on income tax returns. It is essential to depreciate with care and to rely on experts, ensuring that they fully understand the current government rules and regulations.

FAQS

What is depreciation?

It is an allocation of the cost of an asset over a period of time for accounting and tax purposes. Depreciation is charged against earnings, on the basis that the use of capital assets is a legitimate cost of doing business. Depreciation is also a non-cash expense that is added into net income to determine cash flow in a given accounting period.

What is straight-line depreciation?

One of the two principal depreciation methods, it is based on the assumption that an asset loses an equal amount of its value each year of its useful life. Straight-line depreciation deducts an equal amount from a company's earnings throughout the life of the asset.

What is accelerated depreciation?

The other principal method of depreciation is based on the assumption that an asset loses a larger amount of its value in the early years of its useful life. Also known as the 'declining-balance' method, it is used by accountants to reduce a company's tax bills as soon as possible, and is calculated on the basis of the same percentage rate each year of an asset's useful life. Accelerated depreciation also better reflects the economic value of the asset being depreciated, which tends to become increasingly less efficient and more costly to maintain as it grows older.

What can be depreciated?

To qualify for depreciation, assets must:
- be used in the business
- be items that wear out, become obsolete, or lose value over time from natural causes or circumstances
- have a useful life beyond a single tax year

Examples include vehicles, machines and equipment, computers and office furnishings, and buildings, plus major additions or improvements to such assets. Some intangible assets also can be included under certain conditions.

What cannot be depreciated?

Land, personal assets, stock, leased or rented property, and a company's employees.

MAKING IT HAPPEN

In order to determine the annual depreciation cost of assets, it is necessary first to know the initial cost of those assets, how many years they will retain some value for the business, and what value, if any, they will have at the end of their useful life.

For example, a company buys a lorry to carry materials and finished goods. The vehicle loses value as soon as it is purchased, and then loses more with each year it is in service, until the cost of repairs exceeds its overall value. Measuring the loss in the value of the lorry is depreciation.

Straight-line depreciation is the most straightforward method, and is still quite common. It assumes that the net cost of an asset should be written off in equal amounts over its life. The formula used is:

(original cost – scrap value) / useful life (years)

For example, if the lorry cost £30,000 and can be expected to serve the business for seven years, its original cost would be divided by its useful life:

(30,000 – 2,000) / 7 = 4,000 per year

The £4,000 becomes a depreciation expense that is reported on the company's year-end income statement under 'operation expenses'.

In theory, an asset should be depreciated over the actual number of years that it will be used, according to its actual drop in value each year. At the end of each year, all the depreciation claimed to date is subtracted from its cost in order to arrive at its 'book value', which would equal its market value. At the end of its useful business life, any un-depreciated portion would represent the salvage value for which it could be sold or scrapped.

For tax purposes, some accountants prefer to use accelerating depreciation to record larger amounts of depreciation in the asset's early years in order to reduce tax bills as soon as possible. In contrast to the straight-line method, the declining-balance method assumes that the asset depreciates more in its earlier years of use. The table below compares the depreciation amounts that would be available, under these two methods, for a £1,000 asset that is expected to be used for five years and then sold for £100 in scrap.

While the straight-line method results in the same deduction each year, the declining balance method produces larger deductions in the first years and far smaller deductions in the later years. One result of this system is that, if the equipment is expected to be sold for a higher value at some point in the middle of its life, the declining-balance method can produce a greater taxable gain in that year because the book value of the asset will be relatively lower.

The depreciation method to be used for a particular asset is fixed at the time that the asset is first placed in service. Whatever rules or tables are in effect for that year must be followed as long as the asset is owned.

Depreciation laws and regulations change frequently over the years as a result of government policy changes, so a company owning property over a long period may have to use several different depreciation methods.

Declining-balance Method

Year	Annual Depreciation	Year-end Book Value
1	£1,000 40% = £400	£1,000 – £400 = £600
2	£600 40% = £240	£600 – £240 = £360
3	£360 40% = £144	£360 – £144 = £216
4	£216 40% = £86.40	£216 – £86.40 = £129.60
5	£129.60 40% = £51.84	£129.60 – £51.84 = £77.76

Straight-line Method

Year	Annual Depreciation	Year-end Book Value
1	£900 20% = £180	£1,000 – £180 = £820
2	£900 20% = £180	£820 – £180 = £640
3	£900 20% = £180	£640 – £180 = £460
4	£900 20% = £180	£460 – £180 = £280
5	£900 20% = £180	£280 – £180 = £100

TRICKS OF THE TRADE

- With rare exceptions, it is not possible to deduct in one year the entire cost of an asset if that asset has a useful life substantially beyond the tax year.
- To qualify for depreciation, an asset must be put into service. Simply purchasing it is not enough. There are rules that govern how much depreciation can be claimed on items put into service after a year has begun.
- It is common knowledge that if a company claims more depreciation than it is entitled to, it is liable for stiff penalties in a tax audit, just as failure to allow for depreciation causes an overestimation of income. What is not commonly known is that if a company does not claim all the depreciation deductions it is entitled to, it will be considered as having claimed them when taxable gains or losses are eventually calculated on the sale or disposal of the asset in question.
- While leased property cannot be depreciated, the cost of making permanent improvements to leased property can be (refurbishing a leased office, for example). There are many rules governing leased assets; they should be depreciated with care.
- Another common mistake is to continue depreciating property beyond the end of its recovery period. Cars are common examples of this.
- Conservative companies depreciate many assets as quickly as possible, despite the fact that this practice reduces reported net income. Knowledgeable investors watch carefully for such practices.

RECOMMENDED LINKS

Business Owner's Toolkit:
www.toolkit.cch.com
Encyclopedia.com:
www.encyclopedia.com

SEE ALSO

Accounting (p. 487)
Calculating Amortisation (p. 177)

Calculating EBITDA

WHAT IT MEASURES
A company's earnings from ongoing operations, before net income is calculated. The acronym stands for 'earnings before interest, tax, depreciation, and amortisation'.

WHY IT IS IMPORTANT
EBITDA's champions contend it gives investors a sense of how much money a young or fast-growing company is generating before it pays interest on debt, tax collection, and accounts for non-cash changes. If EBITDA grows over time, champions argue, investors gain at least a sense of long-term profitability and, in turn, the wisdom of their investment.

Business appraisers and investors also may study EBITDA to help gauge a company's fair market value, often as a prelude to its acquisition by another company. It also is frequently applied to companies that have been subject to leveraged buyouts—the strategy being that EBITDA will help cover loan payments needed to finance the transaction.

EBITDA, and EBIT, too, are claimed to be good indicators of cash flow from business operations, since they report earnings before debt payments, taxes, depreciation, and amortisation charges are considered. However, that claim is challenged by many—often rather intently.

HOW IT WORKS IN PRACTICE
EBITDA first appeared as leveraged buyouts soared in popularity during the 1980s.

Its formula is quite simple. Revenues less the cost of goods sold, general and administrative expenses, and the deductions of items expressed by the acronym, or:

revenue – expenses (excluding tax and interest, depreciation, etc.) = EBITDA

or:

revenue – expenses (excluding tax and interest) = EBIT

This formula does not measure true cash flow. A communications company, for example, once reported £698 million in EBIT but just £324 million in cash from operations.

TRICKS OF THE TRADE
- A definition of EBITDA isn't as yet enforced by standards-making bodies, so companies can all but create their own. As a result, EBITDA can easily be manipulated by aggressive accounting policies, which may erode its reliability.
- Ignoring capital expenditures could be unrealistic and horribly misleading, because companies in capital-intensive sectors such as manufacturing and transportation must continually make major capital investments to remain competitive. High-technology is another sector that may be capital-intensive, at least initially.
- Critics warn that using EBITDA as a cash-flow indicator is a huge mistake, because EBITDA ignores too many factors that have an impact on true cash flow, such as working capital, debt payments and other fixed expenses. Interest and taxes can and do cost a company cash, they point out, while debt holders have higher claims on a company's liquid assets than investors do.
- Critics further assail EBITDA as the barometer of choice of unprofitable firms because it can present an overly optimistic view of a company's future. *Forbes* magazine once referred to EBITDA as 'the device of choice to pep up earnings announcements'.
- Even so, EBITDA may be useful in terms of evaluating firms in the same industry with widely different capital structures, tax rates and depreciation policies.

RECOMMENDED LINK
The Motley Fool UK:
www.fool.co.uk

SEE ALSO
Accounting (p. 487)

Calculating Economic Value Added

WHAT IT MEASURES
A company's financial performance, specifically whether it is earning more or less than the total cost of the capital supporting it.

WHY IT IS IMPORTANT
Economic Value Added measures true economic profit, or the amount by which the earnings of a project, an operation, or a company exceed (or fall short of) the total amount of capital that was originally invested by the company's owners.

If a company is earning more it is adding value, and that is good. If it is earning less the company is in fact devouring value, and that is bad, because the company's owners (shareholders, for example) would be better off investing their capital elsewhere.

The concept's champions declare that EVA forces managers to focus on true wealth creation and maximising shareholder investment. By definition, then, increasing EVA will increase a company's market value.

HOW IT WORKS IN PRACTICE
EVA is conceptually simple and easy to explain: from net operating profit, subtract an appropriate charge for the opportunity cost of all capital invested in an enterprise—the amount that could have been invested elsewhere. It is calculated using this formula:

net operating profit less applicable taxes – cost of capital = EVA

If a company is considering building a new plant, and its total weighted cost over ten years is £8 million, while the expected annual incremental return on the new operation is £1 million, or £10 million over ten years, then the plant's EVA would be positive, in this case £2 million:

£10 million – £8 million = £2 million

An alternative but more complex formula for EVA is:

(% return on invested capital – % cost of capital) × original capital invested = EVA

TRICKS OF THE TRADE
- EVA is a measure of pound surplus value, not the percentage difference in returns.
- Purists define EVA as 'profit the way shareholders define it'. They further contend that if shareholders expect a 10% return on their investment, they 'make money' only when their share of after-tax operating profits exceeds 10% of equity capital.
- An objective of EVA is to determine which business units best utilise their assets to generate returns and maximise shareholder value; it can be used to assess a company, a business unit, a single plant, office, or even an assembly line. This same technique is equally helpful in evaluating new business opportunities.

RECOMMENDED LINK
Stern Stewart & Co:
www.sternstewart.com

SEE ALSO
Accounting (p. 487)

Calculating Elasticity

WHAT IT MEASURES
The percentage change of one variable caused by a percentage change in another variable.

WHY IT IS IMPORTANT
Elasticity is defined as 'the measure of the sensitivity of one variable to another'. In practical terms, elasticity indicates the degree to which consumers respond to changes in price. It is obviously important for companies to consider such relationships when contemplating changes in price, demand, and supply.

Demand elasticity measures how much the quantity demanded changes when the price of a product or service is increased or lowered. Will demand remain constant? If not, how much will demand change?

Supply elasticity measures the impact on supply when a price is changed. It is assumed that lowering prices will reduce supply, because demand will increase—but by how much?

HOW IT WORKS IN PRACTICE
The general formula for elasticity is:

elasticity = % change in x / % change in y

In theory, x and y can be any variable. However, the most common application measures price and demand. If the price of a product is increased from £20 to £25, or 25%, and demand in turn falls from 6,000 to 3,000, elasticity would be calculated as:

- 50% / 25% = - 2

A value greater than 1 means that demand is strongly sensitive to price, while a value of less than 1 means that demand is not price-sensitive.

TRICKS OF THE TRADE
There are five cases of elasticity:
- E = 1, or *unit elasticity*. The proportional change in one variable is equal to the proportional change in another variable: if price rises by 5%, demand falls by 5%.
- E is greater than 1, or just *elastic*. The proportional change in x is greater than the proportional change in y: if price rises by 5%, demand falls by 3%.
- E = infinity, or *perfectly elastic*. This is a special case of elasticity: any change in y will effect no change in x. An example would be prices charged by a hospital's emergency room, where increases in price are unlikely to curb demand.
- E is less than 1, or just *inelastic*. The proportional change in x is less than the proportional change in y: if prices are increased by 3%, demand will fall by 30%.
- E = 0, or *perfectly inelastic*. This is another special case of elasticity: any change in y will have an infinite effect on x.

There are more complex formulae for determining a range of variables, or 'arc elasticity'.

Elasticity can be used to affirm two rules of thumb:
- demand becomes elastic if consumers have an alternative or adequate substitute for the product or service
- demand is more elastic if consumers have an incentive to save money

RECOMMENDED LINK
Investopedia.com:
www.investopedia.com

SEE ALSO
Accounting (p. 487)

Calculating Interest Cover

WHAT IT MEASURES
The amount of earnings available to make interest payments after all operating and non-operating income and expenses—except interest and income taxes—have been accounted for.

WHY IT IS IMPORTANT
Interest cover is regarded as a measure of a company's creditworthiness because it shows how much income there is to cover interest payments on outstanding debt. Banks and financial analysts also rely on this ratio as a rule of thumb to gauge the fundamental strength of a business.

HOW IT WORKS IN PRACTICE
Interest cover is expressed as a ratio, and reflects a company's ability to pay the interest obligations on its debt. It compares the funds available to pay interest—earnings before interest and taxes, or EBIT—with the interest expense. The basic formula is:

EBIT / interest expense =
interest coverage ratio

If interest expense for a year is £9 million, and the company's EBIT is £45 million, the interest coverage would be:

45 million / 9 million = 5:1

The higher the number, the stronger a company is likely to be. Conversely, a low number suggests that a company's fortunes are looking ominous. Variations of this basic formula also exist. For example, there is:

operating cash flow + interest +
taxes / interest =
cash-flow interest coverage ratio

This ratio indicates the firm's ability to use its cash flow to satisfy its fixed financing obligations. Finally, there is the fixed-charge coverage ratio, which compares EBIT with fixed charges:

EBIT + lease expenses / interest +
lease expense =
fixed charge coverage ratio

'Fixed charges' can be interpreted in many ways, however. It could mean, for example, the funds that a company is obliged to set aside to retire debt, or dividends on preferred stock.

TRICKS OF THE TRADE
- A ratio of less than 1 indicates that a company is having problems generating enough cash flow to pay its interest expenses, and that either a modest decline in operating profits or a sudden rise in borrowing costs could eliminate profitability entirely.
- Ideally, interest coverage should at least exceed 1.5; in some sectors, 2.0 or higher is desirable.
- Interest coverage is widely considered to be more meaningful than looking at total debt, because what really matters is what an enterprise must pay in a given period, not how much debt it has.
- As is often the case, it may be more meaningful to watch interest cover over several periods in order to detect long-term trends.
- Cash flow will sometimes be substituted for EBIT in the ratio, because EBIT includes not only cash but also accrued sales and other unrealised income.
- Interest cover also is called 'times interest earned'.

RECOMMENDED LINK
The Motley Fool UK:
www.fool.co.uk

SEE ALSO
Accounting (p. 487)

Calculating Marginal Cost

WHAT IT MEASURES
The additional cost of producing one more unit of product, or providing service to one more customer.

WHY IT IS IMPORTANT
Sometimes called incremental cost, marginal cost shown how much costs increase from making or serving one more, an essential factor when contemplating a production increase, or seeking to serve more customers.

If the price charged is greater than the marginal cost, then the revenue gain will be greater than the added cost. That, in turn, will increase profit, so the expansion in production or service makes economic sense and should proceed. Of course, the reverse is also true: if the price charged is less than the marginal cost, expansion should not go ahead.

HOW IT WORKS IN PRACTICE
The formula for marginal cost is:

change in cost / change in quantity

If it costs a company £260,000 to produce 3,000 items, and £325,000 to produce 3,800 items, the change in cost would be:

£325,000 – £260,000 = £65,000

The change in quantity would be:

3,800 – 3,000 = 800

When the formula to calculate marginal cost is applied, the result is:

£65,000 / 800 = £81.25

If the price of the item in question were £99.95, expansion should proceed.

TRICKS OF THE TRADE
- A marginal cost that is lower than the price shows that it is not always necessary to cut prices to sell more goods and boost profits.
- Using idle capacity to produce lower-margin items can still be beneficial, because these generate revenues that help cover fixed costs.
- Marginal cost studies can become quite complicated, because the basic formula does not always take into account variables that can affect cost and quantity. There are software programs available, many of which are industry-specific.
- At some point, marginal cost invariably begins to rise; typically, labour becomes less productive as a production run increases, while the time required also increases.
- Marginal cost alone may not justify expansion. It is best to determine also average costs, then chart the respective series of figures to find where marginal cost meets average cost, and thus determine optimum cost.
- Relying on marginal cost is not fail-safe; putting more product on a market can drive down prices and thus cut margins. Moreover, committing idle capacity to long-term production may tie up resources that could be directed to a new and more profitable opportunity.
- An important related principle is contribution: the cash gained (or lost) from selling an additional unit.

RECOMMENDED LINK
The Motley Fool UK:
www.fool.co.uk

SEE ALSO
Accounting (p. 487)

Calculating Payback Period

WHAT IT MEASURES
The length of time it will take to earn back the money invested in a project.

WHY IT IS IMPORTANT
The straight payback period method is the simplest way of determining the investment potential of a major project.

Expressed in time, it tells a management how many months or years it will take to recover the original cash cost of the project—always a vital consideration, and especially so for managements evaluating several projects at once.

This evaluation becomes even more important if it includes an examination of what the present value of future revenues will be.

HOW IT WORKS IN PRACTICE
The straight payback period formula is:

cost of project / annual cash revenues = payback period

Thus, if a project cost £100,000 and was expected to generate £28,000 annually, the payback period would be:

100,000 / 28,000 = 3.57 years

If the revenues generated by the project are expected to vary from year to year, add the revenues expected for each succeeding year until you arrive at the total cost of the project.

For example, say the revenues expected to be generated by the £100,000 project are:

	Revenue	Total
Year 1	£19,000	£19,000
Year 2	£25,000	£44,000
Year 3	£30,000	£74,000
Year 4	£30,000	£104,000
Year 5	£30,000	£134,000

Thus, the project would be fully paid for in Year 4, since it is in that year the total revenue reaches the initial cost of £100,000.

The picture becomes complex when the time-value-of-money principle is introduced into the calculations. Some experts insist this is essential to determine the most accurate payback period. Accordingly, present-value tables or computers (now the norm) must be used, and the annual revenues have to be discounted by the applicable interest rate, 10% in this example. Doing so produces significantly different results:

	Revenue	Present Value	Total
Year 1	£19,000	£17,271	£17,271
Year 2	£25,000	£20,650	£37,921
Year 3	£30,000	£22,530	£60,451
Year 4	£30,000	£20,490	£80,941
Year 5	£30,000	£18,630	£99,571

This method shows that payback would not occur even after five years.

TRICKS OF THE TRADE
- Clearly, a main defect of the straight payback period method is that it ignores the time-value-of-money principle, which, in turn, can produce unrealistic expectations. Put simply, this theory states that £1 now is worth more than £1 in the future—everyone wants their money sooner rather than later!
- A second drawback is that it ignores any benefits generated after the payback period, and thus a project that would return £1 million after, say, six years, might be ranked lower than a project with a three-year payback that returns only £100,000 thereafter.
- Another alternative to calculating by payback period is to develop an internal rate of return. This basically indicates whether an investment is worth pursuing.
- Under most analyses, projects with shorter payback periods rank higher than those with longer paybacks, even if the latter

project higher returns. Longer paybacks can be affected by such factors as market changes, changes in interest rates, and economic shifts. Shorter cash paybacks also enable companies to recoup an investment sooner and put it to work elsewhere.

- Generally, a payback period of three years or less is desirable; if a project's payback period is less than a year, some contend it should be judged essential.

RECOMMENDED LINK
Business Owner's Toolkit:
www.toolkit.cch.com

SEE ALSO
Accounting (p. 487)

Calculating Return on Assets

WHAT IT MEASURES

A company's profitability, expressed as a percentage of its total assets.

WHY IT IS IMPORTANT

Return on assets measures how effectively a company has used the total assets at its disposal to generate earnings. Because the ROA formula reflects total revenue, total cost, and assets deployed, the ratio itself reflects a management's ability to generate income during the course of a given period, usually a year.

Naturally, the higher the return the better the profit performance. ROA is a convenient way of comparing a company's performance with that of its competitors, although the items on which the comparison is based may not always be identical.

HOW IT WORKS IN PRACTICE

To calculate ROA, divide a company's net income by its total assets, then multiply by 100 to express the figure as a percentage:

net income / total assets $\times$ 100 = ROA

If net income is £30, and total assets are £420, the ROA is:

30 / 420 = 0.0714 $\times$ 100 = 7.14%

A variation of this formula can be used to calculate return on net assets (RONA):

net income / fixed assets + working capital = RONA

And, on occasion, the formula will separate after-tax interest expense from net income:

net income + interest expense / total assets = ROA

It is therefore important to understand what each component of the formula actually represents.

TRICKS OF THE TRADE

- Some experts recommend using the net income value at the end of the given period, and the assets value from beginning of the period or an average value taken over the complete period, rather than an end-of-the-period value; otherwise, the calculation will include assets that have accumulated during the year, which can be misleading.
- While a high ratio indicates a greater return, it must still be balanced against such factors as risk, sustainability, and reinvestment in the business through development costs. Some managements will sacrifice the long-term interests of investors in order to achieve an impressive ROA in the short term.
- A climbing return on assets usually indicates a climbing stock price, because it tells investors that a management is skilled at generating profits from the resources that a business owns.
- Acceptable ROAs vary by sector. In banking, for example, a ROA of 1% or better is a considered to be the standard benchmark of superior performance.
- ROA is an effective way of measuring the efficiency of manufacturers, but can be suspect when measuring service firms, or companies whose primary assets are people.
- Other variations of the ROA formula do exist.

RECOMMENDED LINK

MSN Money:
www.moneycentral.msn.com/investor

SEE ALSO

Accounting (p. 487)

Calculating Return on Investment

WHAT IT MEASURES

In the financial realm, the overall profit or loss on an investment expressed as a percentage of the total amount invested or total funds appearing on a company's balance sheet.

WHY IT IS IMPORTANT

Like return on assets or return on equity, return on investment measures a company's profitability and its management's ability to generate profits from the funds investors have placed at its disposal.

One opinion holds that if a company's operations cannot generate net earnings at a rate that exceeds the cost of borrowing funds from financial markets, the future of that company is grim.

HOW IT WORKS IN PRACTICE

The most basic expression of ROI can be found by dividing a company's net profit (also called net earnings) by the total investment (total debt plus total equity), then multiplying by 100 to arrive at a percentage:

net profit / total investment $\times$ 100 = ROI

If, say, net profit is £30 and total investment is £250, the ROI is:

30 / 250 = 0.12 $\times$ 100 = 12 %

A more complex variation of ROI is an equation known as the Du Pont formula:

**(net profit after taxes / total assets) =
(net profit after taxes / sales) $\times$
sales / total assets**

If, for example, net profit after taxes is £30, total assets are £250, and sales are £500, then:

**30 / 250 = 30 / 500 $\times$ 500 / 250 =
12% = 6% 2 = 12%**

Champions of this formula, which was developed by the Du Pont Company in the 1920s, say that it helps reveal how a company has both deployed its assets and controlled its costs, and how it can achieve the same percentage return in different ways.

For shareholders, the variation of the basic ROI formula used by investors is:

**net income + (current value –
original value) / original value $\times$
100 = ROI**

If, for example, somebody invests £5,000 in a company and a year later has earned £100 in dividends, while the value of the shares is £5,200, the return on investment would be:

**100 + (5,200 – 5,000) / 5,000 $\times$ 100
= (100 + 200) / 5,000 $\times$ 100 =
300 / 5,000 = .06 $\times$ 100 = 6% ROI**

TRICKS OF THE TRADE

- Securities investors can use yet another ROI formula: net income divided by shares and preference share equity plus long-term debt.
- It is vital to understand exactly what a return on investment measures, for example assets, equity, or sales. Without this understanding, comparisons may be misleading or suspect. A search for 'return on investment' on the web, for example, harvests everything from staff training to e-commerce to advertising and promotions!
- Be sure to establish whether the net profit figure used is before or after provision for taxes. This is important for making ROI comparisons accurate.

RECOMMENDED LINK

Investopedia.com:
www.investopedia.com

SEE ALSO

Accounting (p. 487)

Calculating Return on Sales

WHAT IT MEASURES

A company's operating profit or loss as a percentage of total sales for a given period, typically a year.

WHY IT IS IMPORTANT

ROS shows how efficiently management uses the sales pound, thus reflecting its ability to manage costs and overheads and operate efficiently. It also indicates a firm's ability to withstand adverse conditions such as falling prices, rising costs, or declining sales. The higher the figure, the better a company is able to endure price wars and falling prices.

Return on sales can be useful in assessing the annual performances of cyclical companies that may have no earnings during particular months, and of firms whose business requires a huge capital investment and thus incurs substantial amounts of depreciation.

HOW IT WORKS IN PRACTICE

The calculation is very basic:

operating profit / total sales × 100 = percentage return on sales

So, if a company earns £30 on sales of £400, its return on sales is:

30 / 400 = 0.075 × 100 = 7.5%

TRICKS OF THE TRADE

- While easy to grasp, return on sales has its limits, since it sheds no light on the overall cost of sales or the four factors that contribute to it: materials, labour, production overheads, and administrative and selling overheads.
- Some calculations use operating profit before subtracting interest and taxes; others use after-tax income. Either figure is acceptable as long as ROS comparisons are consistent. Obviously, using income before interest and taxes will produce a higher ratio.
- The ratio's operating profit figure may also include special allowances and extraordinary non-recurring items, which, in turn, can inflate the percentage and be misleading.
- The ratio varies widely by industry. The supermarket business, for example, is heavily dependent on volume and usually has a low return on sales.
- Return on sales remains of special importance to retail sales organisations, which can compare their respective ratios with those of competitors and industry norms.

RECOMMENDED LINK

Investopedia.com:
www.investopedia.com

SEE ALSO

Accounting (p. 487)

Calculating Working Capital Productivity

WHAT IT MEASURES
How effectively a company's management is using its working capital.

WHY IT IS IMPORTANT
It is obvious that capital not being put to work properly is being wasted, which is certainly not in investors' best interests.

As an expression of how effectively a company spends its available funds compared with sales or turnover, the working capital productivity figure helps establish a clear relationship between its financial performance and process improvement. The relationship is said to have been first observed by the US management consultant George Stalk while working in Japan.

A seldom-used reciprocal calculation, the working capital turnover or working capital to sales ratio, expresses the same relationship in a different way.

HOW IT WORKS IN PRACTICE
To calculate working capital productivity, first subtract current liabilities from current assets, which is the formula for working capital, then divide this figure into sales for the period.

$$\textbf{sales / (current assets – current liabilities) = working capital productivity}$$

If sales are £3,250, current assets are £900 and current liabilities are £650, then:

$$\textbf{3250 / (900 – 650) = 3250 / 250 = 13}$$

In this case, the higher the number the better. Sales growing faster than the resources required to generate them is a clear sign of efficiency and, by definition, productivity.

The working capital to sales ratio uses the same figures, but in reverse:

$$\textbf{working capital / sales} \times \textbf{100\% = working capital to sales ratio}$$

Using the same figures in the example above, this ratio would be calculated:

$$\textbf{250 / 3250 = 0.077} \times \textbf{100\% = 7.7\%}$$

For this ratio, obviously, the lower the number the better.

TRICKS OF THE TRADE
- By itself, a single ratio means little; a series of them, several quarters' worth, for example, indicates a trend, and means a great deal.
- Some experts recommend doing quarterly calculations and averaging them for a given year to arrive at the most reliable number.
- Either ratio also helps a management compare its performance with that of competitors.
- These ratios should also help motivate companies to improve processes, such as eliminating steps in the handling of materials and bill collection, and shortening product design times. Such improvements reduce costs and make working capital available for other tasks.

RECOMMENDED LINK
The Motley Fool UK:
www.fool.co.uk

SEE ALSO
Accounting (p. 487)

Defining Assets

WHAT THEY MEASURE

Collectively, the value of all the resources a company uses to conduct business and generate profits.

Examples of assets are cash, marketable securities, accounts and notes receivable, inventories of merchandise, buildings and property, machinery and office equipment, natural resources, and intangibles such as patents, legal claims and agreements, and negotiated rights.

WHY THEY ARE IMPORTANT

No business can continue for very long without knowing what assets it has at its disposal, and using them efficiently. Assets are a reflection of organisational strength, and are invariably evaluated by potential investors, banks and creditors, and other stakeholders.

Moreover, the value of assets is also a key figure used to calculate several financial ratios.

HOW THEY WORK IN PRACTICE

Assets are typically broken down into five different categories:

- Current assets. These include cash, cash equivalents, marketable securities, inventories, and prepaid expenses that are expected to be used within one year or a normal operating cycle. All cash items and inventories are reported at historical value. Securities are reported at market value.
- Non-current assets, or long-term investments. These are resources that are expected to be held for more than one year. They are reported at the lower of cost and current market value, which means that their values will vary.
- Fixed assets. These include property, plants and facilities, and equipment used to conduct business. These items are reported at their original value, even though current values might well be much higher.

- Intangible assets. These include legal claims, patents, franchise rights, and accounts receivable. These values can be more difficult to determine. FR10, published by the Accounting Standards Board of the Institute of Chartered Accountants for England and Wales is essential reading for dealing with this issue.
- Deferred charges. These include prepaid costs and other expenditures that will produce future revenue or benefits.

TRICKS OF THE TRADE

- Assets do not necessarily include everything of value, such as the talents of individuals, an organisation's collective expertise, or the value of a customer base.
- Classic definitions of assets also often exclude or undervalue trademarks, even though there is universal agreement that these, for example, the three-point star of Mercedes-Benz or Coca-Cola's red logo, can have enormous value.
- Fixed assets are valued at their original cost, because of the prevailing opinion that they are used for business and are not for sale. Moreover, current market value is essentially a matter of opinion.
- Determining the value of patents can be challenging, because a patent has a finite lifespan, its value declines each year, and its useful life may be even shorter.
- Some experts contend that the principal assets of 'knowledge-based' businesses such as consulting firms or property development companies are, in fact, its people. In turn, their aggregate value should be calculated by subtracting the net value of assets from market value.

RECOMMENDED LINK

Investorwords.com:
www.investorwords.com

SEE ALSO

Accounting (p. 487)

MARKETING YOUR IDEA

Choosing Your Marketing Strategy

GETTING STARTED

Defining and implementing a rock solid marketing strategy is probably the single most important factor that will contribute towards the long-term sustainable success of any business venture, yet most businesses don't have one. Even if businesses do have a strategy, it is often then not followed and implemented 100% from top to bottom. For that reason, small businesses that do have the vision to create a dynamic, customer-focused marketing strategy, and also the determination to implement it, usually have the competitive edge. It is these businesses that will have a real opportunity to do something special. They will create the 'buzz' that will set them apart from their competitors.

This actionlist gives more information about how to choose, implement, and maintain a dynamic marketing strategy. A book that you may find useful to read on the subject is *101 Ways to Market Your Business*, written by Andrew Griffiths, and published by Allen & Unwin.

FAQS

What is a marketing strategy?

Having a marketing strategy is different from having a marketing plan. A marketing strategy involves choosing a realistic, measurable, and ambitious goal that you think your business can achieve on a sustainable basis. With a marketing strategy, each marketing tactic you use is 100% focused on reaching and surpassing that overall goal.

What is a marketing plan?

A marketing plan will include all of the tactics and actions that are designed to achieve the overall strategic goal. It will also include a timetable for their implementation. In other words, the plan will detail what you will do to make the strategy happen.

Why don't most businesses have a strategy?

The vast majority of businesses in all sectors market themselves in the same way as their competitors. They use supply-driven marketing messages based on product features; they design unfathomable websites; they create bland straplines and statements about what their business does. They do this because it is easy. Businesses also do this because their owners/managers know their products and services better than anyone else; as a result, they promote themselves in terms that they understand, but that their customers don't. They also do it because they look at what their competitors are doing and fall into the trap of doing the same things. Instead, what they should be doing is differentiating themselves by creating a unique proposition that gives them a real competitive edge.

MAKING IT HAPPEN
Set your sights

The first thing to do is to decide on your ultimate goal. Every business will have different strategic objectives for its own specific situation. No matter how high you set your sights, your marketing strategy should drive everything that your business does to achieve that objective.

You might aim to double turnover in twelve months; to maximise the value of your business in three years in order to sell it; or to increase your market share three fold in six months. You will only make the most of your chances of achieving or surpassing your goal by following a well thought out, meticulously implemented marketing strategy. With your business's marketing efforts accurately aimed and 100% focused on the needs of the target market, you are far more likely to succeed. If the aim is wrong, and your understanding of the market is wrong, you will achieve mediocrity, or fail altogether.

Choose the right marketing strategy

Your business can achieve competitive advantage if it chooses a marketing strategy that sets your business apart from everyone else. There is no magic formula for doing this. You cannot just import or implant an off-the-shelf strategy into a business. It is down to you to choose and define your marketing strategy in your own business situation.

However, there are a number of key factors that will help you choose the right strategy. You need to know exactly who your customers or target prospects are, and where they are located. You also need to know exactly what these people want and need, why they need it, how they need it, and when they need it. You will have to be confident enough to develop or create a unique selling proposition (USP) that you can offer to completely fulfil your customers' needs. You must then ensure that you test your proposition in your chosen market first. Once the proposition is tested, you will need to analyse the results, and use them to refine the proposition until you are sure it is right.

Implement your strategy

You should only attempt to implement your strategy fully when you are absolutely sure that your unique selling proposition is right. Your task then is to get your message across to your market. You need to ensure that your unique selling proposition is articulated in all of your marketing messages, campaigns, and sales channels. It is important that you recognise when your proposition is working so that you can then market it fast, first, and aggressively in your sector. Only in this way will you achieve an unassailable lead over your competitors.

Keep ahead of the game

In the 1990s everyone spoke about being 'market-led'. Today, market conditions change at bewildering speed. Any number of factors can play a part in this, including technology, customers' tastes, fashions, trends, media influences, and so on. If you want your business to survive in the 21st century, you must make the right choice of target market. You then need to focus everything the business does on providing unique value and benefits to meet the needs of that chosen market, and you need to do this better than your competitors.

Your business and your marketing strategy cannot stand still. What is unique today is widespread tomorrow, and unwanted the day after that. The vital ingredient in a truly dynamic marketing strategy is to strive continually to discover new and better ways to add value for your customers, and keep your proposition unique in your chosen market.

Every single time you put your strategy into action, you will also learn something new about your customers' needs, and whether your proposition is right for them. The implementation of your marketing strategy should be a continuous process of creating a proposition to satisfy your customers; testing it; and learning from it. You can learn from it by recognising what is right and doing more of it, or changing what is wrong as soon as you realise it isn't working.

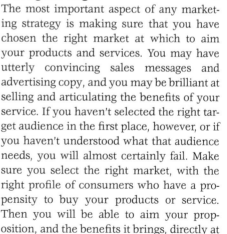

WHAT TO AVOID
Missing the target

The most important aspect of any marketing strategy is making sure that you have chosen the right market at which to aim your products and services. You may have utterly convincing sales messages and advertising copy, and you may be brilliant at selling and articulating the benefits of your service. If you haven't selected the right target audience in the first place, however, or if you haven't understood what that audience needs, you will almost certainly fail. Make sure you select the right market, with the right profile of consumers who have a propensity to buy your products or service. Then you will be able to aim your proposition, and the benefits it brings, directly at them.

Standing still

To succeed in your market you need to keep up to date with changes in customer preference and buying patterns. You also need to keep up with the seemingly relentless changes in technology and other external forces. If you don't make the effort to move forward constantly, your competitors will steal your market share, your biggest customers, or your intended new market, before you have a chance to do anything about it.

Lack of focus

The biggest mistake is to stop focusing on your market. You have to ensure that you are continuing to provide the unique value and benefit your customers need and expect from your service. Take your eye off the marketing ball for a second, and your strategy will fall flat on its face.

RECOMMENDED LINKS

Business Link:
www.businesslink.org
Chartered Institute of Marketing:
www.cim.co.uk
Internet marketing:
www.it-advice.org

SEE ALSO

Market Research and Competitor Intelligence (p. 526)
Profiling Your Competitors (p. 218)
Researching the Size of Your Market (p. 209)

Researching the Size of Your Market

GETTING STARTED

It's important to find out what potential your business has to generate revenues and profits in your chosen market sector, and the only way to do this is to carry out thorough market research. The better the data you have about your market, the better equipped you will be to make informed decisions about your business. Good market research will help you establish the most important objective of all—in other words, your sales targets. Your financial backers, business partners, key staff, and other key stake holders will also have a keen, if not vested, interest in your sales potential and the market share you believe you can realistically achieve.

Before you can estimate the share of the market you want to attain, you'll need to have researched the *overall* size of the market. Its size could be calculated in terms of its volume (that is to say, the number of buyers), and its value (in terms of annual total spend), or both. This actionlist will help you to do this. A book which you may find useful on the subject is *Marketing Research Toolbox: A Concise Guide for Beginners*, published by Sage Publications.

FAQS

What do I need to know about my customer group?

Assuming you have already accurately profiled the customer group that you consider to be your ideal market audience, you need to know how many potential buyers the group consists of, and how much they currently spend.

What else do I need to know before I set my sales targets?

Once you have found out how many potential buyers you have, and how much they spend at the moment, you need to find out whether your market is growing or declining. You then need to decide what sales levels you are going to aim for.

MAKING IT HAPPEN

Find out the number of potential buyers

Your target audience will comprise groups of businesses, groups of individuals, or both. Calculating the size of this overall market, that is to say the number of people who could potentially buy from you, will only be possible once you have considered who they are, their unique characteristics, and where they are located. It may be the case in your business situation that your potential customers live close to you. For example, you may offer a service that people generally will travel only a short distance to purchase.

For some services, people are prepared to travel a reasonable distance, for example, up to an hour, to buy something. In other instances, distance is not an issue, as consumers will purchase by mail order or via the Internet.

You need to ask yourself whether location or proximity to your service is an issue for your target audience. This will help you to scope the potential size of your market when you add this factor into the profile of your customers' buying characteristics. This is important to help you target the number of buyers you think you can reach with your marketing.

Research how much buyers spend in the market

Establishing how many buyers there are for your service is only part of the equation. You will also need to understand how much these buyers are prepared to spend on a product or service such as yours, in terms of each time they buy, and in terms of how frequently they buy.

Knowing your market size is meaningless unless you can attach a value to the volume of potential buyers you have. That value is also meaningless unless you understand the repeat purchase rate, in other words how many times they buy or use your service in weeks, months, or over a year. This information is vital when forecasting sales revenues for your business plan or forthcoming budget.

Establish if the market is expanding or declining

Having established the number of buyers, the amount they spend, and their frequency of purchase, you will need to understand the market potential. You should ask yourself whether your market will be the same size in six or twelve months' time. Look at the trends, to see If they suggest that your customers will be spending more, the same, or less. Try to predict whether there will be any more buyers seeking your type of product and service.

There may also be other target audiences with similar buying characteristics and needs that you will be able to access through your marketing. It is vital that you do not just settle on the information you have about the size of your market now, and miss opportunities to reach a wider audience in a year's time, without even realising it. Similarly, a trend showing a decline in the number of buyers, or their purchase rate must be identified and acted on before it is too late.

Analyse what share of your overall market you want to achieve

The target market share you set for your business will help you determine the precise marketing effort, methods, channels, and budget you require to achieve it. However, it is not as simple a matter as just having good data about the volume or value of your market, or the underlying trends. There are also your competitors' activities to take into consideration. You need to ask yourself whether there is likely to be more competition in a year's time. Find out what the trends are. Try to predict whether your competitors will have new, better value, more innovative services than yours. You will need to keep a very close eye on their marketing activities, for example, special promotions, free gifts, guarantees, after-sales service, and so on. This might give them the edge over your business, and a chance to steal a greater share of the market you have targeted or established for yourself.

Find information about market size and trends

Business and market information is available from a variety of sources. Some is free, but you will probably have to pay for more in-depth statistics, trends, and forecasts. The reference section of your local library will have a business section carrying published market reports on hundreds of sectors. They will also have government statistics, trade magazines, and national and local business directories. If they do not have the publications themselves, they should have a directory of them, together with details of their costs and where you can source them. If you want local population or business information you should contact your local council.

The Internet is also a good place to start, although if you are not an experienced researcher this could be time consuming, or you may end up not finding what you really want. However, employing one of the main search engines and carrying out a search using terms containing the name of the market sector you are in, the type of information you need, a product name, geographic area, and suppliers' or competitors' names, should bring up a good range of relevant websites for your business.

For information on market trends in the United Kingdom, try Mintel, KeyNote, or Euromonitor—or National Statistics Online gives information about statistics and trends (website addresses are given below). For details of potential business buyers, there are a number of good directories including Thomson Directories, Yellow Pages, and the British Chambers of Commerce. If you are just starting up, or are a newly established business, try Enterprise Quest. The website addresses for all of these are given below.

WHAT TO AVOID
Not being up to date

It is vitally important to ensure that your estimates of the size of your market are based on current data and trends. If you make decisions based on out-of-date information, or fail to spot the trends in your sector, you will either miss the opportunities to obtain a greater share of the overall market, or your competitors will steal your market share.

Taking your eye off the target

Do not make this research a one-off task. If you fail regularly to research what is happening to the size and structure of your market, you will lose touch with your existing audiences and potential new customers.

Failing to spot the trends

You must continually try to look at the bigger picture in your sector, and not just one particular aspect of the market, or the statistics relating to it. Look for trends in terms of potential buyers you could reach, the average value of purchase they make, and how often they are buying. Keep an eye out for new entrants in your sector, and the share of the overall market they are taking.

RECOMMENDED LINKS

Chambers of Commerce:
www.chamberonline.co.uk
Chartered Institute of Marketing:
www.cim.co.uk
Enterprise Quest:
www.enterquest.net
Euromonitor:
www.euromonitor.com
KeyNote:
www.keynote.co.uk
Mintel:
www.mintel.co.uk
National Statistics Online:
www.statistics.gov.uk
Thomson Directories:
www.thomweb.co.uk
Yellow Pages:
www.yell.com

SEE ALSO

Choosing Your Marketing Strategy (p. 206)
Market Research and Competitor Intelligence (p. 526)
Profiling Your Competitors (p. 218)

Focus On: Planning Marketing
Malcolm McDonald

GETTING STARTED

Most managers accept that some kind of procedure for planning a company's marketing helps to sharpen their focus, making the complexity of business operations manageable and adding a dimension of realism to the business's future plans. This procedure is known as marketing planning. It is a managerial process with a logical sequence of activities leading to the setting of marketing objectives and the formulation of plans for achieving them.

As with any plan, it needs to be as clear and simple as possible. This also needs to be reflected in the sales approach, which has to be as straightforward for customers as possible and remove any obstacles to actually making the sale. This actionlist explains how to cope with market uncertainty by:

- developing a *strategic* marketing plan
- developing a *tactical* marketing plan
- reviewing current thinking about markets and marketing

FAQS

Why is it important to plan marketing?

The contribution of marketing planning to the success of a business, whatever its size or area of activity, lies in its commitment to detailed analysis of future opportunities to meet customer needs. It offers a wholly professional approach to selling to well-defined market segments those products or services that deliver the desired benefits. Such commitment and activities shouldn't be mistaken for budgets and forecasts, which have always been a commercial necessity. Marketing planning is a more sophisticated approach concerned with identifying what sales are going to be made in the longer term and to whom, in order to give revenue budgets and sales forecasts a real chance of being achieved.

What are the main features of marketing planning?

Successful marketing planning is the cornerstone of developing strong, durable, and robust businesses. Overcoming an organisational culture that acts as a barrier to effective marketing planning is essential if performance is to be optimised and long-term goals are to be achieved. Given the complexity of the rapidly changing business environment and the high number of vari-

ables that influence business performance, it is necessary for managers or owner-managers to have an effective means of making the situation manageable. Thorough and detailed analysis of how to meet future customer needs provides a sophisticated and reliable method for building long-term success. Marketing planning enables your business's vision to become a reality.

Review current thinking

From an extensive review of the current research into strategic marketing planning, five principal conclusions emerge.

- There is a clear consensus about the benefits of the strategic marketing planning process.
- Strategic marketing planning and the marketing orientation that accompanies it are clearly associated with improved performance across most market situations.
- In unsuccessful companies, the process of strategic marketing planning is poorly adhered to in practice, and is frequently used as a pretext for inadequate budgeting and tactical programmes.
- The primary barrier to strategic marketing planning lies in the culture of the company and the values that stem from that culture.

- Although the degree of formality of the process can range from a highly creative, entrepreneurial approach to the more structured, rational process described here, there is universal consensus among strategic thinkers and planners that some kind of managerial planning process has to be used to manage the link between a business and its environment.

In large, multi-national, multi-product, multi-cultural businesses, then, it is usual to find a structured process for marketing planning; in smaller businesses with fewer complex products or markets, the management of the process outlined here tends to be much less formal and structured. The process and the steps, however, are the same in all consistently successful companies.

Understand the level of marketing plan

There are two principal kinds of marketing plan.

The strategic marketing plan. A strategic marketing plan is a plan for three or more years. It is a written document outlining how owner-managers or managers perceive their own position in the market relative to their competitors (with the advantage they have over their competitors accurately defined), what objectives they want to achieve, how they intend to achieve them (strategies), what resources are required (budget), and what results are expected. Three years is the most common strategic planning period. Five years is the longest, but is becoming less common because of the speed of technological and environmental change. Strategic marketing-driven plans are not to be confused with scenario planning or the kind of very long-range plans formulated by a number of Japanese companies (which often have planning horizons of between 50 and 200 years!).

The tactical marketing plan. A tactical marketing plan is the detailed scheduling and costing of the actions necessary for achieving the first year of the strategic marketing plan. The tactical plan is thus usually for one year.

Develop the contents of a strategic marketing plan

The contents of a strategic marketing plan are as follows:

- mission statement, setting out the raison d'être of the business and covering its role, business definition, distinctive competence, and future indications.
- financial summary, summarising the financial implications over the full planning period.
- market overview, providing a brief picture of the market, including market structure, market trends, key market segments, and (sometimes) gap analysis.
- SWOT analysis, analysing the strengths and weaknesses of the business compared with competitors against key customer success factors, and considering opportunities and threats, usually for each key product or segment.
- issues to be addressed, derived from a SWOT analysis (of strengths, weaknesses, opportunities, and threats) and usually specific to each product or segment.
- portfolio summary, offering a pictorial summary of the SWOT analysis that makes it easy to see at a glance the relative importance of each of the four elements; it is often a two-dimensional matrix in which the horizontal axis measures the organisation's comparative strengths and the vertical axis measures its relative attractiveness.
- assumptions, listing the underlying assumptions critical to the planned marketing objectives and strategies.
- marketing objectives, usually consisting of quantitative statements (in terms of profit, volume, value, and market share) of what the business wishes to achieve; they are usually given by product, by segment, and overall.
- marketing strategies, stating how the objectives are to be achieved; they often involve the four Ps of marketing: product, price, place, and promotion.
- resource requirements and budget, showing the full planning-period budget, giving in detail the revenues and associated costs for each year.

Develop the contents of a tactical marketing plan

The contents of a tactical marketing plan are very similar, except that they often omit the mission statement, the market overview, and SWOT analysis, and the plan goes into much more detailed quantification by product and segment of marketing objectives and associated strategies. An additional feature is more detailed scheduling and costing of the tactics necessary to achieve the first year's planned goals.

Complete the process of marketing planning

This involves:

- identifying what sales will be made in the longer term and to whom, in order to turn revenue budgets and sales forecasts into reality.
- analysing your strengths and weaknesses compared with competitors' against key customer success factors, and similarly reviewing the business's opportunities and threats.
- completing the strategic marketing plan before the tactical plan. Write your strategic marketing plan to cover three or more years, defining competitive advantage, objectives, strategies, and budgets.
- building marketing strategies round the four Ps of marketing: product, price, place, promotion.

- writing a tactical marketing plan, detailing schedules and costing for the specific actions necessary to achieve the first year of the strategic plan.

WHAT TO AVOID
Failing to implement the marketing plan successfully

A business's culture is the biggest barrier to implementing effective marketing planning. People may simply want to do what they have always done, or they may misunderstand (or not be told) why a new approach is needed. The solution is to keep everyone informed about the marketing plan: what it is, how it will work, and why it will succeed.

Disorganised planning

The output of the process (the plan) needs to spell out how a business expects to achieve its objectives; however, people may view the planning process as an academic exercise, or they may not have the skills or experience to plan effectively. Also, strategic marketing planning needs to precede tactical marketing planning. The planning process is universal, although how formal its implementation is will vary from business to business.

RECOMMENDED LINK
Market Research Society:
www.marketresearch.org.uk

Focus On: Marketing—The Importance of Being First
Al and Laura Ries

GETTING STARTED

Most managers believe the basic issue in marketing is convincing a prospective customer that you have a better product or service. Not true.

The basic issue in marketing is creating a new category you can be first in.

Marketing is not a battle of products, it is a battle of *perceptions*. To win the battle of perceptions you have to become the leader in a category. Prospects assume the leader must be better because 'everybody knows the better product or service will win in the marketplace'. How do you become the leader? You launch a new category you can be first in. It doesn't have to be a big technological advance. Sometimes the simple ideas are the easiest to get into the mind. And where do you win the battle? You win the battle inside the mind of the prospect.

This actionlist explains how to dominate your market sector.

FAQS

For a small company, how do the principles of marketing differ from those that apply to a large company?

The principles are exactly the same, only a small company usually manages to stay small by ignoring these principles. The truth is, every large company was once a small company that became big by doing the right things. The biggest mistake a small company can make is thinking of themselves as a small company instead of thinking of themselves as a big company in its gestation period.

How does a market leader achieve its leadership?

Not by introducing a better product or service. Invariably the leader in the category got to be the leader by being the first brand in a new category. Some examples:

- Coca-Cola, the first cola.
- Dell, the first personal computer sold direct.
- Domino's, the first home delivery pizza chain.
- Red Bull, the first energy drink.

What big companies introduced these brands? None. They were all started by small entrepreneurs like Tom Monaghan (Domino's Pizza) and Dietrich Mateschitz (Red Bull). Most of these companies started small, then grew up over an extended period of time.

Some consultants have called this leadership phenomenon 'the first mover advantage', but that is not so. It's an advantage, but it's not the reason that most leader brands were first in their categories. It's the 'first minder' advantage. That is, the brand that gets into the mind first is the winner, not the brand that was first in the category. Du Mont made the first television set; Hurley, the first washing machine; Red Rock, the first cola; the MITS Altair 8800 was the first personal computer, but these and many other brands failed to get into the minds of their prospects. You don't win in the marketplace. You win in the mind.

If you weren't first in your category and you can't win by being better, what can you do?

The answer is obvious: start a new category you can be first in. Marketing is more a battle of categories than it is a battle of products. Winning companies think category first and product second. They try to categorise what they do, not in terms of being better, but in terms of being different.

When Procter & Gamble introduced Tide many years ago, they could have called the product a 'new, improved soap'. Tide was a soap then, and Tide is a soap today, in the sense that soap is a 'cleansing agent'. But Tide was made from synthetic materials rather than the fats and lye found in traditional cleaning products like Ivory, Oxydol, and Rinso. Tide could have been called a synthetic soap, but that would have nailed the brand to the soap category. So Procter & Gamble called Tide the 'first detergent', a totally new category, and even today Tide is the leading brand of detergent in the United States.

MAKING IT HAPPEN
Create a new category you can be first in

When Michael Dell set up the Dell Computer Corporation, he could have sold his 'better' products through conventional computer retailers, but he didn't. Instead he launched the first brand of personal computer sold direct by phone. Today Dell is the world's largest selling brand of personal computer and still doesn't sell any computers through conventional computer retailers.

Get the launch right

Before you launch (or relaunch) a new product or service, ask yourself:

- What is the name of the category? Not a name that you might like, but a name the industry gives the category.
- What is the brand name of the leader in the category? Not necessarily the sales leader, but the brand that customers perceive to be the leader.

If there is no dominant brand, or at least not a dominant brand in the mind of most prospects, jump right in with your product or service and try to quickly establish your leadership. Cut prices, cut deals, hire sales people, launch massive publicity campaigns, do everything you can to seize the leadership position before someone else does.

Promote your brand as the leading brand. 'It's so easy to use', says AOL, 'no wonder it's number one'. Leave no piece of marketing material or website or TV advertisement or radio commercial without mentioning your leadership. Leadership is the most important aspect of any marketing campaign. Why? Prospects assume the better product or service will win in the marketplace. Therefore, if you are the leader, you must have the better product.

If there is a dominant brand, then move on and set up a new category you can be first in. But make sure you have a new name to match the new category. You can get in serious trouble if you try to use an existing name.

You can't dictate the category name. Only the industry and the media can do that. Therefore, you have to launch your new brand with publicity and get the media to establish the category name for you.

Avoid falling into the 'better product' trap

Odd as it might seem, a small company is more likely to make the 'better product' mistake mentioned above than a large company. Cynical marketing people who don't really care about 'building a better product' often populate large companies. Their focus is on marketing, distribution, packaging, display, and other sophisticated ways to hype sales. It's the small company entrepreneur who believes deeply in the superiority of his or her product that is most likely to bet the ranch on this strategy.

However, unless you are already the leader in some aspects of what you do, these programmes are bound to fail. People just naturally assume that the leader must have the better product or service.

WHAT TO AVOID
Failing to establish a new category or product sector

There's almost always a way to set up a new category. Unfortunately, most companies refuse to even consider the possibility of a new category because 'there's no market'. Of course, there's no market. If there were, it wouldn't be a new category. That's the most difficult thing to overcome. You have to have faith that you can succeed in getting acceptance for a new category. Furthermore, a new category doesn't necessarily represent a big, technological advance. Soapsoft, the first liquid soap, was a big commercial success. How difficult is it to take a tub of soap and liquefy it?

Using an existing name for the new product sector

How difficult is it to take regular beer and add water? Miller Lite, the first light beer, was a big success, but ultimately paid a big penalty for it. Instead of creating a new brand to match the new category, the company used a line extension name which just about killed their regular beer brand (Miller High Life) and caused them to lose their light beer leadership to the competition. A new category needs a new name.

RECOMMENDED LINK
Market Research Society:
www.marketresearch.org.uk

SEE ALSO
Raising Awareness of Your Brand (p. 282)

Profiling Your Competitors

GETTING STARTED

Competitor information helps you protect and grow your business. You need to build a detailed profile of your direct competitors, their strengths, weaknesses, and relationships with customers, as well as thinking more widely about competition for your customers and their spending. To help you do this, compare the performance of your business with that of your main competitors by measuring factors that are important to quality of service and use the comparison as the basis for a programme of performance improvement.

Whether you sell yourself or you have a sales team, competitor information can be obtained from many different sources. Publications, the press, and the Internet have information readily available that can help you compile intelligence on competitors, and corporate brochures and annual reports are also excellent sources of published information. Maintain a file of press cuttings on your competitors' activities, using their trade publications as a source.

Published industry surveys can provide a useful insight into purchasing patterns and competitors' websites can provide valuable information on their resources, plans, and capabilities.

FAQS

Why is competitor intelligence so important?

Competitive activity can have a significant impact on your own plans. If you are about to run a marketing campaign or new product launch, competitive activity could limit its effectiveness—so you need to know about it. You may also identify growing threats to important accounts. Unless you monitor activity and take appropriate action, your business faces an unknown risk.

Who are my competitors?

Many small companies already know their main, direct competitors. Often they have worked with them or encountered them at trade events or heard of them through customers. It is dangerous, however, to assume you know all the competitors.

It is often useful to think laterally about who might be in competition for your customers. Many products and services could be classed as non-essential and so customers may be choosing to spend their discretionary budget between two very different market sectors. In addition, as a specialist, you could find yourself in competition with a larger company which gives away a competing service as a promotional device.

Should competitor research be carried out internally or by an independent research company?

You can carry out the research internally, provided you have the resources. Much of the source material is in the public domain, so you should be able to obtain it yourself and you must never ignore the wealth of information you already have in your company or can gain through your own contacts. However, if you wish to research customer attitudes (to compare your company to the competition), you may need to use an independent research organisation. Customers may not be completely honest with your own representatives.

How reliable is published competitor information?

You have to make assumptions about the accuracy and quality of any published information that is used for research. Much of the material will be published to provide information for customers, so it is unlikely to be misleading. However, realistically, you can only use the latest and best information that is reasonably available.

MAKING IT HAPPEN
Identify the competitive threat

Competitor information helps you to identify how you can protect your most important business and, more positively, how you can strengthen your position with customers in situations in which your competitors are currently holding a larger share of the business than you. These are the main questions:

- How many competitors do you have? Are they direct or indirect?
- Who are your major competitors—those that threaten your most important customers?
- How much of your business do they threaten? Quantifying the threat helps you prioritise.
- Where are your main competitors located? How do they compare in size? Are they growing? Map them and track them.
- How do your products compare with competitive offerings? What about price? Distribution? Image and reputation? Service quality?
- What are customers' attitudes towards your competitors and towards your own company?
- Which customers might switch to competitors and why?
- How strong are competitors' relationships with key customers or key decision-makers? How long have competitors been dealing with them?
- Have you got the skills and resources to overcome the competitive threat?
- Are any competitors making inroads into businesses in which you are currently the dominant supplier?
- Who are your competitors' main customers?
- Have your competitors invested in links with customers that would make it difficult for other suppliers to make inroads?
- Can you (or your customers) identify weaknesses in your competitors?
- Which of your competitors' customers do you want to win?

Compare key competitive factors

Listed below are a number of factors that are important to meeting customer needs. You can score these factors (0–10, where 10 is the best in the market) to see how your business and your main competitors compare. The results should be used as the basis for a programme of performance improvement. As far as possible you should give priority to the things that matter *to your customers* rather than your own opinion:

- evidence of an excellent service culture, for example, problems quickly resolved by frontline staff rather than reference to higher managers
- high levels of after-sales service and support offered
- product adapted readily to meet customer specifications
- evidence of commitment to quality measurements such as ISO 9002, Investors in People or similar industry schemes
- promises made to customers, for example in sales literature offering money-back guarantees or precise delivery schedules
- evidence of feedback encouraged, for example comment forms or Freephone telephone number made widely available
- flexible approach to pricing such as the use of price incentives or finance schemes to appeal to different types of customer. Willingness to negotiate prices for important customers
- staff knowledgeable about the product and willing to share this knowledge and give advice to customers
- good reputation with agents, distributors or other intermediaries
- overall reputation. For example, how do your staff or customers rate the company?

Use the salesforce

If you have one, the salesforce can obtain competitor information from many different sources. By talking to customers, salespeople can find out about competitors' direct sales calls, marketing campaigns, special offers, and new developments. They can also obtain similar information from retailers or distributors. Crucially, they can get a feel for the customers' awareness and attitude towards your competitors..

Analyse published information

Information is readily available from publications, the press, and the Internet that can help you compile intelligence on different aspects of competitors' business, including:

- main markets
- customers
- resources and financial performance
- product range
- new products
- plans for growth

Obtain competitor literature

Corporate brochures and annual reports are available for some companies. You can sometimes obtain copies from exhibitions and customers or as downloads from competitors' websites. Often just visiting your competitors' offices you can pick up brochures and leaflets.

Monitor the press

Maintain a file of press cuttings on your competitors' activities, using their trade publications as a source, or, depending on your budget, you might consider using a press cuttings agency to gather material for you. Smaller companies can give a member of staff (for example, a sales person) responsibility for gathering and keeping data on a particular competitor.

Analyse industry reports

Published industry surveys can provide a useful insight into purchasing patterns in different market sectors. You can sometimes obtain information on competitors, market share, and industry trends.

Check the Internet

Competitor websites can provide valuable information on their resources, plans, and capabilities. As well as checking the company information and product pages, you should read any customer case studies on the site and monitor the news section to find out about new developments. Trade publications are increasingly available in electronic editions, making it easier for you to monitor the press.

Visit exhibitions

Competitors' exhibition stands can be valuable sources of information. Most organisations only participate in exhibitions that are important to their current or future business plans.

Monitor competitors' promotional activities

Analysing competitors' promotional activities will help you to respond to their activities. By monitoring their advertising, promotions, exhibition presence, press activities, and Internet information, you can assess possible strategies. These are some of the possible scenarios:

- heavy advertising expenditure could indicate a competitor trying to win greater share or attempting to remedy losses in that market
- price promotions may indicate that your competitors want to be perceived as value-for-money suppliers or it may be an emergency response to declining sales
- press announcements about new production facilities could indicate that your competitors are trying to increase their business significantly. They may become more cost-effective and able to offer lower prices, or may be taking on additional overheads that they must finance
- announcements about new branch or dealership openings could mean that competitors are expanding into new territories
- recruitment drives may signal a change in direction, a growth strategy or a sudden loss of staff

All of these can mean that your competitor is spending more money and you might compare this with published accounts (available at Companies House or through credit reference agencies) to gain an indication of their financial health.

Marketing and trade publications can be useful sources of information on competitor marketing activity.

Appoint a research company

If you do not have the internal resources to monitor competitive activity, you can use an independent research company to carry out all the tasks outlined above. You can also ask them to explore customer attitudes to competitors. Customers may be more willing to provide this information to an independent organisation.

Consider benchmarking

Benchmarking compares your performance with that of other, similar companies. Competently done, it will give you a baseline assessment of your company's efficiency and some insight into where competitors may be gaining competitive advantage over you.

WHAT TO AVOID

Overlooking the obvious sources

Some competitor intelligence is freely available from the Internet, the press, and other published sources, and, most of all, from your staff, your customers, and your competitors themselves. Information from these sources can provide a valuable starting point for developing detailed competitor profiles.

Ignoring competitor information

Competitor information is only valuable if you use it to refine your own strategies or take defensive action to protect your business. Simply gathering information without analysis or action is wasteful.

Acting on incomplete information

Be cautious about acting on competitor intelligence. Published sources can only provide a partial picture, and more strategic information is likely to be confidential. This means that you may make incorrect assumptions in planning your response to competitor action.

Using out-of-date information

Records should be carefully checked and maintained. Using poor quality data can ruin the best campaigns.

RECOMMENDED LINK

Market Research Society:
www.marketresearch.org.uk

SEE ALSO

**Choosing Your Marketing Strategy
 (p. 206)**
**Researching the Size of Your Market
 (p. 209)**

WORKING WITH CUSTOMERS

Carrying Out Market Research

GETTING STARTED

Businesses of all sizes need to keep on top of changes or developments in their chosen markets so that they can make sure that the product or service they offer fits the bill. This actionlist gives you some ideas on how to carry out different types of market research.

Telephone interviews are a quick and cost-effective way to obtain opinions from a sample of customers. This type of research can be used to assess your customers' reaction to a change in the product or service, or to measure awareness of a company or product. One of the downsides of this approach, however, is that can be difficult to reassure people that you are carrying out legitimate research—most people will think you're trying to sell them something!

Postal surveys are ideal for customer satisfaction surveys or detailed surveys that take time to complete. However, it can be difficult to obtain a worthwhile rate of response, and you, as the researcher, have little control over the process. Incentives may be needed to improve response and there is a risk of incomplete responses.

Group discussions or focus groups are ideal for identifying issues of concern to customers and assessing customer reactions to potential changes. This type of research is open-ended and can highlight important customer issues that the researcher may not be aware of. However, group discussions are not representative and can be influenced by a dominant member of the group.

The personal interview is ideal for obtaining detailed information on attitudes to products and services or getting feedback from specific individuals. Personal interviews allow in-depth discussion of complex topics and give you greater control over the response.

An omnibus survey is a cost-effective method of researching several topics at the same time. The same survey is used to carry out regular research on a number of different products by telephone or personal interview. You should check that the other topics in the survey are compatible with your own products.

FAQS

Can we carry out market research ourselves, or should we use a consultancy?

Market research is a professional discipline and depending on your industry and what you need to find out, you may get more meaningful results by using a consultancy. They are trained to detect possible errors in research results, and their independence is reassuring to people who are being interviewed. The main problem for small businesses is, naturally, the expense. Review your budget and see if you can afford outside help.

You can carry out a limited amount of research yourself, developing and mailing questionnaires or carrying out limited telephone interviews. Again, there is a risk that people may feel that your research is a thinly disguised sales pitch.

How do I carry out quick and effective research?

Without incurring great costs, you often have the opportunity to research your own customers. Every time you or a member of your staff meet a customer you can discover important information. Record this information and create opportunities to share it.

More formal research may include a space on delivery notes or invoices, enclosures with products, or follow-up phone calls to ask customers' opinions. Be cautious about asking for too much (or too personal) information.

How reliable are the results from focus groups?

The results are as reliable as the quality of the participants and the people who run the sessions. It is easy for individual participants to dominate a group and influence the course of discussions. If the person running the discussion asks the wrong questions, the resulting discussion may prove worthless. Make sure those in charge are well briefed.

We have limited resources for research. Should we participate in an omnibus survey so that we can make the best use of our budget?

An omnibus survey is an ideal way to share expensive research resources and reach a large audience. However, you must be sure that the audience is relevant to your company's business. Ask for a profile of the research audience and check the names of other organisations which have used the survey. If there is a reasonable match to your own business, it could be a cost-effective solution.

MAKING IT HAPPEN
Interview customers by telephone

Telephone interviews are a quick and cost-effective way to obtain opinions from a sample of customers. They can be used to assess customer reaction to a change in the product or service, or to gauge satisfaction ratings compared to competitors. The make-up of the sample is crucial; it is more important to know the views of valuable customers.

Speed up research

The main benefit of telephone research is speed. A large number of interviews can be conducted in a short space of time, and data can be gathered and processed quickly. Telephone interviews also cost considerably less than personal interviews. As long as they are brief and to the point they are non-intrusive and easy to arrange. A customer may be too busy for a personal interview, but willing to spend a short time on the phone.

Be careful about a senior decision-maker being contacted by a junior member of staff or an independent researcher, though, and always bear in mind the effect on the customer's relationship with you.

Don't confuse telephone research with selling

Telephone interviews have limited scope because people may not be prepared to spend a long period of time on the telephone. It can also be difficult to get across complex concepts by telephone.

Follow industry guidelines:
- define the target audience
- draft a questionnaire and test it with colleagues
- make the calls at times likely to be convenient for the target audience, but check when you call that it is convenient; if not, offer to call back
- identify the purpose of the call and give an indication of the likely duration
- use faxes, if necessary, to send more detailed information for discussion

Use postal surveys or questionnaires

Questionnaires are very difficult to compile well. Postal surveys are delivered directly to customers and they can be a quick and relatively inexpensive method of obtaining information. They are ideal for customer satisfaction surveys or detailed surveys that take time to complete. However, it can be difficult to obtain a reasonable rate of response and you cannot assume that the responses will be representative of all customers.

Assess the value of postal surveys

Postal surveys are relatively inexpensive. The costs include outward and return postage and stationery. They are precise and can be targeted at specific customers or prospects. They are also voluntary, because there is no pressure on the customer. The main problem, however, is the low response rates; incentives may be needed to improve it. There is also a risk of questionnaires and survey forms returned incomplete or incorrectly completed. You may face a slow response because there is no time pressure on the customer so you must take this into account in your planning.

Improve the response from postal surveys

Response rates can be influenced by many different factors. For many consumer goods markets less than 5% would be normal and 15% or more would be extremely high. For highly involved customers in some sectors you might anticipate much more. If you need to improve response think about:

- offering an incentive, such as entry into a prize draw, for returned questionnaires
- simplifying the questionnaire
- reassuring the customer that information will be kept confidential
- enclosing a stamped addressed or business reply envelope

Hold a group discussion

In group discussions, or focus groups, customers and prospective customers are invited to discuss a particular topic, usually under the guidance of a researcher. They are ideal for exploring and, possibly, identifying issues or problems which concern customers, and assessing customer reactions to potential changes.

There is no limit placed on what the group can discuss, and this format can highlight important customer issues that the researcher may not be aware of. Many customers welcome the opportunity to discuss products and services with their colleagues and have an opportunity to contribute to change. The disadvantages are that group discussions are not representative, and they can be biased or influenced by a dominant member of the group. It is also difficult to quantify results.

You need to be cautious in planning group discussions. By and large they should not be used to identify only what is wrong with a product or service and it may cause problems to have several, important, customers in the same room. Groups composed entirely of customers with grievances will also have limited value.

To set up a group discussion:

- invite eight to ten customers; this number is controllable, but with fewer people it may be difficult to maintain discussion
- thank customers for participating and put them at their ease
- record the discussion if possible, using a tape recorder
- advise people that their comments are being recorded and that all material will be treated in confidence
- if conducting a group amongst consumers (not your customers) you might consider providing participants with a gift for taking part
- consider using more than one group to gather a range of views

You could also consider using an independent researcher to run the discussion.

Conduct personal interviews

In a personal interview, a customer and an interviewer work through a series of predetermined questions. The personal interview is ideal for key customers and for obtaining detailed information on attitudes to products and services, or initiating the process of getting feedback. The interview can take place in a customer's home or office, or in a public place. It can be prearranged by telephone, post, or personal contact.

Personal interviews allow in-depth discussion of complex topics and give you more control over the response. They offer greater accuracy, and results are easy to analyse. Meeting people in a working environment can give an indication of their real purchasing intentions. The main disadvantages are the time and cost of recruiting interviewers and conducting interviews and the risk of interviewer bias.

Before you carry out personal interviews, you should identify the groups or individuals you wish to contact. You should advise the customer about the length of time the interview is likely to take and respect the confidence of the customer.

Carry out an omnibus survey

An omnibus survey is a cost-effective method of researching several topics at the same time. The same survey is used to carry out regular research on different products by telephone or personal interview. They are suitable for measuring attitudes and behaviour towards different types of products and services or monitoring changes in attitude among groups of consumers.

Before participating in the survey, you should check that the other topics in the survey are compatible with your own products and that the overall length of the survey is not excessive. It may reduce costs, but the audience may not give enough attention to all topics.

WHAT TO AVOID

Asking obvious questions
Be aware that you may already know much about your customers and their attitudes and behaviour. In a business-to-business market, you may know more than your customer. Before undertaking research, be sure it is necessary.

Assuming formal market research is necessary
For many smaller companies, and some quite large ones, expensive research does not meet their needs. Companies with just a handful of very important customers would do better to concentrate on their relationship with these key accounts. For example, local retailers will often know their own area well and may simply need to engage their regular customers in conversation.

Not planning properly
Market research may generate considerable amounts of data and you will need to have the time and resources to analyse and turn it into useful information. Alternatively, if you set out without a thorough plan you may find that you have missed a crucial piece of information and face the embarrassment of having to revisit customers.

Choosing the wrong research technique
Each research technique has different applications, benefits, and disadvantages. You have to decide whether you need depth of information, speedy results, or cost-effective research. A market research consultancy may be able to provide advice on a suitable approach but you need to have a very clear picture of your needs, and how the information will be used.

Relying on limited results
For reasons of cost or time, some research programmes may provide limited results. It is important to put the research findings in context and take account of the limited findings when you are making important decisions. Market research consultancies use proven techniques to evaluate results and should advise you to use their findings with caution.

Using research to sell
Too many companies contact customers and prospects claiming to be carrying out market research. During the course of the research, the company then attempts to sell a product or service on the basis that the respondent has expressed an interest. This is a betrayal of trust and can prove damaging to valid research.

RECOMMENDED LINK
Market Research Society:
www.marketresearch.org.uk

SEE ALSO
Getting More Feedback from Customers (p. 228)

Getting More Feedback from Customers

GETTING STARTED
Customer feedback is essential for improving products and services, and for identifying and correcting any problems at an early stage. Offer customers a choice of feedback methods to encourage them to respond, but make sure that all methods are as easy to use as possible. For high-value goods, a structured follow-up mechanism encourages customer comments on purchases.

FAQS

What is the best feedback mechanism?
For customers, the choice of feedback mechanism is probably a matter of personal preference. Some may prefer the anonymity of a postal questionnaire or response through a website. Others may wish to discuss their concerns and get an immediate response over the telephone. To ensure that you get as much feedback as possible, give customers a choice.

Do we need to use incentives to encourage feedback?
Customers may provide feedback if they feel strongly enough about an issue. Someone who has a serious complaint is likely to let you know. However, customers who have less pressing comments may not bother, feeling that their feedback is unimportant. Incentives may encourage them, but only if the incentives are appropriate.

Should we use an independent research organisation to obtain feedback?
Using an independent research organisation demonstrates to customers that you take their feedback seriously, and provides an objective, independent channel for comments. You may also find that customers are willing to talk to a research organisation about issues that they might be reluctant to discuss with your company directly. You must, however, be sure that the costs of employing a market research company are justified in the light of what you may discover. You and your own staff (if you have any)—especially field staff and sales

people—may already know a great deal about customer opinion.

MAKING IT HAPPEN

Find out what customers think
It is essential to find out what your customers think about your products, your service, and your company. This information can be vital for identifying problems before they become serious. It can also provide valuable input into the product development process. You can use the feedback to:

- improve products
- tailor products and services to the needs of individual customers
- identify new product opportunities
- highlight potential problems
- develop focused marketing and customer service plans
- strengthen customer relationships
- reduce customer losses

You can also use the feedback as part of your promotional message.

Ask customers before you develop a new product
By explaining your plans and involving customers in product development, you can strengthen relationships and provide a service that is mutually beneficial. Questions could include:

- How can we improve the current product?
- What problems need to be overcome?
- What new features would customers welcome?
- Do the plans represent an improvement?
- Would customers make more use of a product that included the features they have highlighted?

Ask about purchasing experience

When a customer buys a product, include a brief questionnaire with it, asking about the customer's buying experience. Questions could include:

- Where did you buy the product? How often do you buy it?
- Why did you choose the product?
- What other (competing or complementary) products do you buy, and how often?
- Why did you choose the retail outlet?
- Where did you hear about the product and retail outlet?
- How did you find the service offered by the retailer?
- Would you visit the retailer again?
- Do you have any specific comments about the product or retailer?

The questionnaire could take the form of a reply-paid card, and should be brief.

Follow up a product sale

If the product is a reasonably high-value one, you could set up a follow-up mechanism to find out about the customer's experience in using the product. Typical intervals would be a week after purchase, a month after purchase, and six months after purchase. The first follow-up would check that the customer had no initial problems, while the subsequent follow-ups would ask about the customer's experience in using the product. Having a scale such as 1–5 (where 1 is 'very poor' and 5 is 'very good') enables comparisons to show improvement over time.

Follow up servicing and maintenance

The standard of after-sales service can be critical in determining overall customer satisfaction with your company. After every service or maintenance visit, contact customers to ensure that they were satisfied with the standard of service they received. Questions could cover:

- convenience of booking a service
- punctuality and response times
- standard of service
- attitude of staff
- availability of spare parts

It is a good idea to use scales as described above to enable comparisons over time. This kind of follow-up can be handled by reply-paid questionnaire or telephone call.

Set up a customer satisfaction programme

Customer satisfaction has become one of the most important issues facing businesses in every market. Customer satisfaction programmes are known by many different names, such as customer service, customer satisfaction, and customer focus. Their common theme is meeting the customers' requirements and ensuring that all aspects of the business contribute to customer satisfaction. The intention is to build repeat business. If customers are satisfied with the product and the standards of service they receive, they will return to the business or the retail outlet again and again for both major and minor purchases.

Measure satisfaction regularly

A customer satisfaction index takes the results from a number of satisfaction surveys, and allocates a numerical value to key customer satisfaction indicators. A local outlet is then given an overall index of performance which can be compared with other outlets and measured on a year-on-year basis. The survey questionnaire asks customers to respond to questions with a scale of satisfaction: fully satisfied, very satisfied, satisfied, not satisfied, very dissatisfied. Alternatively, customers can be asked to respond on a numerical scale, where, for example, 1 is very dissatisfied, 10 is very satisfied. They can also provide written comments on aspects of the service and, in some cases, ask for specific actions, such as an explanation from a departmental manager.

Set up a customer hotline

As well as formal mechanisms, you should also set up facilities to encourage customers to provide feedback at any time. A telephone hotline allows customers to call with queries or complaints about any aspect of your products or service. Calls to the hotline should be free, and the telephone number should be included in all your customer communications. The hotline should be staffed by people trained in customer handling techniques, and it should be continuously monitored to ensure that customers receive a suitable response. All calls should be recorded so that the call patterns can be analysed to identify any recurring problems.

Include a feedback mechanism on your website

You should include a simple feedback mechanism on your website. This provides a similar function to the telephone hotline, and provides customers with an alternative, easy-to-use channel for complaints, queries, and other issues. Users should have to complete only minimal personal details, such as name and e-mail address, before submitting their comments. Alternatively, you can allow users to submit their comments anonymously.

Use incentives to encourage feedback

You will increase response if you offer an incentive such as a free gift. You could also set up a regular prize draw for visitors who submit comments.

Establish a user group

You can encourage feedback and build a sense of community by setting up a user group. The user group would operate as a forum for discussing all issues of concern to customers, such as quality, performance, standards, and future developments. The group would include representatives from your own company and from a cross-section of your customers. The comments from the user group provide valuable feedback on current performance, and help to identify needs that can be met through new product development.

Respond to feedback

Let visitors know that you have received their comments, and thank them for their feedback. When you have taken corrective action, tell them what you have done so they see that their effort is not wasted. This can encourage further feedback. If a visitor highlights a serious problem, keep them informed on progress.

WHAT TO AVOID
Failing to act on feedback

The most important way to encourage feedback is to demonstrate that you can respond. The point of gathering feedback is to identify concerns and problems before they become serious; however, unless you act on that feedback, the exercise will be wasted. Industry experience indicates that customers who have a problem resolved are far more likely to remain customers than those who receive no response. If you act on customer input during the product development process, it indicates a high level of partnership and helps to strengthen customer relationships.

Making it difficult to provide feedback

If you want to encourage feedback, make it easy for your visitors. Calls to telephone hotlines should be free. Postal surveys and questionnaires should also have the return postage paid. Any questionnaires should be brief, and should not ask for much personal information. You should also provide facilities on your website for customers to provide feedback or submit a response to a survey using an electronic form.

Poor complaints management

If you do not record and analyse complaints and other feedback, you may not spot emerging trends. A series of complaints on the same issue indicates a recurring problem that could be dangerous to your company if it is not resolved quickly. Set up a formal mechanism for recording all feedback.

RECOMMENDED LINK

Chartered Institute of Marketing:
www.cim.co.uk

SEE ALSO
Carrying Out Market Research (p. 224)
Involving Customers in Product or Service Development (p. 231)

Involving Customers in Product or Service Development

GETTING STARTED

For some people 'new product development' means inventing something wonderfully new. In reality, though, the vast majority of new products are modifications of existing ideas. In some cases, 'new product development' can also mean adding an element of service onto a (physical) product.

The power of new product development is that your business may be able meet a customer's need more closely than the competition. Involving customers creates the possibility of your product or service being tailor-made for them, thereby encouraging loyalty.

FAQS

Is there a risk in letting customers evaluate new products before launch?

There are two risks. Firstly, the customer may be extremely disappointed with the product if quality is poor. Secondly, there is a risk that competitors could find out about your plans indirectly. The quality issue is one that you should deal with: if a product is not right, it should not be given to customers in any form—it is not enough simply to promise future improvements. The security risk of a leak to competitors can be minimised through disclosure and confidentiality agreements, although these provide no real guarantee. However, the advantages of involving customers outweigh the risks, so evaluation is worthwhile.

How practical is it for customers and suppliers to collaborate on product development?

There are different levels of collaboration. Some may involve regular meetings to provide input and review progress. These meetings can be held on site or remotely, using video-conference links. In some cases, customer staff may work alongside the supplier team for all or part of the project. Secondment like this can provide other benefits for the customer by improving the technical knowledge of their staff.

Does pre-announcement put new product launches at risk?

Some companies, particularly in the IT sector, have put themselves under unnecessary pressure by trying to meet a series of pre-announced release dates. The schedule may not allow proper time for development, resulting in failure to meet the date, or the release of a product that is not ready. Both are potentially damaging.

MAKING IT HAPPEN
Ask customers before you launch your product

If you are planning a new product or redeveloping an existing one, ask your customers for their views on the existing product and what they would like to see in a new one. By explaining your plans and involving customers in product development, you can strengthen relationships and provide a service that is mutually beneficial. Questions could include:

- How is the product used?
- How can we improve the current product?
- What problems have been encountered?
- What new features would customers welcome?
- Do the plans represent an improvement?
- Would customers make greater use of a product that included the features they have highlighted?

Set up a user group

You can encourage feedback and build a sense of community by setting up a user group, which can be online and may allow customers to share experiences or solve one another's problems. The user group can operate as a forum for discussing issues of mutual concern to customers such as quality, performance, standards, future developments, and customer concerns. The group would include representatives from your own company and from a cross-section of your customers. Comments from the user group provide valuable feedback on current performance and help to identify needs that can be met through new product development.

Ask customers to evaluate new products

Customer evaluation, or beta testing, is well established in the software industry. Customers test new products or upgraded versions before they are released to the market. They identify any problems in using the software, thus providing valuable feedback on product performance.

Issue new product announcements

Another valuable practice from the IT industry is to pre-announce new products. For example, a company will set a number of release dates during the coming year when it will release new versions of products. The company outlines the new products and gives customers the opportunity to provide input to the development process. The major benefit for customers is that they can align their own business development plans to the release dates.

Work in partnership with customers

Product development can be a joint initiative where you work closely with specific customers to develop products that meet their specific needs. This approach is a valuable one where:

- your customers have developed partnership sourcing to take advantage of your technology
- your customers have technology and technical skills that complement your own, and a joint project can produce more effective results
- you want to strengthen relationships with key customers by working in partnership on joint development projects

Understand your customers' markets

The new products you develop could enable your customers to improve their competitive performance, so it is important to understand their markets. Tell customers about your product plans and ask them for input to your development process. By building a detailed picture of their markets, you can align your own plans with them, and develop products that are tailored to their needs.

- What are their main markets?
- What is their position in the marketplace?
- Who are their main competitors?
- How are their products regarded in the marketplace?
- What are the key success factors in the market?
- What are the long-term product trends?
- What new technical developments will be needed to succeed?
- Could innovation by you help your customers to succeed?
- Are your customers considering entry into new markets?
- Do you have product development plans that are relevant to the new market?

Understand customer strategies

It is equally important to understand your customers' business strategies: their corporate direction and key objectives, and how they aim to succeed. By aligning your product development objectives with theirs, and showing how your products or services can help them to achieve their strategic business objectives, you can improve the chances of your new products being successful.

There are two possible approaches to customer-focused product development. In a situation where your customers want to become market leaders through innovation, your new product programmes can help them to develop the right level of innovation without investment in their own skills. Where, on the other hand, they want to succeed through competitive pricing, you can help them reduce overall costs by developing cost-effective products.

Assess the value of your products and services

Products that help your customers to meet their strategic business objectives can increase the chances of new product success. The more your customers depend on your new product, the more demanding they will be. If you can keep up with their demands, try to anticipate and meet them and you'll not only help yourself but also create barriers for your competitors.

For example, if your customer must develop new products quickly in order to retain and protect market share, your own new products can be critical to their product development programme.

Analyse your customers' technical requirements

In assessing new product development opportunities, you should analyse how your products can help your customers. They can use your skills in a number of ways:

- improving the performance of their own products and services by using your design and development skills. They may gain privileged access to your technical skills to improve their own competitive performance.
- using your technical expertise to enhance the skills of their own technical staff, enabling them to make a more effective contribution to their own product development process
- using your technical resources to handle product development on a subcontract basis. This provides your partners with access to specialist resources or to additional research and development capacity to improve the performance of their product development programmes
- using your technical expertise to develop new products that they could not achieve themselves. This provides your customers with new technology, and allows them to diversify in line with your specialist skills
- using your design skills to improve through-life costs (the total cost of owning and using a product, including purchase price, maintenance, and any other related costs). By carrying out value engineering studies on your customers' products, you may be able to reduce overall costs and improve reliability by designing components that are easier to assemble and maintain.

WHAT TO AVOID
Not involving your customers sufficiently

Product development should be focused on customer needs. Although most companies carry out research before development, the research may not provide the detailed input that is essential. Product development may also be driven by technology, with no clear market focus. The more your customer depends on your product, the more likely it is to succeed.

Ignoring user groups

There are many examples of companies who have set up user groups in response to a crisis and then failed to use them. This can be frustrating for customers and wasteful for the companies. User groups provide a valuable perspective on products and services, and their feedback can provide real benefits for the product development process.

Failing to understand customer strategies

Where the supplier/customer relationship is that of a partnership, products are developed and customised to help customers meet their business objectives. You must understand customers' markets and business strategies so that your product plans can be integrated with theirs.

RECOMMENDED LINK
Chartered Institute of Marketing: **www.cim.co.uk**

SEE ALSO
Getting More Feedback from Customers (p. 228)
Retaining Existing Customers (p. 237)

Converting Leads into Sales

GETTING STARTED

If you are trying to grow your business, finding leads (that is, potential new customers), is just the beginning. Before they can benefit you in any way, you need to turn the leads into sales. This actionlist offers a systematic approach to doing this and to making sure that the leads are of the right kind in the first place, which will cut down on wasted time and resources.

FAQS

How far can services such as telemarketing take over from the salesforce?

These services can be used to handle many of the sales team's routine functions: carrying out initial research, qualifying prospective customers, making appointments, and maintaining regular contact. They should not be used as a substitute for face-to-face selling if that is important to your customer relationships.

What is the best way to measure lead conversion?

Measuring sales as a percentage of initial leads is too simplistic an approach: it is more effective to measure at each stage of the process. For example, only 50% of initial leads may turn out to be suitable prospective customers. If the leads have been well qualified, the sales team may be able to convert 20% of the final prospect list. Measuring results at each stage helps you focus the right level of resources and plan future lead-generation programmes.

Should we try to get as many leads as possible?

The quality of the leads is as important as the number. Following up a large number of unsuitable leads is a waste of resources, but getting as many good leads as possible is important to any company that wants to expand its business.

MAKING IT HAPPEN
Qualify your leads

Your lead-generation programme may have given you large numbers of leads, but not all of them will convert to sales. Some may be poor prospects, while others may simply be gathering information rather than planning a purchase. Good prospects have the following characteristics:

- the financial resources to purchase your product
- the authority to make a purchase decision
- a genuine need for your product or service
- the desire to learn more about your product
- plans to make a purchase in the near future

Telemarketing can be used to qualify the leads. Call the contact and ask for more details of their inquiry so that you can send information tailored to their needs. Just sending a brochure, with no accompanying letter and no understanding of the prospective customer's needs, is a waste of money.

Qualifying questions can include:

- Are you the person who makes the purchasing decision? If not, who does?
- Is your company currently buying this product?
- What quantities do you buy, or how much do you spend on the service?
- When are you likely to make your next purchase?
- What information do you need on our product and company?

Choose a one-step or two-step process

In the case of some products and services, the lead-generation and sales conversion processes can be combined. These are known as one-step programmes, and are equivalent to direct selling operations. They are suitable for:

- inexpensive products
- information services such as newsletter or magazine subscriptions
- office supplies

- software
- low-value financial offers

In a two-step programme, the prospective customer (prospect) requests initial information. You send the information and then continue following up until the prospect is ready to buy. Two-step programmes are suitable for:

- expensive offers
- complex technical products
- professional services
- high-value financial services

Plan the conversion process

Lead conversion can be a long-term continuous process, the duration of which depends on the complexity of the product and of the decision-making process. For example, how many people are involved or how important is the product to the customer (or the customer's business)?

For a complex product, the process could be:

- identifying key decision-makers
- sending information to key decision-makers
- arranging meetings with decision-makers
- providing sample products for evaluation by the customer
- bidding for a contract against competition
- final negotiations
- purchase
- after-sales service and support

You must decide how you will handle each stage of the process, who will be involved in the sales team, and how you will manage communications with the prospect.

Another example could be where the product and the purchasing process are simpler, but the prospect is reluctant to change suppliers. The conversion process could take a long time, so you must plan a programme to maintain contact and move the prospect away from the existing supplier. Actions could include:

- personalised direct mail with product information
- regular updates on new developments in the company
- targeted special offers to encourage the customer to try the product

Allocate responsibility

Normally, the marketing department generates leads and the sales department follows up. It is important for the two departments to work together to integrate their activities and ensure that the company focuses on the kind of high-quality prospects it really needs. Sales departments frequently complain about the quantity and quality of leads. They want as many leads as possible so that the final number of new sales is high; however, they may also complain if too many of the leads are of poor quality and do not meet the right criteria. Collecting a large number of high-quality leads can be a difficult balancing act. Some sales teams prefer to do their own qualifying, while others prefer to leave that to others so that they can concentrate on face-to-face meetings with prospects.

Back the sales team with telemarketing

Telemarketing can be used to enhance the performance and productivity of the salesforce. The telemarketing team can be responsible for following up sales leads, qualifying prospects, setting up appointments, and maintaining contact with longer-term prospects. This frees the salesforce for increasing the number of face-to-face meetings and for concentrating on the most likely prospects. The integration of telemarketing with the salesforce can play an important part in reducing overall sales costs. The cost of keeping a sales team on the road continues to soar, and it may not always represent the most cost-effective way of reaching the right people.

Maintain a contact diary

A contact diary can help you plan the conversion process and make sure that the sales team does not miss any important contact opportunities. It also ensures that the sales backup team integrates its follow-up activities with the field salesforce. Computer software is available which allows sales teams to operate a sales diary and record details of meetings and other follow-up activities. The same software can be used by the management team to monitor progress and ensure that no important contacts are overlooked. Contact diaries can include details on the customer, the customer's likes and dislikes, availability for meetings or telephone calls, their buying limits/authorisation, and even personal information that helps maintain a relationship with them.

Track progress

It is essential to track progress at each stage of the conversion process. If the prospect is important, you may wish to allocate additional resources to win the business. If a prospect is of only minor importance but is taking time and resources, you may want to refocus the efforts of the salesforce. The progress from initial lead to customer goes through a number of stages:

- raw lead: an initial enquiry from any source
- suspect: an enquiry that has been qualified and has the potential to become a paying customer
- prospect: a lead that has been qualified in more detail
- inactive lead: a prospect who will not buy now but has future potential
- dead lead: a prospect who has little potential to become a customer
- customer

You might also include lapsed customers in this process as a source of qualified leads.

Choose the right contact frequency

A single mailshot, telephone call, or direct response advertisement may produce results, but a series of quality contacts will have greater impact and ensure you meet your response targets. Multiple direct marketing activities raise levels of awareness with each contact, follow up contacts who have not responded, and move individual respondents further along the decision-making process.

Use personalised contact

Personalised one-to-one mailings are an ideal form of communication for companies with detailed information on their prospects. The letter reflects the individual prospect's main interests and concerns, and the offer can be tailored to the prospect's needs. Subsequent mailings can build an individual relationship with the prospect.

WHAT TO AVOID
Focusing on the wrong prospects

Sales teams have a natural tendency to deal with friendly prospects and avoid the difficult ones. From a business perspective, however, they may be dealing with the wrong people. The qualifying process should be used to identify the most important prospects in order to improve the targeting of the salesforce.

Poor management

Lead conversion can be a long, complicated process, so it is essential to monitor progress and manage the programme carefully. Lead conversion can use a lot of salesforce and telemarketing resources, and careful planning can make sure that it is carried out effectively.

Putting all the burden on the salesforce

In some organisations, the salesforce is given total responsibility for generating leads, qualifying them, and converting them into sales. This may not represent the best use of salesforce resources. Telemarketing or other tools can be used to supplement the salesforce and take over routine tasks.

RECOMMENDED LINK
Institute of Professional Sales:
www.iops.co.uk

SEE ALSO
Handling Customer Inquiries (p. 245)

Retaining Existing Customers

GETTING STARTED

Just about every business will depend to a certain extent on repeat sales from customers that have already bought from them. In fact in some cases, repeat sales from existing customers will be the biggest revenue-generating source. However, many business owners do not realise or understand that establishing a long-term relationship with a loyal customer base is as important, if not more important, than getting sales from new customers in the first place.

If your business is one of those where customers are likely to come back and buy the same product or more products from you over again, then it will be vital that you do everything you can to keep them satisfied and loyal to your business for as long as possible. This actionlist contains some ideas on how to ensure that this is the case. One book on the subject you may also find useful is *The Loyalty Effect: The Hidden Force Behind Growth, Profits and Lasting Value* by Fredrick Reichheld, published by Harvard Business School Press in 1996.

FAQS

Why do I need to bother with customers when they've already bought from me?

Having profiled and targeted your ideal market audience and made those all important first sales, your business will only really outstrip those of your competitors in the long term when you truly understand why those customers have bought from you. Only by recognising this will you have a unique opportunity to persuade them to buy from you again and again.

How can I gain the edge over my competitors?

Even if you are lucky enough to be the first into a new market it won't be long before someone else follows suit. What can you do to ensure customers stay loyal to you as long as they are in the market for your service? Can you create a unique selling proposition (USP) that will lock them into your business and not that of your competition? The vast majority of businesses concentrate on achieving a profit from first time or single sales and fail to appreciate that meeting the needs of their customers over the longer term will reap far greater benefits.

MAKING IT HAPPEN

Identify what unique benefits you can offer

People do not buy products for their features. They buy to satisfy their needs and will seek to purchase an outcome that they perceive as giving them the value that will benefit them personally. To succeed in your marketing and create a long-term loyal customer base you will need to identify the unique value that you can provide over and above your basic product or service offering. It is this value, the unique combination of benefits to your customers, that must be at the core of your marketing strategy, and which your competitors will not be able to match.

Offer value that will make customers loyal to you

The key to this is not to think about individual features of your service, but to concentrate on how the benefit within that product or service impacts on your customers' long-term personal needs. These needs often fall into the following categories.

- **A feeling of belonging.** People like people, and they like to do what other people like themselves are doing—for example, being in associations, or in membership schemes. They like being part of a cause and surrounding themselves with people they consider to be their equals. Can you offer something to your customers to satisfy their sense of belonging? Is there something that they can join as part of their purchase of your service? Could you set up a user group? Can you publish a top sellers' list for your products?

- **Self improvement and self esteem.** Just as with belonging, people will often choose to purchase something that makes them feel better, fitter, healthier, or just more important. Do you recognise something in your customer's requirements where your product or service can help them satisfy this need? Can you include this in your USP and marketing message?
- **Being reminded that they have made a good choice.** For customers in many situations the purchase decision is fraught with fear of making the wrong choice. Look for ways you can remind or reward your customers for making the right purchase by buying from you. Can you think of ways to make it a risk free, 100% secure experience for the buyer, for example through extended warranties, money back guarantees, or free after-sales support for long periods? Can you make this better than what your competitors are offering?
- **A sense of achievement.** Is there a way that you can make your customers feel that, by buying from you now and in the future, they are going to put themselves in a much better situation or position than they were in before? Can you create something unique in your after sales service? Is it possible to offer some form of loyalty points scheme, future discounts, or reward scheme that delivers more benefits the longer they remain as your customer?
- **Being educated about your service.** Do you go out of your way to tell customers regularly and in detail about the wise decision they have made in buying from you? Do you let them know how they can get even more benefits by buying again, or can access special offers in the future only available to loyal customers of your business? Publishing a customer newsletter with informative, interesting, and relevant information about how they can make best use of and get more value from your service, is a very popular method of achieving this.
- **Getting a personal and relevant service, exactly when they need it.** More than any-

thing else your purchasers will place the greatest long-term value on your business and your product if they feel they will continue to receive personal attention and care from you whenever they need it. They must be made to feel that they are your most important customer every time they deal with you. Are there ways you can make the sales experience with your firm more fun, more exciting, more rewarding, more personal, and more relevant than it is at the moment? More importantly, can you make this a better experience than is being offered by your competition?

Make sure that your USP aims to keep them loyal

Gaining loyalty and the trust of your customers can only be achieved if they feel you are fulfilling their exact needs, and that they will continue to receive value from you that meets their needs in the future. Your USP needs to communicate the loyalty building value that your service will provide and that your competitors cannot match. Every time your customer wants to re-purchase your type of product or service, your marketing proposition must make it as difficult as possible for them to say no to you. Does your USP express this value strongly enough? Think of the services that you repeatedly buy from other suppliers yourself. Why do you remain loyal to them? What is it that makes you want to keep on purchasing from them? If you can recognise what this is, you should aim to replicate the same value in the service you provide to your own customers.

WHAT TO AVOID
Letting customers forget

You have done all the hard work and built up a solid customer base, but a fatal error will be to let them forget why they bought from you or the extra value they can receive by continuing to buy from you in the future. Your loyalty building strategy should look for continual ways to communicate with and educate your customers about the benefits of your service, competitions, special offers, new product lines, open days, and so on. A newsletter, especially by e-mail, is a very popular and cost-effective way of doing this. If you let them forget you are there, or what you can offer them, they will eventually buy from someone else instead.

Failing to make them feel appreciated

Each customer must feel as if he or she is the most important one you have. Failing to recognise this is an opportunity for them to try a different service, and you may lose their loyalty in favour of your competitors. If you have the names and addresses of your customers, aim to write to them and thank them for their custom on a regular basis. When they first buy from you, ask them if they would like to receive advance details of special offers or new products in the future. If they agree, ask for their telephone number, e-mail, or other contact details and ensure you communicate with them regularly.

Whenever possible, reward them with loyalty building discounts and offers for repeat purchases, or ask them individually—as one of your most valued customers—for their views and opinions about how they use your service and how you can improve it for them. If they feel appreciated, their loyalty and their trust in you and your service will almost certainly follow.

RECOMMENDED LINK
CRM Daily (online customer relationship management magazine):
www.crmdaily.com/perl/section/lylt/

SEE ALSO
Communicating Customer Service (p. 243)
Corporate Hospitality (p. 254)
Involving Customers in Product or Service Development (p. 231)
Public Relations (p. 542)
Selling and Salesmanship (p. 546)

Extending a Product with Service

GETTING STARTED

Service is frequently relegated to maintenance and problem solving. However, done properly, service can be a key differentiator between you and the competition. Meeting customer requirements in the most appropriate and efficient way adds enormously to the perceived value of your product and can sometimes increase the profitability of your relationship.

FAQS

My product is a market leader. Why would services be important?

Services can add further value to a product, providing incremental income and increasing customer loyalty. Services provide you with an opportunity to continue dealing with a customer long after the initial sale and raise barriers around your customers.

I already offer free installation and maintenance with my products. Does that add value?

Yes. But whilst some customers may expect this, others may not or may not value this service. Many companies have recognised the importance of service to certain customers, and have changed their service strategy accordingly. Instead of offering free service to everyone, they have upgraded the services, increased the range of services offered, and therefore, in some cases, started charging customers. Although customers may initially object to being charged for something that seemed to be free, they may see the value of a service that now more closely meets their needs.

I don't have the skills or resources to deliver services. How can I offer my customers a service?

You can either build your own service team through recruitment and training or work in partnership with a specialist organisation which will deliver service on your behalf.

My customers have their own internal service people. Why should they want to use my services?

Many companies have internal service departments. They can be expensive to maintain, however, and are sometimes lacking in essential skills, for example, they may not be trained in the latest software. By demonstrating the potential savings and benefits of outsourcing a service, you can persuade them to switch to you.

MAKING IT HAPPEN
Differentiate your product with service

Service is proving to be a key differentiator in many market sectors. In many companies, however, the role of the service department should be more than simply maintenance and problem solving. For example, a company supplying industrial dishwashers to the restaurant trade must ensure that they can respond quickly to breakdowns—replacing the machine if necessary rather than simply scheduling a repair visit. So, to take full advantage of the service opportunity, it is important to explain the benefits of effective service to customers, and present your service operations as convenient, cost-effective, and strategically important.

Meet key service attributes

These are some of the key features that customers may be looking for in a service offer:

- one contact point, simplifying contact and service administration
- direct contact with a technical specialist, providing an immediate response to problems or queries wherever the customer is located
- quality support to a standard such as ISO 9000, giving independent reassurance that service standards are high
- support round the clock means that it is

available when the customer needs it, and minimises interruption of their business

- service options give a choice of service levels, which can be aligned to customers' needs
- investment in support means long-term commitment to the customer

Provide one contact point for service resources

Whether your customers have a technical query, a service request, or a product enquiry, or need advice, guidance, or information, they should be able to call one number for direct access to all your support resources. Ideally, you'll have specialists on the spot to deal with their requests. If they can't answer the query straight away, make sure that the right person calls the customer back.

Offer direct contact with technical specialists

Your customers may have a technical query, and want to talk to an experienced specialist straight away. When they call the technical help desk, they should be talking to a highly skilled person with extensive technical support and field experience. It may mean locating support staff in accessible locations to be able to make visits quickly and efficiently.

Provide good support

When your customers have a service request, they should be able to contact a central service point where a service co-ordinator ensures that the right specialist help is available. Service co-ordinators should ensure that customers get the fastest and most effective response to their requests. In some cases, service points can deal with requests directly but if not, they can assign an engineer to visit the customer site within agreed times. All service processes should be assessed to ISO 9000. If customers have any queries, there should be an 'escalation procedure' to move a customer complaint up to a more senior team member if the person dealing with the complaint initially cannot resolve it. This should ensure a prompt resolution of any problems.

Offer flexible service options

You can provide your customers with a choice of flexible service options to suit their operational needs and to increase their loyalty. If your customers have in-house support, you can support their team with an efficient spares delivery service, or manage their spares for them. You can also offer to enhance the skills of your customer's in-house team with training, advice and guidance, technical support, and access to specialists. You may go as far as offering consultancy on a fee basis, utilising your specialist knowledge to help your customer.

Invest in support

High-quality service for your market may require a significant investment in the service infrastructure: the right premises, efficient service communications, and a sophisticated service management system to enable you to enhance your response and performance even further. It may require you to appoint one person with specific responsibility for customer service or, perhaps, develop a dedicated support website.

Add value to a product

Improving your customer service may add value and help to differentiate your products and services from the competition. By analysing the products and services in your range (and those of your competitors), you can add relevant value and improve a customer's perception of your business. Some examples are

- business services that free up customer staff to do more important tasks, or help managers perform their jobs better. Training, for example, can ensure that staff make more effective use of the products the company buys.
- complementary services to make a consumer product more attractive, such as film processing offered with a camera
- convenience services added to a basic service to enhance it. Insurance companies, for example, might add a helpline or list of approved repairers to help their customers recover more quickly from an accident

Develop product/service packages

To add value to products and to increase customer loyalty, put together 'bundles' of products and services that reflect customer needs. The list below shows examples of this.

'Adding-in' services

- specialist package holidays, including flights, hotel, and guides
- a building company includes plans and planning application services

'Leaving-out' services

- 'fastfit' car repair centres, without non-essential services
- specialised conveyancing services without using solicitors

Added value services

- home delivery of fast food or videos
- support and advice through helplines

Changing distribution channels

- direct sales, bypassing retailers, such as organic vegetable 'box schemes'
- electronic delivery, such as delivery of technical drawings and specifications

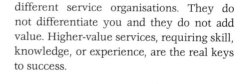

WHAT TO AVOID

Offering only basic services

Basic services such as installation, maintenance, and upgrades are available from many different service organisations. They do not differentiate you and they do not add value. Higher-value services, requiring skill, knowledge, or experience, are the real keys to success.

Failing to invest in a service infrastructure

Customers expect a quality service. That means you have to invest in people and infrastructure. Ideally, your services should conform to recognised industry standards. If you fail to deliver the right standard of service, you could damage customer relationships.

Missing service opportunities

Customers require many different services during the time they own a product. Their requirements could include advice, consultancy, and design before the sale; installation and training, followed by maintenance, upgrading, and other after-sales services. Each of these represents an opportunity to earn incremental income and maintain contact with the customer.

RECOMMENDED LINK

Chartered Institute of Marketing:
www.cim.co.uk

Communicating Customer Service

GETTING STARTED

Your business won't survive without customers, and you need to get across how much you value them. To communicate well externally, you need to have in place a clear, consistent, internal communications strategy too. If you have a team of people working with you, let them know how they each contribute to your business's success, and the way they interact with your customers is a key part of this.

FAQS

Who is responsible for customer service?

Everyone in a business, contributes to overall customer satisfaction, even if their jobs do not involve direct customer contact. Broken delivery promises, inaccurate invoices, or poor telephone handling can cancel out the benefits of a good product or service.

Why are award programmes important to the success of customer service?

Customer service staff are in the front line, facing difficult customers and frequent problems. Award programmes can help to maintain motivation and demonstrate that their contribution is important.

Isn't customer service the same as marketing?

Certain aspects of customer service—understanding customer needs, delivering a service, tailoring the offer to meet customer requirements—are the same, but the scope of marketing is much broader.

Is customer service just a set of personal skills?

Personal skills are important, but a company can put in place processes and programmes that improve the customer's experience and make it easier and more convenient for the customer to do business.

MAKING IT HAPPEN

Communicate clearly

When a company changes its focus towards customer service, it is essential that everyone is involved. Change creates an atmosphere of uncertainty so it is vital that everyone understands the important issues and feels that they can contribute to the success of the change. In an atmosphere of uncertainty, customer service levels can be adversely affected.

Build understanding

Organisational changes can have a significant impact on employees, suppliers, and distributors—so it is vital that they are thoroughly briefed. Change can be a powerful positive factor rather than a cause for concern, and change can demonstrate that a business is committed to improvement and progress.

Encourage commitment

Implementing a customer service policy requires commitment and involvement from all employees. Before implementing a programme, it is sensible to find what the level of commitment is and to include staff in discussion. The most important part of the process is the follow-up. Too many employees believe views will be ignored.

Encourage improvement

As far as possible, training should be offered to all staff to help them understand the importance of customer care. A customer satisfaction guide could be issued, describing the most important elements of customer service and the standards which apply.

Maintain motivation

Motivation and award programmes can help to maintain high levels of interest in the customer service programme and build a high level of commitment to the programme's success. Award programmes that reward continued improvement in levels of customer satisfaction maintain momentum and give customer service programmes a high profile. They are therefore valuable in building team spirit and a commitment to excellence.

Provide a vision

Clear visions and strong, motivating language focus attention on the importance of customer service programmes. It is also essential that the programme is led from the top. A key figure should be involved personally in every aspect of the programmes—talking to groups of employees and using every public relations opportunity to raise the profile of the programme.

Develop champions

The leader cannot achieve all the objectives alone, so it is essential that other people with influence can take on the role of supporting the message throughout the business. Management commentators often call these people 'champions'. Their task is to build commitment and enthusiasm for change. They may be the very people who could undermine change if left out of the process, though.

WHAT TO AVOID
Treating customer service as a departmental function

Customer service is left to those staff who are directly involved with customers. This is too limited a view, because customer service is relegated to a sales or complaints handling process.

Managing customer service at departmental level

If customer service is treated as a line management function, staff will not appreciate its critical importance to the success of the business. Customer service must be led from the top, with the direct involvement of a senior manager.

Failure to develop customer service skills

It's a common misconception that customer service quality depends solely on personal skills. Customer service standards can be improved through training and through the introduction of related programmes.

Low recognition

Customer service has long suffered from low perceived status. Motivation and reward programmes, together with leadership from the top, can help to redress the balance.

RECOMMENDED LINK
Chartered Management Institute:
www.managers.org.uk

SEE ALSO
Corporate Hospitality (p. 254)
Handling Customer Inquiries (p. 245)
Handling Customer Problems (p. 248)
Retaining Existing Customers (p. 237)

Handling Customer Inquiries

GETTING STARTED

Businesses need mechanisms to cope with inquiries or requests for help from both existing and potential customers. This actionlist offers some information on the different options open to you.

Helplines are essential for delivering support, service, advice, and information to customers and add value to a business. To provide the best service, use staff with extensive, up-to-date product knowledge and train them in customer service techniques to ensure they can deal effectively with different types of query or problem. To maximise the benefit to users of the service, deal with queries immediately where possible, or arrange to call the customer back on more complex queries, and ensure that the customer is satisfied with the response at the end of the conversation.

FAQS

Should helpline services be offered free to customers?

Helpline services fall into a number of categories: support, help with problems, advice, and useful information. The support categories should be free because they are essential for customer satisfaction. The information services also can be seen as a customer service, something that adds value to the original purchase. You may feel it strengthens customer relationships to continue offering them free. Information services offered to the general public are valuable services that can be charged, usually through a premium rate number.

Which staff should work on the helplines?

Trained customer service staff can help customers report a problem effectively and may be able to offer advice or help up to a certain level. When the query goes beyond their level of knowledge, you should have a two-stage process in which the customer service representative takes the initial call and arranges for a specialist to call the customer back within an agreed time.

Can a helpline service be handled by an external organisation?

Provided the external organisation's team undergoes thorough training, there is no reason why the helpline cannot be out-sourced. The practice is common in the computer industry.

MAKING IT HAPPEN

Set up a helpline

The most important thing about a helpline is that it really needs to *help*, so there are a number of rules to remember when setting one up.

- Make it convenient: offer customers a Freephone facility to encourage contact, and set opening times to suit customer calling patterns.
- Get the right staff: use staff with extensive, up-to-date product knowledge, and make sure that they are trained in customer service techniques so that they can deal effectively with different types of query or problem.
- Provide the right back-up: helpline staff need to have access to any existing product, technical, or service databases, as well as guidelines on the actions they can take to deal with different types of complaint. Make sure they also have lists of contacts for authorisation of different types of action and information.
- Make the service fast and reliable: deal with queries immediately or arrange to call the customer back on more complex queries, and operate an 'escalation procedure' (see below for more information) to deal with complaints that cannot be resolved within agreed time scales.

- Check and double check: follow up to make sure that if a customer was promised a return call within an agreed time scale, it did happen and that he or she is satisfied with the response.

Plan helpline staffing levels

There's nothing worse that getting to a helpline but then being kept on hold for a long time. It really is crucial to get your staffing levels right, so ask your telephone supplier to provide a report on the number of calls to the helpline number, as well as the average waiting time, and then analyse the pattern of calls during the day/week/month/year, identifying the peaks and troughs. This will help you to determine the current and planned level of calls per day; the ratio of staff to calls, and therefore how many helpline staff you need.

If you have very marked peak and off-peak periods, decide whether you can meet demand using current staff resources, or whether it might be beneficial to use technologies such as voicemail to handle some of the incoming calls. If you can afford it, you could also consider using an external call handling service to manage overload or peak traffic.

Identify helpline skills

Make sure that your staff meet a checklist of appropriate helpline skills. These might include product knowledge, telephone technique, and technical, product service, administrative, and customer service skills.

Develop helpline skills

Regardless of how good your staff are, there are always ways in which you can help them improve and develop their skills. Assess the skills required for different types of helpline service, compare these with the current skills of your helpline staff, and identify the areas that need to be improved. Implement training and monitor performance improvements, ensure that staff know how to use any new technology, and obtain customer feedback to evaluate performance.

Provide customer information for helpline staff

Your staff will be able to provide a prompt response and personal service if they've been given enough customer information. Make available the information you already have, such as existing customer records, data generated by responses to advertisements or promotional activities, and so on, and make sure it is checked and updated. Take the opportunity to capture customer information each time a customer calls, and add further information that is appropriate to the helpline service, such as service records. Use a simple code to access information quickly, for example, name, account number, and postcode, and include prompts to contact customers with details of new products and services.

Set up helpline escalation procedures

There are always some calls that cannot be dealt with immediately, so you need to have an escalation procedure in place to make sure they don't slip through the net. Identify critical types of helpline requests, including technical support, complaints, and breakdowns, and set target response times for such queries. Appoint a supervisor to monitor conformance to target response times; escalate any queries that exceed target times to a designated manager, and monitor the responses to escalated queries.

Record helpline usage

In order to make sure you are meeting demand properly, you need to record helpline usage. How many calls does your helpline receive: per day; per week; per month; per year? What types of call does it receive and what is the volume of each type of call? Which customers are the most regular helpline users? Which media generate most inquiries to the helpline? What is the impact of promotional campaigns on helpline activity? Which products receive most/least complaints, queries, or requests for support? What are the most frequent complaints, queries, and requests for support? Which type of request uses most resources?

What is the average call time for different types of request?

Promote the helpline service

Above all, make sure customers know what help is available to them. Include the helpline number in advertisements, publications, website pages, and other promotional material, as well as on invoices, delivery notes, instructions, user guides, and other product documentation.

 WHAT TO AVOID

Putting the wrong people on the helpline

The people who run the helpline should have good customer handling skills and a level of product and technical knowledge that enables them to provide the right answer or put the customer in contact with the right specialist.

Inadequate resources on the helpline

When customers call a helpline, they are looking for a quick response. Phones that go unanswered for long periods of time show poor customer service. Putting a customer in a queue of other callers is satisfactory only for a short period of time.

Failing to call the customer back

If you cannot deal with queries immediately, let the customer know when someone will get back to him or her, and then check that the return call has been made.

RECOMMENDED LINK

Call Centre Association:
www.cca.org.uk

SEE ALSO

Communicating Customer Service (p. 243)
Converting Leads into Sales (p. 234)
Handling Customer Problems (p. 248)

Handling Customer Problems

GETTING STARTED

Even the most professional service companies will inevitably face a problem with a customer that, if left unresolved, may lead to a loss of business. Customers who know that their problems are taken care of are more likely to be be fully satisfied with the services that are available. A key factor in resolving customers' problems is the ability to reassure them that help is on the way. Having in place a process to respond quickly and effectively to a problem enables a company to deliver the highest standards of customer care at a time when the customer most needs it.

   This process, sometimes called incident management, is particularly suitable for larger companies or if the customer is likely to suffer a great deal of inconvenience because of the incident. However, the principles can be applied to any business, however small.

- In developing a response and support strategy, you should set a wide range of business objectives.
- The incident management approach is to appoint one person, trained in customer service skills, to deal with a customer throughout an incident.
- The role of the personal incident manager is to take responsibility for the provision of appropriate services.
- An incident management programme has two main elements—the infrastructure to deliver the service and the personal skills to provide the right level of customer care.
- Skilled staff are essential to the effective delivery of the service and training may be necessary.
- Many equipment manufacturers use incident management techniques to support their customers after a disaster.

FAQS

Should incident management form part of all service offerings?

It depends on the type of service that is offered. If the service is critical to the customer's business process—telecommunications or computing, for example—incident management would be important. Disruption to those services could damage the customer's business.

Why is a personal incident manager necessary?

During an incident, effective co-ordination of support services and regular communication with the customer are essential. By appointing a single person to take responsibility for co-ordination and communication, you can guarantee continuity and reassure the customer by giving them a single point of contact.

Is it possible to plan for future incidents?

It isn't just possible; it is essential. Industry research indicates that a high proportion of companies who did not have a documented plan failed to recover lost business. Planning is just as important as quality support services.

MAKING IT HAPPEN

Deal with customer incidents

Customers who know that their problems are taken care of are more likely to be fully satisfied with the services that are available and will be happier to deal with the same company in the future. Quality experts found that a key factor in delivering time-guaranteed services was the ability to reassure customers that help was on the way. Customers would then be prepared to wait until help or support arrived, even if there was a long gap between reporting the incident and having it resolved. Other research has shown that customers whose complaints are satisfactorily dealt with are likely to be more loyal than those who had no complaint in the first place.

Identify opportunities for incident management

A number of scenarios can be used to identify situations where support like this could be valuable.

- The customer could suffer a great deal of inconvenience and stress as a result of the incident. Reducing the stress and inconvenience would help to demonstrate high levels of care and increase customer satisfaction.
- The incident could threaten the efficiency of the company business, and measures must be taken to limit the damage.
- The customer does not have the skills and resources to resolve the problems on the spot and is dependent on external forms of support.
- The customer has paid for a support package and has agreed to a certain level of response. The company must respond within the agreed levels.
- The speed of response is seen as a competitive differentiation and is positioned as an integral part of the service package.
- Failure to deal with the incident quickly could have a critical effect on the customer's business or personal activities.
- The incident could have legal implications, and the customer needs high levels of advice and guidance.

Set objectives for incident management

In developing a response and support strategy, you should set a wide range of business objectives:

- to provide the highest levels of quality response and customer support throughout an incident
- to minimise inconvenience for the customer
- to ensure that incidents are resolved promptly within agreed time scales
- to ensure that support resources are

deployed effectively to maximise customer satisfaction

Introduce incident management

The incident management approach is to appoint one person, trained in customer service skills, to deal with a customer throughout an incident.

Incident management can be applied to any service-led organisation where the customer needs to be kept informed, for example, maintenance and support services for vital equipment or disaster recovery services where the customer faces difficult and unfamiliar decisions and needs support.

Appoint a personal incident manager

The role of the personal incident manager is to take responsibility for the provision of appropriate services and to reassure the customer that help and support are on the way. In the smaller company, this may be a senior manager, even the managing director, but whoever takes the role must have the authority to take appropriate action. The personal incident manager:

- takes the incoming calls from the customer, establishes the location, and identifies the form of support needed
- provides individual guidance to the customer on action to be taken with an indication of the support that will be provided
- deals with the customer's immediate queries
- makes detailed arrangements to put support services into operation
- monitors the progress of support services and keeps the customer up to date if possible

Offer disaster recovery services

Many equipment manufacturers use incident management techniques to support their customers after a disaster such as fire, accident, or system breakdown. If the customer loses essential equipment such as computers or telephones for an extended period, this could seriously threaten the future of their business. Industry research shows that only a minority of companies dependent on the computer have a formal disaster recovery strategy and points out that loss of a system for more than a few days could put them out of business.

Plan and implement disaster recovery

A disaster recovery programme has a number of stages:

- helping the customer identify critical activities that should be covered in the event of a disaster
- training staff and managers to prepare for a disaster by simulating the conditions of an emergency
- preparing a contingency plan
- providing replacement equipment and services in the event of an incident
- providing support and project management resources during an incident
- providing full support to restore normal service

Throughout a disaster, the customer would have access to an incident manager who would co-ordinate the rescue and recovery activities, and provide advice, guidance, and support. The principle is similar to that of the personal incident manager, where customers are given reassurance that incidents will be resolved and that they can be sure of the highest standards of support throughout the incident.

Create the infrastructure for incident management

The programme has two main elements: the infrastructure to deliver the service and the personal skills to provide the right level of customer care. The infrastructure requires a significant investment to ensure that the service can be delivered rapidly and efficiently throughout the country. Depending on the complexity of the project, it might include:

- communications to provide a rapid response to customer queries, and put the service into operation
- a trained support team to deliver the service
- quality-controlled suppliers to support the direct response team
- a control centre to manage the operations and co-ordinate the response

- a network of contacts and suppliers to provide the specialist services that form part of the response

Develop the right skills

Skilled staff are essential to the effective delivery of the service. The skills requirements would include:

- incident management skills, to deal with customers who may be in stressful situations
- project management skills, to co-ordinate and implement a response
- technical skills, to deliver the service
- communications skills, to co-ordinate the elements of the programme

WHAT TO AVOID
Failing to communicate with the customer during an incident

Research shows that customers who receive regular progress updates feel reassured that they are getting the right level of support. Anxiety levels are high during an incident, but regular communication helps customers deal with the incident and contributes to overall customer satisfaction.

Having no escalation procedure

A company should have a formal escalation procedure for dealing with customer incidents. If support staff cannot resolve an incident within an agreed time scale, the incident should be reported to a more senior manager, who would then commit more resources. If there is no escalation procedure, the incident can get out of hand and damage customer relationships.

Failure to train staff in customer care

An incident creates high levels of stress in an organisation, and support staff must be trained to deal with this.

RECOMMENDED LINK
Chartered Institute of Marketing:
www.cim.co.uk

SEE ALSO
Communicating Customer Service (p. 243)
Handling Customer Inquiries (p. 245)

Increasing Customer Lifetime Value

GETTING STARTED

'Customer lifetime value' (CLV or LTV) is a way of measuring how much your customers are worth over the time they are your customers. Increases in customer retention can increase sales and profits significantly. It is important to retain customers, but not at the cost of other essential marketing activities.

Putting customers into key categories helps clarify analysis and acts as the basis for marketing activities designed to improve customer lifetime value.

FAQS

What's the difference between customer lifetime value and customer loyalty programmes?

Customer loyalty programmes are designed to retain as many customers as possible, regardless of their real value. The customer lifetime value calculation indicates the contribution individual customers make to profitability.

Why are lapsed customers important?

If they can be 'revived', they tend to behave like new customers and become regular buyers once again, with good potential lifetime value.

Is customer retention more important than acquisition?

Acquisition should never be neglected, because existing business may decline for reasons outside your control. Industry experience indicates, however, that existing customers make a comparatively greater contribution when marketing costs are taken into consideration.

Do we want to retain all our customers?

Not necessarily. Some customers may not be profitable. Using customer lifetime value, you can calculate the cost and contribution of each customer.

MAKING IT HAPPEN

Apply the customer lifetime value concept

Customer lifetime value is a way of measuring how much your customers are worth to you, over the length of time that they remain your customers.

The lifetime for customers will vary from industry to industry, and from brand to brand. The lifetime of customers should come to an end when their contribution ceases to be profitable, unless steps are taken to revitalise them.

Benefits from customer lifetime value

Industry experience indicates that a number of benefits apply.

- A 5% increase in customer retention can create a 125% increase in profits.
- A 10% increase in retailer retention can translate to a 20% increase in sales.
- Extending customer life cycles by three years can treble profits per customer.

Identify categories of customer

Before calculating customer lifetime value, it is possible to analyse your customers according to four key attributes. This can help to clarify analysis and act as the basis for marketing activities to improve customer lifetime value.

- Frequency—how often they purchase (regular customers are more likely to purchase in the future)
- Recency—how much time has elapsed since the last purchase (recent customers are more likely to purchase again)
- Amount—how much they spend (higher spending customers are likely to be more committed)
- Category—what sort of product did they buy (some products will be more profitable

than others and some may be one-off purchases)

Calculate lifetime value

In a consumer business, customer lifetime value is calculated, in practice, by analysing the behaviour of a group of customers who:

- have the same recruitment date
- are recruited from the same source
- bought the same types of product

In a business-to-business environment, a similar approach can be used.

- Isolate particular customers, and examine them individually.
- Analyse the behaviour of different groups, segmenting your customer database by factors such as industry, annual turnover, or staff numbers.

The basic calculation has three stages.

- Identify a discrete group of customers for tracking.
- Record (or estimate) each revenue and cost for this group of customers, by campaign or season.
- Calculate the contribution, by campaign or season.

Refine the calculation

Other factors can be introduced to make the calculation more relevant. In a business-to-business environment, for example, it may be the sales representatives who generate sales. In this case, the calculation should include the representative's 'running costs' and the cost of any centrally produced sales support material.

Evaluate a campaign

The table shows the calculations for a group of customers who were recruited through a direct response advertising campaign that ran in the spring of year 1. The table tracks their expenditure over a five-year period.

Divide the total contribution by the number of customers in the group. Say there are one thousand customers: the average lifetime value per customer is £7. But this compares favourably with a short term analysis which, in the first year, would show a loss of £3 per customer recruited.

Analyse the results

A company may offer different products or brands, which are marketed under different cost centres. If a customer is a customer of more than one cost/profit centre, there is a choice of approaches:

- examine customers of each brand and ignore multi-purchases
- build a more detailed model that combines and allocates the cumulative costs as well as the cumulative profit in the appropriate proportions

Use customer lifetime values to improve marketing performance

There are four important applications:

- setting target customer acquisition costs
- allocating acquisition funds
- selecting acquisition offers
- supporting customer retention activities

In the example above the decision was taken in Year 4 to reduce marketing costs on this group of customers. Equally valid may be an increase in expenditure aimed at reactivating customers—this is a classic retention activity.

Set target customer acquisition costs

If a customer is expected to generate more than one sale, the allowable cost can be greater than the cost allowed for the first

Year	Annual Customer Expenditure	Annual Marketing Costs	Annual Net Contribution
0	£12,000	£15,000	£–3,000
1	£10,000	£6,000	£4,000
2	£8,000	£6,000	£2,000
3	£7,000	£6,000	£1,000
4	£6,000	£4,000	£2,000
5	£5,000	£4,000	£1,000
Totals	**£48,000**	**£41,000**	**£7,000**

sale—the classic loss-leader approach to customer acquisition illustrated in the example table above. However, overspending on customer acquisition can also be ruinous. A reasonable calculation is to recruit only from those sources that yield new customers at less than half the estimated lifetime value. On that basis, the worst sources will have a cost per customer close to a lifetime value, while the average cost per customer should be far lower.

Allocate acquisition funds

Different recruitment sources will provide customers with different lifetime values. After identifying those values, spend more on the best sources.

Select acquisition offers

The lifetime value of a customer may depend on the type and value of their initial purchase. In turn, this can lead to decisions about which products and offers to use when advertising externally, or when considering how to upgrade existing customers.

Support customer retention activities

Once the typical lifetime value of a group of customers is known, companies can decide how hard to work at retaining them. It is not a foregone conclusion that all customers are worth having. Activities should be tailored to the customers who are most valuable.

Increase value with new offers

A financial services company can increase customer lifetime value by cross-selling a range of different products and services.

WHAT TO AVOID

Trying to retain the wrong customers

Customer retention costs money in terms of sales and marketing funds. Moreover, customer lifetime value analysis indicates that it is a mistake to assume that all customers are worth retaining. You should carefully select the customers who are likely to yield the highest returns over a period of time and prioritise the allocation of marketing resources to these.

Offering customers a limited range of products

When you have identified the most valuable customers, you need to have a wide range of products or services to offer them. Cross-selling and up-selling are the best ways to increase customer lifetime value, but this can be difficult with a limited product range. Customers are your company's most valuable asset; think about 'share of customer wallet' rather than just share of market.

Spending too much on acquiring new customers

Customer lifetime value analysis reinforces a traditional marketing rule of thumb, that it costs less to retain existing customers than to acquire new ones. Overemphasis on new business development could prove to be a bad move, since existing customers are easier to sell to.

RECOMMENDED LINK

Peppers + Rogers:
www.peppersandrogers.com

Corporate Hospitality

GETTING STARTED

Corporate hospitality (or entertainment) is widely used by businesses of all sizes as a means of forging and strengthening relationships with people who are important to the success of the business. It can be aimed at internal audiences (staff) through motivational events, or at external audiences (existing clients, potential clients, and even members of the local community) as part of a careful sales and marketing strategy. It provides an opportunity to get to know staff or customers, and to allow them to get to know the manager, business, and product better.

FAQS

What are the advantages and disadvantages of internal corporate hospitality?

Corporate hospitality may be used to improve staff morale, perhaps by motivating a sales team, raising customer awareness, building team working skills, celebrating a special occasion, or increasing business profits. Advantages can include improved communications and understanding, an improved organisational spirit, and a reduction in staff turnover through improved loyalty and greater motivation.

You do, however, need to be aware of some of the disadvantages to this approach. If you're holding a social event, make sure that all employees have an equal opportunity to attend. Give as much notice as you can so that people can make arrangements, such as finding a babysitter if they have children. Also think very carefully about whom you wish to reward. For example, a gift given to one individual may be regarded as favouritism. It's important to exercise discretion and to be aware of the potential risks of damaging staff morale.

Also think long and hard about running a corporate event for employees because you think staff morale is low. There may be more practical reasons for staff discontent, for example salary or promotion problems, or lack of equipment, and team building activities are unlikely to rectify such problems—they could even compound them. Get to the root of the problem first and then decide whether a corporate event is the best way of solving it.

What are the advantages and disadvantages of external corporate hospitality?

External corporate hospitality promotes your business to existing or potential clients, providing an environment to meet clients socially, and using the informality of a social event to find out more about the client's needs. The expectation is that it will help you to develop business contacts, and the business to sell more products and services.

Corporate hospitality can help to increase customer loyalty, differentiate your business from the competition, target the best prospects (your existing customers), increase word of mouth recommendations, raise and maintain the profile of your business, and build positive relationships. The main disadvantages are that external clients may not be able to accept this hospitality, and that there may also be considerable costs involved.

MAKING IT HAPPEN
Types of corporate hospitality event

There are many events and activities on offer to choose from. Make sure the activity is appropriate for your purpose, and put the emphasis on having fun!

Spectator events

A small business is unlikely to have the budget required to entertain clients and/or staff at lavish major spectator events such as the Henley Regatta or Wimbledon. However, you could think about inviting clients and/or staff to popular events such as rugby, golf, football, horse racing, opera, music, or the theatre.

Social events

You may want to invite existing clients to a lunch, dinner, or party. Social events for staff are more likely to be linked to a special occasion, such as Christmas or New Year, or for hitting a specific sales target.

Participation events

Common examples of this type of event include multi-activity days, rock climbing, and sailing. Don't force employees into taking part in physical activities if they don't want to, however—that really will damage morale. It's essential that you obtain adequate insurance cover so that your business is covered in the event of accidents. Unless the client is a personal friend, it's unlikely that a participation event would involve clients—it might be embarrassing if a client was defeated at a sporting event! However, a business meeting could be arranged to take place with a round of golf.

Family occasions

You might also consider showing your appreciation for an employee on a special occasion, for example a wedding or the birth of a child, by offering a gift. Alternatively, you may decide to run a informal family fun day in the form of a small local gathering with side-shows and attractions for the children, such as a bouncy castle or an arts-and-crafts section. Celebrating a family occasion with a client is unlikely as it's usually considered a private affair, outside of the business relationship.

Team-building events

These are a common form of corporate incentive for staff. The traditional outward-bound day may not be suitable, as it places physical rather than mental demands on the participants, and therefore may not be universally popular. Work-related simulation activities, for example running a fictional business, may be more appropriate. The key to the success of such an activity is that the purpose is clearly communicated to all those involved, so explain to everyone why they are doing the activity, and that they are not just having a fun day out. The greatest benefits can be derived from such events when they are followed through and when the lessons learned from the activity are applied to the workplace. While team building is thought of as an employee activity, some companies/suppliers may have a long history of trading with the business so that their employees could also be invited to join in team building events.

Using event organisers

You might enjoy organising small-scale events personally, such as the staff Christmas party or a business lunch, or you might ask another employee to do so. Alternatively, you may decide to engage the services of an event organiser to carry out the planning and staging of larger events. There is stiff competition in this field, with a wide range of event organisers, suppliers, and venues to choose from. The Corporate Hospitality and Event Association (CHA) has a directory of members including caterers, suppliers, event organisers, and venues. Members of the CHA operate to a code of conduct and ensure that customers are dealing with a reputable and responsible business. Event organisers work in close collaboration with outside suppliers, including hotels, tent and marquee hire companies, audio and visual equipment hire companies, and so on. They use a wide variety of venues, ranging from large stately homes to small hotels.

Event organisers usually offer a package tailored to your needs and objectives, timetable, budget, and guest profile. The price depends on the number of people being entertained, the type/number of activities chosen, the duration of the event, and whether catering and accommodation are included. Choose an organiser who offers an inclusive event price and be aware of hidden costs, such as staff accommodation and meals. Ask to see the organiser's terms and conditions so that you know what is in the small print, for example, what happens if an event is cancelled due to bad weather (you can take out insurance to cover this). In addition, check that the event organiser has adequate public liability insurance.

Costs of corporate hospitality

Budget carefully for the cost of providing corporate hospitality and set aside money in your marketing budget at the beginning of the financial year, rather than using surplus money that may be left over at the end. You may need to cut out corporate hospitality altogether if there is a downturn in business. All instances where a client/member of staff has been entertained are a legitimate business expense and should be included in the corporate hospitality budget. These include all business lunches with existing and potential clients, and the staff Christmas party.

Corporate gifts

Corporate gifts can be used as part of your marketing strategy, targeted either at an individual or a group of people. They can be also used to offer a goodwill gesture or to serve as a reminder to customers. Gifts may be given as a staff incentive too, or as a special award. Corporate gifts should be appropriate to the event and reflect something about your business. Typical examples may be a Christmas card bearing your company logo, or a fun item such as a pen or small notebook. It's also often a good idea to leave a reminder of your business name with a client. The gift need not be expensive but should be of appropriate quality. More expensive items may give the impression that the client is valued more highly. However, be aware that local authorities and some private companies do not allow their employees to accept gifts at all, as an extravagant gift may be seen as an attempt to bribe an official or influence a contract. Offering a corporate gift to an employee may be seen by the tax authorities as payment in lieu of wages, or as a bonus.

WHAT TO AVOID

Poor planning

Arrange events well in advance, and choose a suitable time, activity, and location. Don't leave it to the last minute, as this will prove stressful and also mean that not everyone you'd like to attend can come along.

Not arranging insurance

The importance of the employer's duty of care towards their employees cannot be overstated. Make sure you take out public liability insurance.

Not evaluating events

Evaluate each event properly once it's over. For example, you could measure events for your customers for quantifiable results, such as increased sales.

Not taking allowable expenses into account

Contact the Inland Revenue to find out what are considered to be allowable business expenses.

RECOMMENDED LINKS

Association for Conferences and Events (ACE):
www.martex.co.uk/ace
Corporate Hospitality and Event Association:
www.cha-event.co.uk
EventServiceNet:
www.eventservicenet.co.uk
The Inland Revenue:
www.inlandrevenue.gov.uk
Society of Event Organisers:
www.seoevent.co.uk

SEE ALSO

Communicating Customer Service (p. 243)
Managing Key Accounts (p. 257)
Retaining Existing Customers (p. 237)
Selling and Salesmanship (p. 546)

Managing Key Accounts

GETTING STARTED

It's said that 80% of the average business's income will come from just 20% of its customers, so it makes sense to dedicate time and resources to keeping those key accounts satisfied. More than this, you also need to ask yourself how you could better serve the needs of these key accounts, to build loyalty and more business with them.

Your business needs both a commitment and a strategy to manage its key accounts. The first step is to understand and appreciate the need to allocate resources. Research in the United States suggests that larger businesses have been consciously reducing their number of suppliers. The positive side of this is that, if you as a supplier successfully meet your key customers' needs, you're likely to progressively capture more of their business. One of the results is that customers come to rely on your special insight into their needs, and the cost (to them) of changing suppliers then grows.

Your strategy then needs to outline what you want to achieve with your key accounts, and how you plan to achieve this. Make sure that there is a particular person (preferably a senior manager or director) in your business who has the final responsibility for ensuring that each key customer is happy with your service. If you have a formal customer relationship management (CRM) system, this should support your key account strategy by recording the date and nature of all contact with the clients. One book you may find useful for more ideas is *Key Account Management and Planning: The Comprehensive Handbook for Managing Your Company's Most Important Strategic Asset* by Noel Capon, published in 2001 by Free Press.

FAQS

Why is key account management necessary?

The loyalty of your big customers is too important to leave unmanaged. Consider what would happen if the salesperson dealing with a big customer were to resign suddenly and leave certain important duties undone; this could undermine years of trust and co-operation. On a more day-to-day level, your important customers need to know that they can turn to someone senior in your business if there are problems in the business relationship.

How do you identify a key account?

This will obviously depend on how many customers you have, and whether they are evenly spread in terms of the amount that each of them spends with you. As a rule of thumb, you could view any customer who brings in substantially more business than average as a key account. Your challenge will be to see how many of these customers you can treat in a preferential way, given the limits of your time and resources.

Do you need key account managers?

Many small businesses will not have the capacity to appoint a large number of people to work exclusively as key account managers. In reality, you'll probably want to build the job of account manager into jobs that already exist in your business. For instance, as the owner of your business, you'll most likely have an important role to play in managing key accounts; but you'll do this in addition to the various other responsibilities that you have. In the same way, you could get certain senior staff to take on responsibility for other customers, in addition to their core responsibilities.

MAKING IT HAPPEN
Implement a system

To manage your key accounts successfully, you need to build your contact with them into an on-going process, so that:

- someone senior is allocated responsibility for looking after each key account
- regular contact is maintained with—and feedback requested from—each key customer

- targets are set for the revenue expected from each key account
- the health of the relationship with each key customer is monitored regularly

Develop and empower senior staff

Your big customers want to feel that they have the ear of a decision maker in your business. They need to know that if they are dealing with your business through your key account manager, that person must be experienced and authorised to take decisions so that problems are quickly resolved. From your point of view, this requires an on-going effort to develop the management and people skills of your employees. Especially as your business grows, you'll need to delegate these important responsibilities and rely on others to retain your customers' loyalty.

Consider a customer relationship management (CRM) system

As communications technology allows businesses and the individuals within them to become more efficient, you might find it difficult to keep track of each contact with a customer. If you're prioritising the management of key accounts, you may want to build this into a formal CRM system. This is generally provided as a computer program, and can hold contact details of all your customers, as well as details of their orders and communications with your business. The value of these systems is that they allow important information to be shared among different people in your organisation, so there is no duplication of contact with the client and everyone within your business is fully up to date. It's particularly useful when a problem arises and the history of an order needs to be tracked, or when the relevant person is out of the office and someone else needs the latest information on a transaction.

Keep it personal

One of the main advantages of making individuals responsible for managing key accounts is that trust and co-operation can be built up on a personal basis. Even in our high-tech world, it's still true that people prefer to do business with people they like and trust. Being systematic about this relationship need not detract from the person-to-person value.

WHAT TO AVOID
Waiting for complaints

Be proactive in finding out what your key customers feel about your service. Contact them regularly for feedback; do not wait for them to come to you with a complaint. This also creates an opportunity to talk to them about their own activities, and to get early warning of any future work that your business might be able to gain from them.

Becoming complacent

The danger of having a regular customer for a long time is that you can easily take their business for granted, and be complacent in your attitude to them. Make sure that everyone in your business from the receptionist to the book-keeper is aware of who the key accounts are, so that they are particularly well received whenever they interact with the business.

Putting all your eggs in one basket

By concentrating your efforts on your key accounts, you run the risk of paying insufficient attention to your other customers; indeed, it may even detract from your efforts to find and nurture new customers. This makes you over-reliant on just a few customers, where the effect of losing their business could be disastrous. In addition to posing an unacceptable strategic risk for your business as a whole, this situation could also put your key customers in a position of too much strength where they are able to negotiate terms and prices that you would not otherwise accept.

RECOMMENDED LINK
Business Link:
www.businesslink.org

COMMUNICATING WITH YOUR CUSTOMERS

Perfecting Your Pitch: Preparing Presentations

GETTING STARTED

Being able to cope with presentations is a very valuable skill for the owner-manager of a small business. Presentations are useful in many situations, such as pitching for business, putting a case for funding, and addressing staff meetings. Few people like speaking formally to an audience, but there are many real benefits and as you gain experience in giving presentations, you'll probably find that it becomes less of a worry, and even enjoyable. This actionlist will give you some suggestions for preparing the content of your presentation, looking at the objectives for your presentation, the audience you'll be addressing it to, and the best way to get your points across.

FAQS

What objectives should I set?

The starting point for any presentation is to set clear objectives. Ask yourself why you're giving the talk, and what you want your audience to get out of it. Also consider whether using speech alone is the best way of communicating your message, and whether your presentation would benefit from using visual aids and slides to further illustrate its main points. When you're planning and giving the presentation, keep your objectives in mind at all times—they'll focus your thoughts. Having an objective for giving the presentation will ensure that you're not wasting anyone's time, either your audience's or your own.

What do you need to know about the audience?

Before you plan your presentation try as best you can to find out who is going to be in your audience, and their expectations. For example, the tone and content of a presentation to the managing director of another firm will be very different to one addressed to potential users of a product. It's important that you know the extent of the audience's knowledge about the topic you'll be discussing. Their familiarity with the subject will determine the level at which you pitch the talk. Try to appeal to what will motivate and interest these people.

MAKING IT HAPPEN

Write your speech

When it comes to presentations, there is no substitute for detailed preparation and planning. While everyone prepares in different ways, all of which develop with experience, here are a few key points to bear in mind while you're preparing.

Start by breaking up the task of preparing your speech into manageable units. Once you know the length of the presentation— say 15 minutes, for example—break the time up into smaller units and allocate sections of your speech to each unit. Then note down all the points you want to make, and order them logically. This will help you develop the framework and emphasis of the presentation.

Keep your presentation short and simple, if you possibly can, as it will be easier for you to manage and remember. If you need to provide more detail, you can supply a written handout to be given out at the end. A shorter presentation is usually more effective from the audience's point of view, too, as most people dislike long presentations, and will not necessarily remember any more from them.

Avoid packing your talk with facts and figures; you could instead use graphs and charts to illustrate these where they are essential. Aim to identify two or three key points, and concentrate on getting these over in a creative fashion.

Use visual aids and equipment

With any presentation, you'll need to consider whether to use visual aids, such as acetates for an overhead projector (OHP), or a computer presentation package such as PowerPoint. Remember that visual aids should only be used as signposts during the presentation, to help the audience focus on the main point. It's important not to cram too much information on to one visual aid as you'll probably find that you lose the attention of your audience while they try to read everything on it. Make sure the audience can see the information by using big, bold lettering, and bear in mind that images are often far more effective than words.

At its most basic, a personal computer can be used to develop and produce a series of slides which can be printed onto acetates for use on an overhead projector. A more common usage is to link up the PC with a projector in order to show the information on a large screen.

If you're going to use slides, you should try to standardise them to make them look more professional. Use templates where possible to make sure that they don't blend together and again, try not to put too much information onto a single slide, or it will become difficult to read. A sensible guideline is to include no more than six points per slide, and to keep the number of words you use for each point to the absolute minimum. Think of what you're writing as the prompts for what you want to say.

The most common presentation packages are Microsoft PowerPoint and Corel Presentations. These will allow you to develop a presentation using slide templates. You can make full use of charts, graphics, or even photographs to bring your information alive. Packages such as PhotoShop or Paint Shop Pro will allow you to scan in or manipulate photographs, or you could also use some of the available animations for transitions between slides.

You should pay particular attention to the layout and text on the slides and remain consistent throughout. Select a background that contrasts well with the text, and colours that are strong and provide contrast. It may also be a good idea to include the business's logo on all of the slides. It's important, always, to proofread your slides and acetates. There is nothing more noticeable, or more unprofessional, than a typo or grammatical error projected to ten times its size on a screen!

Practise as many times as you can to make sure that you're very familiar with your speech—allow plenty of time for rehearsal before the event. Once you're confident that your presentation is right, resist the temptation to change it. Remember, *you* may have heard the speech many times, but the audience will be hearing it for the first time. It's also a good idea to practise your speech using the equipment you intend to use; slide projectors and video machines should be tested in advance to make sure you know how to operate them. Make sure you have a contingency plan to cope with any unforeseen mishaps. During your rehearsals, it will also be important to time your speech to ensure it's not too long or too short. Remember that you'll probably need to allow time at the end for a question-and-answer session. Resist the temptation to bring your script into the presentation and instead write the main points on numbered cards, known as cue cards, to provide reminders.

Prepare the venue

Make sure that an appropriately-sized room has been organised for your presentation; take into account the number of people you're expecting, and ensure there is enough seating, lighting, ventilation, and heating. It's a good idea to provide some refreshments for participants such as tea, coffee, and water.

You also need to make sure there will be no interruptions, for example by phone calls, fire drills, or people accidentally entering the room. Whether you're presenting at your own office or elsewhere, you must make sure that any equipment or props you need are available and set up properly before the presentation starts. If you're presenting away from your office, for example, at a conference or a client's premises, it's a good idea to visit the site beforehand to make sure it provides the necessary facilities.

WHAT TO AVOID
Not researching your audience

A good knowledge of the audience is absolutely crucial in finding the correct pitch. It's no good blinding your audience with technical jargon if they only have a basic grasp of the subject. Similarly, a very knowledgeable audience will soon switch off if you spend the first few minutes going over the basics.

Long presentations

If your presentation absolutely has to be longer than 20 minutes, it may be a good idea to insert some breaks so that your audience remains fresh and interested.

Not checking the room and equipment

This can be disastrous! Imagine, for example, arriving and finding that there is no facility for delivering PowerPoint presentations, and you have no other method of showing slides. Make sure you're familiar with the environment in which you'll be presenting.

RECOMMENDED LINKS
The Presentation Business:
www.presentationbiz.co.uk
Public Speaking and Speech Writing:
www.speechtips.com

SEE ALSO
Perfecting Your Pitch: Delivering Presentations (p. 263)
Presentation/Speaking (p. 535)

Perfecting Your Pitch: Delivering Presentations

GETTING STARTED

A presentation is an ideal environment for you to promote your business and its products or services. You have a captive audience, are able to provide them with relevant information, and can answer any questions they may have on the spot. For a presentation to be a success you must be able to hold the attention of the audience and leave them wanting to know more.

Giving presentations does not suit everyone, but practice does help. To give a successful presentation you will need to be able to command your audience's attention and speak in an articulate, fluent fashion. Some people are natural presenters, while others find it more difficult, but practice and feedback from previous audiences will help you develop your presentation skills. This actionlist will give you some ideas for structuring, preparing, and delivering your presentation.

FAQS

How should I structure my presentation?

Structure is essential for any presentation. There should be an introduction, a main body, and a conclusion. You can be witty, controversial, or even outrageous if the mood of the presentation allows, but whatever approach you try, your chief aim is to arouse the audience's curiosity, and to get your message across.

What is the best way to introduce my presentation?

The introduction to your presentation needs to attract your audience's interest and attention. A good opening is also for your own confidence, because if you start well, the rest should follow easily. Plan your opening words carefully for maximum impact: they should be short, sharp, and to the point. Let your audience know how long your presentation will take, as this will prepare them to focus for the period of time you expect to speak. Summarise the contents of your presentation, so that your audience can work out how much information they will need to absorb. Explaining the key points in the first few sentences will also help your mind to focus on the task in hand, and refresh your memory on the major points of your presentation. It sometimes helps to get started if you can learn your first few sentences by heart. Let your audience know if you are

happy to interact with them throughout the presentation. Alternatively, inform them that you will be holding a question and answer session at the end.

What should I do in the main body of the presentation?

The main body of the presentation will be dictated by the points that you want to make. Use short, sharp, and simple language to keep your audience's attention, and to ensure that your message is being understood. Include only one idea per sentence and pause after each one, so as to make a mental full stop. Use precise language to convey your message, but make sure that your presentation sounds spontaneous—it shouldn't sound like a chapter from a textbook. You need to convey your message clearly, without masking the salient points with waffle. Stick to your original plan for your presentation, and don't go off at a tangent on a particular point and miss the thread of your presentation. Why not try using metaphors and images to illustrate points? This will give impact to what you say, and help your audience to remember what you have said.

How should I conclude my presentation?

You should close by summing up the key points of what you have covered. The closing seconds of your presentation are as crucial as the opening sentence. Consider what action you would like your audience to take after the presentation is over and attempt to inspire them to do it.

MAKING IT HAPPEN
Think about posture and delivery

There are certain techniques to do with your posture, and the way that you deliver your presentation, that can be used to improve its impact. Maintain eye contact and address your audience directly throughout your presentation. Try to be aware of your stance, posture, and gestures without being too self-conscious. Don't slouch, as you'll look unprofessional. The best way of avoiding this is by always standing when you are doing a presentation. Don't fiddle, for example with a pencil or a piece of paper; try to keep still and avoid moving around excessively. All these things are distracting for an audience, and will mean that they are missing important points in your presentation.

Remember that your audience has come to learn something. Try to sound authoritative, sincere, and enthusiastic. If you don't sound as if you believe in yourself, this will come across to the audience. Think about the way in which you are speaking. Most people need to articulate their words more clearly when addressing an audience. There is usually no opportunity for the audience to ask you to repeat a word they have missed. Aim to sound the vowels and consonants of words clearly. Be aware, also, of your vocal expression. Try to vary volume, pitch, and speed of delivery to underline your meaning and to maintain the interest of your audience. Try not to use too many acronyms that are specific to your business or industry, as you can't be 100% sure that everyone in the audience will know what they mean. If you do need to use them, introduce them and explain them early in your presentation so that everyone can keep up.

Use cue cards, visual aids, and equipment

It's tempting (and, if you're a nervous presenter, comforting) to have the full version of your speech in front of you, but it's best to avoid this and use cue cards instead. These will have a few headings referring to the main subject areas of your speech, and a few key points. In this way you can remember the key points you want to convey, but you have the freedom to talk naturally about them, rather than speaking from an over-rehearsed script, and this will make you seem more spontaneous. You may, however, wish to write the introduction out in full on your first card.

Be careful when using visual aids and equipment in the presentation as these can also be distracting for an audience. Use a pen to point out details on the overhead projector itself, rather than the screen, as this is much clearer. Flipcharts should be written on quickly in long hand, but try not to turn your back on the audience as you write. Commonly available presentation packages often have a facility to enable you to link to specific slides. Additionally, if a specific topic needs further explanation, you could have a built-in series of links so that you can move to some extra slides to explain a particular point. If you intend to use sophisticated technology, then have a technician on hand to help out. It is important to have a contingency plan in case your technology crashes. Make sure you have either a back-up disk, or an alternative presentational medium, or both.

Close your presentation

If you are answering questions at the end of your presentation and you don't know the answer to a question, tell the person you will find the answer and get back to them later. This will save time, and also prevent you from giving an incorrect answer. If the question is a general discussion point, you could always try throwing the question open to the floor; you may be able to get an interesting discussion going between the members of your audience. If you plan to use handouts to add to your presentation's content, make sure that you give these out at the end. Otherwise the audience will be flicking through your handout instead of listening to you.

WHAT TO AVOID
Lack of enthusiasm

If you don't have any interest or excitement in your own speech, then don't expect your audience to have any. Listening to a single voice for 20 minutes or more can be difficult for an audience. You must try to inject enthusiasm into what you are saying. You could consider planning some kind of inter-action with your audience, too, in the form of activities or discussion.

Speaking too quickly

Don't rush your presentation; it is important to take your time. The audience will find it difficult to understand you, or to keep up, if you talk too fast. Make sure you summarise your main points every five minutes or so, or as you reach the end of a section. This will help to clarify the most important issues for your audience, and it is then more likely that they will remember the central issues long after you have finished your presentation.

Not checking equipment

There is nothing more irritating for an audi-ence, who have all made an effort to turn up on time, than to have to sit around and wait while you struggle to get your laptop to work, or sort your slides out. Make sure everything is exactly in place well before your audience begins to arrive. A technician should be on hand if you are planning to use sophisticated technology.

Not interacting with the audience

Be careful not to look at the floor during your presentation, or to direct your speech at one person. Try and draw your whole audience into the presentation by glancing at everyone's faces, in a relaxed and unhur-ried way, as you make your points. Keeping in tune with your audience in this way will also help you judge if people are becoming bored. If you do detect this, you could try to change the tempo of your presentation to refocus their attention.

RECOMMENDED LINKS

The Presentation Business:
www.presentationbiz.co.uk
Public Speaking and Speech Writing:
www.speechtips.com

SEE ALSO

Managing Key Accounts (p. 257)
Perfecting Your Pitch: Preparing Presentations (p. 260)
Presentation/Speaking (p. 535)

Writing a Sales Letter

GETTING STARTED

Most small businesses need to sell by mail in some shape or form. A sales letter is a low-cost selling tool that can be adapted and modified according to circumstances. A good letter by itself can be enough to get the message across, but in most cases sales letters are used in conjunction with other promotional materials such as brochures, samples, and reply envelopes. Some mailings allow for an instant response, often in the form of an order. Others may set the scene for follow-up telephone calls and personal visits in the hope of establishing a longer-term relationship. As the first contact with a client, it's essential that the sales letter sets the right tone and this actionlist explains how to do this.

FAQS

How can I use sales letters?

A sales letter can be used in a variety of ways. It could be the first step in preparing the customer for a phone call or visit, perhaps raising questions that will be answered later.

It may aim just to raise general awareness about the product or service as part of an overall promotional effort. In this case, it doesn't need to contain all of the information the client requires, which can be supplied through other media.

However, if the letter has vague objectives, it will be difficult to measure results. If your business sells to a select group, this type of letter won't appeal and will be a waste of time. Letters to a select group are different from letters to a wider audience. If contacts represent good sales potential, each letter should be written with their particular needs in mind. Letters can also be adapted for a variety of different groups that you might approach at different times.

If you are targeting customers repeatedly, for example, to inform them about new products, new offers, tax-related offers, and seasonal offers, the sales letter should take each offer into account, reinforcing the basic promotional message while providing enough variety so as not to bore the reader or make them feel pestered—they'll simply throw the letter away. Sometimes, a sales letter is used to accompany responses to enquiries requesting information, and this presents an ideal opportunity to sell.

MAKING IT HAPPEN

Planning a sales letter

You need to set down on paper exactly what you want the letter to do. List your points under three headings: Inform, Sell, and Encourage Action.

It's easy to miss out basic information in a letter in an effort to sell the benefits, so remember to include the product name, the price, the business name and address, and order details. If necessary, include more detailed information about the product as well as brochures, other inserts, an envelope, and some sort of reply device.

Be persuasive

In order to sell your product, you have to be persuasive and get customers to view it favourably. Remember, there are limits to what a letter can achieve, and the recipient may need a number of opportunities to decide, so think about making your letter part of a sales drive, including offers, tele-sales, and so on.

Encourage the customer to take further action progressing towards a sale, for example, by reading enclosures, sending or phoning for more information, or placing an order. Follow up enquiries for further information with further mailings or tele-sales and make sure arrangements are in place before the next letter is sent.

Contents of a sales letter

Position key information at the beginning of your letter, and expand on it later. If you have a special offer running, mention it in the first paragraph to attract the reader's attention and make them read on. Make sure you describe how the product works and what it is meant to do in a way that enables the potential customer to visualise it. If you want to draw attention to certain features, why not highlight them with bullet points? You can always expand and give more detailed product information in brochures.

Describe your product's benefits clearly and simply, and try to think of the product from the customer's viewpoint. For example, if the photocopier you offer allows your customer to print documents direct from his or her personal computer so that there's no need to invest in a printer as well, tell them how much money they could save. Don't be afraid to spell out the benefits.

Avoid making exaggerated claims and remember that the customer does not have a chance to ask questions as he or she would in personal selling. If you do make claims, back them up with examples, such as endorsements from current users and case histories. If your business has large or well-known customers, enclose a testimonial from them, but make sure that they are sincere, specific to the product, and signed by the user.

Encourage immediate action wherever possible. Ask for a response, and keep asking for it throughout the letter. Make it easy for the reader to take the next step, by enclosing part filled-out forms, reply-paid envelopes, and Freephone numbers. Give incentives if you can and reward prompt action, for example, with a time-limited discount. Give the reader the option to send for more information, perhaps with samples or a demonstration, and record the details of customers who go to the trouble of doing this, for future sales efforts.

At the end of the letter, reinforce your message by repeating the offer, the guarantee, the cost, and the value of the product or service.

Presentation of a sales letter

Direct mail is a popular method of promotion, and prospective customers are often inundated with it. You must distinguish your business from the others so that its material stands a chance of being read and not put straight in the bin. Materials of an unusual size or colour should stand out. Keep samples of the opposition's mailing materials on file.

Avoid 'Dear Sir/Madam' if possible, and try to find out the recipient's name, taking care to spell it correctly. Alternatively, appropriate titles should be used, for example, if ski equipment is being sold, then 'Dear Skier' could be used. Don't ever use 'Dear Friend', and avoid sexist titles. The top and the bottom of the letter are key attention areas, so a postscript can be useful for announcing or reinforcing a special gift or offer.

A headline will grab initial attention and can be used to state a major benefit of the product or service, and also helps the reader to decide at a glance if the letter is of interest. Break the letter up into short paragraphs with subheadings, which gives the reader an overview of the contents at a glance. The reader can then read the sections that most interest him or her.

Keep the tone of the letter natural, conversational, warm, and easy to read. Use short words and sentences, and avoid jargon and complicated grammar or vocabulary. Use 'you' rather than 'I' or 'we'. Remember that you are addressing an individual person, not a crowd.

Choosing an appropriate typeface will have a big impact on how easy the letter is to read. Black on white is easier to read than the reverse. Avoid using uppercase too much and remember that very small type makes reading difficult. Important words can be emphasised by underlining, italics, bold, and capitals, but take care not to vary the typeface too much or the reader will be distracted by the look rather than the content of the page.

An example sales letter

Mr F Giles
Windy Hill Farm Shop
Nr Cottington
Countyshire
OB29 3YZ

ASHBURY COUNTRY PRESERVES — A TASTE OF SUMMER

Send for our discount sample pack now!

Dear Mr Giles

For a limited period only, Ashbury Country Preserves are providing farm shops in County-shire with an opportunity to test our exclusive range of pure fruit preserves at discount prices.

An Exclusive Product
Made with fresh fruit harvested from our own farm set in the rolling Anyshire countryside, Ashbury Country Preserves are made to Lady Blagington's original recipe. Our preserves provide the traditional real fruit taste that discerning country shoppers are looking for. A growing number of outlets now stock Ashbury Country Preserves. Exclusive food shops in both town and country find this high-quality food product is a reliable seller and an attractive addition to their stock range.

An Attractive Offer
Packed in distinctive octagonal 1kg jars, with attractive floral labels and lid covers, our pre-serves contain only fresh fruit and sugar. Each jar (strawberry, raspberry, and blackcurrant) retails at £2.00. We supply at £1.00 per jar, but discounts are available for long-term purchas-ing commitments. Our introductory pack represents a price of 50p per jar. Supplies are delivered in packs of 36. We will also supply a distinctively-painted wooden display stand to regular customers by agreement. Our brochure and order form are enclosed.

An Elite Market
Ashbury Country Preserves are ideal for the high-quality food retailer. We supply a select group of retail outlets in the Home Counties and London with our exclusive range. Estab-lished customers include Plockington Hall Visitors Shop, the Garlic Sausage Deli chain, and the famous Carrobs department store.

I do hope you will be able to take advantage of our offer, which lasts until March. I will be telephoning you shortly to discuss our products, but if you have any queries in the meantime, please do not hesitate to call.

Yours sincerely

Jenny Jumper
Sales Executive

WHAT TO AVOID

Not treating the mailing package as a whole

Refer frequently to the other parts of your mailing package, to encourage the reader to read the letter several times. It might be a good idea to test a draft letter out on some established customers, and ask for their feedback.

Not making the most of previous mailings

If your business does a lot of direct-mail selling, invest in a personal computer and a laser printer if you haven't got one already. This makes it easier to customise the basic letter for a variety of purposes. You can also keep a mailing database and carry out mail merges so that letters can be personally addressed. Microsoft Word gives helpful advice on creating mail merge documents and once you get the hang of it, you'll find they don't take long at all.

RECOMMENDED LINK

Just Sell:
www.justsell.com

SEE ALSO

Creating Impressive Direct Mail Material (p. 289)
Direct Marketing (p. 503)
Improving the Response to Direct Mail (p. 293)

Selling by Mail Order

GETTING STARTED

Mail-order trading has developed as businesses have recognised it as a good way of getting customers without the overheads of retail premises. Small, specialist catalogues have performed well by using this strategy, particularly in selling niche items like hand-made shirts, kitchen equipment, and luxury and organic foods. This actionlist looks at the advantages and disadvantages of mail-order selling, and also explains some of the legal implications.

FAQS

What are the advantages of selling by mail order?

Selling by mail order is good for cash flow because payment is in advance for goods that the business may not even need to stock, and round payment terms are of 30 or 60 days for purchases. Costs can be kept down because there is no need to rent high street premises, and little or no need for holding stock. Flexible working hours can be introduced, bringing in staff at busy times. If the business is a specialist retail or manufacturing outfit, setting up mail order is a good way of extending your catchment area. Also, mail order can be used with all customer income levels.

What are the disadvantages of selling by mail order?

People may be reluctant to send money to an unknown firm at a distant address. You will need to send frequent mailshots with offers to attract more sales. Mail order also imposes limitations on what product(s) can be sold.

MAKING IT HAPPEN

Choose the product

You need to consider whether there is a market for the item you have chosen; customers should see the advertised product and need it enough to send for it. Try to choose a product that is not generally available and that doesn't require demonstration. You will also need enough of the product to fulfil orders. It should be reasonably cheap, even with postage, and must be straightforward to pack and send. If possible, choose a group or set of products. This encourages people to keep coming back, especially if there is money off future items.

Promote it

Unlike a shop, which will attract passers-by, people need to be told what your mail-order business offers, and how and why they should buy it. There are various ways to get your message across. Direct mail is one. You can rent lists of names and addresses from a list brokerage service until you have built up your own. Data can be broken down specifically, so that tiny sections of the population who are very likely to buy can be targeted.

If you are offering several items, or your product is complicated, then using leaflets or catalogues will be the best means of promotion. Production costs for such materials can be high, so consider charging for catalogues. That way only serious potential customers will request a copy; you can offer to refund the cost if the customer then orders.

Small advertisements are another way to sell. Place adverts in special-interest media to narrow down the target market. Some national papers and magazines have specific sections for small mail-order businesses. To increase the response rate, make sure your timing is right, and don't squeeze too much information into a tiny space. Use a good headline and a few words, with a drawing rather than a photo. Coupons have a good response rate. Respondents fill in a coupon and you send them a more comprehensive leaflet or catalogue.

Give a guarantee; you are expecting customers to buy having seen only a few words and a drawing, so they should be able to send the product back at the business's expense. Don't use box numbers. These

VIEWPOINTS

CONTENTS

Viewpoint: Paula Burrows—Chill Rentals

Chill Rentals is a vehicle rental service based in Widnes, Cheshire. The company was set up in 2002 by Paula Burrows, who has more than a decade's experience in that industry. Offering a wide range of services to both business and private customers, Paula's company aims to offer excellent service and value for money to keep her customers returning. Chill Rentals has a fleet of 12 vehicles, including four seven-and-a-half-tonne lorries (which are refrigerated), cars, and vans on contract hire and self-drive.

STARTING OUT

'I'd been working the vehicle rental business for over 10 years when I decided to set up my own business. I've always wanted to work for myself, and in fact that's why I chose to do a business studies degree at university, as I thought it would help me gain some of the skills I needed.

'Chill Rentals was registered in May 2002, but we bought the first van a few months later in September. By that time, I'd already been working in vehicle rentals for over ten years; while I was studying, I'd had a placement at a local hire firm and as soon as I left university, I was offered the manager's job there. I stayed for 3 years before moving on to become regional manager at a national truck rental company, City Truck Rental Ltd. The head office was in Milton Keynes but I managed five offices across the North.

'In the end, I was spurred into action when City Truck Rental went bust and I was made redundant. I did have other job offers but, bearing in mind how hard I'd been working on someone else's behalf (I used to get up at six o'clock and not get home until eight o'clock in the evening, for example), and realising that there's never really a "good" time to do it, I decided to take the plunge. I was one of the last two people left at the CTR office as the operation was winding down, so I had a bit of breathing space to do some research and come up with a business plan.'

FINDING FUNDING AND ADVICE

'When I first started up, I didn't have capital of my own to invest in the business as my husband and I had not long been married and we'd also bought and renovated a house. As you can imagine, vehicle hire is a capital-intensive business as you have to buy a fleet of vehicles up-front, but fortunately my parents were able to lend me some money to tide me over during the early months. I also visited the Halton Business Forum, which is my local office of the Business Link network, and they advised me to apply for a local authority grant. As part of that process, I had to be willing to locate the business in a particular area of the town that attracted funding. As I was under 30, I also applied to the Prince's Trust for a loan, and received their maximum amount of £5,000.

'Lots of people will offer their advice to you, but be wary of people who seem to promise you the earth. If a package of assistance from a bank or any other backer looks too good to be true, it probably is, so don't pin all your hopes on one source of advice or funding. I found that the best and most helpful advice I received came from my own bank—it was direct, no nonsense, and reliable.

'It takes a lot more than a great idea and funding to make a business a success. You'll find that you'll get knocked back and will need to dust yourself down many times. On the funding front in particular, remember that some grants can take more than 6 months to come through from initial application, so make sure you've some alternative source of funding while you're waiting and in case you are turned down. Also remember that, even when you're up and running, it will take some time before you'll be able to pay yourself anything. It does take a while for the money to come through, I've only have been able to have a proper wage as of June 2003, eight months after we bought the first van.'

WORKING OUT YOUR PRIORITIES

'It is really hard work setting up your own business, and you have to be tenacious and have an unshakeable will to succeed, whatever the knock-backs (and everyone has them). I think having support from friends and family is invaluable too, although you need to remember to see things from their perspective as well and realise that if they sound a bit doubtful at times about what you're doing, it's not because they don't believe in you, but rather that they're worried about you taking on such a lot of risk. Understand where they're coming from, but don't be put off.

'Getting your priorities right is also essential. Don't set up your own business for the money alone—that is part of it, naturally, but just as importantly, you have to be sure that the service or product you're offering is the right one for your customers. We have a lot of repeat customers, which is great, precisely because they know that they're my priority and we'll really put ourselves out for them. To give you an idea, if someone is worried about leaving a vehicle they've rented from us in their drive overnight, we'll go out at 9 o'clock at night to pick it up for them. We've found that that level of personal service is really important.

'Some industries are more women-friendly than others, and it can be annoying when people don't take you seriously at times. Even today, it's still unusual for a woman to be buying or renting vehicles and a fair few times reps have stopped by and assumed I was someone's secretary or personal assistant. One time in particular, a salesman from a local company dropped in and asked when my boss was back, how often did he buy, and if I had a compliments slip with his details on that he could take away. I really enjoyed giving him my business card instead, and letting him know that I was the managing director! Not all men react like this, I hasten to add—I've had lots of great feedback about the business from men and women—but it is something else to be prepared for.'

LOOKING TO THE FUTURE

'I enjoy what I do very much and, as I mentioned earlier, I've always really wanted to do it. There's plenty of variety and no two days are the same. Being your own boss can be stressful at times, especially when things go wrong—for example, a big bite can be taken out of your weekend if you have to sort out breakdowns—but most people have to cope with stress at work, even when they're working for other people. At least when you're running your own business you have a big say in what happens and you don't have suffer as a result of other people's mistakes. Let's face it, nothing's more stressful than being made redundant!

'I see getting through the first few years as the main thing and the business has grown a lot in a short space of time. Although purchasing vehicles takes a big chunk out of the capital, I've got low overheads, and that's a big help. I have a small office here in the business centre, and as many of the vehicles are out on long-term rents we don't need to park them here, although there is a lock-up in the business centre and we have a big drive if needs be!

'I'd love to employ more people eventually, but at the moment I'm concentrating on developing the business and paying off some of the vehicles if I can. My cash flow is fine, and I can pay myself enough to cover the mortgage and a bit more, but I can't really stretch to taking on staff just as yet.

'I do get a lot of support from my husband, Glyn Burrows, though. He's also self-employed and has his own building and roofing business, but he helps me as much as he can, especially at the weekends when we're often in the office. Working for yourself can take a bit of a toll on your home-life, especially where holidays are concerned. We weren't big jet-setters to begin with so it isn't the end of the world, but as we both run our own businesses taking any time off means that we have no income at all. If you're married or have a partner or a family, it's important to talk through all your plans with them and to make sure you'll be able to manage if you don't have a lot of money coming in for a while.

'Even though Glyn and I are both very busy, we see more of each other now than we did when I was working at City because we can now work together a lot of the time. Chill Rentals is a family business with lots of support and help from family and friends. Without that support it would have been ten times as difficult to get through the initial months, but that doesn't mean I wouldn't have done it!

'I used to think that to succeed in starting a business you needed savings in the bank, which was something I didn't have. Now I know that, although it obviously helps to have that money available, there are many other ways round it. Confidence, ability, and the right idea are the main factors people need to succeed; money is the next step.'

Visit Chill Rentals at: www.chillrentals.co.uk

Viewpoint: James Daunt—Daunt Books for Travellers

Setting up and running a successful independent bookshop is a dream for many people hoping to start their own businesses. James Daunt left a career in banking at the age of 24 to do just that, and now owns three bookshops in London. He is based at Daunt Books for Travellers in Marylebone, central London. The bookshop occupies 8,000 square feet in two Edwardian buildings and stocks more than 45,000 books.

THE BUSINESS OF BOOKSELLING

'All in all, bookselling is a good business to be in. It's ostensibly profitable, as publishers will sell you books at a good discount and you can also return books that you buy but don't sell. Having said that, it can be difficult to get a foot in the door. Some publishers don't take independent shops seriously and can be reluctant to send their sales reps to visit you. As much of their time can be spent dealing with larger chains, they often think it's not worth their while to visit smaller shops.

'In comparison to other trades, bookselling is inefficient and not that easy to streamline, but this can work in your favour as a small businessperson—so many people are making a bad job of it that you can do well by just being better than them. Think about what you can get away with doing (or not doing) to survive.

'Independent booksellers have an advantage over the chains which, despite having a bigger structure and more people, are even more inefficient. For example, one very well-known chain was still using an index card system for tracking its stock until a few years ago. When I started the shop, I made sure that all our systems were fully computerised, which meant that we could keep track of things much more easily.'

RETAIL = DETAIL

'To make a success of being in retail, I really feel you need an aptitude for detailed work. You spend a lot of the time dealing with paperwork, such as returns and invoices, and getting behind can cause major problems. If you're a "people person" as well so much the better, as having a persuasive and forceful personality is a great help. The good thing about bookselling is that most people who come into the shop are doing something they enjoy and so are generally in a good mood.'

STARTING UP

'When I was planning to start my business, the (now defunct) Business Expansion Scheme was still running. It really helped those without capital, especially young people, to get up and running as it was virtually impossible to get funding from banks and even if they did fund you, they often foreclosed on a whim.

'Secure funding is essential for a small business, as is good advice. In addition to the Business Expansion Scheme's help, I received funding from some backers who were happy to invest in the business as long as they were given a seat on the board. I found their experience and advice invaluable, especially during bad times—they were much older than me and also one step removed from the day-to-day running of the business, so were able to take a more dispassionate view of things.

'Starting a new business can take up nearly all of your time, at the expense of other areas of your life. For 10 years, I was in the shop 7 days a week and customers who bought books here probably bought them from me in person. You must have a real appetite for work and sustained enthusiasm for it too—you'll often find yourself working 18 hours a day, 7 days a week, so there's a lot of hard labour involved. Don't underestimate how much effort you'll have to put in, and remember that you won't be able to pay yourself much (if anything!).'

GROWING UP

'We've "grown up" as a business in lots of ways. In terms of sales, we've gone from £300,000 worth of books in year one to £3 million in year 15. In terms of employees, for a long time there were just two, but there are now 23. I prefer to employ people with no previous bookselling experience as I feel they have an enthusiasm lost by so many who've been through the (badly-paid) mill in larger chains. We've been able to keep all that experience within the business as the two shops I've recently opened in Hampstead and Belsize Park in North London are being managed by people who used to work here.'

RAINY DAYS

'If your business is going through a difficult time, don't be tempted to spend your way out of it you need to be sensible and run the business as leanly as you can. For example, if the sales just aren't coming in, don't spend £10,000 on a new accounting software package thinking it will help in some way. You probably already have a perfectly good spreadsheet package that comes with your PC, and you'll be much better off keeping that £10,000 to use as contingency for the future. If you don't really need top of the range equipment for what you do, just don't buy it. Having a "bumper" in your budget for the bad times is much more important.

'Finally, don't be put off too easily if you really think your idea will work and you can fund it. Lots of people said I was crazy to even think about setting up an independent bookshop in central London, but I'm still here, the business is growing—and I still enjoy what I do.'

Visit James Daunt's shops at: **Daunt Books for Travellers, 83 Marylebone High Street, London W1M 4AL (Tel: 020 7224 2295)**

Daunt Books, Belsize Bookshop, Haverstock Hill, London NW3 4QL (Tel: 020 7794 4006)

Daunt Books, 50 South End Road, London NW3 2QB (Tel: 020 7794 8206)

Viewpoint: Firetrap Clothing—The Importance of Brand Building

Building a brand is important for businesses of all types, but in the fashion trade its influence can't be over-estimated. **Firetrap Clothing** was launched in 1993 by Steve Atkinson, and its men's collection has firmly established itself in the United Kingdom as a leading brand in the casual wear market, winning the FHM & Menswear Fashion Brand of the Year award in 1999 and constantly making appearances in Top 20 trade monitors. The women's collection, launched in 1998, has also been received extremely well and is now an established competitor within the competitive women's market.

In just ten years, the Firetrap brand has expanded into the key markets of Germany and France and the company also has distributors in Holland, Portugal, Spain, and Greece. Its products are also sold in Switzerland, Denmark, Malta, Cyprus, Japan, the United States, Latin America, and Australia.

How did they do it?

OUR PRODUCTS

'Firetrap is divided into three divisions. We have the men's and women's collections and Firetrap Black Seal, our denim collection. Black Seal is a combination of both men's and women's denim styles, and includes jeans, jackets, skirts, and tops. Although our sales are predominantly within the UK market at present, we expect this to change over the next few years.

'Firetrap product is generally perceived as "strong yet commercial" in terms of styling and pricing, with clever details. The product is not over-designed, and branding is important to both the retailer and the customer.'

OUR CUSTOMERS

'We have a strong appeal for 21-34 year olds who like to make a statement in everything they do, from they way they dress to the car they drive and the music they listen to. We also need to "win back" the 18-20 year old market from competitors such as Topshop and French Connection. This is our focus, but we know that we don't want to lose credibility with our existing customers in the process. Age isn't the "identifier" it once was, though, and we feel that Firetrap lovers are identified more by an attitude of mind.'

OUR BRAND

'Our vision is: *"Where there's Firetrap, there's excitement."* The core of the brand is in its creativity. It is unrestricted and appeals to the independence of the Firetrap wearer, who is free, passionate, and confident in his or her tastes and choices. We feel that our name has immediate resonance in terms of lifestyle, attitude, and fashion. Everyone loves the way it looks!'

OUR MEDIA CAMPAIGNS TO PROMOTE AND STRENGTHEN THE BRAND

'There are different levels of awareness of our brand for men and women and within the United Kingdom and abroad, with the brand at different life stages. Our job is to ensure that Firetrap is at the forefront of our customers' minds and is most definitely seen as a 'destination' brand, that is, one that customers want to aim for.

'The way we've used and focused our marketing campaigns has changed over time. For example, Firetrap is mainly remembered for a series of red cartoon ads that were used in 1996–97. They were innovative, relevant, and humorous. They showed the products in a relatively limited way, but worked well by giving our brand a "personality" — one that was slightly edgy, controversial, had a British feel, and showed that we didn't take ourselves too seriously.

'Since then, we've used a different style and imagery for each season. For Spring/Summer (SS) 1998 and Autumn/Winter (AW) 1998, we tried a campaign featuring computer generated "dogs", then took a different tack in with a different style of illustration used in SS 1999. We changed again for AW 1999, SS 2000, and AW 2000, using ideas based upon the Superheroes theme, which has continued to promote the brand with a twist.

'SS 2002 involved the use of strong fire images to show the energy and strength of the brand when we employed a new creative agency to take us to the next step. AW 2002 saw the brand take a different direction with the building of a Firetrap community. SS 2003 brought a new twist to previous campaigns with an advertising campaign based around a woman who entraps an unsuspecting male for wearing Firetrap product. We also started to advertise on TV for the first time, using MTV to bring the brand to a new media, and supporting this with a viral campaign, which was a huge success for the brand. AW 2003 saw us develop our choices in media, with a TV campaign planned for E4 and MTV in the United Kingdom. The campaign addresses issues about globalisation with a unique and humorous spin.'

Visit Firetrap at: **www.firetrap.net**

Viewpoint: Adam Balon, Jon Wright, and Richard Reed—innocent Ltd

If you're interested in combining work and pleasure by dedicating your business to a product that's good for you, you'd be following in the footsteps of innocent. Formed in 1998 by three college friends, Adam Balon, Jon Wright, and Richard Reed, innocent makes a range of fruit-based drinks that have earned them rave reviews from their industry, their customers, and nutritionists alike. The company has been awarded gold medals at the Great Taste Awards for four years in a row, and has also won:

- Best Soft Drink at the International Food and Drink Expo 2002 (beating other drinks like Tropicana and Coke)
- Small to Medium Sized Business of the Year Award at the National Business Awards 2002
- Investors in People for Small to Medium Sized Business of the Year Award at the National Business Awards 2002
- Marketing campaign of the year for small to medium sized business at the Marketing Society Awards 2003

The company has grown from having zero to 30% market share and this year the turnover will be just over £10 million. As they say in their company literature, '...that's as much of the story as we know so far', but how did they get there?

SMOOTHING THE WAY

'All three of us had full-time jobs when we first thought about setting up a company, but we really wanted to start up a business together. We realised that the right idea was crucial, and had already rejected a few (including a none-too-safe one for a device to automatically fill your bath) before we came up with the idea behind innocent.

'We started thinking about how difficult it was to keep healthy and eat properly while leading a busy life, so thought it might be a good idea to make a totally natural drink from fruit that tasted amazing and did you good all at the same time. We ran the idea past some of our friends, tried out some pretty dodgy recipes, did some serious maths, and then decided that pure fruit smoothies, a blend of fruit and yoghurt, were an excellent idea. Thankfully we also managed to find a private investor who agreed with us, so we were able to move forward.

'In the summer of 1998, we bought £500 worth of fruit, took it to a jazz festival and tried our idea out. We were keen to get some feedback, so we put up a big sign saying "Do you think we should give up our jobs to make these smoothies?" and put out a bin saying "YES" and a bin saying "NO" and asked people to put the empty bottle in the right bin. At the end of the weekend, the "YES" bin was full so we went back to our respective jobs the next day and resigned.

'We then spent a long year of research and development, trying hard to persuade everyone that adding lots of water, sugar, and preservatives to such a great natural product was a bad idea, and the first ever innocent smoothies went on sale in May 1999. We were really nervous and on the first day we waited outside the shop selling the smoothies, piled up lots of milk crates to peer in and see if any of the drinks had been sold. Luckily, the shelf was bare and we went home feeling relieved.'

THE NEXT CHAPTER?

'Things have been going from strength to strength since then. We've found that we were right in our initial idea, and people really do want to buy great-tasting, totally natural drinks to help them stay healthy and don't mind paying premium prices to get them. Over the past four years, we've extended our range of drinks to six smoothies, one of which changes each season, three thickies (yoghurt-based fruit drinks), three great juices, three fruit-flavoured waters, and a fresh orange juice. We've even published a smoothie recipe book called The innocent Little Book of Drinks. And the team has expanded from just three people to thirty five, all based at Fruit Towers in West London.

'We think we offer a fantastic range of top-quality products and have had some great comments; the Sunday Times said we were its 'favourite' health drink, and the BBC 2 programme Food & Drink voted us the best smoothie in the UK. We really try hard not to believe the hype and become over-confident or lazy, but we want to do what we do best—produce lovely drinks.'

FOR THOSE THINKING OF THEIR OWN STORY...

'Be able to condense your business idea down into one sentence that your granny would understand. If you can't articulate your idea simply and clearly, it probably isn't a very good one.

'Keep the main thing the main thing. Have one unifying thought and let it inform every decision you make. And don't compromise on this and let other people water it down. For us, it was about having completely natural unadulterated drinks. While we were setting up, everyone said we could get to market quicker, cheaper, and easier by using concentrates and preservatives and things, but we stuck to our guns. If we hadn't we would have been just another me-too on the market.

'Things definitely take longer than you think they will. Everyone told us this at the time but we didn't believe them. We thought we would get our juices to market in two months—it took nine.

'In terms of qualities, it's important to be very focussed and determined. We wouldn't have made it without being absolutely clear about what we wanted and refusing to compromise. Also, here we don't mind making mistakes. You learn from every mistake and it is inevitable that when you are always trying to innovate and do things in a new way that some things will go wrong along the way. That's why we try and do things by little steps. For example, if we are coming up with a new product we will launch it and then keep looking at it to see if there are any little tweaks that we can do to improve it. That way you always stay one step ahead.'

Visit innocent at: **www.innocentdrinks.co.uk**

Viewpoint: Kalido—Breaking Out of Shell

Sometimes, a new business can be created *within* an established one. **Kalido—originally born out of the Royal Dutch/Shell Group (Shell), and now a successful standalone software company—is a strong case in point. Its founder and chief strategist, Andy Hayler, was working at Shell International when the idea behind Kalido first took root, and indeed the company started out as an 'internal solution' for Shell. When Andy wanted to turn that solution into a viable commercial product, attracting outside expertise and investment was critical to its success.**

'In 1996, while at Shell International, I had just started setting up an information management consultancy practice in Shell when my first internal customer walked through the door. The problem he brought was a thorny one: how can senior management of a large global organisation (such as Shell) get a true understanding of their business performance across multiple operations?

'As you can imagine, Shell had many IT systems in place providing business performance reports, but there were two barriers to obtaining an overall view. First, each country, and sometimes even each business unit, had different business rules, and second, these rules necessarily all altered over time due to changes in each business. No software package on the market could address this dual-edged issue, since traditional approaches all assume that you have to get to one consistent set of data, and hope that change is not too frequent. This approach just does not reflect the real-world view that Shell required. However, innovative research into advanced data modelling was being carried out in a Shell research function, and I realised that if these studies could be made to address 'variance' of business rules over time in a data warehousing application, then we could really be on to something.

'After some initial successful testing I persuaded Shell Lubricants to provide US$1 million funding to develop the idea into a prototype application, which at the time was called Genie, but later became the KALIDO software. The initial prototype was implemented in three countries, and immediately showed its value. The software then began to be rolled out globally, and to attract the attention of other Shell businesses.

'I was driven by a growing conviction that there was a major commercial opportunity for the KALIDO software.

BUILDING AN EFFECTIVE TEAM

'After preparing a business plan to sell the KALIDO software externally I raised money from Shell to develop the product as a stand-alone business. There is a huge difference between an internal application and a robust industrial software product, and it was critical at this point to bring in expertise from the software industry to set up a separate company called Kalido to commercialise KALIDO the product.

'Putting together the team at Kalido has been central to our success, and there have always been three main things that I look for in potential employees. First, I am very happy if they are smarter than me. The role of the leader is to motivate people and remove obstacles, allowing them to progress and to achieve their goals. Second, I look for diversity of thinking. Even though it is more of a challenge to bring together diverse individuals, it is far more rewarding and beneficial to the business if different schools of thought are pooled.

'Third, I look for a spark of passion. I have always tried to provide a shared vision and like to think that my vision sparks employees to strive for success. Persuading experts from companies such as IBM and Oracle to believe in my vision and help me build a software start-up company from within one of the world's largest energy giants was always going to be difficult. However, the effort was worth it and I know all the team were attracted to the proposition because of my vision and the potential they saw in the product.

'Protecting the intellectual property of Kalido was a key step. We applied for a patent on the software design (later granted in the UK) and also trademarked the software and company name in 70 countries. This step has proved critical, as we have already seen three attempts to register our name in other markets, including a major European country. If we had not taken this action then we could have had a major legal problem as we expanded.

BREAKING OUT OF SHELL

'In October 2000 I had a "virtual software company" and a product ready to launch externally. I wrote an updated business plan, this time to complete the separation of the team into an independent company and to construct the sales and marketing arms of the organisation; this involved raising US$ 11 million of funding. A key milestone for Kalido was when we won our first external licence with Unilever; the KALIDO software had developed from being an internal solution into an independent commercial business. In January 2001 Kalido Ltd was established.

'Since that time, Kalido has gone from strength to strength. Our software is now in use in more than 100 countries worldwide. Highlights of this journey include launching a software start-up during the notoriously difficult business conditions of 2001, shifting our revenue base from 100% Shell to over 80% non-Shell from customers such as Unilever, Philips, Cadbury Schweppes, HBOS plc, and United Co-op, and being named by IDC as the world's fastest growing company in the global business intelligence software market in 2001.

LOOKING TO THE FUTURE

'We now have operations in the United Kingdom, the United States, and France and our future plans are focused on continuing our international expansion. To this end, in July 2003 we raised an impressive amount of additional venture capital funding and also recruited a number of high profile senior appointments to the management team. In particular, I brought on board a new CEO,

Bob Potter (formerly of IONA Technologies), to further extend our foothold in the key US market.

'The greatest contributor to our success is our customers. We pride ourselves on providing extremely reliable and effective software to our customers and maintaining open, honest relations with our clients at all times. If we have a problem—and everyone experiences hitches with software from time to time—we are completely frank with our customers about it. Ultimately, customers respect you if you're straight with them. They will buy based on the recommendation of other happy customers, so we put a lot of effort into ensuring that our software is robust.

'We're extremely confident that our software delivers what we promise—it's fast, flexible, and reliable. We're always happy when prospective customers want to test our software head-to-head with our competitors, because no amount of marketing spin can substitute for software which does exactly what it promises to do, and ours does.'

Visit Kalido at: **www.kalido.com**

Viewpoint: Phil Moss—Mailbox Movies

For many people it can take years to come up with an inspirational business idea, and even longer to build up the nerve to actually do something about it. Then there's all the planning and the saving before launch. Not so for Essex lad, Phil Moss. At 26, he's already got two companies under his belt, and is full of bright ideas and ambition for the next move. Since finishing his degree in Product Design, Phil has co-founded Jungle Moss, a website development partnership, and **Mailbox Movies**, an online DVD rental company that provides its customers with an unlimited number of DVDs for a fixed monthly fee.

'If you're young and you have an idea, one of the best times to do it is when you're straight out of university. If you've been in a job for ½ve years and you're used to earning a regular disposable income, it's hard to give that up. But when you walk out of university, you're penniless and quite willing to give up another three years of your life for something you believe in. You're willing to go the lengths that you need in order to make the business work.

'There will always be sacrifices to make, no matter when you decide to set up on your own. But it's about making a better life for yourself—not money, nor anything else—just a better way of life. Will you have a better way of life if you leave your job? Only you can know that. Perhaps you are too afraid because it's so risky. Well, you can stay in the situation you're in now or you can do it yourself. D.I.Y., mate. So, be scared but dive straight in!'

FINDING THE BUSINESS IDEA THAT WORKS

'The first thing you need is a pen and paper. You could be down the pub, you could be sitting on the toilet, you could be doing anything, but at a certain point you'll have a flash of inspiration and you'll think, "That could be something". If you've got them on a piece of paper, you can come back to them and say "Right. This, this, this, this. Which one's a good'un? Okay—let's push on this one, let's put money into that one. Let's do it. Let's put our heart and soul into that and see if it'll work." If it doesn't work, you've still got a list of other ideas to go back to.

'When I came out of university I was excited about setting up Jungle Moss with my friend Mark Durnford (aka Jungle). We started earning money by helping people develop websites for their businesses. We would get our money, they would walk away with a business that we had created online, and that's where it stopped. We kept doing it for three years, but in the back of my mind we knew there was a bigger ½sh which needed frying. Coming up with the idea was the hard part, but we always believed that if we kept going we'd find it. You have to keep your ideas flowing and your mind open. And if the idea gets brought up seven times in a pub, then it's the one. It's something that you lie awake at night thinking about, constantly thinking, "This is it. This is good. Why aren't we doing it?" And eventually, you bow down to it.

'The idea developed out of a mishmash of things. The fact that I'm into movies myself played an important part, of course. Renting from a high street was costing me £3.50 a go and I was in the early days of running a small business, not earning a lot of money. Also, I knew about websites and the Internet. We were developing websites for computer games companies, the property market, big corporations—all sorts of people—so we knew exactly the kind of thing people wanted to see on a website. Originally we said we were just going to do an online DVD rental company, charging £3.50 for 7-day rental, but then we developed the idea and thought of another, better way to do it, involving the set fee and unlimited rental.

WORKING WITH PARTNERS

'Our company started off very small—however, we grew very rapidly over a short period of time and acquired new partners. You cannot run a business without fresh ideas. We were young, keen, and energetic—but there is a lot to be said for a person with a few years on their shoulders. You need vibrant, energetic, blue-sky keenness but you also need someone to pull you down from that balloon, and say "Hang on! You can do it, but let's float up slowly." Radical growth is great, but it needs to be monitored.

'I don't think I could have done it on my own. Jungle and I were always a team. We had different strengths and weaknesses, so we could bounce off each other. You need that. We were friends first before business partners, and I think we've both made an effort to keep the two sides of our relationship separate as far as possible.

'It's gonna be tough if you work by yourself because you've got nobody to rebound off. Without someone else you're somewhere in the desert, and it's... well, it's sandy!'

KIBBUTZ TEAMBUILDING

'There comes a point for a small business when it needs to bring in more hands. It starts to involve more people, and how they're going to live. You may be their boss, but it's the same for them as it is for you: this is their job, their livelihood. If this company folds, they're going to be out of a job. So it almost becomes a community; a kibbutz.

'When you're employing new people, your decision is based on a hunch. That's all it can be. Skills and experience are great, but are they going to get on with me? Are they going to get on with you? Most of it is making sure the team works as a unit. Managing people is not easy. I've never done the training courses, but I've learned from my mistakes. The best way I've found to get the most out of our employees is to involve them as much as we can. If we've got an issue with the business, we bring everyone in— the fulfilment team, the customer service guy, everybody— and we discuss it. They've all got something constructive to say. Make yourself approachable. They are not employees, they are part of the team!'

MAKING FRIENDS AND INFLUENCING PEOPLE

'You can't always get a contract and expect big money. There's got to be a bit of give and take. If you've found a customer that you know could be influential or help you in the future—even if it's simply by improving your portfolio of clients—and they're willing to take you on and give you a chance when you're just starting out without much money or reputation, do them a favour. Don't charge the going rate. If you loosen the string a bit, you know that you can always come back to them at some point and say, "I'm having a bit of trouble here."

'For example, we could charge a well-established business X amount for a web-site, and they're going to think "This is a rip-off, but it's alright", or we could charge them half that, and they'll think "Hey, that's fairly reasonable, and it looks good". They're going to come back again, and again. And then they're going to tell their mates, and their mates are going to tell their mate's mates. Word of mouth is paramount to success—for every business, not just on the Internet. This is the only way to develop your business. It's about respect as well as loyalty. At some point, maybe you're going to need something from them.

'One of the things I've found good about business on the Internet is the fact that you are dealing with everyone—engineers, estate agents, plumbers. So you develop a cross-spectrum of contacts. It's all about making friends and develop-ing relationships. You may do well on one, you may do badly on another, but at the end of the day, it's the see-saw of life. One day you might call upon that per-son, and if that person can help, then you're winning.'

THE ONLY REASON YOU ARE AWAKE

'The thing that keeps you awake at night is paying the next rent bill, paying your bus fare, knowing what you're going to do with your life. Is this business going to work? You don't know. You can't predict it. A business plan is useless if you've got no customers. So know your audience, get a team together, employ the right people, and make sure it works. You have the sleepless nights and you lie awake at night thinking up the next big thing. You get up in the morning and you know it's right because you've thought about it and thought about it. It's all you think about, day and night. The only reason you are awake is to make this business work.

'It does involve a lot of hard work, especially at the start. For us it meant seven-day weeks, enough money to pay the bills and a bit extra if we were lucky, and zero social life. The only way it will work is if you believe in it. We went to see some potential investors, and they thought it was a little bit too much in its early stages for any big investment, so they turned round and said, "If you can get x amount of customers by February then we may be interested. You'll have a rubbish Christmas, but you'll have a great New Year if you can do it." So we showed them, and we did it.

'If it's a good idea, it'll make money, then you're going to get the funding you need. But before you get the funding, you've got to believe in yourself. If you believe in yourself, then other people will believe in you. Luck doesn't come into it. If you've got the right idea, and providing you're willing to put in the hours, it'll work. If it doesn't, then it was a rubbish idea. The difference between a good idea and a good business idea, is one that works and makes you money. Flying to Mars is a good idea, but you can't do it yet, so it's a bad business idea.

'What makes all the hard work worthwhile though, is walking into a shop or restaurant and knowing the money you spend has been earned by you from start to finish, or overhearing a stranger talking about your business, as I did on the Underground one day.

'I love the chaos, the buzz, the whole do-or-die-ness of it all. If you don't work, you don't eat, and that drives you to make it work. You are your own boss. There's a lot of freedom, but there's a lot of chaos thrown in with it: the not knowing how it's going to turn out factor. You could quite easily get a job, get your salary and your five weeks' holiday a year—that's great. But every day you wake up you're going to be making money for somebody else, and doing it on their terms.'

DOT.SERVICE

'The dot.com is dead. It's not dot.com any more, it's dot.service. People want a service and they want a product. They want something in their hands: "I'm paying for this, I'm getting this." The Web is just another way to give them that product. That's why our business works: you log on, you ask for something, and we give it to you, and that's it. It isn't information, it isn't a promise to revolutionise your life—it's a high street shop, but in some ways it's also a life style. Mailbox is an Internet product service of a type never been seen before in this country. It was the new thing. And now lots of other companies are doing it, too. The pied piper comes along and the rats will follow.

'Customer service is the key to success. Everybody fears using the Internet. They feel there's a robot at the other end. In other words, you need to make the business more human: you need to get someone on the end of a phone. The people we brought into the company round it off in this sense. We have become a business as opposed to an Internet business. The difference between the two is waiting seven days for a response. What you want is somebody to respond to your problem within two hours, be that by e-mail or by telephone. Preferably, telephone. This is what keeps us ahead of the competition. You have to look after the people who are paying your salary.

'You are always going to get complaints, but difficult customers are the best parts of the day—looking after them, solving their problems. It's these people who let you know where you are falling down. As long as you make sure 98% of those complaints are catered for, then you're doing well. You're never going to be 100% perfect. Obviously strive for 100%, but I honestly don't believe anyone will ever get there. There'll always be an issue because you're dealing with customers, all with independent needs and standards.'

'FIVE YEARS DOWN THE LINE...

'...we will be the market leader—no question. We will become a household brand name. Game over. Full stop. How? By becoming the best at what we do: having the best customer service, the best product, the best response time. We will give the customer everything they want.

'If you're not keeping up with the latest technology and developments, then it's going to go wrong. You need to keep ahead of the game all the time by thinking: "Okay, we're doing this. The next best thing is going to be that—let's move into that." Keep your business organic: keep growing it, keep moving it, and keep diversifying. We have to make sure we're ahead of the game all the time by reading the papers, reading the news, by finding out what the newest thing is and keeping up. That way, if any client asks me for something, I can say to them: "Okay, we'll do that" or "We'll move into that." I'd like to say we're proactive as opposed to reactive!

'The worst aspect of running your own business is questioning yourself. You have to be very critical of yourself. You have to put yourself up against the big boys—as we did with Jungle Moss. They're charging stupid amounts of money and we're not charging as much. But you've got to keep up or you're nothing. The competition shouldn't scare you. You've just got to do it twice as good. You've got to study your competition hard to better them—it's the only way. You have to befriend people. You have to befriend them. Your best friend's your enemy.

'Believe in your idea from day one. Don't sit on it. Do it. That's it. You can turn the tape recorder off. That's all you need to know.'

Visit Mailbox Movies at: **www.mailboxmovies.com**

Viewpoint: Martin Johnston—Satellite Ltd

29-year-old Martin Johnston can't draw and hates computers, but he is passionate about graphic design and for the past five years has been running his own graphic design company called **Satellite Ltd.** Based in Shoreditch, London, Satellite develops brands and produces creative communication strategies for a wide range of companies in different industries. Most recently, Satellite was shortlisted for the London Olympic bid.

IN THE BEGINNING...

'Like many people who aren't sure what they want to do when they come out of university, I decided to go travelling. Unfortunately, my travels were rather short-lived, though, as I got very ill and was forced to make an early return. Once recovered and back in England, I was faced with a choice: I could either stay at home in Chester where I had a job selling cardboard boxes waiting for me, or move to Oxford where a couple of my friends had a spare room going, and try to find a job in London. Needless to say, I went for the second of these two options, and ended up commuting to London from Oxford whilst working for a well-known magazine as a sales rep selling ad space. After 15 months, as I'd been hitting all my targets, I decided to ask them for a pay rise but was told there was no money. A little disillusioned, I took a week off and approached three companies to see if I could sell for them on a freelance basis. Two of the companies said yes, so I went back to work on the Monday, handed in my notice, and the magazine offered me loads more money and a car. I turned it down because I'd already become excited at the possibility of doing my own thing. My dad runs his own engineering company, so I suppose you could say the idea of setting up on my own was not new or scary. I knew roughly what I'd be taking on.

'So in February 1996 I set up Spinnaker, a freelance sales agency. My dad lent me £800 with which I bought a desk, chair, and second hand Mac (which reminds me, I haven't paid it back yet!) and I started out finding new business for a graphic design company and an engineering company: two completely different markets. I felt it was important to gain as much knowledge of different industries as I could, but in addition, to cover my back in the event that either the marketing communications industry or the manufacturing industry took a downturn. I still hold true to this philosophy today, and Satellite works a lot within the government run education sector which, regardless of whether industry takes a downturn, will always be needed. I tried to sell the graphic design company I was working for into the educational sector for much the same reason, except at that time it was to keep my commission coming in.'

THE BIG IDEA

In the back of my mind, though, I wanted to slowly reverse things so that the company I was going out to find new business for, could become more of a subcontractor helping me to build my business. The work I was doing for the graphic design company was creating opportunities for me to go it alone. Many of my friends were graphic designers and their branding ideas really interested me. I loved the idea that although I couldn't draw myself I could still take part in the creative process and help produce something that people wanted to look at. I really believed, too, that I could sell their ideas. So Spinnaker became Satellite—a graphic design company continuing to do the initial sales process but bringing everything in-house. I work with some of those friends now!

'Luckily, at the beginning with Spinnaker I had no one to manage but myself. But believe me, this is hard enough! On my first day of self-employment I didn't know what on earth to do first, so I gave my flatmate a lift to work, drove home, and then went to the pub with my other flatmate. I knew this couldn't continue— especially as I was hung over the next day! No, but seriously, paying the bills is enough motivation. I'm pretty easily distracted from work, which may sound odd for someone running their own company. I need structure and discipline, but I also need it to be self-imposed. Getting an office certainly helped me with that. For me, work is a means to an end, and the end is not money—it's about getting enjoyment out of life. Since setting up on my own, it feels as though I've had to work a lot less than when I was employed by someone else, which is great— I'm not one of these people who likes to work 15 hours a day (although inevitably there have been times when I've had to do this). However, it has been a lot more stressful.'

MANAGING THE TRANSITION: FROM ONE MAN TO A TEAM
'The financial transition from Spinnaker to Satellite in 1998 was fairly painless because it was organic—most of it was self-investment. I did take a loan of ten grand (which was quickly paid off), but the rest of the money came from the profits of Spinnaker—and this was enough to get the equipment in. Right from the beginning, cash flow, business planning, and development had all been carefully thought out, but as usual in most businesses they change as soon as you start and realise what you're up against. I had little experience of any of these things before, but I learned very quickly that the best plans are the flexible ones!

'This year has been one of growth. Satellite has expanded and we're now a team of four. When I took on Chris and Adam, two excellent graphic designers, we moved offices from Oxford to London—something I'd been meaning to do for ages because the graphic design business here is so much better, but hard to get if you're not within biking distance! Four months ago I also brought Hayley on board, who is an accountant. I've been busy putting the finances into place to allow for sufficient growth resulting, in turn, with more profitability.

'The stress of managing cash flow is probably one of the hardest parts of running a business. When you don't get paid on time by your clients, it's a nightmare. You still have to pay your staff every month—you can't expect them to ride the bandwagon with you. In the past when cash flow was bad, I've had to pay my staff from my own pocket and credit cards! Times like these can make me wonder whether I just want a regular job, but then I remember how much freedom I have, with no one to answer to but myself. I've just spent a month in Peru—something I would not have been able to do in a regular position. Also, every day is different, and you're constantly learning new skills and gathering valuable experience. It would be impossible to pigeonhole my job description.'

LEARNING FROM MISTAKES: WORKING WITH PARTNERS

'Very soon after I'd had the idea to develop Spinnaker into Satellite, bringing the whole process from sales to production in-house, one graphic designer I'd met through the work I'd been doing over the last year convinced me to take him on as a partner. I thought his expertise and experience would be invaluable, being a good deal older than me. Unfortunately though, it didn't work out. I was guilty of thinking I could share the responsibility, workload, and effective running of the company! We both wanted different things and this became apparent very quickly.

'Making bad choices of staff is the single most costly element in running a company. Having had no previous experience of this, it's proved to be one of the hardest things to get right. I would never go into partnership again now. If you are going to go into business with someone, you have to know that person inside out. It's like a marriage. They have to be with you all the way, or not at all. I've had my fingers burned and it's made it very hard to trust anybody again.'

AND NOW FOR THE PHILOSOPHY...

'I believe that graphic design is essentially a cottage industry, and if you can keep yourself relatively anonymous you don't open yourself up to other competitors, but by working hard and building up a good reputation, you can still become well known enough for people to come to you. A lot of the big graphic design companies are very dependent on one or two big clients that may make up 60-80% of the turnover. But rather than set up one business raking in, say, four million pounds, I would rather run four businesses bringing in one million each. By having several businesses working in a range of markets and different places, you can protect yourself from the danger of losing that big client, or suffering in that regional or market downturn. This way you can also hang on to your staff, which I think is vital. If you have one big company, and times get tough, you may have to make redundancies. I just don't think it's good business to take people on, make them part of your business only to have to let them go two years down the line. This is what happened to a lot of big graphic design companies post September 11th. I guess if my degree in economics comes in anywhere, it's here! You've got to protect yourself against adverse cyclical economic forces.

'So five years down the line I'd like to say we'll be in New York and San Francisco, but realistically I would hope that Satellite have an established name where clients come to us for direction and help, and we can focus less on finding clients and more on the projects themselves. It's just starting to happen now, which is great. I want to walk down the street and see our work out there. There's nothing more rewarding than seeing the end product and knowing that your business created it from start to finish. My dream client would be British Airways. I'd love to reinvent their identity—they are such a high-profile company.'

PARTING WORDS OF ADVICE

'What I lacked in experience, I made up for in confidence. I knew that I could make at least enough money to provide myself with a reasonable salary, not to mention a lot more than I was getting in my previous job. I think confidence is vital for anyone thinking about setting up their own company, because people are going to knock you a lot and tell you it's not going to work. You need to have the belief that you can prove them all wrong.

'Anyone can run a business. The hard thing is to run a business that makes money. So in addition to confidence, you need business knowledge, and you must never rest on your laurels. The key to it is continually looking for new markets and new clients. Luck plays no part in running a successful company. If you get opportunities you must have worked extra hard prior to getting them.

'In my particular business, communication is everything, and at every level. At a grass roots level, there's the brand: it's about the effective communication of the thing being sold, be that through cohesiveness, simplicity, etc. If the brand works, the thing more or less sells itself. But then the importance of communication follows all the way down the line, right down to the way you answer the phone to a client.

'Think very carefully about what you want to do. If it's not in your chosen profession then go and learn as much as you can about that industry and working within that industry. So much success in this industry depends on building up a good range of contacts, and the only way to get them is to immerse yourself in it. It's as much about who you know as what you know. Lots of people can do the job, but if the client knows you, they'll give you the chance to prove it.

'Finally, get as much management training as you can before you go it alone, especially with regards to managing other people. This will prove invaluable as you grow!'

Visit Satellite Ltd at: www.satellitelondon.co.uk

Viewpoint: Steven Greenall—Warwick Music

Warwick Music is a music publisher and retail outlet based in the Midlands. The business offers customers specialist books and CDs as well as an extensive range of sheet music across a variety of specialist markets including bands and ensembles, choral, horn, trumpet, trombone, and woodwind—its tenor trombone catalogue alone offers more than 200 titles.

Steven Greenall is a partner in the company, which was established in 1994, and here he tells us more about running a local business with an international outlook.

BUYING INTO THE BUSINESS

'I've always wanted to work for myself. My father worked for a large multinational company for many years and held a very senior position in it, but it put me and my brother off! We both wanted to be our own boss.

'I studied electrical engineering at Warwick University and aimed to use those skills to work in the media. My business partner, Simon, approached me about joining the business, and I bought in (Simon's previous partner had left.) I went back to Warwick and took an MA in business in the arts. I found it really useful and because I was studying part-time I got the best of both worlds—I was able to see the practical application of the theories I was learning.

'Simon is a professional musician, and I think we work very well together. There's a clear division in what we do, in that he's very much more involved in the creative side of the company, whereas I look after the business side, such as dealing with contracts, sorting out copyright arrangements and so on. Warwick Music is now a limited company but it was a partnership initially and Simon and I were equal partners.

'The company had been running for about 2 years when I joined in1996, and like many small businesses, it was a cottage industry and based in Simon's house. We carried on working from home until 1998, but then decided to look for some rented premises via an estate agent. It was a bit of a slog to find the right place, but we rented two office units at first and have since branched out into a third. We're hoping to buy in the next six to 12 months, though, and are looking at some properties in Coventry city centre as it's an area that attracts European Regional Development Fund money.'

MANAGING THE NUMBERS

'We were fortunate in that we didn't need to find external sources of funding when we were starting up, and we're also in a high-niche, ostensibly very profitable business; we make 25–30% profit although our turnover is small. One thing we have taken pains to do is to manage our cash carefully. This is always a problem area for small businesses—you may be making a profit, but if you can't get your hands on the money, it's a real problem and you won't be able to expand. I'm wary about taking out loans too, as you can't tell what will happen to interest rates. That's one of the reasons why we didn't buy premises earlier—what was then the new Labour government had just come in, and things seemed to be in a state of flux, but now they seemed to have settled down.

'We've managed to fund and arrange expansion ourselves so far. Local knowledge helps, I think; both Simon and I are from this area and still live nearby and we've recently joined our local Chamber of Commerce. We're also members of the Federation of Small Businesses (who have a great advice line for legal issues) and the CBI—we've joined them for a year and will see how that goes.

'Keeping on top of your financial affairs is absolutely crucial for anyone running a small business. We outsource all our book-keeping and it's well worth the cost. If you try to do it yourself, you'll just end up putting it off. Also remember that while you may be a great builder, joiner, or designer, you might not necessarily be a good accountant, so it's a good idea to get some professional help. We find that the data generated from the financial reports is really useful as it means that we can think about the big, longer-term numbers rather than the day-to-day small ones. If you can afford it, it really is worth it.'

SELLING ONLINE

'We've invested a lot of money in the website as we do so much business online—between 15–20% of our sales are done that way, and the site features soundclips so that the customers can hear before they buy. We now ship to 30 or 40 countries. The website offers our own publications as well as US imports, and we've a really wide range of specialist CDs too. We're hoping to expand our services, though, to include selling accessories, equipment, and instruments, as not that many outlets stock those items.

'If you are in retail, and music retail in particular, the Internet will be a massive part of the way you do business in the future, and lots of shops are now offering an e-service. If you think that having a website will offer you an income stream, invest in setting one up and having it designed professionally if you can afford it. On the Web, everyone is equal, and you can look as if you're a million pound business even if you're still small. We still get lots of orders through the trade (that is, from other shops), but it's great to have customers coming direct to us as then we don't have to offer such big discounts.'

WORKING WITH YOUR CUSTOMERS

'The way you work and interact with your customers is really important, whatever type of business you're in. Good quality customer service is one of our main priorities. We send all our products by first-class post, but if someone buys on the website with a valid debit or credit card on the website, shipping is free. This is a win-win situation, I think, as we get the money up-front and the customers receive a discount.

'We've had lots of great feedback, which we always appreciate, and we also understand how important it is to keep up the level of customer service when things go wrong, as they're bound to do from time to time. Lots of businesses shy away from apologising as they think it hurts their business, but I don't agree—we don't want to hide away when things go awry, so apologising is the first step and then we concentrate on sorting out the problem. If we've made a mistake, we give the customer a free piece of music as well. Obviously we try to make sure that all our products are the very best they can be in the first place, so we place a lot of emphasis on good quality control to make sure we get it right first time as much as possible. In a way, customers are taking a risk when they buy from us, as we sell relatively new or very new pieces—we don't stock Beethoven and Strauss, for example. The quality has to be top notch so that customers trust us and what we do, and want to come back and buy again.

'I travel a lot with the business, especially to the United States and Europe, and visit as many trade shows as possible. It's good to meet our customers in person and to continue to build on the relationships we have. I've also found that customers have great ideas! One of our bestsellers, a piece for trumpet of which we've sold 4,000 copies, was suggested by a customer originally. We went away, investigated the market and then came up with something that fitted the bill.'

Visit Warwick Music at: www.warwickmusic.com

50 Pearls of Entrepreneurial Wisdom

Inspirational quotes from the people who turned a business idea into a business success.

1 **If you think you can, you can. And if you think you can't, you're right.**

Mary Kay Ash (1915–2001) US entrepreneur, business executive, and founder of Mary Kay Cosmetics. *New York Times* (20 October 1985)

2 **My formula for success is to be found in three words — work — work — work.**

Silvio Berlusconi (b. 1936) Italian media entrepreneur and prime minister. Interview, *Financial Times* (1 August 1988)

3 **Is your company so small you have to do everything for yourself? Wait until you're so big that you can't. That's worse.**

Michael Bloomberg (b. 1942) US entrepreneur, business executive, and Mayor of New York. Bloomberg by Bloomberg (co-written with Matthew Winkler; 1997)

4 **I found that everywhere articles, especially drugs, were being sold at ridiculously high prices... My idea was simply to buy tons where others bought hundredweights or less, thus buying more cheaply.**

Jesse Boot (1850–1931) British entrepreneur and founder of Boots pharmacy chain. 1930. Reflecting on his early success in mass-marketing Epsom salts. Quoted in *Enlightened Entrepreneurs* (Ian Campbell Bradley; 1987), ch. 9

5 **One of the reasons I started this business was I wanted to go to my class reunion in a limo. In school, I knew I was smart...but I was the kid least likely to succeed.**

Terri Bowersock (b. 1956) US furniture company entrepreneur. Quoted in 'Terri Bowersock: Furniture Franchiser', *Women to Watch*, www.womenswire.com (Teresa O'Neil; 1996)

6 **Start with your own money and value your intuition. It's all about endurance in the beginning. Your dream and passion to succeed must be stronger than your fear of failure.**

Terri Bowersock (b. 1956) US furniture company entrepreneur. Advice to would-be entrepreneurs. Quoted in 'Terri Bowersock: Furniture Franchiser', *Women to Watch*, www.womenswire.com (Teresa O'Neil; 1996)

7 **The truth is I started my own company because I could not fill out a job application.**

Terri Bowersock (b. 1956) US furniture company entrepreneur. *Phoenix Business Journal* (1999)

8 **If you can run one business well, you can run any business well.**

Richard Branson (b. 1950) British entrepreneur, business executive, and founder of the Virgin Group. *New York Times* (2000)

9 **I'm Richard Branson, I'm eighteen and I run a magazine that's doing something really useful for young people.**

Richard Branson (b. 1950) British entrepreneur, business executive, and founder of the Virgin Group. Referring to his first business venture. Quoted in *Richard Branson, The Inside Story* (Mick Brown; 1988)

10 **We spend most of our lives working. So why do so few people have a good time doing it?**

Richard Branson (b. 1950) British entrepreneur, business executive, and founder of the Virgin Group. *New York Times* (28 February 1993)

11 **Develop the business around the people; build it, don't buy it; and, then, be the best.**

Richard Branson (b. 1950) British entrepreneur, business executive, and founder of the Virgin Group. Speech to the Institute of Directors, London. 'Growing Bigger While Still Staying Small' (May 1993)

12 **Masters of entrepreneurial judo.**

Richard D'Aveni (b. 1950) US strategist. 'The Mavericks', *Fortune* (June 1995)

13 **You can never be an entrepreneur if you're afraid to lose money. It's like being a pilot who is afraid of bad weather.**

Peter de Savary (b. 1944) British entrepreneur. Quoted in *The Adventure Capitalists* (Jeff Grout and Lynne Curry; 1998)

14 **Being an entrepreneur is about having the will and determination and not being frightened of getting it wrong.**

Jason Drummond (b. 1969) British Internet entrepreneur. *Sunday Times* (October 2000)

15 **I'm a dirt-under-the-nails serial entrepreneur.**

Donna Dubinsky (b. 1955) US IT executive. 'Secrets of the Fastest-rising Stars', *Fortune* (Patricia Sellers; 2000)

16 **First get in, then get rich, then get respectable.**

Bernie Eccleston (b. 1930) British entrepreneur and CEO of Formula 1 motor racing. Referring to his success in developing Formula 1 motor racing. Quoted in *Formula 1, The Business of Winning* (Russell Hotten; 1998)

17 **As entrepreneurs, we have to remember the importance of building bridges...to new opportunities. Those links should reach out to all sorts of folks: artists, engineers, teachers, business owners, writers, elders, singles, couples.**

Gladys E. Edmunds, US travel company entrepreneur. 'Building Bridges to Prosperity', *USA Today* (9 August 2000)

18 **No one can possibly achieve any real and lasting success or 'get rich' in business by being a conformist.**

J. Paul Getty (1892–1976) US entrepreneur, oil industry executive, and financier. *International Herald Tribune* (10 January 1961)

19 **Everything is always impossible before it works. That is what entrepreneurs are all about— doing what people have told them is impossible.**

R. Hunt Greene (b. 1950) US venture capitalist. *Fortune* (27 May 1996)

20 **There are two options: adapt or die.**

Andrew S. Grove (b. 1936) US entrepreneur, author, and chairman of Intel Corporation. Attrib.

21 **To start a business and to run it successfully, you have to like people. You have to care about them.**

Bud Hadfield (b. 1923) US entrepreneur and founder of Kwik Kopy. *Wealth within Reach: Winning Strategies for Success from the Unconventional Wisdom of Bud Hadfield* (1995)

22 **Everything I do I love. An entrepreneur is a big artist.**

Nicolas G. Hayek (b. 1928) Swiss entrepreneur and founder of SWATCH. *Sunday Times* (October 2000)

23 **I think the skills involved in putting together deals are crucial to a start-up. You need wide distribution and many partners.**

Rob Herson (b. 1952) South African business executive. *Marketing* (July 2000)

24 **To me success can only be achieved through repeated failure and introspection. In fact, success represents 1 per cent of your work, which results from the 99 per cent that is called failure.**

Soichiro Honda (1906–91) Japanese entrepreneur, founder and president of Honda Corporation. Quoted in *Thriving on Chaos* (Tom Peters; 1988)

25 **Do you want to spend the rest of your life selling sugared water or do you want the chance to change the world?**

Steve Jobs (b. 1955) US entrepreneur, co-founder and CEO of Apple Computer Company, and CEO of Pixar. Said to John Sculley, then president of PepsiCo, when inviting him to join Apple. *Fortune* (14 September 1987)

26 **Entrepreneurs are simply those who understand that there is little difference between obstacle and opportunity and are able to turn both to their advantage.**

Victor Kiam (1926–2001) US CEO of Remington Corporation. 1990. Quoted in *East Valley Tribune* (2000)

27 **It sounds boring, but anything is easy to start—starting a novel, starting a business…it's keeping the thing going that is difficult.**

Prue Leith (b. 1940) British cookery writer and business executive. Quoted in *The Adventure Capitalists* (Jeff Grout and Lynne Curry; 1998)

28 **The entrepreneurial spirit is alive and well here but it's harder to get funding for your new business if you come from Leicestershire than if you went to Eton and are the son of some banker.**

Isabel Maxwell (b. 1950) British president of CommTouch. Referring to United Kingdom. *Guardian* (22 July 2000)

29 **Running a company is a constant process of breaking out of systems and challenging conditioned reflexes, of rubbing against the grain.**

Mark McCormack (1930–2003) US entrepreneur, founder and CEO of the International Management Group. *What They Don't Teach You at Harvard Business School* (1984)

30 **Today, if someone showed me a five-year plan, I'd toss out the pages detailing Years Three, Four, and Five as pure fantasy…Anyone who thinks he or she can evaluate business conditions five years from now, flunks.**

Mark McCormack (1930–2003) US entrepreneur, founder and CEO of the International Management Group. *Staying Street Smart in the Internet Age: What Hasn't Changed about the Way We Do Business* (2000), Introduction

31 **You do not have to be the son of a rich man to be an entrepreneur. Today kids are far more willing to**

take risks because they've seen high rewards.

Narayana Murthy (b. 1946) Indian founder and CEO of Infosys. *Forbes* (June 2000)

32 **The entrepreneur is...the most important player in the building of the global economy. So much so that big companies are decentralising and reconstituting themselves as networks of entrepreneurs.**

John Naisbitt (b. ?1929) US business executive and author. *Global Paradox* (1994)

33 **I've got an ego and all that, but I know I need help. So I go and hire the very best people.**

H. Ross Perot (b. 1930) US entrepreneur, venture capitalist, and politician. Inc. (January 1989)

34 **Risk is what an entrepreneur eats for breakfast. It's what she slips into bed with at night. If you have no appetite for this stuff, or no ability to digest it, then get out of the game right now.**

Heather Robertson (b. 1942) Canadian author. *Taking Care of Business* (1997)

35 **Risk means not knowing if, or when, you can pay yourself, or anyone else. It means working without health and pension plans, regular promotions, and paid vacations.**

Heather Robertson (b. 1942) Canadian author. *Taking Care of Business* (1997)

36 **Success depends on having a product or a service that catches the consumer's imagination, although at first it may be that nobody but you has ever heard of it.**

Heather Robertson (b. 1942) Canadian author. *Taking Care of Business* (1997)

37 **If I had to name a driving force in my life, I'd name passion every time.**

Anita Roddick (b. 1942) British entrepreneur and founder of The Body Shop. *Body and Soul* (co-written with Russell Miller; 1991)

38 **Three components make an entrepreneur: the person, the idea and the resources to make it happen.**

Anita Roddick (b. 1942) British entrepreneur and founder of The Body Shop. *Body and Soul* (co-written with Russell Miller; 1991)

39 **I wanted to set the world on fire and that would not come about through working for someone else in a nine-to-five job.**

Ian Schrager (b. 1948) US entrepreneur. *Sunday Times* (May 2000)

40 **People who are successful simply want it more than people who are not.**

Ian Schrager (b. 1948) US entrepreneur. *Sunday Times* (May 2000)

41 **It's better to be the head of a chicken than the tail of a cow.**

Stan Shih (b. 1945) Taiwanese CEO of the Acer Group. Referring to a Taiwanese proverb and the preference of entrepreneurs for running their own small business. Quoted in *Giant Killers* (Geoffrey James; 1996)

42 **As an entrepreneur, you have to go against the flow.**

Reuben Singh (b. 1977) British entrepreneur and author. *Management Today* (September 1999)

43 **Money isn't what motivates entrepreneurs; it is acknowledgement— a craving for your ideas to be acknowledged.**

Reuben Singh (b. 1977) British entrepreneur and author. *Management Today* (September 1999)

44 **Start small. If you can succeed with a few thousand pounds, then you can do much better with bigger sums.**

Reuben Singh (b. 1977) British entrepreneur and author. *Management Today* (September 1999)

45 **The younger you are, the fewer responsibilities you have, the more prone you are to take risks and the more commitment you can put into your business.**

Reuben Singh (b. 1977) British entrepreneur and author. *Management Today* (September 1999)

46 **It's one of life's ironies that the more you can prove that you don't need a loan, the better your chances usually are of getting one. This is especially true for start-up businesses.**

Lillian Vernon (b. 1927) US entrepreneur and CEO of Lillian Vernon Corporation. Speech. 'The Entrepreneur and the Professional Manager: Getting the Best of Both Worlds' (1998)

47 **Success is more a function of consistent common sense than it is of genius.**

An Wang (1920–90) US entrepreneur, business executive, electrical engineer, and founder of Wang Laboratories. *Boston Magazine* (December 1986)

48 **To make it in any business, it's not enough to give 100 percent. If that's all you have in you, go work for someone else and give THEM 100 percent. You have to give 200 percent. That's how it happens.**

Lise Watier (b. 1942) Canadian proprietor of a cosmetics chain. Quoted in *Looking Good* (Rosa Harris-Adler; 1997)

49 **My own success was attended by quite a few failures along the way. But I refused to make the biggest mistake of all: worrying too much about making mistakes.**

Kemmons Wilson (1913–2003) US entrepreneur, founder and chairman of Holiday Inn. Speech, Hillsdale College, Hillsdale, Michigan (September 1996)

50 **Sometimes the first step is the hardest: coming up with an idea. Coming up with an idea should be like sitting on a pin—it should make you jump up and do something.**

Kemmons Wilson (1913–2003) US entrepreneur, founder and chairman of Holiday Inn. 'What Makes for Success?', *Imprimis* (March 1997)

These quotations were drawn from *Talking Shop: Over 5,000 Business Quotes to Help You Through Your Working Day*, another title in Bloomsbury's **BUSINESS: The Ultimate Resource** series.

have a low response rate and can give the impression that your firm is being evasive. Keep price and postage separate and give a delivery time (though if you are selling goods zero-rated for VAT, the business could offer 'free postage' and, provided it is VAT-registered, recover VAT from Customs and Excise).

Websites can be used to promote your business and generate orders. It may also be worth investigating taking payment via the site.

Track enquiries

It is important to be able to assess the success of targeting. Make sure that all your coupons are coded with an identifying letter or symbol, to show their origin. If there is not room for this, then a slightly different name or address could be used for each media source.

Keep a record of where each enquiry comes from (media, personal recommendation, direct mailing, and so on), and whether the enquiry becomes a sale. This allows you to determine which adverts lead to sales, as opposed to just enquiries, and to target advertising even more effectively in the future.

Aim to break even on the cost of mailing with your first set of orders. Then convert the requests into regular, loyal customers. This conversion rate should be significantly higher than the initial response rate. If brochures and leaflets are sent out and there is little or no response, some enquirers could be telephoned and asked why.

Get paid

The traditional system of offering cheap credit through agents is declining in popularity; most people want to buy only for themselves. Most small mail-order firms ask for payment with order. It's a good idea to wait for a cheque to be cleared before the goods are sent.

If possible, credit cards should be accepted. Customers prefer this as it is convenient and offers protection: if an individual item bought by credit card costs over £100 but less than £25,000, under the Con-sumer Credit Act 1974 the customer will be reimbursed by the card company should the business go into liquidation.

Package and deliver

Managing the delivery process efficiently is the core element of customer service for mail-order businesses. Test different packaging in Royal Mail conditions by sending items to and from the business. A separate packaging area should be set up with materials to hand. The importance of secure, efficient packaging should be emphasised to staff.

Think about how your business will deliver. Possible offers include free delivery, or free delivery for orders over a specified amount; and guaranteed next day delivery, or a surcharge for guaranteed delivery within 48 hours. Your business needs to decide whether such guarantees can be met, and whether the expense is worth the corresponding increase in customers and customer loyalty.

The British code of advertising, sales promotion, and direct marketing

These codes have been agreed by the advertising industry. They apply to catalogues, circulars, newspaper and magazine adverts, direct mail brochures, and circulars. A catalogue should state that goods can be returned if applicable. It should also give any limitations to the offer. It should state the VAT due, unless the advert is exclusively trade. It should also give an estimated delivery time. Subject to certain exclusions, all orders should be fulfilled within 30 days. If delivery will take over 30 days, customers should be offered a refund. If they choose to wait, either fortnightly reports or a firm date should be given. Written statements of terms and conditions should be provided for customers.

Lists and databases should be run against the Mailing Preference Service (MPS) Suppression File, to ensure their accuracy. Lists that are over six months old should not be used unless they have been corrected. If information will be disclosed to other businesses, consumers should be given the chance to object. Also, personal information should be relevant and not excessive.

Be aware of legal issues

The European Directive on Distance Selling was adopted in May 1997 and covers the supply of goods and services at a distance. Your business should be aware of any changes that this directive makes to existing UK legislation.

The Data Protection Act 1998 covers personal data, that is to say information on a living, identifiable individual. Data controllers must register with the Data Protection Commissioner. There are eight principles of good practice, including that data be fairly and lawfully obtained, that it is held only for the purpose specified in the register entry, and that adequate security measures are taken to prevent unauthorised or accidental access to, alteration, disclosure, or loss and destruction of information.

If credit (subject to certain exemptions) is offered, your business may need a Category A Consumer Credit Business credit licence under the Consumer Credit Act (CCA) 1974.

Consider voluntary protection schemes

Many mail order businesses adopt one of the voluntary codes of practice designed to protect customers' details and money. The Mail Order Protection Scheme (MOPS) covers most adverts in national newspapers that ask for payment with order (excluding most classified advertisements). If the business is cleared, it pays a fee to the common fund based on advertising costs. (This is used to pay customers for goods up to £100 should the advertiser go into liquidation.) To join the scheme you must provide the latest accounts, a bank reference, details of your stock levels, details of advertising agencies used, and your advert and product details.

The Mailing Preference Service allows people to have their details removed from the lists of companies that subscribe. The Mail Order Traders' Association (MOTA) has a code of practice for catalogue mail order that is well worth investigating. Although its members are leading general catalogue companies, its Office of Fair Trading-agreed code has useful guidelines for practice.

WHAT TO AVOID
Not being prepared
Make sure that you have the resources to set up this type of business. It may look like an easy way of selling at first sight, but you need to be certain that you have the right product and that you have pinpointed the right market for it.

Worrying about lack of response
Your business may only get a few replies initially, but if these lead to high-price, high-margin sales, then it can be worth it.

RECOMMENDED LINKS
Advertising Standards Authority (ASA) and Committee of Advertising Practice (CAP):
www.asa.org.uk
Committee of Advertising Practice:
www.cap.org.uk
Direct Marketing Association (DMA):
www.dma.org.uk
Mailing Preference Service:
www.mpsonline.org.uk
Mail Order Traders' Association (MOTA):
www.adassoc.org.uk/members/mota.htm

SEE ALSO
Direct Marketing (p. 503)

Telemarketing

GETTING STARTED

Telemarketing is a marketing strategy that uses telecommunications and computers, or a manual contact system, to make sales calls and build leads for the sale of your product or service. This actionlist looks at the best ways to structure your own telemarketing operation and considers the use of an independent telemarketing agency.

FAQS

How do I set up an in-house telemarketing operation?

Office design can significantly affect performance, so if your budget allows, use a consultant experienced in call centre design. The office should be arranged so that individuals can make or answer calls in private yet still feel part of a team. Good sound insulation is essential. Workstations should be comfortable, and equipment should include lightweight headsets and antiglare computer screens. Workstations and equipment should meet the Health and Safety (Display Screen Equipment) Regulations 1992.

Think carefully about recognition and remuneration. In the case of outgoing calls, you could consider a results-based scheme. For staff handling incoming calls, you could offer bonus payments for hitting cross-selling (selling customers different products within your range) or up-selling (selling customers a higher-priced version of a product they have bought previously) targets. You could run a pilot scheme to evaluate variable factors such as lists, people, markets, equipment, and management, before embarking on a full programme.

How do I introduce a telemarketing programme?

A telemarketing operation won't reach its full potential in isolation, and needs to work with other parts of the business—co-operation is the key to success. Everyone involved in marketing, sales, and production needs to understand the reasons for its introduction, what benefits it will bring, and the impact it will have. Sales people may feel threatened by telemarketing, so you must explain how telemarketing will complement their activities.

The first step is to do an overview of the business operations and then to identify the telemarketing objectives. Then carry out a cost-benefit analysis and draw up a detailed step-by-step plan for implementing and running the operation. Best practice guidelines can be obtained from the Direct Marketing Association. In particular, you will need to be aware of the guidelines in respect of politeness and times of calling, and the use of the Telephone Preference Service if the business is planning to make calls to consumers who are not current customers. Check the provisions of the Telecommunications (Data Protection and Privacy) Regulations 1999.

MAKING IT HAPPEN
Implement a telemarketing programme

First you need to target your telemarketing programme. The targets should be identified for outgoing calls. You can do this by analysing existing customer life-cycles, looking at how recently a customer bought something, how frequently he or she buys, and of what value the purchases are. Prospects can also be identified by geographical location, from lapsed customers, and from bought-in lists of names. Incoming calls are usually generated through advertising, which must itself be targeted. Ideally, rank target groups by potential return on investment.

Second, you must test your telemarketing programme. There are specific methods for calculating how big a sample to try, but for a campaign of any real size it is advisable to work on 500 to 1,000. After determining the sample size, you can work out the level of human and telephone resources needed for the trial period. The trial gives your business a chance to monitor results and modify the details of the programme.

Third, you need to implement your programme, depending, of course, on the test results. Budgets must be set for the programme, and you will need to consider the investment required, operating costs, the cost-saving benefits of the programme, and the extra revenue likely to be produced through additional orders.

Fourth, you should evaluate the programme. You will need to work out costs, and productivity levels in terms of rates of response and conversion (contacts into sales). Telemarketing should produce quantifiable results. With accurate figures, it is possible to establish future activity budgets and be able to compare the cost-effectiveness of telemarketing against alternative sales and marketing methods, or as a support to the existing methods.

Use databases for telemarketing

You will need to purchase or develop a database to store information on customers and prospects. Databases range from simple systems (like a computerised card index system) to relational databases that allow data to be analysed in various ways. Consider what categories of information the database should hold, data entry methods (for example, directly during the customer's telephone call, or later by transfer from paper records), how the information will be accessed, how reports will be generated, and quality standards and procedures (to keep data accurate and up-to-date).

The ideal source of telephone contacts is your business's own database. However, you may wish to buy in contact lists from a specialist agency. It is a good idea to shop around: list-provision is a competitive business. Similar lists may be available through several brokers at different prices. Be aware that lists go out of date very quickly. The quickest way to check the accuracy of a list is by phone.

Telemarketing businesses need to comply with the Data Protection Act 1998. If the business uses a bought-in database, it is important to make sure that it has been screened against the list provided by the Telephone Preference Service; details are available from the Direct Marketing Association.

Call management

Call management affects the service provided to callers and the cost-effectiveness of your telemarketing operation. There are two main methods of managing incoming calls.

1. A Special Automatic Caller Distributor (ACD) transfers incoming calls to the first available person, or plays a message indicating that the caller is in a queue. ACDs also produce useful call-management information for telemarketing operations.

2. Call Sequencers answer calls with a message saying that the call will be taken as soon as possible, or giving the caller an option to leave voicemail for a return call.

ACDs and Call Sequencers can be located on the premises and are available from a number of companies. Additionally, caller-controlled systems let callers select the person or department with whom they wish to speak by pressing buttons on their telephone, or through voice recognition.

Recruit and train for the telemarketing operation

The performance of a telemarketing operation depends on the people on the phones. They must be skilled in creating rapport, overcoming objections, responding to criticisms, and directing conversations. Make an initial evaluation of candidates over the phone. Assess whether they come across as genuine, interested individuals who enjoy contact with people; whether they are clear communicators; and whether they listen well, taking in all the information they are given. You will need to consider whether candidates would work well in a demanding atmosphere without becoming discouraged. This is particularly important, as rejection is part of the job. Training is vital; appropriate courses for telemarketing managers and staff are widely available.

Lead and motivate staff in a telemarketing operation

All telemarketing teams need a leader, someone with excellent interpersonal skills and the ability to motivate staff. Team leaders should start and finish each day with upbeat team briefings. Before making calls, it is important that everyone knows his or her target for the day. At the end of the day, results can be discussed and the day should be closed on a positive note. The team leader should be located near the team, and team members should be encouraged to swap information and raise problems. Calls should be monitored unobtrusively to see who needs help in developing their style and skills.

Think about using using scripts

Telemarketing staff need to direct every conversation in a planned and controlled yet natural way. You will need to develop a script or structured call plan covering all stages of the conversation, from greeting callers and answering questions to taking orders and signing off. Many telemarketing departments provide their agents with computer-based scripts. These often have built-in intelligence; for example, when an answer is filled in by an operator, the computer provides the most appropriate question to ask next. Information from callers can be typed directly onto a form on-screen.

Writing a multi-option telemarketing script is a specialised skill; a professional may be hired to do it. Staff should be allowed to spend time role-playing first. It is useful to tape trial conversations and check that they sound natural. Well-prepared scripts should control the message being delivered and ensure that customers receive correct information. They also ensure that the right information is collected and make it easier to analyse results. However, there can also be drawbacks; in the hands of the inexperienced, scripts can sound false and contrived and they can diminish initiative in more experienced staff.

Use an outside telemarketing agency

Some telemarketing agencies specialise in inbound telemarketing, others in outbound, but many operate in both fields. Make sure you know exactly what services *your* business requires and try to visit each agency in person. Check the agency's client list, and ask permission to contact several clients for references, and also find out about the agency's database system and what management information it can provide. Ask for a written response to your brief, with detailed costing and confirm that the agency has the capacity to handle full implementation if the trial goes well.

Monitoring performance is essential, so arrange for regular reports on all key activities, including lost calls, response rates, and data quality. You could also make some test calls and check that everything is operating within specified timescales. If people are declining an offer, try to find out why— changing the script might help. Finally, reward outstanding results and thank staff personally to keep their motivation high.

WHAT TO AVOID

Not researching thoroughly

It's a good idea to look at the marketing procedures used by the business's competitors, especially telemarketing programmes.

Not getting an 0800 number

It is worth considering getting an 0800 telephone number; 0800 calls are charged to the business. These are available from several telecommunications companies and are popular in telemarketing.

RECOMMENDED LINKS

Chartered Institute of Marketing: **www.cim.co.uk**
Direct Marketing Association: **www.dma.org.uk**
Information Commissioner's Office: **www.dataprotection.gov.uk**
Institute of Direct Marketing: **www.theidm.com**

SEE ALSO
Direct Marketing (p. 503)

Understanding the Uses of a Database

GETTING STARTED

Many small businesses use a personal computer (PC) for administrative tasks like accounts, word processing, and so on. Some form of database package is often run on the same machine. Databases are useful where a lot of information needs to be held in a standardised format.

Most commonly, databases are used to keep a record of existing and potential customers, enabling orders to be processed and direct mail promotions to be carried out. Information is obtained (for example, on an order or enquiry form) and then keyed into the database. Basic databases might be mailing lists categorised according to a variety of criteria (such as location, past customer, or potential customer). At the other extreme, databases can be used to store large quantities of information for reference purposes.

FAQS

What is a database?

A database is in many ways like a traditional card index, but can contain a large number of records in a fraction of the space. A card index is only easily accessible in the order in which it was filed, but database records can be sorted into any order and individual records can be found, viewed, and amended in moments. Databases allow users to carry out statistical analysis to print out sets of records. The information can be carried on computers and transferred to other locations via the Internet.

Most databases have structures based on records and fields. A record is an entry within the database (for example, the details of a single enquiry or individual customer). A field is an item of information within a record (such as an enquiry date, a name, or a postcode). A database can be ordered by a particular field (for example, alphabetically, numerically, or chronologically), and sets of records can be extracted from the main database according to chosen criteria (for example, all current customers who have not placed an order for over three months).

What can a database do?

A database allows you to manipulate and exploit large sets of records far more efficiently than by using manual methods. A database can provide:

- **searching and updating**—individual records can be found quickly, even when the details given are incomplete. They can then be updated as required.
- **grouping and targeting**—sets of records can be selected according to different criteria. This is very useful for targeting groups with different products or different promotions.
- **printing and mail merge**—lists, address labels, personalised letters, and many other customised documents can be generated for selected groups.
- **statistical analysis**—data can be analysed and presented in a form which aids management decision making, such as monthly sales figures, or customer profiles.

Other uses include keeping track of products sold or purchased; stock-control systems linked into bar-code readers; and databases designed to store and analyse the data from questionnaires. Some databases can be used to make the data available to an Internet or intranet website.

MAKING IT HAPPEN

Decide what you need from a database

It is important that you understand your manual systems properly before putting them into a database, so you should analyse your existing procedures. If you have employees, talk to them about how things can be improved. What benefits will using a database provide, over those of a manual system? What do you want to be able to do in the future that you can't do now? Above all, you should look at the paper systems and procedures which will be required to keep the database up to date. You might find that you will need to devote more staff time to data processing than before, though there should be time or cost savings in being able to access and use the data more rapidly.

When the costs of running the system have been evaluated, you should make sure that the benefits of acquiring a database are sufficient. How often will mailshots be done? How many enquiries will be processed daily? How often will reports be required? You should have very specific ideas of the benefits which a database will bring to your business before even starting to look at the technical requirements. It's important to concentrate on the benefits rather than features. If the business runs a network of computers, think about whether the database is a resource that several people may want to share.

Set up a database system

There are a number of essential steps that you will have to take when setting up a database system, all of which will have to be taken into account when working out how long it will be before the business starts to reap the benefits.

Planning and resourcing

Computerising your business's records can fundamentally change work procedures. It is important to plan for the introduction of the new system. Transferring data into a database is time consuming if it is being converted from a paper-based system, so maybe you could consider using temporary staff for the task. Computerised and paper systems could be run in parallel until it is certain that the new system is reliable and everyone is using it correctly.

Designing input systems and screens

It is important to decide exactly what data needs to be stored in the database records, as there is a great temptation to keep more than will be needed. Just remember that the more data you store, the more that has to be gathered, input, and maintained—and there are real costs attached. You should think carefully about what information you really need, and what you will use it for. Input screens should show information in a logical and readable fashion, and the layout should match any paper forms used for data collection.

Data entry and retrieval

Accurate and consistent data input is vital. Standards for data entry should be drawn up before anyone starts to input information— for instance, you need to decide how the system will handle business names (the standard solution is to record a firm's name as it appears on its letterhead). It is also advisable to have consistent rules on spacing between letters and words (otherwise W H Smith could be W. H. Smith, WH Smith or W.H.Smith) —they mean the same to a person, but to a computer they are very different. If a database was searched for an exact match, the entry may be missed if the data entry person was inconsistent (though some databases offer an option to search for the closest matching entry, which should find the record). If codes are to be used to categorise records, it is important to standardise the coding and notify data entry staff in advance. It is usually possible to set the system to reject entries which do not match valid code lists.

Administration

You should have systems in place for keeping data up to date, which may simply involve giving someone responsibility for making changes to the database as they are required. Addresses and contact names should be checked on a regular basis to ensure they are accurate, and defunct records should be deleted regularly so that the system only contains useful information. Employees should be fully trained in the use of the system, and you must make sure that working conditions comply with the Health and Safety (Display Screen Equipment) Regulations 1992. It is also essential to make regular backup copies of data in case the system breaks down. In addition, procedures should be in place to ensure that the only people to access the data are authorised to do so—particularly if information is held on individuals. Compliance with the requirements of the Data Protection Act 1998 is of prime importance, and you can contact the Information Commissioner's Office on 01625 545 745 for details (the website address is given below).

X WHAT TO AVOID
Introducing a database without weighing up the costs and benefits

The business must be committed to computerising the records system and budget accordingly, as new IT systems often involve considerable expense. Computerisation should be seen as an investment which allows the business to do more with the information. The necessary staffing and administrative backup must be in place to ensure the database works properly: there is no point introducing a system which isn't really going to provide major benefits to the business.

Introducing a database system before it is ready

Using a database before it's fully ready can cause many problems, so be sure to plan carefully before implementing a database system to replace any of your manual systems. Also make sure that you have a period where both systems run alongside each other so that you can iron out any problems with the database before abandoning your old system altogether.

RECOMMENDED LINKS
Information Commissioner's Office:
www.dataprotection.gov.uk
UK Online for Business:
www.ukonlineforbusiness.gov.uk

SEE ALSO
Direct Marketing (p. 503)

Complying with Data Protection Legislation

GETTING STARTED

The 1998 Data Protection Act has significantly changed the rules concerning the use of customer data and applies to small companies as much as it does to larger ones. From now on, both paper and computerised records must comply with the Act, which also refers to the use of data for telemarketing.

Companies must also be open about how they use data and must follow sound information-handling practice. Furthermore, data must be available to the individual (usually your customer) who 'owns' it.

All data users must register with the office of the Information Commissioner and comply with the principles of the Act. You (and your company) will then be listed on the register as a 'data controller'.

The key principles of the Act are that data must be:

- fairly and lawfully processed
- processed for limited purposes
- adequate, relevant, and not excessive
- processed in accordance with the data subject's rights
- accurate
- secure
- not transferred to other countries without adequate protection

Companies should use customer data to benefit customers. Many simply hold data without using it. You should reassure customers that you treat their data with the highest levels of confidentiality and use data, within the spirit of the Act, to contact customers with information that you believe may be of interest to them.

Above all, make it clear to consumers how they benefit from giving you information and make it easy for them to respond, change their details, or decline to be contacted.

FAQS

How do I know if my data has to comply with the Act?

Even if you only hold a small number of customer names and addresses, they constitute data under the terms of the Act. By and large, however, the Act is concerned with data relating to private individuals and not companies. You may find that even if your customers are companies you also keep data on individuals within those companies. If in doubt, check.

My company is part of a larger group. Can I pass customer data to other companies in the group?

You should ask the customer's permission before passing data to any other parties, even internal ones.

Do I need permission to collect data?

Yes, you should tell the owner of the data and give him or her the opportunity to opt out of giving you information. Any holding or use of data must be done 'fairly' and usually this means one or more of the following:

- the individual has given his or her consent
- it is necessary for the performance of the contract with the individual
- it is a legal obligation
- it is necessary to protect the vital interests of the individual; or to carry out public functions
- it is necessary in order to pursue the legitimate interests of the data controller or third parties (unless it could prejudice the interests of the individual)

How long can I hold data on a customer?

The Act does not specify a time limit, but recommends that it should not be held longer than necessary. It is in the spirit of the Act that you should not just hold data, but should use it to benefit the customer, for example, by providing him or her with information that you believe is useful.

What happens if data is inaccurate?

According to the Act, data must be accurate and up to date. That puts the onus on you to maintain it properly and check with customers that it is accurate.

Can I use data for telemarketing?

Yes, but again you must ask permission from individuals or companies before sending faxes and individuals have a right to opt out of telephone calls. Companies cannot insist on no telephone calls, but you would be well-advised to consider such a request seriously! Both individuals and companies must give permission before you can use automated call systems—a point not well known.

✔ MAKING IT HAPPEN

Check all your records

The use of customer data changed significantly when the 1998 Data Protection Act came into force. The 1994 Act only covered data held electronically which could be processed on a computer. However, the 1998 version includes paper records.

Remember that paper records must comply as well

In theory, this means that if you have a box of file cards with names and addresses, you should register that information with the Data Protection Registrar (Information Commissioner). Many sales and customer service teams still use this type of filing, even in relatively large companies.

Use data properly

The basic premise behind the Data Protection Act is: if you have data, use it properly. The Act works in two ways.

- Firstly, it places obligations on data users. They must be open about how they use data and must follow sound information-handling practice which is specified in the Act.
- Secondly, the Act gives every individual access to information held about him or herself. It also allows them to have the information corrected or deleted where appropriate if it is wrong, and gives the right to seek compensation for damage and associated distress through the courts.

Register your data

Under the Data Protection Act, all data users must register with the Information Commissioner. Once registered, users must comply with the principles contained in the Act. They must:

- obtain and process personal data fairly and lawfully
- hold the data only for the purposes specified in the register entry
- only hold accurate data which is relevant and not excessive for the purpose for which it is held
- ensure personal data is accurate and, where necessary, kept up to date
- not hold data for longer than necessary

The Information Commissioner has a helpline to find out more: 01625 545 745.

Use customer data to benefit customers

Not all companies comply with the spirit of the Act. According to research, some of the organisations holding most data, particularly in financial services, don't seem to use it at all, resulting in poor communications with customers. Many companies have simply been collecting data and not really putting it to good effect. The data is itself very valuable, but customers may feel that they have handed over a great deal of information on their lives without seeing any benefit. The issue of data collection becomes even more complicated with the growth of the Internet. Not only will data collection be faster; consumers will expect higher levels of service than ever.

Be aware of Internet data

The issue of regulation for the Internet is a difficult one. The World Wide Web is based on principles of freely available information on a worldwide scale. However, consumers need to be protected so that they can use the Internet with confidence.

Check data accuracy

Recent changes to the Data Protection Act mean that companies must ensure the data they hold is accurate and up to date. As part of your commitment to customer service, you should aim to offer customers useful and timely information that meets their individual requirements. To do this you might hold contact details, together with information on customers' personal interests which they have provided in the past. Because circumstances change, make sure that you have your customers' correct details and check that they are happy for the company to continue to contact them.

Customers have a right under the Data Protection Act to ask for a copy of the information you hold on them and to have any inaccuracies corrected.

Get the customer's permission

Ask customers to let you know if they do not wish you to give this information to other parties. Tell them that you would like to continue contacting them. However, if the customer prefers you not to, ask them to let you know. If they do not reply within a specified time frame, tell them that you will assume that it is okay to continue contacting them.

Reassure customers about data

Customers should be assured that you treat their data with the highest levels of confidentiality. You should not disclose their information, without their consent, to third parties, any party within your own business, dealers, or other businesses acting on your behalf.

Use the information to maintain contact

If you have data, you can use it—within the spirit of the Act—to contact customers with information about products and services that you believe may be of interest to them. You can also use the information for marketing, research or sales tracking purposes. Customer names and addresses may also be used to process orders and maintain accounts with the company or its dealers.

Make it easy for customers to respond

Allow customers to respond to requests for permission or change of details by post, fax or e-mail. Let them know that they should reply if they would like you to stop contacting them, or if they want to change contact details. Provide a helpline that customers can call if they need any further information on your data policy or on the data you hold.

WHAT TO AVOID
Storing data and not using it

The Act says that you should not hold data for longer than necessary. Consumer attitudes say that they should see some recognisable benefit for providing the information.

Using inaccurate data

The onus is on the company to ensure that data is accurate. This means contacting customers to ensure that information is up to date and correct.

Failing to register data

The 1998 version of the Act widened the scope of data protection to include paper records. Even small organisations with apparently simple customer records must comply.

Making it difficult for customers to respond

The Act says that you must give customers access to any data you hold on them. That means you must make it easy for customers to contact you.

RECOMMENDED LINK

Data Protection Agency:
www.dpa.gov.uk

SEE ALSO
Carrying Out Market Research (p. 224)

Raising Awareness of Your Brand

GETTING STARTED

Brand awareness is an important factor in customer purchasing decisions. Brand values relate to many areas, from product attributes to less tangible aspects of a company's reputation.

By identifying the key values of your brand you can establish how your products, your services, and your company are perceived by different types of customer.

FAQS

Can a small company use branding?

Absolutely. You have to understand your own brand, since you will have a brand or corporate image in your market whether you like it or not!

Smaller companies increasingly compete with large, well-known brands—sometimes globally—so the aim of branding is to differentiate your company or product and to convey its unique attributes.

How important are brand values?

Branding is frequently perceived as a consumer marketing discipline. However, industry experience indicates that business-to-business purchasing is a complex process influenced by intangible perceptions as much as by hard facts on product performance.

MAKING IT HAPPEN

Identify the most important elements of a brand

The key attributes of a business brand may include:

- fitness for purpose—is it the best at what it does?
- value for money—if not offered at always the lowest price, does it represent a good deal compared to the competition, even if it isn't better?
- quality—is it simply better built or better managed?
- extendability—does the brand work in many related markets?
- company reliability—does the brand come from a good 'stable'?
- proven products—is the brand associated with established successes?

- investment in product development—is innovation significant?

Find out what is important to your customers

Although these brand values can be applied to business products in general terms, it's vital to understand how individual customers rank the values. This can be determined in several ways, described below.

Talk to customers

This is the simplest way to find out what they value, but take care not to talk exclusively about the physical benefits of a product. There will almost certainly be aspects of service that are as important. You should also ask 'open' questions about the competition for example:

- Who else have you looked at?
- What do you think of them?
- What is their biggest strength or weakness?
- What do other people think of them?

Carry out customer surveys

To find out what your customers consider important, carry out a survey; if your budget runs to it, this should be done through a market research company so that respondents feel the survey is independent. It should ask respondents how they rank the different brand values and how they believe your company and a number of competitors compare across these values.

Run a focus group

A focus group can be used to cover the same ground as the customer survey, but it enables you to cover the subject in greater depth and to raise issues that you may not anticipate or that would normally be outside the scope of a survey. Focus groups are ideal for identifying branding issues that concern customers, assessing customer reactions to potential changes, or identifying any problems customers are experiencing.

Review industry trends

Industry associations and publishers produce regular surveys into buying behaviour in their industry sector. These surveys can highlight issues that concern the whole market.

Find out about customer purchasing requirements

An increasing number of business customers use formal criteria to evaluate potential suppliers and monitor their performance. These purchasing criteria indicate the factors that your customers believe are important and can help to identify the key messages you should include in your own brand communications.

Communicate through all channels

Advertising and marketing communications are the most important media for raising awareness. However, there are several other direct and indirect channels, including:

- products—the design and brand symbolism can convey significant brand values
- services—the way you deal with customers can demonstrate your commitment to their needs
- packaging—can carry messages regarding your brand
- distribution facilities—can give an impression of your approach and values
- websites—must be consistent with your key brand values
- customer service facilities—must deliver the promise of the brand

Assess your product branding

Do your products communicate your key brand values? The most important values are listed above but include every aspect of your company that your customer may experience.

If customer research shows that you are perceived as poor in any of these areas, or if customers are not aware of your strengths, you must look closely at your product development programme. Also review your customer communications to see how customers build their image of your brand.

Brand your services

Service capability can also help to differentiate a company.

Many companies have underestimated the importance of service to their customers and have therefore not adequately communicated their service capabilities. Raising awareness of service capability is therefore an important aspect of brand communication. You can increase awareness through product advertising, product literature, direct marketing, and product public relations, as well as through service communications.

Communicate brand values through packaging

Packaging raises awareness of brand values by the way in which it reflects the corporate identity. The right packaging can visually support your brand through the use of your logo, slogans, promises, and company values.

Don't forget to include your branding distribution facilities

Your distribution facilities can affect awareness of your brand. Again, if your budget allows, vehicles, uniforms, and premises should carry the same logo and key messages as other mediums of communication.

Distribution is an area that is frequently overlooked in branding programmes, but it can make an important contribution to customer perceptions of your company. For example, the cleanliness of a delivery van shows a level of professionalism.

Build brand values through your website

An effective e-commerce website is one in which the various technical and design components all work together to generate customer interest, build trust, communicate product value, and support convenient profitable transactions. Even if you don't sell directly from your website, the key is that your customer must feel they have gained something from the visit that exceeds the 'cost' (even if only in time) of visiting.

Brand through customer service facilities

Your customer service facilities have a major impact on the way your customers perceive your company. Customer contact takes place both before and after a sale, and these contacts can prove critical in shaping customer attitudes. When your customer service team handles enquiries, orders, or complaints effectively, it creates awareness of positive brand values.

Monitor levels of brand awareness

Customer perceptions change over a period of time. Continuous research should be carried out to monitor customer attitudes. This type of research is known as tracking research, and it helps to measure the effectiveness of brand communications programmes.

WHAT TO AVOID

Failing to monitor customer perceptions

Regular research is critical. You must know how you are perceived by your customers so that you can plan the way your brand is represented in the future.

Overlooking individual customer preferences

Industry research may give you a broad view of the brand values that are important to customers. However, it's more important to understand how individual customers—particularly your most important customers—rank individual values. This can be achieved only by continuous detailed research into individual customer needs.

Ignoring important communication channels

Brand values are communicated through many different channels, not just advertising and marketing media. Customers' attitudes and perceptions are shaped by packaging, customer service, distribution, and products as well as by other factors. Make sure every aspect of your business reflects the brand values that are important to your customers.

RECOMMENDED LINKS

British Brands Group:
www.britishbrandsgroup.org.uk
Institute of Practitioners in Advertising:
www.ipa.co.uk

SEE ALSO

Planning a Cost-effective Direct Marketing Campaign (p. 285)
Planning an Advertising Campaign (p. 303)
Producing Press Material (p. 296)

Planning a Cost-effective Direct Marketing Campaign

GETTING STARTED

Direct marketing works most effectively when it is aimed at a precise audience that cannot be easily reached by any other medium. A campaign should be carefully planned in accordance with the target market and the product or service concerned. Short-term results can be measured accurately and directly by the level of response, so the effectiveness of a campaign can be assessed quickly.

There are, however, many different factors that can affect the outcome of a campaign, such as product price or the quality of the campaign material. As with any direct approach, it is essential to make it as easy as possible for customers to respond.

FAQS

Is direct marketing the same as direct mail?

No. Direct marketing (DM) is any marketing activity that depends on a direct and measurable response. Conventional advertising can be 'direct', as can telephone, fax, e-mail and, of course, the Internet. Direct mail is direct marketing communication sent by post and therefore often has a poor reputation because of the amount of unsolicited mail that people regularly receive.

Can direct marketing be used to sell products?

There are many situations in which you can use direct marketing to build direct sales. You may not have a salesforce or a retail network, so customers can only buy direct from you. If you want to sell to niche markets, or if your customers are widely spread or even global, direct marketing may be the only cost-effective way of reaching them. If you decide to sell direct, you must ensure that the products themselves are suitable for selling through direct marketing—that is, that they do not have to be demonstrated, or inspected by the customer.

How does direct marketing build relationships with customers?

The stronger your relationship with your customers, the more opportunities you have to influence the future direction and success of your business. If your company depends on a few key customers for most of its business, you can use direct marketing to improve customer loyalty by building long-term relationships with them. You may also need to use it if your customers want to rationalise the number of suppliers, and you want to remain on the approved list.

Is direct marketing only effective for reaching a small audience?

There are numerous examples of successful large-scale mailings. However, the key to direct marketing success is reaching the right people in a cost-effective way. Large-scale mailings based on poorly researched mailing lists may yield results, but there will also be a high level of wastage. The more precise your mailing, the more likely you are to succeed.

MAKING IT HAPPEN

The key stages of a direct marketing campaign are described below.

Set campaign objectives

Direct marketing objectives can be initially expressed in general terms:

- encouraging prospects to buy directly in response to a direct marketing campaign
- generating leads for the salesforce or retail network
- supporting salesforce activity
- improving the effectiveness of other forms of communication

- raising awareness of a company, product, or service among clearly identified customers and prospects
- maintaining effective contact with customers and prospects
- building relationships with customers and prospects

However, these general objectives should be translated into precise, measurable objectives, for example:

- raising awareness of your product range among 35% of technical directors in the mechanical engineering sector
- ensuring that purchasing managers of your ten top corporate customers are contacted at least once a fortnight
- increasing direct sales of supplies by 15%

Define the target market

Do you want to reach all customers and prospects, or are you targeting specific groups? Direct marketing is a precise medium, so your campaign could be aimed at just a few key decision-makers or thousands of potential users. To plan your direct marketing campaign, you should ask questions such as:

- Who buys your type of product?
- Who influences the purchasing decision?
- How many prospective customers (prospects) do you want to reach with the direct marketing campaign?
- How many prospects can you normally convert to customers, and how long does it take?
- How do they currently get information about your products?
- Is direct marketing the best (or only) way of reaching the target audience?

The more information you have about your target audience, the more precise you can make your campaign. In an ideal world, direct marketing would allow you to communicate one to one with every prospect, but, in practical terms, you are more likely to be communicating with groups that share certain characteristics. For example, you could reasonably expect that 'all fleet managers in the North East of England managing more than thirty vehicles' would have similar needs in respect to their day to day job.

Plan campaign timing

A direct marketing campaign can run at any time, so you do not have to consider advertisement publication dates. However, timing may be dictated by other factors—lead times for producing mailing material, seasonal purchasing patterns, product availability, or tender dates. These are some of the factors to consider in planning the timing of your campaign:

- When is your customer likely to be making the buying decision?
- How long is the selling or buying process? How many stages are involved? Who is involved?
- Does your direct marketing campaign have to tie in with the timing of any other marketing activity, such as an exhibition, advertising campaign, or salesforce visit?
- If you are launching a new product, when will the product be available?
- How long will it take to produce the material that is to be mailed?
- When will you be able to follow up the campaign?
- What will you do if you get fewer responses than you need or more than you can handle?

Decide on your contact strategy

A single mailshot, telephone call, or direct response advertisement may produce results, but a series of appropriate contacts will have greater impact and ensure you meet your objectives. There are several benefits from repeated contracts:

- raising levels of awareness with each contact
- educating potential clients about your product/service
- following up those who have not responded
- moving individual respondents further along the decision-making process
- maintaining contact during extended decision-making processes

There is no hard-and-fast rule about the frequency of individual campaigns; a company trying to get a prospect to make a decision may make contact several times a week, while a company aiming to maintain long-term customer loyalty may only need to contact customers monthly or quarterly.

Develop a response mechanism

Action is a vital ingredient of any direct marketing campaign, and it is essential that you make it easy for your prospects to respond. First, decide if your prospects are to place an order, request a sales visit, or ask for further information. Then decide which of the five basic types of response mechanism is the most appropriate: post, telephone, faxback, e-mail, or website address.

Keep track of the campaign

You must be prepared to keep records of every aspect of your campaign. You will have to set up the systems to capture data before your campaign (or test campaign) starts. Aim to know at the very least:

- what was sent (the offer, the pack/letter, and so on) and to whom (the lists used and reason for selection)
- the anticipated response (for example, percentage initial response and percentage purchase)
- the actual response
- the costs and the return—in other words, did your campaign make a profit?

Test the campaign

Part of the flexibility of direct marketing is that you can test your approach before committing resources to the full campaign. There are several variables that can be tested:

- the target audience—the most important element
- the offer—what exactly you are offering for sale (including any incentive)
- the creative approach—the look and feel of the communications
- the response mechanism—how easy it is to respond, for example, using a Freephone number or Freepost
- frequency and timing—including the way you follow up enquiries

The test campaign can be carried out in a number of ways:

- on a sample of the target market
- in a defined sales or geographic territory

- in a particular sector of the target market

The most effective test campaign is the one that achieves the highest response levels, and committed DM organisations test continuously to drive down their costs and drive up response rates. Indeed, every campaign should be considered a 'test' to improve on previous campaigns. Each best-performing campaign then becomes the 'control' against which others can be evaluated.

Plan split campaigns

Testing your campaign may reveal that different approaches work more effectively in different market sectors. If budget allows, you can develop a series of campaigns that vary the offer, the creative approach, frequency, timing, or other factors, but ensure you keep track of these variables so that you can use the best-performing campaign format next time.

Set target response levels

In the long term, a campaign may increase awareness, improve customer relations, or cut the cost of sales. However, the simplest and most immediate measure of a direct marketing campaign is the response level it generates. In setting your target response levels, you should aim for a realistic figure that is within budget. Note that:

- response levels as low as 1 or 2% are regarded as the industry norm for large companies sending mail to 'cold' lists
- response rates in the region of 5% are therefore regarded as high
- response rates in the region of 10–20% have been reported by companies who have integrated other forms of marketing communications
- far higher response rates can be experienced by specialist companies communicating vital information to a very committed list of supporters

Many different factors can affect the level of response, including price, quality of the mailing list, the promotional offer, and quality of copy and design. A test is very often the only way to set an initial target response rate for future campaigns.

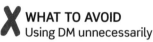

WHAT TO AVOID
Using DM unnecessarily
While the principles of direct marketing can help any company in its communications and selling, sometimes direct *mail* is used when the existing channels are preferable. Customers who are used to a personal visit and face-to-face negotiations may feel aggrieved if you try and deal with them at a distance.

Failing to set measurable targets
The results of a direct marketing campaign can be measured precisely by the number of responses. This makes it a particularly accountable medium. It is therefore important to set realistic, measurable objectives. If your target is to generate leads from 2% of the target audience, this will determine how many people you mail, the type of offer you make, and the response mechanism you provide. It will also tell you very quickly if your budget balances—how many of those leads need to convert into customers to cover your costs?

Poor audience selection
With direct marketing you can communicate with a single prospect or with 50,000. However, there may be more cost-effective ways of communicating with 50,000 prospects. Direct marketing works most effectively when it is aimed at a precise audience that cannot be easily reached by any other medium and, crucially, when you want a response. For example, you may find there is a specialist magazine or newsletter that precisely covers your target market.

No integration with other communications
If your marketing budget is split between different communications activities such as advertising, sales promotion, and press and public relations, it is essential that each activity works as effectively as possible. You can use direct marketing in conjunction with other methods of communication. If you place advertisements in publications that only reach a general audience, you can reinforce the advertisements with personalised communications to selected prospects. If your advertisements include a response mechanism, keeping to direct marketing principles will ensure effective follow-up. You can also tailor your product and corporate literature to the information needs of different market sectors by including direct marketing material.

RECOMMENDED LINKS
The Direct Selling Association:
www.dsa.org.uk
The Institute of Direct Marketing:
www.theidm.co.uk

SEE ALSO
Raising Awareness of Your Brand (p. 282)

Creating Impressive Direct Mail Material

GETTING STARTED

When you are marketing your product or service, you may find you need an effective and precise marketing tool that you can personalise in order to more accurately reflect the needs of customers and prospective customers. If so, direct mail may be what you need. It can be eye-catching and creative, and allows you to include different types of enclosure to provide additional details on the product or service being offered.

Another benefit of direct mail is that its easy to measure its results precisely, so that you can assess how you've done with a particular campaign or approach. As part of this process, you need to include an easy response mechanism for the customer, such as a reply-paid envelope, or contact details such as an e-mail address, so that your customers can give you feedback.

FAQS

Don't customers just throw direct mail in the bin?

No, but attitudes vary enormously. According to research (DMIS Sector Intelligence Surveys and DMIS Business to Business Direct Mail Trends Survey 2000) consumers opened and read over 80% of direct mail items relating to travel, but only 16% of those about home insurance. Business managers opened more than 70% of their direct mail but, on average, filed only 13%.

Is it possible to create effective direct mail?

Like any other marketing activity, work must be directed towards an objective. The more information you have, the more focused the work. Direct mail is a very precise medium, so it is possible to create highly customised and attractive mailings that meet the information needs of your chosen prospective customers (prospects).

How far can personalisation go in direct mail?

Of course, mailings to a small number of customers can easily be personalised, and should be. Provided you have the budget, larger mailings can be personalised down to individual level (one-to-one marketing). As an example, you could write individual letters to each of your prospects, or include an incentive tailored to their individual preferences. Practical financial constraints usually prevent this degree of personalisation, so most companies concentrate on limited customisation, addressing specific sector concerns or tailoring special offers to different types of business.

Can the quality of direct mail creative work be measured?

Direct mail is an extremely accountable medium, and the results can be measured precisely, making it possible to judge whether or not a particular creative approach has worked. However, creative work is only one of the factors that influence campaign success, so many companies test different creative approaches to try to identify how they affect results. Remember, though, that the offer's recipient is more important than the presentation of the offer itself, so targeting should be your priority.

MAKING IT HAPPEN
Create good-quality mailing material

Direct mail is the most precise marketing medium, but campaigns will only be effective if they combine precise targeting with good creative work.

In theory anything can be sent by post, but most mailings consist primarily of printed material—letters, leaflets, and brochures. Three-dimensional objects can be mailed and can stimulate interest, but they must be relevant and cost-effective. A striking envelope design can also add impact to a mailing. The Post Office have a dedicated team to provide all the information you need to ensure your mailings conform to their regulations and to help set up Freepost and Business Reply services.

Use direct mail letters effectively

Letters are a universal communications medium and an integral element of any direct mail campaign. They can be used on their own as a personalised form of communication, and can also be used to support and personalise other standard mailing items. Letters can be customised easily and cost-effectively to meet different sector marketing requirements.

Personalise letters

Personalised one-to-one mailings are an ideal form of communication for companies with detailed information on their prospects. The letter should reflect the individual's main interests and concerns, and the offer can be tailored to the individual prospect. Subsequent mailings can build an individual relationship with the prospect.

The key features of this type of letter are:

- it is personalised to the individual reader
- it offers direct and valuable benefits
- it builds future relationships with the customer by promising regular offers

Letters can also be customised by market sector, offering specific benefits to groups of customers.

Use letters to support other mailing material

Direct mail letters can also be used to accompany other material—a product brochure, management guide, or even an invoice, for example. The letter can customise the mailing by including information specific to the individual prospect or market sector, or by making a further offer to the prospect.

Include enclosures

Enclosures can include:

- catalogues
- sales leaflets or brochures
- price lists
- management reports or surveys

- information on special offers
- samples, free gifts, or incentives

There are a number of criteria for selecting enclosures:

- they should be relevant to the prospect's needs
- they should not make the mailing impractical or costly because of size or weight
- they should improve response, size of order, or frequency of order—if they do not they are an unnecessary cost

Treat envelopes creatively

Postal authorities specify a number of preferred envelope sizes which help them to handle mail more efficiently. Companies that wish to use specific postal response services such as Freepost or Business Reply must use the preferred layouts indicated in the authority's design specification. However, using non-standard envelope sizes can add greater impact to a mailing. Envelopes can be designed in a number of ways to achieve greater impact:

- they can include advertising messages
- addresses can be handwritten to add a personal touch
- they can incorporate corporate design elements such as logos or company colours

But be aware of occasions when a clearly, but wrongly identified envelope may depress response, such as if the item looks like a routine statement.

Create three-dimensional enclosures

Three-dimensional enclosures can add impact and novelty value to a mailing. They can be used to send product samples by mail, to send promotional items, or to improve response by creating interest. However, it is important that they are relevant to the prospect's needs, that they do not make the mailing too expensive, and that they do not contravene postal regulations.

Include a response mechanism

If your mailing is designed to stimulate action, it should include an easy-to-use response mechanism such as a reply-paid card or envelope, or contact details such as a

Freephone telephone number, e-mail address, or website address.

Use professional creative and production services

Quality and impact are essential to the success of a direct mail campaign. Creating an effective direct mail item requires professional skills, and is best handled by suitably experienced people. Although many of the direct mail processes are straightforward, your company may not have the skills or resources to achieve the best possible results. External specialists provide a range of direct mail services, including copywriting and design, printing letters, and producing three-dimensional enclosures.

Specialists include:
- direct mail agencies
- advertising agencies
- marketing communication consultancies
- design consultancies
- creative consultancies
- printers

However, there may be occasions when you decide to create simple direct mail items yourself.

Write persuasive copy

Use a powerful headline to get the attention of the reader. Words such as 'free', 'new' and 'improved' attract attention, while price benefits such as 'sale' and 'reduced' are also useful. Keep your writing style simple, with short sentences and paragraphs; in longer mailing items, use headings and subheadings to make sure that the reader picks up key messages without having to read the complete text. Tell your prospects what they need to know in order to make a decision about your product or service. Your message should deal with your customers' most important concerns and requirements. Describe benefits to the prospect, not features of the product: for example, a power drill that features extremely high operating speeds may be technically interesting, but the benefits to a builder are greater productivity and the opportunity to finish a job quickly. Offer the prospect a clear, powerful proposition. Your copy should encourage the prospect to take action—contact the company for more information, ask for a demonstration, or order immediately to qualify for a promotional offer. Describe your biggest benefit first, then remember that everything that follows should be designed to make the potential customer move on to the next stage.

Create a well-designed layout

Design quality is also important in getting a message to prospects clearly and effectively.
- keep the layout simple to ensure immediate comprehension
- use photographs, diagrams, or illustrations if they help to clarify a point or create impact
- use the most legible type faces and sizes to make text easy to read
- use bold headings or a larger type size for the headline or to emphasise important statements

WHAT TO AVOID ✘
Using mailing unnecessarily

When customers already know your company and do business with you, it can be off putting for them to be treated as 'prospects'. Always check that your mailing is an effective means of communicating.

Producing standard mailing material

Direct mail is a precise medium. You can use that precision to talk to specific customer groups or individual prospects with tailored messages and offers. Too many mailings fail to address prospects' individual needs and concerns. Research will help you to identify the key messages for different prospects, and to build them into your mailing.

Failing to plan

All mailing activity must be planned with sufficient time and resources. Rushing a mailing can lead to embarrassing and costly mistakes. Not anticipating response can lead to disappointed customers.

Failing to measure

Direct mail campaigns are measured on

their results: they should deliver enquiries or sales. If they do not deliver results, even the most creative campaigns should be considered failures. Make sure that you set realistic targets for your campaign. If you do not reach the targets, change the targeting, the offer, the format, or timing until you find one that delivers the results you want.

Making mailings too complex

Some mailings contain so much material they can be daunting to deal with, so the prospect may lose interest.

RECOMMENDED LINKS

The Institute of Direct Marketing:
www.theidm.co.uk
Royal Mail:
www.royalmail.com

SEE ALSO

Improving the Response to Direct Mail (p. 293)
Writing a Sales Letter (p. 266)

Improving the Response to Direct Mail

GETTING STARTED

The simplest and most immediate measure of a direct marketing campaign is the response level it achieves. Many different factors can affect response rates; it is important to test the variables before committing all your resources to a particular approach, and you should aim for a realistic figure that is within your budget.

Define your target market precisely. The more precisely you target, the better your response rates will be. Make it easy for your prospects to respond, and test your approach before committing resources to the full campaign.

FAQS

Why are direct mail responses so low?

The figures quoted are industry averages. They can vary upwards or downwards depending on the industry and the type of mailing. Remember that a small percentage of a mass mailing can provide you with a reasonable level of new prospects. To put the response rates into perspective, compare the response and the cost of response with an equivalent spend on advertising.

Should direct mailing always be tested?

If it is practical, test direct mail on a small proportion of the market. Although direct mail is a precise medium, testing can refine the process even further. With so many variables in a mailing campaign, you can test different elements individually and plan your full campaign on the basis of the best response rate.

Should direct mail effectiveness be measured by response or by sales?

The ultimate test of any marketing campaign is an increase in profitable sales. However, direct mail, on its own, cannot deliver sales. Sales depend on pricing, the quality of your products, sales representatives, customer service, competitive activity, and many other factors. Direct mail should be given a specific role and measured by how it fulfils that role.

MAKING IT HAPPEN

Set target response levels

- Response levels as low as 1 or 2% are regarded as the industry norm.

- Response rates in the region of 5% are regarded as high.
- Response rates in the region of 10–20% have been reported by companies who have integrated other forms of marketing communications.

Define your target market precisely

Do you want to reach all customers and prospects, or are you targeting specific groups? Direct marketing is a precise medium, so your campaign could be aimed at one key decision-maker or thousands of potential users. The more precisely you target, the better your response rates will be.

Integrate the campaign with other marketing activities

Direct marketing campaigns can run at any time. However, performance can be improved by integrating the campaign with other marketing activities such as an exhibition, advertising campaigns, or salesforce calls. With integrated campaigns, overall awareness levels among customers and prospects will be much higher. Your direct marketing offer will have a much higher chance of success.

Choose the right campaign frequency

A single mailshot, telephone call, or direct response advertisement may produce results, but a series of quality contacts will have greater impact and ensure you meet your response targets. Multiple direct marketing activities provide a number of benefits:

- they raise levels of awareness with each contact
- they follow up contacts who have not responded
- they move individual respondents further along the decision-making process

Make it easy for prospects to respond

If you want to improve response rates, it is essential that you make it easy for your prospects to respond. Website or e-mail addresses, Freepost, and Freephone facilities provide easy-to-use response mechanisms that can boost response. You should monitor the response levels from different sources to see which is the most effective.

Test your campaign

To guarantee the success of your campaign, you should test your approach before committing resources to the full campaign. There are a number of variables that can be tested:
- the offer
- the creative approach
- the target audience
- the response mechanism
- frequency and timing
- integration with other communications programmes.

Use split campaigns

If budget allows, you can develop a series of campaigns that vary by offer, creative approach, response mechanism, frequency, and timing.

Improve your mailing lists

Getting the mailing list right is vital. Basic mailing lists simply include names, addresses, job titles, and telephone numbers of customers and prospects. The basic list can be refined by adding information about buying patterns, lifestyle, and many other factors—providing a comprehensive picture of customers and prospects.

Check all internal sources of information

Your customer records are probably your most valuable asset as they invariably generate the highest response rates when they are mailed with relevant information. The most important sources are:
- customer records
- customer correspondence, including records of complaints
- warranty records
- service records
- sales prospect files
- salesforce reports
- records of lapsed customers

Simple segmentation of your internal lists might give you categories such as:
- customers who have bought in the last six months
- lapsed customers
- customers who spend over £X a year

Add external sources of information

Your internal lists are likely to yield high response rates. However, if you are moving into new market sectors, internal lists may not provide the information you need. External lists are available from a number of different sources, including list brokers, magazine publishers, directory publishers, trade associations or professional institutes, commercial organisations, and retailers. To achieve a high response rate, check how closely the list matches your customer profile.

Commission a special list

Standard lists may not give you the degree of match you need. The successful preparation of a tailored list is directly related to the quality of the brief, and you should provide the supplier with a detailed description of your target audience.

Keep refining your lists

- Ensure that the list is kept up to date with new customer and prospect data.
- Include coupons and other reply mechanisms with every form of communication, and add the responses to your lists.
- Encourage the salesforce to provide up-to-date customer and prospect information.
- Maintain an active search programme in appropriate websites, magazines, and newspapers to identify new prospects for your list.

Check the accuracy of lists

To improve response and reduce waste in your mailing campaigns, it is important that your lists are regularly checked for accuracy. The two main problems are:

- duplication, where the same individual appears several times on the same list, possibly in different guises, for example as Ron Smith, R.T. Smith, and Mr Smith
- out-of-date information, where the original recipient has moved, or, for business mailings, changed jobs.

Use personalised letters

Personalised one-to-one mailings are an ideal form of communication for companies with detailed information about their prospects.

If the database or mailing list holds complete names and other information, direct mail letters can be personalised in a number of ways:

- including the name in the address and greeting only: 'Dear Mr Jones'
- including the name throughout the text: '. . . and Mr Jones, you'll be glad to know that you've won a discount. . .'

Use telemarketing

Direct mail response levels can increase significantly when telemarketing is used. It offers a range of benefits:

- selective: contact can be initiated and maintained with all or selected groups of customers and prospects
- precise: the calls can be targeted
- flexible: the offer and the message can be varied

- fast: calls can be made immediately
- responsive: because telemarketing is interactive, it encourages response
- measurable: the effectiveness of a telemarketing campaign can be measured precisely

WHAT TO AVOID
Setting unrealistic response rates

Direct mail is a precise medium. However, it is easy to set unrealistic targets for response. Figures such as 5% or 6% would be seen as extremely high in many industries.

Failing to integrate direct mail with other activities

Direct mail works most effectively when it is part of an integrated marketing campaign. Advertising can be used to raise the company profile; direct mail would be used to reach specific prospects with a targeted offer, and telemarketing could be used to back up the mailing with follow-up calls.

Poor mailing lists

Good response rates depend on high quality mailing lists. If your lists contain duplicate addresses, out-of-date information, or incorrect data, response will be poor.

RECOMMENDED LINK
The Institute of Direct Marketing:
www.theidm.co.uk

SEE ALSO
Creating Impressive Direct Mail Material (p. 289)
Writing a Sales Letter (p. 266)

Producing Press Material

GETTING STARTED

Newspaper, television, trade press, and radio journalists are always looking for stories. Supply information in the form of press releases, feature articles, or advertorials—in the right format and to the right person—and you can gain great publicity for your organisation.

FAQS

Will the press be interested in us?

Journalists are always looking for stories and they work under great pressure so a well-written, informative, and current press release is always welcome. They won't, however, be interested in you unless you have a story to tell. Like customers, editors will want to know what makes your company different from others. Local media will be interested in how you fit in with the community; and the trade press will be more interested in new products and ideas.

It is worth developing a relationship with editors in order to understand how you can help them. By concentrating on the kind of news and story they want, you can save yourself time and increase the chances of your story being published.

Should we produce our own press material or use the services of an external agency?

An external agency can take a more objective view of your press material and may have experience of writing for the publications on your distribution list. That means they can tailor material for individual publications and ensure that it is printed. They may, however, lack product knowledge and require considerable training to achieve the right results. If your company produces complex technical products, you may split the task, keeping technical press releases in-house, and using an external agency to produce company or business material.

Can we use the same press release for all the publications on our distribution list?

You can issue a single release, but you will increase the chances of getting into print if you tailor information to the needs of individual publications. By talking to journalist, reading previous issues and studying publishers' readership data, you can identify the type of material that is likely to be printed or broadcast.

What should we do if an editor does not publish the information in a press release?

There could be a number of reasons for non-publication that are outside your control, such as lack of space, the release missing the copy date, or another story coinciding with your release. Your story may appear in the next issue if space allows. However, the editor may have decided that your information was wrong for the publication or not newsworthy. A quick call to the editor may help you find out the reason. If your material was unsuitable, you may be able to provide something more relevant for future issues.

MAKING IT HAPPEN

Plan your press release

A press release is a piece of information distributed to newspaper, television, or radio journalists which is published or broadcast as a piece of news. It can cover a variety of topics, including:

- information on new products or services
- information on developments in a company
- news of new appointments or promotions

An effective press release should contain news rather than thinly disguised advertising, and it should reflect readers' interests.

The release may be used without modification if it is newsworthy, timely, and if space permits. The press release may be cut to fit the available space without any further reference to you. In some cases, a journalist or editor may contact you for further information and rewrite the item in the style of the publication. It is often a good idea to provide additional background information to help journalists in this task. Information such as product specifications, contact details, or alternative photographs are useful. Some companies offer such information specifically for journalists on a section of their website. Sometimes the information may not be used, because it is not newsworthy or not relevant to the readership. Alternatively, although the main press release may not be used, an accompanying photograph may be used with a caption.

Produce your press release

The following guidelines will help you produce an effective press release:

- Press releases should be typed double-spaced.
- The source of the release should be clearly identified.
- A contact name for further information should be provided.
- Any limitations on use or timing of publication should be clearly highlighted, for example, 'not for publication before. . .'.
- The most important information should be included in the early paragraphs. If an editor is short of space, the press release will be cut as simply and quickly as possible, probably from the bottom upwards.
- Quotes are useful and are frequently used by editors.
- Photographs or diagrams add value to the release and may help to ensure publication.
- The style of writing, even the length of sentences and paragraphs, should match the targeted publication as far as possible.

Distribute your press release

Press releases can be delivered by hand or by post, depending on quantity. They can also be sent by e-mail or placed on a website so that they can be picked up by visiting journalists. Wherever possible, they should be sent to a named individual. Information on editorial contacts, with details of their special interests, is available in the *PR Planner*, which is updated regularly. If you do not want the information published before a certain date for reasons of commercial security, include an embargo—'not for publication before. . .'.

Time your press release

Check the publication dates of magazines or newspapers on your distribution list. This information is available in publications such as *British Rate and Data*, *Willings Press Guide*, or the *PR Planner*. An editorial copy date will be indicated. Ensure that your release reaches the editor by that date at the latest.

Plan feature articles

A feature article, which could be 500–2,000 words in length, is published in a magazine and credited to an organisation. The article may be on technical or business developments in an industry, or on other subjects that provide practical or topical information for readers. The article may form part of an industry survey. This type of feature provides an opportunity for organisations to demonstrate their expertise and professionalism.

Feature articles can cover a variety of topics, including surveys of new industry or technical developments, practical 'how to' articles, or reviews of research projects.

If it is reasonably well written, the article may be used without modification; it will be published when space permits, or may be used as part of a special survey. In some cases, a journalist or editor may contact you for further information and rewrite the item in the style of the publication.

Produce feature articles

An effective feature article should reflect readers' interests and contain information that is useful to them. It should also bring them up to date with recent developments.

The following guidelines should help you prepare a feature article:

- feature articles should be typed double-spaced
- length should be discussed with the editor, but is likely to be between 500 and 2,000 words, with 1,000 words as the average

- a contact name for further information should be provided
- photographs or diagrams, with a caption for every item, add value to the article

Distribute feature articles

Feature articles should only be sent to one publication at a time, although they can be modified for use in other markets. Wherever possible, they should be sent to a named individual. Information on editorial contacts, with details of their special interests, is available in the *PR Planner*, which is updated regularly. In some cases, the initiative may come from the publication and the editor will provide you with details of requirements.

Time feature articles

Check the publication dates of magazines or newspapers on your distribution list. This information is available in *British Rate and Data*, *Willings Press Guide*, or the *PR Planner*. An editorial copy date will be indicated. Ensure that your release reaches the editor by that date at the latest. You should also ask the editor for a list of special editorial features. The article may be suitable for inclusion in a survey.

Produce advertorials

An advertorial is a special category of feature article, combining advertising and editorial, which is used to promote products and services. These are the key characteristics of an advertorial. It:

- may include a reader offer, such as a chance to participate in a competition
- should be identified as an 'advertisement feature'
- is produced in the form of an editorial rather than in a conventional advertisement format, even though the space is paid for

The writing guidelines are similar to those for press releases and feature articles but you are paying for the space and you have considerably more control over what is published. Newspapers and journals will often help with the layout.

WHAT TO AVOID

Writing information that is not suitable for a publication

It is important to study the publications that are on your distribution list. Editors know very quickly what is relevant or interesting to their readers. If your material is not suitable, it will not be used. Study the editorial content and check the readership figures, which are usually available from the publication.

Providing news stories that are out of date

'Old news is no news' and that means a story could be wasted. It's easy to get the timing right with a daily or weekly publication, but it can be tricky to decide on the right date to send a news story to a monthly publication. The publication can provide you with the dates when your copy will be required, but you have to make sure that those dates tie in with your own schedules. If you have to release a sensitive news story early to catch a publication date, you can protect your interests by putting an embargo clause on the release, saying 'not for publication before. . .'.

Confusing editorial with advertorial

A press release or feature article should provide factual, newsworthy information. It should not be a blatant advertisement for the company. Editors are not keen on items that are thinly disguised advertisements.

RECOMMENDED LINK

Institute of Public Relations:
www.ipr.org.uk

SEE ALSO

Raising Awareness of Your Brand (p. 282)

Setting Advertising Objectives

GETTING STARTED

Clear objectives for a communication campaign are essential, whether it is intended to generate leads, raise the awareness of your product or brand, or encourage brand switching. These objectives should be in place well before a campaign begins, so that each campaign has a specific task. In addition, the desired results should be measurable so that you can be sure the campaign is worth the investment.

FAQS

What can communications achieve?

Communications are about influencing the customer or potential customer in the way they make decisions. No matter how good your communications, they cannot overcome the problems caused by poor products, inefficient service or distribution, or uncompetitive pricing, so realise their importance but don't over-estimate it.

Should advertising be judged on sales results?

Advertising should certainly be measured, but there may not be a direct correlation between advertising and sales. Advertising may generate a large number of leads, but the salesforce may not be able to convert those leads to sales, so don't get carried away too early.

Should advertising agencies be judged solely on the results they deliver?

There has been a trend towards judging agencies on measurable results. This has been driven partly by the increasing importance of direct marketing agencies who claim to be driven by results, and partly by the desire of marketing executives to increase accountability. Some agencies have gone so far as to base their fees on results, rather than traditional agency payment. The problem is that results are dependent on so many other aspects of marketing. An agency could claim that it has no control over the performance of the salesforce or the quality of the product. It is essential therefore that you agree on a definition of success before you embark on a campaign.

Is it possible to set a number of different objectives for the same advertising campaign, particularly when budgets are limited?

It *is* possible, but it may not be a good idea. An effective campaign has a single focus with a specific measurable result. By mixing objectives, you may achieve only part of the outcome you want.

MAKING IT HAPPEN
Set the right objective

You must have clear objectives for your campaign. There are many different advertising objectives, so identify a specific task for a specific campaign. This might be:

- raising awareness of a company, product, or service within a clearly identified target market
- communicating the benefits of a product or service
- generating leads for the salesforce or retail network
- encouraging prospects to buy directly through a direct response campaign
- persuading prospects to switch brands
- supporting a special marketing event such as a sale or an exhibition
- ensuring that customers know where to obtain the product
- building confidence in an organisation

Whatever your general objectives, you should be clear about how much of that is dependent on the communications and how much dependent on other aspects of your marketing effort, such as the sales force (if you have one).

Make the objectives measurable

To ensure you design a cost-effective campaign that delivers results, advertising objectives should be translated into precise, measurable targets, as in the following examples.

Consumer product

- target market: 500,000 ABC1 prospects in the South of England
- marketing objective: achieve high level of product understanding
- advertising objective: persuade 15% of targeted prospects to request a free sample

Business product

- target market: 5,000 specialist machinery designers in (specified) industrial processes
- marketing objective: increase market share to 20% (that is, recruit 1,000 new clients)
- advertising objective: persuade 40% of prospects to request product fact file

Raise awareness

This objective is usually the starting point for advertisers and is especially important if your company is entering new markets where you do not have an established reputation, or you are trying to influence important decision-makers who may not be aware of your company. Awareness advertising can also be used if you are launching new products which appeal to specific sectors of your market, or if research shows that customers and prospects are not aware of the full extent of your products and services.

This type of objective would be important for a company launching a new range of products. For example, to raise awareness of its new range, one company planned to advertise in a group of special interest consumer magazines aimed at its target audience. The advertisements included the telephone number of an information line that generated a large number of inquiries. Editorial articles in the same group of publications backed up the advertising by providing more detailed information for consumers. You should, however, be wary of specifying awareness targets. Awareness on its own will not sell products and, if this is

your aim, you will have to integrate your campaign carefully with other elements of your marketing to meet your targets. Likewise awareness amongst the general public is very different from awareness in a very small, specialised market, so you should be clear about who you are trying to reach.

Communicate benefits

Product advertising should lead on benefits. This type of advertising is important when research shows low awareness of product benefits. It should also be used if your products have recently been improved, or if you need to counter competitors who have introduced products with similar or better benefits.

For example, if research shows that your company's products are perceived as old-fashioned or poor value for money, you need to take action to correct this impression and communicate the real benefits of your products.

Generate sales leads

Advertising's role is to provide leads that can be followed up by a field salesforce or telemarketing team. Lead generation is important if marketing success depends on the performance of the salesforce. Sometimes, customers or prospects have a complex decision-making structure and you cannot identify some of the decision-makers. Advertising that generates inquiries can identify the right people and open the door for the sales team. It can also be used to identify prospects when you are entering new market sectors where you do not have an established customer base. The final use for this type of campaign is to generate leads for agents, distributors, or retailers who handle your local marketing.

Sell through direct response

Direct response advertising is the most measurable form of advertising. The advertising budget provides a direct return in terms of incremental sales. This objective can be important if customers can only buy direct from you. In an increasing number of markets, customers prefer the convenience of buying direct and you have to decide whether to bypass your existing distribution channels. If you are targeting niche markets which are not covered by retail outlets, direct response can be used to complement your distribution channels. Selling direct is not always a practical proposition. Where product inspection or demonstration is important, direct response may not be appropriate.

In the personal computer market, for example, manufacturers found that businesses and individuals were willing to buy personal computers 'off the page' or via the Internet. The products were regarded as commodities and the resulting price competition put pressure on margins. The result was a considerable growth in the level of direct sales with manufacturers using large format advertisements or inserts in computer and business publications. Direct selling meant that the manufacturers could reduce prices by avoiding the cost of selling through retail outlets.

Encourage brand switching

Brand-switching advertising plays an important role in winning new customers as the first stage in a customer relationship programme. It helps you to increase market share or maintain share against competitive actions, and is also important if you are introducing new products that offer greater benefits than competitive products.

Support a marketing event

This objective can be important in a number of situations, for example, taking part in an exhibition where an important new product will be launched, or holding a sale, or promoting a seminar or other customer event at which you wish to ensure customer participation. Advertising helps to build traffic for your event and ensures that the event attracts the right prospects. A company that sponsors senior executive seminars as a way of building its credibility could run advertisements in the business press to promote a seminar.

Help customers obtain the product

Advertising can help to drive business to retail outlets or distributors, or improve the performance of your distribution network by showing the range of services available from the outlets. It can also counter competitive action, if, for example customers are using other distributors to obtain spare parts and service. To win back this important business, advertising could show locations of retail outlets and explain why the authorised distributor should be the first choice for customers.

Build customer confidence

Capability advertising or corporate advertising is sometimes dismissed because it is difficult to measure, but is important when a company has been undergoing significant change, or is entering new markets where it's not established. It also provides support when a company is trying to win key account business, or if competitors are threatening important business.

WHAT TO AVOID
Setting objectives that cannot be measured

Advertising objectives should be measurable for two important reasons. First, to ensure that advertising represents an adequate return on investment. Second, to measure the effectiveness of the campaign itself so that future advertising can be improved or modified to deliver better results.

Setting objectives that are too general

A general objective, such as raising awareness, is important, but often is seen as the only objective. Advertising objectives should be closely linked to marketing objectives so that advertising is used to carry out specific tasks within an overall marketing framework. You should be sure that what you want to achieve is possible with communications and acknowledge the importance of other elements of your marketing, crucially the product itself or your pricing strategy.

Failing to integrate communications objectives with other marketing objectives

It is important that some advertising objectives, such as generating more leads, should be integrated with the other activities that will increase sales. It may be necessary to increase salesforce training to improve the team's ability to convert leads into sales. Advertising alone cannot be expected to deliver sales.

RECOMMENDED LINK

Institute of Practitioners in Advertising: **www.ipa.co.uk**

SEE ALSO

Planning an Advertising Campaign (p. 303)
Preparing an Advertising Brief (p. 310)
Selecting and Working with an Advertising Agency (p. 306)

Planning an Advertising Campaign

GETTING STARTED
Any communications campaign needs to have clear, measurable objectives, whether it is designed to communicate product benefits or to support an event. In order to achieve these objectives, it must also be planned carefully. There are eight main stages to consider, from defining the target market to setting a budget.

FAQS

Do I need an advertising campaign?
Often the term advertising campaign is used when the more holistic term 'communications campaign' would be more appropriate. Advertising strictly only refers to paid-for space or time in media such as newspapers or radio. On the other hand, direct mail, sales promotions, exhibitions, or any of a range of communication tools can be used in a campaign to support your marketing. To decide if you need a communications campaign, you should be fairly sure that the problem you want to address can be solved best by communications. For example, finding new customers or prospective customers is often best accomplished by advertising or direct mail, but converting enquirers into customers may be better dealt with by you or your sales team (if you have one) in person.

Who is responsible for campaign planning—the client or the advertising agency?
Both parties contribute. The client sets the overall marketing objectives and the specific communications campaign objectives. The agency develops an advertising strategy based on those, but may seek to modify the campaign objectives. Timings will be determined by the client's product and marketing plans, together with practical considerations such as publication dates and lead times.

Why is it necessary to plan a campaign in so much detail?
To be effective, advertising and communications must meet specific measurable objectives. The objectives affect choice of media,

creative strategy, overall budget, and lead times. Overlooking any of those details could weaken the effectiveness of the campaign.

Should planning be applied to the creative process?
There is an assumption that creative work takes place in a vacuum. Like any other marketing activity, it must be directed towards an objective. The more information a creative team has, the more focused its work.

MAKING IT HAPPEN

Set campaign objectives
It is important to set clear objectives for an advertising campaign. It is essential to identify a specific task for a specific campaign. This might be:

- raising awareness of a company, product, or service within a clearly identified target market
- communicating the benefits of a product or service
- generating leads for the salesforce or retail network

To ensure you design a cost-effective campaign that delivers results, advertising objectives should be translated into precise, measurable targets.

Identify key planning activities
There are eight main stages in planning an advertising campaign:

1. Define the target market
Who is your campaign aimed at?

An understanding of your audience will influence the media you select and the creative treatment of your advertisement. To define your target market, you should ask questions like these:

- Who buys your type of product?
- Who influences the purchasing decision?
- In business buying, who are the important decision-makers?
- Do you need to communicate with the actual buyers or those who influence the purchasing decision?
- How many potential buyers are there?
- How many users are currently buying your product and what is your share of the market?
- Which prospects do you want to reach with the campaign and where are they located?
- What are the characteristics of these people (for example, age, sex, income, job title), and what are their most important considerations in choosing a brand or a supplier?
- What does research tell you about their attitudes towards your company and your products?
- How do they currently receive information about your products?
- What is the role of advertising in reaching the target audience?

2. Select media

There are four important factors to consider in selecting campaign media:

- how closely the audience profile of the medium matches your target audience
- the comparative costs of reaching the target audience through different media
- whether the frequency of the medium matches the timing of your campaign
- the creative opportunities of the medium for the communication of your message

3. Plan campaign timing

When should your campaign run? You have to consider a number of factors first in relation to the purchasing pattern of your products:

- When are your customers making their buying decisions?
- Do you know when your customers hold product/purchasing review meetings?
- If you are launching a new product, when will the product be available?

- Does your advertising campaign have to tie in with the timing of any other marketing activity, for example, an exhibition, direct marketing campaign, or salesforce call?
- How quickly will you be able to follow up the campaign?

You also have to take into account production and media lead times:

- What is the next available publication or broadcasting date?
- When does the mediium owner require your advertisement?
- How long will it take to produce the advertisement?

4. Decide campaign frequency

Campaigns raise levels of awareness with each appearance and increase the number of opportunities to see the advertisement. They also move individual respondents further along the decision-making process and maintain contact during an extended process. Campaigns reinforce the impact of the message by repetition and provide an opportunity to communicate multiple or complex messages about the company or the product range.

Frequency is determined by a number of factors:

- frequency of publication, that is, how often the publication appears
- frequency of broadcast: radio or television commercials can be broadcast many times during the same day, if the budget allows
- your budget, although a number of appearances in the same medium will earn a discount that makes the entire budget go further
- the behaviour of consumers or buyers: if a buying decision is made only annually then timing may be more crucial than frequency

5. Plan creative treatment

To achieve good results, you must develop a comprehensive creative brief. These are the main elements:

- campaign objectives
- description of the target audience
- the main concerns of the target audience: why they buy; what they consider; how they view different products and suppliers

- the main benefits of the product or service: why the product is different from competitive offerings; what is new; why the benefits are important
- the core message or proposition—what the prospect is being offered: the opportunity to sample or buy; further information; a sales visit; an incentive; or a discount
- the planned response: should the prospect contact the company, send off an order, wait for a phone call, or simply absorb the information?
- the media—size and mechanical details
- the supporting activities—telemarketing, advertising, sales follow-up, tie-in promotions

6. Develop a response mechanism

Action is a vital ingredient of any advertising campaign and it is essential that you make it easy for your prospects to respond. First, decide which action your prospects are to take:

- place an order
- arrange a sales meeting
- request further information
- visit a retail outlet
- try the product

Review the cost, convenience, and practicality of response options, including telephone, post, fax, e-mail, and website.

7. Set a budget

A campaign budget will include direct, indirect, and variable costs. Direct costs include the production costs of advertisements, including design, writing and production, and media costs. Indirect costs include the cost of setting up response handling, either by internal resources or an external supplier, and the management costs of planning and controlling the campaign. Variable costs include the cost of handling the campaign response, for example, Freephone costs and telephone resources, or costs of Freepost services; the cost of meeting the response—supplying and distributing the material that is requested; and the cost of servicing the

response—sales or telemarketing costs in dealing with the potential volume of new business.

8. Set schedules

To set a campaign schedule, work back from the launch date and work out how long each individual activity will take.

WHAT TO AVOID
Poor targeting

Without a clear picture of your target, market advertising can be wasteful. You should always aim for the best match between the audience and your ideal customers—subject, of course, to your budget.

Failing to integrate advertising plans with other marketing activities

Advertising must be integrated with other related marketing tasks. Poor salesforce performance, for example, could waste the contribution of a highly successful advertising campaign that provided a large number of sales leads.

Trying to take shortcuts on lead times

Advertising lead times are influenced by a number of factors including publication dates, production lead times, and product availability.

Trying to achieve advertising objectives with inadequate resources

If companies try to achieve targets without committing the right budget, it will mean either that advertisements do not appear frequently enough to have impact, or that production quality is sacrificed.

RECOMMENDED LINK
The Advertising Association:
www.adassoc.org.uk

SEE ALSO
Preparing an Advertising Brief (p. 310)
Selecting and Working with an Advertising Agency (p. 306)
Setting Advertising Objectives (p. 299)

Selecting and Working with an Advertising Agency

GETTING STARTED

If your budget will stretch and you are able to engage an advertising agency to help you spread the word about your product or service, you need to choose an agency that can provide the right selection of services. These can include consultancy, strategy, creative work, media, and integration with other communications activities. Important factors in selecting an agency include its approach, reputation, and financial stability. Careful selection can avoid problems that cause breakdowns in the agency/client relationship.

FAQS

Do I need an advertising agency?

Many small to medium-sized companies don't. However, the skills offered by agencies are just as specialised as those offered by your accountant. Many agencies will be able to offer services other than advertising, including direct marketing, sales promotion, and public relations. Indeed they may not call themselves an 'advertising' agency at all. Agencies that offer a wide range of skills are often called 'full-service' agencies. If you know what you want to achieve, but are not sure if advertising is the best course, discuss the issues with a number of different agencies.

I want to work with a specific agency, but they already handle the account of a competitor. Should I work with that agency?

This problem occurs frequently, particularly when agency mergers occur, and the new group finds that its client lists include conflicting accounts. The decision to continue handling conflicting accounts is sometimes taken by the agency, and sometimes by the clients. It can be particularly difficult if the agency is seen as an industry specialist, with considerable expertise in a particular market. Sometimes the problem can be resolved by handling the conflicting accounts through separate agency teams.

How do I know that an agency can maintain its standards in day-to-day business, once they have won the initial pitch?

Sometimes agencies field a special senior team to win new business, and then hand the day-to-day account to a completely different team. Since a good relationship between agency and client is so important, you should insist on meeting the team who will actually work on the business.

Is it essential to appoint an agency to handle advertising campaigns?

A full-service agency may not be essential, particularly if you have the resources to handle part of the task internally. Creative consultancies, media specialists, or integrated agencies can take on specialist tasks.

MAKING IT HAPPEN
Choose the right type of agency

Depending on the type of agency, you can use a comprehensive service or specific services including:

- initial consultancy
- development of an advertising strategy
- creative proposals, copywriting, design, and production of advertisements
- media planning, negotiation, buying, and administration
- integration of advertising with other communications activities

Whatever you decide, ask to see examples of previous campaigns and for an honest appraisal of their effectiveness.

Work with a full-service advertising agency

Full-service agencies handle all aspects of an advertising programme. You should select a full-service agency if you do not have any internal skills or resources for handling advertising, or if extensive advertising is important to the achievement of your marketing objectives.

Use a media independent

A media independent only handles media planning and buying and so is likely to be interested only if you are spending a considerable amount on buying space in newspapers and magazines or airtime on TV or radio. By concentrating on media, the independents can often negotiate better deals with them than full-service agencies. Many smaller advertising agencies use media independents to handle their media buying. If you can handle campaign planning and creative work in other ways but do not have any internal skills or resources for media planning and buying, then you should use a media independent.

A media independent could prove useful if you spend a large amount of your budget on media, and you want to take advantage of specialist buying skills to get better positions or lower rates. You may find that certain media will not deal with you, because you are an advertiser. In that case, a media agency can provide valuable support.

Choose creative independents

Creative independents only handle creative work such as copywriting and design. By specialising in this way, the independents can often achieve more effective advertising than full-service agencies. You would have to handle campaign planning and media in other ways. There are three types of creative independent:

- freelance staff, either combined writer/art director teams, or individuals
- design consultancies offering advertising as part of a communications service
- specialist creative independents—small agencies that either have their own creative teams, or manage freelance teams

You should consider using a creative independent if you can handle campaign planning and media in other ways but do not have any internal skills or resources for creative work. If advertising is a small part of your marketing activity, you could develop effective campaigns by taking advantage of specialist creative services.

Work with an integrated agency

Integrated agencies handle all aspects of an advertising programme and integrate advertising with other media. Agencies offer integrated services in two forms:

- as a single integrated agency, in which all campaigns are handled by the same team
- as an agency group, in which nonadvertising campaigns are handled by specialist companies within the group

An integrated agency may be suitable if other tools, such as direct marketing, publications, and sales promotion are as important as advertising, and you want all of the activities integrated and handled professionally. Any extra cost incurred will be well worth it.

Use the media's own expertise

One alternative to using an agency is to ask the newspaper, magazine, or radio station to help. Often they will offer basic design or writing services free of charge. However they are rarely as skilled as specialists and you may find it difficult to make your advertising stand out or to maintain consistency over time.

Evaluate advertising agencies

There are a number of important factors in selecting an agency:

- approach: what is the agency's philosophy, and how does it work in practical terms?
- track record: what campaigns has the agency produced, and how effective have they been?
- reputation: does the agency have an established reputation in your market? Are you able to approach other clients to give their assessment of the agency?
- accountability: how does the agency measure the performance of its campaigns?

- client relationships: what is the current client list, and how many of these clients are enjoying long-term relationships? What is the average length of account tenure?
- disciplines: does the agency offer all disciplines from within its own resources, and can it offer the full range of services?
- staff: does the agency have the staff to handle complex, large-scale programmes? What is the consultancy's recruitment and personal development policy?
- financial stability: what is the agency's recent performance? Does it have the stability and resources to sustain an effective level of service over the long term?

Check agency performance

According to Henley Centre research, clients believe the ten most important questions regarding agency performance are:
- Does it take the trouble to understand your business?
- Can it use creativity effectively to sell your products?
- Does it have real creative flair?
- Does it get work done on time?
- Does it have a good understanding of your consumers?
- Does it believe in defining advertising objectives beforehand?
- Does it keep costs within budget?
- Does it use research to aid its creative work?
- Is it strong on media buying?
- Is it thorough and hard-working?

Obtain information about advertising agencies

There are a number of useful sources of information about agencies:
- The Institute of Practitioners in Advertising and the Marketing Communication Consultants Association publish information about agencies.
- Individual agencies provide videos of their agency credentials or will send, or present in person, their portfolio of work. Larger agencies have their details available through the Advertising Agency Register and most agencies have websites or, at the least, brochures available.

- *Campaign*, *Marketing*, and *Marketing Week* magazines publish regular news about agencies and their clients, and your own trade publications may mention agencies which specialise in your market.
- Talk to friends and colleagues, even if in different businesses, to find out which agencies are reliable.

Avoid problems in client/agency relationships

Reports in the trade press highlight a number of factors that create conditions for a breakdown:
- The client believes that the advertising has not delivered results, or not had the planned effect on the marketplace.
- The agency feels that poor results are caused by marketing, product, or management problems on the client side.
- The client does not like the advertisements for subjective reasons.
- The agency fails to understand the client's business.
- A failure of communication means that the agency cannot respond to the client's real needs.
- Frequent changes in the agency team or client team make continuity difficult.
- Poor agency administration can let down good creative work.
- Relationships can become stale.

WHAT TO AVOID
Choosing the wrong size of agency

A large agency may have the resources and scale to support national or international campaigns, but if your account is small, you may get poor service from a junior team. It may be more appropriate to work with a smaller agency, where you will get personal service from the senior people.

Choosing the wrong type of agency

Agencies, like any other business, develop specialities. Their expertise may not coincide with your needs. The most important division is between a consumer and a business-to-business agency but, beyond that, agencies develop expertise in certain industries or markets. Look carefully at the agency's client list to find the right match.

Relying on a creative pitch

Agency selection is frequently made on the basis of a pitch—a presentation that shows how an agency would tackle a specific project. Although the presentation gives an insight into the agency's working methods, it is an artificial guide to potential performance.

Not sharing information with the agency

Clients often expect a lot from a new agency, but can be disappointed when the agency does not know something 'obvious' about the client's business. The agency can only know what you know *if you tell them*. If you are concerned about confidentiality, discuss this and get a signed agreement from the agency management.

Not discussing the budget in enough detail

Agencies work for a fee and, like you, will want to make a profit. You will only get good service when they feel your business is worthwhile for them. From the outset discuss how much you plan to spend and what you want to achieve—competent agencies will tell you from the outset what is possible.

RECOMMENDED LINKS

Institute of Practitioners in Advertising: **www.ipa.co.uk**
Institute of Sales Promotion: **www.prca.org.uk**

SEE ALSO

Planning an Advertising Campaign (p. 303)
Preparing an Advertising Brief (p. 310)
Setting Advertising Objectives (p. 299)

Preparing an Advertising Brief

GETTING STARTED

To get the most from working with an advertising agency, you need to make a start by putting together a comprehensive creative brief. This must cover all aspects of the project: background, objectives, research, competitors, product information, and the target audience. It's worth spending time on making the briefing information as complete as you can, as otherwise you run the risk of wasting time and money on a campaign that has little impact.

FAQS

Why is a detailed brief important?

It will start the campaign on exactly the right foot. An imprecise and undetailed brief may mean that the work is aimed at the wrong audience. Provide the agency or consultancy with as much information as possible so that they can produce a campaign that achieves results.

Who should be involved in setting a creative brief?

The people who evaluate a creative brief should also be involved in setting or approving the brief. It can be difficult to deal with objections and criticism from someone who does not understand the brief. On the client side, the briefing team is likely to include the marketing executive, sales executive, and any relevant marketing specialists such as promotions or direct mail executives. The person who has the final say—whether it is you yourself or your business partner—must be involved in defining the brief. The team should also include product or research specialists to provide detailed information on the product and prospective customers. The agency team should also be involved in preparing the brief, although this does not always happen in practice.

Should an agency brief always have measurable objectives?

The more specific the brief, the easier it is to assess the results of the creative work. It is not always possible to set a measurable objective, but this should be the goal. Agencies may argue that results depend on factors outside their control, but it should be possible to isolate the communications objectives and identify a way of measuring them. A direct response campaign, for example, can be measured by the number of responses, while a corporate campaign could be assessed through attitude surveys conducted before and after the campaign.

MAKING IT HAPPEN

Plan the campaign approach

How will you present your message? Most publications and commercial broadcast media carry high volumes of advertising. Your advertisement must achieve immediate impact to succeed. There are three essential checks that can be applied to creative work in any media:

- it must have immediate impact
- it must meet the needs of the reader or viewer
- it must stimulate a response

Provide background Information

Your briefing of the agency or consultancy should begin with the background to the project:

- What is the overall aim of the project?
- What threats and opportunities does the business face?
- Why is the project being produced?
- How does the project fit into the overall marketing programme?
- Why is it necessary to advertise and what is it intended to achieve?

The background material should include any research that you have carried out or used. You should ensure that the project works in the context of other marketing activities of yours and of competitors.

Produce a comprehensive brief

To achieve good creative results, you must develop a comprehensive creative brief. These are the main elements:

- campaign objectives
- description of the target audience
- the main concerns of the target audience: why they buy; what factors they consider; how they view different products and suppliers
- the main benefits of the product or service: why the product is different from competitive offerings; what is new; why the benefits are important
- the core message or proposition: what the prospect is being offered—the opportunity to sample or buy, further information, a sales visit, an incentive or discount
- the planned response: should the prospect contact the company, send an order, wait for a phone call, or simply absorb the information offered?
- the media: scope and practical details
- the supporting activities: telemarketing, advertising, sales follow-up, tie-in promotions

Information of this kind would enable writers and designers to approach the creative process in a disciplined, logical way. Great creative ideas may occur in a vacuum, but they are more likely to be a response to a clearly defined problem.

The creative brief is important whether you are using external suppliers or carrying out the creative work internally.

Set out objectives

The brief should set out a number of objectives, including the overall corporate objective and the marketing objective. State the communications objectives and how they contribute to the wider marketing objectives. For example you may want to make potential customers in a new region aware of your product in order that sales staff can work more effectively.

The campaign objectives should be detailed and specific. Examples could include:

- generate 3,000 prospects and convert 3% of them

- ensure that key decision-makers understand the product's business benefits
- raise awareness among 20% of the target audience

Provide access to any research information

The creative team should be aware of any relevant research information, including:

- customer surveys, interviews, or analysis
- industry surveys
- competitor analysis
- product reviews
- press comment on the product or company
- feedback from focus groups
- results of previous campaigns

Include information on competitors

The brief should include detailed information on:

- which competitors provide a similar product or service
- how the competitive offering compares
- the product's key benefits against the competition
- how competitors are perceived by customers

This information can help creative teams identify some of the key benefits that will differentiate the product from competitors' offerings. It will also show how other companies have tackled the problem of describing the product.

Provide comprehensive product information

The product or service should be described in detail:

- what it is
- what it is used for
- how it operates
- the main benefits for the customer
- the advantages over competitor products

If the team can use or experience for themselves your product or service in the same way as a customer then this will greatly enhance their understanding.

Describe the target audience

Describing the target audience helps the creative team to focus on the key decision-makers:

- What types of company buy the product?
- Which business sectors are they in?
- How big are these companies?
- Who are the main decision-makers?
- What is their role in the decision-making process?
- What are their business concerns?
- What is their perception of your company and its products?

Establish target perceptions

The creative team should be aware of any key messages that are important to the target audience. The task of the creative team is not to invent these messages; it is to communicate them as effectively as possible. The brief should therefore set out the perceptions that the target audience have now and those they should hold once the campaign is finished.

Get approval of the brief

The brief should be circulated to all members of the group involved in briefing and approving the project. No creative work should begin until the brief has been signed off by everyone involved. Once the brief has been approved, members should not be able to change it without good reason.

Be clear about payment terms

Some agencies will present their ideas without expecting payment, but most would rather not. If you cannot pay for initial ideas, make this clear before expecting anything of value from the team. If, however, you *can* pay, agree the amount and establish who will own the ideas once the initial presentation is finished.

Describe the review process

Let the creative team know how their work will be reviewed and evaluated. This can take place at a number of levels:
- review by the agency and client teams
- evaluation in focus groups
- pilot campaigns in test markets

WHAT TO AVOID
Making the brief too specific

It is possible to make a brief too specific, thereby ruling out creative approaches that may achieve outstanding results. For example, setting out the creative approach in the brief before the creative team has had an opportunity to consider it will produce very limited results. The creative team needs information to focus their attention on the problem, not suggestions on how the problem should be solved.

Not integrating creative work

Although the brief should allow the agency creative team complete freedom, it is equally important that creative work across different media should be integrated. If advertising is the dominant medium, and a team is working on direct marketing, they should relate their approach to the advertising theme. Repetition of the same creative theme across different media reinforces the key messages and can improve overall awareness.

Concentrating too hard on creativity, and not enough on results

Creative work should be accountable. The agency may have a brilliant, award-winning creative idea, but if it fails to produce the intended results it may be a waste of money. The creative team should therefore be aware of the specific objectives of the campaign; it is not enough just to get attention.

RECOMMENDED LINK
Institute of Practitioners in Advertising:
www.ipa.co.uk

SEE ALSO
Selecting and Working with an Advertising Agency (p. 306)
Setting Advertising Objectives (p. 299)

Working with Your Local Community

GETTING STARTED

Corporate social responsibility (CSR) started as little more than corporate philanthropy and involvement in the community. However, CSR is about far more than that. It's about taking a responsible approach to every aspect of your business. It covers almost any activity of a business, so there is a good chance that you may be doing something already. Every business has an impact on society through what it produces, how it employs and develops its staff, how it purchases supplies and sells its products or services, how it affects the environment, and how it acts in the community. Social responsibility can help any business to succeed. It can build sales, develop the workforce, encourage enthusiasm, and increase trust in the business as a whole. Businesses are stronger and work better when they have the support and respect of all their stakeholders; their customers, suppliers, staff, and communities.

This actionlist aims to introduce you to some of the ideas behind corporate social responsibility, and to suggest some ways in which you could take your business forward in this respect. For further information, you may be interested to contact the Small Business Service, which has a Benchmarking Index module that can help you assess your current approach to social responsibility. This can be found on the Small Business Service website (address given below).

FAQS

Is corporate social responsibility relevant to small businesses?

Corporate social responsibility is not just for large corporations—it's essential for all businesses to think about their role in the community and their responsibilities to all of their stakeholders. Corporate social responsibility is about business behaviours that not only deliver commercial objectives, but that also have a positive social impact. It is for their own long-term good, as well as for reasons of principle, that businesses should aim to be responsible in all their activities, and to embrace the principles of sustainable development in their widest sense.

What are the key principles of social responsibility?

Businesses can help to improve the lives of their customers, suppliers, staff, and shareholders by enabling them to share in the wealth the business creates. They should deal honestly with their suppliers and competitors, and act as good citizens in their local communities. Sincerity, truthfulness, and keeping promises not only contribute to credibility, but also to the effectiveness of business transactions. Businesses clearly have to respect the rule of law, but in many cases it makes good economic sense to do rather more than the legal minimum.

Why is corporate social responsibility important?

Customers, suppliers, and employees are all becoming more interested in the way that businesses behave. A good reputation can open doors, win loyalty, and create staff enthusiasm. Social responsibility is about getting business benefits from being a good corporate citizen. It is not random philanthropy. Done well, it raises your profile in the most positive way. Responsible businesses do not just gain respect; they can gain real business benefits too.

Can small businesses afford a social responsibility programme?

Businesses can choose to support community initiatives with money, but in most cases being responsible is simply about ensuring the right behaviour. There may be a cost associated with this, in the sense that behaving irresponsibly is cheaper, but in the long run behaving responsibly will enhance your reputation and do more to help you retain customers and staff.

How do you get the best value for social responsibility?

As with every other aspect of your business, you need to review carefully your activities and ensure that you are getting a return, whether it is in terms of staff feeling more motivated, lower staff turnover, a better reputation locally, or higher sales.

MAKING IT HAPPEN
Reflecting stakeholder needs

Businesses need to provide customers with the highest quality products and services consistent with their specified needs. You need to treat customers fairly, ensure health and safety, and respect human dignity. You can also engage with customers in social projects. This is often called 'cause-related marketing' and can increase customer appreciation of a product while simultaneously delivering a social benefit.

Every business has an interest in being an employer of choice. In a competitive job market, this can be a real advantage. This means paying staff fairly, providing a good working environment, communicating openly and honestly, respecting staff suggestions, avoiding discrimination, and promoting personal development and continuous learning. It increasingly means ensuring that staff can balance their work and the rest of their life, with appropriate flexibility in working patterns.

Businesses have a responsibility to manage assets effectively to provide investors with a fair and competitive return. Different businesses will take different views about what constitutes the most appropriate level of social engagement; but the importance of sustainable behaviour is now being reflected in legal requirements.

Businesses have a responsibility to deal fairly with suppliers. The relationship should be free from coercion and should aim to foster stability in return for value, quality, and reliability. Some businesses, for example, prefer suppliers whose values reflect their own. This can mean avoiding sub-contractors who have poor labour practices. Small businesses often think that this does not apply to them, but you may find yourself caught up by human rights requirements if you supply larger organisations. One obligation that applies to every business is to pay suppliers on agreed terms.

Businesses, of whatever size, see involvement in the local community as part of being a good corporate citizen. It is no longer enough to argue that businesses contribute to society simply by creating jobs and wealth. Enlightened self-interest plays a part; businesses understand they need an educated and healthy workforce to work for them, a healthy business sector to provide suppliers and customers, and a 'licence to operate'.

Community investment is more than just giving money. While that is important, benefits also accrue, for example, from giving away old equipment, or getting staff involved with community organisations. There may be merit in reflecting your business's core competences in the ways in which you become involved in the community. You may want to look for mutually beneficial arrangements, so that you get some return, perhaps in terms of publicity and reputation.

Some basic steps to take

The first thing to do is to look at your own practices systematically. If you don't yet have a statement of business principles, you may like to think about creating one. Ideally, it should insist on honesty, integrity, and fairness in all aspects of your business. You could consider committing the business to an external code or set of business principles that provide a framework for you and your stakeholders to measure your progress on environmental, social, and community issues. You might also consider using some of your marketing budget to associate your business with a social cause.

Consider how your stakeholders feel about the business. Identify your most important stakeholders and their concerns, and relate them to your business interests. Think about ways in which you could be more socially responsible in your relationships with your stakeholders. You could set out to seek mutually beneficial relationships with contractors, suppliers, and customers, as well as with other stakeholders, such as communities and local government. Make sure that you pursue ethical supply-chain management. Remember to promote your business principles at all times.

Review your business's current policies and processes. One good area to think about is waste recycling, and the use of renewable sources of energy and materials. Consider whether there are any ways to avoid materials that are known to be toxic, or to damage the environment. Introduce a social and environmental strategy, and set targets for your business. You could, perhaps, establish an environmental management system (EMS) with objectives and procedures for evaluating progress.

It is important to measure how well you perform, and to make it clear to your staff that you care about this. Any success should be celebrated; remember that people feel good about getting social responsibility right. Make sure that you communicate what you are doing. You could include a passage on this area in your annual review, mention it in newsletters, or even produce a special report. Let people know what you are doing, because it will affect their view of your business.

In order to be socially responsible, you must respect the rights of yourself and your staff. You can do this by providing good and safe working conditions, and introducing health and safety policies. Ensure that all your staff understand these, and adhere to them. It is important to develop and make the best use of the talent of your staff. You should provide training opportunities and

mentoring, so that promotion from within the organisation is maximised. Encourage your staff to be involved in the planning and direction of your company. Your commercial success depends on their commitment and talent. Show staff that you are open to job-sharing, flexitime, and other family-friendly policies.

Encourage staff volunteering in the community, as well as supporting the community with financial contributions and help in kind. Look for opportunities to make surplus product and redundant equipment available to local schools, charities, and community organisations. You can also help your local community by buying from local suppliers.

WHAT TO AVOID
Treating social responsibility as an isolated activity

The most common mistake is seeing social responsibility as an add-on, rather than as an integral part of your business strategy. It is important to regard social responsibility as one of the ways in which you can build the reputation of your business. In other words, you should treat it as seriously as you treat all the other aspects of running your business.

RECOMMENDED LINK
Small Business Service Benchmarking Index:
www.dit.gov.uk/mbp

SEE ALSO
Small and Growing Businesses (p. 478)

GROWING YOUR BUSINESS

Analysing Your Business's Strengths, Weaknesses, Opportunities, and Threats

GETTING STARTED

SWOT analysis (Strengths, Weaknesses, Opportunities, and Threats) is a method for assessing a business, its resources, and its environment. The analysis is often completed as a part of business and marketing plans to understand a business and its markets, and to show potential investors that all options have been thoroughly considered.

The essence of the SWOT analysis is to discover what you do well; how you could improve; whether you are making the most of the opportunities around you; and whether there are any changes in your market—such as technological developments, mergers of businesses, or unreliability of suppliers—that may require corresponding changes in your business. This actionlist will introduce you to the ideas behind the SWOT analysis, and give suggestions as to how you might carry out one of your own. For further information, you might be interested in looking at *Planning to Succeed in Business*, written by David Irwin, and published by Pitman in 1995.

FAQS

What is the SWOT process?

The SWOT process will focus on the internal strengths and weaknesses of you, your staff, your products, and your business. At the same time, it will look at the external opportunities and threats that impact on your business, such as market and consumer trends, changes in technology, legislation, and financial issues.

What is the best way to complete the analysis?

The traditional approach to completing SWOT is to produce a blank grid and then list relevant factors in the appropriate boxes. You may find that some factors appear in more than one box. A factor that appears to be a threat could also represent a potential opportunity. A rush of competitors into your area could easily represent a major threat to your business. However, competitors could boost customer numbers in your area, some of whom may well visit your business.

What is the point of completing a SWOT analysis?

By completing a SWOT analysis, you will be able to pinpoint your core activities and identify what you do well, and why. It will also point you towards where your greatest opportunities lie, and highlight areas where changes need to be made to make the most of your business.

MAKING IT HAPPEN
Know your strengths

Take some time to consider what you believe are the strengths of your business. These could be seen in terms of your staff, products, customer loyalty, processes, or location. Evaluate what your business does well; it could be your marketing expertise, your environmentally-friendly packaging, or your excellent customer service. It is important to try to evaluate your strengths in terms of how they compare to those of your competitors. If you and your competitors provide the same prompt delivery time, then this cannot be listed as a strength. However, if your delivery staff is extremely polite and helpful, and your competitor's staff has very few customer-friendly attributes, then you should consider listing your delivery staff's attitude as a strength. It is very important to be totally honest and realistic. Try to include some personal strengths and characteristics of your staff as individuals, and the management team as individuals.

Recognise your weaknesses

Try to take an objective look at every aspect of your business. Ask yourself whether your products and services could be improved. Think about how reliable your customer service is, or whether your supplier always delivers exactly what you want, when you want it. Try to identify any area of expertise that is lacking in the business. You may find, on consideration, that you need some more sales staff, or financial help and guidance. Don't forget to include location as an aspect to consider. Think about whether your location is right for your type of business, whether there is enough parking, or sufficient opportunity to catch passing trade.

Your main objective during this exercise is to be as honest as you can in listing weaknesses. Don't just make a list of the mistakes that have been made, such as an occasion when a customer was not called back promptly. Try to see the broader picture. The weakness might be that your systems or processes do not ensure that customers are contacted exactly when they need to be.

It is a good idea to get an outside viewpoint on what your weaknesses are. You may strongly believe that your years of experience in a sector reflect your business's thorough grounding and knowledge of all of your customers' needs. A customer, however, may view this wealth of experience as portraying an old-fashioned approach, and an unwillingness to change and work with new ideas.

Spot the opportunities

The next step is to analyse your opportunities, and this can be tackled in several ways. External opportunities can include the misfortune of competitors who are not performing well, providing you with the opportunity to do better. There may be technological developments, such as broadband arriving in your area, or a new process enhancing your products. There may be some legislative changes affecting your customers, offering you an opportunity to provide advice, support, or added services. Changes in market trends and consumer buying habits may provide the development of a niche market,

of which you could take advantage before your competitors, if you are quick enough to take action.

Another good idea is to consider your weaknesses more carefully, and work out ways of addressing the problems, turning them around in order to create an opportunity. For example, a supplier who continually lets you down could be turned into an opportunity by sourcing another supplier who is more reliable. A member of staff who leaves could provide the opportunity for a re-evaluation of duties in a more efficient way, or the appointment of a new member of staff who brings additional experience with them.

Watch out for threats

Analysing the threats to your business requires some guesswork, and this is where the analysis can be overly subjective. Some threats are tangible, such as a new competitor moving into your area. Other threats may only be intuitive guesses that result in nothing. However, being vigilant will mean that if a potential threat becomes real, you can react much quicker, having already considered your options and perhaps put some contingency planning into place.

Think about the worst things that could realistically happen, such as losing your customers to your major competitor, or the development of a new product far superior to your own. Listing your threats in your SWOT analysis will provide ways for you to plan to deal with the threats, if they ever actually start to affect your business.

Use your analysis

After completing your SWOT analysis, it is vital that you learn from the information you have gathered. You should now plan to build on your strengths, using them to their full potential. You can also plan to reduce your weaknesses, either by minimising the risk they represent, or making changes to overcome them. Now that you understand where your opportunities lie, make the most of them and ensure you capitalise on every opportunity in front of you. Try to turn threats into opportunities. Try to be proactive, and put plans into place to counter any threats as they arise.

To help you in planning ahead, you could combine some of the areas you have highlighted in the boxes; for example, if you see an external opportunity of a new market growing, you will be able to check whether your internal strengths will be able to make the most of the opportunity. Do you have enough trained staff in place, and can your phone system cope with extra customer orders? If you have a weakness that undermines an opportunity, it provides a good insight as to how you might develop your internal strengths and combat your weaknesses to maximise your opportunities and minimise your threats.

The SWOT process is to fill in the four boxes, but the real benefit is to take an overview of everything in each box, in relation to all the other boxes. This comparative analysis will then provide an evaluation that links external and internal forces to help your business prosper.

 ## WHAT TO AVOID
Focusing just on a few issues

Don't just focus on the large, obvious issues, such as a major competitor encroaching on your business. You need to consider all issues carefully, such as whether your Internet system provides everything you need.

Completing your SWOT analysis on your own

It is important to encourage other people's contributions to help you complete your

SWOT analysis; don't try and do it alone. Other people's perspectives can be very useful, particularly as they may not be as close to the business as you are and as a result are able to be more objective.

Using your analysis for the next ten years

Don't do a SWOT analysis once and then never repeat the exercise. Your business environment will be constantly changing, so use SWOT as an ongoing business analysis practice to obtain maximum benefit from the exercise.

Relying on SWOT to provide all the answers

Use SWOT as part of an overall strategy to analyse your business and its potential. It is a useful guide, not a major decision-making tool.

RECOMMENDED LINKS
Business Eye (Wales):
www.businesseye.org.uk
Business Gateway (Scotland):
www.sbgateway.com
Business Link (England):
www.businesslink.org
Invest Northern Ireland:
www.investni.com

SEE ALSO
Identifying Opportunities for Your Business (p. 324)
Small and Growing Businesses (p. 478)

Focus On: Competitor Analysis—Turning Data to Insight
Liam Fahey

GETTING STARTED

Competitor analysis (CA) has developed from a simple emphasis on gathering data about competitors, to a much greater in-depth analysis of customers' strategies and actions. The most competitive businesses are those that effectively transform data relating to competitors into 'decision-relevant' insights. The great advantages of in-depth analysis are that it is one means of learning more about the broader competitive environment, generating insights into customers, distribution channels, suppliers, technology, and competitive dynamics. CA is also used to reflect on and learn about one's own business—its vulnerabilities, limitations, and capabilities relative to current and potential rivals.

When you are analysing and understanding competitor's marketplace strategy, it is important to consider three central elements:

- What product-markets does the competitor compete in (or want to compete in)?
- How does it compete in those product-markets to attract, win, and retain customers?
- What does it seek to achieve in those product-markets?

This actionlist explains how a greater awareness and understanding of competitors can help you grow your business.

FAQS

What are the main pitfalls when thinking about competitors?

Insight is sometimes flawed or limited in many firms because too much attention is devoted to *current* large market-share competitors, while far too little is given to other types of current and potential competitors. Critical insight into change in customers' buying behaviours often emanates from analysis of smaller rivals or of functional substitute rivals. Sometimes it is especially useful to 'invent' a competitor that is not yet in the marketplace. This can be used as a reference point to challenge the firm's existing strategy or potential strategy alternatives.

What are the main sources of competition?

Professor Michael Porter of Harvard Business School has identified five forces affecting competition in an industry, and these provide an interesting lens through which to view current and potential competitors. Porter's five forces are:

- **industry rivalry**—direct competition resulting from the activities of companies in the same industry. An example of this is the Cola wars, dominated for much of the 20th century by Pepsi and Coca-Cola.
- **market entry**—new entrants to a market are another source of competition, with firms needing to understand who might enter the market, as well as how and when it will happen. Often the entire product offer provided by the new entrant—including product quality, features, and price—could challenge those already in the market.
- **substitutability**—businesses with products or services that may be substituted with alternatives face competition, especially over price. For example, a train operator may face competition from airlines.
- **suppliers**—these businesses wield significant power if the item they provide is scarce or unique, or if there are only a few suppliers. Suppliers have considerable power to damage a competitive position. One response is to build close relations with important suppliers to secure delivery and to control prices.

- **customers**—the power of the customer is seen as another source of competition. This means considering how dependent the business is on individual customers, the ease with which customers can move to another supplier, the customer's knowledge of the business's competitors, and the conditions (price, quality, overall offer) that are prevailing. An example of customer power is provided by the growth of the Internet as a sales channel, which has empowered customers.

What is it about our rivals that we should analyse?

One of the first challenges we face is to decide the focus of competitor analysis. A central question confronts every business: what do we need know about our current and potential rivals? If you view competitor analysis as much more than this, though, and open it out to see it as a source of learning about both the competitive environment and our own business, you'll find that you also need to learn about:

- the competitor's *marketplace strategy*: how it tries to outmanoeuvre rivals in the marketplace
- the competitor's *activity/value chain*: how it organises itself to develop and execute its marketplace strategy
- the competitor's *alliances and networks*: what other businesses it aligns with and how it manages its network of alliances
- the competitor's *assumptions*: what the competitor assumes about the marketplace and itself
- the competitor's *assets and capabilities*: what enables the competitor to compete
- the competitor's *infrastructure and culture*: the nature of the competitor's business

---

MAKING IT HAPPEN

Understand the factors intensifying competition

You need to be able to spot when competition may arise or when it is gathering pace. Competition can intensify in several circumstances:

- when the market is expanding or new, as with the computer industry over the last 20 years or the telecoms industry during the last ten years
- when the stakes are high and there are major profits to be gained or losses to be suffered, notably when there are relatively few businesses in a large market as, for example, with Coca-Cola
- when the market is set to change, perhaps as a result of developments affecting patents and intellectual property rights (such as when the patent for a clinical drug expires), or as a result of political or legal developments, such as privatization
- when the market is shrinking or when there is over-capacity in the market chasing fewer customers. This is apparent in major manufacturing industries such as ship-building, steel-making, and car production

Increase market awareness

Understanding your competitors will be easier if you develop a keen sense of market awareness, including a sense of how your competitors are perceived in your chosen market and why. Think about their:

- pricing policies and product offers
- brand reputation and recognition
- customers' perceptions
- product quality
- service levels
- product portfolio
- promotional campaigns: timing, nature, and channels used
- customer loyalty

Maintaining an awareness of these issues can help in analysing sources of competitive advantage and disadvantage.

Understand competitors' marketplace strategies

To understand what your competitors are up to, think about:

- **their product and customers,** taking into account the range of products offered, the variety within each product line, the groups of customers reached, and differences across the groups.
- **how the competitor (or competitors) provides value to customers,** taking into account product features, functionality, service, availability, image and reputation, selling and relationships, and price.

All of these issues to take into account are commonly called 'indicators'.

Assess competitors' marketplace strategies

Analysis only generates real insight when it turns to assessing what change in the competitor's strategy indicates about current, emerging, and potential change in the broader competitive context. You need to work out what such change implies for both the firm's current and potential strategy and decisions.

Assessment begins by evaluating the performance of your rival's strategy. For example, is it resulting in market-share gain? Is it leading to a greater share of individual customers? Is it building greater brand name and reputation (that in turn could be the basis of further market-share gain)?

Assessment addresses how well the rival's strategy is performing compared to other rivals or to your own firm's strategy. For example, with regard to specific customer segments, or even individual customers:

- is the competitor or your own firm providing greater value among the modes of competition?
- based upon customers' judgments, who is providing superior functionality?
- who is providing more useful services?
- whose image and reputation is more appealing to customers?

It is important to note that these assessments must be based largely on the judgments of the customers themselves.

WHAT TO AVOID
Not using data from a variety of sources

Think about the wide variety of sources that can provide you with the information on competitors that you need. Start with your own business first—check your IT systems, and ask both your team and your customers. External sources such as analysts, journalists, competitor websites, and publications can also be especially useful. Finally, focus on the competitor and always ask, for example, what a change in a competitor's activity indicates about the potential change in a broader competitive context.

Failing to undertake a process of analysis

The basic process in competitor analysis is as follows. First, identify relevant indicators from competitors' behaviours, actions, and words. Second, draw inferences as to what change among those indicators would imply for what the competitor might do in the future (for example, how it might change its strategy), or what it might suggest about developments in the broader marketplace (such as how fast specific products might come to the market or how quickly other products might penetrate particular customer segments).

Competitor analysis is always about detecting change in and around competitors and assessing what change implies for the competitor itself, for the marketplace in general, or for your own business.

Failing to act

It's vital to use any information gathered to strengthen your own business. Analysing everything you discover will help you assess and learn about your own company's vulnerabilities, capabilities, and future direction.

RECOMMENDED LINK
Management Help:
www.managementhelp.org

Identifying Opportunities for Your Business

GETTING STARTED

The business world today is fast moving, and the pace of change can at times seem bewildering. The environment in which your business operates is changing all the time, and there are many different factors that influence it. There are continual changes in your market, your customers' needs and preferences, the technology you use, your sales channels, and the way you can deliver your products or services. These changes can bring threats to your business, but they will also, undoubtedly, bring opportunities.

It is important that you periodically take a step back and try to analyse the way in which your business currently operates. Think about the factors that may promote change. Try to identify threats, and make sure you are prepared for them. It is also important, however, that you spot the many opportunities that arise. This actionlist will give some advice on how to spot opportunities, and make the best of them.

A book that you might find helpful is *Marketing Plans That Work*, written by Malcolm McDonald and Warren Keegan and published by Butterworth-Heinemann. The website address for the Chartered Institute of Marketing is given below.

FAQS

What am I successful at so far?

Ask yourself what your current business success is based upon. If you can explain how you became successful in the first place, you have more chance of being able to repeat that success again. Carry out an analysis of your current strengths and weaknesses, and try to establish how these are contributing to your current success, or lack of it.

What opportunities can I identify?

Write down a list of the opportunities you think you can exploit. These opportunities might be a natural extension of what you are doing already, or an adaptation of what you currently do. Alternatively, they could involve branching out into something completely different.

Which opportunity can I exploit most quickly, and most profitably?

Most businesses will be able to say that there are many new opportunities for them. It is more difficult to identify those opportunities that have realistic potential. Before you plunge headlong into pursuing every opening that arises, try to identify the one prospect that provides the most immediate, long term, profit-making potential for you. Try to be honest with yourself; decide if the opportunity you are selecting is really the one that will have the greatest impact on your business future. You may find some useful advice in the book, *Targeting Profitable Customers: How to Do It, How to Profit from It* by Malcolm McDonald and Ian Dunbar, published by Palgrave Macmillan.

How can I prepare my business for change?

The needs of the market change continually. Trends can be influenced by technology, fashion, lifestyle, and the economy as a whole. No small business can avoid these effects. Try to identify the trends that are affecting your business now, and over the next 12 months. Try to spot the opportunities those trends will create, as well as the threats they may pose. You need to think about how to prepare your business to adapt its products, prices, marketing methods, sales channels, or overall customer experience in order to make the most of these opportunities.

MAKING IT HAPPEN
Attracting new customers
Look at the way you acquired your existing customers. Make sure that you understand why they buy from you. It may be that you have used different methods to attract customers, so try to identify which is your most productive method of generating business. By doing this, it may be possible to repeat this success. Speak to your existing customers to find out why they buy from you. If you have customers who have bought from you in the past, it may be possible to ask them why they have stopped buying from you now. Try to find out what you need to do to encourage them to buy from you again.

Retaining existing customers
Work out your current client retention rate. Think about ways in which you could improve it. It may be that you already have an existing, loyal customer base, where there is a high degree of trust in the service you provide. However, there may still be potential to offer add-ons to your current service. Look out for opportunities to generate or improve repeat levels of sales. You might consider offering new products, or adaptations of products, or upgrades of your existing service to your customers.

Find out your average sales value per customer, and think about ways in which you can improve it. Try to encourage feedback from your customers and ask if there is anything they need that you currently do not supply. You may be able to build some of these things into your service. It may also be worth carrying out a formal piece of research with a sample of your customers, to help identify opportunities for new services or products.

Expanding your customer base
Think about whether there are customer groups that you do not sell to at present, but who you believe would benefit from your services. Write a list of specific businesses, or business types, you do not currently sell to, then identify reasons why they might buy from you. If you sell to individual consumers, make a list of specific groups of individuals who could benefit from your service. Write down the characteristics that made this group distinctive, for example their age, gender, race, occupation, income, hobbies, membership of clubs and associations, and so on. Write down a list of the benefits that your existing products and services can provide to these groups of people.

Unique selling propositions
A key question to ask yourself when assessing whether you can exploit the opportunities you are facing is how you can make yourself different from your competitors. There must be something about your business, products, or the way that you market your service that sets you apart. You will not be able to exploit your opportunities if you provide the same products and services at the same prices and in the same way that your competitors do.

Identify your unique selling proposition (USP). Make a list of all your main competitors; it may be helpful to do this in the form of a grid. Write down areas where you can do something more, better, cheaper, faster, or just differently from them. Identify any specific locations where your competitors don't operate. Find out if they supply to any customer groups that you currently don't. From your list, try to identify two or three key areas where you can position your service or product as being different, or better, than your rivals'.

The way you differentiate products, prices, customer service levels, marketing messages, money-back guarantees, upgrade offers, or overall company image will ultimately determine whether you will succeed in capitalising on new market opportunities.

Partnerships with other businesses
It is unlikely that any small business on its own will be able to meet all of the opportunities that it is facing, and exploit their full potential. It can often prove really worthwhile to identify other businesses that offer complementary services to your own which are aimed at the same, or similar, customer groups. By doing this you can open the doors to opportunities for your business

that you would otherwise be unable to develop. There are several ways in which you could work in partnership with another business. For example, you could access their products to sell to your existing customers. You could develop a new product or service based on a combination of your own and another business's product. Both businesses could share costs in joint marketing campaigns, for example at trade fairs, in catalogues, or in brochures. Alternatively, another business might be able to sell your product to a customer group that you currently do not reach. These 'piggyback' marketing relationships are increasingly popular, and can help small businesses to develop opportunities very quickly.

WHAT TO AVOID
Spreading yourself too thinly
You must try to avoid a scattergun approach to pursuing the opportunities you are facing. Don't spread your ideas so thinly, that you end up being ineffective in everything you try to achieve.

Being unrealistic
If you are not selective enough, and have not sufficiently considered the full impact on your ability to develop or deliver a new product or service, or carry out a marketing campaign to a new target audience, you will not make the most of the opportunities that exist. If you do not honestly assess what you have done right and wrong in the past, there is a real danger of repeating mistakes and failing to achieve your potential.

RECOMMENDED LINK
Chartered Institute of Marketing:
www.cim.co.uk

SEE ALSO
Analysing Your Business's Strengths, Weaknesses, Opportunities, and Threats (p. 318)
Small and Growing Businesses (p. 478)
Understanding the Effects of Growth (p. 327)
Understanding the Role of Partnerships for Small Business (p. 330)

Understanding the Effects of Growth

GETTING STARTED

All businesses need to plan strategies for growth or run the risk of declining, often suddenly. The most successful approach to growth is an integrated one, in which the business's owner or management team look at how all aspects of the business can work together to reap the benefits of growth. For example, a successful new sales promotion strategy put together by the marketing department has brought in many new customers.

In principle, this is fantastic news, but what will happen if the customer services department hasn't taken on enough new staff to deal with new accounts, or if the despatch department cannot cope with the increased demand in orders? All that effort will be wasted, so put plenty of time into planning and look at the whole picture so that you understand exactly what growth means for your business.

FAQS

How do I keep control of a growing business?

Many businesses that start small get by without a proper plan of exactly whom they will serve, how they will focus their resources, and what they aim to achieve. However, as a company grows, it becomes more difficult to operate effectively without a solid and detailed plan.

It's a good idea to prepare a business plan (or adapt the one you have already written in the past) to plot the future direction of your company and to address the demands of growth. Consult a business adviser for help with this important task—another perspective will be very useful during this process.

How do I make sure that the growth is sustainable?

If your business has tended to grow without specific marketing efforts, you may need to find out more about your market before you can be confident the growth will continue. If you're not sure where the increased customer demand is coming from, you cannot be certain if it will last.

As a start, find out where your most ready markets are and get a better picture of what they want. Look carefully at how your customer base is evolving as it grows; there may be segmentation occurring which requires you to push your product in the direction of new markets.

What are the legal implications of growth?

If your business started life on a 'sole trader' basis (or even as a partnership) you may, after a period of growth, have to consider whether incorporation as a limited company would be more beneficial. This change would involve more paperwork and compliance requirements, but would limit your personal financial liability. This is particularly important to consider as turnover grows and your business's financial requirements and risks begin to dwarf your personal resources.

Issues of contractual liability also become more pressing as the size and number of your transactions increase. In time there will be more at stake, and you need to protect yourself and your business with good contracts and terms—both with your suppliers and your customers.

It's very important that you do your research properly and get good professional advice, preferably from your accountant and a solicitor experienced in commercial law, before you make any major decisions. Discuss your options well in advance of any big change.

MAKING IT HAPPEN
Find finance for growth

Growing a business without the necessary working capital or investment is difficult at best, and at worst could endanger the whole enterprise. Supplying larger orders or providing a service to more customers invariably means investing in productive capacity long before you get a return on that investment. Sources of finance to help you do this will depend on how much you need and what exactly you need it for.

Bank loans are a common form of finance for growing businesses. These range from long-term loans (for property or fixed assets) to overdraft facilities (for short-term fluctuations in cash flow). Getting substantial amounts of investment finance may require you to relinquish part of your ownership—for instance, selling shares in your company or taking in another partner—and could involve venture capitalists or business angels.

Take on new employees

Moving from operating as a sole trader to a partnership or an employer can be a difficult step to take as it represents many changes for the owner-manager. However, if the business is to grow, it may be an essential progression.

Entrepreneurs have to learn to delegate tasks and relinquish control of some business operations in order to create the capacity for growth. The recruitment of appropriately skilled individuals, who are trustworthy, reliable, and dedicated to the job, is important. Success depends on the efforts of others, not just the entrepreneur's motivation.

Taking on employees involves substantial costs. When considering cash flow, you will need to take into account the costs of recruitment, training, pension contribution, employee liability, National Insurance, taxes, health and safety regulations, and personal records, as well as the cost of a salary.

Be selective about who you employ, as it is important to ensure that they will fit in with you or your other employees. Employee dissatisfaction results in low quality products, an unpleasant atmosphere, and general disruption to the flow of business.

An alternative to taking on more employees may be to bring in a partner.

Before establishing a partnership, you will need to decide exactly how responsibilities will be split and how soon the partner will have full business control. It is particularly important that you completely trust and feel able to work with the new partner.

Consider subcontracting some work if you are reluctant to employ people directly, though do make sure you assess the firms to whom you intend to subcontract work carefully; an irresponsible company will damage your reputation. Subcontracting may also be a way to increase your customer base, especially if the subcontracted firm offers parallel goods or services to your own.

Consider relocation

Many small firms are initially run from small, low cost premises—often the home of the owner-manager. As the business expands, so will the work area needed. For some idea of what to expect, consider how expensive it is to move house. For a firm to open additional branches, considerable strategic planning is needed to ensure success. You should be concerned not only with site selection, financing, and staffing, but also with the degree of independence each site will have and the adequacy of information and accounting systems.

Increase efficiency

To deal with the challenges of growth it is essential to run a well-designed operation. If you need to increase capacity, make sure you allow plenty of time to test out new systems and products and ensure that they work properly. It is all too easy for costs to get out of control. Ensure you invest in suitable cost-control systems as you increase capacity—you may need help to do this. Are you working to optimum efficiency? There is no point expanding inefficient systems into bigger ones.

Telework

Teleworking may be an appropriate way to deal with growth. Having employees working from home reduces the pressure on space, decreases overheads, and keeps the office size to a minimum.

WHAT TO AVOID
Not being fully committed to growth
Decide once and for all if you really are committed to further business growth. There is little point in expanding the business if you decide that you prefer working in a small operation. Are you prepared to deal with the challenges of increased responsibility? Don't fall into the grass is greener trap and think that growing the business won't take up that much of your time and energy. It will, and you need to be sure you have the right people and places in place to help you do it (see below).

Not having the capabilities to run a larger team of employees
Expanding the business will mean that you'll have to learn how to develop and manage a larger working team or employ a manager to help you do that. Be brutally honest with yourself and conduct a 'time audit', that is, a detailed breakdown of how you spend your day. Be realistic about how much time you have to spare from the day-to-day running of the business to manage growth. If you think that you can't do it all yourself, think about what new systems and how many new staff you'll need to make

sure you can all cope. If you think you can incorporate the extra responsibilities into your day, you might want to undertake a professional management qualification yourself or attend some courses on managing staff.

Not having enough funds to generate growth
You must make sure that you fund all your plans to increase capacity. Again, be realistic and be prepared to limit your objectives or delay growth plans until you can commit safely to the levels of funding they require.

RECOMMENDED LINKS
Business Eye (Wales):
www.businesseye.org.uk
Business Gateway (Scotland):
www.sbgateway.com
Business Link (England):
www.businesslink.org
Invest Northern Ireland:
www.investni.com

SEE ALSO
Identifying Opportunities for Your Business (p. 324)
Small and Growing Businesses (p. 478)

Understanding the Role of Partnerships for Small Business

GETTING STARTED

Small businesses can enter into partnerships with other businesses working towards a mutually-agreed goal. They can be long-term partnerships (for example, developing a new product), or short-term (for entering a new market). Partnerships are especially useful if you are seeking to exploit the new opportunities and challenges created by today's global marketplace. By teaming up with another business possessing complementary skills, you can achieve the strengths needed to exploit new opportunities and undertake new challenges. Inevitably there are risks involved; however, many of the potential problems can be anticipated and avoided by taking sensible steps in advance.

FAQS

What are the benefits of partnerships?

Clearly the overriding benefit of developing partnerships is obtaining access to the extra resources brought by the other partner, and achieving goals which would not be possible alone. When the partner business is operating in another country from your own, there can be additional benefits of access to international markets or new products to import. There are other important advantages too.

- Businesses who would otherwise only be able to reach a new market by over-committing themselves can do so without risking the rest of the business.
- By pooling resources, smaller businesses have more chance of winning a large contract, as they will be seen as being more secure and reliable.
- Partnerships allow small businesses access to technology, know-how, and customers that they could not have reached on their own.
- Partnerships can increase your databases of customers and contacts.

MAKING IT HAPPEN

There are several steps you will need to take before choosing a partner to work with.

Decide what you want from a partner

What are the general aims of the partnership? Are you aiming to access a new market, develop a new product, or raise its profile in a certain area? Although details can be worked out at a later date, you need to decide if your partner will be expected to input money, technological know-how, publicity, and so on.

For many reasons, joint ventures based on equal partnerships work best, and by teaming up with another small business, each party is able to contribute without either feeling they are working for the other. However, it is important to resist the urge to approach a business which is very similar to yours. It is better to team up with one that offers complementary skills and services so that you can both contribute without being in direct competition. There will also be less disagreement over which business has most to gain from the partnership.

Make inquiries

In England, some Business Links run schemes for finding partners, and the services of a network broker can also assist in establishing a partnership. Similar services are available from Scottish Development International, Invest Northern Ireland, and WalesTrade International.

A listing of European businesses seeking partners to co-operate in research and development activities is available through the European Commission's CORDIS database. Access to these services is through the CORDIS website.

Informal links with local entrepreneurs may develop into partnerships. It may be worthwhile studying the local business community for suppliers/customers who might be interested in a partnership. They may also know of other businesses that might consider the possibility of teaming up.

Some specialist consultancy firms provide support to businesses interested in entering new markets in a specific country or industry sector. Their services often include help in finding and approaching a partner in the new market, and further advice in establishing and developing the joint venture.

Businesses seeking partners sometimes place advertisements in the local press, trade magazines, or on the Internet. You should check these sources for suitable partners, but it is important to investigate any business thoroughly before agreements are signed. If you are a member of a trade association, advisers there may be able to offer you support and advice.

There are also a number of formal joint venture programmes offering support, assistance, and finance for businesses seeking partners. Contact your local Business Link, Business Connect, Small Business Gateway, or Invest Northern Ireland office for information.

Investigate possible partners

Once a likely candidate has been found and a positive response received, you need to make certain checks. Doing this before you finalise your commitment will make sure that a partner can be trusted. Check that there are no court judgments against them, whether they pay suppliers on time, and what their customer service record is like. If you are working with another business, some of its reputation may rub off onto your business, so it is important that it is good.

Assess whether you can work together

Many partnerships, especially between small businesses, break up because of personality clashes. A good working relationship must be developed if the partnership is going to work. In many ways working with someone who has a different business style

can be helpful, for example, one partner may be less cautious, and the other more so. However, it is important that the business ethos of the two firms is similar; for example, if one partner regards employees as his or her greatest asset, whereas the other considers employees just to represent a huge wage bill every month, it may be very difficult to work well together.

Form the partnership

The aim of the partnership should be clear from the outset, and put into writing. You should seek legal advice when drafting the formal agreement. The written plan should not only cover goals, financial contributions (such as profit sharing, purchasing, and expenses), and any joint training, but also factors such as any time limit on the partnership and how to end it if necessary. You should make provision for any intellectual property issues which may occur; joint product development, especially technological development, could leave both parties in joint ownership of a patent or copyright. This could cause problems if the partnership dissolves on a negative footing.

Trust is essential; if partners are continually checking up on each other, there is not much hope for the strength of the venture. You are not obligated to reveal everything about the business to the other party if it is not relevant to the project in hand. However, you should decide on how much information the other business can have access to, for example, will it have access to your existing customer base? It is important not to give away unnecessary information, and to think carefully before revealing anything that is confidential. You should try to ensure that, as far as possible, both parties are making an equal contribution to the project, for example in terms of technology or sales leads.

Work together, not as rivals

It is important that you maintain an open working relationship with your partner and avoid treating them like a rival. As with any project, ample time should be given to strategy, planning, promotion, implementation, and back up such as after-sales care. You should also ensure that employees are given adequate time to get to know the counterparts they will be working with in the partner business, and if possible, joint training should be given to both sets of employees to inform them of the goals of the project. Good communication is also essential—so make sure you keep employees informed of progress so that they can feel a part of any success.

WHAT TO AVOID

Not doing enough research into your potential partner

You really need to find out as much as you can about any potential business partners. If you're not fully aware of the way the other business works and what their objectives are for the partnership, disputes can arise. For example:

- personality clashes develop with other managers—these can be especially invasive in smaller businesses, where the owner of the firm is likely to have imprinted his or her style on the business, working methods, and staff
- one party feels it is contributing more, and effectively carrying the other
- one side takes a disproportionate share of the profits
- there is a mismatch between the two parties in terms of goals
- disputes arise over legal issues such as ownership of copyright material or other intellectual property which has been produced/developed by the partnership

Not putting the agreement into writing

It is easy for different businesses to enter a partnership with differing ideas and goals. Similarly, it is surprising how often two parties will come away from the same meeting with different ideas of what was agreed. Although each may have slightly different aims to achieve, the overall aim of the project should not be in doubt and the best way to achieve this is to have a written agreement signed by both parties.

RECOMMENDED LINKS

Business Eye (Wales):
www.businesseye.org.uk
Business Gateway (Scotland):
www.sbgateway.com
Business Link (England):
www.businesslink.org
Community Research and Development Information Service (CORDIS):
www.cordis.lu
Invest Northern Ireland:
www.investni.com
Scottish Development International:
www.scottishdevelopmentinternational.com
Scottish Enterprise:
www.scottish-enterprise.com
UK Trade & Investment:
www.uktradeinvest.gov.uk
Wales Trade International:
www.walestrade.com

SEE ALSO

Identifying Opportunities for Your Business (p. 324)
Small and Growing Businesses (p. 478)

Timing the Decision to Export

GETTING STARTED

The lure of foreign markets can be tempting for a small business looking for new customers, especially when your national market is becoming saturated. Such an expansion, however, needs to be thoroughly researched and carefully considered to ensure that the timing is right, both for the business and the market being considered. For a start, your business needs to have proved the success of its products or services closer to home, where the risks and costs of entry are generally going to be lower. This should be reflected not just in customer satisfaction but also in the commercial success of your business over a number of years; it is essential to proceed from a strong financial position if you want to develop markets abroad.

You will need to establish the commitment of your management team, based on in-depth knowledge of exactly what will be involved in the export effort. This support will be important in getting over the many (and unexpected) hurdles of entering a market for the first time. Be prepared to hold back on pursuing your ideas until everyone is 'on board'. Once this commitment is solid, you can develop the plans, capacity, and systems for your business to launch an export programme confidently.

Thorough analysis and understanding of the market you want to enter is vital. Your research and PLEST (political, legal, economic, socio-cultural, and technological) analysis should provide you with a reliable insight into your new market to assess whether this is the right time to enter an export market.

FAQS

How long does the planning take?

It is possible to fast-track the export planning and development process so that you can be winning your first export orders within six months. On the other hand, the circumstances of your business might require a year or two before you feel comfortable to start exporting. As a practical guideline, you could aim at achieving some progress within a year, but be aware that unexpected problems might force you to take longer.

Is it important to pioneer new markets?

There is obvious merit to being among the first to exploit a new export market, but the risk of being a pioneer may outweigh the possible benefits. It is usually businesses with deep pockets who venture into uncharted territory, and other businesses following will learn by the earlier mistakes. When considering the timing of a new market entry, be aware of all the unknown factors that could cost you dearly. Start with small orders, for instance, and make sure all agreements are in writing and signed by both parties.

Where can I find out more about the impact of the euro on UK exporters?

Twelve countries in Europe (Austria, Belgium, Finland, France, Germany, Greece, Ireland, Italy, Luxembourg, The Netherlands, Portugal, and Spain) have adopted the euro as their single currency and become the 'eurozone'. While the United Kingdom is not part of this group, many of its businesses are affected by it, especially those who trade with partners in the 'eurozone' or those whose supply chain passes through there.

There is a good deal of information for you to tap into if you are unsure of how the euro affects you. Tradepartners UK (address below) is an excellent source of advice and it offers many links to other sources, including the Treasury's Euro Information site: **www.euro.gov.uk**, which aims to provide businesses of all types with relevant information on this topic. The 'Business Impact' section of this site offers an interactive assessment of how your business is, or may be, affected and also provides access to a series of factsheets for further reading. The Department of Trade and Industry (**www.dti.gov.uk** and Business Link (**www.businesslink.org** or 0845 7567765) also offer advice.

MAKING IT HAPPEN
Conduct a PLEST analysis
A PLEST analysis—standing for political, legal, economic, socio-cultural, and techno-logical—of the market you plan to enter will ensure that you appreciate all the important factors that impact on your work there.

- **Political factors.** The political arena influences the regulation of businesses and the spending power of consumers and other businesses. Consider issues like: How stable is the political environment? What is the government's overall economic policy? Is the government likely to change tax regulations soon? What is the government's position on marketing ethics? Does the government have a view on culture and religion? Is the government involved in regional trade agreements?

- **Legal factors.** Every country has its own legal structure and legislation. You need to make sure that your products or services will not be infringing any legislation and that your exporting processes fully comply with customs regulations. Other issues to consider could include packaging and related environmental legislation; and your marketing strategy, as many countries over recent years have adopted new advertising constraints, covering issues such as advertising certain products like alcohol and tobacco, and advertising directly aimed at children.

- **Economic factors.** Consider the state of the economy you are planning to enter. This is especially important when planning for international marketing. You need to look at issues like interest rates, the level of inflation, the employment level per capita, long-term prospects for the economy, and gross domestic product.

- **Socio-cultural factors.** The social and cultural influences on business vary from country to country, so you should consider

questions like: What is the dominant religion? What are the attitudes to foreign products and services? Does language affect which products make it into the market? How much time do consumers have for leisure? What are the respective roles of men and women within society? What is the average life span? Are the older generations wealthy? Does the population have a strong opinion on green issues?

- **Technological factors.** Technology is vital for your competitive advantage, so consider these questions: Will technology help reduce the cost and quality of products and services? Do the technologies offer consumers and businesses more innovative products and services such as Internet banking and new generation mobile telephones? How is distribution changed by new technologies? Does technology offer businesses a new way to communicate with consumers?

Set time-bound objectives
Within the constraints of your particular business and sector, set some time frames that you can work towards. You need to take into account the level of funding available to implement your plans; the revenue that you expect from your capital outlay; the extent to which your export business will strengthen its position, and the extent to which exports further the overall mission of your business.

Test and modify your product first
In your export development plan, give yourself time to test your product in the market and to make any modifications that might be necessary. Do this before launching a full-scale marketing campaign so that you can deliver, from the start of proper trading, a final product closer to local requirements.

Build up skills and capacity
From your market research, you will develop sales forecasts to use in developing production and supply plans. When timing your export launch, make sure you give yourself enough time to employ and train

the necessary people, and to install the systems you will need to meet the demand you expect. You will be working hard to get these new export customers, but you will not be able to keep them if you have not developed the capacity to deliver on new order levels.

Choose the moment

There may be factors peculiar to your new market that you need to consider when timing your entry. If certain trade barriers or customs duties are being changed or removed, this could present a good opportunity to start trading with a lead on competitors. There may also be certain times of year that see more trade in your sector, particularly if it is seasonal. You would need to consider the conditions on the supply side (for instance, if you are exporting fruit when it is in season at home) and the demand side (where you would want to enter the new market at a time when those fruits are in short supply).

WHAT TO AVOID
Rushing in

The size of a market is no guarantee of its willingness to let in new entrants. Indeed, large markets are often those most heavily contested by big and small players because of the high stakes. Take your time in doing

your research and in finding the best point of entry.

Unrealistic expectations of quick returns

Most small businesses will be constrained in their export efforts by their limited funds and resources, so your export plan will be tailored to take account of your individual situation. With this in mind, be careful not to expect miracles from a new market. If you are working through an agent or distributor, they might give an overly optimistic forecast of what they might sell; you need to know enough about the market to make a realistic assessment of these forecasts, so that you do not expect too much, too soon. This can be particularly dangerous if your export effort is drawing on cash or resources that are vital to your core, local market.

RECOMMENDED LINK

UK Trade & Investment (the Government export promotion agency):
www.uktradeinvest.gov.uk

SEE ALSO
Exporting for the First Time (p. 339)
Small and Growing Businesses (p. 478)
UK Trade & Investment—A Quick Guide (p. 349)

Exporting—Methods of Market Entry

GETTING STARTED

Many first-time exporters feel unsure about the best way to approach their export market and how to manage a complex marketing and distribution process from a distance. This actionlist explains the various ways to approach market entry and also suggests how to choose a sensible market entry method for your business.

FAQS

What do the terms 'direct' or 'indirect' exporting mean?

Direct exporting means actively developing your venture into overseas markets. This approach requires a great deal of preparation and considerable investment of time. You could employ someone to take charge of part of the process, or to act as a representative in the chosen market. Alternatively, you may choose to manage the whole process yourself. Examples of direct exporting include joint ventures, using agents, or selling via trade fairs.

Indirect exporting usually means exporting via customers in the United Kingdom, which may eliminate the need for travelling abroad and dealing with complex export processes. However, it still requires considerable commitment. It can be a useful route into selling abroad for small-to-medium enterprises (SMEs), and provides a means of testing product viability in new markets.

Where can I go for advice and information on exporting?

UK Trade&Investment offers a range of market research, programme planning, and promotional support to exporters. Export Explorer is a scheme that aims to help new or inexperienced exporters take part in export missions into western Europe. Support and assistance is also delivered through local business advice organisations such as Business Links and Chambers of Commerce, in conjunction with commercial teams in British Embassies abroad.

The British Exporters Association (BExA) aims to link first-time exporters with professional services. It can also give details of regional Export Clubs, groups of business people who meet informally to discuss exporting issues. Members may be able to recommend agents or give advice on methods they have used. The embassies and Chambers of Commerce often have local expertise and contacts in certain markets. They are a useful source of practical information on import and export legislation. TradeUK is a DTI, Foreign and Commonwealth Office, and Dialog Corporation PLC venture. It is an export information service alerting UK businesses to export and import opportunities around the world. Registration is free.

Trade associations often have links with international groups or lists of contacts in export markets. Some have well-developed export services and can arrange joint ventures and trade fair visits, as well as provide general advice. All the major banks have international divisions that should be able to provide useful contacts and give general advice on the financial implications of particular export options.

Many solicitors have specialist expertise on contract law abroad and should especially be consulted when signing up an agent or distributor. Freight forwarders are an important part of the distribution process and can also provide advice on terms and paperwork. It may also be helpful to consult the national and trade press of the proposed export market and any international export journals. Often export representatives seeking customers will advertise in these publications.

MAKING IT HAPPEN
Choose an exporting method

Look carefully at your proposed market and

customers. Clarify the existing channels of distribution for your business's particular type of product. A trade visit will provide a good opportunity to study the local business structure. Are there any legislative issues which will affect sales, such as restrictions on choice of representatives? How do existing customers prefer to do business? For example, many large organisations are not keen on unsolicited approaches but channel all their buying through an agent.

In many cases, the nature of the product or service being exported will determine the selection of entry method. Make a list of any factors that may affect the way the product should be sold, using experience of the UK market where applicable. For example, what level of technical backup and promotional investment will be required? Think about your available resources, such as staff time, language skills, technical and marketing resources, as well as finance. How will domestic business be affected if technical staff are busy dealing with problems abroad?

Find out about methods of entry

Commission agents seek orders on behalf of a client in return for an agreed commission on each order. The agent is briefed on appropriate prices and terms and then approaches businesses within a designated area. Agents legally bind the business they represent to any contracts they sign for product orders. They generally seek sole agency rights for a country or region. Agents do not deal with shipping or payment, which must be arranged separately from the United Kingdom. An agent will accept no credit risk on stock unless they are a 'del credere' agent, charging a higher commission to compensate for the credit risk involved.

Distributors hold stocks of products from which they fulfil local orders. Unlike agents, they usually take legal title to the goods, buying from a business and selling on their own account at prices that they fix themselves. They usually also oversee the export process. It is normal to grant the distributor an agreed area of operation and to take orders from that area through them only.

Sell direct using the business's own resources

It is possible to sell direct to individual customers or outlets abroad. This may be appropriate where the customer base is narrow or limited, for example, luxury goods stocked by a small number of exclusive outlets, and when there is little need for servicing or after sales care. However, selling direct will involve considerable resources of time and money.

Attend trade fairs

Fairs and exhibitions are held throughout Europe and beyond, attracting customers and suppliers involved in various trades. If your business is considering exhibiting, contact the relevant trade association. Even if your business doesn't exhibit, there will be opportunities to make contacts, research the market, find agents or wholesalers, and develop sales leads.

Consider franchising

Franchising involves selling a business as a ready-made package to local operators in return for fees and other income, for example a percentage of annual profits. Franchising is a means of expanding rapidly while limiting management responsibility. The operation must be unique in some way to be a viable franchise. The franchisee contributes towards capital and resources as well as paying a licence fee, whilst the business is expected to provide a range of support, including training and technical services.

Consider licence agreements

A business can grant another firm the right to use its product names, technical specifications, processes, or patents, by drawing up a licence agreement. A fee (which may or may not include royalties) is charged for the licensed rights. Licensing may depend on the business securing protection for intellectual property rights in the country concerned and may also require government approval.

Consider joint ventures

There are many types of joint venture. It may be possible to identify a suitable UK firm that is willing to enter into a partnership to begin exporting. This provides an opportunity to pool resources and expertise, but it is important to find a firm with strengths that balance your existing weaknesses. Export clubs can be a good means of locating potential partners.

You could make an arrangement with a compatible business abroad. You might agree to manage each other's export trade, or combine in an operation to enter a specific market or markets. This often involves joint investment. Another option is to work with an international firm. Large international companies, whether UK-based or in the export market, often seek new products for their sales portfolio. If initial research indicates that a product could work well within a particular business's range, this 'piggy back' method is worth exploring.

Investigate export houses

Export houses are firms with a detailed knowledge of international sales who specialise in financing and servicing exports. The price paid for the product on offer will reflect their costs, but in some cases the importer pays the export house fees.

Export consultancies are generally small and specialise in particular markets and services. They usually accept responsibility for all aspects of export administration or will offer specific services and support.

Export merchants buy products outright from the manufacturer and sell them abroad. They usually take delivery and make payment in the United Kingdom, and often specialise in certain products. When dealing with a new product, they will require an agreement to protect their investment in building overseas sales, and they may also request product or packaging changes to meet their market requirements.

Confirming houses place orders with manufacturers and suppliers on behalf of overseas organisations and attend to all transport arrangements. They can also act as agents for UK manufacturers.

The Crown Agents

The Crown Agents make purchases on behalf of the public sector, for example, foreign governments, armed forces, and transport authorities. They are responsible for paying UK suppliers.

Buying houses

Large overseas businesses often have buying houses in the United Kingdom. These have huge purchasing budgets, and, although businesses usually still have to deal with the physical process of exporting, they are guaranteed fairly large-scale sales.

WHAT TO AVOID
Not researching thoroughly

Different markets and countries operate in different ways. In many countries, government regulations may dictate the choice of representation, and may stipulate the level of commission. It is important to remember that the best method in one market may not work in another. Many businesses which export to a number of markets deal directly in some areas, while using UK intermediaries to sell to other territories.

RECOMMENDED LINKS

British Exporters Association (BExA):
www.bexa.co.uk
Export Credit Guarantee Department (ECGD):
www.ecgd.gov.uk
The Institute of Export:
www.export.org.uk
Invest Northern Ireland:
www.investni.com
Scottish Development International:
www.scottishdevelopmentinternational. com
TradeUK:
www.tradeuk.com
UK Trade & Investment and Export Information Centre:
www.uktradeinvest.gov.uk
WalesTrade International:
www.walestrade.com

SEE ALSO
Exporting (p. 512)

Exporting for the First Time

GETTING STARTED
Exporting can be a rewarding way for a small firm to develop and grow. At the same time, it presents challenges and risks that are different from those in the domestic market. This actionlist will help you identify potential problems and plan for them.

FAQS
Why should I export?
There are many reasons why small firms seek to export. These might relate to the personal aims of the owner or manager (new challenges, credibility, added wealth, and so on). They might also relate to the commercial needs of the business (increased turnover and profits, reduced reliance on the home market, and so on).

When is the right time to begin exporting?
Exporting should be seen in the wider context of the strategic business plan. The potential rewards are massive, but a substantial investment is required to achieve them. Beware of overstretching your resources. Often, additional finance and evidence to show that the investment will pay off may be required.

Before you commit your business to the additional costs of export activity, carry out a business 'fitness check', to assess whether it is in a condition to sustain the additional effort required (or, indeed, to maintain current levels of activity properly).

Five areas that should be of particular concern are: your knowledge of the market; your production, distribution, and sales capacity; your flexibility to meet market needs; the financial resources available to you; and management, staffing, and skills resources.

MAKING IT HAPPEN
Know the key factors for success
Successful exporters demonstrate management commitment to exporting and will have carried out thorough research and planning. They will have conducted market visits and research validation and will have developed contacts and relationships. They will have a feel for foreign cultures and languages and an eye for detail in export documentation and procedures. They will also have put the emphasis on quality.

Avoid potential problem areas
A number of problems can arise that may not appear to be directly related to exporting. The added challenge of exporting, whether successful or not, can show up the flaws in a business. Growing firms can find it hard to recruit staff with the right knowledge and experience. Recognise your limitations and be prepared to use appropriate external advisers for a different perspective. They can provide strategic guidance, commission research, and act as a sounding board for problems.

The cost of breaking into foreign markets is frequently underestimated. The venture should be seen as an investment, covering the initial costs of research, developing contacts, and the losses incurred before sales begin to cover the extra cost. It may be necessary to explore separate financial arrangements in order to support any exporting ventures.

Pricing is another potential problem area. Having established the market potential for the product or service, the price the market will bear is crucial in determining how profitable the returns will be.

Accepting substantial new business without thinking through all the implications can be risky and may cause operational problems. Cash-flow problems destroy many promising firms, and payment can take longer for exports. Stock control is a particular issue in terms of capital and prompt delivery. The administration of orders, insufficient production capacity, and extensive transit times may produce delays unacceptable to the customer.

All investment of management and staff time, money, and costs must be taken into account. It will be necessary to consider: UK factory costs; export packing; inland transport and handling costs; export transport costs; insurance costs; overseas handling and transport costs. There are also taxes: any customs duties payable overseas, including VAT; freight forwarders' charges, inclusive of documentation; any direct office costs, including any salesperson's commission; overseas agents' charges; advertising; cost of money and credit, and the cost of cover against exchange rate risk when applicable.

Work with other organisations

A lot of advice, information, and support is available to exporters through business support organisations, much of it free or subsidised. UK Trade & Investment, the new Foreign Office and Department of Trade and Industry (DTI) export agency, provides a number of useful market research, export counselling, and trade mission services. Points of contact include: the local Business Link in England; Scottish Development International; WalesTrade International, and Invest Northern Ireland.

There are also organisations that can provide the necessary expertise to help a business to develop an export market. Chambers of Commerce provide specific export training and services, for example, documentation, letters of credit, and certificates of origin. They also undertake trade missions, often sponsored by UK Trade & Investment, and act as host to local export clubs. Export consultancies are, usually, small consultancies specialising in particular markets and services. They take on all aspects of export marketing and administration, or provide particular services, for example, training, to assist with exporting issues.

Commission agents will seek orders on behalf of the business and charge an agreed commission on all orders from their territory, even if they did not obtain the order. Agents also generally seek sole agency rights for a country or region. Distributors act as agents and hold stocks of the product, from which local orders are supplied. Often distributors buy from the business and sell for their own account, at local prices, which they fix themselves.

Buying houses are often specialised, buying products outright from the manufacturer and undertaking to sell them abroad. They usually require an agreement that protects their investment in building up the overseas sales of the product. Confirming houses place orders with manufacturers and suppliers on behalf of overseas organisations and attend to all the shipping arrangements. They may also act as agents for United Kingdom manufacturers, and often seek orders from their overseas contacts and principals.

Crown Agents make purchases on behalf of overseas governments, and a number of large organisations. Customs and Excise will provide technical advice and information on export procedures, duties, restrictions, refunds, and product classification.

Think about transportation and distribution

There are many unfamiliar issues involved in the exporting of goods, including aspects of transport and distribution that may have not been a problem in the past. The following paragraphs cover some of these issues.

Freight forwarders offer comprehensive documentation and transportation services, not necessarily using their own transport. They undertake door-to-door services for shipments. An efficient freight forwarder will take advantage of the keen competition between transport operators to secure the best prices. The British International Freight Association can assist with finding a local forwarder. You might also consider using a freight forwarder to deal with documentation. Simple typing errors can lead to long and costly delays at overseas customs. The United Kingdom network of Chambers of Commerce offers a comprehensive export documentation and certificates of origin service.

Suitable packaging should be used to ensure that goods reach their destination undamaged at the most economical cost. For export, packaging may have to be tougher and/or meet specific legal standards. Particular attention should be paid to any printed descriptions on the packaging. Another issue is the terms of delivery. The point at which the business's responsibility for the goods ends and that of the overseas buyer begins is determined by the contract terms. As there is a wide range of options available, it is essential that the business is fully aware of its responsibilities regarding insurance and contractual obligations.

Manage the risks

If you explore foreign markets directly, reduce the initial financial investment and risk by focusing on one market. In exporting it is even more important that delivery promises are kept and products are acceptable and reliable. The administration, documentation, and physical distribution of products can be handled efficiently by external companies. Marketing can be contracted out to specialists.

There are various risks to consider when exporting. Insurance will cover straightforward commercial risks such as those encountered during transportation. More critical is the risk that an overseas buyer may refuse to accept delivery of goods ordered, or may take delivery, refuse to pay, and disappear. It is therefore essential to put all of the terms (Incoterms) of the contract in writing, and select a secure method of getting paid which is appropriate to the risk involved.

Political risks can vary from political instability (military coups) to the sudden imposition of restrictions by a government on import payment. Currencies may fluctuate wildly or cease to be convertible into other currencies, making them effectively valueless. Assessments of political and economic risks can be obtained through discussions with British Embassy commercial staff overseas.

Interest rate risks can be especially important in the case of high-value capital ventures, where there is a long period between initial planning and final payment for the product. In such cases, costings should take account of the charge for the money required. There is also a risk that the rate of exchange between sterling and the buyer's currency will change between agreeing terms and completing the deal. Hedging mechanisms enable exporters to protect themselves from exchange rate changes, and banks can provide further details.

WHAT TO AVOID
Exporting when your business is unfit
Exporting can put pressure on a business. It is essential that your business is running efficiently before taking on the added complications of exporting.

Not getting the right advice
Take full advantage of the free advice and information available. Some of the subsidised services can assist with finding partners who can give the right type of support for your particular products and markets.

Providing inadequate training
Training for both management and employees, is essential. It will enable your business to make an informed decision about which foreign markets to investigate.

RECOMMENDED LINKS
British Exporters Association:
www.bexa.co.uk
British International Freight Association:
www.bifa.org
Scottish Development International:
www.scottishdevelopmentinternational.com
Simpler Trade Procedures Board (SITPRO):
www.sitpro.org.uk
WalesTrade International:
www.walestrade.com
Invest Northern Ireland:
www.investni.com
UK Trade & Investment:
www.uktradeinvest.gov.uk

SEE ALSO
Export Documentation (p. 342)
Exporting (p. 512)
Timing the Decision to Export (p. 333)

Export Documentation

GETTING STARTED

To the small business exporter, the documentation required can seem daunting, but it is worth getting documentation right; having the correct information, knowing where and when to send it, and to whom, speeds up the processing of individual transactions and inspires confidence in the business. Indeed, where letters of credit are involved, correct documentation is essential to receive payment. Export documentation is subject to frequent change and amendment, and requirements vary from country to country.

FAQS

Why would I need to use export documentation?

Documentation is used to reduce delayed shipment and delivery; to describe cargo; for customs clearance; to indicate the ownership of goods for collection purposes or in the event of dispute; and to obtain payment. Documentary requirements often depend on the Incoterm used. (Incoterms are standard trade definitions most commonly used in international sales contracts, and help traders in different countries to understand one another. Information on the Incoterms is found on the International Chamber of Commerce website, the address of which is given below.)

What types of export documentation are there?

Most export documentation falls into one of five broad categories: commercial, official, transport, insurance, and financial documents.

Many export documents are now a part of the United Kingdom Aligned System of Documents, managed by the Simpler Trade Procedures Board (SITPRO). This system implements the United Nations Layout Key for Trade Documents. It basically means that the same piece of information is in the same place on all documents. This makes the completion, checking, and comparison of related documents much easier.

Who can I ask for assistance with export documentation?

SITPRO (Simpler Trade Procedures Board) has developed a range of systems for preparing paperwork quickly, cheaply, and accurately without repetitive retyping, and offers advice to individual businesses on export needs. HM Customs and Excise advises on export documentation requirements for United Kingdom or European Community purposes, VAT, controlled goods, and legislation. Customs officers oversee the key aspects of export transactions, such as documentation, legislative standards, and duty.

Local Chambers of the Chambers of Commerce can help with information and advice on all aspects of export/import documentation, and will usually have experienced staff to advise on specific problems. The Department of Trade and Industry's Export Control Organisation can tell you if your particular product is exportable only under licence, can give details of any restrictions, and tell you how to obtain the relevant licence.

Freight forwarders offer a range of services covering the physical transportation of goods for export, usually including packing and documentation. The British International Freight Association (BIFA) can help you contact such companies. Export management and documentation services are also an option; the British Exporters Association (BExA) can help in finding sources of assistance.

MAKING IT HAPPEN

Commercial documents

There are three types of commercial document. The commercial invoice is a bill for the goods, a basis for the assessment of import duty, evidence of value in case of an insurance claim, and in some cases a contract of sale. It describes the product, including shipping marks, price, and so on. It must be completed according to the requirements of customs authorities in the export market.

The pro forma invoice may be needed in advance if the importer has to get an allocation of foreign exchange, or an import licence. It can also be used to send commercial samples and other 'free of charge' consignments. Blank or nil value pro formas are illegal in all countries.

Finally, there is the Export Cargo Shipping Instruction (ECSI). This is the instruction from the exporter to the forwarder or carrier. It sets out the terms and conditions for the movement of goods, and who is responsible.

Official documents

There are many different kinds of official documents. The Single Administrative Document (SAD) is known as the C88 in the United Kingdom. It is used for exports, imports, and goods transiting the European Union.

Export licences are required for certain goods to be exported legally, for example drugs, chemicals, antiques, military-related items, high-technology industrial goods, and scientific instruments, under the Export of Goods (Control) Orders. It is the exporter's responsibility to ensure that their goods are covered if necessary. The Department of Trade and Industry's Export Control Organisation can be contacted for further information. Contact the Department of Culture, Media, and Sport for specific information related to antiques and works of art.

Certificates of Origin (C/O) are required by some countries when goods are imported. They are available from Chambers of Commerce for goods of EU origin. Documentary proof of origin (usually the manufacturer's invoice) must also be submitted to the Chamber. Movement Certificates are required where goods are being exported from the European Union to a country covered by EU trade agreements. These certificates ensure preferential tariff treatment. They must be stamped by UK Customs before dispatch. Certificates of Health are often required for food, livestock, agricultural, and horticultural products. These certificates are issued by a state-appointed veterinary inspector or health board, this being DEFRA (Department for Environment, Food, and Rural Affairs) in the United Kingdom.

The Clean Report of Findings (Pre-Shipment Inspection Certificate) applies mainly in developing countries, where foreign currency is rationed, and where priority may be given to medical supplies, food, and so on. The report is issued by an independent inspection house, appointed to check that the goods being shipped are those on the pro forma invoice, and that they conform to quality, price, and quantity requirements. Checks are also made once shipment is complete. Contact the inspection agency as early as possible if you believe that inspection may be required.

Individual countries have their own very specific requirements relating to import licences and special requirements. Many require import licences for certain goods, and some for all imports. Others prohibit certain goods entirely. Although it is normally the customer's responsibility to comply with import documents, it makes sense for you to confirm that they are doing so.

Transport documents

The maritime bill of lading is issued and signed by the designated carrier once the goods to be exported have been placed in its care. It serves as evidence of a contract between the exporter or importer and a shipping company to transport the goods; it also acts as a receipt for goods. It may describe the condition of the goods when transferred to the shipper, and it also serves as a document of title indicating the person, or business, who has the right to possess the goods.

The bill should show relevant information, for example, the date and point of dispatch, and the shipper's name and destination port. The reverse side gives details of the terms on which the transporter is carrying the goods, and indicates limitations on its liability. Bills are usually completed in sets of two or three, one being forwarded immediately, another sent later in case of loss, while a number of copies are kept as records.

Goods can be consigned 'to order', which means the importer can give someone else authority to collect them on arrival. In this case, the bill of lading will be endorsed by the exporter. If the consignee (importer) is named, the goods will only be released to them.

Bills of lading can be issued in several forms, for example a 'shipped' or 'shipped on board' bill signifies that the goods have been received and placed on board ship, while a 'received for shipment' bill indicates that the goods have been received by the ship owner, but have not been placed on board. Other types of bills cover 'combined transport', for example, over land as well as sea, and containerisation.

The sea waybill serves the same purpose as the bill of lading except that it is not a document of title.

An air waybill receipt is issued by an airline when goods are received for transport, which travels with the cargo. It is similar to a bill of lading, but cannot serve as a document of title.

A parcel post receipt is issued by the Royal Mail as proof of dispatch. It is not a document of title. A similar receipt would be issued by Parcelforce Worldwide.

The CMR (Convention relative au contrat de Transport International de Marchandises par Route) accompanies goods transported by road. The CIM (Convention International de Marchandises par Chemin de Fer) accompanies goods dispatched by rail. Neither is a document of title, but both function as receipts and evidence of the contract of carriage.

The dangerous goods note (DGN) is required when shipping hazardous, or potentially hazardous, goods. The exporter must provide the transporter—that is the shipping, haulage, or air company—with full details of the goods, including the official 'class' of danger to which they belong. You should also be aware of packing and marking requirements for hazardous cargoes. A new version of DGN came into force in July 1999, which implemented various changes including new declarations, updated completion guidelines, and so on. For air transport, the International Air Transport Association (IATA) Dangerous Goods Declaration should be used.

The standard shipping note (SSN) is usually completed by the exporter and is the receiving document for ports and container bases in the United Kingdom. It advises recipients of the necessary information to handle the goods. The SSN was also amended in July 1999. The note may now be used for goods classified as hazardous by a mode of transport other than that for which the SSN is being used, for example goods classified as hazardous under the IATA Dangerous Goods Regulations.

ATA (Admission Temporaire, or Temporary Admission) Carnets are particularly useful where the exporter is taking goods through a number of countries, for example to a trade fair, but will bring them back to the United Kingdom. Carnets are issued by selected Chambers of Commerce on payment of a fee and relevant security, and serve as a 'passport' for the goods. Export and import restrictions, including licence requirements, must still be observed under the Carnet system. The maximum period of validity of Carnets is one year, but they can cover a number of journeys.

Insurance documents

Arrange freight insurance through a broker with a thorough knowledge of exporting. The insurance policy should cover goods for at least their full value (110% is common), should carry all details of quantity and route, and should provide for time extensions and trans-shipments where necessary.

A Certificate of Insurance is issued by the insurance company or underwriters to certify that insurance has been arranged for the goods being exported. It should detail the degree of protection, and list the policy number and all relevant details, for example, dates, destination, transport method, route, description of the cargo, and the value for which it is insured.

Electronic Data Interchange is increasingly important to the international exchange of commercial information. It greatly reduces the time taken for document exchange and increases accuracy by eliminating transcription errors. EDI systems use conventions and standards of formatting for correct data delivery. International standards have been devised so that various documents can be exchanged between companies, for example, invoices and orders. Their precise layout makes them simpler to use for trading partners in different countries without a common language.

EDI involves a computer with a modem and communications software (to provide data translation) at either end of a telephone line. Many businesses use a Value Added Network supplier (VAN) to handle connections and forward documents. To use EDI, the exporter should set up a Trade Interchange Agreement with the customer(s). This replaces the terms and conditions of trade which normally appear on the back of a purchase order. HM Customs operates a system for exporters which allows paperless export declarations to be made.

The Internet can also be used as a means of sending documentation. Benefits include speed, accuracy (supported by database files), and the ability to send to a large number of recipients using one system. Disadvantages include problems of providing adequate security, and dealing with global orders without knowing the integrity of the person doing the ordering.

WHAT TO AVOID

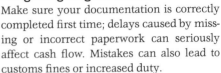

Not getting it right first time
Make sure your documentation is correctly completed first time; delays caused by missing or incorrect paperwork can seriously affect cash flow. Mistakes can also lead to customs fines or increased duty.

Not getting the right advice
Take as much advice as possible when dealing with paperwork. Talk to SITPRO, an export counsellor, the Chamber of Commerce, the agent or distributor, and so on, to ensure that you are fully prepared.

RECOMMENDED LINKS
British International Freight Association:
www.bifa.org
British Exporters Association (BExA):
www.bexa.co.uk
Department of Culture, Media and Sport:
www.culture.gov.uk
The Export Control Organisation Helpline:
www.dti.gov.uk/export.control
The Institute of Export:
www.export.org.uk
International Chamber of Commerce:
www.iccwbo.org
Simpler Trade Procedures Board (SITPRO):
www.sitpro.org.uk

SEE ALSO
Exporting (p. 512)
Exporting for the First Time (p. 339)

Importing for the First Time

GETTING STARTED

Importing is the process of bringing goods from one country into another. The main reasons for importing are either to obtain goods or materials from a source which is the cheapest available or of the highest quality for a given price, or to obtain raw materials, components, or finished goods that are not available in this country.

This actionlist explains why you might consider importing, how to go about it, and some of the common pitfalls you should be aware of. If your business is unfamiliar with import procedures, it is a good idea to employ a clearing agent who will deal with procedures on the business's behalf.

FAQS

How might I find sources of supply?

One way is to respond to advertisements placed by would-be suppliers, for example in the trade press or on the Internet. If a supplier is required for particular items, advertise in the appropriate overseas publications and via your business's website. Research possible sources thoroughly, and make a personal visit to each supplier on your shortlist.

There are numerous directories of products and services, of which the best known is *Kompass*. Available in book form or on CD-ROM in almost 70 countries, including all the main trading nations, this publication can be found in most main libraries and Chambers of Commerce. If direct access to information on suppliers in a particular country proves problematic, the country's embassy in the United Kingdom may be able to help. There may also be a joint Chamber of Commerce that encourages trade between the United Kingdom and the country of interest.

Sometimes, an individual or organisation overseas can be appointed to act as an agent and manage deals with suppliers on your behalf. However, payment of a fee or commission will usually be required, unless the individual or organisation works on an export programme run by the foreign government.

MAKING IT HAPPEN

Arranging to import

The simplest way to import is to do it indirectly, which means that someone else handles the importation process, and goods are simply purchased from them. These importers can be wholesalers or import merchants; commission agents or distributors working for the overseas manufacturer; or a UK subsidiary of the overseas business. Indirect importing can be less risky as it usually involves buying from a UK registered business covered by UK company law, and payment is usually in sterling. It usually costs more than direct importing, however.

Direct importing is when the business is in personal contact with the overseas suppliers. It gives the business more control over the process, and may even prove to be more profitable. However, it will be necessary to find the right overseas suppliers and to handle negotiations, regulations, and paperwork personally. Regulations covering imports from the specific countries of interest can be obtained from HM Customs and Excise and the Department of Trade and Industry's Import Licensing Branch.

Potential pitfalls of importing

An importer often holds the linguistic advantage over a buyer, and language can be a significant barrier. Specify that any correspondence, particularly quotations and contracts, must be in English. Making initial contact overseas will be easier if the manager or an employee of the business can speak the other language.

The physical distance in moving goods increases the risk of delays and means that client-customer servicing is more expensive. These risks need to be built into planning, especially if the business is run on a Just-in-Time basis. The total cost of the goods bought has the potential to be much higher than the price agreed for the actual items. Additional costs may include packing, transport, insurance, and customs duty. The business will therefore need to ensure that allowances have been made for such costs in budget calculations, or that they are included in the total contract price that will be paid.

It is essential to consider which currency is to be used in the transaction. A foreign supplier is often much more comfortable dealing in their own currency and may be able to quote a more competitive price. However, you will need to pay for the exchange, and money may be lost if the exchange rate fluctuates between placing the order and making the payment. If the transaction is in pounds sterling it will be easier to ascertain how much will be paid, but the supplier may ask a higher price for the privilege. The further into the future the transaction is, the greater the uncertainty, and the more it is likely to cost. If orders are likely to be large and frequent, then buying in the foreign currency may be preferable, hedging any risk by agreeing a forward exchange contract with a bank.

The single European currency (the euro), introduced on 1 January 1999, affects UK businesses wishing to import goods. Current European Union member countries that have joined are Austria, Belgium, Finland, France, Germany, Ireland, Italy, Luxembourg, Netherlands, Portugal, and Spain, collectively known as the euro zone. As of January 1999, businesses in these countries became entitled to trade with each other without any exchange rate risk. In January 2001 Greece also joined the single currency. If a UK business is obliged to deal in euros, then exchange rate risk could be an important issue to consider.

Import quotations and orders

State your requirements clearly and consistently when requesting quotations, so that responses can be easily compared. Ensure that you specify the quantity, expected order date, and expected payment terms (for example, form of payment, currency, and payment date). Be clear about details such as specific packaging, labelling, and transport requirements (including terms of, and responsibility for, arranging delivery). State your requirements for goods to meet specific quality, technical, or safety standards, and the requirements that are related to the business's legal obligations (these will be of particular importance). It is important to agree under which country's legislation any trading contract is made.

The more professional the request looks, the more willing a company will be to do business. The name and title of the person to whom responses should be sent, and also the business's full address, with phone and fax numbers and e-mail addresses, should be provided.

Agreeing payment terms can be difficult until business creditworthiness has been proven. Signify good intentions by giving the supplier the name of the business's bank and inviting them to ask for a reference (the bank must be informed about this first). There are a number of ways to pay, ranging from cash in advance to cash on delivery. Two of the safest methods for the business and the supplier are letters of credit and bills of exchange. The bank will be able to give advice regarding the details.

Once a supplier has been chosen, the order placed should include the same details as the quotation, with any agreed amendments. It is also important to specify any conditions of purchase. To avoid contract disputes, the supplier must agree to all of the terms of the order, in writing.

Import controls

Import sanctions, quotas, and other controls can be imposed in the United Kingdom, which is also subject to European Union restrictions, or alternatively may be put in place by the export regulations of the supplier's country. Importers should check with the supplier to find out if an export licence from the supplier's country will be required. The main government departments involved with import licensing include the Department of Trade and Industry's Import Licensing Branch; the Health and Safety Executive; and the Department for Environment, Food, and Rural Affairs. The range of goods subject to controls is extensive, and your business should check with its regulatory body.

HM Customs and Excise collects duty and VAT, and can also provide details of what is expected regarding an importer's responsibilities. For example, the Harmonised System is an internationally recognised way of coding imports so they can be recognised in trade statistics, and for the charging of duty. The full code number should be agreed and quoted on all documents by both importer and supplier.

Transport and delivery when importing

Terms of delivery may be encountered in abbreviated form and come from an internationally recognised list, known as 'Incoterms'. In some cases the definitions of the terms may vary by country, so you should seek advice from the local Chamber of Commerce.

The terms of delivery should always be agreed in quotations and orders. They determine what the price includes, where delivery of the goods takes place, and where possession passes from the exporter to the importer. These points are important because they will affect decisions such as final cost and insurance responsibility. The choice of transport used will depend upon the type of goods, and the quantity, urgency, and cost. The route options of air, sea, road, or rail all have advantages and disadvantages. For some goods it may also be possible to use postal services.

In many cases, when importing for the first time it is a good idea to use the services of a freight forwarding company. They usually have agents overseas and can therefore arrange most aspects of overseas transportation and insurance.

WHAT TO AVOID
Not understanding the business from an exporter's point of view

As an importer, your business may be requested by its overseas contacts to trace goods or services in the United Kingdom and then export them. A willingness to fulfil such reciprocal requests will help to build a good working relationship and will also result in an improved knowledge of the supplier.

Not taking all costs into account

If price is a factor, businesses should carefully consider whether importing works out cheaper, especially in cases where payment of duty, transport costs, agent's commission, and so on, are required. Other factors, such as reliability of supply, may also be an issue.

If the business is re-exporting imports to outside the European Union, it may qualify for Inward Processing Relief. HM Customs and Excise can be contacted for further information.

Not inspecting goods that are received

It is essential that any goods received are inspected promptly, in case it is necessary to reject them or make an insurance claim.

RECOMMENDED LINKS

British International Freight Association (BIFA):
www.bifa.org
Euro Information (The Official Treasury Euro Resource):
www.euro.gov.uk
HM Customs & Excise (HMCE):
www.hmce.gov.uk
Kompass:
www2.kompass.com
RBS Small Business Clinic:
www.rbs.co.uk/Small_Business

SEE ALSO

Exporting (p. 512)
UK Trade & Investment—A Quick Guide (p. 349)

UK Trade & Investment—A Quick Guide

GETTING STARTED

Government support for exporters now comes under the general heading of UK Trade & Investment. (Until November 2003 Trade Partners UK and Invest UK covered export and investment issues respectively.) UK Trade & Investment makes use of the information gathering and representational potential of the commercial teams in over 200 overseas diplomatic posts operated by the Foreign and Commonwealth Office (FCO). This is linked with the UK-based resources of the Department of Trade and Industry (DTI), Scottish Development International (SDI), WalesTrade International, and Invest Northern Ireland. This actionlist briefly describes how UK Trade & Investment can help you as the manager or owner of a small or medium-sized business, how you can get in contact with the organisation, and how to make the most of what it has to offer.

FAQS

How can UK Trade & Investment help my business?

A number of schemes and services managed by UK Trade & Investment are designed specifically for small and medium-sized businesses. Other schemes aim to assist trade associations and other intermediaries, who in turn help groups of businesses to explore opportunities in foreign markets. Some services are free, others are charged for. It is therefore advisable to check with the local provider for up-to-date costs. There are a variety of services available, many of which can be tailored to the needs of your business. Some of these services are described in more detail in the next section. The exact nature of what is on offer, and the associated charges or financial support, are subject to review.

How do I approach UK Trade & Investment?

The first points of contact for anyone seeking assistance from UK Trade & Investment are the local Business Link (in England), Scottish Development International, Wales Trade International, and Invest Northern Ireland. All website addresses are given below.

MAKING IT HAPPEN

Help with exporting

UK Trade & Investment offers a number of 'Country Reports'. These provide a description of the services and publications available to assist with exporting to certain countries, and much of this information is accessible via the Internet (the website address is given below). UK Trade & Investment also publishes *Overseas Trade*, a magazine which provides exporting information to small and medium-sized businesses.

The Export Explorer scheme is also part of the UK Trade & Investment service. This scheme aims to help smaller businesses that are considering exporting to western Europe. There are two aspects to the scheme: Market Explorer and Trade Fair Explorer. Both of these include visits to a given country, as well as advice and information on export issues.

Commercial officers at embassies and other missions overseas can produce tailor-made reports for companies. Reports can include basic market information, identification and assessment of potential agents and distributors, customised local contact lists, market assessments for products and services, advice on market approach, information about potential local business contacts, and general information on local investment opportunities.

Help with market research

There are a number of services aimed at helping would-be exporters to assess markets for their product or service overseas. An excellent starting point is the UK Trade & Investment website, an online gateway which provides a wide range of start up information, useful links and contacts, checklists for new exporters, frequently asked questions, an events list, enquiry service, and sales leads from around the world. A number of 'Market Desks' provide collated market advice and information on specific countries. The Export Promoter Initiative helps small and medium-sized enterprises to win business overseas. Export promoters are industry experts seconded to the Department of Trade and Industry. They are market specialists or generalists who provide their services free of charge.

The UK Trade & Investment information centre provides resources for people to undertake their own market research at a specialist library. The information held includes business statistics, country reports, foreign trade directories, market reports, and guides to doing business. This service is administered by the British Chambers of Commerce (the website address is given below).

For people who cannot visit the information centre, the UK Trade & Investment Support for Export Marketing Research allows a business to employ an experienced researcher to do the work. You will need to discuss your information requirements over the telephone, and the cost of obtaining it is quoted (charged per half hour of research time). Results can often be supplied the same day.

It may be more appropriate for you to obtain the advice of a professional export marketing research adviser. He or she can advise you on whether specific marketing surveys are needed and how to get started. They can also point out to you any financial support available for approved marketing research studies undertaken overseas. The advice might include considering using professional consultants, training up your business's own staff, purchasing published market research, and using research commissioned by trade associations.

It is possible to commission tailored market information from Commercial Officers at embassies and other overseas missions. Research will be commissioned through the local UK Trade & Investment service. Such reports might include advice on the suitability of a particular product, information about local competition, advice on marketing methods, tests of local response to products, and lists of suitable contacts and agents. These reports, and the research time spent on them, are charged for. For reports costing more than £600, the business may be eligible for a grant of up to 50%. This grant must be used on a visit to the chosen market within six months of receiving the report.

Help with export promotion

A broad range of assistance is available to help with the promotion of a business and its goods or services, within an export market. This can be anything from a tailored programme of publicity in an overseas market (including an introductory press release), to financial help to enable attendance at trade fairs in target countries, including subsidised trade missions via Chambers of Commerce, and so on.

Help with identifying appropriate contacts

Help can be provided in identifying appropriate contacts in the target country to act as representatives of the business, for example, import agents. Using information about the products or services, an investigation can be carried out to help identify the most suitable representative for your organisation. If your business has already identified a potential representative, or one has approached you, suitability checks can be arranged. You must remember, however, that these often will not advise on creditworthiness.

UK Trade & Investment also provides information about trade fairs and exhibitions held in the United Kingdom (the website address is given below) which can help organisations to identify contacts, business opportunities, or potential export partners.

Guidance on countering problems with the language barrier

The National Languages for Export Campaign can assist your business to develop effective language and cultural strategies needed to succeed in non-English speaking countries. The Campaign offers a range of practical services to enable businesses to make more informed choices about communication needs, including a national database of language trainers, translators, and interpreters; how-to-do-it guides and expert software; and a subsidised on-site communication review.

Pointing out potential export opportunities

TradeUK is UK Trade & Investment's export information service. It alerts UK businesses to opportunities around the world. Trade-UK's Exporters Database gives the United Kingdom's businesses a free Internet entry on the government's official National Exporters Database. The database currently contains over 57,000 UK business entries. This means that anyone with Internet access can contact a company if they are interested in its goods and services. Trade-UK Export Sales Lead Service supplies UK businesses with current, detailed export enquiries automatically via e-mail. TradeUK can also provide information about electronic commerce.

 WHAT TO AVOID
Not keeping up to date
It is a good idea to check the current services provided by UK Trade & Investment, as there may be updated schemes or services in development which are more suitable for your business's requirements. It is also important to keep up to date with, and check, the current prices of information and services with the relevant organisations.

Not getting the right advice
The local Business Link (in England), Business Gateway (in Scotland), Business Connect (in Wales), Invest Northern Ireland office, Learning and Skills Councils (LSCs) in England and the National Council for Education and Training in Wales, and Local Enterprise Company (LEC) or Enterprise Agency can all offer help and guidance. The website of UK Trade & Investment is also invaluable, since it provides businesses with instant information, market reports and opportunities, and so on.

RECOMMENDED LINKS
British Chambers of Commerce:
www.britishchambers.org.uk
Business Eye (Wales):
www.businesseye.org.uk
Business Link (England):
www.businesslink.org
Business Gateway (Scotland):
www.bgateway.com
Department of Trade and Industry:
www.dti.gov.uk
Invest Northern Ireland:
www.investni.com
Scottish Development International:
www.sti.org.uk
UK Trade & Investment:
www.uktradeinvest.gov.uk
UK Trade & Investment Information
  Centre:
**www.uktradeinvest.gov.uk/information_
  centre/home/welcome**
UK Trade & Investment also provides
  information about trade fairs and
  exhibitions held in the United Kingdom:
www.exhibitions.co.uk
TradeUK:
www.tradeuk.com
WalesTrade International:
www.walestrade.com

SEE ALSO
Exporting (p. 512)
Exporting for the First Time (p. 339)
Importing for the First Time (p. 346)
Timing the Decision to Export (p. 333)

WORKING ONLINE

Setting Up a Basic Website

GETTING STARTED

A website is a way of informing customers and other groups such as suppliers, journalists, or employees about your company. A basic website involves delivering essential information that is easy to read and well laid out. In website design, simplicity is always best. A website must also be actively promoted to make people aware of its existence. When approaching website design, ask yourself the following important questions:

- Who are the people that I want to communicate with (your target market)?
- How am I going to structure my information so it is easy to navigate and read?
- How am I going to let people know that my website exists?
- How am I going to keep my website updated and keep people informed of new content?

FAQS

How much information should I include on a website?

Provide the information that your visitors are likely to read. Don't fill your website with irrelevant and/or repetitive information as it will clutter your site and make the important information hard to find.

How often should I change website content?

You should change your content whenever you have something new and important to say, and whenever content already on the site is out of date. Ideally you should try to publish fresh content every week.

Can I transfer printed copy to the website?

Printed copy can be used as a starting point for web copy, but the structure and length would probably be unsuitable. People like to read short, punchy copy on the Web, so snappy headings and summaries are important. For a website to be truly effective, you must also use links (known as 'hypertext') so that people can click through for further information if they need it.

MAKING IT HAPPEN

Know who you want to reach

Before you do anything, decide who you want to reach. Prioritise your information for your most important audiences. Ask yourself:

- Do I want to reach new customers? In new markets?
- What can I say on my website that will turn a potential customer into an actual one?
- Do I want to offer support for existing customers?
- Do I want to provide information to attract new staff?

Keep it simple

Website design is about the design and delivery of information, not about graphic design. Only a small proportion of Internet users have access to broadband, so it is best to avoid fancy graphics and moving images. They slow down a site and frustrate visitors looking for information. Good website design has simple layout and rich content that is well organised. The best, most successful websites in the world (Yahoo, Microsoft, Amazon) don't employ fancy gimmicks; neither should you. Keep it simple. Maximise the content and minimise the presentation.

Structure your information well

When people come to your website, they want to find information quickly. They have come for a purpose and they are probably impatient and sceptical. It is therefore essential to make your website as accessible and easy to navigate as possible.

A well-structured website needs good links that allow the visitor to navigate to other sections of the site. Without these links, a page becomes a dead end.

Include important website sections and links

You should have at least some of the following sections on your website. Links to these sections should be provided in a set of essential links placed prominently on every page of the website.

Home page

The home page is the first page on your website and the most important, as it is usually the first page visitors see. From a linking point of view, the home page is referred to as 'Home'. It should always be the first link in your set of essential links. The home page itself should be full of punchy, attention-grabbing headings and summaries that quickly inform the visitor of, for example, what you do, what you have to sell, or what special offers you have. The Microsoft home page (**www.microsoft.com**) is a great example of using a home page well.

What's New

This section contains information on important news, events, and press releases. Always keep this section updated, and make sure that you date each entry. You should plan to add an entry for this section at least once a week, but remember to remove old items too.

About

This section should contain essential information about your business or organisation. If the section contains a lot of information it should be broken down into manageable subsections. 'About' information includes the following:

- mission: a short description of the organisation and what it seeks to achieve.
- key strengths: key products, market position, manufacturing, skills, distribution
- company background
- management team: pictures and short biographies of key members of the management team
- financial information: annual results
- contact and location details: this should link to the Contact section on your website

Products

This is the core part of your website, containing the things you have to sell. It should contain a brief overview of products and services and links to detailed information on specific products or services, containing:

- product/services description
- product applications
- business case and ROI (return on investment): how using your product can make and/or save money
- specifications
- purchase and delivery details
- frequently asked questions (FAQs)
- pricing (be sure to specify currency);
- product reviews
- where you sell to (specify the countries or regions you do or do not sell to)

Purchase

This is an essential link if you have a facility that allows people to buy direct from your website. Ideally you should also create a small graphic to be displayed prominently, particularly on the home page, informing customers that they can purchase your products online.

Customers

People want to know who your customers are. Include a list of your key customers and a selection of quotes and case studies.

Partners

If you have a number of partners and joint ventures, you should have a section describing them, explaining how they allow you to deliver a better service.

Contact

This section should contain all your essential contact information including:

- e-mail address
- postal address and map of location
- telephone and fax

Search

If your website has more than 50 pages, you need a search facility to enable visitors to find information. Aim to have a search box on every single page of your website, preferably near the top.

Offer an e-mail newsletter

Every website should offer an e-mail news-letter. If visitors give their e-mail address on their first visit, you can send them a regular weekly or monthly e-mail newsletter to tell them what's new.

Use metadata

Every web page should have a title. Where appropriate, you should create 'metadata' for your content. This is a method of describing your content and it should include: classification (type of information), page title and headings, summary, date of publication, author name, and keywords that appear in the text. Search engines use this metadata to index your website prop-erly, so that visitors can find quickly what they are looking for.

Make sure you have proper footer information

The bottom of every page should have footer information containing:

- a list of the essential links for the website
- essential contact details: main address, telephone and fax, e-mail
- the copyright notice
- your privacy policy

Remember to promote your website

Promotional strategies include:

- registering with the major search engines (Alta Vista, Google, Yahoo), as well as search engines specific to your industry or sector
- making sure that your website and e-mail address are on all your promotional literature

Decide whether to do it yourself or get a design company

If you are a competent computer user, you may well be able to do most of the work yourself, using packages such as Microsoft FrontPage or Macromedia's Dreamweaver, but you may require a graphic designer to help you with design issues.

WHAT TO AVOID

Being too clever

Some sites try too hard to entertain without providing hard information. Animation, multimedia, video clips, and other tricks can obscure important data. Many visitors are deterred immediately by a home page that features animation.

Poor classification, navigation, and search

Good classification, navigation, and search are essential for a successful website. Cus-tomers expect easy access to the informa-tion they want. If they can't find it easily on your site, they will go somewhere else. Structure is critical because it helps people find their way around.

Content that is difficult to read

Many websites try to impress by using lots of colour, but the easiest text to read is black on a white background. Keep paragraphs, line lengths, and documents short.

RECOMMENDED LINKS

Builder.com, a detailed source of information on design:
www.builder.com
Webmonkey, a dynamic, contemporary source of detailed information on design:
www.webmonkey.com

SEE ALSO

Computers, Information Technology, and E-commerce (p. 499)
Coping with Computer Viruses (p. 362)
Writing Well for the Web (p. 370)

Outsourcing Your Website

GETTING STARTED

As your business grows, you may become dependent on a larger and more sophisticated website. Running a large website is a complex operation that requires substantial IT architecture and support. This can take the focus of your business away from its core business of selling, marketing, and supporting your products and services. It will also tie up any technical staff on your team. Outsourcing involves hiring third party professionals to manage and run your website's operations for an ongoing fee.

When approaching outsourcing, remember to:

- develop a proper strategy: outsourcing needs a serious approach
- ensure that a comprehensive contract is in place, and that there are proper metrics and management structures
- make sure that you choose a robust, well-funded outsourcing vendor with a good track record for service and support

FAQS

What are the key factors that drive outsourcing?

- The need to focus on core business activities rather than on building up a large IT function.
- Lack of sufficiently skilled staff to run complex web operations.
- Flexibility: a quality outsource vendor can respond more quickly to rapid changes in customer demand.

MAKING IT HAPPEN

Develop an outsourcing strategy

When considering the outsourcing of Web functions, think about exactly why you want to outsource.

Do you want to outsource:

- to reduce costs?
- to give greater flexibility?
- because you can't find the right IT skills?
- to guarantee a more reliable service?
- to focus better on your core business?
- to keep your IT department as small as possible?
- to reduce staffing levels?

You should have a clear strategy of your vision and objectives long before you start discussions with vendors.

Be prepared

Deciding on an outsourcer is a complex and time-consuming process, so you must think very carefully about what you want to achieve and why. When developing your strategy, it is best not to be too open with outsourcing vendors. They will naturally want to sell you what they have, and may try to shape your thinking in a way that is not appropriate. It is better initially to go to a quality independent consultant who will help you think through all the issues.

When you finally engage with your short-list of outsourcing vendors, they will have many detailed questions on how your operations are currently run. If you cannot answer these questions you will slow the whole process down, and will encourage the vendor to put forward a less fully and clearly defined contract than if it had had all the required information.

Choose a robust, well-funded outsourcer

Choose a company that has a good reputation, is well funded, and has a good track record. When choosing an outsourcing partner, ask the following questions:

- How stable and well funded is it?
- Has it got a satisfied customer base?
- Has it successfully dealt before with the same needs as mine?

Make certain that you receive the right service and support

The more you outsource, the more dependent you become on your outsourcer, so it is vital that your chosen vendor delivers comprehensive service and support.

Remember that choosing an outsourcing vendor takes time

Outsourcing is a major strategic move involving much research and negotiation, so do not impose tight deadlines on yourself.

Ensure that a comprehensive contract is in place

An outsourcing contract should be precise, and should describe exactly what is to be delivered. It should state penalties for non-delivery. Legal expertise should be brought in early in the process, ideally when the RFP is being developed, so that everyone understands the legal implications of everything that is being asked for and promised. However, the IT environment is constantly changing, and the contract must recognise this. Quality contracts are designed to facilitate later change and renegotiation.

Avoid long-term contracts. Vendors will argue that, because they have to bear a high upfront cost, you should sign a five to ten year contract with them. This does not make sense in a rapidly changing IT and e-commerce world; a two-year contract is a more reasonable option.

Determine how this relationship will be managed and measured

You must develop a set of metrics to measure how the outsourcer is meeting the objectives set by the contract. By doing this regularly, and addressing issues as they arise, major disputes can be avoided.

Outsourcing is as much about managing the day-to-day relationship between you and the outsource vendor as it is about managing the technology. While a contract is important, prevention, by management that keeps a regular track of what is expected and what has been delivered, is better than cure.

Have a corporate technology strategy

You are outsourcing your technology, not your technology strategy, and will always need skilled in-house resources to help you plan your direction from a technological point of view. Your outsourcer cannot do this; if they do, their recommendations will reflect their own strategy rather than yours.

Remember that outsourcing is outsourcing

You cannot have the same level of control over the day-to-day running of your IT infrastructure after you outsource it, but some businesses forget that and try to achieve such control. This is counter-productive. You chose your outsourcer because—you hope—they do the job better and more efficiently than you do.

Consider the security issues

Outsourcing creates an increased security risk. You must establish that the outsource vendor will adhere to your security policy, and that all work done integrates proper security procedures. Ask yourself:

- What is the outsourcer's security policy?
- What are its data backup and disaster recovery procedures?
- How is your data safeguarded from its other customers?
- How is your data safeguarded from its own employees?
- How is it insured in relation to security breaches?

WHAT TO AVOID
Outsource vendors who promise too much

Outsource vendors have been known to over-promise and under-deliver.

Getting rid entirely of the internal IT web operation

Some internal IT resource is necessary to take a more strategic view of the web operation in order to plan its future evolution.

Going for the lowest price

Going for the lowest price rarely works out well in the long term. Service and support are critical elements in outsourcing, and the outsourcer that offers the lowest price is also, generally speaking, the one who will offer the least support.

Not being able to deliver the right information

To deliver an outsourcing service, the vendor requires very detailed information on your current IT and web setup. If you can't provide this information, you slow the whole process down, which results in imperfect solutions.

Badly framed contracts

Long-term contracts are too often developed on the basis of short-term financial goals, such as cost cutting. What invariably happens is that the contract is unsuitable and renegotiation is required.

RECOMMENDED LINKS

Firmbuilder.com:
www.firmbuilder.com/home.asp
Outsourcing Center:
www.outsourcing-center.com

SEE ALSO

Computers, Information Technology, and E-commerce (p. 499)

Managing E-mail

GETTING STARTED

E-mail is a powerful communications tool. Used properly, it can allow a business to work more efficiently and to communicate more actively with customers. E-mail is fast and cost-effective; however, it is too often treated in a casual manner. Like every other business tool, the use of e-mail needs to be managed and this can seem overwhelming if you don't have that much experience of the online world. This actionlist sets out to give you some pointers, though, so bear in mind the following

- Because e-mail is such an easy form of communication it is often misused, thus leading to e-mail overload.
- If your business has a website, it's important to implement and monitor a policy for responding to e-mails so that you can keep on top of them all.
- Writing good e-mails is a skill that is too often absent in e-mail communication, but it can be learned.

MAKING IT HAPPEN

Manage e-mail overload

E-mail has revolutionised the way business is done today, but so many e-mails are sent that there is a danger that important messages may be swamped.

It is estimated that by 2005 there will be 36 billion e-mails sent every day. To prevent your business from succumbing to e-mail overload, you need to establish standards on how e-mail is sent and replied to. Training may well be required in order to ensure that you (and your staff, if you have any) understand and implement best practice in e-mail management.

E-mail management on a website

If you have a website, show contact details prominently. A key part of such contact is e-mail. You must decide how many e-mail addresses you will have: will each department have its own special e-mail address, for example, sales@mycompany.com; support@mycompany.com? If you have staff to help you deal with e-mails, decide who e-mails should go to. What happens if the addressee is unavailable? Should managers be cc'd on all incoming e-mails? How will e-mail communication be tracked?

You also need to think about setting some standards for replying to messages. Studies indicate that many businesses are unprofessional at responding to e-mail communications, and those that would never dream of leaving a phone to ring unanswered behave in a lackadaisical manner when it comes to replying to e-mail, so work out a time limit for replying to received messages, stick to it, and monitor it. You may also decide to have an automatic reply message for all your addresses; this will inform the sender that the e-mail has been received, and that a response will be given within X hours.

Write and reply to e-mails

When you're writing or replying to an e-mail, bear the following points in mind.

- Respond quickly, but only respond—or write in the first place—when you have something worthwhile to say.
- Make the subject line interesting, if it's not interesting, then the chances of your e-mail being opened are diminished.
- If you are replying to an e-mail, change the subject line as appropriate.
- Although the writing style for e-mails is—in general—casual, it should not be over-casual. Don't try to be too friendly. Always strive to be polite. It is good manners to address the person you are communicating with, and to sign/type your name at the end.

- Check your spelling; e-mails that are filled with spelling or grammatical errors reflect poorly on the sender.
- Keep e-mails short. Get to the point. Long e-mails put people off.
- Avoid attachments, unless they are essential. A general rule is never to send an attachment to someone who is not expecting it.
- Don't reply in anger. It is very easy to respond to an e-mail that makes you angry. Don't. Count to at least ten before replying. Remember, e-mail is a rather distant medium of communication, and it is very easy for misunderstandings to occur.
- Be careful what you write. Write nothing in an e-mail that you can't defend in a court of law.

SEE ALSO

Computers, Information Technology, and E-commerce (p. 499)
Coping with Computer Viruses (p. 362)
Using E-mail Marketing Effectively (p. 373)

Coping with Computer Viruses

GETTING STARTED

Computer viruses are a growing threat on the Internet, and if your business operates online they are something you need to bear in mind as they cost companies billions of pounds globally every year. By September 2001, it was estimated that one in every 300 e-mails contained a virus, up from one in every 700 in October 2000. In addition, it is now possible to get a computer virus by visiting a website or simply by opening an e-mail. To combat computer viruses:

- ensure that you have the very latest antivirus software and that you scan your entire computer regularly
- ensure that you have the very latest software security patches for your computer
- immediately delete e-mails that you are in any way suspicious of
- don't download anything from the Internet except from reputable websites
- back up your data regularly

MAKING IT HAPPEN
Understand computer viruses, Trojan horses, and worms

In its simplest form, a computer virus attaches itself to computer files, and then seeks to replicate itself. Viruses can infect all sorts of files, from program and system files to Word documents and HTML files. The Internet enables viruses to spread with extraordinary speed.

What is known as a 'Trojan horse' pretends to serve a useful function, such as a screen saver. However, as soon as it is run, it carries out its true purpose, which can be anything from using the computer as a host to infect other computers, to wiping the entire hard disk of the computer. Never download software over the Internet unless you are sure of its authenticity.

A computer worm does not try to damage the files it infects. Its objective is rather to replicate itself as quickly and as often as possible. Computer worms are a major drain on the Internet because they clog up bandwidth.

Remember that prevention is much better than cure

Viruses can be extremely difficult to get rid of. You may think you have cleaned them out with your antivirus software, but they may well have inserted hidden code in your operating system that is almost impossible

to detect. It is, therefore, essential to stop viruses from getting into your computer in the first place. You do this by:

- making sure that you have the very latest antivirus software; popular antivirus software types include McAfee and Norton
- joining an e-mail list that will inform you of new virus attacks. As soon as you hear of them, check your vendor for the latest updates.
- scanning your entire computer for viruses at least once a week
- always making sure that you have the very latest security patches for your computer software. Viruses are always at their most potent in the first hours and days after their release, so it is vital to implement software patches as soon as they become available.
- if you use recent releases of Microsoft Windows, regularly checking www.microsoft.com/security//for news and updates. Microsoft also has a service that will check your computer for security weaknesses. It can be found at: www.microsoft.com/technet/mpsa/start.asp
- only downloading software from reputable websites
- deleting e-mails you are in any way suspicious of

Act immediately if you become infected

Deal with the threat immediately. Never

wait, as the longer the virus is on your computer the more files it can infect. Some viruses, such as Code Red, open up your computer system to potential hacking. There is no guaranteed way to know that your system does not contain some malicious code that will be used at a future date, even when the offending virus has been deleted. If a virus such as Code Red has indeed infected your system, and if you want to be absolutely safe, reformat your hard disk and reinstall all your software again.

Cope with virus hoaxes

The Internet is full of virus hoaxes that waste time. If you get an e-mail about a new virus, go to the website of your antivirus software provider, and check if the warning is real. In order to judge whether it's a hoax, ask yourself the following questions:

- does the message come from a reputable source?
- does it ask you to e-mail it on to anyone you know? If it does, it's probably a hoax.
- does it have a reputable link for more information?

RECOMMENDED LINKS

McAfee antivirus software:
www.mcafee.com
Norton antivirus software:
www.norton.com

SEE ALSO

Computers, Information Technology, and E-commerce (p. 499)
Making Your Website Secure (p. 394)
Managing E-mail (p. 360)
Setting Up a Basic Website (p. 354)

Understanding the Key Principles of Internet Marketing

GETTING STARTED

If you work online, you need to think about Internet marketing and what it can do for your business. Internet marketing is about giving, rather than getting, attention. An adjunct to traditional marketing, it supports and enhances the overall marketing message by providing comprehensive information that answers consumers' questions about a particular product or service. Internet marketing also exploits the networking capabilities of the Web by leveraging online community activities, linking, affiliate marketing, viral marketing, e-mail marketing, and loyalty programmes. When approaching Internet marketing, keep the following in mind:

- when visitors come to a website they are already aware of the brand. They want information.
- use Internet technology to understand the needs of your customers, so that you can offer them just the right information and products
- remember that the Internet empowers the consumer. A dissatisfied consumer can use the networking capabilities of the Internet to undermine your brand.

FAQS

What sort of products and services is Internet marketing best suited to?

Internet marketing is best suited to:

- products and services that require a lot of information to sell. For example, travel and books are ideal for the Internet. Travel is a very information-intensive product. People want times, prices, and information about the destination. When buying books, they are strongly influenced by reviews, opinions of other readers, tables of contents, and sample chapters.
- products and services that people feel strongly about, such as books, music, and films. Fans network with other fans in online communities to discuss their favourite artists. Much of the huge success of *The Blair Witch Project* was credited to fans getting together on the Internet and promoting it through enthusiastic reviews and dialogue.
- products and services that are bought by the Internet demographic. Although the Internet demographic has broadened, it is still generally the domain of the well educated and better off. Those working in technology and academia are very well represented.

What about online advertising? Does it work?

As a pure branding tool, online advertising does not have the same impact as television or glossy media, because of bandwidth restrictions. Studies indicate that most consumers avoid interactive ads because they simply take too much time to download.

However, the real power of online advertising does not lie in mass marketing but, rather, in its ability to reach niche markets and target just the right consumer with just the right product. Advertising success is claimed by opt-in e-mail-based marketing, where consumers request information on a particular product or service. In online advertising, the scattershot approach is out and laser point focus is in.

MAKING IT HAPPEN
Recognise that Internet marketing is part of the overall package

The objective of Internet marketing should be to integrate it into the overall marketing strategy, where it supports and is supported by offline marketing activities. However, that is not to say Internet marketing doesn't have its own unique characteristics. Internet marketing is not about a big idea, some compelling graphics, and a killer catch-phrase. Offline marketing brings consumers to the website with such approaches. Their interest has been aroused. They have questions. Internet marketing answers those questions by having comprehensive information on offer. Remember, if people have read the brochure offline, they're not coming to the website to read it again.

Understand the consumer better

Effective Internet marketing focuses on getting to know the consumer better. The objective here is to understand consumers' exact needs so that exactly the right products and services can be offered to them at exactly the right time and in exactly the right way. The strength of the Internet is also its weakness, though. While people want information, they also suffer from massive information overload. The Internet marketer who can cut through the overload and bring to time-starved consumers the information they need is much more likely to succeed. Find websites and e-mail databases that attract the exact type of consumer you wish to target. Analyse statistics generated as a result of consumers visiting your website and react appropriately to key trends that these statistics throw up. With more sophisticated websites, you can customise consumers' experiences through personalisation systems, whereby a unique and finely targeted set of information and products is presented to each individual visitor.

Back it up with e-mail marketing

Since the Web was launched, perceptive marketers have been stressing that every website should have an e-mail marketing strategy. Consider that consumers must actively decide to go to a website, but with e-mail they join a database in which they can be regularly informed of products, services, and offers that the organisation has. The key to e-mail marketing success is getting people who want the information to join a database from which they will receive regular e-mail alerts and newsletters. Of course, the information they receive needs to be of a type and quality that they signed up to get.

Tap into the networking ability of the Internet

The Internet is a community and it offers a tremendously powerful means for people and organisations to network. Linking is one of the simplest yet most effective Internet marketing devices there is. It underpins affiliate marketing efforts by websites such as Amazon.com. Linking is like embedded word of mouth. If another website links to you, it is essentially recommending you to its own visitors. Viral marketing is a network effect, whereby groups of consumers create a buzz about a product or service by e-mailing friends and/or creating their own websites. Consumers gain a power through Internet networking that they traditionally did not have. There are hundreds if not thousands of websites and activist groups set up by disgruntled consumers with the objective of attacking particular organisations.

Make advertising and promotion highly focused

A website, because it is not a physical store, faces a constant challenge to achieve and maintain awareness among its target market. Traditional offline marketing, such as press advertising or direct mail, plays a key role here, but so too do specific online marketing strategies. Registration with a commercial search engine is an obvious one. This is not some simple, one-off task but an ongoing activity because the rules by which search engines classify sites are constantly changing. Banner ads can be effective, if properly targeted. Banner ad design needs to apply the unique characteristics of the medium, and not simply apply traditional advertising principles. A specialist agency can advise on suitable creative approaches. Getting other websites to link can be very effective, but this is a slow process, the rewards of which are delivered over time. E-mail signature files can promote a website effectively.

Remember that affiliate marketing and loyalty programmes can deliver

There is no better example of the success of affiliate marketing than that of Amazon .com. Literally hundreds of thousands of websites offer books and other products to their visitors using Amazon's affiliate programme. It's a win-win situation. The web site in question offers an extra service that is easy to establish and delivers a certain amount of revenue. The affiliate sponsor opens up a new channel every time another website hooks into them.

However, like all marketing techniques, it's not some magic formula. It needs to be thought through properly and applied professionally.

Loyalty programmes can work on the Internet, though they have been over-hyped. Key elements in the management of loyalty programmes are the use of customer databases and the tracking of customer purchasing behaviour. The Internet facilitates such activities, and can thus be a medium through which loyalty programmes can be run. Getting the incentive structure right is critical to the success of loyalty programmes.

Use online communities to build loyalty

Using chat, discussion boards, and e-mail mailing lists to bring people together to discuss issues of interest can enhance brand loyalty. It can also be a source of unique and cost-effective content. However, it doesn't work in all situations, and online communities that are not properly managed can quickly lose momentum.

Remember that some old marketing tricks still apply

Discounts, competitions, and free offers work as well online as they do offline. While perhaps too much has been offered free on the Internet in order to build business, properly used, these traditional marketing techniques can be effective on websites.

 WHAT TO AVOID
Being flashy
Although the Internet has been around

since 1996, it is amazing how many marketers still think it's TV on a computer screen. On the Web, visitors don't really care about the graphics; they just want the information. Splash screens, audio, video and Macromedia Flash animations should be kept to an absolute minimum.

Not building and leveraging a customer database

Bringing people to a website without strongly encouraging them to join some sort of a database is a serious mistake. Studies indicate that many consumers will visit a website once, rarely if ever to return. It's vital to get them into a database so that ongoing communication can be set up.

Focusing on volume of visitors rather than quality targeting

In the early years of the Web there was a frantic rush to build visitor traffic to a website, without any real focus on issues such as revenue per visitor, numbers who joined databases. Acquisition costs for visitors were high, and as the large number of visitors did not translate into valuable customers, the business model collapsed for many websites.

Focusing purely on purchase activity on a website

There is a need to understand how a website contributes to the overall purchasing process. For example, a great many people visit car websites before they make a purchase, but very few will actually make the purchase online. The key is to forget about measuring by crude visitor volume numbers and focus on the quality of the targeting, along with the influence that the website and e-mail communications have on purchase behaviour.

RECOMMENDED LINKS

Adventive e-mail mailing lists:
www.adventive.com
Web marketing information centre:
www.wilsonweb.com/webmarket

Promoting Your Website Effectively

GETTING STARTED

Launching a website is like opening up a shop at the North Pole or the Sahara Desert. Nobody will know that you are there unless you promote yourself! Website promotion is not some one-off event that occurs at launch. It is an ongoing activity that demands a keen understanding of promotional techniques that are unique to the Web. It also requires full integration into offline marketing and promotional activities. When approaching website promotion, consider the following:

- it requires a range of promotional strategies, both online and offline
- it's an ongoing activity
- it should be fully integrated into the overall promotional and marketing strategy

FAQS

Why is website promotion of such importance?

In the property business people talk about 'location, location, location'. Well, a website doesn't really have a location. It's not on a high street where thousands of people walk by every day. Without such physical visibility, a website has a major problem attracting consumers. That is one reason why a clicks-and-mortar strategy (combining physical stores with an Internet presence) is deemed so essential for the success of a website. In a physical store, and in its related marketing and promotional activity, consumers can be exposed to the benefits of the website constantly.

What is banner advertising and does it promote a website well?

Banner advertising is the use of rectangular advertisements or logos across the width of page on an Internet site. Businesses often place advertisements of this type on a third party's site to attract users to visit their own.

The jury is still out on the effectiveness of banner advertising. However, prices for banner advertising have dropped significantly in recent years and there is certainly value to be had. It's really down to the target market you are after and whether that accurately matches the profile of visitors coming to a particular website. Online advertising systems allow for a level of targeting and measurement that is impossible in much offline media. So, if you can get to the right target market at the right price, then the equation makes sense.

Does online advertising and promotion have to cost a lot of money?

No. Online ads have dropped significantly in price and, with proper investigation, very good value can be had. Online promotion requires dedication, but a few hours spent every week can deliver real results in the longer term.

MAKING IT HAPPEN

Get linked

Linking is one of the most powerful means of promoting a website. A link from another website is essentially embedded word of mouth, a recommendation from that site to its visitors also to visit you. The Web is huge, with millions of websites, many of them of poor quality. People who use the Internet have become very sceptical and conservative in their behaviour. Building credibility is thus of key importance to online success. There is no better way to build such credibility than to have hundreds—ideally thousands—of other websites linking to you.

Google, perhaps the Web's most popular search engine, achieved popularity because its search results were seen as more relevant than those of other search engines. The way it achieved better results was by analysing a website and seeing how many external websites had linked to it. The more links the website had, the higher in the results Google placed it. Thus, if you want your website to feature prominently with Google, the more links you can get the better.

But linking is not simply about getting placed higher in search engine results. Think of each link as another 'road' to your website; another way that the visitor can get to you. Getting links is not easy. It involves finding websites that attract your target market and convincing them to include a link to you. Usually, they will not do this unless you have valuable content that could be of interest to their customers. Another approach is to pay for a link, either through monthly fees or through what is called 'click-through payments'—you pay for every visit that results from a particular link.

Get registered with search engines

Because so many people use commercial search engines, it's extremely important that your website is properly registered. Keep the following in mind:

- there are hundreds of search engines and directories but only a handful that really matter. These include: Yahoo, Google, Alta Vista, Microsoft Network, Excite, Lycos, Go, HotBot, All The Web, Direct Hit, Look Smart, Northern Light.
- there may well be specialist search engines and directories for your particular industry. You should register with them.
- all search engines used to be free to register with, but this is no longer the case for an increasing number. You need to consider if the fee is worth it.
- an increasing number of search engines sell special placements in their search results. You can choose a keyword and when that keyword is input by a searcher, a short promotion for your website will appear.
- search engines need to be monitored regularly, as they can change the rules by which search results are presented. A set of keywords needs to be drawn up and the search engine regularly searched using these keywords. If you find your website is dropping down the results page, you may need to re-register. Also, if you launch a new product or service, you should consider registering that.
- don't register popular keywords with a

website just for the sake of increased visitors. It achieves very little, and some search engines will remove websites that continuously abuse search registration processes.

Use banner and other online advertising

As stated above, banner advertising doesn't work for everyone, but it may work for your business. It's particularly useful where a new website, product, or service is being launched. Banner ads can be paid for either on a cost-per-thousand (CPM) basis or per click-through, where the seller gets paid wherever a visitors clicks on an ad. Online ads should be a call to action, with the key objective being to get the person to click on the ad. There are a variety of online advertising options:

- banner advertisements. These ads can go across the top or bottom of the page or down the side, like wallpaper.
- interstitials. These are ads that appear before the actual web page loads. They certainly get the visitors' attention but can be very frustrating.
- pop-under ads. These ads launch in a separate browser window and have been controversial.

Consider e-mail as a form of advertising

E-mail can be a very effective form of advertising, particularly when the advertiser is reaching a targeted list that has opted in to receive information on particular products or services. The thing to watch out for in e-mail advertising is spam. Spam is mass-distributed e-mail that is unsolicited by the receiver. People are increasingly annoyed at receiving spam, and anti-spam legislation has been enacted or is pending in many countries. It's not simply about whether spam is legal or not—but it is certainly unethical, and no reputable organisation should use such an approach.

Remember e-mail signature files

An e-mail signature is the text at the bottom of an e-mail that contains information about the sender. It is also possible to place a short, two-line ad there (e-mail signatures should not be longer than five lines). E-mail signature promotion was used very effectively when Andersen Consulting changed its name to Accenture. For a period after the name change, every time one of Accenture's 60,000 employees sent an e-mail, there was a short e-mail signature ad notifying the receiver of the change of name.

Integrate with offline marketing and promotion

Every single piece of offline literature should contain the website address and, where appropriate, an e-mail address. This includes: all stationery (letterheads, business cards, compliment slips, receipts, invoices); all product packaging; training and support manuals; all ads that are placed in print, radio, or television. If the organisation has physical stores, then promotional material should be placed prominently within these stores informing visitors of the website. When planning new offline promotional and marketing activities, you should seek ways to get consumers to go to the website. For example, the website could be the place where the consumer enters a competition.

Include competitions and free giveaways

Consumers are as likely to react positively to quality web-based competitions and special promotions as they do to such tactics in the offline world. Competitions and special offers give the website a sense of vibrancy. A key objective of such promotions should be to get consumers to join databases, used in the future to inform people of other special offers and relevant information.

Use your home page

A key objective of a home page is to promote important content, products, and services situated deeper in the website. That's the job of sharp, punchy headings and summaries, supported on occasion by small graphics. The Microsoft website (www.microsoft.com) is a perfect example of how to use a home page to promote key

events, special offers, product launches, upgrades, and so on.

WHAT TO AVOID

Seeking quantity of visitors over quality

In the early days of the Web there was a mad rush—fuelled by venture capital—to drive as many visitors as possible to websites. A stream of new brands emerged, each one seeking to out-do the next with ad spend. There is still a tendency to consider quantity over quality when it comes to building visitor numbers to a website. This is a serious and expensive mistake.

Focusing purely on search engines

Search engines are important, but they should still be only a part of an online promotional strategy. Also, abuse of search engines by bombarding them with popular keywords and other visitor-generating techniques merely serves to bulk up visitor figures. It does little or nothing for the bottom line.

Lack of integration with offline marketing

Organisations miss vital and cost-effective ways of promoting their websites by not fully utilising offline resources.

Lack of ongoing commitment

Too many websites have been launched enthusiastically, only to be left to wither in the wilderness of cyberspace. To be successful, promotion must be an ongoing activity.

RECOMMENDED LINK

Google:
www.directory.google.com

SEE ALSO

Applying a Viral Marketing Approach on the Internet (p. 376)
Computers, Information Technology, and E-commerce (p. 499)
Delivering the Benefits of Affiliate Marketing on the Web (p. 378)
Understanding the Key Principles of Internet Marketing (p. 364)
Using E-mail Marketing Effectively (p. 373)

Writing Well for the Web

GETTING STARTED

People read differently on the Web, so you need to write differently for the Web. Surprisingly, very few websites take the time to lay out their content in a way that will maximise its readability. Don't forget that it is more difficult to read on a screen than from paper, so you must write and lay out your content in a more simple, straightforward manner than you would in print. If you want to ensure that your content has the best chance of being read, focus on:

- shorter sentences, shorter paragraphs and shorter documents
- plentiful use of short, punchy, and descriptive headings and summaries
- larger font sizes and sans serif fonts, because they are easier to read
- straightforward, factual prose

FAQS

In what way do people read differently on the Web?

They scan, moving quickly across text, always looking in a hurry for the content they need. They are very fact-oriented. People don't read on the Web for pleasure— they read to do business, to be educated, to find out something—so they like to read content that gets to the point quickly.

People like reading short documents with links to more detailed information as appropriate. If a document is long, and people really have no choice but to read it, a significant number of them will print it out. In general, however, long documents tend to go unread.

Why do so many people regard web content as poor quality?

People don't trust the content they read on the Web because they come across so many websites with poor publishing standards. The Web gives everyone access to the tools of publishing, but giving someone a word processor does not make them a good writer. Too many websites lack proper editing standards. They also translate documents that were prepared for print directly to the Web; this may save money in the short term, but if people don't read the content, it is pointless. Some websites deliberately try to mislead people with their content. All this gives a poor impression to people who use the Web.

Is writing for the Web a difficult skill to learn?

It is not easy to learn how to write well, no matter what the medium is. However, writing for the Web is about concentrating on the facts. You don't need flowery prose; instead, you must be able to communicate the really important information in as few words as possible. This is not an easy thing to do, but with practice most people can master the basics.

MAKING IT HAPPEN

Recognise that if you're not read, you're dead

The connection between writing and reading is one that is not always considered: a surprising number of organisations create vast quantities of content without asking some obvious questions:

- Is anyone interested in reading this content?
- Is it written in a way that is understandable and easy to read?
- How are we going to let people know that we have just published this content?

Realise that less really is more

Writing is rarely about quantity, but it should always be about quality. It is easier to write 5,000 words of waffle than 500 words that are succinct, but 500 words is what is needed on the Web; less is definitely more.

Editing is essential

One of the primary functions of editing is to

get a long draft into shape. As George Orwell said: 'If it is possible to cut a word, always cut it.' We all have pet phrases that we love to put into sentences whenever we can. They may sound good to the writer, but very often add nothing to the meaning of what is being communicated. The Web is about functional writing; get to the point as quickly as you can and then stop.

Keep it short

When writing for the Web:

- documents should rarely be longer than 1,000 words: 500 to 700 is a good length to aim for
- paragraphs should be between 40 and 50 words
- try not to let your sentences go over 20 words

Write for the reader, not your ego

When writing, always keep in mind who it is you are writing for. Is it the sales rep, the technician, the support staff, the customer, the investor? Will they understand what you are writing about? Don't write to please yourself—write to please your reader and be clear and precise.

Focus on the headings

Headings are important on the Web for two central reasons. First, people scan, so the first thing they often do is to look for headings; if the heading doesn't attract their attention, then they probably won't read any further. Second, people use search engines a lot, and the most prominent things in a page of search results are the headings. The heading really has to sell the web page and convince the person to click for more information.

Writing headings well is an art, but here are a few rules that will help you get the basics right:

- keep them short. A heading should not be longer than five to eight words.
- make your point clear. For example, 'Nasdaq crashes to record low' is more informative than 'Apocalypse now for investors!'.
- use strong, direct language. Don't be sen-

sational, but at the same time don't be vague, and don't hedge.
- don't deceive the reader, for example by using 'Microsoft' in a heading just because you think people will then be more likely to read it. Remember, the job of the heading is to tell the reader succinctly what is in the document.

Use subheadings

In longer documents it is always a good idea to use subheadings, as they break up the text into the more readable chunks that readers like. Subheadings should be used every five to seven paragraphs.

Summarise the who, what, where, and when

Next to the heading, the summary is the most important piece of text. It should be descriptive, not wandering or indirect. Tell the reader what the document is about, and who, where, and when the information relates to.

Get down to write

'No man but a blockhead ever wrote. . .except for money,' according to Samuel Johnson. Sound advice. Writing is not easy but someone has to do it. The first rule of writing is reading: if you are asked to write a technical paper, read how other people write them. Read how they are written on your own website, on competitors' websites, in industry journals. Find a style that works well and copy it; use its techniques and approach to structure. Don't plagiarise, but never feel ashamed of finding good-quality writing and learning from it.

Learn how to edit

Even if you have an editor, you still want to send him or her a well-written draft. Here are a few steps to follow.

- Get a first draft written and don't throw it away.
- Leave it for a while—have a cup of tea— then print it out, or make the font size larger so that the text stands out more.
- Read it as if someone else wrote it. Be severe. Is it written in a way that the reader

can easily understand? What is the writer trying to say here? Is this sentence or paragraph necessary? Has the writer covered all the essential facts?

- First drafts are often too long. When preparing the second draft, cut ruthlessly, maybe by as much as half.
- Use your word count carefully. When you are asked to write something, always ask how many words are required. If you are not given a word count then decide on one yourself. Keep it as low as possible.

Explore collaborative writing

Computers and the Internet make collaborative writing far easier, and as a result it is becoming an increasingly popular approach to writing content. Collaborative writing works well if:

- the writers spend time working through the objectives of the writing exercise, and reach agreement on such necessary matters as the style, tone, and length of the piece
- there is a lot of content to be written that can benefit from the input of multiple disciplines
- people can be given defined segments of content to write, and/or the different skills of different people can be used, for example, when one person understands the subject well, while another is a good writer
- there are professional processes in place to facilitate collaboration
- the writers know and respect each other

✖ WHAT TO AVOID

Not focusing on the needs of the reader
A surprising number of websites fail to consider who their reader is, simply adding content for its own sake. If you ignore the needs of your reader, then your reader will ignore you.

Putting non-web formats onto the Web
Translating a 40-page Word document into HTML is a simple task; persuading someone to read it is another job entirely. Have you ever tried reading an Adobe PDF file on a screen? It's a painful experience. How many of your customers have read that Power-Point presentation you translated into HTML?

Putting every piece of content you can find on the Web
The Web is not a dumping ground for content. You might have 50,000 documents, with only 5,000 suitable for your website. Publishing the other 45,000 simply wastes your readers' time—not something you want to do.

Poor editing
It is almost impossible to create quality content without sending it through a professional editorial process. No matter how good the writer, his or her content will always benefit by being checked over by an editor.

Long, rambling documents
If, after reading the heading and summary, the average web reader hasn't understood what exactly you are trying to communicate to them, then chances are they will click the Back button. Readers on the web have become ruthless about their time.

RECOMMENDED LINK
Clickz Writing for the Web:
www.clickz.com/design

SEE ALSO
Computers, Information Technology, and E-commerce (p. 499)
Setting Up a Basic Website (p. 354)

Using E-mail Marketing Effectively

GETTING STARTED

E-mail should be an essential part of any Internet marketing strategy. If you have someone's e-mail address, you can send them information directly. But with e-mail it is important that the recipient wants the information you are sending. When considering e-mail, keep the following in mind:

- e-mail is a relatively cheap, but powerful communications tool—you can send thousands of e-mail newsletters in a simple, cost-effective way
- e-mail allows you to keep in regular contact with customers and to build up a rapport with them
- never send unsolicited e-mails (spam). E-mail should only deliver worthwhile information.

FAQS

How often should you contact customers by e-mail?

E-mail is a fast, simple, and cost-effective form of communication, so it is tempting to use it at every opportunity. However, unless the information is valuable, this can become annoying for customers. As a general rule, you should not send e-mail to people more than once a week, unless there is a specific and defined need. People are overloaded and if they see too many e-mails coming from you they will turn off. Whatever the frequency, make sure that you stick to your schedule, as people will be expecting it.

Should newsletters be free or chargeable?

It depends on the focus of your business. If you are publishing information, then it is hard to see how a business model can be developed that is advertising only. However, if you are using the information you send to help sell some other product or service, it is highly unlikely that anyone will be willing to pay for it.

What is spam?

Spam is mass-distributed, unsolicited e-mail. Spam is a major problem on the Internet today in that it is easy to buy a database of millions of e-mail addresses and send out unsolicited e-mails to them. If you want to be seen as a reputable business, you should avoid sending spam. Legislation is pending in a number of countries to make sending spam illegal.

What do the terms 'opt-in' and 'double opt-in' mean?

An opt-in approach is where someone actively decides to give you their e-mail address so that you can send them e-mail. However, the emerging convention is double opt-in. What happens here is that when a person receives a request to subscribe to an e-mail address, they reply to that address for verification that the request did in fact come from there. This ensures that the e-mail address was not maliciously set up by a third party.

Is it better to buy software or can it be rented?

Very often it is better to rent. There are a number of organisations that offer professional e-mail management services. To get a list of such companies, go to **www.directory.google.com/Top/Computers/Internet/Mailing_Lists/Hosting_Companies**.

MAKING IT HAPPEN
Isolate the information need

The first step in any e-mail strategy is to isolate the information need of your target market. What sort of information would they find useful? Would they like information on new products and special offers? Would they like information on trends within your industry? What sort of information would make them want to give you their e-mail address?

Define your publication scope and schedule

Once you have defined an information need, you must make clear what the scope of your e-mail publication is. What exactly will the person get if they subscribe? Unless you are delivering very time-sensitive information, a weekly publication is usually sufficient.

Make the subscription process prominent on your website

Getting people to subscribe is vital to the success of your e-mail strategy. There should therefore be a prominent subscription box on your website encouraging people to subscribe. Also, include subscription details in every mailing that you send out. Don't ask too many questions in the subscription process.

Many successful e-mail newsletter providers only ask for the e-mail address of the subscriber. That makes it a very easy and quick process for the potential subscriber. You can always ask for more information later on, when you have established a stronger relationship with the subscriber. As a rule, the more valuable the information is to the potential subscriber, the more information you can ask of them.

Make the unsubscription process as easy as possible

It is equally important to ensure that the unsubscription process is easy to use. People can get frustrated and angry if they find it difficult to unsubscribe from a service, and some might think you have started spamming them.

If you're offering a paid-for subscription service, offer a free 'teaser' subscription

If you plan to offer a commercial service where you charge people to subscribe, then it is a good idea to offer a free e-mail that contains brief summaries of what is included in the commercial offering. It may also be an idea to offer a free trial period, so that the subscriber can get an understanding of what you have to offer.

Decide whether you want a plain text or HTML version of your e-mail

There are two basic options for the format you can use when delivering an e-mail to your subscriber base: plain text and HTML. Plain text is just like a normal e-mail, and is the simplest and easiest to produce. HTML is like sending a web page in an e-mail. It will deliver a lot more impact and colour, but it is more expensive to produce, and a number of older e-mail systems find it hard to read HTML. If you do decide to use an HTML e-mail approach, it's a good idea to offer a plain text version as well or a significant number of people may be unable to subscribe to your service.

For plain text e-mail layout keep the line length of text between 65 and 70 characters to avoid breaking lines, which make the layout look very ugly, and keep paragraphs nice and short—five to six lines is optimum. Use capitals for headings. Because plain text e-mails do not allow the use of bold or font sizing, capitalising is the only way to give emphasis. Use a nonproportional font such as Courier, because it remains constant regardless of the e-mail package being used.

Keep the e-mail short and punchy

Think of what you are doing as delivering a publication. You're trying to get people to read something that will make them want to act—to buy your product or use your service, for example. The scarcest commodity today is people's time. Nobody will read an e-mail that goes on and on, so focus on having punchy headings and short summaries. Avoid having articles that are longer than 500–600 words. The entire e-mail should not contain more than 1,500 words, unless you have a dedicated audience that you know is willing to read longer pieces. So keep things short, and always have some sort of call to action.

Have a strong subject line

The subject line is what subscribers see first

when they download their e-mail. Because people are so busy they often scan the subject line and, if it's not interesting, delete the e-mail. However, if you are sending out a regular publication you may wish to include the title of the publication and date in the subject line. In the body of the e-mail itself, it's a good idea to have a table of contents near the top that lets the reader know what to expect from the rest of the e-mail.

Use hypertext and e-mail addresses

It's a good idea to use a hypertext to link back to your website, in order to encourage the subscriber to get more information, purchase your product, and so on. However, when writing out a hyperlink (URL) always use the full URL. For example, don't use 'www.mycompany.com'; instead, use 'http://www.mycompany.com'. The reason is that some older e-mail packages will not automatically turn the URL into a link unless you include the full URL. Also, if you have a URL that is more than 65 characters long, put it in angle brackets (< >). Otherwise, a number of e-mail packages will break the URL onto two lines and make it unusable. If you are including an e-mail address, put in a 'mailto': before the e-mail address, as this will turn it into a link to the subscriber's e-mail package. For example: 'mailto:tom@mycompany.com'.

Include the essential things every e-mail mailing should have

Every e-mail you send out should contain the subject line (title) and date, subscription and unsubscription information, copyright and privacy policies (or links to these on the website), e-mail contact details (telephone and address may also be included), links back to the website, and brief information on the publication schedule and scope.

WHAT TO AVOID

Using a 'bait and switch' approach

Be very clear to the potential subscriber about what exactly they are subscribing to. If you specialise in special offers, e-mail and tell them so. Don't pretend that you're going to send valuable updates on a particular industry, and then just send a blizzard of special offers.

Not meeting a real information need

Ask yourself the question: why would anyone want to read this? Too many e-mail mailings are full of useless, repetitive, or out-of-date information.

Not keeping to a publication schedule

If you say you will deliver an e-mail every Wednesday, do it. Being late risks losing credibility and subscribers.

Not managing the subscription and unsubscription process professionally

Make it difficult for someone to subscribe and they just won't bother. By the same token, if you make it difficult for people to unsubscribe, they'll become frustrated and with good reason.

Spamming people

Never subscribe people against their will or without them knowing. Sending unsolicited e-mail is a 'get rich quick' strategy. It will damage your long-term reputation.

RECOMMENDED LINK

Clickz e-mail marketing section:
www.clickz.com/em_mkt/em_mkt

SEE ALSO

Applying a Viral Marketing Approach on the Internet (p. 376)
Computers, Information Technology, and E-commerce (p. 499)
Delivering the Benefits of Affiliate Marketing on the Web (p. 378)
Promoting Your Website Effectively (p. 367)

Applying a Viral Marketing Approach on the Internet

GETTING STARTED

Viral marketing is really another name for word of mouth on the Internet environment. Viral marketing can work in mysterious ways, but what is clear is that the Internet is a medium that offers significant potential for such strategy. Yahoo did little or no advertising in its early years—people told other people that it was a great resource. News about music-swapping services such as Napster, and the independent film *The Blair Witch Project*, grew like wildfire within universities. Viral marketing works well when:

- the product is new and genuinely different, and is something opinion leaders want to be associated with
- the benefits are real—people are telling their friends; they are putting their reputations on the line
- the product is relevant to a large number of people, and it is relatively easy to communicate the benefits

MAKING IT HAPPEN

Consider incentives

Some viral marketing campaigns use an incentive-based approach. This involves rewarding people if they inform their friends and a percentage of these friends purchase the product or fill out a questionnaire, for example. It is important to have a cap on the number of people that the first person is asked to inform. For example, ask him or her to tell no more than five people. If the process is open-ended then it's very easy for spam to occur, where someone sends out thousands of e-mails to people they don't know in order to increase their rewards.

Create useful information that will be quoted and passed on

People see the Internet as an information resource. A powerful way of building a brand is to publish information that you allow people to quote and redistribute. There is no better way to enhance your reputation than for someone to pass your newsletter on to a friend, recommending that they should read it. The objective is that you be seen as an expert on a particular subject that is directly related to a product or service you offer. To facilitate such a process, create an 'e-mail-to-a-friend' function on your website, which allows someone easily to e-mail information on something they have just read.

Recognise that linking is viral marketing

Linking is another form of word-of-mouth. It's one thing for someone to send an e-mail praising your product or information, but the effect is much better and longer-lasting if that person publishes a positive review on their website and links back to you.

Remember that viral marketing works well when there is something free

People love to tell their friends when there is some great new service that is free. The Hotmail free e-mail service and the Geocities free website service grew quickly with little or no marketing spend. The appeal of what is free may be losing some of its lustre as the Internet matures, but it is still a powerful driver of behaviour.

Emulate the Hotmail approach

Hotmail was a pioneer of viral marketing. Its success was not simply based on the fact that it was a free service. It embedded viral marketing into the product itself. Every time someone using Hotmail sent an e-mail, at the bottom of the e-mail was the compelling message: 'Get your private, free e-mail at http://www.hotmail.com'. With Hotmail and other communications services such as ICQ, the very use of the product became a vehicle for marketing and promotion.

Be wary of inappropriate viral marketing

Done inappropriately, viral marketing can be seen as pyramid selling, chain-letter selling, and/or spam. Every e-mail sent needs to make clear that the business is not involved in spamming or other unethical practices or you'll become tarred with the same brush. If you do attract adverse attention from an irate recipient, remain calm and respond to the complainant in a professional manner.

Some viral marketing campaigns involve people sending e-mail addresses to the business, which then carries out the actual communication. It's important that these e-mail addresses are only used for a one-off mailing, and that they are not added to a database for ongoing communication. Also, when sending out the e-mail, remember to state clearly who referred the recipient to you. Bear in mind that a referral does *not* mean that someone has agreed to receive ongoing communication from you.

RECOMMENDED LINK

Business2.0:
www.business2.com

SEE ALSO

Computers, Information Technology, and E-commerce (p. 499)
Delivering the Benefits of Affiliate Marketing on the Web (p. 378)
Promoting Your Website Effectively (p. 367)
Understanding the Key Principles of Internet Marketing (p. 364)
Using E-mail Marketing Effectively (p. 373)

Delivering the Benefits of Affiliate Marketing on the Web

GETTING STARTED
Affiliate marketing is about paying for performance. In short, it is a type of marketing in which one company induces others to place banners and buttons on their websites in return for a commission on purchases made by their customers. Amazon.com is the pioneer of affiliate marketing. It allows other websites to publish information of their own choices of books. When people click through to Amazon and buy these books, the website in question gets a commission. Affiliate marketing can open up new channels to market for the affiliate sponsor, and be a source of extra revenue for the affiliate website. When investigating affiliate marketing, remember that:

- affiliate marketing is more suited to products than services
- you'll need to work hard with your affiliates if you want it all to work
- a well-designed compensation package will be critical to success

MAKING IT HAPPEN
Work out if your business is suited to affiliate marketing
Keep the following in mind:

- There needs to be a substantial number of websites that are attracting your target market. These websites need to show a willingness to join an affiliate programme. You might be selling medical supplies but that doesn't mean that hospital websites will become affiliates.
- Affiliate marketing is better suited to products than to services. It is much harder to track whether another website sent you visitors who, after prolonged negotiation, decide to pay you for your services.
- Is the market already saturated with affiliate programmes? It would be difficult to set up an affiliate programme today that offered commission on book sales.

Have a strong value proposition
As with all good ideas, there are a huge number of companies offering affiliate programmes. How is your programme going to attract new members? The level of compensation/commission you will offer will be important. However, on its own it will rarely be enough. You will need to work hard with your members by organising regular competitions, special offers, and other incentives that make for an attractive value proposition both for your affiliate members and the end customer.

Keep in regular touch with your affiliates
Keeping in regular communication with your affiliates is essential in order to build their enthusiasm and trust. You should plan for an e-mail affiliate newsletter. Your affiliate members are your partners, and unless you treat them as such by working closely with them, they will drift away.

Agree a compensation approach
Critical to the success of your programme will be how the affiliate is compensated. There are various compensation approaches:

- You might pay commission only; for smaller-price items such as books and music, commission is a popular option.
- For more expensive items such as cars, compensation may be based on paying for qualified leads.
- If brand building is also an important objective, then you might also offer compensation every time a visitor clicks through from an affiliate.

When making payments you will need to decide how often you do it. Every month? Every quarter? A problem you may face with partners is that some of them will have achieved very little revenue for a particular period, and it will not be cost-effective to send them a cheque. So you need to inform partners that there is a certain threshold before payment is made, and that commission earned in one period, if below the threshold, will be added to the commission for the next period. You will need an affiliate agreement that will cover these and other relevant issues.

Innovate, analyse, test, and adapt

There is a need to innovate constantly so as to find the best approach. Affiliate software delivers substantial data and this needs to be carefully analysed. New initiatives need to be properly tested and you need to be willing to keep adapting and refining your offer until you find something that works for both you and your affiliates.

Decide whether to outsource or buy software

Organisations can have the choice of outsourcing much of the running of the affiliate programme or purchasing software and designing it in-house. It is better to outsource, as it allows you to focus on what you do best—selling and marketing your products and services.

RECOMMENDED LINKS

Affiliate Marketing Resource Centre:
www.affiliatemarketing.co.uk
Associate Programs:
www.associateprograms.com

SEE ALSO

Applying a Viral Marketing Approach on the Internet (p. 376)
Computers, Information Technology, and E-commerce (p. 499)
Promoting Your Website Effectively (p. 367)
Understanding the Key Principles of Internet Marketing (p. 364)
Using E-mail Marketing Effectively (p. 373)

Getting the Best from E-marketplaces

GETTING STARTED

An e-marketplace is an Internet-based environment that brings together business-to-business buyers and sellers so that they can trade together more efficiently. Used properly, e-marketplaces can make for more efficient purchasing processes, saving time and money for everyone involved. When considering involvement in an e-marketplace, keep the following in mind:

- An e-marketplace gives the smaller company access to many more sales opportunities and allows it to compete on equal terms with larger companies.
- The technology is still relatively new, as are many of the companies involved. Caution is necessary before any major decisions are made.
- There are different types of e-marketplaces and you need to decide which is right for you.
- E-marketplaces should not simply focus on getting the lowest price. Collaboration and the supply of quality information are key benefits they can deliver.

FAQS

What are the key benefits of becoming involved in an e-marketplace?

Reduced sales costs, greater flexibility, saved time, better information, and better collaboration.

What are the key drawbacks of e-marketplaces?

The key drawbacks are inertia and resistance to change among key players, costs in changing procurement processes, the cost of applications and set-up, the cost of integration with internal systems, and transaction/subscription fees.

What types of e-marketplaces are there?

There are three distinct types of e-marketplace:

Independent: These are public e-marketplace environments that seek to attract buyers and sellers to trade together. Many simply didn't attract a critical mass of buyers and sellers and folded quickly. Such marketplaces have found most success in commodity-based industries, where there are buyers and sellers.

Consortium-based: These are set up on an industry-wide basis, typically when a number of key buyers in a particular industry get together. They often drive an industry-wide move to achieve common standards for the transfer of information.

Private: These are established by a particular organisation to manage its purchasing alone. The organisation retains full control, though technology costs can be significant.

MAKING IT HAPPEN
Remember that there's more to it than buying and selling

The early e-marketplaces were little more than auction environments. However, as they've evolved, they have sought to help businesses trade more efficiently with partners. This has involved optimising communication and collaboration; improved time to market as information flows more quickly between parties involved; and better stock control, through better market feedback.

Consider joining an independent e-marketplace

The advantages of joining an independent e-marketplace are:

- you can find new trading partners that you might otherwise not have been aware of
- it's useful if you need to reduce inventory
- it can work well when marketing commodity products
- independents should embrace open infra-

structure standards, making them easier to plug into than private e-marketplaces, which may use more proprietary technology.

The disadvantages are:

- a volatile environment, with many independents going out of business
- they are not really suitable for developing long-term trading relationships
- confidentiality and security can be an issue
- many suppliers see such marketplaces as a way to drive down prices and are wary about getting involved. This limits the buying options.

Consider joining a consortium-based e-marketplace

The advantages are:

- less expensive than establishing a private e-marketplace. Charges are usually in the form of subscription fees and/or commission.
- more choice of buyers and sellers
- cheaper prices, though this isn't always the case
- enhanced ability to work on industry-wide issues such as achieving common data standards

The disadvantages are:

- you are setting up a trading environment with your competitors
- less control than with a private e-marketplace
- it won't generally integrate as well into backend technology and processes as a private e-marketplace
- it's more open and thus more generic. If buying/selling relationships are key to your competitive edge, then a consortium-based e-marketplace will not be a huge benefit.
- governments may view such e-marketplaces as cartels or monopolies, depending on the members and their power within the overall marketplace

Bear in mind that you don't have to stick with one type of e-marketplace

Depending on the complexity of your needs, you may decide to use a number of e-marketplaces. For example, you might use a consortium-based one for most of your needs, but, when you have unusual demands, use an independent to give yourself greater choice. A trading partner you meet in an independent e-marketplace may end up migrating into your private e-marketplace.

Recognise that confidentiality is key

One of the major worries regarding involvement in either an independent or consortium-based e-marketplace is confidentiality. Over time, a picture will be built up of how an organisation trades; this is important information, which could be very valuable to competitors. It's essential that proper security procedures are in place.

Consider content management

Content management is an important part of an e-marketplace environment. The system will need to deal with requests for proposals (RFPs), quotations, product diagrams and specifications, pricing and delivery information, and so on. It will need to be able to archive everything in an easily accessible way, and to deal with version control so users can receive the most up-to-date on the Webdate information.

Train and educate your staff

E-marketplaces invariably introduce new ways of doing things. There may be resistance within the business and this will require ongoing education and evangelism. Training will be required for the staff who are expected to operate the e-marketplace.

Seller beware

Sellers have been very cautious about getting involved in e-marketplaces because of their initial tendency to focus primarily on price. Some e-marketplaces have encouraged reverse auctions, whereby sellers bid against each other to sell to a particular customer. However, the right e-marketplace can have benefits for a seller, opening up new markets and customers, and providing a way of reducing excess stock.

Consider general issues

- What is the procedure if you want to develop a one-to-one relationship with a trading partner you meet within an e-marketplace?
- Will the e-marketplace have any role to play in shipping and logistics?
- What is expected of you as a participant? How, for example, do you deliver content and updates?
- What integration work is involved? And if it doesn't fully integrate, what are the costs involved in new processes?
- How are payments to be made?
- How are the request for proposal (RFP) and quotation processes handled? Does the e-marketplace offer software that makes these processes more efficient?
- Is there a certification process in place to ensure that you are dealing with reputable entities?

WHAT TO AVOID

Forgetting about corporate inertia

The expectation by e-marketplace providers that businesses would suddenly change their buying and selling habits upon the arrival of new technology was a serious mistake. Relationships and habits build up over years and change only slowly in most situations.

Ignoring the fact that there's more to buying and selling than price

Product quality, support, and personal relationships are still key in business-to-business situations. E-marketplaces that simply focused on pitting seller against seller found that that approach simply didn't work and have had to rethink their strategy.

Delays in getting the e-marketplace up and running

E-marketplaces are a lot more complex than was originally predicted for many reasons. The more partners involved, the more difficult it becomes to synchronise the information and business processes between each entity. Delays in making some of the best-known e-marketplaces fully functional have hurt the image of the industry.

Failing to provide a robust payments process

Many e-marketplaces lack a process whereby the participants can immediately settle the whole transaction. The fact that some of the trade must then be completed offline means that both offline and online processes need to be maintained, reducing efficiencies and savings in costs as well as time.

RECOMMENDED LINK

B2business.net:
www.b2business.net/eMarketplaces

SEE ALSO

Computers, Information Technology, and E-commerce (p. 499)

Getting the Best from Loyalty Programmes on the Web

GETTING STARTED

Loyalty programmes reward customers who spend more and/or stay longer with a business. Like much else about the Web, loyalty programmes were a gigantic trend that crashed pretty severely. However, much of what went wrong does not reflect an inherent fault in the loyalty model itself, but rather in the vastly overhyped expectations of what loyalty programmes can deliver. When considering using loyalty programmes on the Web, keep the following in mind:

- you should implement loyalty programmes on the Web only after you have your e-commerce fundamentals solidly in place.
- loyalty programmes are long-term projects: it can be disastrous to start a loyalty programme and then stop it within six months.
- getting the level of incentive right is critical to success—too much and your profits will be hurt; too little and you won't attract members.

MAKING IT HAPPEN

Make sure your e-commerce fundamentals are in place first

Top of the list for consumers are service, comprehensive information, appropriate returns policies, and good support. Unless these fundamentals are fully addressed, consumers will see loyalty points only as gimmicks.

Remember that loyalty programmes are long-term projects

A critical issue with regard to loyalty programmes is that, by their very nature, they have to be there for the long term. Loyalty programmes ask two key things of consumers: to collect points that will be redeemed at some future date; and to give their loyalty. There is no better way to antagonise a consumer than to start a loyalty programme and then six months later— as the member has collected half the points required for that coveted flight—to stop the programme. Don't start a loyalty programme unless you're in it for the long haul.

Find out what makes your customer loyal

If you don't know what makes your customers loyal then you cannot develop a programme that will enhance their loyalty. It is also critical to focus on making your most profitable customers more loyal.

Choose the right type of loyalty programme

The following is a selection of loyalty programme approaches:

- points systems—a very popular approach that gives points to customers based on what they purchase
- premium customer programmes— customers who spend certain amounts of money and are repeat purchasers of a product or service gain special status. This may involve their receiving special service offers, discounts, exclusive offers, gifts, and so on. The important thing here is to make the customers feel special—make them feel that they are getting things that those who are not part of the programme don't get.
- buyers' clubs—when a certain number of consumers get together to buy a particular product, they will be offered a special volume discount

Get the switching cost right

If you offer too much in your loyalty programme then your margins will be squeezed, and you will be running to stand still from a profitability point of view. If your incentives are too low then the switching cost for your customer will remain low, and the very purpose of the loyalty programme will have been negated. It would seem that the problem with a lot of loyalty programmes on the Web was that, fuelled by venture capital, major incentives were offered in the hope of attracting huge numbers of members.

Create a loyalty path for the customer

Customers can take loyalty programmes very seriously. Some customers see it as an important achievement that they have a 'Gold Card', or are seen as a 'Premium Customer'. There needs to be a clear loyalty path to tap into this sort of loyalty psychology. The customers need to see that the more they spend and the longer they stay with you, the more rewards and better treatment they will get.

Keep the customer informed

Customers need to be able to check up on their status easily—to see, for example, how many points they have currently accumulated. Keep in touch. Send loyalty club members a regular bulletin that creates a continuing buzz about the loyalty programme, announcing competition winners, new competitions, special offers, and so on.

RECOMMENDED LINK

Business 2.0:
www.business2com

SEE ALSO

Building Loyalty Through Online Communities (p. 385)
Computers, Information Technology, and E-commerce (p. 499)

Building Loyalty Through Online Communities

GETTING STARTED

Online communities allow consumers to engage with one another and with your business through use of interactive tools such as e-mail, discussion boards, and chat software. (Broader and more social online communities are not the topic of this actionlist.) They are a means by which you can take the pulse of consumers to find out what they are thinking, and to generate unique content. As a stand-alone business, online communities have been found to be weak: they work best when they are supporting the need for the business to get ongoing feedback. Online communities:

- allow the consumer an ongoing voice, thus facilitating greater feedback
- require moderation and care if they are not to fizzle out, or turn negative
- offer different options for interaction that reflect the varying ways in which people like to communicate

MAKING IT HAPPEN
Keep it moderated

Online communities rarely work if you simply install some discussion board software on a website and walk away. The discussion will either quickly dry up, or else drift off to topics that have nothing to do with the company and may well be libellous or illegal. Thus, to make a success of an online community, quality moderation is essential. Moderators need to combine editorial and chairperson-type skills. They need to be knowledgeable about the subjects being discussed, be enthusiastic, and encourage debate and quality discussion. They require an understanding of legal (particularly libel and copyright) issues, and should have the ability to deal with negative situations where members become overly virulent. Most of all, they need to care and want to make the community work for everybody involved.

Set up e-mail mailing lists

E-mail mailing lists are an excellent way to discuss complex topics over a longer period of time. Members can be drawn from anywhere in the world and come together to share information and experience on a particular theme or subject area. The success of an e-mail mailing list is down to the quality of the contributions and moderation. Done

right, it is a powerful way of transferring knowledge. An e-mail mailing list works as follows:

- A moderator establishes a list with mailing list software (this can be bought or rented; renting is usually the best option).
- The theme and focus of the list is published, and people join up, using a website form and/or e-mail address.
- The moderator invites contributions and these are duly published by e-mail.
- Subscribers react to the initial publication with their opinions and feedback; a selection of these reactions then gets published in the next e-mail sent out.
- If successful, a feedback and opinion loop is created, with new topics of discussion being introduced as older topics have received sufficient discussion.

Set up discussion boards

Discussion boards (also known as newsgroups, discussion groups, or bulletin boards) are areas on a website that allow people to contribute opinions, ideas and announcements. They tend to be more general in nature than e-mail mailing lists, and are more suited to casual, one-off interactions. People require less commitment to participate in such boards. They can generally review a discussion topic without subscribing, although they do have to subscribe if they want to contribute something themselves. Moderation is not as essential here, although it is important to watch out for the emergence of 'off-topic' subjects—contributions that are unnecessarily negative and perhaps libellous—and copyright infringement.

A prime example of the success of the discussion board approach is how Amazon.com uses it to allow consumers to publish book reviews. Discussion board software is relatively cheap and easy to install.

Set up online chat

Online chat is real-time, text-based communication. Online chat can be effective when:

- there is a specific event occurring that is of interest to people
- an expert can be made available to talk about a subject or product and answer queries.

To be productive, online chat needs to be well moderated. It is really only suited to small groups of people (2 to 20) at any one time so that all participants can have their say. Online chat software is relatively cheap and easy to install.

SEE ALSO
Computers, Information Technology, and E-commerce (p. 499)
Getting the Best from Loyalty Programmes on the Web (p. 383)

SELLING ONLINE

Establishing an Enterprise Portal

GETTING STARTED

If your business has grown and you employ a number of staff, you may want to investigate enterprise portals. Put very simply, these are websites that assemble a wide range of content and services for staff. Some of this content is published by the organisation itself, and some will be acquired from third-party publishers. The principle is to bring together all the key information that staff require to do a better job. When considering developing an enterprise portal, keep the following in mind:

- the word 'portal' means different things to different people: to some, it's a souped-up intranet, to others it's a nascent o marketplace; others will see it as part of a customer relationship management strategy
- enterprise portals, while great in theory, are complex to develop and expensive to manage
- an enterprise portal can easily fall into the trap of trying to provide all the information staff could possibly need and providing none of it very well.

MAKING IT HAPPEN
Exploit the extra potential

In many ways, an enterprise portal (sometimes referred to as an enterprise information portal) is a fancy name for an intranet. The key difference is that an enterprise portal manages not just internal content, but also external content that may be useful to staff. Such external information could include, for example, specialised news feeds, or access to industry research reports.

Learn from the public portals

On the Web everyone is a publisher, but that doesn't mean that everyone is a good publisher or that people will want to read what they publish. Very few public portals have survived, because they have not been able to build a viable business case.

Another portal sector that has seen great change is the much-vaunted 'vortal'. A vortal, or vertical portal, provides information that is organised around a vertical market sector, such as pharmaceuticals or plastics. Vortals and e-marketplaces have a lot in common, and in many markets may be one and the same thing. Most of these vortals, if they haven't evolved into e-marketplaces, are probably no longer in business.

The lessons that need to be learned from public portals and industry vortals include:

- people are very conservative in the way they consume content. The majority of people go to a few trusted brands
- running portals is expensive; many have not survived because they did not have a proper business model

Don't get complacent about having a captive audience

The enterprise portal would seem to have a captive audience—employees. But it's not as simple as that. Staff who use an enterprise portal demand high publishing standards. High publishing standards are expensive to maintain, and many enterprise portals are dying because they don't have enough quality content, the content is not being kept up to date, and the whole environment is not properly organised and structured. What many organisations are discovering, to their cost, is that providing all this related information is wonderful in theory, but expensive and difficult to manage in practice.

Know your employees' content needs

Ask the following questions:

- How are employees' information needs being met at present?
- Are any of these needs not being satisfied properly?
- Can I fill this gap cost-effectively?

- Will my staff trust me to fill this gap?
- Where's the return on investment?

Related information is all well and good, but the key question must be: where is the return on investment? If a member of staff can just as easily get this related information somewhere else, why duplicate the effort? Unfortunately, organisations rarely take the time to examine which content drives the business forward, and which has little effect. But having a website is being a publisher, and if you don't understand the impact of your content, you don't understand publishing.

RECOMMENDED LINK
Business2.0:
www.business2.com

SEE ALSO
Computers, Information Technology, and E-commerce (p. 499)

Managing Payments Online

GETTING STARTED

If your business sells its products or services online, it's absolutely essential you're your online payment system works well, and works safely. The system must be easy to use, as consumers dislike having to go through long, cumbersome processes to purchase products, but it must also be as secure as possible; it's estimated that fraud costs an online business three times as much as an offline one. Remember that:

- consumers may be wary of giving credit card details and other personal information online. Your first step must be to gain their trust.
- fraud and chargebacks are critical issues that can seriously affect an online business
- there is a wide range of online payment services available, so shop around to make sure you get the best one for you

FAQS

What is the most common form of payment on the Internet?

For consumer commerce it is the credit card. In the United States it is claimed that over 90% of all online payments are made by credit card. In Europe, the figure is estimated at 70%. For most business-to-business transactions, payment is usually made offline. New forms of payment are emerging, such as prepaid accounts and payments via mobile phone.

What are the key issues facing online payments?

- Fraud is a critical concern that must be addressed comprehensively.
- There is no cross-border integration of payment systems.
- People develop payment habits, and are reluctant to change them.
- Can traditional payment methods adapt to the new environment, or is a brand new payment system required?
- There is still no comprehensive hard data on how people pay online.

What is a payment culture?

Within any particular country, and sometimes within states or regions of a country, there are distinct approaches to payment, depending on:

- the range of payment options available locally
- local payment habits
- local/national payment regulations

MAKING IT HAPPEN

Understand your marketplace

Depending on the country, or the region/state within a country, people pay for things in different ways. Different countries also have different payment processing approaches and legal obligations.

Understand the types of payment option available

It is important to understand the range of payment options available before choosing a particular payment method. The options available include the following:

- credit or debit card payment
- credit transfer
- electronic cheques
- direct debit
- smart cards
- prepaid schemes
- loyalty scheme points-based approaches
- person-to-person payments
- mobile phone schemes

The approach you choose will depend on your target market. For example, where a website targets young people, who often have no credit cards, a prepaid scheme can work well. A particular website may use a variety of payment approaches, depending on its needs, but the ability to process all the major credit and debit cards is almost always essential.

Check the characteristics of an online payment system

An online payment system should have these key characteristics:

- efficiency and ease of use: a central advantage of doing business online is that it saves time and cuts costs
- robustness and reliability: because payment is such a critical function, it is essential that a payment system is fully reliable. Payment systems cannot afford to be down for any length of time
- authentication: much online fraud is caused by the absence of proper authentication
- integration: a payment system must be able to integrate properly with relevant internal information systems, so that, for example, a record of the payment can be added to the account details
- insurance: facilities such as escrow services must be available to ensure that the seller gets the money and the buyer gets the goods

Select an online payment service

The most suitable type of online payment service will depend on the volume of business you intend doing and the margins you make on each sale. There is a wide choice of payment services, so it is important to shop around to find the best one. However, whatever service you choose must be able to verify the credit card, process the transaction, and deposit the money in your account.

Key factors you must consider are set-up fees, ongoing charges, and software and hardware expenses. Most banks offer some form of online payment service, and can be a good choice. When looking beyond banks, make sure you are dealing with reputable organisations. Those that advertise extremely low charges usually have expensive hidden extras.

Offer a choice of credit card payment methods

There are two distinct methods by which credit or debit card payments are made for Internet purchases: payment directly online, and payment by phoning or faxing credit card details. The first method is by far the most popular (88%), but it is advisable to offer both options to potential consumers.

When implementing an online credit card system, a comprehensive security system using a secure server with encryption technology is essential. It is equally important to have comprehensive security procedures for the storage of the information. A database containing confidential information on thousands of individuals is far more attractive to a criminal than acquiring a single credit card number.

Keep the process simple and fast

Whatever the payment system you choose, make sure to keep the process as simple and fast as possible. Studies have indicated that many consumers abandon the online purchase process, often because it is too long and difficult to understand. Streamlining the purchasing process is extremely important where repeat business is concerned. Amazon.com, for example, has implemented a patented '1-Click' purchase process for repeat customers, avoiding a lot of form filling.

Consider business-to-business (B2B) payment options

While there is a wide range of effective business-to-consumer online payment options, payment for B2B transactions is generally made offline. One reason for this is that the amounts of money involved are usually large. However, one of the key reasons businesses embrace online B2B and join e-marketplaces is to reduce costs and to make transactions more efficient. Not being able to complete the payment online adds cost and inconvenience. A range of systems is available for B2B payment online; they focus on ensuring security and authenticity, and some also offer digital signature facilities.

Think about offering online escrow services

Online escrow services offer to hold payments while the buyer examines the products purchased. If the buyer is satisfied with the products, they then authorise the payment. An online escrow service incurs extra cost because a fee is charged, but it may be worthwhile if it is essential to give the buyer as much confidence as possible.

The system operates by giving the escrow service a tracking number for the delivery. You must agree the time period allowed to the buyer for examination of the merchandise; you must also establish who pays the carriage fees if the product is returned.

Remember that fraud and chargebacks are major issues

Some studies estimate that e-tailers are losing as much as 5% of their margin to fraud— a rate three times higher than for businesses operating offline. For e-tailers on small margins this is a very serious issue. There are many different types of fraud, but a particularly common online form is identity theft, where fraudsters acquire confidential information on an individual and use it to purchase products. Clearly, e-tailers must take great care in this area, otherwise their profits will be eaten away. Fraud detection software is available and should be used.

Chargebacks (disputed payments) are also a major concern. MasterCard claims that, while online purchases represent 4% of total retail transactions, they account for 40% of all chargebacks. Credit card companies have initiated chargeback limits for e-tailers, and penalties are imposed for those who exceed them.

Understand how payment systems work

This is how the process works:

- customers visit your site anytime, during or outside normal business hours
- they view products and brief descriptions
- they select products and put them into an electronic shopping basket
- customers are offered payment options, ideally in their own currency
- online payment is handled securely, probably by a specialist payment processor
- payment is approved and confirmed to you and the customer
- purchases are delivered to the customer

Choose the right system

An effective payment system allows your customers to buy online and allows you to manage the process efficiently. A complete payment system includes all the facilities to display products, accept payments, and manage your business. You can also choose systems that can be integrated with existing product display and business management systems. The system should allow you to:

- display products that customers can buy from your website
- calculate any taxes due
- calculate shipping or delivery charges
- provide a quick, simple ordering mechanism
- provide a secure customer payment mechanism
- accept payment by credit card, debit card, and cheque
- handle transactions from customers with approved accounts
- handle payment for small and large purchases
- accept payment in local currencies from all the countries where you have customers
- accept payments in multiple currencies
- protect your customers and your business against fraud
- handle customer refunds
- receive settlement from the payment processor
- automate stock control
- simplify administration and accounting
- expand in line with growth of business
- minimise the cost of handling transactions

Select a payment processor

You can set up your own payment processing facilities, but if you only handle a small number of transactions or if your transaction requirements are complex this may not be practical. Payment processors can provide you with an established proven system that can grow in line with your business, and services of this type are offered by banks and independent specialists.

Using an external provider offers you a number of advantages: there is no need for capital investment from you; there are no hardware, software, and support requirements; high levels of security for your business and your customers are provided; there is a reliable operation, round the clock; and services can expand in line with your business.

Apply for a payment account

Many businesses, particularly smaller and medium size operations, can be put off by the complexity of the application process but bear in mind that some suppliers have simpler processes than others. For commercial and security reasons, no company can cut out initial checks but some suppliers have gone out of their way to make the application process as simple as possible. The process varies in a number of areas:

- some independents can make their own internal risk assessment without referring to banks
- you may or may not have to provide a detailed trading history
- the proportion of successful applications varies by supplier—independents generally accept a higher proportion of applicants than banks

Make sure you complete the application forms fully and return all essential documentation, including a customer agreement, direct debit mandate, bank details, and balance sheet.

Offer a clear payment page

Simplifying payment is an important part of the online shopping experience. A clear, easy-to-use order form allows customers to place their orders quickly. The form should include:

- customer details
- delivery requirements
- product details
- quantity
- price
- delivery charges
- total cost
- payment option
- account details, if appropriate

- mechanism to submit the order
- acknowledgment of the order and payment approval

Check the operation of the payment page and ensure that any changes to the page layout reflect customer experience and feedback. Also make sure that the page is easy to navigate and simple to complete.

WHAT TO AVOID ✗
Not understanding payment cultures
While credit cards may be very common in the United States, they are not as widely used in Europe. Different countries have different payment habits and payment legislation. Not understanding these is a serious obstacle to online business.

Not securing peace of mind for the consumer
Consumers are very concerned that their credit card numbers will be stolen on the Internet. They are equally concerned that confidential information that they give to a website will not be properly protected. Websites that fail to show clearly the steps taken to protect customer information are likely to lose potential business.

Underestimating fraud
Fraud is a pressing issue on the Internet, and can have a serious impact on profit margins.

RECOMMENDED LINKS
E-payment Systems Observatory:
www.epso.jrc.es
Epaynews.com:
www.epaynews.com

SEE ALSO
Computers, Information Technology, and E-commerce (p. 499)
Making Your Website Secure (p. 394)
Understanding Legal Issues in E-commerce (p. 400)

Making Your Website Secure

GETTING STARTED

Internet security is a critically important issue. The Internet is, by definition, a network; networks are open, and are thus vulnerable to attack. A poor Internet security policy can result in a substantial loss of productivity and a drop in consumer confidence. When developing such a security policy, keep the following in mind:

- be continuously vigilant: the perfect Internet security system will be out of date the next day
- combine software and human expertise: security software can only do so much; it must be combined with human expertise and experience
- secure internally as well as externally; many security breaches come from inside the business

FAQS

What are examples of best practice in Internet security?

Consider the following as best practice:

- have an Internet security policy
- if your system has been compromised, seek immediate independent expert help
- for complete safety after an attack, the best course of action is to reformat the hard disk
- strip your computer system down to its bare essentials. The more features, options, and software your system has, the more open it is to attack. This is particularly true for Internet-related software and functions
- for personal computers, be very careful about always-on connections provided by many broadband suppliers. An always-on connection to the Internet is always open to probing and attack by a hacker.
- do not download software from the Internet unless you are totally confident that it is from a reputable source

Are cookies a security threat?

Cookies collect information on how you browse the Web, and are a relatively low security risk. However, cookies can encourage lazy security practices, since they remember user-names and passwords.

Can you get a virus by opening an e-mail?

Yes. It used to be impossible to be infected by a computer virus transmitted by e-mail unless you opened the e-mail attachment. However, more recent viruses such as Nimda simply required the opening of the e-mail itself. Be very careful about unexpected e-mails from unfamiliar sources. If in doubt, delete without opening.

MAKING IT HAPPEN
Develop an Internet security policy

Keep the following in mind when developing your Internet security policy:

- many security breaches are internal. The fewer people with access to the inner workings of the system, therefore, the better. Those who are allowed access must be recorded and given specific access rights. Immediately delete revoked and inactive users, or users who have left the business
- put in place a rigorous procedure for granting and revoking rights of access
- streamline hardware and software: a complex system is more open to attack. In your server software, for example, strip away as many of the optional features as possible.
- have a password policy. Do not allow simple or obvious passwords. Make sure passwords are changed regularly.
- have procedures for data backup and disaster recovery
- have procedures for responding to security breaches
- be vigilant. The Internet security threat is constantly changing, and constant vigilance is the best security.

- have your security policy audited by an external professional organisation, and have them on call should a major breach occur

Consider the benefits of firewalls

A firewall is software that polices the space between your computer system and the outside world. The design and management of firewalls has become more complex since the advent of the Web because of the vast increase in activity between computers and the Internet. If the firewall is too stringent, it slows everything down and prevents people from carrying out certain legitimate activities; if it is too lax, however, it opens the computer up to attack.

Deal with viruses

Computer viruses are becoming more sophisticated and widespread. By September 2001, it was estimated that one in every 300 e-mails contained a virus, up from one in every 700 in October 2000. It is essential to have antivirus software and to keep it up to date. It is equally vital to upgrade your computer with the latest software security patches. For Microsoft software, more information on such patches is available at **www.microsoft.com/security**.

Deal with hackers

The main objective of a hacker is to gain unauthorised access to another computer. This is done by probing for vulnerabilities on the computer, perhaps the result of flaws in the computer software and/or poor security procedures. The Web is more open than a stand-alone computer, so many hackers now focus on web-based applications. Many of these applications are still relatively new and have not developed robust security measures. Security breaches can range from the hacker changing the pricing in a shopping cart to the theft of credit card numbers. The only way to deal with hackers is to implement rigorous security procedures and to monitor activity on the network constantly.

React rapidly to a security breach

After a security breach there are two basic objectives. First, find out what happened so that you can stop it happening again. Second, find out who did it so that you can prosecute or otherwise deal with them. It is very difficult to prosecute a security breach without hard evidence, and very easy to contaminate or destroy such evidence. In dealing with security breaches, make sure that:

- you get professional advice, particularly if it is the first time your security has been breached
- you protect all log information tracking activity on the system
- the information collected is technically accurate
- information is collected from various sources to develop an overall picture of what happened
- no information is tampered with or modified

In monitoring for security breaches:

- check access and error log files for suspicious activity
- be alert for unusual system commands
- be alert for repeated attempts to enter a password

Guard against denial of service attacks

Denial of service attacks do not seek to break into a computer system, but rather to crash a website by deluging it with phony traffic. They are difficult to defend against, and have been directed at some of the best-known websites, such as CNN and eBay. Firewalls can be designed to block repeated traffic from a particular source.

Make sure you have a secure web server

A web server is potentially an open door into your network: if someone can break into your server, they are closer to breaking into your entire computer system. Before you set up a web server you must ensure that you understand and deal effectively with the various security issues. By definition, web servers interface with the World Wide Web and its potential hazards. They are large, complex software programs that embrace open architecture and that have often been developed at great speed.

From an e-commerce perspective, a secure server is a prerequisite. A secure server uses encryption when transferring or receiving data from the Web. Without a secure server, credit card information, for example, could be easily targeted by a hacker. A secure server will encrypt this information, turning it into special code that will then be decrypted only when it is safely within the server environment.

Equally important is what happens to the confidential information once it has reached the server environment. Once the information has been acted on, it should be stored in encrypted form. In the case of sensitive information, such as credit card details, it should be deleted.

Restrict access to your website

You can restrict access to part or all of your website in a number of ways. The most common is by implementing a user-name and password system. However, you can also restrict access by IP (Internet) address, so that only people connecting from a certain address or domain can access information. Perhaps the most powerful approach is to use public key cryptography, whereby only the person with the assigned cryptography key can request and read the information.

Consider the security implications of outsourcing

Outsourcing creates an increased security risk. You must establish that the outsource vendor will adhere to your security policy, and that all work done adheres to proper security procedures. Specific questions that you need to ask your outsourcing vendor include:

- What is its security policy?
- What are its data backup and disaster-recovery procedures?
- How is your data safeguarded from that of other customers?

- How is your data safeguarded from the vendor's own employees?
- How is it insured with regard to security breaches?

WHAT TO AVOID ✗

Not being continually vigilant

There is no such thing as a perfect security system. Without constant vigilance, computer systems become an open invitation for hackers and viruses. An essential part of such vigilance is having the very latest security patches and antivirus software installed.

Thinking that you won't get a virus

Viruses are becoming increasingly common. If you haven't had one so far, either you are tremendously lucky or you have excellent antivirus procedures.

Thinking that you are anonymous on the Internet

In general, you are not. When you visit a website, you will provide some or all of the following information:

- IP address
- time of access
- user-name (if a user-name and password are used)
- the URL requested
- the URL you were at just before you visited the website
- the amount of data you downloaded
- the browser and operating system you are using
- your e-mail address

RECOMMENDED LINKS

CERT Internet Security Center:
www.cert.org
Computer and Internet Security:
www.loc.gov/global/internet/security.html

SEE ALSO

Computers, Information Technology, and E-commerce (p. 499)
Coping with Computer Viruses (p. 362)
Managing Payments Online (p. 390)

Collecting Consumer Data on the Internet

GETTING STARTED

If your business has a website, you'll find that Internet technologies offer a wealth of ways in which information on consumers can be gathered. Such information can either be collected directly as a result of consumers providing details, or indirectly by analysing consumers' behaviour while on a website. If you decide to gather information on consumers this way, keep the following in mind:

- privacy is a central concern of people who use the Internet, and they are becoming increasingly wary of websites that seek personal information
- the benefit to the consumer needs to be made clear. Consumers are much more willing to offer personal information when a clear benefit to them can be articulated.
- it is one thing to gather information on consumers but another to analyse it properly and use it productively

FAQS

Why has privacy become such a burning issue on the Internet?

The Internet has lacked a common and comprehensive legal infrastructure and this has led to an unfortunate situation in which basic consumer rights have been exploited. Websites have gathered information on visitors in a surreptitious manner. Personal data has been sold on to third parties without making the consumer aware. This behaviour has resulted in a consumer backlash.

What are the key benefits of collecting consumer data?

Getting to know consumers better results in offering them products and services that are more in tune with their needs. This is a key competitive advantage in an information-driven economy. With more and more products becoming increasingly similar in their physical makeup, competitive advantage is achieved through finding out exactly what the consumer wants and meeting those needs precisely.

Why is it so important to collect information on how a website is performing?

A website is not like a bricks-and-mortar shop in which a manager can walk around and observe what is happening. People may be dropping out in the middle of a purchase process on a website, but unless proper data is coming through and being analysed, no one will know. The number of people visiting the website may be dropping off. How will this be known without proper data? Websites, like offline stores, need to monitor their performance continuously and adapt where appropriate. Without proper data and thorough data analysis this cannot be done.

MAKING IT HAPPEN
Use website logs to analyse consumer behaviour

Website logs (server logs) track activity on a website. For an average website, such log software is simple to install and can be purchased fairly cheaply, though for larger websites it is more complex and expensive. It is strongly advisable to use log software, as it delivers vital information on website performance.

Unless the website is hooked into a personalisation system, website logs are not able to identify who exactly has visited the website. Instead, such logs collect general website activity information. Such information includes:

- total number of visits to the website during a defined period of time
- visitor frequency. Information on the number of people who visited only once during the period (unique visitors), and those who have visited more than once.
- page impressions/views. Information on

the total numbers of complete web pages visited during the period. This is a key measure for advertisers.

- hits. One of the most abused statistics on the Internet, and a totally unreliable measure of website visitor activity. Every web page is made up of a number of components—graphics, text, programming elements. Some pages may have anything from ten to 20 components. Each of these components is counted as a 'hit'. Therefore, the total number of hits is generally very high and bears little or no relation to the actual visitor activity.
- most frequently visited pages

Website logs can deliver a mind-numbing array of data. This will seem very exciting when you first install the software but can become tedious to wade through every day. It's thus important to isolate what are the key measures required to deliver a better picture of how the website is performing.

Use cookie software to track consumers

Cookies are small files that are sent to reside in consumers' browsers in order to track those consumers the next time they visit the website. Cookies are an important component in personalisation. A typical example of the use of cookies can be seen when people have subscribed to a service on a website. Cookies allow the website to remember the user-name and password information, so that they don't have to keep filling it out every time they revisit. This is clearly a benefit for most people. However, cookies have been abused, collecting information on people without their knowing. When using cookies, clearly explain to people why they are being used and how they benefit them.

Be cautious about using web bugs that track website usage

An alternative technology to cookies is what has become known as web bugs. Web bugs are not detectable by standard browsers, although there is software that can be downloaded to detect them. Web bugs have been controversial because they are often used in a surreptitious manner. Their very design

reflects a desire not to let the person know that they are being tracked. Web bugs are adding fuel to the belief that people's privacy rights are being constantly abused on the Internet.

Collect information through the use of website forms

Website forms are used to collect information from a consumer in a structured manner. The following are guidelines to follow when designing a form:

- keep the forms as short as possible. If you make the form too long, consumers will simply not fill it out, or will skip over large sections of it.
- if forms have to be long, break them up. However, inform the person clearly of how many sections there are in the form.
- clearly mark mandatory fields. In every form there will be fields, such as e-mail addresses, that must be filled out. The convention is to mark the text associated with these fields in red and/or to place a red asterisk beside the field. At the top of the form, a clear statement needs to be made relating to the mandatory fields.
- don't demand information a consumer can't give. Offer an alternative, for example: 'If you don't have a ZIP code, please write "None".'
- ask opinion-type questions first. Where the objective of the form is to collect opinion-type information, start off with these questions. People tend to be more open to giving opinion rather than personal information.
- isolate errors that are made. Everyone makes mistakes, particularly when they are filling out long forms. Never say, 'There's an error in your form. Go back and fill it out correctly.' Rather say, 'It seems you have not filled out your e-mail address. Please fill it out here.'
- make sure the fields are of sufficient size. Don't, for example, give people a tiny field when you want their street address, which may be quite long.
- make sure it's accessible to all. Offer an alternative approach for people with disabilities to complete the information

requested. Minimum accessibility standards are increasingly required by law.

- test regularly. It's not simply a good idea to test forms to see how user-friendly they are before they are launched.
- Forms break. As part of website maintenance, forms should be tested regularly with sample data.

Follow best practice in consumer data collection

People have become rightly uneasy about the abuse of personal information on the Web. To assuage fears and create a win-win situation, put into practice the following:

- clearly inform people why the information is being collected and what purposes it will be used for
- never use this information in a way that was not originally intended
- allow the consumer to find out what information has been collected on them
- allow them to delete any or all of this information if they desire
- publish a comprehensive privacy statement in a prominent position on the website

Protect consumer data

Hackers—people who break into computer systems—love to target consumer databases. The reason is that these databases may contain credit card information (it is not advisable to store credit card numbers on a website). More usually, hackers know that publicising the theft of consumer databases will be hugely damaging and embarrassing to the organisation. It is therefore vital that any consumer data collected is properly protected and backed up.

Take care when collecting consumer data on children

The rules for collecting consumer data on children are quite naturally a lot stricter than for adults. While the law is evolving, numerous companies have been fined for collecting too much information on children who visit their websites. It's not enough simply to check your national legislation on this issue. The Web is international and your websites should adhere to international standards when it comes to children's privacy rights.

WHAT TO AVOID ✗
Surreptitiously collecting data

People have become very wary about their privacy on the Internet. Too many websites have collected data on consumers without them knowing. This may produce short-term benefit but has led to an inevitable backlash.

Collecting too much data

Software today can deliver seas of data, and websites with large numbers of visitors can easily get flooded. Not focusing on what is the really important data to collect is a common problem. It's important to remember that analysing data takes time, and that if tangible benefits are not delivered then it will be wasted time.

Not protecting consumer data properly

There are numerous high-profile cases in which hackers broke into websites and exposed confidential consumer data. Make sure that your consumer data is properly protected.

RECOMMENDED LINK
Information Commissioner's Office:
www.dataprotection.gov.uk

SEE ALSO
Computers, Information Technology, and E-commerce (p. 499)

Understanding Legal Issues in E-commerce

GETTING STARTED

In any e-business strategy, it is important to address comprehensively the key legal issues. At a basic level, these are matters such as copyright and libel; at a more advanced level, such things as unique restrictions pertaining to the sale of your product within particular jurisdictions need to be dealt with. When addressing legal issues on the Web, keep the following in mind:

- Prevention is better than cure. Establishing a sound legal structure early on is much easier than trying to firefight legal problems as they occur.
- Legal systems are getting a grip on the Internet. More and more laws are being passed that deal with doing business online.
- While you can't deal with the unique legal aspects of every jurisdiction, you still need to isolate the key jurisdictions for your online business and make sure you adhere to their relevant laws.

FAQS

Why should you address legal issues from the start?

Because it's important to guard against unpleasant consequences if you get legal things wrong, or just ignore them. Some early e-commerce businesses adopted the latter approach, believing that cyberspace was a kind of laissez-faire utopia beyond the reach of terrestrial governments.

Is it not the case that many laws do not apply online?

Nobody believes that fallacy any more. Which is fortunate, because courts and governments around the world have shown no hesitation about claiming jurisdiction over online activity—in some cases, even when the website in question is hosted on another continent. They have applied civil sanctions (such as injunctions and damages) and criminal penalties (fines and even imprisonment) in certain instances.

Is there a pragmatic approach to dealing with legal issues online?

Yes. The practical approach is to get legal advice on three specific types of territory for your website:

- the country (or countries) in which your web operations are principally based, which will often, but not always, be where the site is hosted

- the countries that are the primary target market of the website
- any other countries which may claim authority over the website, and the breach of whose laws might cause unpleasant consequences. The United States is by far the best example of this: its legal regime has a dauntingly long reach

MAKING IT HAPPEN
Understand the different kinds of website

While there are many different types of website, they can broadly be divided into those with the following attributes:

- shop window websites, which provide information about a company and its products, but without encouraging any significant visitor interaction—rather like an online company brochure
- contributed content websites, which allow visitors to contribute content, such as information about their identity, or postings on message boards
- full e-commerce websites, through which visitors can purchase goods or services, either physical products which are delivered offline, or digitised material which is available for download

Recognise shop window website issues

Even shop window websites have legal issues to address. They comprise various types of digitised content, such as graphics, text, images, music, and coding, that raise issues which apply to all forms of website.

Website owners must assume that all such content is protected: either by copyright—which, in effect, disallows its inclusion in another website without the copyright owner's permission; or, in some cases, by moral rights—which require the author to be attributed, and that the work should not be significantly modified without the owner's permission.

These clearances can take the form of a licence or an assignment of copyright from the relevant rights holder, which might be a third-party website designer, photographer, journalist, or (in the more difficult case of music) two or more rights-holding organisations.

In addition, you must ensure that content on your website satisfies other requirements, including:

- Using the registered trade marks of a third party as part of your website's metadata will generally constitute trade mark infringement. Even a straightforward reference on a website to a third party's trade mark can constitute an infringement.
- Hypertext linking, particularly by means of deep linking or framing, to third-party websites without the consent of those websites should be avoided.
- Misleading price indications, for example where online prices have not been updated, can incur penalties.
- Incorrect product descriptions, where inaccurate statements are made as to the quantity, size, fitness for purpose or performance of goods, can also cause repercussions.
- Unfair comparative advertising, such as comparisons between goods or services that are not intended for the same purpose, must be avoided.

As well as guarding against infringement of third parties' rights, it is important for owners to include wording in the terms and conditions of their websites which protects their own copyright and other rights. Usually this is done by means of terms which appear directly on the home page or, more

commonly, are linked to/from the home page, as well as at the bottom of every other page on the website.

Appreciate contributed content website issues

Websites that encourage visitors to interact are exposed to several additional forms of legal risk. One of the most basic means of facilitating visitor interaction is a discussion board or chat room. Such environments can pose legal problems, as they are often unchecked and allow visitors to post information without any apparent restriction. You need to recognise that you can find yourself liable, either as a civil matter (where a third party's rights have been infringed) or, more extremely, under the criminal law, unless steps are taken to control material which appears on your website.

Some of the most obvious problems here include:

- defamatory statements
- infringement of copyright material
- obscene, blasphemous, threatening, racially discriminatory, and other legally objectionable material

To avoid liability for such material, you need to establish one or more of the following safeguards:

- proactive moderation of material before it appears on the website
- a documented 'notice and take down' procedure, under which infringing content is removed from the website as soon as it has been notified
- regular reviewing of material which has been posted, and removal of any which appears problematic

These issues all need to be addressed in your website's terms and conditions, so that visitors (and potential third-party complainants) are aware of the steps taken to prevent infringement. Many prudent owners also require visitors to register with the website before they can post messages. This allows the owner to contact the visitor if a problematic posting is made by the visitor, and, in certain circumstances, to provide that visitor's personal and contact information to a wronged third party, or to a law enforcement authority.

Account for full e-commerce website issues

Clearly, there is a wide variety of goods and services which are capable of being traded through a website. Further, the seller can be either the website owner or a third party trading through the website, as in an online auction service.

It is impossible to cover here all the issues which the various kinds of products can raise. Many have specific regulations which have been imposed by governments for social, ethical, and fiscal reasons. Examples of these include:

- sale of alcohol
- sale of medicines, particularly prescription-only medicines
- financial services
- betting, gaming, and lotteries
- auctions, particularly in various European countries

Depending on the jurisdiction and type of product being sold, a website may need to adhere to regulations such as:

- provision of clear information to consumers before the conclusion of a contract, including: the identity of the supplier; the main characteristics of what's being sold; payment and delivery arrangements; and the principal terms and conditions of the contract between seller and purchaser
- a minimum period during which a consumer may withdraw from the contract for any reason, and reject whatever has been purchased

Whatever you sell through your e-commerce website, it is important that you form a legally binding contract with the purchaser. For example, you might ensure that such a contract is formed by requiring the visitor to scroll through your terms and conditions and click on an 'I accept' button.

WHAT TO AVOID

Doing nothing because you think it's just too complicated

It is certainly true that there is a dizzying array of legal issues to ponder when trading over the Web. However, that's not an excuse for doing nothing. There is a basic minimum that can and should be addressed. The key is to understand the legal issues that, if not addressed properly, can have a major impact on your business.

Assuming that the long arm of the law does not reach online

This is a false assumption. Yes, it is often more difficult successfully to prosecute an organisation that is trading over the Web. However, that does not mean that governments and legal systems are ignoring those who they feel are breaking their laws, just because they happen to be on the Web.

Failing to deal with copyright and libel issues quickly

If a third party accuses you of libel or copyright infringement, it is imperative that you deal with it urgently. In many courts of law, the longer the libel remains published on the website, the greater the penalties.

RECOMMENDED LINKS

British and Irish Legal Information
  Institute:
www.bailii.org
LLRX.com:
www.llrx.com

SEE ALSO

**Computers, Information Technology, and
  E-commerce (p. 499)**
Managing Payments Online (p. 390)

MANAGING YOURSELF AND OTHERS

Managing Your Time

GETTING STARTED

Time is a man-made concept. Animals do not understand the idea. They live *in* time; they are in the moment; the present is all that counts. Remembering this can be useful in the business world: being able to focus on the present is often an effective way of getting through laborious tasks and not worrying about the past or future.

In business, time is money. Paradoxically, as technology proliferates (with the promise that it will increase productivity), it simultaneously adds complexity to workloads, frequently with fewer staff to complete the work. The only realistic way out of such a paradox is to make better use of time.

FAQS

How can I be a better time manager?

The *desire* to be good at time management is half the battle, but you need to be aware of the choices you have to make. These relate to your overall life balance and the values you hold.

As a first step, look at what you need to do and why. If some requests are outside your area of responsibility or expertise, work with your partner(s) and team (if you have one) to clarify the boundaries. Delegate as much as you can. Although this might seem difficult in a small business environment, it's a really useful skill to develop and it will benefit the business as whole—things will get done rather than sit on your desk.

You'll also need to be more realistic about your strengths and capabilities. Set realistic deadlines and build in some slack in the schedule to give yourself the best possible chance of meeting deadlines.

I run a very efficient team. One of my team members seems incredibly disorganised. What can I do?

A good team leader often needs to work with individual team members to help them to understand what is expected. Set realistic goals and give them adequate time and resources to complete the work. Additionally, if possible, ask them to examine their performance objectively and identify patterns of behaviour that contribute to being disorganised. Often time management requires a change in habitual behaviour. This can only be achieved by building awareness, charting a clear route, and rewarding success.

I've recently invested in a hand-held organiser but find I am still using a diary as well. How can I get away from using redundant systems?

Plan the time it will take to learn the new technology and transfer your information. Ask for a tutorial from someone who has made the leap already. Then, over a period of a month, wean yourself off the dual system by omitting the diary. You will soon find the computerised method more versatile and convenient than anything you have used in the past. Remember to back up your data regularly to avoid losing vital information due to battery or power failures, which can be distressingly common.

MAKING IT HAPPEN

Conduct a 'time audit'

You may find it useful to conduct a 'time audit' on your life. What is the balance between the demands placed upon you at work and those that define your private life? Does this balance satisfy you, or do you find yourself sacrificing one element for another? One key to good time management is being aware of the wider world in which you live and the interrelationships between its component parts. Another key is prioritising—if in fact there is not enough time to satisfy all competing demands—and then choosing how you apportion your time.

Take a large sheet of paper and write your

name in the centre. Write all the demands of your life around it. Include work hours, commuting, socialising, eating, sleeping, household duties, and family commitments. Remember that taking time for family and friends, exercise, hobbies, holidays, and just plain fun is important. Mark the number of hours that you dedicate to each of these areas throughout the day, month, or year. This chart graphically represents your life, in terms of the choices and tradeoffs you have made in areas that are important to you.

Ask yourself, is this how I want to live my life? You may decide to sacrifice some important areas in the short term, but be aware of what might happen when a particular phase of your life comes to an end. For example, how will you manage if you get married or divorced; when children grow up and leave home; if your business takes off and starts to demand much more of your time; if you have an accident or long-term illness; when you retire?

Evaluate what action needs to be taken

Take a highlighter and mark those areas on your chart that need attention. If, for instance, you are spending too much time at work, you need to review your professional objectives and decide how to achieve a better balance.

Life is all about choices. You may find that you can win more time by working from home, if your employer will permit it and your family will respect the necessary home-work boundaries.

You will probably find that there are other ways to prune hours from the day that are otherwise wasted. For instance, if you like to play sport or keep fit, consider finding a club near work where you can go early in the morning, instead of having to fit this in during the evening.

Look for patterns in the way you use your time. You may find that you are constantly in meetings that run late or that you pick up a lot of work that is not really profitable, or not what you really want to do because you are not assertive enough in saying no. If you don't have enough time and your own behaviour is contributing to the shortage, change your patterns of behaviour.

Learn to use the right tools

Time-management tools and techniques are only as useful as the time you invest in using them. Some commercially available tools and techniques include:

- handheld organisers, also known as personal digital assistants (PDAs)
- organisers, both computer-based programs and paper diaries or schedulers
- 'to do' lists
- prioritising work according to its importance, and focusing only on the essential
- shared diaries—team, secretarial, professional groups

If you are a person more accustomed to focusing on 'the moment' rather than the 'big picture', it may be a good idea to learn to stand back and look at time as a continuum, in terms of past, present, and future. Doing so gives you a sense or order, structure, and perspective.

If too much work is the issue, look at your workload, prioritise, and refer back to how it fits your job description. Decide, perhaps in

Some dos and don'ts of time management

Do	Don't
Undertake a 'time audit'	Spend time on unnecessary activities or those that do not serve your purpose
Be honest about how long things take	Try to undertake the impossible
Build in time for reflecting and learning	Blame others for your disorganisation
Build in time for yourself	Get hung up on process
Delegate wherever you can	Make commitments that you can't meet
Anticipate the pressure of commitments	Expect others to make up for what you can't do
Communicate with others where you have time conflicts	Give up
Plan ahead	

consultation with partners, which of your tasks add value to the business and its potential, and which would be better delegated to others.

WHAT TO AVOID
Buying a new gadget but still relying on old time-management tools
If you're going to buy a new device to help you plan your time better, you need to plan the time to learn to use it competently! Don't buy something and try to pick it up as you go along as this will make you very frustrated *and* inefficient.

Expecting too much of yourself and becoming disenchanted
Change is difficult and often requires a new set of skills. The principles of time management sound completely logical and straightforward, but in fact we lead extremely complex lives, and these simple principles are hard to put into practice. Don't overwhelm yourself by trying to change everything at once. Instead, establish a series of small, clear goals, and achieve them one by one.

Not being prepared to break bad habits, and not asking for help
Old habits do die hard, and one of the hardest to break is the way we structure and use our time. Everyone knows people who are always late or always early, who jump right onto tasks or are terrible procrastinators, who are stressed-out workaholics or who always seem miraculously refreshed and relaxed. The choices we make in managing our time are connected to the way we view ourselves and the world: making different choices affects our sense of identity and our relationships. Take it slowly, look to family, friends, and work colleagues for support in making these changes, and don't rule out taking workshops or looking for a consultant to help you.

RECOMMENDED LINK
Mindtools.com:
www.mindtools.com/pages/article/ newHTE_03.htm

SEE ALSO
Delegating (p. 412)
Managing Pressure (p. 407)

Managing Pressure

GETTING STARTED

Pressure is increasingly a way of life for managers and executives, and when you are running or growing a small business, you may feel as if you have to soak up the stress that in larger businesses would be shared among a larger team. This actionlist sets out to help you to identify different types of pressure and find ways to cope with them.

FAQS

My business partner thrives on pressure and expects me to do the same, but I work more effectively in a less intense environment. How can we work well together?

This is a common problem. If you can find a way to work together, however, your differing styles can actually complement each other. Try to broach this issue with your partner, and put together a plan of action.

I work well under pressure and have no problem with it, but it is now affecting my relationships with others who don't. What do I do?

Although pressure often gives us the boost we need to get a job done well and on time, it can, however, become so habitual that we fail to recognise its constant presence in our workplace. While people can become very focused in such an environment, they may also begin to neglect other parts of their lives such as their relationships with friends and family, or even their health. In the long term, pressure is not a desirable permanent fixture in working life.

How do I maximise the benefits and minimise the downside of pressure?

Pressure can improve our performance, but sometimes it can be at the detriment of other factors such as relationships. Under pressure people often become highly task-orientated and focus on the immediate areas. Other people become very short-term orientated. Observe your own behaviour, seek feedback, and evaluate whether you believe there is an issue or not. The earlier you recognise it, the easier it is to ensure that the negative impact of pressure is alleviated.

MAKING IT HAPPEN

Work towards a work/life balance

Managing pressure is about achieving some balance in your life and activities. It is usually in the workplace that we are most susceptible to pressure, but be aware that pressure sometimes stems from home or the social environment. Pressure can make us do or say things that, on reflection, we wish we hadn't. Where possible, try to make sure that work is not the central focus of your life. For example, take advantage of your allotted number of holidays, take exercise regularly, and maintain your relationships with friends and family. Having hobbies and interests that help you to 'turn off' is also very useful. Try to raise your concerns with someone you trust.

Recognise the symptoms of pressure

Symptoms of pressure fall into four main categories:

- **physical**—headaches, sweats, panic attacks, raised blood pressure, sickness, sleeplessness, palpitations
- **physiological**—over-production of adrenalin, leading to tension, aggression, feelings of stress in the so-called 'fight or flight' syndrome
- **emotional**—depression, feelings of inadequacy, loss of confidence, detachment, denial
- **behavioural**—focus on short-term tasks, loss of temper, dismissive behaviour, self-centredness, irritability, impatience with others

Know the causes and types of pressure

There are numerous causes of pressure in the workplace today, many of which are linked. Some of the most obvious are:

- insufficient resources—not enough time, funds, or staff to get the job done properly
- insufficient *appropriate* resources—skills gaps in certain areas
- unreasonable demands—customers expecting you constantly to be at their beck and call
- improper staffing or staff direction—failure to understand what different people are capable of
- insufficient training
- poor planning
- promising to do too much too quickly

There are also many *types* of pressure. The most common is time pressure—too much to do and too little time to do it in. However, there are plenty of coping strategies to help manage it. For example:

- Anticipate where the pressure may come from.
- Plan and resource what needs to be delivered and when.
- Prioritise actions to ensure that things are done efficiently.
- Communicate progress to other stakeholders in the task and manage expectations. For example, if a task will take longer to complete than originally thought, be upfront. The sooner you alert people to potential problems, the sooner you can work together to plan for contingencies.
- Understand how others respond to pressure and work with them.

While this may not alleviate time pressure by actually extending your deadline, it will allow you to feel more in control.

Where time pressure continues to be an issue, it may indicate that you need to re-evaluate your role and its demands and resources. Are you delegating enough? Have you prioritised your actions? Are you promising to do too much too quickly?

Find a solution

Solutions fall into two areas:

- organisational—structure, planning
- personal—intellectual, behavioural, physical

Organisational solutions

Where pressure exists, it could be as a result of the nature of the job, or of how the role fits in with the rest of the business. In the small company environment, responsibilities may not be as clearly defined as in a larger concern. Your role or job may need to be renegotiated with different boundaries put in place. Clearer lines of responsibility, as well as better delegation and prioritisation, will help reduce pressure.

Better planning, with the ability to anticipate pressure points, can help ensure that resources are in the right place at the right time. Sometimes pressure is unavoidable, but certainly more bearable if it is for short periods of time.

Personal solutions

On a personal level, we may put ourselves under pressure when we lose confidence in our ability. Having a good self-awareness and understanding of our real skills is important. Building and supporting confidence is also invaluable.

Be aware of how you respond to pressure. Some symptoms you display may be positive and motivating, others not. Know your balance and how others respond. At the same time, be aware of pressure in others. No two people respond to pressure in the same way.

Physically there are things we can do to help manage pressure. Exercise is good from a health viewpoint, and may allow pent-up frustration to be exercised out. Even stretching in your chair, going for a quick walk, or talking to a friend or confidante are good remedies for relieving pressure. Try to take a break through regular holidays.

Most important to remember is that you are not alone in managing pressure; there are others in your life who want you to succeed and will help you if you let them. Having a sense of humour can help, as can remembering to step back from a situation. It is important to tackle the underlying causes of pressure if you can, rather than just dealing with the symptoms. Above all, remember that you're not alone. Don't hesitate to confide in a friend or colleague or seek counselling if you need help.

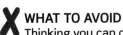

WHAT TO AVOID
Thinking you can do it all alone

People sometimes take on too much, thinking that they can cope without additional support. Perhaps you think you are saving your business money by covering a number of responsibilities—but in reality you could be wasting money in missed opportunities or inefficiency. Often, under pressure, the one thing we become incapable of doing well is delegating work appropriately. Better communication and prioritising objectives are therefore essential. Working on identifying better resource management, prioritising the work load, building in time/slack, anticipating pressure points, and monitoring progress are all important in dealing with pressure.

Never saying 'no'

Perhaps you're one of those people who are capable of sustaining high levels of activity over a long period of time, and it has become expected that you always perform at that pitch. The solution is about being assertive and saying no when the pressure is too great. Like a car, you can't stay in fifth gear all the time; you have to vary your speed and occasionally have a 'pit stop'.

Succumbing to a 'long hours culture'

Sometimes people assume that the longer they work, the better, and that longer hours equals great productivity. It's just not true.

When you are your own boss, there'll be times when you've so much to do you think you should stay up all night to finish the tasks at hand, but try not to do this if you can. Anything you write, create, or produce when you're half asleep you'll just have to do again when you've had some sleep. Try instead to adjust the way you think. Shift your focus from the hours that you work and concentrate instead on the achievement of your goals or tasks.

Taking it out on others

Pressure is no respecter of boundaries. Pressure from one aspect of your life will eventually affect all other elements of your life, too. Be aware of how these pressures may affect your work performance. Try not to transfer them to those who are not part of the problem. Work on the causes and not the symptoms. Compartmentalisation will only work in the short term.

RECOMMENDED LINKS
About.com site:
http://stress.about.com
Mindtools.com:
www.mindtools.com/smpage.html
UK National Work-Stress Network:
www.workstress.net

SEE ALSO
Delegating (p. 412)
Managing Your Time (p. 404)

Focus On: Managing Projects
Robert Buttrick

GETTING STARTED

The progress of companies has always relied on the management of projects. New plants, new methods, new ventures all require dedicated teams working to strict timetables and separate budgets. However today, managers may spend as much time in interdisciplinary, cross-functional project teams as they do in their normal posts—project management has now become a core competence for all managers. This applies not only to projects undertaken for customers (external projects), but also to those undertaken for the development of the business itself (internal projects).

All businesses, regardless of size, have problems and opportunities they need to address. These may be related to introducing new technology, developing people, or introducing new products, processes and systems; there is always something, somewhere that needs to be created or improved.

Project management is the key tool for tackling change, and is well suited to meet the needs of modern businesses, big or small. Unfortunately it's too often thought of as something 'for techies', rather than the powerful business tool it is. In addition, it's often said it is 'too much of an overhead for small businesses'. Nothing could be further from the truth. Project management may be as formal or informal as you want—that is your choice. But underlying both formal and informal approaches are the same set of principles, which, if you apply them correctly, will give you the results you need.

In small businesses, project management does not need sophisticated tools and system—often a big wall, paper, and Post-it stickers are all you need for planning and control.

FAQS

What exactly is involved?

Understanding the scope and complexity of project management is an essential first step to achieving success. Project management involves the following key elements:

- making sure your projects are driven by your strategy
- using a staged approach to manage your projects
- placing high emphasis on the early stages
- engaging your 'stakeholders' (that is, everyone potentially involved or affected by a project, such as staff, customers, and suppliers)
- encouraging teamwork and everyone's commitment
- ensuring success by planning for it
- monitoring against the plan
- formally closing the project

How can I make sure that a project runs smoothly?

Your project will run much more smoothly if you focus on a few basics.

- Define strategies clearly so that you are better able to eliminate low-value projects.
- Plan through progressive stages: proposal, initial investigation, detailed investigation, development and testing, trial, operation, and closure.
- Concentrate on the early stages of the project, when the decisions you take can have a far-reaching effect on the outcome.
- Analyse the project, determine which are the intrinsically risky parts, and act to reduce, avoid, or, insure against the risks.
- To make projects succeed, tip the balance of power towards the project and the person appointed as project leader away from your company's normal management structures.
- Focus progress monitoring more on the

future than on completion of activities, which doesn't predict that future milestones will be met.

MAKING IT HAPPEN
Be aware of your business vision
Don't waste time on unnecessary projects. Be clear about your company's 'vision' (that is, what you want to achieve, how, and when) or you'll risk wasting precious resources on ideas that are ultimately worthless and which will risk the business's overall performance.

Use a staged approach to manage your projects
It's very rare to be able to plan a project completely to its conclusion when you've just started work on it. However, it's usually possible to at least plan the next steps in detail and prepare a rough plan for the remainder.

As you progress through the project you gather more information, risk is reduced, and confidence in delivery increases. These progressive steps are called 'stages'. Companies have their own names for these, but typically they are:

- **Proposal:** identifying the idea or need.
- **Initial investigation:** having a quick look at the possible requirements and solutions.
- **Detailed investigation:** undertaking a feasibility study of the options, choosing a solution and defining it.
- **Develop and test:** building the solutions.
- **Trial:** piloting the solution.
- **Release:** putting it into practice and closing the project.

You should use the same generic stage names **for all your projects**. This makes the use and understanding of the process very much easier, avoiding confusion and the need to learn different terms for various types of project. What differs is the content of each project, the extent to which each stage is used, the level of activity, the nature of the activity, the resources required, the stakeholders and decision-makers needed.

Concentrate on the early stages
Decisions taken during the early stages of a project have a far-reaching effect on the outcome. Creative thinking and solutions can cut delivery times in half and reduce costs dramatically. On the other hand, once development is under way, it's seldom possible to make savings of anything but a few percent whilst introducing changes later can be very costly. Up to 50% of the project life can be usefully spent on the investigative stages before any final deliverable is physically built. Sound investigative work means objectives are clearer and plans more robust; work spent on this is rarely wasted effort.

Engage your stakeholders and understand their needs
As mentioned above, a stakeholder is any person involved in or impacted by a project. The involvement of stakeholders, such as staff, customers, and suppliers, adds considerable value at all stages of the process. Viewed from a stakeholder perspective, a particular project may be just one more problem they have to cope with as well as fulfilling their usual duties; it may appear irrelevant to them, or even regressive. If their consent is required to make things happen, you ignore them at your peril!

Encourage team work and commitment
If you have a team of people working with or for you, involve everyone so that they all work together. This approach really will deliver the best results. If you are managing the project, be as open as you can with your team and they'll appreciate it.

Smaller business often have an advantage over larger organisations in this area as larger businesses have to draw on people in more (and necessarily separate) departments to collaborate on projects, and this can cause all manner of internal problems. As there are fewer line managers in small businesses, the projects are 'business-led' not manager-led, leading to effective delivery. In time, this will also lead to effective change which can be managed as the business grows and matures.

RECOMMENDED LINK
Project Workout:
www.projectworkout.com

Delegating

GETTING STARTED

If you have a team working with you, delegation is a key skill to acquire or develop. Delegation is not just about giving tasks to others—it's about getting staff to take full responsibility for certain key functions or tasks. In order for a business to grow (and for employees to find new paths of development) new people must be employed to take over established functions, allowing others to develop different aspects of the business.

Owner managers tend to like being in control of everything. They find it difficult to let go of things that they have created and nurtured, yet this is exactly what they must do if the operation is to grow and develop.

FAQS

Why do people find it difficult to delegate?

There are many reasons why you may find it difficult to delegate. Often, it seems quicker to perform the task yourself rather than bother to explain it to somebody else and then correct his or her mistakes. You might worry that the person will make a bit of a hash of it and it'll take a long time to put right the mistakes they make. On the other hand, you may feel threatened by the competence of an employee who is quick on the uptake and does well. There is a fear that the employee may take over the role of being the person the rest of the staff goes to with their problems. They may even find something wrong with the way *you* do things.

If you lack confidence, you may find it hard to give instructions and you'll put off delegating. If you do delegate, and problems arise because the employee fails to do what you've asked him or her to do, you may doubt your own ability to confront the person about his or her actions. If staff have been given increased responsibilities and have done well, you may not be confident of being able to reward them sufficiently. Conversely, you might be reluctant to delegate tasks that you think are too tedious.

Finally, you may realise that delegation is necessary, but you don't know where to start, or how to go about it. You need some kind of method to follow. The following paragraphs will help put you on the right track.

How can delegation help me?

Delegation offers many benefits. Done well, it will allow you to concentrate on the things you do best and also give you the time and space to tackle more interesting and challenging tasks in the future. You'll be less likely to put off making key decisions and you'll be much more effective. Your staff will benefit too; everyone needs new challenges, and by delegating to them, you'll be able to test their ability in a range of areas and increase their contribution to the business. Staff can take quick decisions themselves and they'll develop a better understanding of the details concerned. Done well, delegation should improve the overall productivity of employees.

It's all too tempting to withdraw into 'essential' tasks and not develop relations with your team. The bottom line is that it is wasteful for senior staff to be given high-level compensation for doing low-value work, and passing tasks down the line is essential if the business is to grow. Not knowing how to do this is recognised as one of the biggest obstacles to small business growth. By delegating, you'll have much more time to think strategically about business growth.

Delegation doesn't make things easier (there will always be other challenges), but it does make things more efficient and effective. Essentially, it represents a more interactive way of working with a team of people, and it involves instruction, training, and development. The results will be well worth the time and effort you invest in doing it properly.

When should I delegate?

Delegation is fundamental to successful management—look for opportunities to do it. If you have too much work to do to complete all the tasks at hand, or if you don't have enough time to devote to important tasks, delegate. When it's clear that certain staff need to develop, particularly new employees, or when an employee clearly has the skills needed to perform a specific task, delegate.

What tasks should I delegate?

Begin with any routine administrative tasks that take up too much of your time. There are likely to be many small everyday tasks which you have always done—you may even enjoy doing them (for example, sending faxes)—but they're not a good use of your time. Review these small jobs and delegate as many of them as you can. Being your company's point of contact for a particular person or organisation, which is important but can be time consuming, is also an excellent task to delegate.

On a larger scale, delegate projects that it makes sense for one person to handle; this will be a good test of how the person manages and co-ordinates the project. Give the person something he or she has every chance of completing successfully, rather than an impossible task at which others have failed and which may well prove a negative experience for the person concerned. Tasks for which a particular employee has a special aptitude should be delegated.

Who should I delegate to?

Make sure you understand the person you are delegating to. He or she must have the skills and ability, or at least the potential, to develop into the role and must be someone you can trust. It's a good idea to test out the employee with small tasks that will help show what he or she can do. Also make sure that the employee is available for the assignment—beware of overburdening your

effective workers. Delegation should be spread out among as many employees as possible, so think about the possibility of assigning a task to two or more people.

MAKING IT HAPPEN
Be positive

Think positively: you have the right to delegate, and you must delegate. You won't get it 100% right the first time, but you'll improve with experience. Be as decisive as you can and if you need to improve your assertiveness skills, consider attending a course or reading one of the many books on the subject. A positive approach will also give your employees confidence in themselves, and they need to feel that you believe in them.

If you expect efficiency from the person you delegate to, organise yourself first. If there's no overall plan of what is going on, it will be hard to identify, schedule, and evaluate the work being delegated. Prepare before seeing the person (but don't use this as a ploy to delay!). Assess the task and decide how much responsibility the person will have. Assess the person's progress regularly and make notes.

Discuss the task to be delegated

When you meet the employee or employees you are delegating to, discuss the tasks and the problems in depth, and explain fully what is expected of them. It is crucial to give people precise objectives, but encourage them to seek these out themselves by letting them ask you questions and participate in setting the parameters. They need to understand why they are doing the task, and where it fits into the scheme of things. Ask them how they will go about the task, discuss their plan and the support they might need.

Set targets and offer support if necessary

Targets should be set and deadlines scheduled into diaries. Summarise what has been agreed, and take notes about what the employee is required to do, so everyone is clear. If the person is given a lot of creative scope and is being tested out, you may decide to be deliberately vague, but if the task is urgent and critical, you must be specific.

How much support you offer and give will very much depend on the person and your relationship with them. In the early stages you might want to work with the person and to share certain tasks, but you'll be able to back off more as your understanding of the person's abilities increases. Encourage your staff to come back to you if they have any problems—while it is important to have time alone, you should be accessible if anyone has a problem or the situation changes. If an employee needs to check something with you, try to get it back to him or her quickly. Don't interfere or criticise if things are going according to plan.

Monitoring progress is vital—it's very easy to forget all about the task until the completion date, but in the meantime, all sorts of things could have gone wrong. When planning, time should be built in to review progress. If more problems were expected to arise and nothing has been heard, check with the employee that all is well. Schedule routine meetings with the person and be flexible enough to change deadlines and objectives as the situation changes.

How did it go?

When a task is complete, give praise and review how things went. If an employee's responsibilities are increased, make sure he or she receives fair rewards for it. On the other hand, there may be limits on what can be offered, so don't offer rewards you can't deliver. Also bear in mind that development can carry its own rewards. Such career development issues can be discussed with the employee in appraisals, and the results of delegated tasks noted for this purpose. If the person has failed to deliver, discuss it with them, find out what went wrong, and aim to resolve problems in the future.

WHAT TO AVOID
Expecting employees to do things like you do

Managers often criticise the way things are done because it isn't the way they would have done it themselves. Remember that people prefer working in different ways and concentrate on the results rather than the methods used to obtain them.

Not giving people a chance

If you are giving a person something new to do, you must be patient. It will take time for employees to develop new skills, but it is time that will pay off in the end. Have faith in the people around you.

Delegating responsibility without authority

It's unfair to expect results from someone with one hand tied behind his or her back. If you are going to delegate responsibilities, make sure that those involved know this, and confer the necessary authority upon the person you are delegating to.

SEE ALSO
Developing Leadership Skills (p. 444)
Managing Pressure (p. 407)
Managing Your Time (p. 404)
Small and Growing Businesses (p. 478)

Staff Planning

GETTING STARTED

As your business grows, it will naturally require more people to carry out the work and new skills will be required to handle a wider range of business activities and developing technology. You'll need to have new employees in place in good time to meet increased demand, and you should provide opportunities to develop, train, and promote existing staff. Future salary and training costs need to be built into the cash-flow forecast and financial plan. It is important to foresee these requirements and to plan accordingly.

This actionlist looks at the main issues that a small business needs to address as it plans for its staffing requirements.

FAQS
What is the best way to approach staff planning?

A number of statistical methods have been developed to help businesses to analyse, predict, and plan future staffing requirements. Each business is different, so there is no single answer to how best to plan. In basic terms, though, you'll need to forecast sales and plan future production levels, estimate the amount and type of work that will be required, identify who can do this work and how training and recruitment can fill the gaps, and then implement the plan and review its success.

Link staff planning to the wider strategic planning process. Your staffing plan should develop from the long-term forecast for the development of sales and the required increase in working capacity that this represents. The various types of work must be identified and quantified. Costs may then be attached, enabling budgets and finance to be planned. You will need to plan for the long term (for example, five years), the year ahead (relating to the annual budget), and possibly month by month to show how change may be phased in during the year ahead (coinciding with the cash-flow forecast). All this should feed back into your main strategic plan for business development.

MAKING IT HAPPEN
Estimate future work requirements

In addition to estimates for future levels of output, you need information about how work is done, who does it, and what the options are for making changes.

The first step is to analyse jobs by clarifying the main job elements and determining how much work is required to carry them out. Don't make too many assumptions about what people do and how they do it. Your staff are more in touch than you are with how things are really done. A minor task may take much longer than you think. Another task may be so boring that it seriously threatens effectiveness and job satisfaction. While a scientific 'work study' can be useful, informal discussion and team meetings are a much more diplomatic way to look at how work is done.

You then need to estimate how workloads will increase. From sales forecasts you can work out the required level of production from month to month. These estimates then need to be shown in terms of staffing levels. The number of workers required will often increase in proportion to the volume of work, for example, double the work (usually) requires double the workers. In some cases the workload might be helped by further training or the introduction of different working methods. Nevertheless, it is often helpful to create estimates based on the amount of work required to produce one unit of production (sometimes known as the Workload Method). The work required to produce one unit is split into its constituent parts. Each part is given a time value. These can then be multiplied by the number of units required, giving the total amount of work of each type. For example:

Types of work	Time/unit	@180/month	@200/month
Assembly	1.0	180hrs (24 days)	200hrs (26.6 days)
Testing	0.4	72hrs (9.6 days)	80hrs (10.6 days)
Packaging	0.2	36hrs (4.8 days)	40hrs (5.3 days)

Fluctuations in demand are important in many industries. In some cases you may need to employ some people on a casual basis in order to meet peak demand. Some industries work to annualised hours whereby an employee will work a set number of hours per year but with a staggered working pattern. This may mean that the majority of their hours are in the summer months (for example) but their wages are evenly spread throughout the year. This removes problems of overtime payments for the business and removes the need to be continually training casual workers. It may also help to switch resources or to build up stock in order to even out these fluctuations. On the whole, most organisations will not want extra stock on the premises because of storage costs, fire risks, and so on.

Analyse the workforce

It can be helpful to profile the people you employ by summarising and collating information about individuals into a single quick-reference document. For example, you could look at what each person does, areas of competence, qualifications, and development options. If these can be presented on a single sheet it can help you identify the various options for development. Include also the basic information in your staff audit, such as salary and length of service.

You can also profile your workforce as a whole, by identifying some key measures for the way it has been developing. For example, you could look at staff turnover (number leaving divided by total workforce) and growth (number of staff year on year). Other measures might include supervision (number of staff per supervisor/manager) and promotion (number of managers from the workforce compared to the number of managers recruited from outside). You could also consider the annual recruitment cost (include the time required to interview and coach new staff), annual training costs, and productivity (turnover divided by number of staff). Also consider the average time that employees stay with the company, and staff stability (this can be measured by a staff stability index, which looks at staff with long service and provides an indication of their tendency to stay with the organisation).

Staff planning is not an exact science. Comparative information may be available through your trade association. Key measures are mainly useful to help you understand the present situation, to set targets, and to measure success. There may be limits to what can be achieved (for example, in your competitive environment, promotion opportunities may be limited or salary development may be very difficult).

Relate tasks to individuals

Adjusting individual work roles can become very complicated. Where a large team is working on a variety of projects, changing one factor can have an impact upon everyone else. You need a simple way to look at who does what, and then to look at what happens if you change who does what, and how this will develop over a period of time. A computer spreadsheet is especially useful for this, enabling you to reconsider values without having to recalculate totals every time.

One approach is to create a matrix that sets individuals against specific work areas. For example, calculating on an average of 18 working days (allowing for sickness and holiday) per full-time employee per month, the diagram shows how work (shown in days) is split between a number of employees, for an estimated level of activity in each area.

An overview chart for the year ahead is useful. A month-by-month chart showing fluctuations in production requirements will help you to plan for change in good time to meet your future commitments.

Types of work	Amount	Ali	Jim	Aisha	Helen	Justin	Omar
Sales and Admin	18	3	12	3			
Research	47		4	15	16	6	6
Edit/Proofing	28		2		2	12	12
DTP	15	15					
Total Days	108	18	18	18	18	18	18

Consider staff development issues

Staff planning provides an opportunity to put into action your plans for developing individuals. Your personnel policy document should be a useful framework to help you take decisions that will affect individual employees.

Job design and job satisfaction are two important areas to consider. As the business and the individuals change and develop, new jobs need to be defined. Roles and job descriptions must be clear cut. Look for activities that complement each other and suit the skills and experience of the people concerned.

Be open minded about what people can achieve; do not assume that certain individuals can't take on new responsibilities. To provide scope for staff to develop, aim to take new people on at the most junior level, promoting existing staff into new positions of responsibility when more senior vacancies arise.

If you are facing new skill requirements, could existing staff be trained to meet them? The cost of training should be offset against the benefits of being able to use someone familiar with the business and who is not an unknown quantity. Training is a benefit to staff and is also a motivator.

Some kind of plan for pay increases should be considered. If pay is improved ad hoc, you may risk not being able to provide fair long-term benefits across the board. A clear pay structure will also help long-term financial planning. Seek to compete with similar rates in the industry if you wish to retain your experienced staff. Lower pay may keep your prices competitive, but you will not be able to hold on to the best staff available. Seek information about standard rates of pay, and create salary bands related to skill and responsibility.

Consider recruitment lead times

Make adequate provision for the time it takes for new people to settle in; even the most competent people take time to learn about the job and to gain the trust of their colleagues. If you do need to recruit, the lead times for advertising, selection, notice periods, training, and induction can be long. You may need to start the whole process as much as six months in advance of the time when the person's full workload will be required. Recruitment is also a significant workload for managers, and should be accounted for in your forward planning.

WHAT TO AVOID
Making it complicated
Use simple analysis and planning methods for the best results.

Not thinking about your own staff first
Remember to talk to your staff first about how jobs, individuals, and teams can be developed and improved. Aim to develop and retain your existing workforce before thinking of recruitment from outside.

RECOMMENDED LINKS
Chartered Institute of Personnel and Development (ePolitix website):
www.epolitix.com
Chartered Management Institute:
www.managers.org.uk

SEE ALSO
Conducting Interviews and Making Job Offers (p. 423)
Employee Benefits/Compensation (p. 505)
Handling Resignations (p. 454)
Understanding the 2003 Changes to Employment Law (p. 420)

Focus On: Finding and Keeping Top Talent
Philip Sadler

GETTING STARTED

Just as businesses have changed dramatically in nature over the last 20 years, so have people's attitudes to their employers—and the attitudes of the most talented people are no exception. Furthermore, knowledge is more important than ever before and a major source of competitive advantage. Attracting, finding, and retaining talented people is therefore vital for success. Not only are people the most decisive and expensive resource, they also determine the success of every activity within the business

This actionlist explains how to find and keep the best people—a challenge that involves:
- understanding the characteristics of talent-intensive businesses.
- choosing the best ways to attract, recruit, and retain the most talented people.
- building the right work environment and culture.

FAQS

What are the characteristics of talent-intensive businesses?

Businesses that are rich in talent can be spotted in the following ways.
- Their principal assets (that is, their talented people) do not appear on the balance sheet (although they are, or should be, the main determinants of the company's market valuation).
- These key assets are mobile. They can, despite contracts of service, simply walk away.
- Talent-intensive businesses rely particularly on creativity and imagination.
- The success criteria for talent-intensive organisations stretch far beyond the accountants' bottom line. For example, winning an award for innovation may weigh far more than profit or cash-flow.

MAKING IT HAPPEN

Find the best people

Don't assume that finding top talent will be expensive or lengthy: it need not be, even for the most senior appointments. If you have a vacancy, first of all ask your current team to see if they know anyone who might be a good candidate. Because they understand you, the role, and the business, they are best placed to find a good candidate. There may be other people in your company's network that could also suggest a candidate: shareholders, suppliers, customers, and professional advisers may all be able to recommend good people.

Make sure you allow enough time to make the right appointment, and to ensure that others meet the preferred candidate. Time pressures and isolation are two key factors that can lead managers to make appointments that are flawed.

Choose the best way to recruit

The recruitment activity itself can be separated into two quite distinct processes. The first is attracting people whose talent has already been established and recognised elsewhere. This can be called the 'transplanting' type of recruiting, equivalent to digging up and repositioning a mature tree or shrub in the quest for an instant garden.

The second process is the 'seed bed' or 'nursery' approach, recruiting young people straight from school or university, nurturing or developing their emerging talents and bringing them to fruition. This is clearly a longer-term approach and can be a bit risky For example, you may give too much weight to academic qualifications. Less risky, however, is the process of finding talent among existing employees. Assuming they've been in employment for some time, a well-designed appraisal and development procedure can be a good way of finding promising candidates.

Keep the best people

Remember that keeping top talent is as much about the people, the job, and the business as it is about the specific individual. Ask yourself at regular intervals the following key questions:

- who are my key people?
- what makes them exceptional?
- how are they feeling? Positive (for example, stimulated, challenged, valued) or negative (under pressure, concerned, struggling to perform at their best)?
- are their working environment and terms and conditions of employment competitive?
- do they know how much I value them?
- what are their aspirations and are they realistic? If so, what am I doing to support them? Do they know I'm doing this?

Finally, it is worth remembering that whether you are trying to find or to keep someone, pay remains important for most people, if not for its own sake, then for the sense of recognition that it brings to the individual.

Build a culture that retains talent

As mentioned above, when it comes to retaining talent within your business, the need for an adequate rewards package goes without saying. What makes the real difference in keeping talented employees loyal, however, is the extent to which the company provides them with a working environment favourable to creativity, self-expression, and the exercise of initiative. Small business have an advantage over larger organisations here, as bigger companies are hierarchical, bureaucratic, and conformist in order to achieve efficiency and uniformity, yet it is just these characteristics that turn off highly creative people.

The chief characteristics of a culture that nurtures talent are:

- effective teams
- authority residing in expertise and competence rather than rank or status
- talented people respecting and recognising the contribution of the colleagues who support them
- respected leadership—talented people are critical people who do not follow blindly, and know when the emperor has no clothes.
- freedom, autonomy, space, and flexibility.
- openness and trust.
- encouragement of risk-taking

WHAT TO AVOID
Thinking that money is everything

Companies often make the mistake of assuming that cash is the most important factor in attracting or retaining someone, which often puts small businesses at a disadvantage. An outstanding performer in any field is unlikely to move from one business to another if it involves a drop in pay, but there are other factors to consider. In the case of highly talented people, for example, a key influence on the decision whether or not to move jobs is the reputation the recruiting business has in its particular field. Is it at the leading edge? Does it set the pace for its industry? Does the individual feel flattered by being approached? Reputation building, therefore, is a key element in recruiting strategy.

Failing to distinguish between recruiting and finding talent

The distinction between recruiting talent and finding it is important; sometimes a business looks outside for new talent when the potential for outstanding performance already exists unnoticed among the existing team.

RECOMMENDED LINK
Leaders Direct:
www.leadersdirect.com

SEE ALSO
Assessing Your Entrepreneurial Profile: Do You Have What It Takes? (p. 6)

Understanding the 2003 Changes to Employment Law

GETTING STARTED

When your business employs people, it must comply with a number of legal requirements. Many of these are there to protect the rights of your employees, while others relate to aspects such as employees' tax, National Insurance, working time, and health and safety.

Employment legislation is changing all the time and 2003 has been a particularly busy year for new legislation. It is important that you keep up to date with what is going on in the field of employment law to ensure your employees are treated fairly and to avoid potentially costly employment tribunals. This actionlist contains a brief guide to the most important recent developments, and tells you where you can go for help and advice.

FAQS

Where can I get advice on employment law?

There are many sources of help and advice you can access, the most important of which are listed below.

Department of Trade and Industry—TIGER website: The DTI's Employment Relations Directorate has developed a website devoted to certain aspects of employment law. TIGER stands for Tailored Interactive Guidance on Employment Rights. Currently the site has sections on the national minimum wage, maternity rights, paternity rights, adoption rights, and flexible working rights. All of these areas have seen massive changes in related legislation during 2003 and the site provides comprehensive guidance on all the changes.

Department of Trade and Industry—Employment Relations Directorate: The Employment Relations Directorate is actually responsible for producing employment legislation. It produces guidance on all employment legislation, which can be ordered through DTI Publications or can be downloaded free from the Directorate's website. The website also has a 'Hot Topics' page which gives details of the latest legislation and potential legislation which is being consulted on or currently going through parliament. The DTI does not provide information on individual cases.

Advisory, Conciliation, and Arbitration Service (Acas): Acas works to prevent and resolve employment disputes, conciliates in actual or potential complaints to employment tribunals, provides information and advice, and promotes good practice. Acas has several offices throughout the United Kingdom which can be contacted for advice. There is also a central telephone helpline (on 0845 747 4747) which can deal with enquiries on employment legislation. Acas has its own publications service, which provides a wide range of free and priced publications covering several aspects of employment law, for example, recruitment and selection, discipline and grievance procedures, and handling redundancy. Many of these are available for download free from the Acas website.

Commission for Racial Equality: The Commission provides advice and assistance on equal opportunities policy and practice to many organisations and businesses, large and small. The Commission has produced an 'Employment Code of Practice' and provides information on how to ensure that job advertisements comply with the Race Relations Act 1976. The Commission has a number of offices throughout the United Kingdom and general enquiries can be made to its head office on telephone number (020) 7939 0000.

Equal Opportunities Commission: The Commission is the expert body on equality between women and men in the United Kingdom. It provides information on implementing equal opportunities policies in the workplace and compliance with sex discrimination laws. The Commission has offices in England, Wales, and Scotland, and a national inquiry line (on 0845 601 5901). Its website provides a wide range of free information and publications which can be downloaded.

Disability Rights Commission: The Disability Rights Commission (DRC) has been set up to provide information and advice to disabled people, employers, and service providers about their rights and duties under the Disability Discrimination Act 1995 (DDA). The DRC's comprehensive website provides practical guidance about the best ways to ensure that disabled people are treated fairly, and the Commission can also provide advice on recruiting disabled people and providing equal treatment in the workplace. The DRC can be contacted via a national helpline (0845 762 2633) or through its website.

Other sources of help and advice: Your solicitor will be able to keep you updated on changes in employment law. In addition, advice can be obtained from your local Business Link, Small Business Gateway, Business Connect, or Invest Northern Ireland office.

MAKING IT HAPPEN

There have been a large number of changes in employment law during 2003 and there are more to come. Here is a summary of the major changes.

Working time—young workers

Under the Working Time (Amendment) Regulations 2002, from 6 April 2003, workers aged between the minimum school leaving age and 18 must not work longer than 40 hours per week and 8 hours per day. These hours cannot be averaged out and there is no opt-out. Young workers may work longer hours where this is necessary either to maintain continuity of service or production, or in response to a surge in demand for a service or product—*provided* that there is no adult available to perform the task, and the employer ensures that the

training needs of the young worker are not adversely affected.

Flexible working

Under the Employment Act 2002, from 6 April 2003, parents with children aged under six or disabled children aged under 18 will have the right to request a flexible working pattern, and their employers will have a duty to consider their applications seriously. The right enables parents to request to work flexibly. It does not provide an automatic right to work flexibly, as there will always be circumstances when the employer is unable to accommodate the employee's desired work pattern. The employee has a responsibility to think carefully about his or her desired working pattern when making an application, and the employer is required to follow a specific procedure to ensure requests are considered seriously.

Parental rights

From 6 April 2003, several new rights were provided regarding maternity, paternity, and adoption leave.

Maternity leave—The length of ordinary maternity leave has been extended to 26 weeks. In addition, a woman can take up to 26 weeks additional maternity leave. A woman who intends to return to work at the end of her full maternity leave entitlement is no longer required to give any further notification to her employer. Statutory maternity pay has increased to £100 per week.

Paternity leave—Providing an employee meets certain conditions, he is able to take one or two weeks paid paternity leave following the birth of his child. Employees must inform their employer of their intention to take paternity leave by the end of the 15th week before the baby is expected. They are entitled to £100 statutory paternity pay per week.

Adoption leave—Adopters are entitled to up to 26 weeks ordinary adoption leave, followed immediately by up to 26 weeks additional adoption leave—a total of up to 52 weeks leave. Adopters are required to inform their employer of their intention to take adoption leave within seven days of being notified by their adoption agency that they have been matched with a child for adoption. They are entitled to £100 per week statutory adoption pay during ordinary adoption leave.

Equal pay

The equal pay questionnaire, which came into effect on 6 April 2003 under the Equal Pay (Questions and Replies) Order 2003, is intended to help employees who believe they may not have received equal pay, to request key information from their employers to establish whether this is the case and, if so, the reasons why. The point of the questionnaire is to help establish whether an individual is receiving less pay and whether the employer agrees that the people being compared are doing equal work. The information should help to establish key facts early on and make it easier to resolve any disputes in the workplace.

Potential changes

Other changes to employment law likely to occur during late 2003 include:

- reforms to the employment tribunals system
- dispute resolution regulations to move the focus of resolving disputes in the workplace away from employment tribunals, placing an obligation on employees to raise grievances with employers before applying to a tribunal
- reforms to the Transfer of Undertakings (Protection of Employment) Regulations 1981 (TUPE). These reforms will improve and simplify the effects of TUPE and ensure compliance with the EC Acquired Rights Directive
- regulations to prevent discrimination on

the grounds of sexual orientation, religion, or belief

WHAT TO AVOID
Assuming you know everything about employment law

If you are not aware of changes in employment law you cannot comply with them. If you fail to comply, you are at risk of being taken to an employment tribunal by a disgruntled employee and could be liable for large fines if you are found in breach of the law.

RECOMMENDED LINKS

Advisory, Conciliation and Arbitration Service (ACAS):
www.acas.org.uk
Business Eye (Wales):
www.businesseye.org.uk
Business Gateway (Scotland):
www.bgateway.com
Business Link (England):
www.businesslink.org
Commission for Racial Equality:
www.cre.gov.uk
Disability Rights Commission:
www.drc-gb.org
DTI—Tailored Interactive Guide on Employment Rights:
www.tiger.gov.uk
DTI Employment Relations Directorate:
www.dti.gov.uk/er
DTI Publications:
www.dti.gov.uk/publications
Equal Opportunities Commission:
www.eoc.org.uk
Invest Northern Ireland:
www.investni.com

SEE ALSO
Employment Law (p. 506)
Staff Planning (p. 415)

Conducting Interviews and Making Job Offers

GETTING STARTED

There are two main purposes to any job interview: the first is to find out whether the candidate is suitable for the job and the second is to provide the candidate with information about the job and the business. It's very important that the interviewer gives every candidate the same opportunities to give the best presentation of him or herself. The candidate should be free to demonstrate his or her suitability and to ask questions about the business and the job. It is also important that the interviewer knows exactly what he or she is looking for in the candidate, and has prepared questions to elicit information that will help in the final selection process. This actionlist gives advice on preparation for the interview, interview technique, and what to do after the interview is over.

FAQS

What information should be provided before the interview?

Before the interview, give the prospective interviewees clear instructions on how to get to your place of work and also tell them who they should ask for when they arrive. Also tell them what they should bring with them (such as pens, paper, or a calculator), roughly how long the interview is likely to last, and whether they will be reimbursed for travel expenses. If you are going to give them a test (for example, a short proof-reading test if you are hoping to recruit an editor), it's polite to let the candidates know first.

Who should carry out the interview?

As a small business owner, you may be the only manager and therefore the sole interviewer. If you do work with others, though, you might like to ask a colleague to join you so that you get another opinion on each candidate. If the interviewee will be working for someone other than you, involve the candidate's prospective line manager or supervisor as much as possible. If possible, you might also want to involve someone in the business who has specialist technical knowledge related to the job vacancy.

How long should the interview take?

There are no hard and fast rules, but generally interviews last between 30 and 60 min-

utes, including time for the candidate to ask questions of the interviewer. Schedule a break of about 20 minutes between interviews to give you time to make notes on the last interview and briefly prepare for the next. Interviewing is a tiring process, so don't schedule more than four or five interviews in a day.

MAKING IT HAPPEN
Prepare for the interview

Decide what questions you are going to ask, and base these on the selection criteria for the job. Include general questions on the candidate's experience and skills, as well as questions which probe more directly into how well they are suited to the job description. You should also prepare questions specific to each candidate, such as queries about gaps in their curriculum vitae, or any issues that are not clear on their application forms. Take the time to read over their applications thoroughly.

As well as preparing questions, you also need to give some thought to where the interviews are to be conducted. Find a place where there will be no interruptions and make sure that you've made any adjustments needed to accommodate an interviewee who has indicated a disability.

Conduct the interview

The first thing to do is welcome the candidate and introduce yourself, and any other interviewers who may be present. Follow this by giving a brief outline of how the interview will be structured, and also some background about the organisation and the job.

Start the interview with easy 'getting to know you' questions, which will help put the candidate at his or her ease. These questions can also be used to build up to more probing, in-depth questions. Ask about the candidate's skills and experience first. When you have covered these, move on to why the candidate thinks they are suitable for the job, and what his or her ambitions and expectations are.

While you are conducting the interview, observe the candidate's behaviour. This is often a good indication of his or her general level of confidence, as non-verbal behaviour is usually a subconscious use of the body to telegraph meaning. It goes without saying that you shouldn't jump to conclusions and make snap judgments, but watch the interviewees' reactions to a range of questions and see how they react under pressure.

Towards the end of the interview, ask the candidate whether they have any questions. It is a good way to find out how much homework about the business the candidate has done, and whether he or she is really interested in the job. Also ask them if they can briefly summarise for you what *they* understand the job to be—this will help you to check that they have grasped the outline you've given them and that you have explained it unambiguously. Finally, remember to thank the candidate for coming to meet you and explain to them what the likely next steps are (for example, if there are likely to be second interviews) and when they should expect to hear from you.

Questioning techniques

Try to ask open-ended questions that can't be answered by just saying 'yes' or 'no'. When you want more information, make sure you probe for specific answers. If a candidate seems to be avoiding a topic, use follow-up questions to try to fill in the blanks. Encourage candidates to expand on descriptions of their skills, and to demon-

strate how they relate to the requirements of the job. Use questions that will encourage the candidate to sell him or herself to you. For example, you could ask questions such as, 'Why should I hire you?', and, 'Why do you want to work here?'

It is often a good idea to ask situational questions. These involve the interviewer describing a situation or case related to the business; the interviewee then has to propose a solution to handle the situation. This is a useful way to test problem-solving and reasoning ability. For example, you might ask the interviewee, 'Your boss tells you to do a certain task. Shortly afterwards a colleague says they need your help for a high-priority project. What do you do?'

Remember to keep your tone mild and non-judgmental, particularly when asking difficult questions. Keep to a logical sequence of questions so that the candidate does not become confused. Make sure that you allow pauses in the conversation, to give the candidate time to think. It might be difficult, especially if a candidate is struggling with a particularly tricky question, but try not to interrupt—give each candidate the opportunity to get his or her point across.

Assess the interviewee

It's essential that you give yourself time after the interview to make notes on anything said that is directly relevant to your decision. Do this as soon as you can so that the conversation is still fresh in your mind. If you've prepared properly before the interview, you'll already have decided on key selection criteria; the final decision should be based on how closely each candidate matched the person specification for that particular job. You may find that a marking system, which gives a score to each candidate for each of the areas highlighted in the job specification, makes it easier for you to make your decision.

After the interview

Once you've selected the person you want to recruit, let them know as soon as possible, preferably by telephone, as there is always the possibility that they will have other interviews to attend. Discuss salary (or other benefits) with them at this point and address any queries the successful candidate has thought of since they saw you.

Follow up your conversation with a letter formally confirming the job offer and containing details of start dates and basic terms and conditions. If the selection has been narrowed down to two or three people, they can then be asked to come back for a second interview. Finally, write to unsuccessful candidates informing them of the outcome of the interview as soon as the decision has been made. Some candidates may request feedback on their interview, so be prepared to answer their queries (you might like to arrange another time to telephone them so that you have your notes in front of you).

Draw up an employment contract

You may want to add extra weight to the confirmation letter mentioned above by drawing up an employment contract—understandably, employees want some protection from being dismissed at will, and, without an employment contract, they may feel that they're at the whim of employers who don't need legal, concrete reasons for terminating them. From an employer's point of view, without a contract of employment, those you recruit aren't necessarily bound to allegiance or secrecy, and could defect to a competitor company without you having any legal recourse. Having a contract might also discourage less than honourable people from applying, knowing that your recruitment and employment practices would probably turn up something about their past and the baggage they bring with them.

If you are putting together a contract for the first time, here is a list of key elements to include. If you are thinking of overhauling your recruitment procedure and are thinking of rewriting contracts for future employees, the list may include things that have been missing in the past, or that might help avoid future conflicts:

- name of employee and the company
- name of the job and job description
- dates (starting and ending if the contract is

for a limited duration)
- the salary or rate of pay, plus details about its calculation and when paid
- company benefits (health and medical, holiday entitlements, sick leave, bonuses, retirement, and so on)
- terms and conditions of employment—probationary period, place, hours, flexitime, and so on
- options for termination and notices required
- process for filing a grievance and recourse for appealing disciplinary action
- confidentiality, non-disclosure, and non-compete clauses (so that essential information cannot be taken to any new jobs that the employee takes up in the future with competitors)
- ownership rights to property and product (intellectual and real) developed while employed

WHAT TO AVOID
Asking discriminatory questions
Legally, there are many questions that you must not ask because they are considered to be discriminatory. Three of the more obvious ways in which your questions could be seen in this light are described below:

- **Sex discrimination.** Obviously everyone should avoid making sexists comments, but you must also avoid questions such as 'Are you planning to start a family?'. If you refuse to employ someone because they say that they are, you are being discriminatory, and the candidate can lodge a complaint against you.
- **Racial discrimination.** Similarly, you must not discriminate on grounds of race. This covers both ethnic background and country of origin. Do not ask candidates if they have any religious affiliations.
- **Disability discrimination.** If the candidate discloses a disability, you cannot use it as a reason not to employ him or her unless it is justified. For example, somebody who is visually impaired would not be able to take up employment as a driver; he or she could take up a variety of roles in an office setting with the right equipment. If it will only take small adjustments for a disabled

person to do a job and that person is the best-qualified candidate, then you have to make the adjustments. Any questions relating to disability have to be carefully worded and must centre on how you can enable the candidate with the disability to do the job, rather than on why the disability would exclude the candidate.

Making unjustified assumptions

It's very easy for stereotype assumptions to creep into the interview process. In particular, you should beware of rejecting candidates on the grounds of a 'gut feeling', or the idea that they would not 'fit in'. Employment tribunals are increasingly suspicious of such comments, as they are seen to be based on discriminatory assumptions, and they may lead to complaints and legal challenges.

Causing the candidate to believe they have been offered the job

It's very important that you avoid making statements during the interview that could be alleged to create a contract of employment. It's easy to find yourself saying 'you' when you are describing what the successful candidate would be doing in his or her job (for example, 'You would be liaising with partners on a variety of projects.'). Try to avoid this as much as you can, and use more general terms such as 'the post-holder'.

You should also avoid making excessive assurances about job security. Courts have, on occasion, held that promises made during interviews created contracts of employment.

RECOMMENDED LINKS

Chartered Institute of Personnel and Development (CIPD)—found by searching the ePolitix website:
www.epolitix.com
Commission for Racial Equality:
www.cre.gov.uk
Disability Rights Commission:
www.drc-gb.org
Equal Opportunities Commission:
www.eoc.org.uk

SEE ALSO

Employee Benefits/Compensation (p. 505)
Staff Planning (p. 415)

Running a Payroll System

GETTING STARTED

As soon as your business starts to employ people (including company directors), you will need to set up and manage a payroll system. This will allow you to make the correct deductions from staff wages or salaries, make the necessary payments to the Inland Revenue on time, and maintain an orderly system of pay-related records.

This actionlist explains the requirements for administering staff wages, including the deduction of tax and National Insurance (NI) contributions. At first glance, the process might look rather complicated, but actually it is quite simple, if a little time consuming.

FAQS

What must I deduct from employees' pay?

The deductions you are required to make from your employees' pay are usually for income tax, and for National Insurance contributions under the Pay As You Earn scheme (PAYE). You then pay these deductions to the Inland Revenue in the month (or quarter, if you qualify as a PAYE small employer) after the staff have been paid.

You may also deduct pension contributions, and you may pay tax credits to your staff through the payroll. You are also expected to administer Statutory Sick Pay (SSP), Statutory Maternity Pay (SMP), and the Student Loan Deductions Scheme, if any of these apply to an employee.

How do I calculate net pay?

Many businesses use computerised payroll systems, but if your business has only a few employees, you may want to do the calculations manually. Even if you use a computer, it will be helpful to understand the principle of how to calculate pay and tax. The Inland Revenue provides forms and tables that simplify the calculations. There are four basic steps you need to follow.

- Add up the gross pay. This comprises the amount that you intend to pay your employee, together with any additional payments such as Statutory Sick Pay and Statutory Maternity Pay.
- Calculate the tax and National Insurance contributions. Inland Revenue forms make this process straightforward.
- Add tax credits, or deduct student loan payments if applicable.

- Prepare a payslip for each employee, pay the employee, and send the deductions to the Inland Revenue.

At the end of each year, you will need to give each employee a summary of their pay and deductions for the year and send copies to the Inland Revenue, together with a reconciled statement of gross pay, deductions, and amounts sent to the Inland Revenue during the year.

How much tax must I deduct?

Explaining how to calculate an employee's tax is probably best done by using an example. If an employee earns £12,000 a year (gross), they will be entitled to a certain amount of tax-free income, normally the single person's allowance of £4,615. They will then pay tax of 10% on the first £1,960 of taxable pay, 22% on further taxable income up to £30,500, and 40% on the balance. The calculation is as follows:

Gross income	£12,000
Tax-free allowance	£4,615
Taxable pay	£7,385
Tax payable on first £1,960	
(10% of £1,960)	£196
Tax payable up to £30,500	
(22% of £5,425)	£1,194
Total tax	£1,390
Net pay	£10,610

Staff will normally be paid monthly, fortnightly, or weekly. Deductions can either be calculated based on the annual amount (as a computer does) or you can use the tables provided by the Inland Revenue.

How much National Insurance must I deduct?

Both employers and employees make National Insurance contributions. Except for some special cases, the amount depends solely on the level of the employee's salary, not on their personal circumstances (as in the case of income tax). The amount to be deducted can be easily determined from the tables provided by the Inland Revenue.

MAKING IT HAPPEN
Written pay statements

You must provide a written pay statement (payslip) to every employee when you pay them, setting out how their pay has been calculated. It must show gross pay, the amount of any deductions and the purpose for which they are made, and take-home pay. The table below shows an example of a pay statement.

Statutory sick pay

Employers have to pay Statutory Sick Pay (SSP) to employees who satisfy certain conditions and who have been sick for at least four consecutive days (including weekends and bank holidays). Statutory Sick Pay is paid to the business by deduction from National Insurance contributions. For the employee, it is treated as earnings. It is subject to tax and National Insurance contributions from the employee and employer.

There are various rules that need to be followed for periods of incapacity for work and qualifying days. The first three 'qualifying days' are known as waiting days and do not qualify for Statutory Sick Pay. There is now one standard rate of pay for Statutory Sick Pay. An eligible employee is entitled to £64.35 per week up to a maximum of 28 weeks in one spell of absence, but you should note that spells of at least four days with eight weeks or less between them are counted as one spell.

The employer must keep proper records to justify any claims. There is no prescribed form, although the Inland Revenue can provide form SSP2 to be used. The employer must record the dates of each reported incapacity, details of agreed qualifying days, Statutory Sick Pay paid, and dates when Statutory Sick Pay was not paid, with reasons.

The business may qualify for the Percentage Threshold Scheme, designed to reimburse employers who have a high percentage of workers off sick at any one time. If, in the tax month (which runs from the sixth of one month to the fifth of the following month), your Statutory Sick Pay is more than 13% of the total gross Class 1 National Insurance contributions liability, you can claim back the difference.

You may decide to pay sick employees a higher amount than the Statutory Sick Pay, for example, full salary for a month, and dropping after that. This is not compulsory and is not subject to the payment and reimbursement provisions outlined above.

Statutory Maternity Pay

Employers have to pay Statutory Maternity Pay (SMP), which works in much the same way as Statutory Sick Pay. The employer pays it to the employee for up to 18 weeks; most of this can be reclaimed from the government by way of deductions from National Insurance contributions. The employer can (but is not obliged to) add to

Employee		Number		Employer	
Jane Smith		***		Smith and Sons	
Payments		**Deductions**		**To Date**	
Gross:	£1,000.00	PAYE:	£115.83		£1,000.00
		NI:	£69.00	TAX:	115.83
				NI:	£69.00
Total:	£1,000.00	Total:	£184.83	**NET PAY:**	**£815.17**

PAY DATE: 25/05/03   TAX CODE: 461L

TAX PERIOD: 1   NI No: NZ-**-**-**-*

this amount, although only the statutory element is recoverable. Female employees absent from work to have a baby are usually eligible to claim Statutory Maternity Pay. Statutory Maternity Pay is paid at 90% of weekly earnings for the first six weeks, then £100 per week for the next 20 weeks (or, if the employee earns less than £100 per week, 90% of average weekly earnings).

You can reclaim 92% of Statutory Maternity Pay contributions, although firms qualifying for Small Employers' Relief (SER) can claim back 100%, plus a further 5% of Statutory Maternity Pay paid to cover employers' National Insurance contributions. The Inland Revenue should be contacted for details of eligibility.

Tax credits

Lower paid staff might be entitled to tax credits. From April 2003, these are the Child Tax Credit and the Working Tax Credit (these replaced the Working Families Tax Credit, Disabled Person's Tax Credit, and Children's Tax Credit). You are required to add the tax credit amount (as notified by the Inland Revenue) to the employee's net pay. Tax credits are offset against the combined total of PAYE tax, National Insurance contributions, and student loan deductions paid to the Inland Revenue. If credits exceed the total deductions, you may apply to the Inland Revenue for funding.

WHAT TO AVOID
Not doing your homework

Make sure you find out exactly what is required of you. The Inland Revenue has a good website with a great deal of informa-

tion and all the current rates. It also publishes a number of guides which you may find helpful: *BIF 15 An Introduction to Tax, National Insurance and VAT, BIF 241 A Guide for First Time Employers, CA30 Statutory Sick Pay Manual for Employers, E15 Pay and Time Off Work for Parents, E6 Working Tax Credit Paid with Wages,* and the *Employer's Annual Pack (Covering National Insurance, PAYE, SSP, etc)*. These can be ordered via the Employers' Orderline (0845 764 6646). The Inland Revenue also runs three helplines: for the newly self-employed (0845 915 4515); for new employers (0845 607 0143); and for employers (0845 714 3143).

Not getting the right advice

It is important to run a payroll system correctly, so make sure you get the proper advice. PAYE and National Insurance calculations are usually easy to work out. However, if you are having difficulties, seek advice from an Inland Revenue helpline, your local enterprise agency, or your accountant. If employees want to understand more about their entitlements, the Department of Work and Pensions has a website with information that will help. Website addresses are given below.

RECOMMENDED LINKS
Department of Work and Pensions:
www.dti.gov.uk
Inland Revenue:
www.inlandrevenue.gov.uk

SEE ALSO
Employee Benefits/Compensation (p. 505)

Complying with the National Minimum Wage Act 1998

GETTING STARTED
All businesses in the United Kingdom must comply with the National Minimum Wage Act 1998, which requires them to pay workers aged 18 or over at least the national minimum wage. This actionlist gives the current national minimum wage rate, explains who it applies to, and lists the exceptions. It also describes which elements of workers' pay are included in the minimum wage, and stresses the importance of keeping relevant records.

FAQS

How much is the national minimum wage?
As at October 2003, the minimum hourly rate for adult workers aged 22 or over is £4.50 before deductions. The minimum 'development rate', for 18 to 21 year olds and those on accredited training courses, is £3.80 per hour. The minimum wage has increased annually since its introduction in 1999, and this may continue if economic conditions remain favourable.

Who does the national minimum wage apply to?
All workers aged 18 or over working in the United Kingdom are entitled to the national minimum wage (subject to certain exemptions given below). No employer is exempt from paying the national minimum wage, whatever the size of their business. All types of workers are covered (whether full- or part-time), including casuals, temporary workers supplied through employment agencies, sub-contractors, trainees (with certain exceptions), and homeworkers.

Any employer refusing to pay a worker the minimum wage will be committing a criminal offence and can be fined. Fines can be up to £5,000 and employers may be ordered to make back-payment to employees. Employers must keep sufficient records to prove that they have paid their employees the minimum wage. The legislation applies equally across the United Kingdom (but not in the Channel Islands or the Isle of Man).

Workers aged 22 or over on accredited training courses, can be paid the development rate for only the first six months of a new job with a new employer. The employer must have agreed in writing to provide 26 days of accredited training before the end of the first six months of employment. After this period they must be paid the standard rate. Accredited training includes training for National Vocational Qualifications, Scottish Vocational Qualifications, and General National Vocational Qualifications; verified in-house training; and vocational training undertaken as part of the New Deal programme for 18 to 25 year olds.

Who is exempt from the national minimum wage?
Workers under 18 do not need to be paid the national minimum wage. Apprentices and Modern Apprentices under the age of 19 do not qualify for the national minimum wage, nor do apprentices under 26 who are in the first 12 months of their apprenticeship. Further exclusions include people working and living as part of a family, such as au pairs, friends, neighbours, and family who help out with household chores. Also exempt are non-employed trainees on government-funded training schemes, students working as part of sandwich courses, and teacher trainees placed in schools for work experience as part of their course. Homeless people who take part in a scheme for which they are provided with shelter in return for doing some work are exempt; so are voluntary workers who work for a charity, voluntary organisation, charity shop, school,

hospital, or similar body, who receive any reasonable expenses or benefits in kind, or are placed by a charity or similar body with another charity and receive money for subsistence. All the people listed above can legally be paid less than the minimum wage.

How many hours must a person work to qualify?

There is no minimum period that a person must work before they qualify. The minimum wage is payable for the time when a worker is required to be at work or available for work. This includes time spent training and travelling for the purposes of the job (this does not include commuting to and from work).

As an employer, you must pay an average hourly rate of no less than the minimum wage appropriate to the worker. This is true for all types of workers, including those paid by output rather than time. Piece workers, for instance, must be paid no less than the minimum wage on average for the period they work, regardless of their output or the piece rate. It is the employer's responsibility to ensure that a worker is paid the national minimum wage over the period of time they work, regardless of how pay is calculated.

What makes up the minimum wage?

Elements that count towards the minimum wage include tips collected by an employer for employees and paid through the payroll, incentive payments, and bonuses. Elements that do not count towards the minimum wage include tips paid directly to workers by customers, and any loans, advances, pension payments, redundancy payments, awards by a court, or awards under staff suggestion schemes. Benefits in kind, such as meals or luncheon vouchers, and premium payments for overtime or shift work, are not included. Neither are allowances that are not consolidated into pay (for example, regional allowances), or the use of a company car and petrol.

Some elements may be deducted without reducing the amount paid to an employee for the purposes of the minimum wage. These include penalties imposed upon an

employee for misconduct, where the employer is permitted to make the deduction under the terms of the contract. Also included are the repayment of any loans, advance of wages, or purchase of shares, and repayments of any accidental overpayment of wages. Payments made by an employee to the employer for goods or services purchased may be deducted, as may the cost of accommodation provided by the employer, up to a limit. The cost of items related to the worker's employment (for example, uniforms and tools) can also be deducted. It is a good idea to get advice on these deductions, as they can be complicated.

MAKING IT HAPPEN
Keep good records

As an employer, you must keep records to prove that your workers have received at least the minimum wage. The legislation does not define exactly what records should be kept, as this will vary from employer to employer. Examples include general records kept for tax and National Insurance purposes, as these will usually detail how much the employee has been paid, and over what period.

If any queries arise about minimum wage payments, it is up to the employer to prove they have paid the minimum. It is not the employee's responsibility to prove that he or she has not been paid it. Records must be kept for a minimum of three years after the relevant pay reference period. The records must be produced on request, whether this request is by the worker, Inland Revenue, employment tribunal, or civil court. Under most circumstances, an employer has 14 days to produce the records following a request from the worker. Failure to do so may result in a penalty.

Understand employee rights concerning the minimum wage

The worker has three main rights. First, if a worker has reasonable grounds to believe that he or she has not been paid the national minimum wage, they have the right to see and copy the employer's records relating to them. They must make a written request to the employer who has to provide the records within 14 days. Second, employees can not be dismissed just because they have become eligible for a higher rate of pay under the minimum wage legislation. Where an employer fails to comply with the legislation, workers may enforce their rights by complaining to an enforcement agency; this agency may be the Inland Revenue, an employment tribunal, or a civil court. If this happens, the employee making the complaint must continue to be treated the same as all other employees. Third, a worker cannot agree to accept less than the minimum wage if they are entitled to it.

Know how the minimum wage is enforced

The Inland Revenue has overall responsibility for enforcing the national minimum wage. It has the power to serve enforcement and penalty notices, and to carry out visits to employers' premises to determine that the minimum hourly rate has been paid.

The Low Pay Commission (LPC) was established to recommend the coverage and initial level of the national minimum wage. The LPC has recently submitted a third report recommending a number of changes concerning the development rate, compliance and enforcement, and future increases in the national minimum wage rate.

 WHAT TO AVOID
Not keeping employees informed

You should display details of the national minimum wage prominently in your workplace so that your employees know their rights.

Refusing or neglecting to pay

Refusing or wilfully neglecting to pay the national minimum wage is a criminal offence and is punishable by a fine of up to £5,000.

Not getting the right advice

The Department of Trade and Industry's TIGER website (address given below) provides advice on how to calculate wages in compliance with the national minimum wage. The National Minimum Wage Helpline publishes two guides, *A Detailed Guide to the National Minimum Wage* and *National Minimum Wage—A Short Guide for Employers*, which may be helpful. It also has a number of telephone lines: 0845 600 0678 for enquiries, 0845 845 0360 for information and publications, and 0845 602 4027 for information in large print, in Braille, and on audio cassette.

RECOMMENDED LINKS

Department of Trade and Industry (DTI):
www.tiger.gov.uk
Low Pay Commission (LPC):
www.lowpay.gov.uk

SEE ALSO

Employee Benefits/Compensation (p. 505)
Employment Law (p. 506)

Setting Up Job Shares

GETTING STARTED

Job sharing is an arrangement in which two employees share the responsibility of one full-time position with the salary, paid leave, pension rights, and fringe benefits divided between them, according to the time each works. This actionlist looks at some of the advantages and disadvantages of job sharing, and provides a brief guide to setting up a job-sharing scheme.

FAQS

What are the advantages of job sharing?

Job sharing enables employees to retain the responsibility and status of full-time work while being able to work shorter, and often more flexible, hours. Job sharers are usually better paid, more highly skilled, and have better prospects for promotion than most part-time workers.

Job sharing benefits the employer too. Job sharing schemes can help you to retain skilled and experienced staff who are unable or don't want to work full-time but do not wish to leave their present job. It can also help to reduce absenteeism, as each job sharer has a greater amount of free time to organise other commitments and domestic responsibilities. As job sharers work fewer hours, there may also be less time taken off for stress-related disorders.

Job sharing can ensure greater continuity of work. When one job-share partner is off sick or on holiday, at least one half of the job is still being done, and it may be possible to organise the job-share agreement so that both partners can be present at peak times. Job sharing also enables employers to get the best of two people's skills and experience for the price of one. Job sharers can organise their workload to take advantage of respective strengths and weaknesses, so that their capabilities are used to the full.

What are the disadvantages of job sharing?

Job sharing usually increases administrative costs. However, recruitment will often be for one worker to make up the job share (as you'll normally have one person on your team already), and if two workers are employed at once, costs such as advertising, induction, and so on, can be combined for the two.

Poor communication can be a problem, and it may be difficult to call meetings. Address this by making sure that both job sharers are kept properly informed of all developments, and, if possible, incorporate an overlap period, even if it's just a few hours a week, so that sharers can discuss their work. Ask both sharers to keep good records of what they do, have done, and are expecting to do so that everyone is clear and work isn't duplicated.

The job share may make extra work for managers in terms of allocating work, co-ordinating the work of the sharers, and communicating requirements. This will vary with the type of job and the way your business is structured. The division of responsibilities of the post will also need careful consideration, but time used in planning will be well-spent.

MAKING IT HAPPEN
Start a scheme

Before you implement a job-share scheme, make sure that everyone in your business understands, approves of, and accepts the principles of job sharing, especially those who will have contact with the job sharers. Be aware of prejudices against part-time workers, who may be regarded as less committed to the company. Other considerations that you need to bear in mind are discussed in more detail below.

Create a job description

A detailed job description, clearly defining the duties and responsibilities of the post, will make it easier to divide responsibilities according to requirements. Many clerical posts can be split by hours, providing continuous coverage. Management and professional posts can be split by client, referral, project, and areas of expertise. Some jobs may have quite autonomous responsibilities, for example, different client caseloads, whereas others may require both job-share partners to contribute to the same project. In that case, if the job involves making important decisions, it will be necessary to decide if one partner's decisions must be upheld by the other.

Working hours
Job shares can be split in a variety of ways. Common patterns of work include split days, with one employee working in the morning and one in the afternoon; split weeks, where one employee works one half of the week and one the other; alternate weeks; or no fixed schedule, which is a less formal arrangement. Work out which pattern will suit the requirements of the job and the employees involved. Jobs may not always be split equally; one sharer may want to work fewer hours than the other. Bear in mind, however, that if one sharer only has very few hours, it may be difficult to replace that person if he or she leaves.

Overlap periods
Most job shares incorporate an overlap period for sharers to discuss developments and communicate problems. The length and frequency of the overlap periods will depend on the pattern of hours worked and the splitting of responsibilities; job sharers in a secretarial post may only need five minutes a day to discuss unfinished work, whereas partners who share a job as environmental consultants will obviously need more time to discuss clients and workloads.

Workspace
Job sharers will often share the same working area. However, if there are significant periods of overlap, it may be necessary to provide extra accommodation.

Training and induction
If possible, job sharers should attend induction training together. This will help to develop a working relationship and ensure that both receive the same training. Further training can either be undertaken individually, according to areas of expertise and interest, or together, in areas of shared training needs.

Management and supervision
Job-share posts will require more management time, with an emphasis on good verbal and written communication. Meetings could be alternated between job sharers, and every third meeting could be with both in attendance.

Promotion
It is usual to allow job sharing 'units' to apply for promotion on equal terms with full-time employees. Some organisations only consider the sharers together, and either appoint or reject them both; others will consider them individually as well as together, and appoint the best person for the job.

Holidays
Job sharers usually receive the same amount of holiday as full-time workers, but they are paid in proportion to the number of hours worked. For example, where a job-share partner works the equivalent of half a full-time job, working five half-days a week, he or she may be allowed to take 25 days holiday, the same as other employees, but only 12.5 of those will be paid holiday. Public holidays may cause some difficulties, as they usually fall on a Monday and therefore mostly within one job-share partner's working period. Public holidays are usually split into hours and divided between partners, with the time taken elsewhere by one partner.

Pension schemes
Pensions are usually paid pro rata, depending on the number of hours worked by each individual.

Recruiting job sharers

Decide which jobs will be open to job sharing and how they will be advertised. In many cases these will be internal applications, and it will be important to decide whether or not those wishing to job share must identify a partner before applying. Consider whether separate application forms are required from each partner, whether they have to justify why they want to job share and demonstrate how they are compatible to do so on the application form, and whether they will be interviewed together, or separately, or both. Decide how applications from job sharers without a partner should be treated. Careful selection is necessary when recruiting two people for a job share. Their qualifications, experience, and skills should be compatible, and they should appear capable of forming a close working relationship. You must also consider whether you will make the position a full-time job, if you are only able to recruit one partner.

Employment rights

Job shares usually consist of two people sharing the workload normally assigned to one person. This usually involves a weekly workload spread over between 15 and 20 hours. The workers have the same rights as full-time employees according to the Employment Rights Act 1996. The rights of job sharers have been further extended by the introduction of the Part-time Workers (Prevention of Less Favourable Treatment) Regulations 2000, which came into force in July 2000. Under these regulations, job sharers receive the same hourly rate as full-time workers, and the same hourly rate of overtime as comparable full-time workers once they have worked more than the normal full-time hours. The regulations also cover the rights of employees not to be excluded from training simply because they work part time, and to have the same entitlements to annual leave and maternity/parental leave on a pro rata basis as their full-time colleagues. They should also have equal access to pension schemes. If an employee feels they have been less favourably treated, they can request a written statement for this from their employer, who must respond within 21 days. The new regulations should encourage more people to consider working part time as their circumstances change.

What to do if one partner leaves

If one job-share partner leaves, many organisations choose to offer the job on a full-time basis to the remaining partner. If he or she does not accept the offer, the next step is to advertise the post as a job share, detailing the number of hours available. If no suitable replacement is found within a reasonable length of time (usually between three and six months), the remaining partner may be offered a part-time post or be redeployed elsewhere, if possible.

WHAT TO AVOID ✗
Not keeping people informed
Inform all employees and management about the principles behind job sharing, and how it differs from part-time work, before a scheme is implemented.

Not getting the right partners
How well a job share works depends on the people involved, so extra care will need to be taken with recruitment and selection procedures. It is important that both partners are able to communicate and interact well with each other, as well as with other employees, managers, and outside contacts.

RECOMMENDED LINKS
Department for Work and Pensions:
www.dwp.gov.uk
New Ways to Work:
www.new-ways.co.uk
Recruitment and Employment Confederation:
www.rec.uk.com
The Stationery Office:
www.legislation.hmso.gov.uk

SEE ALSO
Employment Law (p. 506)

Employing People with Disabilities

GETTING STARTED

As an employer, you have a general duty not to discriminate against any employee. The Disability Discrimination Act 1995 (DDA) specifically prohibits discrimination on the basis of disability, although this currently applies only to businesses with more than 15 employees. By October 2004, all businesses will be required to comply with the employment aspects of the DDA.

This actionlist explains what is expected of employers when they interview and employ a disabled person. It describes the legal requirements and also suggests ways to improve the employment environment to accommodate disabled staff.

FAQS

What is a disability?

The Act defines a person with a disability as someone with a physical or mental impairment that has a substantial or long-term adverse affect on their ability to carry out normal day-to-day activities.

What are my legal obligations?

The Act requires employers to consider the ability of the person and to make reasonable adjustments in working arrangements or to the physical features of the premises. You need to take fair steps to prevent these arrangements or features placing the disabled person at a disadvantage. These will vary from situation to situation. You will need to consider how effective the adjustments will be in helping the disabled person, whether they are practical to implement, how much they will cost, and whether you can afford them. You will also need to check whether there is any financial assistance available to help you make the adjustments.

How do these rules apply in Northern Ireland?

The Disability Discrimination Act applies in the same way in Northern Ireland as it does in the rest of the United Kingdom, but there is a separate Northern Ireland Code of Practice for eliminating discrimination against disabled people (available from the Stationery Office).

In Northern Ireland, the Disablement Advisory Service provides services and programmes for disabled people equivalent to the Jobcentre Plus in England, Scotland, and Wales. Disability Employment Advisers are known as Disablement Employment Advisers.

The Employment Service Disability Symbol does not apply in Northern Ireland, but the province has an equivalent programme to Workstep, called Employment Support. The Northern Ireland Training and Employment Agency is an executive agency of the Department of Economic Development and is responsible for the development and implementation of the training and employment functions.

MAKING IT HAPPEN
Prevent discrimination when recruiting

If you're using advertisements to recruit new staff, it's good practice to welcome applications from people with disabilities. Provide information about the job in an accessible format such as large print (which people with learning disabilities or sight difficulties will find easier to read) or with illustrations. If you place your advert with the Disability Employment Adviser at the Jobcentre or Jobcentre Plus, you can guarantee that disabled people will see it. You can also mail your vacancy bulletins to local specialist agencies and offer job-share vacancies to allow applicants flexible working arrangements.

Some people with learning disabilities can fill in an application form themselves; others will need help from a supporter.

Consider allowing candidates to submit an application in different formats, such as by telephone, audio-tape, or e-mail. It's good practice to include a question on the application form to ask applicants if they would have any special requirements at an interview.

Make your workplace friendlier to disabled staff

If any physical feature of your premises, or any arrangements made by you, causes a substantial disadvantage to a disabled person compared with non-disabled people, you have to take reasonable steps to address this. Physical features include things like a building's design or construction, access to a building, fixtures, fittings, furnishings, equipment, or materials. For example, the design of a workplace may make it difficult for someone with a hearing impairment to hear.

The Act gives a number of examples of steps that you may have to take. You may have to make adjustments to premises, such as providing a wheelchair ramp, or allocate some of the disabled person's duties to another employee. Another step might be to transfer the person to fill an existing vacancy, or to assign the person to a different place of work. Other examples include altering the person's working hours, or allowing him or her to be absent during working hours for rehabilitation, assessment, or treatment. You may be required to arrange for training for the person, to acquire or modify equipment, or to provide a reader, interpreter, or extra supervision.

Avoid discrimination against disabled people

Take care that your actions, or lack of them, do not lead to what is known as 'constructive dismissal', a situation in which a disabled employee's job is made too difficult for them to continue. Your employee can then take legal action if you did not make reasonable adjustments to enable them to do their job.

If an employee complains of, or shows signs of, physical pain, such as back pain caused by lifting, or stress related to work,

it's best to talk to him or her about it and see if anything can be done to remedy the situation. Record all interviews of this kind, even if the employee says that it's not a problem.

Adopting good practice can help minimise or avoid the risk of costly litigation. There is a Code of Practice on the employment provisions of the Act. Good practice is about looking beyond the disability to what the person can actually do, sometimes with a bit of adjustment to the workplace or working practices.

Find out about support for employers of disabled staff

Effective and practicable adjustments for disabled people often involve little cost or disruption. However, if you think you may not be able to afford the necessary changes, the Government Access to Work scheme might assist. This is a grant for any extra costs incurred by an employer resulting from the disability of an employee. It gives financial support for a variety of areas, such as aids and adaptations.

The funding available depends on the employment status of the disabled person at the time of the application. For disabled people already employed, you can receive a maximum of 80% of the costs of special equipment or adaptations costing between £300 and £10,000, and 100% of costs over £10,000. It can cover 100% of approved costs for unemployed disabled people taking up employment, for disabled people who have been in work for less than six weeks, and for disabled people who are self employed.

Other support agencies and initiatives include Jobcentre Plus (part of the Department for Work and Pensions), which can advise on benefits and employment. The Jobcentre Plus service has set up Employer Direct customer service centres with one central number to help you find candidates to fill vacancies. There is also New Deal, the Government's flagship initiative to move socially excluded people into work. There are several New Deal programmes aimed at helping individuals improve their employability and find work. If you offer jobs to people with disabilities you also receive practical support and help from New Deal personal advisers, including advice on their eligibility for additional funding through the Access to Work scheme. Disability Employment Advisers can advise about the New Deal programmes available to employers, and your nearest Jobcentre can help you contact them.

The Job Introduction Scheme (JIS) provides a weekly grant towards the cost of employing a disabled person for a trial period. You usually receive a grant of £75 a week over a trial period of six weeks (although it can be extended for up to 13 weeks). The job can be full or part time, but must be expected to last for at least six months after the JIS grant ends. You must apply for JIS before the person begins paid work.

Supported Placement Schemes (SPS) enable you to provide job opportunities for severely disabled people to work alongside other employees. The scheme works as a three-way partnership between a contractor, a host, and the employment service. Contractors are organisations that provide employment opportunities and are often voluntary bodies or local authorities. The host provides the work environment, and the Employment Service provides the finances.

WHAT TO AVOID
Not getting the right advice
The Job Introduction Scheme (JIS) can help you if you're thinking of recruiting someone with a disability. You can discuss any practical concerns to do with taking on someone with a disability with a Disability Employment Adviser (DEA). They will then decide whether JIS can help you. Further information can be found in your local Jobcentre Plus office or Jobcentre.

Not demonstrating your commitment to equal opportunities
Show that you have a commitment to equal opportunities. Mention disability explicitly in any equal opportunities policy and reassure any disabled applicants that their needs will be met. Make sure all your staff implement such policies.

RECOMMENDED LINKS
Department for Work and Pensions (responsible for delivering support and advice through a network of services to people of working age, employers, pensioners, families, children, and disabled people):
www.dwp.gov.uk
Department of Trade and Industry:
www.dti.gov.uk
Disability Rights Commission (an independent body set up by the government to help secure civil rights for disabled people):
www.drc-gb.org
Disability Service Team (part of Jobcentres):
www.jobcentreplus.co.uk
Employers' Forum on Disability (national employers' membership organisation focused on training and employment of people with disabilities. It has contact information on consultants and trainers active in this field):
www.employers-forum.co.uk
Employers' Forum on Disability (Northern Ireland):
www.efdni.org.uk
The Stationery Office:
www.hmso.gov.uk

SEE ALSO
Employment Law (p. 506)

Modern Apprenticeships

GETTING STARTED

Modern apprenticeships were introduced in 1995 and are designed to provide support for businesses recruiting and training 16 to 24-year-olds. As part of its youth guarantee policy, the government gives priority to those between the ages of 16 and 18.

The responsibility for modern apprenticeships falls on the following training organisations: in England, Learning and Skills Councils; in Wales, National Councils for Education and Training; in Scotland, Local Enterprise Companies; in Northern Ireland, Local Training and Employment Agencies.

Two publications which might be useful to you are: *Evaluation of Modern Apprenticeships*, by Economic Research Services Ltd, published by Prentice Hall/Harvester Wheatsheaf in 1999; and *Modern Apprenticeships: A Survey of Employers*, by C. Hasluck, T. Hogarth, M. Maguire, and J. Pitcher, published by The Stationery Office (website address given below).

FAQS

How does apprenticeship work?

There are two levels of apprenticeship: Foundation and Advanced. Foundation modern apprenticeships result in the attainment of National Vocational Qualification (NVQ) Level 2. The advanced modern apprenticeship is based on the attainment of the minimum of a National Vocational Qualification Level 3, and the development of key skills such as communication, information technology, team working, and problem solving. Many of the advanced level apprenticeships now also include study for a technical certificate relevant to the apprentice's specific vocation.

The apprenticeships usually run for three to four years, depending on the skills the young person already has. Applicants are usually expected to have at least five GCSEs at grade C or above. They must be at least 16 and be able to complete their training programme by their 25th birthday.

Apprenticeships are available in over 80 industry and business sectors, including engineering, construction, information technology, business administration, catering, accountancy, retailing, hairdressing, and hospitality.

What are the benefits of this scheme for employers?

Recruiting modern apprentices may help you find and train people to have exactly the skills you need to build your business and to remain competitive within your chosen industry. You can also enrol people who work for you already on to the scheme, which will assist in their development and may also help you retain the skills your business can call on. You'll receive financial assistance for funding the scheme too—see below for more information.

What are my obligations as an employer to the modern apprentice?

At the start of an apprenticeship, the employer, the apprentice, and the Learning and Skills Council (or equivalent) sign a 'pledge'. The employer agrees to provide training and experience to industry-recognised standards; the apprentice agrees to be hard working and loyal.

A training schedule is drawn up. This will specify the skills the apprentice needs to develop, how and where the training is to be delivered, and the qualifications that will be attained. The skills identified can be general (such as communications and numeracy) or specific (such as learning a foreign language). Employers tend to work closely with the Learning and Skills Council to develop the training programme.

MAKING IT HAPPEN

Recruit modern apprentices

Apprentices are recruited using a variety of methods, usually through colleges, Learning and Skills Councils (or equivalent), or the Careers Service, all of which might provide support in the recruitment process. Other methods include newspaper advertising and word of mouth.

Apprentices can be selected using guidelines for the business sector, as well as personal criteria. An apprenticeship programme may be run without recruiting new staff, as long as the business has employees under the age of 24.

Fund modern apprenticeships

Apprentices are usually employed by an organisation. In rare cases where employment is not possible, the apprentice will be linked to one or more employers and paid an allowance. Arrangements regarding wages and/or allowances will be made between the parties concerned.

The Department for Education and Skills (DfES) provides the funds for the apprenticeships. They are channelled through the Learning and Skills Councils (or equivalent), which will agree funding levels with individual employers according to local arrangements. Employers will normally have to meet the cost of wages, and may also be asked to contribute towards training costs.

The national minimum wage does not need to be paid to apprentices who are under the age of 18. People who start apprenticeships aged 16 or 17 and continue until they are 18 will not need to be paid the national minimum wage until they are 19.

WHAT TO AVOID

Not thinking ahead

Remember that you need to plan staffing to meet future as well as current business needs, so that you don't get caught on the hop. Also bear in mind that you need to include the cost of training in your budgets.

Not getting the right advice

If employing under-18s, it is important to check if your local authority has any relevant by-laws and guidelines.

The range of modern apprenticeships is being expanded to cover more business and industry sectors. Trade associations and the training organisations mentioned in the introduction can provide details of apprenticeships relevant to your business.

RECOMMENDED LINKS

Department for Education and Skills (DfES):
www.dfes.gov.uk
Department for Employment and Learning (Northern Ireland):
www.teaonline.gov.uk
National Council for Education and Training (Wales):
www.elwa.ac.uk
Scottish Enterprise:
www.scottish-enterprise.com
The Stationery Office:
www.hmso.gov.uk

SEE ALSO
Employment Law (p. 506)

Working Time Regulations 1998

GETTING STARTED
The Working Time Regulations were introduced to lay down the minimum health and safety requirements for the organisation of working time. They implement a European Council Directive on the Organisation of Working Time (commonly referred to as the Working Time Directive). The Regulations also implement parts of the European Community Young Workers Directive, which specifically contain sections defining young workers. This actionlist explains how you are affected by these regulations.

FAQS
What types of business are affected by the Working Time Regulations?
The Working Time Regulations 1998 apply to all sectors, both public and private. Industries which are excluded include air, rail, road, sea, inland waterway and lake transport, sea fishing, and the activities of doctors in training, the armed forces, and police force. The self-employed are also excluded.

When did the Working Time Regulations come into force?
The Working Time Regulations came into force on 1 October 1998. The regulations were amended in 1999 to add in further provisions that apply to workers whose working time is partly measured, predetermined, or determined by the worker, and partly not. The regulations were also amended on 5 October 2001 to include the entitlement of four weeks' annual leave for all workers.

Who enforces the Working Time Regulations?
The responsibility for enforcing the regulations lies with different bodies. The Health and Safety Executive is responsible, for example, for administering the 48-hour limit and health assessments for night workers in sectors including factories, fairgrounds, farms, and building sites. Local authorities have responsibility for retailing, offices, hotels and catering, sports, leisure, and consumer services. Employment tribunals cover problems relating to employee rights, for example, leave and rest breaks. They also provide workers with the opportunity to present complaints, any breach of the regulations, and related cases of unfair dismissal. The Health and Safety Executive has the power to ensure that an employer complies with the regulations. If you fail to do so, you could be faced with a fine or imprisonment.

What is the purpose of the Working Time Regulations?
The regulations are intended to provide protection to the most vulnerable employees, and to lay down the minimum health and safety requirements for the organisation of working time. They also offer flexibility for an employer and worker to make arrangements that suit them both. They establish guidelines for minimum periods of daily and weekly rest, annual leave, breaks, and maximum weekly working time. This helps to ensure an alert work force, which may reduce the risk of an accident occurring or a mistake being made. They also cover aspects of night work, shift work, and overall patterns of work.

What do the terms used in the Working Time Regulations mean?
The term 'workers' covers those with a contract of employment, plus a wider group who undertake work under other forms of contract, for example, agency and temporary workers, and freelancers. However, it does not cover the self-employed. 'Young workers' refers to workers who have reached school-leaving age but are not over 18 years old.

The term 'working time' in relation to a worker refers to any period during which he or she is working, at the employer's disposal, and carrying out his or her activities and duties. In relation to young workers, it also includes any time spent doing in-house training or work experience, for example, on a National Traineeship or New Deal scheme.

The term 'rest period' is any period of time that is not classed as working time.

'Night time' is a period of not less than seven hours, which must include the hours between midnight and 5am. Under the regulations, this is defined (in the absence of other industry agreements) as the period between 11pm and 6am. A 'night worker' is any worker who works at least three hours of their daily working time as part of night time. It also applies to those who are likely to work a certain proportion of annual working time during night time.

The term 'shift work' applies to the organisation of work according to shift patterns where workers need to work at different times over a period of days or weeks. A 'shift worker' is any worker who is employed to do shift work.

MAKING IT HAPPEN
Realise opt-out agreements are voluntary

As an employer, you are obliged to take all reasonable steps to ensure that workers are not required to work more than an average of 48 hours per week. The exception to this is when a worker has signed an opt-out, which allows him or her to work longer than the 48-hour limit. Signing an opt-out agreement must be voluntary on the part of the worker. The opt-out agreement needs to be in writing and signed by the worker. There is no need for it to be renewed. Workers have the right to cancel the opt-out agreement when they want. However, they are obliged to give you a minimum of seven days' notice, or as long as three months, if appropriate.

Know working time limits

You must be familiar with what counts as working time and what does not. It will also be useful to have an understanding of how average weekly working time is calculated. The Department of Trade and Industry's publication *Your Guide to the Working Time Regulations* may be useful in this regard.

Remember night workers

It is important that you comply with the regulations if you employ workers who can be classified as night workers. Employers should be aware of how many hours night workers normally work, and how they may be able to reduce the hours of work of those night workers who normally work more than eight hours in any 24-hour period. It is essential to give special consideration if a night worker does work involving special hazards, or heavy physical or mental exertion.

Night workers are entitled to a free health assessment before they commence work and at regular intervals following employment—although workers are not obliged to have a health assessment. A health assessment comprises two parts: a questionnaire and a medical examination, which is only necessary if the worker's fitness for night work is in question. Seek help from a qualified health professional when drawing up and assessing the questionnaire. Those suffering from problems related directly to working at night should be transferred to day work where possible. The suitability of certain vulnerable groups of people for night work, especially new or expectant mothers and young workers, should be given special consideration.

Give time off and rest breaks

Check how working time has been arranged in your organisation, and that workers are able to take the time off they are entitled to. Employers need to be familiar with the special provisions that apply to young workers. You are also obliged to check whether there are any exceptions that apply to workers taking time off.

You should also be informed about who is entitled to annual leave. Each worker (including part-time) is now entitled to four weeks' paid annual leave. Annual leave may not be replaced by remuneration in lieu, except where the employment contract is terminated. There is no statutory right to bank holidays, and as such, the annual leave requirement includes them. Employers have the right to stipulate rules for when annual leave should be taken, for example, over the Christmas period.

Employees must be able to take the rest breaks that they are entitled to. You need to be familiar with the different rest break periods that apply to young workers. As an employer, you are also obliged to check whether there are any exceptions that apply to workers taking rest periods. It is possible for employers and workers to agree to vary their entitlement to rest periods, with the workers receiving 'compensatory rest'. This is a period of rest that is identical in length to the period of rest that the worker has missed.

Keep records

You are obliged to keep records to show that you have complied with the working time limit per week within your organisation. It is the responsibility of each employer to decide what records need to be kept to fulfil this obligation. Existing records, which are currently employed for other purposes, may be used, or alternatively, you may choose to compile and maintain new records. It is important to keep up-to-date records of workers who have signed an opt-out agreement to work more than 48 hours a week. Records of regular health assessments of night workers also need to be kept. Records must be kept for two years. Keeping records of rest breaks, days off, and annual leave is not required.

Be aware of exemptions from the regulations

Certain professions, for example, managing executives, family workers, or those in office at religious ceremonies and religious communities, cannot completely comply with the regulations due to the nature of their job. These are people whose time cannot be measured and can only be determined by the workers themselves. They are exempt from the provisions in the regulations relat-

ing to weekly working time, night work, rest periods, and breaks.

Further situations that cannot fully comply include: workers whose place of employment and place of residence are distant from each other; security and surveillance activities that require permanent presence; activities involving continuity of service or production, for example, hospitals, residential institutions, dock and airport workers, media, ambulance, fire and civil protection services; and activities in which there is a potential surge of activity, for example, agriculture, tourism, and postal services. Workers in these situations must be provided with periods of compensatory rest.

WHAT TO AVOID
Not seeking the right advice

Consult a solicitor or legal adviser if you have any queries about how the business may be affected. You can also contact The Health and Safety Executive and the Advisory Conciliation and Arbitration Service for further information—local offices are listed in the phone book.

Not keeping staff informed

Members of staff who are affected by the changes should be identified and all staff provided with a brief outline of the new regulations.

RECOMMENDED LINKS

Advisory Conciliation and Arbitration Service (ACAS):
www.acas.org.uk/publications/pub_ab_changing.html
Department of Trade and Industry:
www.dti.gov.uk/er/work_time_regs
Employment Tribunals Service:
www.employmenttribunals.gov.uk
Health and Safety Executive (HSE):
www.hse.gov.uk

SEE ALSO
Employment Law (p. 506)

Developing Leadership Skills

GETTING STARTED

There are many myths about leaders—'leaders are born and not made' being a prime example. Owner-managers of small businesses might not necessarily have been in a leadership role before they started their company, and while some people are naturally better suited to leadership roles than others, the good news is that the necessary skills *can* be learned.

FAQS

Now that my business is growing I've been on a leadership course and understand the theory of being a good leader. How do I put this into practice?

Being an owner-manager will give you plenty of opportunities to put your new skills to the test, but remember that leadership capability does not emerge overnight; it takes time and practice, so don't expect too much of yourself too soon. Why not make a start, though, by leading a new project, where you can test out the skills you've acquired? Make sure you plan carefully for resources and support. Taking this first step will give you the opportunity to test out your responses to this new situation. In turn, you'll then be able to evaluate what has worked and what hasn't, and help you plan what to do or avoid doing next time.

I seem to command an audience easily when I make presentations, but will I make a good leader?

Commanding an audience is a great skill and many leaders have it, but it's not the sole requirement. Leaders also need to be problem-solvers and have originality and flair, confidence and self-knowledge, strong interpersonal skills, the ability to listen, visioning capability, good organisational skills, and so on. Your ability as a speaker suggests that you're articulate and self-confident. If you possess the other qualities too, you are well on the way to being the leader your business needs.

MAKING IT HAPPEN

Understand the different facets of leadership

There are different types of leadership styles—**leadership from the front, supportive leadership**, and **interactive leadership**. For leaders to exist, there must be followers, and the needs of followers change depending on the context. Knowing how to apply different leadership styles can help you respond equally effectively in many different kinds of situations.

Another school of thought recognises four leadership styles: directive, process, creative, and facilitative, each one related to a personality trait. So, being more relaxed doesn't necessarily mean you can't be a leader. You simply have natural tendencies for a certain type of leadership. And you may be able to learn other styles—more dominant, intuitive, or structured—as you become more confident and practised in leadership. Try to work with your preferred style until you are comfortable enough to branch out.

Evidently, certain styles are suited to particular situations. A structured leader, for example, is likely to succeed in a situation where process is important, for example, in running an operation. The relaxed or facilitative leader may be one who manages a professional group of people. Dominant leaders may be needed in businesses where there is a real drive for change.

Get some training

If your budget permits, a leadership course will help you gain a fuller understanding of what leadership is, and, by extension, how it will work for your business. Courses usually range from business theory to developing strategy to understanding business risk.

Having well-developed commercial awareness and a good business education will not only give you confidence, but will also help command respect from others.

Build self-awareness

Your leadership style is the means by which you communicate. The more self-aware you are, the more effectively it will work for you. This means knowing:

- what you are like
- what your preferences are
- what your goals are
- how other people perceive you and your goals
- how you are motivated to achieve them

Numerous tests and questionnaires can be used to help you explore your personality and preferences; they are widely available from books, the web, consultancies, and other sources. Surveys are also useful. Business schools have valuable data on expected leadership behaviours. You can combine information from all these sources to establish a benchmark for yourself.

Apply leadership skills

Leadership opportunities are often thrust upon us unexpectedly, but in a small business environment you'll come across them more frequently. As in most situations, your best bet is to start with an analysis of the situation. Decide what is needed, and how you can best achieve it.

Some leadership positions require you to set the objectives for others to follow. In these situations, scheduling, consultation, and team building are essential to success. Leaders often need to work as intermediaries between two groups—those wanting the results (boards, investors, etc.), and those who will deliver the results. In this case you need to establish good communication channels with both parties. Try to pick teams that have a good balance between competent managers and energetic, loyal team members. Teams need consistent, positive energy levels to sustain momentum, so choose a team by the mix of talent required, rather than by friendships or politics.

WHAT TO AVOID
Mirroring other leaders too closely

People new to leadership roles may try to copy a leader they respect, because the person provides an easy model. This can create a false impression of what you are really like, or, worse, make you look foolish for trying to mimic a style incompatible with your own personality. Leadership behaviours come from within. Understand what it is you respect in the other leader and think about how you can best display that attribute. If it doesn't work, don't be afraid to try a new approach.

Not working at it

Many people hope that they have natural leadership skills, and accept leadership positions without proper training or mental adjustment. This sink-or-swim approach works sometimes, but not always! Building up leadership skills, increasing awareness of yourself, and evaluating what you do have much more potential for success. It will also give you more room to make mistakes without losing credibility.

RECOMMENDED LINKS

Emerald (trading name of MCB University Press):
www.managementfirst.com/experts/leadership.htm
Entrepreneur.com:
www.entrepreneur.com (management tab)
The Leadership Trust:
www.leadership.co.uk
University of Exeter, Centre for Leadership Development:
www.ex.ac.uk/leadership

SEE ALSO
Delegating (p. 412)

Focus On: Win–win Performance Appraisals
Patrick Forsyth

GETTING STARTED

As your business grows and you recruit employees, you or your office manager will need to conduct performance appraisals. These face-to-face discussions (ideally undertaken annually) are an opportunity for an employee's work to be discussed and reviewed, and should aim to improve motivation and performance during the coming year. Unfortunately, many managers dislike conducting appraisals and worse, many employees rate their appraisals as worthless—or something even less flattering. In reality, appraisals are a major opportunity for both managers and staff.

This actionlist will review:

- why appraisals are necessary and will examine the benefits to managers and staff. Primarily, they ensure and improve future performance.
- how effective appraisals should be planned and undertaken to maximise their positive impact while avoiding negative pitfalls.
- the impact of appraisals on the long-term success of the business. Appraisals provide considerable opportunity for improving on-going operations, effective management, and catalysing change.

FAQS

What are the reasons for performance appraisals?

There are many positive reasons why appraisals are necessary. They give managers an opportunity to review individuals' past performance, plan their future work and role, and set and agree specific individual goals for the future. Making time to hold a meeting with the person to be appraised also allows for on-the-spot coaching, which in turn can identify development needs and set up development activity.

In addition, appraisals can:

- allow the exchange of feedback
- reinforce or extend the reporting relationship
- act as a catalyst for delegating work
- focus on longer-term career progression
- underpin or increase motivation

Often a negative reason is the close relationship between appraisals and employment legislation (for example, lack of appraisal may make it impossible to terminate someone's employment). This is also a factor to keep in mind.

Overall the underlying intention is to improve future performance. The good appraisal presupposes that even the best performance can be improved, and seeks to increase the likelihood of future plans being brought to fruition.

How should the appraisal be organised?

For a successful and well-organised appraisal, there are a number of things you can do. You need to:

- allow enough time. You need to do the job and also to reflect the importance of the occasion. Few appraisals will be accomplished properly in less than an hour; some may last two or three hours or more—and will still be time usefully spent.
- allow no disturbances. Pausing to take even one telephone call sends out the wrong signals.
- create a suitable environment. Appraisals should be held somewhere private, comfortable, perhaps less formal than across a desk, yet suitably business-like.
- put the individual at ease. Remember that, even with good communication beforehand, appraisals may be viewed as somewhat traumatic. Anything that can be done to counter this is useful.

MAKING IT HAPPEN
Prepare throughout the year

Unsurprisingly, the key to effective appraisals is preparation by both parties. The manager must:

- spend sufficient time with staff during the year.
- communicate clearly and thoroughly the purpose and form of the appraisal so that people know what to expect. Employees should understand the need for appraisal, its importance, the specific objectives it addresses, and how both parties can get the best from it.
- prepare throughout the year, keeping clear records. Keeping an appraisal collection file means you don't have to rely on memory. In this, you should note matters that can usefully be raised at appraisals, making notes and filing copies of documents that will assist the process.

The appraisee (or team member) should keep running records and should plan in detail the kind of meeting he or she intends to have.

Successful appraisal is the culmination of a year's worth of thinking. Recalling every detail of an employee's working year is difficult, but you can only appraise properly by being informed.

Relevant background information needs checking: for example, the appraisee's job description (which may need amendment after the appraisal), specific past objectives, possible changes to the job, its responsibilities, or circumstances, and the records of any previous appraisals.

Prepare carefully and plan

- Prepare written notification. As well as confirming mutually convenient timing, this should recap the purpose of the appraisal and highlight background information. Distribute copies of any documents or forms you intend to use or refer to during the meeting.
- Study the appraisee's file, making sure that you have all the information you need about what was supposed to happen during the year and what actually did happen. Make notes of points needing discussion

and ensure that you can move between the documents easily as the meeting progresses.

- Review agreed standards and identify any that are no longer relevant or that need to be changed.
- Draft a provisional assessment. Brief notes can provide a starting point, prompt the agenda, and link to the system. Don't prejudge the discussion or make decisions prematurely.
- Assess your initial thoughts. Check your rationale, asking yourself a why question about anything noted at this stage. If no clear answer comes, more research may be necessary.
- Consider specific areas of the appraisal. It may be clear that some training is necessary, for example. Again without prejudging, it may be useful to check out what might suit and formulate a suggestion before the meeting.
- Think ahead. Remember that the most important part of the discussion will be about the future. You may need to plan particular projects and tasks, taking both development and operational considerations into account.
- Consult with others. Speak to those who work or deal with the appraisee to get a complete picture.
- Be clear about the link with a pay review. Many managers feel this should be kept for a separate occasion. Otherwise it can be difficult to stop appraisees from thinking all that matters is the potential increase.

Handle the appraisal effectively

Before you go any further, make completely sure that everybody being appraised understands the need for appraisal, its importance, its objectives, and its mutual benefits. When the appraisal starts:

- explain the agenda and how things will be handled. Remember to ask what the appraisee's priorities are.
- act to direct the proceedings. Do not, however, ride roughshod over the appraisee.
- ask questions. Open questions prompt and focus discussion.

- listen. The meeting is primarily an opportunity for the appraisee to communicate. In a well-conducted appraisal, the appraisee should do most of the talking; the manager's job is to make that happen.
- keep primarily to agreed performance factors. Don't indulge in amateur psychology or attempt to measure personality factors. Also, keep primarily to performance factors, getting the appraisee to do most of the talking—while you listen hard.
- use the system. Use systems and appraisal forms to guide the meeting; working through the form systematically will ensure most of what needs to happen does.
- encourage discussion. Consider the appraisee's personal strengths and weaknesses, successes and failures, and their implications for the future. Concentrate the appraisal process on future performance, and don't confuse it with discussion of remuneration.
- set out action plans. Describe those that can be decided there and then (who will do what, when); note those needing more deliberation in terms of when and how action will be taken. Deal with each factor separately, for example, by devoting time to development action.
- conclude on a positive note. Always thank the appraisee for the role he or she has played and for the past year's work. Link this to any subsequent documentation.
- follow up appraisals promptly, sending all necessary written material to the appraisee and flagging any opportunity for further discussion.

 ## WHAT TO AVOID

Treating appraisals as an end, rather than a means to an end

Appraisals achieve most when placed in a long-term context and linked to ongoing operations. Bear in mind:

- the ongoing management relationship: an effective appraisal should make all management processes through the year easier.
- the link with training and development: consultation, counselling, mentoring, and informal discussions are all just as important extensions of appraisal as formal training.
- motivation: appraisals must themselves be motivational, and what stems from them must assist ongoing motivational activity for the employee.

Dwelling too much on the past

This should not really account for more than 60% of the discussion at most; you also need to discuss future activities, priorities, development needs, and objectives.

Being too directive, highly critical, or being perceived as being critical

Successful appraisals are dynamic, positive discussions, not a witch-hunt or a chance to heap blame and ignominy on someone. (If you do need to tackle a problem, do it when the problem arises, and don't just store it up for the appraisal!)

Giving comments and feedback poorly

The appraiser must be clear, honest, and open in his or her comments at all times. The more appraisers hedge, the more chance there is that misunderstandings will creep in.

Failing to follow up after the meeting

There is one key action here: to complete all documentation and confirmations that are necessary promptly after the meeting. Send copies to the appraisee, flagging any opportunity for further discussion and asking for comments. If your business is big enough to have a personnel department, send a copy there too.

RECOMMENDED LINKS

Institute of Management Excellence:
www.itstime.com/index.html

Focus On: Mentoring
Max Landsberg

GETTING STARTED

Mentoring suits smaller organisations especially well. It can build productively on the small-world environment in which 'everybody knows everybody else' to enhance professional skills and relationships. It can also make up for a potential lack of advanced HR systems—systems the smaller firm might be unable to afford.

- Mentoring is crucial to developing employees and retaining them.
- Mentors give advice on a spectrum of topics, ranging from specific skills to broader issues of career direction.
- Mentees gain advice, access to established networks, and broader personal and professional perspectives.
- Though mentoring happens naturally to some degree, it can be boosted by programmes which match seasoned employees to colleagues who are new either to the business or to their role. These programmes are designed to have a measurable impact.

This actionlist offers advice on how to get the best from a mentoring relationship, whether you are a mentor hoping to keep a valued member of staff, or a mentee aiming to build your role in a small business.

FAQS

What is mentoring?

Mentoring is the process by which wisdom and experience is shared between two people, one of whom (the mentor) is typically senior to the other (the mentee). The advice that the mentor conveys to the mentee supports development of the mentee's skills, career, and networks.

Most of us have probably acquired our mentors more by luck than through planning, but with the erosion of traditional career ladders and the increasingly organic and unstructured composition of the modern firm (especially small firms), individuals and companies alike are seeing ever greater merits to this once informal relationship.

What is the scope of a mentoring relationship?

In a business setting a mentoring relationship focuses on skills, career, and personal development. At the start of their relationship, neither the mentor nor the mentee can anticipate all the issues that they'll end up discussing. Nevertheless, both parties should be aware of the topics which they might usefully discuss, or which might emerge anyway. These topics fall into two broad categories: helping the mentee to achieve learning and career goals, and building the mentee's confidence and self-awareness.

Career issues typically include:

- whether the mentee's career vision and goals seem relevant and viable
- how to 'decode' the business's feedback to the mentee, for example, from an annual appraisal or from a promotion received or missed
- what experience and expertise to acquire in the short and long term
- where to find role models with whom the mentee can identify
- how the mentee should best interact with his or her manager
- whether to accept an internal (or external) job offer
- how best to promote an initiative within the business that the mentee has conceived
- how to react to unacceptable behaviour experienced by the mentee, for example, apparent bias, favouritism, or harassment
- how to deal with the effects of a personal or family problem

Issues of **confidence and self-awareness** may include:

- how the mentee can make a frank review of his or her own strengths and weaknesses
- whether feedback received by the mentee about his or her personal style is accurate or not
- how to overcome apparent career set-backs, or feelings of isolation or depression

Despite this great breadth of role, mentoring relationships do have limits. If you are a mentor, remember to:

- focus on advice rather than 'rescue'
- *not* build a nepotistic relationship in which you try to exert undue influence in favour of your mentee
- direct the mentee to a professional counsellor if needed

MAKING IT HAPPEN
Understand different types of mentoring

There are four main types of mentoring which an individual may seek, or which a business may wish to promote. Note that these four models are not mutually exclusive, and also that most people have more than one mentor, each of whom may play complementary roles.

Informal or **'natural'** mentoring happens when a more experienced person decides to take a less experienced person under his or her wing, often to give career advice. Such relationships form spontaneously and are usually based on a similarity of interests, expertise, or personal history. These relationships tend to grow and flourish and often continue after one or both the people leave the business.

Situational mentoring is the providing of advice for a specific circumstance, such as when the mentee has to implement a new computer system, or set up a new office. Although these relationships are often short-term, they can develop into a longer term mentoring connection.

Positional mentoring occurs when the mentor is the manager of the mentee. All good managers mentor their team members to some extent, but there are natural constraints to the effectiveness of this approach.

Firstly, the mentee may find it difficult to raise issues of switching jobs or roles. Secondly, the mentor will not provide an impartial view of their relationship as superior and junior. Thirdly, the manager may be accused of favouritism, if one of his or her mentees advances more rapidly than others.

Formal mentoring programmes emerged during the 1990s in an attempt to gain the advantages of natural mentoring while recognising the limitations of positional mentoring. They are discussed in more detail below.

Understand the benefits for all parties

Mentees are the most obvious beneficiaries of mentoring—they receive advice, guidance, access to contacts and networks, reassurance, and a broader perspective on their careers. Mentors also benefit, however. They typically strengthen their interpersonal skills, find insights into the workings of their business and teams, and have the satisfaction of seeing others grow. Finally, businesses benefit through better recruitment, induction, and retention of staff; better communication across all areas of the business, faster learning within the company, and a stronger overall culture.

Excel as a mentor

As a mentor, you will sometimes need to be a coach, sometimes a motivator, or guide, counsellor, role model, or provider of contacts. To excel in these roles, you will need to:

- help the mentee to focus his or her efforts, and to clarify goals
- prompt the mentee to develop effective strategies, and act as devil's advocate to challenge them
- help the mentee to identify appropriate resources, contacts, and role models
- share knowledge and wisdom based on your own experiences
- act personally as a source of inspiration and motivation, while maintaining confidentiality

To accomplish this, ask penetrating questions that help the mentee distinguish 'real' issues from apparent ones; accept the mentee unconditionally, asking 'how' or 'what' rather than 'why'; listen actively to the mentee's feelings as well as to the words; and volunteer your observations where appropriate. Having said that, don't aim to become a personal 'fixer' of your mentee's problems. Instead, help your mentee learn how to develop problem-solving skills which will feed into his or her overall development.

Excel as a mentee

If you are being mentored by someone else, be open, take initiatives, and show your consideration for your mentor's time.

In terms of openness, be open about your objectives and aspirations, but also be open to feedback or other observations made by your mentor. If your mentor finds that any frank comments are met with defensiveness, the relationship will soon wither.

In taking initiative, be proactive in meeting with your mentor, and in relating to him or her: arrive at your meetings fully prepared and with clear objectives, and take the lead in suggesting new ways of viewing your issues. Actively follow up on any ideas generated in the meetings, and let your mentor know of progress you make.

Finally, show consideration for the mentor's investment of time. This involves: identifying what the mentor wants to derive from the relationship; accommodating the mentor's schedule when arranging meetings; and providing feedback, praise, and thanks in an appropriate way.

Get the best from mentoring programmes

Larger businesses increasingly use formal programmes to encourage mentoring and to reap its benefits. Compared with natural mentoring (see above), formal mentoring tends to be based on more specific objectives. It also aims at more measurable impact (e.g., employee retention); runs for a more limited period; typically involves discussions of more prescribed structure; and is based on pairing that is balanced more in favour of the mentee.

Such programmes require focus, and typically aim to support employees who are new to the business, new to a role, or who are part of a group that is in some way specialised or disadvantaged. Efforts to provide mentoring for *all* employees in a business rarely succeed, if those efforts are based purely on formal programmes. The broader objective of 'mentoring for all' is best tackled as part of a wider programme of cultural change, which should also examines how the company's day-to-day business is conducted.

WHAT TO AVOID
Not building the right programme for your business

It's important to tailor any mentoring programme to your own business's needs—what might work somewhere else won't necessarily work for you. Here are some key elements to consider.

- decide whether to adopt a formal programme, or one that includes some element of natural mentoring
- have simple criteria for people's eligibility to be mentees and mentors, and for the maximum number of mentees per mentor
- agree whether mentees choose mentors (recommended), or vice versa; establish a matching process that is seen as fair by everyone
- explain the ground rules clearly, for example, a commitment to a duration of one year, the ability to terminate the relationship at any time with no blame, and complete confidentiality
- provide training for mentors and mentees, and set out the expected benefits
- plan how you will check whether the programme is working. Monitor it periodically. reward, praise or thank the mentors
- do not over-design the programme: make it clear to potential mentees that the quality of mentoring they receive will in large measure depend on their own ability to attract mentors

---

RECOMMENDED LINK

Institute of Management Excellence:
www.itstime.com/index.html

Focus On: Building Great Teams
Meredith Belbin

GETTING STARTED

The problem about the word 'teamwork' is that it has become too popular and has therefore lost its meaning. A person thought to be good at teamwork is all too often someone who fits into a group and keeps out of trouble. Complying with majority decisions and being willing to do anything that's required is seen as being ideal behaviour, but if everyone behaved like that, a team just wouldn't work effectively—a flock of sheep may hang together well, but their only accomplishment is to eat grass.

Teams and team-based working has developed into the normal way of structuring organisations of all sizes and undertaking tasks, yet it is a difficult aspect of leadership and is usually developed through experience. In the context of a small business, you as the owner or owner-manager, are likely to be the leader of your team. Every leader has his or her own style, and when developing a high performing team this needs to combine with an understanding of:

- the benefits of team-building—what it can achieve and what the leader should be striving for
- team roles and dynamics—how teams work and achieve their greatest success
- the key stages of team development—what they are and how to support the team in each stage
- the features of a successful team and team leader
- how to avoid potential problems and pitfalls

FAQS

What makes a good team leader?

Leadership, in broad strokes, is the capacity to establish direction and motivate others towards working for a common aim. Successful teamwork depends on the team leader's ability to make sure all team members know their common aim and what they each need to do to achieve it.

Naturally, all teams are different and have their own dynamic and all leaders develop their own style for forming, developing, and leading them, but there are some general characteristics of a good team leader. For a team to work, it's essential that all members are committed, so leaders must be supportive, enthusiastic, and motivating people to work with. They must organise and communicate well in order to co-ordinate team efforts both *within* the team and with others *outside* the team. During difficult or stressful times, team leaders need to be approachable, good listeners who can offer feedback and advice.

What are the features of a good team?

It goes without saying that successful teams are ones in which people do not waste time trying to achieve success at the expense of others. Instead, they work at understanding each other, and communicate honestly and openly. They are committed to the team's success and are respectful and supportive of each other by sharing information and experience.

Conflict is unavoidable in most work situations, but a good team will work through it and reach an understanding by generating new ideas. A good team also acknowledges the role of the leader and understands when he or she needs to act and make a decision (i.e. in an emergency or if there is a major problem or disagreement).

MAKING IT HAPPEN
Focus on the work

For anyone interested in productive teamwork, it's often better to start with the work rather than the team. First of all, think about whether the job in hand really does need a team to tackle it. Some types of work, such as repetitive or unskilled tasks and, at the other extreme, specialist activities, are best performed by loners. Rounding up such people and making them members of a team risks producing a double disadvantage: their personal productivity falls and their privacy is invaded. While it's currently popular to strive for such an 'all inclusive' approach in the workplace and some people argue that isolated workers need a social dimension to their work, there are often few benefits to forcing this set-up on someone.

Enable the team to succeed

The team approach for organising work depends on empowerment, that is, making sure that each person is allowed to perform to the best of his or her abilities. This relies on trust and also depends on how well members of a group have developed an understanding of each other's strengths and weaknesses. That's why, if your budget allows, training in teamwork is so important and why it helps to understand the language of team roles.

Reward teams at the right time

All teams need to be assessed, but how should it be done so that it is positive and constructive? One way is to set objectives for teams and judge how well these have been met. This view is popular in the 'top-down' school of management, where senior managers make all the decisions and these are then passed down through the ranks to employees. In larger organisations, this approach is given added impetus by performance-related bonuses.

The argument put forward is that teams need fixed incentives to perform well, an assumption linked with the converse view that without such an incentive the team will not perform satisfactorily. I believe this approach is likely to backfire. Success in meeting given criteria depends partly on circumstances and contingencies, and may not be commensurate with effort or skill. Objectives may be too easy to reach or too difficult. In the end, people may focus more on the shortcomings of the incentive than on the sense and purpose of their work. Retrospective awards for good team performance are better received than prospective rewards for teams given set targets.

Stick to the essentials of effective teamworking

Again, start with the work and think about whether it really calls for a team at all. If you do decide that a team is the best way to tackle a task, work out who will be doing what; also, decide which responsibilities can be assigned to individuals, and make them subject to personal accountability.

If possible, train your team so that it plays to the best strengths of its individual players. Make sure each person is allowed to develop ownership, pride, and maximum commitment to the team's responsibilities.

WHAT TO AVOID
Misunderstanding people

While it's obviously crucial that you understand the nature of the work being undertaken, you also need to be aware of the skills, experience, and approach of those doing the work. Taking account of people's strengths and motivations can certainly help to build or break teams.

Misunderstanding teams and what they need to succeed

Don't become too glib about the terminology and remember to spend time on evaluating whether you really need a team to complete a given task before you embark on a team exercise, and if you do go ahead bear in mind that not everyone flourishes in a team—some people will need more support than others.

If you are the team leader, remember that you have to allow team members the freedom to do what their role entails—empower them. Give them all the information they need and set boundaries to make sure that things happen.

RECOMMENDED LINKS
Belbin Associates:
www.belbin.com

Handling Resignations

GETTING STARTED

Although it is disappointing to lose key people, especially in a small business environment where some of your employees will have been with you from the start, resignations give companies a chance to plan ahead and recruit people who will assist in the growth of the business. They provide the opportunity to take a fresh look at what is working and what is not, and whether or not changes need to be made.

From the employees' standpoint, resignations allow people to move on in their careers, learn new skills, and take on new responsibilities. An individual leaving a company is not necessarily withdrawing his or her loyalty or influence over its future direction. Indeed, past employees may well be instrumental in instigating joint projects or ventures that will change the fortunes or organisation of the business at which they once worked.

FAQS

My second in command has just handed in her resignation. How can I convey this information to the rest of the team without risking a drop in morale?

You might find that calling the team together, along with the person who has resigned, allows an open discussion to take place in which you can address both the resignation and its implications. By showing your concern about their feelings and asking for input, you will ensure their involvement and give them a sense of control. It will also give you an opportunity to discuss any structural or resource issues that may arise from the departure.

I run a team of specialists who are hard to replace, and as soon as one left the others started to follow. What can I do to prevent talent from haemorrhaging out of the business?

This indicates one or more things: perhaps terms and conditions for their employment are more favourable elsewhere, or perhaps conditions in your business have deteriorated substantially without you noticing. By conducting an exit interview with them, you may pick up on the reason for their exodus and start structuring a solution. Involve those that remain and allow them to contribute to the discussion on improving conditions. This may also be a time to look at your succession plans for the company. Are you preparing others for these specialist roles, and what are the routes to them? Can you do something to clear the path for succession?

A member of my team wishes to leave full-time employment and become a contractor to the business on a project basis. Is this a good idea?

Increasingly, businesses are using contract employees to suit many different circumstances. Doing so allows more flexible working arrangements, and also reduces the direct cost of employment. In many instances, contract employees are responsible for the cost of their own office space off premises as well as funding their own benefits such as health insurance, pensions, taxes, and so on. However, contract employees will often charge more for their services than they were paid as an employee. The key issues are costs and benefits. Another part of the equation is how you manage the situation with others in the team, so that there is no ambiguity about how work is to be done and who has responsibility.

I was handed a resignation by someone whom I was happy to see leave. However, he then changed his mind and asked to stay. How do I handle this?

If you feel strongly that your business would be better off without this person, you're within your rights as the supervisor to deny his request. If you think the person might be suited for a job elsewhere in your company, you could advise him to discuss the matter with the human resources department. It is not unusual for people to panic when leaving a role they know well, so this may just be pre-leaving nerves rather than anything more serious.

MAKING IT HAPPEN
Be prepared
Most small and growing businesses value a stable workforce, but it's inevitable that a certain percentage of the workforce will move on each year, picking up skills and experience in your company and taking them elsewhere. Whatever position the employee leaves, it is desirable that his or her departure is handled well. These people will speak of your business after they leave, and they can help build, or destroy, its reputation in the marketplace.

Acknowledge the intention to leave
Verbal notice may be acceptable, but it's usual for a resignation to be submitted in writing so that the process of removing the employee from the payroll and the final account and allocation of benefits may begin.

Confirm the leaving date
Notice periods vary according to the role/ job and the seniority level of the departing employee. You may find that the person who is leaving wants to negotiate an early departure, so this will have to be considered alongside their role demands and the volume of work pending. If work priorities allow, you may be willing to sanction this.

Hand over
Depending on the nature of the work that the departing employee was engaged in, there will need to be a programme to ensure the smooth handover of projects and responsibilities. This could be a simple plan developed jointly by the employee and his or her manager, or it may involve a wider group of people who will be affected by the resignation.

Increasingly, organisations use 'natural attrition' to reduce their workforce. Where departing employees may find that there are no plans to replace them, their responsibilities would be reallocated to other members of the team.

A handover programme may be quite involved. Time is needed to brief colleagues, tie up administrative loose ends, and perhaps instigate some training in areas where special skills are required.

If the person who is leaving has a network of business relationships crucial to your business—clients or customers, for example—these will also need attention. Meetings between the client and the new person on your team, perhaps with the departing employee also present, will improve the chances that continuity in service will be maintained. If the person leaving developed personal relationships with key clients or suppliers, this can be a difficult time. The client and former employee may wish to remain in touch with one another. Loyalty to an individual instead of to an organisation means that such departures leave the company vulnerable to loss of business, especially if the former employee becomes your competitor in the marketplace.

Conduct an exit interview
Exit interviews are a good idea, and are usually conducted with a member of the human resources team. During the interview, the person leaving should be encouraged to discuss all aspects of the role/job that they are vacating, their reasons for leaving, and any issues that contributed to that decision.

The exit interview should be a positive experience, although grievances may be aired. If this is the case, it is important to listen to what the person has to say. Sometimes, things that haven't been said before this point are relevant for those remaining at the company. Grievances can vary, but if the same information is being heard repeatedly at exit interviews, there is clearly a need to change something within the organisation to make it a better place to work.

Remember other considerations

There may be circumstances when the employee will be asked to leave immediately upon resignation—for example, when the employee has access to confidential information and is leaving to join a competitor. It may also occur where there is a risk of disruption or sabotage, where the health of the employee may not be good, or where work has dried up. In these cases, it is usual to pay the salary equivalent in lieu of notice.

Leaving a job—even under the best of circumstances—is not always comfortable, so handling someone's departure sensitively makes the experience easier. Of course, there will be those who are desperate to move on and who share their euphoria freely, but in most instances, it's customary to host a farewell event of some kind and give a gift to show appreciation for the work done.

WHAT TO AVOID
Taking it personally

Taking a resignation personally can lead to distress on both the employee's and employer's side. People decide to leave for a wide variety of reasons; it is not necessarily an act of betrayal. Try and be open to hearing the reasons behind the decision and explore the options, if there are any.

Ignoring the implications of the resignation

Ignoring the prospect of someone's departure can leave you vulnerable. Everyone involved needs to pitch in to make sure that the leaving causes as little disruption as possible, so try bringing those affected by the move together to create a smooth transition.

Showing that you're pleased he or she is going

No matter how unlikable, annoying, disruptive, or incompetent the employee has been, try not to show your delight that he or she is leaving: it's disrespectful to the departing employee and demoralizing for those who remain. Behave with professionalism from the moment you receive the resignation throughout the exit process, and leave your ego to one side.

RECOMMENDED LINK

I-resign.com:
**www.i-resign.com/uk/resignationkit/
exit_interview.asp**

SEE ALSO
Staff Planning (p. 415)

RETREATING WITH DIGNITY

Deciding Whether to Sell Your Business

GETTING STARTED

The reasons behind selling your business will determine how you approach the task, and will also affect your expectations of the transaction. If you are selling so that you can retire, for instance, you could sell at any time over a number of years to get the best offer available. Selling due to ill health may require a quicker sale, but if the business is in a good state it need not be immediate. If the business is in financial crisis, a low selling price may be necessary for a quick sale before you lose too much money. A forced sale may also be due to changed market circumstances or technological changes. As well as business-related reasons for sale (such as diversification, receivership, or bankruptcy), you may also have personal reasons for wanting to sell up, such as a death in the family, or the breakdown of a partnership.

One useful book that you may find helpful on the subject is *How to Sell Your Business and Live Happily Ever After* by Gary Morley, published in 2002 by Management Books.

FAQS

When is the best time to sell?

Ideally, you should sell your business after a number of consecutive profit-making years, so that prospective buyers can be sure that the business is a viable concern and that they can make realistic estimates of future earnings. The selling value of your business will tend to be based largely on what the purchaser expects to earn in the few years immediately after acquiring the business. Depending on the sector you are in, and the expectations of investors in that sector, the purchaser will want to be sure that the business delivers a minimum rate of return so that they can recover the purchase price within a number of years.

If the business is not yet profitable, or has been through an unprofitable patch, consider building it up for a few years before putting it on the market. This is often the only way of retrieving some value from your business for all the investment you have made in product development, market recognition, customer loyalty, and sweat equity. Without some hard evidence of profit-making history or potential, you could find it difficult to put a realistic sale value on your business.

What are the alternatives to selling?

If you are selling because of financial problems, consider whether the prospects for the business really are so bad. Have you considered the options? For example, could a manager or partner be taken on to help you cope, or to address the main problems? Could particularly troublesome aspects of the operation be minimised?

It is important to compare realistically the costs of selling up with the costs of keeping going. What is the most likely outcome from the sale, for instance, and will this be a financial solution? Look at alternatives like:

- selling assets (such as land and machinery) and then leasing them back to the business to improve cash flow
- taking on a partner who will contribute capital and take on some responsibilities
- scaling down operations to focus on the most profitable work

Should I sell all or part of the business?

Raising cash is often the motivation behind the sale of a business. But selling your whole business is a big step, and will often prevent you from building on your experience in that sector (you will usually be required to sign a 'restraint of trade' agreement preventing you from competing with your old business for a number of years). This may undermine your own position, and make it difficult to develop your career the way that you would like. One way around this is to sell only part of your business to raise some capital, and use this to strengthen the portion that you keep.

MAKING IT HAPPEN
Prepare the business for sale

There are a few aspects of the business that you can usefully focus on in preparation for a sale—the most important of which are listed below.

- **Reduce discretionary expenditure.** This is expenditure not necessary to keep the business going. You don't necessarily have to eliminate discretionary expenditure, just highlight it to potential buyers. Common areas of discretionary expenditure include travel and entertainment, and running expensive company cars.

- **Reduce costs.** Other expenditure can also be reduced, but it is important not to cut back in vital areas. Buyers will often look for consistent expenditure trends. A sudden reduction in expenditure will be very noticeable and potentially negate the positive effects you were hoping it would have on potential buyers.

- **Maintain your property and assets well.** If you have leasehold property, security of tenure and rent reviews should be obtained. Keep machinery in good condition, using maintenance contracts if necessary.

- **Improve your working capital position.** For instance, reduce excess stock levels and make better use of creditors.

- **Keep employees informed.** Most businesses hinge on the skill and experience of certain key workers. The sale may unsettle them, so keep them informed and secure their loyalty (it might be necessary to consider incentives).

- **Make sure you have the loyalty of key customers and suppliers.** This can often be done with long-term contracts, as buyers will be keen to ensure continuity of supply. If the business operates under licence, it is important that you ensure the licence is transferable to potential buyers.

Determine a price

Valuing a small business can be difficult, as there is no publicly trading share price that can be simply multiplied by the number of shares issued. Determining the value will involve the hard figures such as assets,

liabilities, historical earnings, and cash flow, as well as more subjective figures such as projected earnings, know-how, quality of management, and goodwill. External factors also need to be considered, such as current market conditions and industry popularity. Ultimately, however, what a business is worth comes down to what both parties agree it is worth. Get some expert help to make sure that you get the best price possible.

Check the legal status

The legal status of the business for sale is very important to bear in mind, mainly because it defines exactly who owns the various assets to be sold. If you operate as a sole trader, you own all the assets of the business and it is up to you if, and how, they are sold. Similarly, partners will own their share of the assets, and any sale must be agreed according to the provisions of the partnership agreement. A limited company is a separate legal entity from its owners. In this case, selling the business may simply be a matter of selling shares in the business, or the shares might be retained while the equipment, premises, and goodwill are sold.

WHAT TO AVOID
Waiting too long

Perhaps the worst time to sell a business is once it is deep in debt. If you are forced into a sale, the chances are that you will not get a reasonable price—even if your business is still potentially profitable. By taking on debts, and perhaps even a loss-making enterprise, a purchaser is also taking on the substantial financial risk that the business will not respond to remedial action. The purchaser will therefore want to reduce this risk by paying a lower purchase price and keeping cash in reserve to fund possible future losses. For your part, you need to plan as far ahead as possible to anticipate what trading conditions might be like at the time you wish you sell. It is easier to demand a premium price when business is growing; that way, a purchaser is more likely acknowledge some 'blue-sky' value and pay for it.

Setting an unrealistic asking price

When determining your asking price, do not get carried away by the theoretical prospects of your business. While there may well be potential for a new investor to exploit, this must be weighed against the hard realities of what is possible within your business and within your particular market. The financial history of your business will be the foundation on which valuations are based, so build your arguments on that.

Ending up in protracted negotiations

Keep your negotiations about selling as short as possible. If you can, set yourself some deadlines for certain key decisions about who to sell to, under what terms, and at what price. This will avoid the danger of letting the selling process drag on for too long. There is inevitably going to be a feeling of insecurity among staff and customers, so it is best for all parties to conclude a deal as quickly as possible. Bear in mind that a successful sale might not be agreed, in which case everyone is expected to return to business as usual; this is often difficult after months of uncertainty.

RECOMMENDED LINKS

Daltons Business (a useful selling guide):
www.daltonsbusiness.com/sellguide.asp
Deloitte and Touche (online guide to selling your business):
www.deloitte.com

SEE ALSO

Bankruptcy and Business Failure (p. 493)
Finding Potential Buyers for Your Business (p. 467)
Management Buyouts (p. 522)
Understanding the Legal Ramifications of Winding Up a Business (p. 473)
Venture Capital (p. 554)

Knowing the Value of Your Business

GETTING STARTED

Knowing the value of your business is very important if you are considering selling it or looking for external investment into your venture. Ultimately, the value of a business comes down to what both parties agree it is worth. A company which has shares listed on the stock exchange has a clear value in the number of shares in the company, multiplied by their value set by the exchange. The share value in a small business, however, is harder to calculate and must take into account such elements as assets, liabilities, profitability, customer base, goodwill, and trading history.

This actionlist provides some general 'rules of thumb' on how to value your business, or how to check that it has been properly valued by someone else.

FAQS

Who should value the business?

If you're using a business broker, it will be down to them to value your business. However, it would still be wise to value the business yourself so that you can relate to the price that the broker has specified. For whatever price they place on your business, you should establish how they arrived at this figure so that you can agree that the price is fair.

Likewise, if you use an accountant to value your business, you should still value the business yourself so that you can satisfy yourself that they have given a reasonable and fair value. After all, who knows your business better than you do?

It may be that you decide to value the business alone, without the assistance of professionals; however, their input could add valuable credibility to your arguments when it comes to negotiating a final price and terms with prospective buyers.

How is a business valued?

Valuation is not an exact science. It is difficult to set the value of a business at a single figure, as so many factors should be taken into account. Hard figures such as assets, liabilities, historical earnings, and cash flow must be accounted for, but more subjective figures such as projected earnings, know-how, quality of management, and goodwill should also be used. External factors should be considered, such as current market conditions and industry popularity. What you consider to be the value of your business and its final selling price may differ considerably depending on the circumstances surrounding the sale or investment into the business. Is the buyer keen to buy quickly? Is there more than one investor/buyer interested? What form will the payment or investment take? What is the level of risk involved for the buyer or investor? How urgently do you want to sell?

Do you need to compare your business with similar businesses?

Before proceeding with the valuation, you should compare the financial results of your business with those of similar organisations within the same industry. This will help you determine whether there should be a premium added or discount given over the value of comparable businesses. Financial comparisons should be made using several measures, including: sales growth; gross margin; earnings before tax as a percentage of sales; return on assets; current ratio, and debt-to-net-worth ratio. What is the growth rate of the business compared to the industry as a whole? Is the business gaining or losing market share?

MAKING IT HAPPEN

Value the business

The final valuation figure will depend on the technique adopted. There are effectively three methods of valuing a business—net assets, multiple of earnings, and standard formulae.

Calculate net assets

Valuing a business by calculating its net assets is the most easily understood method, and the one most commonly used for small businesses. The net assets (the net worth of the business) are shown on the balance sheet. If everything was sold at the value recorded on the balance sheet, the amount of money realised would be equal to the net assets. Sometimes buyers are reluctant to pay much more than net asset value, as it is very difficult to make a suitable allowance for intangible assets such as goodwill. The value of other intangibles can also be considered, such as ownership of patents, trademarks, and copyrights; the value of long-term contracts, licence agreements, and so on.

The net-assets figure may need to be adjusted to reflect the true worth of the assets. Buildings, for example, may be worth more than shown on the balance sheet. Equipment, especially computers, may be worth far less. You may need to enter into negotiations about how assets will be valued, but take into account replacement value and realisable value.

Calculate the earnings multiple

The earnings multiple calculation for valuing a business is based on the price/earnings ratio (P/E ratio). The P/E ratio is the price of one share to the earnings (that is, the net profit after tax) attributable to that share. The P/E ratio gives an indication of how much investors are prepared to pay to buy the shares.

If, for example, a company has earnings per share (EPS) of 18.5p and one share costs £5 then it has a P/E ratio of 27 (500 divided by 18.5). You can apply this to any business. Take the net profit, apply a suitable multiplier, and that gives you the value of the business. Try selecting a suitable multiplier by looking at the P/E ratios for quoted companies, usually printed in the financial sections of newspapers. However, you will need to apply a discount to take account of the smaller size, the greater risk, and the difficulty for investors wishing to sell shares in private limited companies. Typically, you should apply a discount of 30–40%, though if your profit is less than £1 million, the discount should probably be at least 50%.

For example, you have achieved earnings of £100,000 per annum over a number of years and can show that this trend is likely to continue. If, in your business sector, the average P/E ratio is 12, you then need to apply a discount of 50%, which then gives a multiplier of 6. This implies that the business is worth £600,000. You should remember to exclude non-recurring expenditure (such as one-off purchases) when you calculate the earnings for a particular year.

Understand standard formulae

Standard methods of valuing a business have become established in some industry sectors. For example, the valuation of a milk round depends on the average daily delivery; and insurance brokers often multiply their gross commission one to two times to work out the value of their business. There may be an accepted formula applied in your business sector, and it may be worth investigating this further before committing yourself to any valuation process.

Divide the shares

Valuing the business only gives you a starting point. If you are looking for an external investor, you then have to negotiate the proportion of shares that might be exchanged for a certain amount of finance. The owners of a business will have invested their own finance—though this should, in effect, be reflected in the valuation. They will also have invested considerable time and effort to build up the business to the point where they are seeking additional equity. This, too, should be recognised and rewarded.

One way of doing this is to add a notional amount to the net asset valuation to represent the 'sweat equity'—that is, the hard work and effort which has already been applied to build the business up to its current position but which is not reflected in the valuation of the business. If, for example, a business has a net asset valuation of £50,000, a further £50,000 might be added as sweat equity. An investor providing an additional £50,000 would then receive 33% of the shares.

Understand the buyer's valuation

The value that you place on your business, whichever method you choose, is very unlikely to be the price that you receive: it merely forms the starting point for negotiations. You should therefore add a little to the price, say 5–10%, as you can always expect the buyer to try and negotiate a lower price, even if they feel they have found a bargain.

The buyer will not value the business until they have seen the business inside and out. After this, they will probably involve their accountant or broker in order to help them to reach a realistic value for your business. It's likely that they will use a different valuation method from the one you have used, as quite often buyers will find a value that compensates for the expected return they hope to receive by investing in the business.

Buyers will always have a keen eye on the future performance and profitability of your business. You should therefore prepare to be offered an amount that reflects how profitable your business is expected to be in the future.

In basic terms, you have to acknowledge one important rule of valuation: a business is only worth what someone is willing to pay for it.

WHAT TO AVOID

Having unrealistic valuations

You are aiming for an achievable valuation to which both parties can agree so you need to be realistic. If you're using the P/E ratio as the basis of your valuation, make sure you select a realistic ratio and a discount which is appropriate for the size of your business.

Getting the wrong advice

The first common mistake is hiring the wrong adviser. For example, many sellers decide to hire a solicitor but will often be attracted to the first contact they find and consequently overlook the more qualified and experienced people. This leads to the wrong decisions and advice being made at crucial moments in the selling process. The same scenario can be applied to business brokers and accountants.

RECOMMENDED LINKS

Business Eye (Wales):
www.businesseye.org.uk
Business Gateway (Scotland):
www.bgateway.com
Business Link (England):
www.businesslink.org
Invest Northern Ireland:
www.investni.com

SEE ALSO
Bankruptcy and Business Failure (p. 493)
Management Buyouts (p. 522)
Venture Capital (p. 554)

Knowing When and How to Liquidate a Business

GETTING STARTED

If your business is experiencing financial difficulties and there is an imminent likelihood of insolvency, you may decide to cease trading to avoid adding to the debt. You have a legal duty to stop trading when there is no chance of your business recovering and paying back its debts.

To make a reasonable judgment about this, you need to have up-to-date information about your finances and the immediate prospects. Your business accounts need to be current, and you need to be able to take into account the commercial effect of future contracts. You also need to have an accurate account of your business assets, as these would be off-set against debts if you decided to wind the enterprise up.

FAQS

Where can I get advice about winding up a business?

There are many sources of professional help available, and it is crucial that you seek the right advice in order to achieve the best possible outcome for your business, your customers, and your staff:

- **Solicitors**—Sourcing and listening to good legal advice is vital during this type of business process. A solicitor will also be required to draft legal documents relating to the dissolution of the business.
- **Accountants**—Your accountant will provide essential advice on financial planning and tax aspects of the dissolving or sale of your business. An accountant should be consulted as early in the proceedings as possible. He or she will also be able to help when drawing up the business package for prospective buyers.
- **Insolvency practitioners**—These specialists will advise you on the implications of insolvency for your business, and how to embark on a winding-up process.
- **Companies House**—This government agency can advise on the processes of dissolving a company. It also produces a wide variety of business booklets on key aspects of company law, which are available both in hard copy and in a PDF downloadable format online.
- **Business advisers**—Your business adviser will provide a range of commercial information and assistance on all aspects of the decision to cease trading. Seeking the advice of an impartial adviser often helps keep the processes in perspective and can present an objective outside view at what can be a very difficult time for a business.

MAKING IT HAPPEN

Check whether you are solvent

Do a detailed analysis of your business's financial position, asking yourself a series of questions—it's important to be realistic about the answers. Is the business able to pay its debts at or near the time they are due? Are the assets of the business worth more than the liabilities? (Make sure you consider the liabilities you are likely to incur in the future, and also any liabilities that you may incur unexpectedly.) If the business were liquidated now, could it meet all its liabilities in full? (Remember to include the cost of debt collection and liquidation.)

Dissolving a limited company

The best route is a members' voluntary liquidation (MVL) which allows a solvent company's members to pay off its creditors and wind the company up. A majority of the directors must make a statutory declaration of solvency not more than five weeks before the passing of the winding-up resolution. The declaration must contain a statement that the directors are confident that the company will be able to pay all debts within a period of not more than 12 months from the date of winding up, and a statement of company assets and liabilities, which should be as up to date as possible.

Shareholders in private limited companies are in effect part-owners of the business. If you are a director of a company, you have a duty to be honest with your shareholders and not to mislead them. If the company is to be wound up and creditors paid, the principle of limited liability means that shareholders are only liable for company debts up to the value of their shares.

Dissolving a partnership

As a partnership has no separate legal identity, it may be dissolved by an agreement between partners or by notice of dissolution given by one partner to the others. The partnership agreement may provide for dissolution after a specified period of time, or on other set terms.

Once an agreement has been reached, dissolution may proceed in the normal way—usually handled by the partners themselves. Partnership accounts are prepared and the dissolution will be advertised. All clients must be given notice that the business has been wound up—issuing of this notice represents the end of the partners' authority to bind the firm.

The mutual responsibilities of partners in the event of dissolution of their business should be set down in the partnership agreement. It is important to note, however, that when a partnership is wound up, any premiums (fees which may have been paid by new partners on joining) are usually treated as priority debts.

Duties of a director

As a result of the Insolvency Act 1986 and the Company Directors Disqualification Act 1986, it is important for directors of a company to be able to demonstrate that they acted properly in the event of the company becoming insolvent. Both of these acts have been amended by the Insolvency Act 2000, insofar as it strengthens the rules covering the disqualification of unfit directors.

Regular board meetings should be held, all decisions properly documented, and the minutes circulated to all of the directors. Under the Insolvency Act 1986, the directors may be held personally liable for a company's debts where that company has gone into insolvent liquidation, and if at some time before liquidation the directors knew, or ought to have concluded, that there was no reasonable prospect of the company avoiding liquidation. This is the civil offence of 'wrongful trading'. Resigning as a director in advance of insolvency if it might have been expected, will not absolve responsibility—although if a director lodges written disapproval of the business continuing to trade wrongfully it can be taken into account during any legal proceedings resulting from wrongful trading.

A director will not be liable if it can be shown that every step was taken that ought to have been to minimise the loss to the creditors. Directors should therefore ensure that they are always aware of the company's trading position and financial status, and should minute the discussions at meetings and the consideration they give to the company's future prospects.

Directors have unlimited liability for fraud or negligence. However, it is possible, and slowly increasing in popularity, for directors to take out some insurance cover to protect themselves against liability to the company, shareholders, and third parties. Directors' insurance cover is a relatively new trend, with some prohibitive costs involved, so professional advice should be sought before taking up this option.

Responsibilities to employees when winding up a business

Debts which a business owes to employees for wages or services rendered during the four months prior to its insolvency, and all accrued holiday pay (up to a total of £800) are designated as 'preferential' debts and should be settled before any other claims.

If immediate payment is not forthcoming, employees have the right to apply direct to the Secretary of State for payment of a designated portion of what is owed from the National Insurance Fund.

It is important during winding up or liquidation that employees are kept informed of what is happening to try and retain as much loyalty as possible while the process is being worked through. Employees working in the finance area are particularly important during this phase, due to their knowledge of the business accounting procedures, financial filing and archiving systems, and so on.

WHAT TO AVOID
Not drawing up a partnership agreement
When a business partnership is formed, it is vital to draw up an agreement which is a legally binding document. The agreement will set out the procedures to be followed during liquidation or winding up.

Not keeping employees informed about the state of the business
It is important to keep employees informed of what is going on and to try to give them as much notice as possible of any changes, especially if they risk redundancy as a result of any decision. This will enable them to look for other work if necessary.

RECOMMENDED LINKS
Companies registry:
www.companiesregistry-ni.gov.uk
Insolvency Service:
www.insolvency.gov.uk/index.htm
Registrar of Companies for England and Wales (for Scotland, telephone (0870) 333 3636) :
www.companieshouse.gov.uk

SEE ALSO
Bankruptcy and Business Failure (p. 493)
Management Buyouts (p. 522)
Venture Capital (p. 554)

Finding Potential Buyers for Your Business

GETTING STARTED

If you've decided to sell your business, potential buyers could come from a number of sources including competitors, suppliers, customers, and new market entrants. While you might want to reach as many potential buyers as possible, you will probably want to keep your dealings confidential until you decide to inform employees, suppliers, and customers.

For many small businesses, networking is one of the most effective ways of communicating with parties who may be interested in buying you out. However, if you need to be more proactive about the process, and do not have the time to pursue it yourself, you could employ the services of a business broker (see below for more information). A broker will actively seek out interested parties, either directly or through networking with other business brokers. Your broker could also advise and support you through the negotiation and sale of your business. To advertise your business yourself, the most effective media are newspapers, magazines (both in your sector and specialist publications advertising businesses for sale) and the Internet. The Internet is fast becoming one of the most popular ways to advertise a business for sale, its main advantage being that it can reach a wide and global audience quickly. Although not the best source of advertisements for all businesses (for example, those with a very defined, local appeal), it's highly recommended for small businesses with a wider appeal.

FAQS

What is a sales memorandum and why use one?

A sales memorandum is a detailed description of your business that you can provide to prospective purchasers. It outlines the history, products and services, assets, and market and financial performance of your business. It needs to include your reason for selling and your asking price. The memorandum should also include a detailed business plan for the next few years, and the likely outcomes of that plan. The aim of the memorandum is to inspire interest from prospective buyers, as well as to anticipate some of the questions that they may want answered.

What could a business broker do for me?

A business broker will research the market for prospective purchasers of your business. She or he will work with you to establish a list of businesses or individuals who might be interested in finding out more about your business. Your broker will arrange the signing of confidentiality agreements, and hold preliminary discussions with some or all of the interested parties. He or she will then process the responses and advise you on

which options are worth pursuing, leaving you with more time to get on with running the business.

How do I keep the process confidential?

When you advertise your business in a newspaper or magazine, or on the Internet, do not mention your business name. Simply describe the sector you are in, your turnover and your asking price, as well as your regional location (but do not give the exact town or city). Give the interested parties a PO Box or an e-mail address to reply to. Before you provide any information to an interested party, get a confidentiality letter or agreement signed by the interested party (this usually only relates to information that is not publicly available). You can then release a sales memorandum with a request for a response on a given date.

What is a qualifying buyer?

When you consider the replies to your adverts, you need to sort out those expressions of interest that are serious from those that will only waste your time. Draw up a list of qualifying buyers, and limit your distribution of sales memoranda to this group only.

MAKING IT HAPPEN
Spend time preparing the business for the sale

Spending some time preparing the business for sale can enhance the price. Issues to consider include: reducing discretionary expenditure (for example travel and entertainment); reducing business costs without cutting back on vital areas (buyers will look for consistent spending patterns and sales figures); making sure that any property and equipment is well maintained; and reducing excess stock levels to improve the level of working capital.

Decide what type of buyer you want

If you want cash from a deal, it may rule out buyers below a certain size. If you're looking for a friendly purchaser who will safeguard future employment of staff and management, there is little point talking to known 'asset strippers', that is, those who set out to acquire a company and sell its assets for a profit without regard for the acquired company's future business success.

In conjunction with your professional advisers, you should put together a list of possible buyers. You may well hold market information about prospective trade buyers, but do not rule out prospective new entrants to the sector. Non-executive directors, or specialist professional advisers, should have the ability to identify 'non-trade' buyers who may be prepared to pay a premium to enter your market.

Keep your target list to manageable proportions. If you have to advertise, the time drags on and you end up sending out the wrong signals to the industry as well as receiving time-wasters.

Prepare a sales memorandum

It is advisable to prepare your sales memorandum with an adviser or accountant, or with the business broker who is helping you sell your business. You could consider preparing a summary of the main points of interest as well as a more comprehensive document.

Select qualifying buyers

Look for buyers who want to add to their own business profiles; these are generally the most likely to put in a serious offer. They will often be players already in your sector, so they will understand how your business would contribute to their own. They will also have a good idea of the financial benefits they could derive.

It is important that you try to establish whether the interested party has the finance necessary to purchase your business. Otherwise, this might become a problem as your negotiations proceed.

Send out confidentiality letters

Once you have identified those parties that you believe to be serious about buying your business, you need to send confidentiality letters to them. Make sure that the letters are professionally drafted. They will need to be signed and returned before you send out the sales memoranda.

It is a good idea to give a deadline of about a fortnight. This will also help you establish which parties are prepared to give priority to the matter.

Send out sales memoranda

This can be done in two phases. The first phase involves sending out a summary. Distribution of the full sales memoranda should then be limited to those parties who have read the summary and have requested a full document. This indicates that they are genuinely interested in finding out more about your business.

WHAT TO AVOID
Releasing too much information to competitors

One of the dangers of putting your business up for sale is that it presents your competitors with an opportunity to gain access to sensitive financial information. In this respect, it is useful to have the input of a business broker. Your broker can advise you on whether your competitors' interest is genuine or not, and will also maintain your anonymity right up to the stage of narrowing down to a few genuinely interested parties. You will need carefully to balance the need for interested parties to see your financial history, with the possible commercial advantage that a competitor could gain from this information.

Spending too much time with time-wasters

There are bound to be a number of responses to your advertisements which simply do not warrant following up. It is important that you identify these as early as possible, as you will probably need to spend a considerable amount of time with each of the interested parties in the near future. You should only pursue expressions of interest from parties that look like serious businesses with enough finance to make a rea-

sonable offer. Carrying out a credit check, or sourcing a company report, can provide useful insights into your potential buyers.

RECOMMENDED LINKS

Byabiz:
www.byabiz.com
Companies for Sale:
www.companiesforsale.uk.com
UK Business Base:
www.ukbusinessbase.com

SEE ALSO

Bankruptcy and Business Failure (p. 493)
Deciding Whether to Sell Your Business (p. 458)
Management Buyouts (p. 522)
Venture Capital (p. 554)

Selling Shares

GETTING STARTED

People sell shares in their companies for a variety of reasons. They may be hoping to raise additional finance, or alternatively could be hoping to dispose of the company by selling all or most of the shares. Shares can be sold to business angels, venture capitalists, individuals, and other businesses—the motive for buying shares may well be different, depending on who buys them, and purchasers' expectations of dividends and exit routes will also differ.

This actionlist provides a rough guide to the main points you need to take into account when considering whether to sell shares.

FAQS

What are shares?

Shares in a company represent a proportion of the ownership of that company. Initially, shares are exchanged for cash and that cash is then available to the business. This pot of cash is known as the 'equity capital' or as the 'share capital'. Shares can be sold by the owner of a company, though in a small, unquoted, business there are regulations governing the way in which the shares can be sold.

Can a company sell shares at any time?

Companies set an authorised amount of share capital in their Memorandum of Association (MOA), that is, the total number of shares that the company is permitted to sell. The authorised share capital can be raised at any time by the shareholders, and the company can then sell the additional shares. Unquoted companies normally include a 'pre-emption' clause in their Articles of Association (AOA) requiring that any additional shares are first offered to existing shareholders before being offered to potential new investors.

Are there different types of shares?

Companies can create different classes of shares. The main, voting shares are known as 'ordinary shares'. Companies also often create 'preference shares' in order to raise equity capital. In the event of a company being wound up, the preference shares are considered for repayment before the ordinary shares.

Preference shares usually attract a fixed dividend (provided, of course, there is enough profit to cover the dividend). Sometimes these shares are cumulative—if the dividend is missed one year, it is carried forward until such time as there is sufficient profit to pay it. Dividends on ordinary shares cannot be paid until the dividend on the preference shares is paid. Preference shares are usually redeemable, meaning that the company can buy them back and cancel them, if it so desires. Usually they are repaid at par (that is, for the amount for which they were bought), but the repayment amount can be varied. The values for redemption are normally set out in the company's AOA.

What is internal rate of return?

You may have heard talk of equity investors expecting high levels of return—typically 35–40% internal rate of return. That return does not come solely from dividends, but includes the return achieved when the shares are eventually sold. The total rate of return, from income and capital growth, on an annualised basis, is known as the internal rate of return.

What is private equity?

Private equity is simply the term used for finance from venture capitalists, seed funds, and business angels in exchange for a share of the business.

What is an exit route?

The term 'exit route' is used to describe the way that a business angel or venture capitalist exits from an investment. In general, there are just three routes: flotation of the company; a buy back from the founders of the business; or a trade sale. In practice, early investors may also exit by selling shares to a bigger investor. For example, a business angel might exit when a venture capitalist decides to invest and provides an exit route for the business angel by buying his or her shares.

What is an IPO?

An initial public offering (IPO) is the term used if you sell shares to the public through a stock exchange, such as OFEX or the Alternative Investment Market (AIM), which trades in shares of small or emerging companies that are not eligible for listing on the London Stock Exchange.

MAKING IT HAPPEN
Sell a business

In order to sell your business you will need to make sure that you have up-to-date accounts, and be willing to spend time talking to prospective purchasers. If your objective is to sell your business, say, because you want to retire, or want the money to start a new venture, then in most cases your best bet will be to use a business transfer agent, who will help you advertise the business and seek prospective buyers. It is worthwhile, though, mentioning your intention to sell your business to local accountants and business support organisations, as they may well have clients who would be interested in buying.

You may want to stay in the business, or buyers may wish you to stay, at least for a period, so think about whether this is of interest. Some buyers may want to structure a deal over two or even three financial years; this improves their cash flow and maintains a period of stability and continuity in the business, but may also help your tax position. Some buyers may want an earn-out, whereby at least part of the price is dependent on future profit levels—so it is important to be realistic about future prospects.

Raise equity for investment

If your objective is to raise money to reinvest in the business, then you need to do much more work. You need to consider what makes the business attractive to an equity investor—do you have proprietary intellectual capital; do you have the potential for high returns; is there an attractive exit route; and, perhaps most important of all, do you have the management team in place to make it all happen? If the answer to these questions is yes, then you need to prepare a detailed business plan setting out the business's prospects for the next three to five years. You need to demonstrate, too, that you have the determination and commitment to succeed.

Find an investor

The hardest part is finding potential investors. The best starting point is to talk to your local business support organisation. The advisers there will be able to help you prepare your business plan, but will also be able to give advice on approaching business angels and venture capitalists.

WHAT TO AVOID
Exaggerating the figures

Be realistic in valuing your business—but also make an allowance for the sweat equity that you have put into your business.

Not spending enough time on your proposals

Venture capitalists receive hundreds of plans for every one in which they invest—so you need to work hard to capture their attention and persuade them that your business should be the one to receive their money. Regard this as a marketing exercise. You need to grab their attention—and then you need to build on that by making a solid case for investment.

Being overly optimistic

Don't over-estimate your chances of success; be realistic about the size of the market and about how long it will take you to win customers.

RECOMMENDED LINKS
British Venture Capital Association:
www.bvca.co.uk
European Business Angels Network:
www.eban.org/services.htm
National Business Angels Network:
www.nationalbusangels.com

Venture Capital Report:
www.vcr1978.com

SEE ALSO
Bankruptcy and Business Failure (p. 493)
Management Buyouts (p. 522)
Venture Capital (p. 554)

Understanding the Legal Ramifications of Winding Up a Business

GETTING STARTED

Winding up or liquidation is the process of gathering in the assets of a business, to settle the corporate debts. Once this process is completed, the business is then dissolved. It is important to take advice about whether this is the best route for your business. If it is insolvent with serious debts, there may be no choice—creditors can petition for its liquidation. Where the operation is solvent, however, or you as the owner confidently expect to be able to pay off debts, then the potential options for voluntary dissolution should be explored. This actionlist deals with some of the key issues.

FAQS

How is a partnership wound up?

As a partnership has no separate legal identity, it may be dissolved by an agreement between the partners, or by notice of dissolution given by one partner to the others. The partnership agreement may provide for dissolution after a specified period of time, or on other set terms.

Once an agreement has been reached, dissolution may proceed in the normal way—usually handled by the partners themselves. Partnership accounts are prepared and the dissolution will be advertised. All clients must be given notice that the business has been wound up—issuing of this notice represents the end of the partners' authority to agree to contracts and transactions with clients.

How is a private limited company wound up?

Liquidation is a legal process resulting in a company ceasing to exist. Liquidation involves distributing a company's assets to pay off its creditors' debts. The company's assets are placed in the hands of an insolvency practitioner (a licensed person who specialises in insolvency, authorised by a professional body or the Secretary of State). Following liquidation, the company is wound up. A company may be wound up either voluntarily by its shareholders, or through the courts by creditor petitioning.

MAKING IT HAPPEN

Be aware of the legal implications when a partnership is wound up

The law on partnership insolvency comes from the Insolvency Act 1986, the Insolvency Rules 1986, the Insolvency Act 1994, the Insolvency Act 2000, and the Insolvent Partnerships Order 1994 (as amended). Insolvency, under the 1986 Act, means being unable to pay, provide security, or come to an acceptable arrangement for the payment of a debt of £750 or more, within three weeks of a formal demand for payment.

Where a business is insolvent and partners cannot pay its debts, it may be treated as an unregistered company, to be wound up (usually in the County Court), under the terms of the Insolvency Act 1986. Under the principle of unlimited liability, however, once partnership assets have been exhausted in the payment of creditors, each partner can be made bankrupt and creditors may lodge petitions against the partners' individual estates. Wealthier partners may find that partnership creditors will pursue their assets before those of their co-partners.

When joint bankruptcy orders are made against partners, an official receiver immediately becomes trustee of the partners' separate estates and trustee of the partnership. The partnership is then wound up—that is, assets will be gathered in and used to settle business debts, and the partnership dissolved.

Appraise the assets of the partnership

Unlike sole traders, whose personal and business assets are counted together for the purposes of creditors in bankruptcy, in a partnership, separate accounts must be kept of the joint (partnership) estate, and of each partner's individual estate. Once a partnership is dissolved, separate statements of affairs for joint and individual estates must be lodged with the court.

It is an offence to have disposed of valuable assets within five years before the bankruptcy, either by giving them away or selling them cheaply to relatives or friends, unless it can be proved that the disposal was an innocent transaction.

Bank accounts will be frozen at the point of bankruptcy, and the trustees will sell assets as they think fit. A spouse who has a joint interest in property will normally be protected for a year, but after this period, the court puts the interests of the creditors first.

Pay creditors

Through unlimited liability, a situation may arise where two sets of creditors are chasing payment of debts from partners—creditors owed money by the business, and personal creditors of individual partners. In this case the partnership assets pay off partnership debts, and partners' individual estates are used to pay off their personal debts. Any surplus in the joint estate then goes to the partners' estates in proportion to their share in the partnership, while any surplus from partners' estates goes to the joint estate to pay off partnership debts.

Certain 'secured creditors' may have direct claims on specific assets which will be satisfied first of all. Other creditors may be designated 'preferred', 'ordinary', or 'deferred', being paid according to their status.

A shortfall in the partnership estate may be 'proved for' (claimed) in the individual estate equally with the individual creditors' claims.

Understand the legal implications when a private limited company is wound up

The main legislation covering company insolvency comes from the Insolvency Act 1986 (as amended). The Insolvency Rules 1986 will also apply, as will the Insolvency Regulations 1994.

Consider voluntary liquidation

If a company is facing serious financial trouble, its members/directors may decide that liquidation is the only option for the business. Two types of voluntary liquidation exist:

1. Members' voluntary liquidation (MVL) may be initiated by solvent companies, that is when a company has sufficient assets to meet all its debts. The directors of the company sign a declaration of solvency, which must include a statement that they will be able to pay off all creditors within 12 months following commencement of liquidation. The declaration must also include an up-to-date account of all the company's assets and liabilities. Members must hold a meeting to pass a resolution to wind up the company voluntarily and to appoint a liquidator who will handle the affairs of the company and distribute assets to pay off creditors.

2. Creditors' voluntary liquidation (CVL) occurs when shareholders vote for a voluntary liquidation, despite the majority of directors having not made a solvency declaration. Unlike an MVL, the company may already be insolvent. In order to vote for a voluntary liquidation, shareholders must hold a general company meeting and pass a voluntary winding-up resolution stating that they cannot continue to trade due to their liabilities. A creditor meeting must also be held to inform them of the company's financial position. Creditors are given the opportunity to nominate somebody to act as liquidator, and their decision will generally take priority over that of any nominations made by the company.

Consider compulsory liquidation

Compulsory liquidation occurs when a court orders a company into liquidation. This normally happens following a winding-up petition from a creditor, or group of creditors (who must be owed at least £750). However, the company itself or its directors may also file a winding-up petition. Following a court order, an official receiver will be appointed as liquidator by the court to handle the winding up of the company and investigate the possible causes of the liquidation.

Remember employees' rights when a business is wound up

An employer may owe debts to employees for wages, salary, or accrued holiday pay. If it is solvent when it ceases trading, employees may also be entitled to redundancy payments. Where insolvency leads to winding up, up to £800 of the sum owed to an employee for the previous four months can be designated as 'preferential' debts, to be settled before the claims of ordinary creditors. The remainder is designated as ordinary debts.

 WHAT TO AVOID

Not drawing up a deed of partnership when setting up

When forming a partnership, a deed of partnership should be drawn up. It should specify arrangements to be followed in insolvency. Otherwise the partnership is subject to the relevant provisions of the Partnership Act 1890, which may not best suit the needs of the business.

Providing the wrong information

The court and any insolvency practitioners should be provided with all the information they require—omissions or false statements can result in criminal proceedings.

RECOMMENDED LINKS

Companies House:
www.companieshouse.gov.uk
Companies Registry:
www.companiesregistry-ni.gov.uk
Insolvency Service:
www.insolvency.gov.uk/index.htm

SEE ALSO

Bankruptcy and Business Failure (p. 493)
**Deciding Whether to Sell Your Business
 (p. 458)**
Management Buyouts (p. 522)
Venture Capital (p. 554)

ESSENTIAL
INFORMATION
DIRECTORY

Small and Growing Businesses

BOOKS AND DIRECTORIES
Beating the Odds in Small Business
Tom Culley
London: Simon & Schuster, 1998
320pp ISBN: 0684841835
This book is a survival manual for new businesses, and systematically explains and analyses every key 'survival priority', upon which the sustainability of a new business is dependent in the critical first years. The author shows how the odds can be turned in your favour by avoiding the distractions of chasing easy success in order to get rich quick, and instead focusing only on the harsh realities of the business jungle.

Business Development: A Guide to Small Business Strategy
David Butler
Oxford: Butterworth-Heinemann, 2001
192pp ISBN: 0750652470
This book aims to help owner-managers of small businesses draw up a plan for the long-term future. The subjects covered include: reviewing performance, resource implications, sales and marketing strategy, market expansion, staffing, and financial performance. The standards for business development established by the Small Firms Enterprise Development Institute (SFEDI) are appended.

Business Grow How: The Stepping Stones to Successful Growth
Alan Baines, Raj Sinhal
London: Accountancy Books, 1999
250pp (Bottom Line Business Guides)
ISBN: 1853559431
The authors set out the DIAMOND model of growth, detailing seven key stages which all successful companies go through: dreaming, initiating, attacking, maturing, overhauling, networking, and doing it all over again. The topics they cover along the way include: the start up process; business plans; marketing; delegation and empowerment as the company grows;

financing the business; risk management; adding value; and selling the business.

Business Planning: A Guide to Business Start-Up
David Butler
Oxford: Butterworth-Heinemann, 2000
276pp ISBN: 075064706X
This book contains all the factual information required to produce a successful business plan for presentation to a potential source of finance or for use in an NVQ portfolio. It is in line with the major syllabuses for business start-up and can be used as a course guide for anyone completing a formal NVQ level 3 qualification in this area.

Capitalizing on Success
Neil Coade
London: Thomson Learning, 2001
195pp (Smart Strategies Series)
ISBN: 1861527659
This book takes a practical approach to the process of business development. After discussing the stages of business growth, it considers the challenges that face emerging businesses and may prevent them from reaching their potential. As means of meeting those challenges, it stresses the importance of effective leadership, good management practice, and creative people able to move the business forward.

Effective Small Business Management 7th ed
Richard M. Hodgetts, Donald F. Kuratko
Thomson Learning, 2000
700pp (Dryden Press Series in Entrepreneurship)
ISBN: 0030319390
Intended for students and lecturers as well as owner-managers, this book provides an introduction to the world of small business and the fundamentals of effective small business management. Its contents include: opportunities for getting into small

business; start up concerns; managing operations; marketing goods; finances and inventory control; and current issues in the field.

The E-myth Revisited: Why Most Small Businesses Still Don't Work and What You Can Do About Yours Rev ed
Michael E. Gerber
London: HarperCollins, 1995
268pp ISBN: 0887307280
First published in 1986, this best-selling book provides information and guidance on starting and maintaining a small business or franchise. 'E-myth' stands for 'entrepreneurial myth' and refers to Gerber's belief that entrepreneurs do not necessarily make good business people. The book shows the reader how to simplify the systems involved in running a business, and instead create a tightly organised and regimented plan, so that the systems can more or less run themselves, freeing the entrepreneur's mind to focus on long-term strategy.

Enterprise and Small Business: Principles, Practice and Policy
Sara Carter, Dylan Jones-Evans
Harlow: Financial Times Prentice Hall, 2000
608pp ISBN: 0201398524
This book provides a comprehensive introduction to small businesses, covering the environment in which they operate, the nature of entrepreneurship, and the techniques of practical management. Its authors draw on the work of leading academics in the United Kingdom and Europe and cover the latest thinking and research in the field.

Entrepreneur's Ultimate Start-up Directory
James Stephenson
Entrepreneur Media, Inc, 2001
428pp ISBN: 1891984330
This book offers an extensive listing of business ideas, covering more than 1,300 potential start-ups across over 30 industries. It covers new and traditional business areas,

including working from home and working via the Internet. Each entry is rated according to the following criteria: ease of start-up; estimated cost and potential income; possibility of exploiting the idea online; skills required; whether the start-up could be run part-time; and licensing/franchising opportunities.

Essence of Small Business 2nd ed
Colin Barrow
Harlow: Prentice Hall, 1998
216pp (The Essence of Management Series)
ISBN: 0137486413
This guide offers an introduction to setting up and managing a small business. The topics it covers include: forming a business; sources of finance; franchising; market research; financial management; general management; business planning; and winding up a business.

Financial Management for the Small Business: A Practical Guide 5th ed
Colin Barrow
London: Kogan Page, 2001
253pp (Business Enterprise Series)
ISBN: 0749435003
The author provides practical advice on proper financial planning and control for the small business. The three main sections cover key financial statements, financial analysis tools, and business plans and budgeting. A list of further reading and sources of information is included.

Finding Your Perfect Work: The New Career Guide for Making a Living, Creating a Life
Paul Edwards, Sarah Edwards
Penguin Putnam, Inc, 2003
480pp ISBN: 1585422169
This book is aimed at those in the crucial first phase of setting up a business: assessing yourself. Considering what you really want to do and get from your own business is explored in depth here, and the book contains worksheets to help the reader pinpoint his or her own strengths, weaknesses, and goals.

Go It Alone: The Streetwise Secrets of Success
Geoff Burch
Oxford: Capstone, 2003
336pp ISBN: 1841124702
An easy-to-read, practical guide to those thinking of starting their own business, packed with anecdotal advice. The author's very original and humorous approach helps get across his wealth of experience in entrepreneurship and sales.

Growing a Private Company: Commercial Strategies for Building a Business Worth Millions
Ian Smith
London: Kogan Page, 2001
180pp ISBN: 0749432802
This book is aimed at owners of private companies and provides guidance on strategy, operational efficiency, growth techniques, venture capital, acquisitions, and exit options.

Growing Business Handbook: Strategies for Planning, Funding, and Managing Business Growth 5th ed
Richard Willsher, Adam Jolly, eds
London: Kogan Page, 2002
320pp ISBN: 07493600X
Designed to help businesses with an established market position, this handbook presents a range of practical strategies for managing growth. The contributors, who come from a variety of backgrounds, provide advice in areas including funding options, competition, managing the risks, making the most of IT, external relations, and competitive purchasing.

Grow Your Business
Mark Henricks
Waterloo, Ontario: Entrepreneur Press, 2001
450pp ISBN: 1891984209
Author Mark Henricks guides the reader through a wide portfolio of issues that includes: assessing a business's strengths, setting targets, managing risks, negotiating bureaucracy, and handling the competition. Focused on the contemporary business climate, which has witnessed a growing number of new businesses, Henricks takes the fledgling business from infancy and helps it to maturity.

How to Help Your Clients Start a Successful Business: Using the National Standards of Good Practice
Ruth Lowbridge
Small Firms Enterprise Development Initiative, 2001
42pp ISBN: 1903225086
This publication is designed to help those advising people on how to start a business. It offers guidance on the advice process, including asking the right type of question, and on key issues for consideration when starting a business. The advice framework is based on the common Standards for Business Support and the National Standards for Business Start-up.

How to Set Up and Run Your Own Business 16th ed
Helen Kogan
London: Kogan Page, 2000
293pp (Daily Telegraph Guide)
ISBN: 0749433086
This book provides basic information for anyone interested in starting up a business and guides its readers through the major issues that they need to consider. These include: preparing a business plan; finding finance; choosing premises; seeking help from government aid schemes; getting to grips with tax, self-assessment, and National Insurance; marketing and selling a product or service; meeting legal responsibilities; getting into export; and using information and communications technology.

Improving Your Business: The Standards for Business Development
Small Firms Enterprise Development Initiative, 2001
258pp ISBN: 1903225132
The full text of the standards for business development drawn up by the Small Firms Enterprise Development Initiative (SFEDI) is given, together with details of how to use the standards to review a business, identify weaknesses, develop plans, and work

towards improvement. The standards cover all aspects of running a business including sales and marketing, customer relationships, developing products and services, using information technology, managing finance, personnel issues, and health and safety.

ISO 9001 2000 for Small Businesses 2nd ed
Ray Tricker
Oxford: Butterworth-Heinemann, 2001
460pp ISBN: 0750648821
This book explains the requirements of the new ISO 9001 2000 standard and looks at how smaller companies can benefit from it and set up their own quality management systems. Background information on ISO 9001 and the importance of quality control and quality assurance is provided.

Kick Start Your Dream Business: Getting It Started and Keeping You Going
Romanus Wolter
Berkeley, California: Ten Speed Press, 2001
304pp ISBN: 1580082513
This book contains practical advice for anyone thinking about starting a small business, as well as supportive real-life examples of successful entrepreneurship.

The Legal Advice Kit for Your Business: Setting Up a Limited Company
Mark Fairweather, Rosy Border
London: Stationery Office, 2000
82pp (Simply Legal)
ISBN: 0117023515
This is a practical guide to the procedures for setting up a limited company in the United Kingdom. The text covers: considering the options; roles and responsibilities; and completing the required forms. Sample letters, minutes, resolutions, and articles of association are included in the text and on floppy disk. Listings of frequently asked questions and useful contacts are also provided.

Limited Company Guide
London: Law Pack, 2000
92pp ISBN: 1902646584

This guide aims to explain how to set up your own limited company. Valid in England, Scotland, and Wales, it describes the essential procedures and incorporates examples of forms from Companies House, articles and memoranda of association, and directors' resolutions.

New Venture Adventure: Succeed with Professional Business Planning
Ueli Looser, Bruno Schlapfer eds
London: Texere Publishing, 2001
217pp ISBN: 1587990032
This manual, written by consultants from McKinsey, offers professional advice on starting up a business. The book opens with an overview of the stages a typical start-up company will go through and a consideration of what constitutes an attractive business idea. The main focus is on the preparation of a professional business plan and an example of a business plan is provided. The book also covers the questions of how to value a start-up business and how to raise equity.

The Next Level: Essential Strategies for Achieving Breakthrough Growth
James B. Wood
Cambridge, Massachusetts: Perseus, 2000
224pp ISBN: 0738201596
An accessible guide to planning and managing the stages of company growth, *The Next Level* centres around the use of a powerful, field-tested diagnostic tool, the Inc Growth Strategy Analysis. James Wood carefully shows entrepreneurs and established business leaders alike how to analyse their organisation's growth potential, identify the key constraints to future growth, and put into practice the strategies that will enable them to arrive at new levels of expansion and profit generation.

Outsmarting Goliath: How to Achieve Equal Footing with Companies That Are Bigger, Richer, Older and Better Known
Debra Koontz Traverso
London: Kogan Page, 2000
215pp ISBN: 0749432985

The author presents practical advice on how to present a professional image, produce high-quality marketing materials, and win contracts that may seem out of reach for a small company. The book also outlines a number of innovative ways to enhance company profile.

Setting Up and Running a Limited Company: A Comprehensive Guide to Forming and Operating a Company As a Director and Shareholder 4th ed
Robert Browing
Oxford: How To Books, 2003
189pp ISBN: 1857038665
This guide is aimed at anyone thinking of establishing a limited company and addresses statutory requirements as well as advising on best practice. The book includes information on: the responsibilities of shareholders and directors; setting up your business; preparing financial records; sourcing venture capital; and retreating gracefully if things don't go to plan.

Small Business Management
Frank Dawes, ed
Dublin: Blackhall Publishing, 1999
178pp ISBN: 1901657590
This book features contributions from a number of staff at the Bolton Institute, who run the first, and as yet only, accredited MBA in Small Business Management. It covers: challenges facing the small business; managerial style and competence; team-working in the small business; performance and profitability; business growth and failure; the competitive environment; and challenges of strategy and leadership.

Small Business Marketing Management
Ian Chaston, Terry Mangles
Basingstoke: Palgrave, 2002
275pp ISBN: 0333980751
This book is designed to give undergraduate and postgraduate students an understanding of the small business marketing process, including positioning, competitive advantage, product management, pricing, and distribution. The impact of e-commerce and the Internet, the marketing of services,

and international marketing are also covered. The text is supported by real-life case studies and published research findings.

Small Time Operator: How to Start Your Own Business, Keep Your Books, Pay Your Taxes, and Stay Out of Trouble 25th ed
Bernard B. Kamoroff
Willits, California: Bell Springs Publishing, 2000
200pp ISBN: 0917510186
Kamoroff presents the reader with the essentials of building a business, from obtaining initial permits and licenses, to seeking financing, locating the right business area, establishing an accounts and book-keeping system, and taking on new staff. Continually updated, Kamoroff is conscious of reflecting the very latest thinking in tax and business management.

Spare Room Tycoon: Succeeding Independently—The 70 Lessons of Sane Self-employment
James Chan
Nicholas Brealey Publishing, 2000
224pp ISBN: 1857882474
Written by a entrepreneur with over 20 years' experience of working from home, this book is aimed at anyone thinking of setting up a home-based business. It offers support and tips on how to avoid isolation and to spread the word about your business. The book focuses on 'soft' skills, such as work/life balance, building confidence, and coping with the emotional demands of being your own boss, and offers reassuring anecdotal advice.

Starting Your Own Business: How to Plan and Create a Successful Enterprise 3rd ed
Jim Green
Oxford: How To Books, 2000
192pp ISBN: 1857036522
This practical guide examines the steps that need to be taken before starting a business. These include preparing a business plan, raising finance, and developing marketing

strategies. The role of the Internet is also considered. The book includes a directory of sources of advice and information.

Start Up: An Entrepreneur's Guide to Launching and Managing a New Business 5th ed
William J. Stolze
Franklin Lakes, New Jersey: Career Press, 1999
288pp ISBN: 1564144231
This book is aimed at those setting up or expanding a business and is a practical guide to launching and managing a new enterprise. It includes various case studies and sample business plans.

The Startup Garden
Tom Ehrenfeld
Maidenhead: McGraw-Hill, 2001
220pp ISBN: 0071368248
Ehrenfeld identifies a current trend toward entrepreneurship, and in this book he shows his readers how they can construct their own perfect job. *The Startup Garden* takes the reader through the processes involved in starting a company and shows how this is matched to the reader's hopes and dreams, demonstrating the link between your personal life and your business drives.

Tolley's SME Handbook
Paul Andrews, Graeme Forbes
Croydon: Tolley, 2001
436pp ISBN: 0754512754
This book provides practical guidance on the legal and regulatory compliance issues facing owner-managers, directors, and advisors of small and medium-sized enterprises in the United Kingdom. The book is laid out in a user-friendly format with bullet points and checklists.

Understanding and Negotiating Business Contracts: Master the Small Print and Get a Better Deal
Jonathan Rush
Oxford: How To Books, 2002
166pp ISBN: 1857037987
This book offers clear, easy-to-read guidance for small businesses on the basics of

drawing up contracts. The chapters are structured along the lines of a contract and avoid complex terms and jargon.

Understanding the Small Family Business
Denise Fletcher ed
London: Routledge, 2002
224pp ISBN: 0415250536
This book offers an overview of current research in the small family business sector, with the main focus on the relationship between work and family and the tensions and contradictions that can arise. The contributions are organised in three sections relating to rationality discourse, resource-based discourse, and critical discourse. It is more useful background than a practical guide.

What No One Ever Tells You about Starting Your Own Business: Real Life Start-up Advice from 101 Successful Entrepreneurs
Jan Norman
Chicago, Illinois: Upstart Publishing, 1999
224pp ISBN: 1574101129
Drawing on the experience of, and mistakes made by, 100 business people, this book contains helpful and practical advice on how to start your own business without headaches.

Your First Business Plan: A Simple Question and Answer Format Designed to Help You Write Your Own Plan 4th ed
Joseph Covello, Brian Hazelgren
Naperville, Illinois: Sourcebooks, 2002
160pp ISBN: 1402200021
This popular book contains practical advice on writing an impressive business plan, including useful information on the constituent parts of a business.

WEBSITES
Benchmark Index
www.benchmarkindex.com
Affiliated to Business Link, this website offers help and advice on benchmarking to businesses, advisors, and networks. It aims to help businesses understand their current position and plan effectively for the future.

BizMove.com
www.bizmove.com

This US-based site features the Small Business Knowledge Base, a range of free information resources for small businesses. It offers advice on government grants, a free business plan template, subscription to its e-zine, and an e-book entitled *101 Tips and Strategies to Small Business Success.*

Business Eye (Wales)
www.businesseye.org

Launched in September 2003, Business Eye (Wales) replaces Business Connect as a free information service for all businesses in Wales. The service is managed by the Welsh Development Agency and has more than 30 local offices across Wales. Business Eye (Wales) does not provide business support or grants itself, but instead aims to 'signpost' users towards the best sources of help for their particular needs. The website offers a gateway to numerous resources for Welsh entrepreneurs, including links to useful sites across over 20 key topics, a business forum, business news, information on courses and training, a support directory, and contact details of the local branches in North, Mid-, West, and South-East Wales.

Business Europe
www.businesseurope.com

This site offers advice, information, and news for all small businesses based in the United Kingdom. It is packed with features. The site provides access to a extensive range of practical guides to challenges in the areas of finance, technology, people, e-commerce, sales and marketing, and transport. A detailed directory enables users to search for suppliers by name, location, and industry type, and businesses may also register to appear in the directory themselves. There is also a forum in which users may ask questions of experts or register to answer others' questions if they have an area of expertise. A series of 'zones' covering starting up, imports/exports, and learning offer information and case studies.

Business Gateway (Scotland)
www.bgateway.com

Aimed at both start-ups and existing businesses in Scotland, Business Gateway (Scotland) is in partnership with Scottish Enterprise, Scottish Executive and Scottish local authorities. There are local offices ('Gateways') in 13 regions across Scotland, but the website offers a range of help and advice to the user, including a business information service, start-up and high growth start-up services, and a business growth service.

Business Link
www.businesslink.org

The UK Small Business Service runs this site to provide advice for small business owners and anyone thinking of setting up a small business in England. The site is packed with helpful information and is easily navigable. Business Link offers a telephone support line on 0845 600 9006 and also has a network of 45 operators across the country which puts you in touch with an experienced adviser.

Business Owner's Toolkit
www.toolkit.cch.com

The toolkit is provided by CCH Incorporated, a leading provider of business, legal, and tax information in the United States, and includes model business plans and documents for downloading, plus information from the SOHO guidebook.

Community Interest Companies (CICs)
www.dti.gov.uk/cics

Between March and June 2003, the Department for Trade and Industry consulted on a new legal framework for both companies and charities ('Enterprise for Communities—Proposals for a CIC'). The results, available on the DTI website, would be of particular interest to those planning on starting a business with social, ethical, or environmental aims.

Department for Trade and Industry
www.dti.gov.uk/for_business.html

This site contains links to all UK government departments and also offers a variety of helpful information, including taxation advice, sources of finance and legal requirements, and more generally useful 'best practice' guides for small businesses from the Small Business Service.

Dowling Kerr
www.dk-business.com
An agency that deals in businesses for sale, from retailers to nurseries. This site offers free access to lists of businesses as well as additional fee-based services, such as finding a business that meets your specification.

Environment Agency
www.environment-agency.gov.uk/ netregs
This government website aims to help small businesses get to grips easily with the environmental legislation with which they are legally obliged to comply.

Formationshouse.com
www.formationshouse.com
A company-formation service that guides you through the process of forming and registering a limited company. This site offers a name-search facility and a fast-track service that will help you set up a company within eight working hours (provided your application is not held up for unforeseen reasons).

Inc.com
www.inc.com
Inc.com is the online version of the magazine *Inc*. The website provides information, products, services, and online tools—accumulated from a variety of sources—for many business or management tasks. This information has also been organised into categories to help the user find quickly what he or she needs.

Invest in Northern Ireland
www.investni.com
This site offers practical advice on how to establish a business in Northern Ireland. It has an excellent section of sources of further information made up of weblinks to key

organisations and industries in the area. The site is colourful and well designed, featuring key facts about Northern Ireland and a list of the top 10 reasons to invest there.

Jordans Limited UK
www.jordans.co.uk
An online company-formation service that also offers additional services such as search functions and debt recovery.

Scottishbusinesswomen.com
www.scottishbusinesswomen.com
Part of the Scottish Enterprise Network initiative, this website is aimed at women in Scotland who either run their own business or who are thinking about establishing one. It offers support and advice on how to grow and develop existing businesses and also contains practical help and valuable sources of information for start-ups.

smallbusinessadvice.org.uk
www.smallbusinessadvice.org.uk
Smallbusinessadvice.org.uk is a free and independent source of information and advice for entrepreneurs, owner managers, and the self employed, starting or running a business with fewer than 10 staff and based in England. The website operates a business enquiry service which links users to over 200 accredited business advisers. It also offers online guides to various aspects of business planning, a resource centre, e-business advice, discussion boards, and help for students.

Smallbusiness.co.uk
www.smallbusiness.co.uk
Sponsored by Lloyds TSB, this website offers extensive help on a variety of key small business issues. The site is divided into seven main areas (starting up, finance, people, technology, legal, property) that are then subdivided into more detailed sections.

Small Business Research Portal
www.smallbusinessportal.co.uk
Intended for academics, policy makers, and support agencies, the portal provides a collection of links to small business sites

under categories that include news, publications, research, institutes, and conferences.

UK Company Registration
www.uk-company-registration.co.uk
Another site which helps users set up companies online. The site is easy to navigate and has a helpful list of frequently asked questions.

UK National Work-stress Network
www.workstress.net
An informative site that aims to educate users about the causes of work-stress and various ways of coping with it. While the site does not offer stress counselling, but offers helpful sources of, and links to, sources of further information and support.

UK Online
www.ukonline.gov.uk
UK Online is a government sponsored website run by the Office of the e-Envoy, which falls under the jurisdiction of the Cabinet Office. The UK Online site covers a variety of topics, and has a separate section on setting up and running a small business. It includes jargon-free explanations of taxes and other relevant regulations and also offers a series of checklists and sources of information about first steps.

ORGANISATIONS
British Chambers of Commerce
1st floor, 65 Petty France, London, SW1H 9EU
T: +44 (0) 20 7654 5800
F: +44 (0) 20 7654 5819
E: info@britishchambers.org.uk
www.britishchambers.org.uk
This is an umbrella body for a network of some 150 locally-based chambers of commerce serving local businesses and providing advice on importing and import services to member companies.

European Small Business Alliance
Logos, Rue Vautier 54, B-1050 Brussels, Belgium

T: +32 2 639 62 31
F: +32 2 644 90 17
E: secretariat@esba-europe.org
www.esba-europe.org
The ESBA was formed in 1998 by a group of organisations representing small businesses in European countries to protect and promote the interests of small-scale entrepreneurs within the European Union. It works with European institutions and other bodies to create a favourable environment for small businesses.

Federation of Small Businesses
Whittle Way, Blackpool Business Park, Blackpool, Lancashire, FY4 2FE
T: +44 (0) 1253 336000
F: +44 (0) 1253 348046
E: ho@fsb.org.uk
www.fsb.org.uk
The FSB, which has 160,000 members in the United Kingdom, represents the interests of small businesses with up to 200 employees. It organises an annual conference, publishes a bimonthly magazine, *First Voice*, and lobbies on policy issues, while its local branches provide networking and research facilities in addition to general support services for members.

Forum of Public Business
Ruskin Chambers, Drury Lane, Knutsford, Cheshire, WA16 6HA
T: +44 (0) 1565 634467
F: +44 (0) 1565 650059
E: fpbltd@fpb.co.uk
www.fpb.co.uk
The FPB aims to influence laws and policies affecting UK private businesses and provide support for its members.

The Prince's Trust
18 Park Square East, London, NW1 4LH
T: 0800 842 842
F: 020 7543 1200
E: info@princes-trust.org.uk
www.princes-trust.org.uk
The Prince's Trust was established by the Prince of Wales in 1976 to help young people realise their full potential. Aimed at those aged between 14–30 (or 14–25 in

Scotland), the Trust offers support and financial assistance across a range of core programmes including business start-ups. Since 1983, the Trust has helped over 50,000 businesses and its business programme currently offers: a low-interest loan of up to £5,000; a marketing grant of up to £250; advice lines and seminars; access to a volunteer business mentor.

Small Business Bureau

Curzon House, Church Road, Windlesham, Surrey, GU20 6BH
T: +44 (0) 1276 452010
F: +44 (0) 1276 451602
E: info@sbb.org.uk
www.smallbusinessbureau.org.uk
The Small Business Bureau was founded in 1976 to promote the interests of small businesses in the United Kingdom. Its activities include an annual conference and a quarterly magazine, *Small Business News*. The organisation has also set up Women into Business to encourage more women to choose business and business ownership as a career.

Small Business Service

Kingsgate House, 66–74 Victoria Street, London, SW1E 6SW
T: +44 (0) 845 001 0031
E: gatewayenquiries@sbs.gsi.gov.uk
www.sbs.gov.uk
The Small Business Service is a UK government agency which coordinates support and advice for small businesses.

Small Firms Enterprise Development Initiative

5th Floor, S1 St James's, Vicar Lane, Sheffield, Yorkshire, S1 2EX
T: +44 (0) 114 241 2155
F: +44 (0) 114 241 2166
E: info@sfedi.co.uk
www.sfedi.co.uk
The SFEDI has been appointed by the UK government to identify standards of best practice for small businesses and to work with providers of small-business training, education, and advice to raise standards of support.

SEE ALSO
Entrepreneurs (p. 510)

Accounting

BOOKS AND DIRECTORIES
The Best Small Business Accounts Book (Blue Version)
Peter Hingston and Stuart Ramsden
Hereford: Hingston Publishing Co., 2000
64pp ISBN: 0906555124
There are three versions of this book, all designed for the UK tax system. This blue version, which has a monthly layout, is ideal for non-VAT registered credit-based businesses. Updated since its initial publication in 1991, this book allows the small business owner to keep the accounts in one compact book. It provides full instructions and worked examples to help the user to book-keep correctly and effectively, including 16 columns to analyse cheques and an easy-to-do monthly bank statement check.

The Best Small Business Accounts Book (Yellow Version)
Peter Hingston and Stuart Ramsden
Hereford: Hingston Publishing Co., 1991
64pp ISBN: 0906555116
There are three versions of this book, all designed for the UK tax system. This yellow version, which has a week-to-page layout, is ideal for non-VAT registered cash businesses. Initially published in 1991, this book enables the small business owner to keep complete accounts in one compact book, offering detailed instructions and worked examples along the way.

Book-keeping & Accounting for the Small Business: How to Keep the Books and Maintain Financial Control Over Your Business

Peter Taylor
Oxford: How To Books, 2003
192pp ISBN: 1857038789
Aimed at both students and anyone running
or responsible for the accounts of a small
business, this guide offers structured advice
on the essentials of book-keeping.

Excel 2002 for Dummies

Greg Harvey
Chichester: John Wiley, 2003
384pp ISBN: 0764537563
This book gives the reader key advice and
help on how to get to grips with this useful
computer package. It covers the basics of
setting up a worksheet to creating
formulae, charts, graphs, and spreadsheets
so that all your essential business
information can be safely stored and
effectively used.

Finance for the Non Specialist

Janet Walker
London: CIMA Publishing, 1998
166pp ISBN: 1874784736
This introductory text is designed for non-
specialist managers and students who
need an understanding of the basic
principles of financial and management
accounting. The topics covered include
accounting statements, profit and loss
accounts, cost analysis, and budget
planning and control.

The Finance Manual for Non-Financial Managers: The Power to Make Confident Financial Decisions

Paul McKoen, Leo Gough
Harlow: Financial Times Prentice Hall, 1999
319pp (Smarter Solutions Series)
ISBN: 0273644939
The book aims to give the non-financial
manager a practical introduction to
financial management and control. It
explains the basics of accounting and
financial reports, with separate chapters
covering costing, pricing, project analysis,
corporate taxation, financing, and risk
management. The accounting implications
of acquisitions are also discussed.

The Green Bottom Line: Environmental Accounting for Management Current Practice and Future Trends

Martin Bennett, Peter James, eds
Sheffield: Greenleaf Publishing, 1998
432pp ISBN: 1874719071
The editors have brought together a
collection of papers on research and best
practice in the area of environmental
management accounting, with a strong
focus on the analysis of financial costs and
the benefits of environmentally-friendly
behaviour in business. The papers are
grouped in four sections: general concepts;
empirical research; case studies of
individual companies; and practical
suggestions on how environment-related
management accounting can be
implemented.

How to Read a Financial Report 5th ed

John A. Tracey
Chichester: John Wiley, 1999
192pp ISBN: 0471327069
Tracey provides guidance on interpreting
company accounts (with relation to US
practice), with particular reference to the
three essential parts of every financial
report—the balance sheet, the income
statement, and the cash-flow statement. His
explanations are illustrated with many
examples.

How to Understand and Use Company Accounts 4th ed

Roy Warren
London: Random House Business Books, 1998
136pp ISBN: 071267764X
This is a practical guide intended to
help anyone in business to understand
and interpret company accounts. It
describes the construction of accounts
and their content, and explains how to use
them.

Intermediate Accounting

Donald E. Keiso, Jerry J. Wygandt, Terry D.
Warfield
Chichester: John Wiley, 2001
1438pp ISBN: 0471363049

The book is used in over 70% of the intermediate accounting courses taught in post-secondary institutions in the United States. It covers the conceptual framework underlying financial accounting, financial reporting standards and statements, and more complex topics and transactions that are encountered in today's business environment. Specific guidance is provided for numerous topics including accounting for cash and receivables, inventory, intangible assets, current and long-term liabilities, income taxes, leases, shareholders' equity, and revenue recognition.

Introduction to Bookkeeping and Accounting in a Week
Roger Mason
London: Hodder and Stoughton, 1998
96pp (Business in a Week Series)
ISBN: 0340712031
Mason provides a practical introduction to book-keeping and accounting. He explains the basic principles of book-keeping, the different types of account and various ledgers, the preparation of accounts, the profit and loss account, and the balance sheet.

Pocket Accounting
Christopher Nobes
London: Economist Books, 2001
202pp ISBN: 1861973667
This pocket guide to accounting is divided into three. Part one is a collection of short essays covering such topics as setting standards in the 1990s, accounting for goodwill and brands, and international differences in accounting. Part two provides a dictionary of key terms. Part three consists of appendices covering abbreviations, the world's largest accountancy firms, useful addresses, and UK accounting standards.

Teach Yourself Book Keeping
Andrew G. Piper, Andrew Lymer
London: Hodder Arnold, 2003
356pp (Teach Yourself)
ISBN: 0340859423

This book aims to demystify the area of book-keeping, essential for small business owners and managers. Offering plenty of examples to help explain key terms and concepts, the book covers the double-entry system, the processes of recording purchases, and different types of transactions. Profit and loss accounts and balance sheets are also explained. The book also includes helpful completed exam pages with worked examples.

Teach Yourself Small Business Accounting
Mike Truman
London: Hodder Arnold, 2003
176pp (Teach Yourself)
ISBN: 0340859415
This practical guide is for the small business owner with no aptitude for figures or interest in book-keeping or accountancy. It provides jargon-free step-by-step instructions, using examples of real businesses, on how to record each transaction, as well as advice on pricing goods and services. It also offers an alternative, easier, and less time-consuming system to that of double-entry book-keeping.

Test Your Financial Awareness
John Hodgson, Liz O'Neill
London: Hodder and Stoughton, 2000
93pp (Test Yourself Series)
ISBN: 0340782870
If you are responsible for the way in which assets are utilised, sales revenues earned, or expenses incurred, then this book is intended to sharpen and consolidate your financial skills. The authors provide an introduction to basic financial awareness, help you assess your understanding with a before-and-after test, explain how to calculate key financial measures, and discuss how to make better business decisions based on financial input.

Unlocking Company Reports and Accounts
Wendy McKenzie
Harlow: Financial Times Pitman, 1998
400pp ISBN: 0273632507

McKenzie provides a key to understanding company reports and accounts from first principles, explaining every point through the use of worked examples. She takes extracts from published accounts, including those of overseas companies, to illustrate accounting presentation, and enables the reader to understand and analyse a company's accounts and so build a comprehensive picture of its financial state.

WEBSITES
Accounting Web
www.accountingweb.co.uk
This site is an extensive UK-based online resource. It contains material from a number of providers intended for accountancy and finance professionals. It has received an award as the New Media Business Website of the Year.

Financial Accounting Standards Board
www.fasb.org
This is the website for the Financial Accounting Standards Board, the independent private-sector entity that establishes generally accepted accounting principles (GAAP). The Board issues formal accounting guidance on the treatment and reporting of financial transactions and performance.

ORGANISATIONS
Association of Accounting Technicians
154 Clerkenwell Road, London, EC1R 5AD
T: +44 (0) 20 7837 8600
F: +44 (0) 20 7837 6970
E: aat@aat.org.uk
www.aat.co.uk
The AAT awards qualifications in accounting at NVQ levels 2, 3, and 4. An accounting technician is qualified to a slightly lower level than a fully qualified accountant.

Association of Chartered Certified Accountants
29 Lincoln's Inn Fields, London, WC2A 3EE

T: +44 (0) 20 7396 7000
F: +44 (0) 20 7396 7070
E: info@accaglobal.com
www.acca.co.uk
The Association is a professional and examining body in accountancy, recognised under the Companies Act 1989 by the UK Department of Trade and Industry.

Chartered Institute of Management Accountants
26 Chapter Street, London, SW1P 4NP
T: +44 (0) 20 7663 5441
F: +44 (0) 20 7663 5442
www.cimaglobal.com
CIMA is the leading UK professional organisation for management accountants.

CIPFA (Chartered Institute of Public Finance and Accountancy)
3 Robert Street, London, WC2N 6RL
T: +44 (0) 20 7543 5600
F: +44 (0) 20 7543 5700
www.cipfa.org
CIPFA is a professional accountancy body whose main aim is to train managers to understand public finance and manage public money. Its members are drawn from both the public and private sectors. In addition to providing membership services, running courses, and awarding certification, it organises conferences and produces publications.

Institute of Chartered Accountants in England and Wales
Chartered Accountants' Hall, PO Box 433, Moorgate Place, London, EC2P 2BJ
T: +44 (0) 20 7920 8100
F: +44 (0) 20 7920 8547
E: debds@icaew.co.uk
www.icaew.co.uk
The Institute is the largest professional accountancy organisation in Europe with over 120,000 members, is responsible for educating and training chartered accountants and maintaining standards of professional conduct among its members.

Institute of Chartered Accountants in Scotland
CA House, 21 Haymarket Yards, Edinburgh, Scotland, EH12 5BH
T: +44 (0) 131 347 0100
F: +44 (0) 131 347 0105
E: enquiries@icas.org.uk
www.icas.org.uk

ICAS is the leading professional accounting body in Scotland, and the oldest professional body of accountants in the world.

SEE ALSO
Budgeting (p. 494)
Reading a Balance Sheet (p. 161)
Taxation (p. 549)

Advertising

BOOKS AND DIRECTORIES
Advertising: What It Is and How to Do It 4th ed
Roderick White
Maidenhead: McGraw-Hill, 1999
264pp ISBN: 00770794581
This informative and detailed introduction to all aspects of advertising is aimed at organisations new to advertising, as well as people training in the area. It discusses the necessity and cost of advertising, the use of agents, the definitions and theories of advertising, planning advertisements, the media, and international and multinational advertising. Further sources of information are also listed.

Copywriting 2nd ed
Jonathan J. Gabay
London: Hodder and Stoughton, 2003
336pp (Teach Yourself Series)
ISBN: 0340867280
The author offers a step-by-step guide to writing powerful copy. All aspects of creative advertising and promotion are covered, including direct mail, the Internet, radio and TV, business-to-business, the press, public relations, charities, and posters. The book is written for both the beginner and the more experienced copywriter.

The Elements of Copywriting: The Essential Guide to Creating Copy That Gets the Results You Want
Gary Blake, Robert W. Bly
Harlow: Longman, 1998
184pp ISBN: 0028626303
A tightly written overview of copywriting, this book concentrates on the use of words that have exceptional impact on consumers, as proved by market research. It is an especially useful text because it addresses several direct-marketing forms that are still comparatively new—press releases, electronic messages, and web advertising. It also deals with traditional marketing forms such as brochures, catalogues, and print ads.

Managing Advertising
Margaret Allen, ed
Dublin: Blackhall Publishing, 1999
192pp (Advertising in Action)
ISBN: 1901657515
The entire advertising process, from strategic marketing thinking to the appraisal of production quotes, is examined in order to help the reader understand and manage it successfully, including working with the advertising agency. A glossary and list of contact organisations is provided.

My Life in Advertising and Scientific Advertising: Two Works
Claude C. Hopkins
Maidenhead: McGraw-Hill, 1986
336pp (Classic Reprint Edition)
ISBN: 0844231010
This book is a classic in the advertising genre. Originally published some 80 years ago, its succinct advice on reaching customers effectively has never been bettered—which accounts for its dominance in the field. *Scientific Advertising* is the more

important of the two reprints here: it details methods for copywriting and test marketing, and introduces many more ideas that have come to be accepted as the building blocks of successful advertising campaigns. Hopkins coined the phrase, 'Advertising is salesmanship'; these texts are the touchstone for all advertising texts that followed.

WEBSITES

AdForum
www.adforum.com
This gateway website offers links to advertising agencies, press releases, videos of advertisements in production, advocacy agencies, consultants, the trade press, and more.

The British Codes of Advertising and Sales Promotion
www.cap.org.uk/codes
The latest edition of The British Codes of Advertising and Sales Promotion.

ORGANISATIONS

The Advertising Association (AA)
Abford House, 15 Wilton Road, London, SW1V 1NJ
T: +44 (0) 20 7828 2771
F: +44 (0) 20 7931 0376
E: aa@adassoc.org.uk
www.adassoc.org.uk
The AA is a federation of 26 trade associations and professional bodies representing advertisers, agencies, the media, and support services. Its remit is to promote and protect the rights, responsibilities, and role of advertising in the United Kingdom.

European Advertising Standards Alliance
10a rue de la Pépinière, 1000 Brussels, Belgium
T: +32 2 513 7806
F: +32 2 513 2861
www.easa-alliance.org
The Alliance is a co-ordinating body for 28 self-regulatory organisations within Europe.

Its main task is to administer a cross-border complaints procedure.

Institute of Practitioners in Advertising (IPA)
44 Belgrave Square, London, SW1X 8QS
T: +44 (0) 20 7235 7020
F: +44 (0) 20 7245 9904
E: info@ipa.co.uk
www.ipa.co.uk
The mission of the IPA is to serve, promote, and anticipate the collective interests of advertising agencies, and, at the same time, to define, develop, and help maintain the highest possible standards of professional practice within the advertising business.

International Advertising Association (UK Chapter) Ltd (IAA)
166 Finchley Road, London, NW3 6BP
T: +44 (0) 20 7431 7701
F: +44 (0) 20 7431 7098
www.iaaukchp.co.uk
The Association promotes the critical role and benefits of advertising as the vital force behind all healthy economies and the foundation of diverse, independent, and affordable media in an open society.

Outdoor Advertising Association of Great Britain Ltd (OAA)
Summit House, 27 Sale Place, London, W2 1YR
T: +44 (0) 20 7973 0315
F: +44 (0) 20 7973 0318
E: enquiries@oaa.org.uk
www.oaa.org.uk
The OAA is the central reference point for the outdoor advertising industry. It seeks to advance and protect the interests of its members, promote standards of best practice in the industry, and encourage the growth of business.

SEE ALSO
Direct Marketing (p. 503)
Marketing Management (p. 523)
Market Research and Competitor Intelligence (p. 526)
Product and Brand Management (p. 537)

Bankruptcy and Business Failure

BOOKS AND DIRECTORIES
Buying a Company in Trouble: A Practical Guide 2nd ed
Ian E. Walker
Aldershot: Gower, 1992
144pp ISBN: 0566072890
This book provides practical guidance for those planning to buy a company that is formally insolvent or close to insolvency. It considers the reasons for buying such a company and discusses how to recognise a company in trouble, decide when to buy, and negotiate the offer, as well as the other matters that should be taken into account.

Corporate Insolvency: Law and Practice 3rd ed
David Milman, Chris Durrant
London: Sweet and Maxwell, 1999
290pp ISBN: 0421656409
The authors provide an overview of insolvency law and procedure in the United Kingdom for the benefit of practitioners. The areas covered include the qualification and responsibilities of insolvency practitioners, the appointment of receivers, liquidations, claims against company assets, and the responsibilities of directors of insolvent companies.

Insolvency in Business: How to Avoid It, How to Deal With It
Paul Finn
London: Cassell Educational, 1989
123pp ISBN: 0304317977
The author provides a practical guide to corporate insolvency for small business owners and, in particular, examines and assesses possible alternatives to liquidation or bankruptcy.

Introduction to Corporate and Personal Insolvency Law
Fiona Tolmie
London: Sweet and Maxwell, 1998
429pp ISBN: 0421598506
This introductory text covers personal and corporate insolvency in the United Kingdom.

It summarises the relevant legislation and explains how it works in practice. Key policy issues and areas where the law may be changed in the future are also highlighted.

Phoenix Factor: Lessons for Success from Management Failure
David Clutterbuck, Sue Kernaghnan
London: Weidenfeld and Nicolson, 1990
215pp ISBN: 0297811231
The authors provide an insight into business failure, identifying and analysing the attitudes and behaviours which contribute to it. They also present the results of a survey of lending institutions and receivers, and case studies of failing companies.

WEBSITES
Business Bankruptcy Info
www.creditworthy.com/topics/ bankruptcy.html
This website, hosted by Creditworthy Co., provides links to business bankruptcy information covering the United States, Canada, and the United Kingdom. It includes information on, and links to, US bankruptcy courts, an overview of the US Bankruptcy Code, and statistics and research on bankruptcy filings.

InsolvencyAsia
www.insolvencyasia.com
This site, based in Hong Kong, provides insolvency-related news together with information on bankruptcy legislation and listings of consultants, associations, and regulatory authorities in Asian countries.

Insolvency.co.uk
www.insolvency.co.uk
This website is the major Internet source of information on bankruptcy and insolvency in the United Kingdom. It provides access to databases of companies in liquidation, receivership, and administration, and of specialist legal firms. It contains links to legislation and other relevant sites, as well as offering a range of services including news, FAQs, mailing lists, and training courses.

Insolvency Services
www.insolvency.gov.uk
This government-sponsored site provides practical information and advice on personal and corporate insolvency in the United Kingdom, including statistics and a database of insolvency practitioners.

InterNet Bankruptcy Library
www.bankrupt.com
This site, sponsored by the Bankruptcy Creditors' Service and the Beard Group, is aimed particularly at creditors. It includes a news archive, a database of bankruptcy professionals, information on legal rules in US states, and details of publications, as well as providing access to discussion groups.

World Internet Insolvency and Bankruptcy Resources
www.insolvency.com
This site includes a listing of US and UK mailing lists and newsgroups connected with insolvency.

ORGANISATIONS
Bankruptcy Association of England and Wales
4 Johnson Close, Abraham Heights, Lancaster, Lancashire, LA1 5EU
T: +44 (0) 1524 64305
F: +44 (0) 1524 389717
E: bankruptcyassociation@ gbandi.freeserve.co.uk
www.theba.org.uk
The Association was founded by John McQueen in 1983 to provide information and advice to debtors and bankrupts in the United Kingdom and to campaign for reform of insolvency legislation.

Insolvency Practitioners Association
52–54 Gracechurch Street, London, EC3V 0EH
T: +44 (0) 20 7623 5108
F: +44 (0) 20 7623 5127
E: secretariat@ipa.uk.com
www.ipa.uk.com
The IPA, founded in 1961, is a professional organisation for insolvency practitioners. Its main objectives are to promote training and education in insolvency administration and to maintain the standards of performance and conduct of those working in the field.

R3, The Association of Business Recovery Professionals
4th Floor, Halton House, 20–23 Holborn, London, EC1N 2JD
T: +44 (0) 20 7831 6563
F: +44 (0) 20 7405 7047
E: association@r3.org.uk
www.r3.org.uk
R3 (Rescue, Recovery, Renewal), founded in 1990 and formerly known as the Society of Practitioners of Insolvency, is a professional organisation for insolvency practitioners and turnaround managers which places a growing emphasis on reconstruction, turnaround management, and corporate recovery. Its activities include courses, conferences, and producing publications— including the quarterly journal *Recovery*.

SEE ALSO
Accounting (p. 487)

Budgeting

BOOKS AND DIRECTORIES
Better Payment Practice: A Guide to Credit Management
Department of Trade and Industry
London, 1998
39pp
The payment of bills on time is good business practice and both buyers and suppliers have a part to play in it. This booklet offers guidance and advice to small businesses from the perspective of both the supplier and the buyer. The section for suppliers looks at preventive measures, risk-reducing techniques, and collecting the cash. The buyers' section offers guidance to all purchasing organisations on how to overcome the problem of late payment.

Budgeting for Non-financial Managers: How to Master and Maintain Effective Budgets

Iain Maitland

Harlow: Financial Times Prentice Hall, 1999
204pp (Smarter Solutions Series)
ISBN: 0273644947

This book takes you through each stage of the budgeting process, explaining all you need to know about it. From understanding the procedures for making budgets and forecasts to developing realistic contingency plans, it shows how to turn your budgeting strategy into a valuable management tool. It also contains a wide range of model forecasts, forms, and budgets, and comes complete with checklists and case studies.

Cash Flows and Budgeting Made Easy: How to Set and Monitor Financial Targets in Any Organization 4th ed

Peter Taylor

Oxford: How To Books, 2002
160pp ISBN: 1857038037

This practical guide aims to cover the whole budgeting process, and contains information on planning financial requirements, forecasting, VAT, managing cash flows, and using IT to help make your financial life easier.

Costing, Pricing and Credit Control: How to Improve Profitability and How to Get Paid Promptly 2nd ed

Keith Kirkland, Stuart Howard

London: Kogan Page, 1998
189pp (Simple and Practical Series)
ISBN: 0749429305

The book aims to provide a sound understanding of how to work out the cost of a product or service, fix the right price for it, work out the break-even point, handle price discounting, deal with loss-making activities, formulate a credit control strategy, control debt, and recover bad debt through the courts.

Credit Risk Management: A Guide to Sound Business Decisions

H. A. Schaeffer, Jr

Chichester: John Wiley, 2000
288pp ISBN: 0471350206

This book examines the steps leading to a sound business credit decision. It is divided into four main sections: analysis for creative credit management; building up essential business credit information; considering all factors that affect the business credit decision; and making a decision or recommendation. Twelve detailed case studies are provided, illustrating common problems along with their solutions.

Handbook of Budgeting 4th ed

Robert Rachlin

Chichester: John Wiley, 1998
976pp ISBN: 0471183504

Targeted at controllers and budget directors, this book demonstrates how to create a broad range of budgets, from the traditional budget to the activity-based budget. The handbook is divided into five major categories that cover the budgeting process, tools and techniques, preparation of specific budgets, budgeting applications, and industry budgets.

Keys to Managing Your Cash Flow

Joel G. Siegel, and Jae K. Shim

Hauppauge, NY: Barrons, 1992
153pp (Barrons Educational Series)
ISBN: 0812047559

Aimed at business people who want to learn more about making the company's cash work harder, this book contains practical information on liquidity, credit control, dealing with surplus cash, preparing a cash budget, and much more.

Managing Budgets

Stephen Brookson

London: Dorling Kindersley, 2000
72pp (Essential Managers Series)
ISBN: 0751307718

This introductory guide to managing budgets explains the technique of budgeting and examines the processes of preparing, writing, and monitoring a budget.

Managing by the Numbers

Chuck Kremer, Ron Rizzuto, John Case

Cambridge, Massachusetts: Perseus, 2000
224pp ISBN: 0738202568

This is a handy and practical guide to reading and using balance sheets, income statements, and cash flow statements to drive business growth and profitability.

Mastering Spreadsheet Budgets and Forecasts: How to Save Time and Gain Control of Your Business
Malcolm Secrett
Harlow: Financial Times Prentice Hall, 1999
260pp (Smarter Solutions Series)
ISBN: 0273644912
This step-by-step, jargon-free guide demonstrates the advantages and potential of using spreadsheets to prepare and present budgets and forecasts. It includes examples of budgets and forecasts, followed through completely from beginning to end.

Successful Credit Control in a Week
Roger Mason
London: Hodder and Stoughton, 1999
96pp (Business in a Week Series)
ISBN: 0340747528
In this practical, step-by-step introduction to the essentials of credit control, Mason explains the precautions to take when opening an account, the effective use of the telephone, and how to overcome excuses, source good information, and use the courts effectively.

Total Business Budgeting: A Step-by-step Guide with Forms 2nd ed
Robert Rachlin
Chichester: John Wiley, 1999
321pp ISBN: 0471351032
Rachlin provides an introduction to a wide range of budgetary techniques and applications, and shows how to analyse outside influences, develop performance targets and budgeting segments, and administer the right budgeting processes. He includes detailed instructions, forms, examples, schedules, and formats.

WEBSITES
Accounting Web
www.accountingweb.co.uk
This site is an extensive UK-based online resource. It contains material from a number of providers intended for accountancy and finance professionals. It has received an award as the New Media Business Website of the Year.

Credit to Cash
www.credit-to-cash.com
This UK portal provides a wide range of financial information and advice, specifically on credit management and policy, debt recovery, cash-flow control, and other issues of interest to small businesses.

The Dyer Partnership
www.netaccountants.com
The site provides a wide range of information on UK tax and accounting matters and other business issues of interest to owners and managers of UK businesses.

ORGANISATIONS
Association of Chartered Certified Accountants
29 Lincoln's Inn Fields, London, WC2A 3EE
T: +44 (0) 20 7396 7000
F: +44 (0) 20 7396 7070
E: info@accaglobal.com
www.acca.co.uk
The Association is a professional and examining body in accountancy, recognised under the Companies Act 1989 by the UK Department of Trade and Industry.

Chartered Institute of Management Accountants
26 Chapter Street, London, SW1P 4NP
T: +44 (0) 20 7663 5441
F: +44 (0) 20 7663 5442
www.cimaglobal.com
CIMA is the leading UK professional organisation for management accountants.

Institute of Chartered Accountants in England and Wales
Chartered Accountants' Hall, PO Box 433, Moorgate Place, London, EC2P 2BJ
T: +44 (0) 20 7920 8100
F: +44 (0) 20 7920 8547
E: dsbds@icaew.co.uk
www.icaew.co.uk
ICAEW, the largest professional accountancy organisation in Europe with over 120,000 members, is responsible for educating and training Chartered Accountants and maintaining standards of professional conduct among its members.

Institute of Chartered Accountants in Scotland
CA House, 21 Haymarket Yards, Edinburgh, Scotland, EH12 5BH

T: +44 (0) 131 347 0100
F: +44 (0) 131 347 0105
E: enquiries@icas.org.uk
www.icas.org.uk
The Institute is the leading professional
accounting body in Scotland, and the oldest
professional body of accountants in the
world.

Institute of Credit Management
The Water Mill, Station Road, South
Luffenham, Oakham, Leicestershire, LE15
8NB
T: +44 (0) 1780 722900
F: +44 (0) 1780 721333
E: info@icm.org.uk
www.icm.org.uk
The Institute of Credit Management (ICM) is
the largest organisation of credit
professionals in Europe, and the focal point
in the United Kingdom for all matters
relating to credit management and its
ancillary functions. The ICM sets
professional standards and tests and assesses
those who wish to gain its professional
qualification. It also provides advice to
government and other national bodies.

Institute of Financial Accountants
Burford House, 44 London Road, Sevenoaks,
Kent, TN13 1AS
T: +44 (0) 1732 458080
F: +44 (0) 1732 455848
E: mail@ifa.org.uk
www.ifa.org.uk
The Institute of Financial Accountants,
established in 1916, is the largest
professional body of its type in the
world. It represents members and
students in more than 80 countries
around the world and provides a
qualification and continuing professional
development for those who want to
become financial accountants. It also sets
both technical and ethical standards
within the profession, and provides
guidelines for maintaining those
standards.

SEE ALSO
Accounting (p. 487)
Controlling a Budget (p. 116)
Controlling Costs (p. 119)
Drawing Up a Budget (p. 122)

Business Plans and Planning

BOOKS AND DIRECTORIES
The Business Plan Workbook
Colin Barrow, Paul Barrow,
Robert Brown
London: Kogan Page, 2001
382pp ISBN: 0749434996
The processes and procedures required to
write a business plan are brought together
in this workbook, and are illustrated with
examples from actual business plans. The
seven-phase approach focuses on: the
business history and position to date;
market research; competitive business
strategies; operations; forecasting results;
business controls; and writing up and
presenting your business plan. Appendices
give market research information sources
and sources of finance for new and small
businesses.

By the Numbers: Using Facts and Figures to Get Your Projects, Plans, and Ideas Approved
Joseph McLeary, et al
New York: AMACOM, 2000
286pp ISBN: 0814404995
The authors demonstrate how to present a
winning business case based on figures.
They explain how to research a company
strategy, determine whether an idea is in
keeping with industry trends, build alliances
and support before a formal presentation,
and prepare answers to critical questions.

The Complete Book of Business Plans: Simple Steps to Writing a Powerful Business Plan
Joseph A. Covello, Brian J. Hazelgren
Naperville, Illinois: Sourcebooks, 1994
320pp ISBN: 0942061411

This classic business text presents the key questions to bear in mind when writing a plan for a new business, and encourages the reader to look for the answers to the kinds of questions that investors ask, to develop marketing strategies and financial presentations, and to find ways to stay ahead of the competition. Written in the early 90s, it retains all of its initial impact today.

The Definitive Business Plan: The Fast Track to Intelligent Business Planning for Executives and Entrepreneurs
Richard Stutley
Harlow: Financial Times Prentice Hall, 2001
332pp ISBN: 0273659219
This text is written for both the newcomer and the experienced planner. It provides a concise guide to the business planning process, and focuses attention on strategic planning and strategic and operational controls. The practical aspects of constructing various types of business plan are explained in some detail.

How to Prepare a Business Plan: Planning for Successful Start-up and Expansion
Edward Blackwell
London: Kogan Page, 2002
190pp (Sunday Times)
ISBN: 0749437472
A highly-recommended title that takes the owner/manager through the process of developing a business plan for start-up or expansion. This book covers financial forecasting and planning and gives useful case studies of businesses preparing and following business plans.

How to Write a .com Business Plan: The Internet Entrepreneur's Guide to Everything You Need to Know about Business Plans and Financing Options
Joanne Eglash
Maidenhead: McGraw-Hill, 2001
191pp ISBN: 007135753X
Written for entrepreneurs, business owners, and website owners, this text provides a practical guide to developing a business plan for an Internet-based business. Eglash focuses on the factors which distinguish online businesses from conventional enterprises, and covers the areas of mission statements and company descriptions, competition, markets and customers, products and services, marketing and sales, operations, financial projections, and financial management. A sample business plan and an extensive directory of helpful websites are included.

The Successful Business Plan: Secrets and Strategies 4th ed
Rhonda M. Abrams
Palo Alto, California: Running R Media, 2003
409pp ISBN: 0966963563
This book is designed to help readers create a business plan that will attract the funding they need to get started. It presents insights from some 200 business owners, venture capitalists, and CEOs, but, in addition, contains worksheets and sample business plans, provides tools to help in number-crunching, and offers guidance on the length of an ideal plan and the way it should be worded and formatted.

Successful Business Plans in a Week 2nd ed
Iain Maitland
London: Hodder and Stoughton, 1998
93pp (Business in a Week Series)
ISBN: 034071199X
This step-by-step guide to the process of compiling and writing a business plan explains how to identify goals, make preparatory notes, compile the financial and commercial sections, and present the plan.

WEBSITES
Business Planet
www.bizplanet.com
BizPlanet provides a range of resources including a newsletter, a virtual business plan, and reviews of business planning software and books.

Business Plan Guide
www.business-plans.co.uk
This site, sponsored by Miller Consultancy, provides information on business planning

resources. It includes books, links to websites, articles, and an e-mail newsletter.

Business Plans
www.bplans.com
This site, created by Palo Alto Software, offers planning advice for small businesses and a substantial range of sample plans, which subscribers to bplans' software can download and edit. It also includes a resource centre with links to other websites, as well as an 'ask the experts' section.

More Business
www.morebusiness.com
This site has a lengthy business and marketing plans section and provides some useful sample business plans.

Venture Associates
www.venturea.com/business.htm
Produced by an investment banking and management consulting firm, the site provides freely available information on various aspects of business planning. It also includes a useful business plan outline.

Venture Capital Resource Library
www.vfinance.com
This site provides a business plan template, general articles, and texts of SEC and UCC rules and regulations, as well as leads to sources of venture capital.

SEE ALSO
Budgeting (p. 494)
Small and Growing Businesses (p. 478)

Computers, Information Technology, and E-commerce

BOOKS AND DIRECTORIES
Absolute Beginner's Guide to Computers and the Internet
Michael Miller
Indianapolis, Indiana: Que, 2002
471pp ISBN: 0789780121
This book sets out to equip readers with the knowledge they need to carry out the most popular IT and Internet-related tasks, such as sending e-mail, Web surfing, online banking, and downloading music. Readers' basic skills are developed and these can then be applied in more specialist or business-related areas.

The Beginner's Guide to Computers and the Internet
Susan Holden, Matthew Francis
Chichester: Summersdale Publishers, 2002
395pp ISBN: 184024061X
This is a guide to the basics of using computers. Avoiding technical jargon, the book explains key terms and concepts and shows a range of time-saving shortcuts for those unfamiliar with computers. E-mail and the Internet are also covered.

E-business for the Small Business
John Fisher
London: Kogan Page, 2001
162pp (Business Enterprise Guide)
ISBN: 074943479 1
E-business presents many new opportunities for businesses of all sizes. This guide takes you through the necessary steps for building a successful and sustainable e-business. It deals with: finding the funds; getting the right equipment; setting up a website; legal issues; online marketing and advertising; business-to-business opportunities; and developing an e-business plan.

E-commerce Law for Business Managers
Charles Chatterjee
Canterbury: Financial World Publishing , 2002
338pp ISBN: 0852975643
Aimed specifically at smaller businesses, this is a reference guide to the legal issues of launching a commercial Internet site. Some of those issues include: e-commerce security; corporate identity; service provision; intellectual property rights;

domain names; and email marketing. Many well established businesses have been caught out by the requirements of the Data Protection Act, and so this book seeks to help readers to understand the legal status of electronic money, signatures, privacy, and consumer rights. It provides this advice in a clear, practical, and user-friendly format, so that all types of manager can gain an understanding of key UK legislation and EU directives.

IT Investment: Making a Business Case
Dan Remenyi
Oxford: Butterworth-Heinemann, 1999
160pp (Computer Weekly Professional Series)
ISBN: 0750645040
The author presents clear arguments for preparing an IT business case and includes model questionnaires and forms that managers can use in preparing a case of their own. He stresses in particular the importance of demonstrating the improvements an IT project can make to business processes, practice, and efficiency, and introduces a five-factor model which ties the project into an organisation's corporate strategy.

Learning to Succeed in Business with Information Technology
Tim Lane, David Snow, Peter Labrow
Manchester: NCC Education, 2000
192pp ISBN: 1902343328
Aimed at managers within industry, this book addresses the reasons why it is important to invest in the IT skills of the workforce. Changes within the workforce, business attitudes to IT education, IT certification and accreditation, and methods of learning are examined in detail. The authors also make recommendations regarding best practice in IT skills training in organisations and for the IT training industry.

Learning Web Design
Jennifer Niederst
Farnham: O'Reilly UK, 2003
488pp ISBN: 0596004842

Aimed at those new to Web design, this book is a comprehensive introduction to the fundamentals. The book is accessible in both tone and lay-out and is split into four sections: an overview of the Web design process; an introduction to HTML, the coding that makes up the background of Web pages; a guide to Web graphics; and advice on design. Jargon-free and full of practical tips, this book is ideal for beginners.

The Mini Rough Guide to Personal Computers: How to Choose and Use a PC
Peter Buckley, Duncan Clark
London: Rough Guides, 2001
432pp ISBN: 1858286577
A pocket-sized guide to the basics of choosing the best PC for you and understanding how it works. The book covers five main sections (computer hardware, computer software, the Internet, Windows, and troubleshooting) and sets out to demystify the world of computers for beginners.

The Really, Really, Really Easy Step-by-step Computer Book: For Beginners of All Ages
Robynn Hofmeyer, Gavin Hoole
Cape Town: Struik Publishers, 2001
80pp ISBN: 1868726827
As the title would suggest, this illustrated book is aimed at the absolute beginner. It offers step-by-step advice and information on a variety of essential skills, including choosing the right PC for you, getting to know your machine, creating and saving documents, and using e-mail.

The Rough Guide to the Internet
Peter Buckley, Duncan Clark
London: Rough Guides, 2003
540pp ISBN: 1843531011
One of the most popular guides to the Internet for beginners, this book explains how to get to grips with the online world. It gives information on how to search, shop, browse, play, and communciate online as well as on how to create a Web page. Fully updated, some of the book's new features

include a glossary to define complex terms when they first appear in the text, information boxes to anticipate common mistakes, and a variety of exercises so that readers can test their newly-gained skills. This book will be a boon to all new or unpractised Internet users.

Small Business Guide to the Internet: A Practical Approach to Going Online
Richard Lewis
Dublin: Oak Tree Press, 1999
308pp ISBN: 1860761461
This practical guide to electronic commerce for small businesses examines both strategic issues—for example, which businesses are most likely to succeed with electronic commerce—and practical considerations such as getting online, designing and marketing an effective website, and the true cost of doing business online. Listings of ISPs and online resources are included.

Small Business Websites That Work: Get Online to Grow Your Company
Sean McManus
Harlow: Prentice Hall, 2001
240pp ISBN: 0273654861
A guide to help you get to grips with the essentials of website design and management. This book will be particularly helpful if you are outsourcing your website and need to learn not only how to brief people effectively so that you save time and money, but also how the basic technology behind the Web works.

WEBSITES
Beginners.co.uk
www.beginners.co.uk
This website offers a range of advice for absolute beginners as well as those with some IT knowledge. The site offers a range of free tutorials as well as a range of online training courses to help those who would like to gain or expand their IT knowledge for work or personal use. The site is easy to navigate even for Internet novices.

@Brint.com
www.brint.com
This extensive portal and community network for e-business, information, technology, and knowledge management contains news, articles, book reviews, and links to relevant websites in the featured areas.

CMC Information Sources
www.december.com/cmc/info
This site, which focuses on computer-mediated communications, offers a set of links to essential websites concerned with computer training, applications, technology, and culture.

E-commerce focus
www.ecomfocus.com/cgi-bin/library/list.asp?sector=12
This site offers useful guidance on e-commerce and its importance for businesses and also provides a list of contacts for further information.

Which? Online
www.which.net
A subscription website, *Which?* Online offers access via the Internet to the wide range of information contained in the range of *Which?* magazines, including *Computing Which?*. The site offers a tour and a 30-day free trial. Subscribers gain access to thousands of reports contained in the print versions of all *Which?* magazines, searchable guides, and interactive features.

PC Magazine Online
www.pcmag.co.uk
This easily navigable site offers a range of helpful services to the user. These include an 'e-shopper' facility which allows you to compare specifications and prices on IT products and a forum whereby users can pose questions to the magazine's editors. There are also a series of information centres on news, products, downloads, advice, and careers as well as subsections on e-business, communications, business hardware, business software, security, personal computing, and gaming.

ORGANISATIONS
British Computer Society
1 Sanford Street, Swindon, Wiltshire, SN1
1HJ
T: +44 (0) 1793 417424
F: +44 (0) 1793 480270
E: bcshq@hq.bcs.org.uk
www1.bcs.org.uk
Founded in 1957, the British Computer
Society is a professional and learned society
with members from both the United
Kingdom and overseas. It aims to provide a
voice for the IT industry in discussions with
the UK government. In addition, it offers
both its own qualifications and others
accredited by the Engineering Council that
can lead to Chartered Engineer status.

National Computing Centre Limited
Oxford House, Oxford Road, Manchester,
M1 7ED
T: +44 (0) 161 242 2121
F: +44 (0) 161 242 2499
E: info@ncc.co.uk
www.ncc.co.uk
Founded in 1966, the National Computing
Centre is an international, membership-
based organisation that aims to promote the
effective use of IT and computers. Its areas
of particular interest include systems
design, computer security,
communications, and training.

Contracts and Contracting

BOOKS AND DIRECTORIES
Business Contracts Kit for Dummies
Richard D. Harroch
New York: Hungry Minds, 2000
330pp ISBN: 0764552368
This kit comprises a book and a CD-ROM
providing a reference guide to business
contracts, with almost 200 sample
documents and contracts.

Commercial Contracts: A Practical Guide to Deals, Contracts, Agreements and Promises
C.P. Thorpe, C.L. Bailey
London: Kogan Page/Institute of Directors, 1999
246pp ISBN: 0749428422
This is a guide to the basic principles of
contract law. It places them into a
commercial context, illustrated with
examples. Topics covered by the book are:
entering into a contract, standard terms and
conditions; contract interpretation; invalid
contracts; and the involvement of third
parties.

Concise Business Guide to Contract Law
Charles Boundy
Aldershot: Gower, 1998
295pp ISBN: 0566079216

Aimed at all managers, this book introduces
the principles of UK contract law and the
way in which they apply to key elements of
business. The book also covers the planning
of contracts, the use of standard forms, the
international dimension, and what to do
when things go wrong. A glossary of legal
terms is included.

Contract Law 3rd ed
Catherine Elliott, Frances Quinn
Harlow: Longman, 2001
327pp ISBN: 058243818
This is a popular student textbook on UK
contract law. The authors present a clear
explanation of the law of contract, and make
reference to contemporary cases and topical
issues in the media. They also present
guidelines on answering typical
examination questions, together with more
general advice.

Contract Negotiation Handbook 3rd ed
P.D.V. Marsh
Aldershot: Gower, 2001
320pp ISBN: 0566080214
This textbook sets out a structured approach
to all stages of negotiation. It covers the
entire process: preparing to negotiate, the

opening and development of negotiations, and the closing and recording of the bargain.

The Law of Contract 10th ed
Sir Guenter H. Treitel
London: Sweet and Maxwell, 1999
1010pp ISBN: 042163460X
This text explains and analyses the law of contract, and provides a detailed and clear examination of many areas of controversy and difficulty. New cases, and new and prospective legislation, are examined.

Managing Contractors: A Guide for Employers 2nd ed
Health and Safety Executive
Sudbury, 1997
49pp ISBN: 071761195
The use of contractors within industry is increasing. Many are used for specialist tasks, often involving hazardous activities. This guide helps managers understand the best ways to manage contractors, and offers practical advice for action. It includes a series of checklists and action plans to emphasise the key issues which have to be addressed.

One Stop Contracts 2nd ed
John Wyborn
London: ICSA Publishing, 2000
246pp (One Stop Series)
ISBN: 1860721230
This book is an introductory text that includes coverage of contract law, drafting contracts, and standard contracts. It also gives advice on negotiating contracts, and on issues of procurement, outsourcing, and intellectual property.

WEBSITES
Contracting and Organizations Research Initiative
http://cori.missouri.edu
CORI is a research initiative at the University of Missouri. Its mission is to improve understanding of how the economic system works by facilitating empirical research on contracting and organisational structure. It has created a collection of contracts that researchers can use.

ORGANISATIONS
European Institute of Advanced Project and Contract Management
Epci, Prof. Olav Hanssensvei 10, 4021 Stavanger, Norway
T: +47 51 87 66 72
F: +47 51 87 17 11
E: epci@epci.org
www.epci.no
EPCI was founded in 1994 and has an international membership of companies and academic institutions. Member organisations form a network aimed at developing competence in project and contract management.

SEE ALSO
Employment Law (p. 506)
Outsourcing (p. 532)

Direct Marketing

BOOKS AND DIRECTORIES
2,239 Tested Secrets for Direct Marketing Success
Denny Hatch, Don Jackson
Maidenhead: McGraw-Hill, 1999
368pp ISBN: 0844203491
Divided into topic sections for easy reference, this book is an excellent source of

direct marketing advice drawn from the experience of experts.

Commonsense Direct Marketing 4th ed
Drayton Bird
London: Kogan Page, 2000
392pp ISBN: 0749431210
This is a practical textbook, introducing

direct marketing, that is packed with international case studies and demonstrations of successful strategies. It covers the following topics: the role of the marketing department; how to acquire and keep customers; how to achieve objectives and evaluate results; what you should sell; how to position products effectively; how to choose an agency and how to do without one; and the Internet, the direct marketer's new tool.

Direct and Database Marketing

Graeme McCorkell
London: Institute of Direct Marketing/Kogan Page, 1997
315pp ISBN: 0749419601
The best UK introduction to direct marketing, this book was written to be read from cover to cover and contains some good small business examples. This text is also useful to dip into for examples of how direct marketing campaigns are measured and evaluated.

Direct Marketing: Strategy, Planning, Execution 4th ed

Edward L. Nash
Maidenhead: McGraw-Hill, 2000
600pp ISBN: 0071352872
This updated edition is a classic in the direct marketing industry. The author, a direct marketing company executive, presents a thorough overview of all aspects of direct marketing, including strategic planning, media-specific marketing techniques, the economics of direct marketing, and direct marketing considerations for Internet and global marketing.

Enterprise One-to-One

Don Peppers, Martha Rogers
London: Piatkus Books, 1998
451pp ISBN: 0749918144

Written by the champions of customer relationship marketing, this is a best-selling guide to using new technology in your quest to get ahead, and stay ahead of the field.

Making It Personal: How to Profit from Personalization without Invading Privacy

Bruce Kasanoff, Don Peppers, Martha Rogers
Cambridge, Massachusetts: Perseus, 2001
240pp ISBN: 0738205302
This book is a study of how the forthcoming growth in the use of personal information will affect the corporate world. Using research carried out in real life, the author investigates the contradiction that exists in some areas between increasing profits through personal interaction and not invading privacy.

WEBSITES

The Direct Marketing Association
www.dma.org.uk
The Direct Marketing Association is a trade association serving the needs of direct marketing users and suppliers. Its website provides comprehensive information on direct marketing. This includes: conferences and seminars; professional development; industry guidelines, such as ethics guidelines and online tutorials; directories of direct marketers listed by name and type of service; privacy information; research; and legislative issues.

Royal Mail
www.royalmail.com
The Business Mail section of this website offers information on principles of best practice in direct mail, as well as lots of useful help on creating, planning, and budgeting a campaign.

Federation of European Direct Marketing
Tervurenlaan, Avenue de Tervuren 439,
B-1150 Brussels, Belgium
T: +32 2779 42 68
F: +32 2779 42 69
E: info@fedma.org
www.fedma.org
A membership organisation for national
direct-marketing associations, FEDMA aims
to promote, protect, and provide
information about the European direct-
marketing industry.

Information Commissioner's Office
Wycliffe House, Water Lane, Wilmslow,
Cheshire, SK9 5AF
T: 01625 545745
F: 01625 545748
E: data@notification.demon.co.uk
www.dataprotection.gov.uk

The Information Commissioner is
responsible for enforcing the eight
principles of good practice regarding the
processing of personal data in the United
Kingdom as set out in the Data Protection
Act 1998 and the Freedom of Information
Act 2000.

Institute of Direct Marketing
1 Park Road, Teddington, Middlesex,
TW11 0AR, United Kingdom
T: +44 (0) 20 8977 5705
F: +44 (0) 20 8943 2535
E: enquiries@theidm.com
www.theidm.co.uk

SEE ALSO
Marketing Management (p. 523)

Employee Benefits/Compensation

BOOKS AND DIRECTORIES
Company Cars
Industrial Society
London, 1999
64pp (Managing Best Practice 58)
This survey of UK personnel and HR
specialists investigates company policy on
the provision of company cars. It considers
the rationale for providing company cars
and the issues of entitlement and status and
perk cars. Case studies of Asda, Cable and
Wireless, Origin, the RNIB, and Surrey
County Council are presented and sample
documentation from these organisations is
reproduced.

Flexible Benefits
Industrial Society
London, 2000
64pp (Managing Best Practice 75)
This booklet presents the results of a survey
of flexible benefits schemes carried out
among UK human resource managers in
June 2000. Topics covered include: how
common flexible benefits are; how costs are
calculated and controlled; and the
drawbacks of flexible benefits schemes.

Case studies of Cable and Wireless,
Cadbury, PriceWaterhouseCoopers, and the
Spring Group are used, and consultancy
advice and sources of further information
are also provided.

Flexible Benefits: A Practical Guide
Russ Watling
Hitchin: Technical Communications, 1996
*76pp (Busy Manager Series—Best Practice
Management Reports)*
ISBN: 1859530613
This publication examines the strategy that
should underlie a benefits programme and
identifies the key issues to be considered in
any feasibility study of the subject. These
include the design of flexible benefits, the
ways in which benefits can become flexible,
and the employment benefits strategy. A
case study of Mercury Communications is
provided.

The HR Book: Human Resources Management for Small Business
Lin Grensing Prophal
Naperville, Illinois: Sourcebooks, 1999
280pp ISBN: 1551802414

This book is a 'complete guide' to human resource management for the small business. Although written from a US perspective, its message is useful for small businesses all over the world.

Managing Pensions Change
Industrial Society
London, 2001
64pp (Managing Best Practice 81)
The results of a survey of best practice in the area of managing change conducted among human resource specialists are presented here, along with case studies of six organisations, AMP UK, the BG Group, C and J Clark, Rexam, Thorn, and the Universities Superannuation Scheme. The booklet also offers consultancy advice, a review of legal provisions that employers must take into account in the United Kingdom, and details of further sources of information.

Pensions for Today
Confederation of British Industry
London: Caspian Publishing Ltd in association with the CBI, 2001
80pp (Business Guide)
ISBN: 1901844218
This Confederation of British Industry guide explains the key issues within the changing pensions market place, including the introduction of stakeholder pensions, pan-European pension provision, the changing world of work, communicating the benefits, and pension provision in the future.

WEBSITES
BenefitsLink.com
www.benefitslink.com
This large US site is aimed at employers and provides news, compliance information, a question and answer service, links to articles, and a database of speakers.

Employee Benefit News
www.benefitnews.com
This site provides news and analysis of benefits issues and an e-mail newsletter. Registration is required.

Employee Benefits Interactive
www.employeebenefits.co.uk
The site includes a knowledge bank of articles from *Employee Benefits* magazine and a directory of service providers.

Employee Benefits Survey
www.bls.gov/ncs/ebs
This site provides access to data from the US Bureau of Labor Statistics Employee Benefits Survey in PDF format.

Smart Benefits
www.smartbenefits.com
Information and links for benefit administrators are available on this site, including advice on choosing a plan.

SEE ALSO
Employment Law (p. 506)

Employment Law

BOOKS AND DIRECTORIES
Butterworths Employment Law Handbook 11th ed
Peter Wallington, ed
London: Butterworths, 2000
2000pp ISBN: 0406963045
This is a comprehensive reference source of statutory and non-statutory material relating to employment law in the United Kingdom. The text takes account of changes according to the following legislation: Employment Act 2002, the Fixed Term Employees (Prevention of Less Favourable Treatment) Regulations 2002, the Paternity and Adoption Leave Regulations 2002, the Statutory Paternity Pay and Statutory Adoption Pay (General) Regulations 2002, and the new regulations on flexible

working. It also incorporates updated codes of practice, such as the Employment Practices Data Protection Code and the Commission for Racial Equality Code of Practice on the duty to promote racial equality.

Collective Labour Law
Gillian Morris, Timothy J. Archer
Oxford: Hart Publishing, 2000
623pp ISBN: 1841131776
A masterly book on collective labour law which is suitable both for specialists and for those with no detailed prior knowledge. Trade union and worker rights and obligations are dealt with in detail along with coverage of the law relating to industrial action. The book takes full account of the Human Rights Act and of relevant European law. Appendices include comprehensive information to assist further research.

Contracts of Employment: Law, Practice and Precedents
Michael Duggan
Welwyn: EMIS Professional Publishing, 2001
424pp ISBN: 1858112397
As well as providing samples of complete employment contracts, this book provides hundreds of clauses for special situations, with commentary to explain points to be considered and the reasons behind the suggested wording. It comes with a CD-ROM in an innovative format (PCs only) specially designed to make it easy to compile complete contracts tailored to suit various situations.

Employment Law Checklist 7th ed
Erich Suter
London: Institute of Personnel and Development, 2000
196pp ISBN: 0852928491
The fact that this book is now into its seventh edition gives an indication of its usefulness. It provides alphabetical and chronological listings of employment legislation and summarises the contents, scope, and effects of each Act in a clear,

comprehensible manner. This edition has been updated to include pivotal legislation such as the Employment Relations Act 1999 and regulations on the minimum wage and working time.

Essentials of Employment Law 7th ed
David Lewis, Malcolm Sargeant
London: Institute of Personnel and Development, 2002
389pp ISBN: 0852929390
Lewis and Sargeant have put together a comprehensible introduction to the main statutory and common-law rules in the United Kingdom that govern such issues as contracts of employment, discrimination, and union rights. Other areas covered include the sources and institutions of employment law, the national minimum wage, working time regulations, parental and maternity rights, dismissal and redundancy, health and safety, data protection, trade union recognition, and sex, race, disability, and age discrimination.

Law Society Employment Handbook
Daniel Barnett, Henry Scrope
London: Law Society Publishing, 2002
320pp ISBN: 1853287164
This is a comprehensive general employment law book with a companion website. In addition to a clear exposition of the law, the book includes a final section devoted exclusively to employment law on the Internet and incorporating an extensive directory of relevant websites, both free and subscription-based. Based on law at 1st October 2001.

Tolley's Employment Handbook 2003
Elizabeth Slade
London: Butterworths Tolley, 2003
648pp ISBN: 0754523551
This handbook seeks to explain the legislation in its context, along with the common law and EC law on employment matters. It is intended to serve as a comprehensive handbook on employment law.

Welfare Benefits and Tax Credits Handbook

Child Poverty Action Group
London, 2003
1784pp ISBN: 1901698513
This book is excellent value for money. Fully updated and revised to incorporate information on the wide-ranging changes to the UK benefits system launched in April 2003, the book offers comprehensive information on all means-tested and non-means-tested benefits.

WEBSITES

British Employment Law
www.emplaw.co.uk
This is an extensive site concerned with British employment law, in easily accessible A-Z format. The site has a substancial free area, but to get the most from it you need to purchase a password. It has a free 'employment law super portal' of hundreds of indexed employment law related links, including direct links to employment law source material on official EU and British sites.

Butterworths
www.butterworths.com
Butterworths, part of the Reed Elsevier group, is one of the leading and longest established legal publishers in the UK. Their online subscription services include two employment law sites, based respectively on their *Tolley's Handbook* and on a combination of *Harvey*, their definitive five volume loose-leaf service, and their IRLR and All England law reports. The search engine on the Butterworths site is particularly good.

CompactLaw
www.compactlaw.co.uk/emp.html
The CompactLaw document centre provides an extensive range of free factsheets, articles on recent aspects of employment law, and an employment law question-and-answer section.

Direct Access Government for Business
www.dag-business.gov.uk
This is a one-stop shop for business, developed by the Small Business Service. There are links to regulatory guidance and forms published on a range of government websites. Access is by department and subject indexes, and there is a search facility.

emplaw.co.uk
www.emplaw.co.uk
This site offers information and services to those seeking advice on employment law as well as professionals. A free area gives information on current regulations and a series of links is available to subscribers. There is also a map showing the location and contact details of employment law specialists throughout the United Kingdom. Users may register for a free monthly e-mail which brings them up to date with new initiatives.

Incomes Data Services
www.incomesdata.co.uk/brief/law.htm
The site offers news, reports, and guidance on a wide range of employment law issues. There is some free information; otherwise you are directed to the extensive range of IDS published products.

OneClick HR
www.oneclickhr.com
A truly comprehensive site on all matters concerned with HR management and personnel issues which includes a useful employment law section. The site offers a wide range of services, including specimen letters and forms (some of which are free) for use in situations from recruitment to dismissal. There is also a free daily e-mail news service.

Sweet & Maxwell
www.smlawpub.co.uk/online
Formerly CCH/Croner BELS service, Sweet & Maxwell now offers various online subscriber services, including daily case reports from the New Law online service, printed case report booklets (monthly) and journals (fortnightly) at discount prices, as well as e-mail alerts.

UK Department of Trade and Industry
www.dti.gov.uk/er
This government site contains a wealth of useful information on a wide range of issues affecting people at work. There are links to sections on employment relations, including a series of employment rights factsheets (www.dti.gov.uk/er/regs.htm), and tailored interactive guidance on employment rights. The main site covers recent consultations and press notices. The other part of the DTI website relevant to employment law is at www.dti.gov.uk/employment.

ORGANISATIONS
Advisory Conciliation and Arbitration Service (ACAS)
Rita Donaghy OBE
Brandon House, 180 Borough High Street, London, SE1 1LW
T: +44 (0) 20 7210 3613
www.acas.org.uk
ACAS is a nationwide organisation (with its head office in London) of employment relations experts. It has been working with employers, employees, trade unions and other representatives for more than 25 years. The organisation has a network of telephone helplines giving free help and information, and the Advisory Service works with hundreds of companies every year to develop a joint approach to problem-solving. Most cases going to an employment tribunal are first of all referred to ACAS to see if there is a less damaging and expensive way of sorting the problem out. The organisation also runs workshops and seminars around the country, targeting small businesses without specialist personnel sections.

Chartered Institute of Personnel and Development
Geoffrey Armstrong, Director General
CIPD House, Camp Road, Wimbledon, London, SW19 4UX
T: +44 (0) 20 8971 9000
F: +44 (0) 20 8263 3333
E: cipd@cipd.co.uk
www.cipd.co.uk
Formed in 1995 from the amalgamation of the Institute of Personnel Management and the Institute of Training and Development, the CIPD is a professional body for personnel and training professionals which aims to promote good practice in the management and development of people.

SEE ALSO
Contracts and Contracting (p. 502)
Employee Benefits/Compensation (p. 505)

Entrepreneurs

BOOKS AND DIRECTORIES
Against the Odds: An Autobiography
James Dyson
London: Texere Publishing, 2000
341pp ISBN: 1587990148
The story of man and machine, this book charts the path to the shops of James Dyson's innovative vacuum cleaner.

Boo Hoo: A Dot-com Story
Ernst Malmsten, Erik Portanger, Charles Drazin
London: Random House Business Books, 2002
416pp ISBN: 0099418371
A cautionary tale of life at the height of the dot-com boom, this book details the rise and fall of boo.com, an online fashion site. While only portraying one side of the story, this is an entertaining tale that, if nothing else, reminds the reader of the importance of backing up fantastic-sounding plans with action and funds.

Entrepreneurship 5th ed
Robert D. Hisrich, Michael P. Peters
Maidenhead: McGraw-Hill, 2001
640pp ISBN: 0071123512
This comprehensive textbook is in four sections: the entrepreneurial perspective, which provides a theoretical and historical background; creating and starting the venture, which includes a consideration of the legal issues and information on developing business, marketing, and finance plans; financing the new venture; and managing, growing, and ending the new venture. It includes a glossary and case studies.

Fostering Entrepreneurship
Organisation for Economic Co-operation and Development
Paris: The Brookings Institution, 1999
286pp ISBN: 9264161392
This book explains the importance of entrepreneurship and its benefits in terms of job creation and economic growth. It looks at ways of removing impediments and developing the conditions that enable entrepreneurs to flourish. A second section provides country-by-country information on the entrepreneurial climate, and summarises the lessons that can be learned from their experience.

Generation Entrepreneur
Stuart Crainer, Des Dearlove
Financial Times Business, 2000
266pp ISBN: 0273649205
This title looks at the future of business in the hands of 'Generation X'. This inspirational book suggests that entrepreneurship is now a 'lifestyle choice' for young people wise in the ways of e-commerce, but there are lessons here for more traditional businesses.

The HP Way
David Packard
London: HarperCollins, 1996
224pp ISBN: 0887308171
In this book, Packard charts the emergence of his technology business: Hewlett Packard. He attributes the company's success to the unique outlook of the firm, 'The HP Way', which promotes a combination of openness, honesty, and flexibility. The book should interest both entrepreneurs and technologists alike, in demonstrating the growth of a major contemporary technology company.

Inside Intel: Andy Grove and the Rise of the World's Most Powerful Chip Company
Tim Jackson
New York: Plume, 1998
432pp ISBN: 0452276438
Most of today's computers operate using Intel chips, and this book provides an account of how the company under CEO Andrew Grove rose to such global dominance. In using both public and private documents and a number of selected interviews, *Financial Times* columnist Tim Jackson charts the story of Intel from its conception to the present day.

Marketing and Entrepreneurship in SMEs: An Innovative Approach
David Carson, Stanley Cromie,
Pauric McGowan, Jimmy Hill
Upper Saddle River, New Jersey: Prentice-Hall, 1996
296pp ISBN: 0131509705
Combining entrepreneurial theory and research with marketing knowledge to give a new perspective on the small business, this book is useful as both a reference book and as a support to general business education.

Matsushita Leadership: Lessons From the 20th Century's Most Remarkable Entrepreneur
John P. Kotter
London: Simon & Schuster, 1997
320pp ISBN: 068483460X
This book chronicles the life of Japanese entrepreneur Konosuke Matsushita, founder of the Matsushita Electric Corporation and Panasonic. It pays particular attention to his visionary management and leadership style, and highlights his views on the social responsibility of business.

The MouseDriver Chronicles
John Lusk, Kyle Harrison
Cambridge, Massachusetts: Perseus, 2002
256pp ISBN: 0738205737
Lusk and Harrison, MBA graduates, narrate their experiences of starting their own company, and the problems they encountered along the way. Their product was the MouseDriver, a computer mouse fashioned as a golf club head, which experienced mixed fortunes in a volatile technology market. Lusk and Harrison describe the events leading up to the product's conception, and how they managed to support it in a continually changing market place.

WEBSITES
Entrepreneur.com
www.entrepreneur.com
This is a magazine site sponsored by Entrepreneur Media, Inc, offering a comprehensive range of practical information for owners of small businesses. The information includes a search engine, business tools, databases, newsletters, and message boards.

Entrepreneurial Edge
www.lowe.org
The Michigan-based Edward Lowe Foundation provides information and resources for entrepreneurs: news, articles, and an e-mail newsletter.

EntreWorld
www.entreworld.org
This is a collection of resources for entrepreneurs provided by the Kauffman Center for Entrepreneurial Leadership in Kansas City. Three sections focus on starting, growing, and finding support for a business. The site includes articles, a glossary, practical advice, an e-mail newsletter, an events calendar, and a bookshop.

eWeb
http://eweb.slu.edu/eweb.htm
This website is provided by Saint Louis University, and provides information on entrepreneurial education programmes, organisations, research centres, and assistance for entrepreneurs, including advice on business planning.

Global Entrepreneurship Institute
www.gcase.org
The site sponsored by this non-profit, non-governmental organisation provides open source material for entrepreneurs and managers of small businesses, and includes articles and book lists.

ORGANISATIONS
National Federation of Enterprise Agencies
Trinity Gardens, 9–11 Bromham Road, Bedford, Bedfordshire, MK40 2UQ
T: + 44 (0) 1234 354055
E: enquiries@nfea.com
www.nfea.com

The NFEA is a network of independent, non-profit local enterprise agencies for the support of small and growing businesses, especially startups and micro-businesses. The organisation aims to identify the needs of such businesses, encourage the government and others to provide the conditions for them to flourish, and provide a forum for members to share best practice. The British Volunteer Mentors Association is an initiative of the NFEA.

Small Firms Enterprise Development Initiative
5th Floor, S1 St James's, Vicar Lane, Sheffield, Yorkshire, S1 2EX
T: +44 (0) 114 241 2155
F: +44 (0) 114 241 2166
E: info@sfedi.co.uk
www.sfedi.co.uk
The SFEDI has been appointed by the UK government to identify standards of best practice for small businesses and to work with providers of small-business training, education, and advice to raise standards of support.

UK Business Incubation
Aston Science Park, Holt Street, Birmingham, West Midlands, B7 4BB
T: +44 (0) 121 250 3538
F: +44 (0) 121 250 3542
E: info@ukbi.co.uk
www.ukbi.co.uk

UKBI is a public/private sector initiative set up by the Department of Trade and Industry and HM Treasury to provide information and support for the incubator industry in the United Kingdom. The organisation runs the incubation network in the UK, lobbies on behalf of the industry, produces publications, and provides consultancy and networking opportunities.

Young Enterprise UK
Peterley House, Peterley Road, Oxford, Oxfordshire, OX4 2TZ
T: +44 (0) 1865 776845
F: +44 (0) 1865 775671
www.young-enterprise.org.uk
Young Enterprise is a national educational charity founded in 1963 to develop links between schools and industry, and to encourage young people to learn and succeed through involvement in enterprise. Programmes organised by Young Enterprise involve thousands of young people and volunteer advisors from local and national businesses. The programmes include the Company Programme, Team Enterprise, and the Entrepreneurship Masterclass.

SEE ALSO
Small and Growing Businesses (p. 478)
Venture Capital (p. 554)

Exporting

BOOKS AND DIRECTORIES
Exporter's Checklist: A Step-by-step Guide to Successful Exporting 2nd ed
Harry Twells
London: Lloyds of London Press, 1995
403pp ISBN: 1850448647
The guide takes managers through each stage of the export procedure, highlighting the pitfalls, presenting the alternative areas of action, and showing where to get help. 26 sections cover every aspect of exporting,

identifying the essential elements, and presenting them in a checklist format for ease of reference.

The Export Handbook
Harry Twells, ed
London: Kogan Page, 1998
368pp ISBN: 0749421576
Published jointly with the British Chambers of Commerce, this handbook provides an easy-to-use guide to export procedures and

documentation. It also includes a directory of suppliers of export services.

Finding Export Markets: A Guide to Methods and Information Sources in the UK and Worldwide for British Exporters 2nd ed
Douglas Tookey
Peterborough: Trade Research, 1995
38pp ISBN: 0904783340
The contents of the guide include: how to find export information—where to begin; finding markets; export buyers in the United Kingdom; sending goods abroad; Department of Trade and Industry and Foreign and Commonwealth Office services to exporters; other information sources in the United Kingdom; and export information sources listed by country.

Global Jumpstart: The Complete Resource for Expanding Small and Midsized Businesses
Ruth Stanat, Chris West
Cambridge, Massachusetts: Perseus, 2000
198pp ISBN: 073820160X
This book is a useful resource guide for companies of the size mentioned in the title who have reached any stage of the expansion process. It provides in-depth analysis of business opportunities around the world, while also giving a valuable insight into the pitfalls in international markets for small companies.

Principles of Management in Export
James Conlan
Oxford: Blackwell Business, 1994
325pp (Principles of Export Guidebooks)
ISBN: 0631191941
Using the syllabus of the Institute of Export as a basis, the author shows how all areas of export practice can be integrated. The emphasis is on profitable export management, covering the core topics of running and structuring an export business, and including all the necessary techniques and measuring and benchmarking systems for assessing profitability, setting strategic goals, and creating quantifiable reporting and control systems.

WEBSITES
British Chambers of Commerce
www.britishchambers.org.uk
The site offers an extensive range of services to member companies covering all aspects of exporting. It also provides links to all 150 local chambers.

Business Advice Online
www.businesslink.org
This is an online service provided by the Small Business Service of the UK Department of Trade and Industry. It provides an extensive range of general information for small businesses, as well as details of the services available through the network of 150 local Business Links. The latter provide face-to-face advice on exporting and importing for small businesses.

Market Access Database
www.mkaccdb.eu.int
The Market Access Database is provided by the DG Trade, European Commission. Certain parts of the site are open only to people having an ISP connection located in Europe but the section on trade barriers is open to all Internet users. The site contains details about trade barriers by market sector and country, import formalities by country and import duties by product code and by country.

Thomas Global Register
www.tgrnet.com
Formerly the American Export Register, this comprehensive web-based directory run by Thomas Publishing gives details of some 500,000 manufacturers and distributors across 22 countries, divided into 10,500 product and service classifications.

ORGANISATIONS
British Chambers of Commerce
Manning House, 22 Carlisle Place, London, SW1P 1JA
T: +44 (0) 20 7565 2000
F: +44 (0) 20 7565 2049
E: info@britishchambers.org.uk
www.britishchambers.org.uk

This is an umbrella body for a network of some 150 locally-based chambers of commerce serving local businesses and providing advice on importing and import services to member companies.

Export Credits Guarantee Department

PO Box 2200, 2 Exchange Tower, Harbour Exchange Square, London, E14 9GS
T: +44 (0) 20 7512 7000
F: +44 (0) 20 7512 7649
E: help@ecgd.gov.uk
www.ecgd.gov.uk
This government department provides export credit insurance and reinsurance for exporting companies and companies investing overseas.

HM Customs and Excise

New King's Beam House, 22 Upper Ground, London, SE1 9PJ
T: +44 (0) 845 010 9000
www.hmce.gov.uk
Her Majesty's Customs and Excise is the department responsible for administering and collecting all import duties as detailed in the Customs Tariffs. It also has specific responsibility for enforcing all prohibitions and restrictions on the export (and import) of certain classes of goods.

Institute of Export

Export House, Minerva Business Park, Lynch Wood, Peterborough, Cambridgeshire, PE2 6FT
T: +44 (0) 1733 404400
F: +44 (0) 1733 404444
E: institute@export.org.uk
www.export.org.uk

This professional membership body aims to raise standards in international trade management and export practice.

UK Trade and Investment

Kingsgate House, 66–74 Victoria Street, London, SW1E 6SE
T: +44 (0) 20 7215 8200
F: +44 (0) 20 7215 4699
www.uktradeinvest.gov.uk
Established in November 2003, this organisation combines the roles of Trade Partners UK and Invest-UK, which separately covered its remit prior to that time. UK Trade & Investment offers a wide variety of help to businesses or individuals who do business overseas (or are hoping to begin doing so).

World Trade and International Trade Rules

Trade Policy Directorate, Kingsgate House, 66–74 Victoria Street, London, SW1E 6SE
T: +44 (0) 20 7215 4557
F: +44 (0) 20 7215 4556
E: worldtrade@dti.gov.uk
www.dti.gov.uk/worldtrade/import.htm
The Department of Trade and Industry is responsible for UK trade policy at international, European, and national levels, and for harmonising customs tariff levels with European Union member states. It is also responsible, in conjunction with several other government departments, for policy on all UK export and import prohibitions and restrictions.

SEE ALSO
Importing (p. 517)

Franchising

BOOKS AND DIRECTORIES
Buying a Franchise
Phil Stone
Oxford: How To Books, 2000
63pp ISBN: 1857036182
This concise book offers advice on the various pros and cons of buying a franchise and suggests key points to consider. It covers: the basic concept of franchising; selecting the right franchise for you; evaluating a franchise; cost considerations; and what to do once the purchase is complete.

The Daily Telegraph Guide to Taking Up a Franchise 13th ed
Colin Barrow, Godfrey Golzen, Helen Kogan
London: Kogan Page, 2000
344pp ISBN: 0749433108
This book introduces the concept of franchising and summarises its advantages and disadvantages. It goes on to discuss a range of issues that need to be considered before taking up a franchise, including contracts, finance, legal and tax matters, and training, and to offer practical guidance on evaluating opportunities. Useful organisations and publications are listed, and an overview of UK franchises and international opportunities is also provided.

The Franchise Bible: How to Buy a Franchise or Franchise Your Own Business
Erwin J. Keup
Waterloo, Ontario: Entrepreneur Press, 2000
314pp ISBN: 1555715265
Aimed at both existing and prospective franchisors, this book offers practical information on what franchising entails and the benefits it can offer. Checklists and worksheets are included.

Franchise World Directory 2004: The UK Annual Directory 20th ed
Franchise World
London, 2003
208pp ISBN: 14618893
This is a comprehensive directory that provides a guide to franchises in the United Kingdom and contains a collection of articles for prospective franchisees and franchisors written by leading franchise specialists. Specimen contracts are also included.

Franchising for Dummies
Michael Seid, Dave Thomas
New York: Hungry Minds, 2000
378pp ISBN: 0764551604
A simple-to-follow but detailed guide to entering the world of franchises, this volume presents the basics, ranging from initial research, selecting locations, training employees, and running and developing the business. One of the authors is the late Dave Thomas, founder of the ultra-successful *Wendy's International*; the other is a consultant with more than 20 years of hands-on experience. Their book provides practical advice on the major issues facing those who decide to follow this route to self-employment.

The Guide to Franchising 6th ed
Martin Mendelsohn
London: Cassell, 1999
384pp ISBN: 0304704830
The author introduces franchising by describing its history and development and deals with fundamental questions such as: why franchise your business; why take up a franchise; and what can be franchised. He also provides essential information on the legal aspects of the franchise contract. Profiles of the British Franchise Association and the Franchise Consultants Association are included.

Tips and Traps When Buying a Franchise 2nd ed
Mary E. Tomzack
Oakland, California: Source Book Publications, 1999
236pp ISBN: 1887137122

The second, revised edition of this guide provides those new to franchising with information on the right questions to ask at the outset, how to find the right location, where to get loans, how to find and train employees, and the ins and outs of buying equipment. It contains war stories and success secrets from a wide variety of franchisees operating in different industry sectors.

WEBSITES
British Franchise Association
www.british-franchise.org
The British Franchise Association's site offers a comprehensive range of advice and information on all aspects of franchising from the perspectives of both franchisors and franchisees, including risk assessments and sources of finance. It also provides useful links to other relevant sites.

Entrepreneur
www.entrepreneur.com
This site is a good source of information for those interested in going into business for themselves for the first time, with an informative page on franchising as well as pages covering management, advertising and marketing.

Franchising.org
www.franchising.org
This is a useful US site with links to many other franchise organisations. Articles, advice, and information are also provided.

Franinfo
www.franinfo.com
This site provides an overview of franchising, as well as advice and guidance. It contains two self-tests to determine whether you are suited to being a franchisee.

International Franchising
www.franchiseintl.com
This is a guide to international franchising and offers detailed profiles of a number of franchisors.

Nolo-Law for All
www.nolo.com
This is a good source of legal information, some of which is specifically related to franchising.

Small Business Administration
www.sba.gov
This US government site provides information about resources available to those who need help with their entrepreneurial efforts, including finding, financing, and locating workshops and training.

ORGANISATIONS
British Franchise Association
Thames View, Newtown Road, Henley-on-Thames, Oxfordshire, RG9 1HG
T: +44 (0) 1491 578050
F: +44 (0) 1491 573517
E: mailroom@british-franchise.org.uk
www.british-franchise.org
The BFA was formed in 1977 to promote high standards of practice in franchising; member companies adhere to a code of ethics drawn up by the Association. It also provides a comprehensive range of information to both member and nonmember organisations through its extensive website and publications. It is affiliated to the World Franchise Council and the European Franchise Federation.

European Franchise Federation
Avenue 179, B-100, 1070 Brussels, Belgium
T: +32 2 520 16 07
F: +32 2 520 35 17
E: eff-franchise@euronet.be
www.eff-franchise.com
The Federation is an international non-profit organisation, founded in 1972, that aims to promote franchising in Europe and the interests of the national franchise associations or federations that make up its membership.

SEE ALSO
Small and Growing Businesses (p. 478)

Importing

BOOKS AND DIRECTORIES
Building an Import/Export Business 2nd ed
Kenneth D. Weiss
Chichester: John Wiley, 1997
288pp ISBN: 0471177873
This is a user-friendly guide to starting and building a successful import or export business. It gives guidance on potential areas of concern, such as operational procedures, trade agreements, and marketing techniques. It also provides practical advice on how best to tap into the lucrative global markets. It includes bibliographical references and an index.

The Importer's Handbook: A Practical Guide to Successful Importing 2nd ed
Jack Butler
Hemel Hempstead: Woodhead Faulkner, 1994
163pp ISBN: 0859419134
This handbook explains the structure and regulation of international trade, and deals with best practice in importing, import administration and documentation, and the impact of new technology.

Import/Export: How to Get Started in International Trade 3rd ed
Carl Nelson
Maidenhead: McGraw-Hill, 2000
340pp ISBN: 0071358714
This book is aimed at those wanting to make a start in international trade. Fully revised and including a section on e-commerce, it sets out to guide beginners through the myriad challenges of importing and exporting.

WEBSITES
Business Advice Online
www.businesslink.org
This is an online service provided by the Small Business Service of the UK Department of Trade and Industry. It provides an extensive range of general information for small businesses, as well as details of the services available through the network of 150 local Business Links. The latter provide face-to-face advice on exporting and importing for small businesses.

Kelly's Directory
www.kellys.co.uk
This online searchable database lists over 140,000 UK manufacturers and service organisations under 50,000 product headings. A print media version of the database may also be purchased.

Kompass
www.kompass.com
This online searchable database lists some 1.6 million companies in about 70 countries under approximately 50,000 product/service codes. The databases for individual countries may also be purchased in printed format.

Market Access Database
www.mkaccdb.eu.int
The Market Access Database is provided by the DG Trade, European Commission. Certain parts of the site are open only to people having an ISP connection located in Europe, but the section on trade barriers is open to all Internet users. The site contains details about trade barriers by market sector and country, import formalities by country, and import duties by product code and by country.

Thomas Global Register
www.tgrnet.com
Formerly the American Export Register, this comprehensive Web-based directory run by Thomas Publishing gives details of some 500,000 manufacturers and distributors across 22 countries, divided into 10,500 product and service classifications.

ORGANISATIONS
British Chambers of Commerce
Manning House, 22 Carlisle Place, London, SW1P 1JA
T: +44 (0) 20 7565 2000
F: +44 (0) 20 7565 2049
E: info@britishchambers.org.uk
www.britishchambers.org.uk
This is an umbrella body for a network of some 150 locally-based chambers of commerce serving local businesses and providing advice on importing and import services to member companies.

Department of Trade and Industry
Trade Policy, Kingsgate House, 66–74 Victoria Street, London, SW1E 6SE
T: +44 (0) 20 7215 4557
F: +44 (0) 20 7215 4556
E: dti.enquiries@dti.gsi.gov.uk
www.dti.gov.uk/worldtrade/import.htm
The Department of Trade and Industry is responsible for UK trade policy at international, European, and national levels, and for harmonising customs tariff levels with European Union member states. It is also responsible, in conjunction with several other government departments, for policy on all UK export and import prohibitions and restrictions.

HM Customs and Excise
New King's Beam House, 22 Upper Ground, London, SE1 9PJ
T: +44 (0) 845 010 9000
www.hmce.gov.uk
Her Majesty's Customs and Excise is the department responsible for administering and collecting all import duties as detailed in the Customs Tariffs. It also has specific responsibility for enforcing all prohibitions and restrictions on the export (and import) of certain classes of goods.

Simpler Trade Procedures Board (SITPRO)
Oxford House, 76 Oxford Street, London, W10 1BS
T: +44 (0) 20 7467 7280
F: +44 (0) 20 7467 7295
E: info@sitpro.org.uk
www.sitpro.org.uk
SITPRO is dedicated to giving practical help to UK exporters and importers. In addition the site offers ElecTra toolkits for paperless international trade and is currently preparing a WebElecTra system.

SEE ALSO
Exporting (p. 512)

Intellectual Property

BOOKS AND DIRECTORIES
Copyright Theft
John Gurnsey
Aldershot: Gower, 1995
208pp ISBN: 0566076314
Gurnsey's book attempts to cover all forms of copyright theft. It reviews both commercial and domestic theft, incorporating the experiences of a wide range of organisations. Book, electronic, database, audio, video, games, and multimedia publishing are all considered, as is the question of whether existing laws can effectively serve a rapidly changing industry.

From Ideas to Assets: Investing Wisely in Intellectual Property
Bruce M. Berman, ed
Chichester: John Wiley, 2001
624pp ISBN: 0471400688
Based on the experience of expert contributors, the book argues that corporations need to understand what their intellectual property assets are and how to protect their rights to them. It covers such topics as maximising returns on intellectual property assets, valuing those assets, and discerning performance variables.

How to Prepare a UK Patent Application

Patent Office
Newport, 1999
28pp
This pamphlet provides a layman's guide to the preparation of an application for a UK patent. Guidance on the subsequent procedures is also given.

Patent It Yourself 9th ed

David Pressman
Berkeley, California: Nolo Press, 2002
512pp ISBN: 0873378016
As an experienced patent attorney and former patent examiner of the US Patent and Trademark Office (PTO), David Pressman has developed a very useful guide containing all the instructions and forms necessary to patent an invention in the United States. The book offers comprehensive and up-to-date advice for obtaining a high quality patent and presents the information in a user-friendly, jargon-free, and well-illustrated way.

Patent Protection

Patent Office
Newport, 1999
24pp
This publication provides a brief introduction to the system for obtaining patents in the United Kingdom. An outline of the procedures involved in applying for European and international patents is also given.

Protecting Intellectual Property 2nd ed

Richard R. Halstead
Hemel Hempstead: ICSA Publishing, 1995
192pp ISBN: 1872860931
This book explains the different types of intellectual property rights available, such as trade marks, registered designs, and copyright. It covers the practical issues of how businesses can protect and exploit intellectual property rights, including how to avoid infringement, and what happens during court proceedings. This revision takes account of the UK Trade Mark Law and the Community Trade Mark.

Protecting Your #1 Asset: Creating Fortunes from Your Ideas—An Intellectual Property Handbook

Michael A. Lechter
London: Warner Books, 2001
276pp ISBN: 0446678317
Placing its emphasis on protecting intellectual property (IP), this book makes the case for understanding developments in this arena. It covers topics including identifying and benefiting from IP assets, using IP assets to build barriers to competition, licensing IP assets, and using IP assets to attract investors and raise capital.

Registering a Trade Mark

Patent Office
Newport, 1999
24pp
This publication is intended as an official guide to the legal and regulatory procedures for registering a trade mark in the United Kingdom.

Understanding Copyright in a Week

Graham Cornish
London: Hodder & Stoughton, 2000
96pp (Business in a Week Series)
ISBN: 0340782412
This introductory text, written in friendly, accessible language, will help you understand what copyright is, why it is important to respect it, and how you can make use of copyright law in business, management, and everyday life.

What is Intellectual Property?

Patent Office
Newport, 1997
15pp
This booklet provides an introduction to the different types of intellectual property rights that give legal recognition and protection from exploitation to the owners of new ideas, inventions, and brand names. The areas covered include copyright, patents, trade names, and design rights. Together, all the Patent Office booklets mentioned provide comprehensive coverage of IP issues.

WEBSITES

Copyright and Fair Use: Stanford University Libraries
http://fairuse.stanford.edu

The site provides a quick search facility and overview of copyright law, with links to Internet resources, current legislation, cases, judicial opinions, and regulations.

Copyright Clearance Center
www.copyright.com

Copyright Clearance Center, Inc, the largest licenser of text reproduction rights in the world, was formed in 1978 to facilitate compliance with US copyright law. It provides licensing systems for the reproduction and distribution of copyrighted materials in print and electronic formats throughout the world.

The Copyright Licensing Agency
www.cla.co.uk

The Agency is the United Kingdom's reproduction rights organisation—the UK equivalent of the US Copyright Clearance Center.

Intellectual Property
www.intellectual-property.gov.uk

This site gives information and advice on patents, trademarks, design, and copyright with links to the relevant government departments. It also addresses key questions on protection, permissions, and enforcing rights.

International Intellectual Property Alliance
www.iipa.com

Sponsored by a private-sector coalition formed to protect US copyrighted material around the world, the site offers articles on a variety of IP topics and country-specific copyright information.

UK Patent Office
www.patent.gov.uk

The website of the UK government department responsible for intellectual property—copyright, patents, designs, and trade marks—has a section of links to government, academic, and general IP sites.

United States Copyright Office
www.loc.gov/copyright

The US Copyright Office is located in the Library of Congress. The site has a section for FAQs and another for requests relating to the Freedom of Information Act, besides material on copyright legislation and an international section with links to the WIPO.

United States Patent and Trademark Office
www.uspto.gov

The PTO promotes industrial and technological progress in the United States and strengthens the national economy by administering the laws relating to patents and trademarks, and advising the US government on patent, trademark, and copyright protection, and on trade-related aspects of intellectual property.

World Intellectual Property Organization
www.wipo.org

WIPO is a Geneva-based specialised agency of the United Nations whose mandate is to promote the protection of intellectual property worldwide. It administers 21 treaties in the field of intellectual property—15 covering industrial property and six covering copyright. The first general group of treaties defines internationally agreed basic standards of intellectual property in each of the 177 member states.

Logistics and Distribution

BOOKS AND DIRECTORIES
Fundamentals of Logistics
Douglas M. Lambert, James R. Stock,
Lisa M. Ellram
Maidenhead: McGraw-Hill, 1997
640pp ISBN: 0256141177
This book offers a unique take on the area
of logistics, approaching the topic from
both a marketing and customer service
perspective. The text emphasises concept
and context over actual system design
proposals. The book is considered
noteworthy for its insistence that logistics is
much more than solving transportation
problems—it is a fully integrated science
demanding customer service and internal
organisational attention.

The Handbook of Logistics and Distribution Management 2nd ed
Alan Rushton, John Oxley, Phil Croucher
London: Kogan Page, 2000
582pp ISBN: 0749433655
Written to appeal to both students and
experienced managers, this handbook
explains the basics of modern logistics and
distribution. The authors explain the
fundamental concepts of logistics and
include discussions of warehousing,
transport, and information and control
systems.

WEBSITES
Digital Neighbors
**www.digital-neighbors.com/news/
industry/logistics.htm**
This website is updated regularly
throughout the day. It focuses on logistics
industry news, cataloguing logistics news
from the United States as well as stories of
international interest. The site is searchable
by city, country, and industry, so any
specific questions about logistics capacity in
certain regions can generally be answered
in a timely way.

The Logistics Network
www.logisticsnetwork.com
This site offers a wide selection of
information for the logistics manager,
including a discussion forum, news,
employment information, and
recommended readings.

Logistics World
www.logisticsworld.com
This site provides a directory of logistics
resources, including subsites devoted to
a range of issues, including freight,
transportation, supply chain management,
warehousing, and distribution. It is also
home of the WWW Virtual Library of
Logistics.

Loglink
www.loglink.com
This is a gateway website featuring
hundreds of links to providers of logistics
support, from freight, air, and rail transport,
to straight logistics, to providers of logistical
software, to warehousing and distribution
services.

ORGANISATIONS
European Logistics Association
Avenue des Arts 19/ Kunstlaan 19, B-1210
Brussels, Belgium
T: +32 2 230 02 11
F: +32 2 230 81 23
E: ela@elalog.org
www.elalog.org
The ELA is a federation of 36 Western
European national logistics associations. It
aims to provide a link and an open forum for
any individual or society concerned with
logistics. The ELA formulates European
logistics education standards and has
established a vocational qualification
procedure to enable the standards to be
accepted by businesses on a pan-European
basis.

Institute of Logistics and Transport
Logistics and Transport Centre, PO Box
5787, Corby, Northamptonshire, NN17 4XQ
T: + 44 (0) 1536 740100
F: + 44 (0) 1536 740101
E: enquiry@iolt.org.uk
www.iolt.org.uk
The Institute exists to promote professional
excellence and social responsibility in the
fields of transport and supply-chain

management. Formed in 1999 from the
integration of the Institute of Logistics and
the Chartered Institute of Transport, the
IoLT offers members a range of activities
and benefits, including development
programmes and information services. A
number of special-interest groups
enable members to network and share
experiences with like-minded
individuals.

Management Buy-outs

BOOKS AND DIRECTORIES
The Art of M&A: A Merger Acquisition Buyout Guide
Stanley Foster Reed, Alexandra Reed Lajoux
Maidenhead: McGraw-Hill, 1999
1011pp ISBN: 0070526605
Presented in a question-and-answer format,
this book looks at over 1,000 aspects of
mergers, acquisitions, and buy-outs.
Questions covered range from locating a
suitable target to closing and post-merger
integration. The book gives real-world
insights through synopses of dozens of
landmark cases and includes sample forms
and checklists.

Buyout: The Insider's Guide to Buying Your Own Company
Rick Rickersten, et al
New York: AMACOM, 2001
304pp ISBN: 0814406262
This book gives you the tools and strategies
you need to lead a successful management
buy-out. It includes everything from how to
select the company you want to buy,
through due diligence issues and finding
equity partners, to running the company
when you succeed in your buy-out.

Management Buyout: A Guide for the Prospective Entrepreneur 2nd ed
Ian Webb
Aldershot: Gower, 1990
176pp ISBN: 0566028107
This book provides an introduction to the
process of achieving a successful buy-out
and considers the financial and legal issues

involved. It reviews the development of
the buy-out market in the United Kingdom
and considers the relevance of an
entrepreneurial mindset to buyout
situations. Five case studies are included.

Successful Acquisition of Unquoted Companies: A Practical Guide 4th ed
Barrie Pearson
Aldershot: Gower, 1999
168pp ISBN: 0566080990
This practical guide is designed to help
anyone who undertakes the acquisition of
an unquoted company or a subsidiary of a
quoted one. It explains the process of
investigating a potential acquisition, and a
checklist is provided. Management buy-outs
and buy-ins and the process of selling a
business to maximise shareholder value are
also covered.

WEBSITES
Are You Management Buyout Material?
www.cfo.com/Article?article=2117
Management buy-outs are not for everyone.
It takes the right team with appropriate
backing. This checklist can help you
determine whether you have what it takes
to be successful.

Survey of the Economic and Social Impact of Management Buyouts and Buyins in Europe
**www.pwcglobal.com/fr/pwc_pdf/
pwc_economic_impact_of_buyouts.pdf**

This site contains the full text of a report based on a pan-European survey conducted by the Centre for Management Buy-Out Research (CMBOR) on behalf of the European Private Equity and Venture Capital Association.

ORGANISATIONS
Centre for Management Buyout Research
Nottingham University Business School, Jubilee Campus, Wollaton Road, Nottingham, Nottinghamshire, NG8 1BB
T: +44 (0) 115 951 5493
F: +44 (0) 115 951 5204
E: margaret.burdett@nottingham.ac.uk
www.nottingham.ac.uk/business/Cmbor

The CMBOR was founded by Barclays Private Equity Limited and Deloitte & Touche at the Nottingham University Business School in March 1986 to monitor and analyse management buy-outs in a comprehensive and objective way. A database of MBOs in the United Kingdom and Europe has been developed, and quarterly reviews and research papers are published.

SEE ALSO
Venture Capital (p. 554)

Marketing Management

BOOKS AND DIRECTORIES
The 22 Immutable Laws of Marketing: Violate Them at Your Own Risk!
Al Ries, Jack Trout
London: HarperCollins, 1994
132pp ISBN: 0887306667
Designed by marketing strategists for marketing strategists, this illustrated book contains 22 practical rules aimed at promoting the readers' success in global marketing.

101 Ways to Market Your Business
Andrew Griffiths
London: Allen and Unwin, 2001
272pp ISBN: 1865083860
Packed full of practical yet simple marketing ideas for business owners, this book will be a huge help to anyone thinking of setting up or running a small business. The book steers clear of theory and concentrates instead on easy-to-follow advice that should reap rewards.

The Anatomy of Buzz: Creating Word of Mouth Marketing
Emanuel Rosen
London: HarperCollins, 2001
320pp ISBN: 0006531601

Rosen discusses the benefits of 'word of mouth' marketing, and explores the capacity of large companies to exploit this strategy.

Direct and Database Marketing
Graeme McCorkell
London: Institute of Direct Marketing/ Kogan Page, 1997
315pp ISBN: 0749419601
The best UK introduction to direct marketing, this book was written to be read from cover to cover and contains some good small business examples. This text is also useful to dip into for examples of how direct marketing campaigns are measured and evaluated.

The End of Marketing As We Know It
Sergio Zyman
London: HarperCollins, 2000
257pp ISBN: 0006531849
In this title, the author argues that for marketing to be truly efficient, it must sell the product and not merely focus on advertising image. The book contains several stories concerning campaigns at Coca-Cola, where Zyman was chief marketing officer.

Getting Business to Come to You

Douglas Edwards
New York: J P Tarcher, 1998
686pp ISBN: 087477845X
A popular book aimed at helping businesses expand their customer base and increase their market. Although written from a US perspective, the tips and examples offered work well wherever your business is located.

Gonzo Marketing: Winning through Worst Practices

Christopher Locke
Oxford: Capstone Publishing/Perseus, 2001
256pp ISBN: 1841121665
This book is a knuckle-whitening ride to the place where social criticism, biting satire, and serious commerce meet—and where the outdated ideals of mass marketing and broadcast media are being left in the dust. As master of ceremonies at the wake for traditional one-size-fits-all marketing, Locke has assembled a unique guest list of expert witnesses, from Geoffrey Chaucer to Hunter S. Thompson, to guide us through the revolution that is rocking business today, as people connect on the Web to form powerful micromarkets. These networked communities, based on candour, trust, passion, and a general disdain for anything that smacks of corporate smugness, reflect much deeper trends in our culture, which Locke illuminates with his characteristic wit.

Guerilla Marketing for the Home-based Business

Jay Levinson, Seth Godin
Boston, Massachusetts: Houghton Mifflin, 1995
240pp ISBN: 0395742838
From the authors of the acclaimed *Guerilla Marketing*, this book offers advice on the most productive marketing strategies and techniques for home-based businesses. Aimed at anyone thinking of starting a business for the first time, or those in business already, the book focuses on the importance of customer service, direct mail, word-of-mouth marketing, and positioning.

Guerrilla Marketing with Technology: Unleashing the Full Potential of Your Small Business

Jay Conrad Levinson
London: Perseus, 1997
224pp ISBN: 0201328046
A good introduction to the 'guerrilla' concept for SMEs, this book takes a simple question-and-answer approach to implementing innovating and exciting ideas.

Inside the Tornado

Geoffrey A. Moore
Oxford: Capstone, 1998
264pp ISBN: 190096158X
This book addresses the ever-changing face of market-focused business, aiming to highlight the importance of adapting to keep up with competitors. Moore uses examples from inside the industry to discuss a range of managerial strategies, and how they can be usefully applied in today's marketing world.

It's Not About Size: Bigger Brands for Smaller Business

Paul Dickinson
London: Virgin Books, 2001
203pp (Virgin Business Guides)
ISBN: 0753505932
This book aims to address comprehensively the issue of branding and its importance for small businesses. It covers a range of key challenges, including finding out what is best for your customers, which media will get your message across best, how to use advertising to differentiate yourself from your competitors, and how to increase profits through canny branding.

Kotler on Marketing: How to Create, Win, and Dominate Markets

Philip Kotler
London: Free Press, 1999
257pp ISBN: 0684850338
In this title, Kotler discusses his ideas on how marketing programmes should be approached by executives. The book is divided into several sections addressing strategy, tactics, administrative issues, and

transformational marketing. The latter is a term the author uses to describe the effect of new technology, such as the Internet and cable TV, on marketing practice.

Marketing Warfare

Al Ries, Jack Trout
Maidenhead: McGraw-Hill, 1997
224pp ISBN: 0070527261
A 'military' approach to the world of marketing—Ries and Trout aim to teach marketers tough strategies, both defensive and offensive, to deal with the competition in an objective, tactical manner.

Permission Marketing: Turning Strangers into Friends, and Friends into Customers

Seth Godin, Don Peppers
London: Simon & Schuster, 1999
255pp ISBN: 0684856360
In this title, the authors claim that traditional forms of advertising such as magazines and radio are no longer sufficient in themselves. They assert that what is most important is to find a way of luring the customers into giving some of their time, and then creating a lasting relationship with them. The book backs up this theory concerning what they call 'permission marketing' by discussing the techniques and tactics of some of the companies who use it.

Real Time: Preparing for the Age of the Never Satisfied Customer

Regis McKenna
Boston, Massachusetts: Harvard Business School Press, 1999
224pp ISBN: 0875847943
In this book, McKenna addresses the issue of what customers expect from the modern world. In order to fulfil customer expectations, he argues, companies must be prepared to adapt to the increasingly rapid modes of global communication (e-mail, fax, etc). McKenna aims to clarify the abstract notion of collecting and using 'real time', with the view that this can lead to greater organisational success and consumer satisfaction.

Relationship Marketing: Successful Strategies for the Age of the Customer

Regis McKenna
Harlow: Addison Wesley Publishing, 1993
242pp ISBN: 0201622408
McKenna focuses on the importance of building strong bonds in the marketing world, in order to gain success and become dominant in the marketplace. He provides industry examples to help outline ways of achieving market ownership.

Selling the Invisible

Harry Beckwith
London: Texere Publishing, 2001
272pp ISBN: 1587990660
Selling the Invisible is aimed at marketers who work to promote a service ('the invisible') rather than a tangible product. The book contains a large range of practical suggestions and ideas, addressing some new developments in marketing, and discussing how an organisation can use them to best effect.

Successful Direct Marketing Methods 7th ed

Bob Stone, Ron Jacobs
Maidenhead: McGraw-Hill, 2001
579pp ISBN: 0658001450
This newly updated edition provides a classic guide to direct marketing, combining new media with traditional marketing strategies to provide effective direct marketing to consumers. The content includes identifying and meeting consumers' needs, business-to-business marketing, and e-commerce techniques, such as branding strategies for Internet sites.

Successful Marketing for the Small Business 5th ed

Dave Patten
London: Kogan Page, 2001
271pp (Business Enterprise Guides)
ISBN: 0749435240
An updated edition of this popular book, which aims to show how organisations can benefit from tackling marketing effectively. Aimed at those thinking of starting a

business or those running one already, this book is full of practical advice on a range of key issues including advertising, market research, promotion, launches, and exporting.

WEBSITES
Guerrilla Marketing
www.gmarketing.com
This is the online home of the very successful 'Guerrilla Marketing' series of books. Users may subscribe to a free weekly newsletter offering marketing tips.

ORGANISATIONS
Chartered Institute of Marketing
Moor Hall, Cookham, Maidenhead, Berkshire, SL6 9QH

T: +44 (0) 1628 427500
F: +44 (0) 1628 427499
E: marketing@cim.co.uk
www.cim.co.uk
The CIM is the main organisation for professional marketers in the United Kingdom. It runs courses, holds examinations, produces publications, and offers information services covering all aspects of marketing.

SEE ALSO
Advertising (p. 491)
Direct Marketing (p. 503)
Market Research and Competitor Intelligence (p. 526)
Public Relations (p. 542)
Selling and Salesmanship (p. 546)

Market Research and Competitor Intelligence

BOOKS AND DIRECTORIES
Managing Frontiers in Competitive Intelligence
Craig S. Fleisher, David Blenkhorn
Westport, Connecticut: Quorum Books, 2000
328pp ISBN: 1567203841
This book is a nice balance of the theoretical and the practical aspects of Competitive Intelligence (CI). While describing the best practices in the industry, the authors present the steps necessary to counter CI. They provide information on how to improve your intelligence collection process, methods, and tools. Significantly, they tie CI back to the needs of the business and point out its interface with finance, research and development, and product development.

Marketing Research 7th ed
David A. Aaker, V. Kumar, George S. Day
Chichester: John Wiley, 2000
768pp ISBN: 0471363405
This text adopts a 'macro-micro-macro' approach towards marketing research and its uses within organisations. The authors initially explore the uses and place of

marketing research in managerial decision making, as well as the industry itself (briefly examining both suppliers and users) at macro-level. The authors also examine the processes of marketing research in more depth, including industry examples to fulfil the micro phase of the text. Provides coverage of the most recent research techniques.

Marketing Research for Managers
Sunny Crouch, Matt Housden
Oxford: Butterworth Heinemann, 2003
352pp ISBN: 0750654538
This is one of the leading UK texts for managers seeking to understand market research. Rather than proffering over-detailed explanations of how to undertake research, this book explains enough for managers to be able to commission worthwhile research from professionals.

Market Research Matters: Tools and Techniques for Aligning Your Business
Robert Duboff, Jim Spaeth
Chichester: John Wiley, 2000
320pp ISBN: 0471360058

The authors explain the value of market research and forecasting techniques to successful business strategies. They describe the tools and techniques that enable analysts to anticipate marketplace shifts and the methods of using them. Among other topics, they discuss customer loyalty, brand management, competition, distribution channels, employee performance and loyalty, and the Internet. Diagnostic material to allow readers to assess the progress of their business in each area is also included.

The Market Research Toolbox: A Concise Guide for Beginners
Edward F. McQuarrie
London: Sage, 1996
172pp ISBN: 0803958579
The book is aimed at less experienced market researchers who want to link market research to their business decisions. It defines market research and explores some of its different types, as well as exploring what beneficial results can be expected from meeting objectives. In describing six main market research techniques, the author examines a range of details from how they work to cost. He also discusses recent, less traditional types of market research. Finally, he details five common business applications that can be addressed using a combined research strategy.

Market Research Using Forecasting in Business
Peter Clifton, Hai Hguyen, Susan Nutt
Oxford: Butterworth-Heinemann, 1992
294pp ISBN: 0750601531
The book is written from the viewpoint of people who are responsible for forecasting business results in large companies on the marketing side. It indicates the resources available to in-house forecasters, such as company sales figures and collections of industry statistics, and provides a comprehensive guide to the tools of analysis and statistics. Above all, it stresses the role of the analyst as a supporter of the entrepreneur in the tasks of fostering

growth in new or unfamiliar areas and effectively exploiting new opportunities when they are offered.

Millennium Intelligence: Understanding and Conducting Competitive Intelligence in the Digital Age
Jerry P. Miller
Medford, New Jersey: Information Today, 2000
240pp ISBN: 0910965285
Miller has assembled a thinktank of practising experts in Competitive Intelligence (CI). Together they lay out the reasons for conducting a planned and thought out CI programme for your company. Their book details the skills required, the tools and methods available for gathering and analysing the information, and the reasons and methods to do so in an ethical and legal manner.

Proven Strategies in Competitive Intelligence: Lessons from the Trenches
John E. Prescott, Stephen H. Miller, eds
Chichester: John Wiley, 2001
288pp ISBN: 0471401781
The editors have assembled a collection of articles that identify and explore proven practicable approaches to competitive intelligence that can be applied across a variety of business areas. Once the concept of competitive intelligence has been introduced and its legal and ethical boundaries have been explored, further contributions from leading executives and market leaders highlight the best techniques that can be used to outwit and outperform current, emerging, and potential competitors.

The WarRoom Guide to Competitive Intelligence
Steven M. Shaker, Mark P. Gembicki
Maidenhead: McGraw-Hill, 1998
240pp ISBN: 007058057X
This book is written for managers who want to use information more intelligently, with a view to improving corporate strategies. The authors advise business leaders on gathering and analysing information in

order to become more competitive within the industry. They also explore ways of creating a 'WarRoom' within an individual organisation in which to collate information for future use.

WEBSITES
ECNext
www.ecnext.com
This is a site offering online access to a database of business and market intelligence from global publishers.

Esomar Glossary
www.esomar.nl/EGlossary.htm
This glossary of market research terms seeks to explain frequently used marketing research terms in language that someone new to the industry can easily understand.

Euromonitor International
www.euromonitor.com
In-depth strategic analysis and up-to-date market statistics and market reports are all available to purchase online from this site.

Key Note Market Information Centre
www.keynote.co.uk
This site is run by suppliers of market research reports, which are available for purchase, and provides free executive summaries.

Market Research.com
www.marketresearch.com
Collecting reports from all over the world, marketresearch.com is one of the largest collectors of published research on the Web. Reports can be bought and managed with a personal account, and the site has other features such as an e-mail update service.

@ResearchInfo.com
www.researchinfo.com
This site is a remarkable collection of information on the market research industry. It includes the Market Research Roundtable, a directory of research companies, software reviews, and market research calculators.

ORGANISATIONS
Association of European Market Research Institutes
35 Perrymead Street, London, SW6 3SN
T: +44 (0) 20 7736 4445
F: +44 (0) 20 7371 9542
E: info@aemri.org
www.aemri.org
The Association is a representative organisation for market research institutes in Europe and other parts of the world.

British Market Research Association
Devonshire House, 60 Goswell Road, London, EC1M 7AD
T: +44 (0) 20 7566 3636
F: +44 (0) 20 7689 6220
E: admin@bmra.org.uk
www.bmra.org.uk
The BMRA aims to represent and promote the professional and commercial interests of its members, to increase the professionalism of market research, and to promote confidence in the market research industry generally.

EFAMRO
26 Chester Close North, Regent's Park, London, NW1 4JE
T: +44 (0) 20 7224 3873
www.efamro.org
EFAMRO is a federation of market research agency associations in the European Union founded in 1992. Its aims are to represent the interests of its members and to maintain high standards in the industry. Members adhere to the ICC/ESOMAR International Code of Marketing and Social Research Practice.

Market Research Quality Standards Association
6 Walkfield Drive, Epsom Downs, Surrey, KT18 5UF
T: +44 (0) 1737 379261
F: +44 (0) 1737 351171
E: gwareing@lineone.net
The main aim of the Association is to develop minimum standards for market research.

The Market Research Society
15 Northburgh Street, London, EC1V 0JR
T: +44 (0) 20 7490 4911
F: +44 (0) 20 7490 0608
E: info@mrs.org.uk
www.mrs.org.uk
The MRS sets and enforces the ethical standards to be observed by research practitioners. Its framework of qualifications and membership grades reflects the education, knowledge, and competence required for the effective conduct of market research.

Negotiation

BOOKS AND DIRECTORIES
Business Negotiation: A Practical Workbook
Paul T. Steele, Tom Beasor
Aldershot: Gower, 1999
270pp ISBN: 0566080729
This practical textbook provides a step-by-step guide to acquiring key negotiating skills and the techniques for using them successfully, as well as identifying the key topics in negotiation. Each chapter includes a checklist of the key points made and exercises for applying what has been learned.

Difficult Conversations
Douglas Stone, Bruce Patton, Sheila Heen
London: Penguin, 2000
272pp ISBN: 014027782X
This book aims to help readers to become calm and assertive in difficult situations (such as asking for a pay rise, or experiencing problems with colleagues). In discussing the different emotions and requirements that arise from such conversations, the book aims to pinpoint ways of managing them more effectively.

Negotiating in a Week
Peter Fleming
London: Hodder & Stoughton, 2003
96pp (In a Week)
ISBN: 0340849541
A revised edition of this popular book, this aid to negotiation aims to provide a framework for successful negotiation. The book includes information on how to research, prepare an argument, summarise, and conclude.

Negotiating Skills
Tim Hindle
London: Dorling Kindersley, 1998
72pp (Essential Managers)
ISBN: 0751305316
A helpful introduction to the art of negotiation, including information on how to prepare your argument, brief a team, maintain good relations, and close a deal. The book is full of practical advice on how to achieve the best result.

The Negotiation Toolkit: How to Get Exactly What You Want in Any Business or Personal Situation
Roger J. Volkema
New York: AMACOM, 1999
208pp ISBN: 081448008X
This book offers a guide to negations aimed at helping people build the skills and self-confidence to become good negotiators. It explores the golden rule of negotiation, explains when not to negotiate, discusses the issue of tough negotiators and how to deal with them, describes the tactics, skills, and behaviours of star negotiators, looks at cross-cultural negotiations, and provides ways to measure your own skills.

The Power of Nice: How to Negotiate So Everyone Wins—Especially You!
Ronald M. Shapiro, Mark A. Jankowski, James Dale
Chichester: John Wiley, 2001
304pp ISBN: 0471080721
This book is based on Shapiro's belief that negotiation works best if two negotiators can build a common bond between them. In exploring this theory, Shapiro offers advice

on various types of negotiation, and on creating effective proposals.

Thinking on Your Feet in Negotiations: Rapid Response Tactics
Jane Hodgson
Harlow: Prentice Hall, 1999
252pp ISBN: 0273644998
This is a manager's guide to the latest techniques for developing negotiation skills, thinking creatively in situations which need a quick response, building a good rapport with colleagues and clients, dealing effectively with conflicts, and solving problems.

WEBSITES
Interneg – For and About Negotiation
http://interneg.org/interneg/links/learning.html

This site is a directory of resources for the negotiation field with links to numerous other sites, covering areas from training and teaching materials to games to programmes and seminars.

Mediate.com
www.mediate.com
This site provides articles and news on mediation, conflict resolution, and arbitration. It also includes information about training, events, organisations, and academic courses in this field.

SEE ALSO
Pricing (p. 537)

New Product Development

BOOKS AND DIRECTORIES
Developing New Product Concepts
Christopher Miller
Harrisburg, Pennsylvania: Pennsylvania Chamber Educational Foundation, 1999
151pp ISBN: 1929744048
This is a workbook useful for individuals or small groups in the early stages of the development process. It has more than 125 pages of exercises, checklists, fill-in pages, and sample forms to guide you through the practical steps of creative problem-solving.

Managing the Design Factory: The Product Developer's Toolkit
Donald Reinertsen
London: Free Press, 1997
256pp ISBN: 0684839911
This book applies product development principles and integrates them with management theories. In short, it shows how the two sides of the coin must work together for successful product launching. Management theories and principles are not always incorporated well in practice with a design team. Reinertsen has practical ideas about how to make sure the entire creative team is 'speaking the same language' as a product launch moves from idea to reality.

Marketing the Unknown: Developing Market Strategies for Technical Innovations
Paul Millier
Chichester: John Wiley, 1999
248pp ISBN: 0471986216
How do you make a product successful? This is one of the basic questions that this practical book sets out to answer. It also discusses what is the best process to follow, and how you choose or transform markets so as to ensure a successful launch. It paves the way for marketing, for R and D, and for project managers in industrial organisations to launch and market innovations successfully in a very competitive field, and outlines strategies for further development.

Product Juggernauts: How Companies Mobilize to Generate a Stream of Market Winners

Jean-Philippe Deschamps, P. Ranganath Nayak
Boston, Massachusetts: Harvard Business School Press, 1995
472pp ISBN: 0875843417
The authors cite stories from real companies around the world to illustrate guidelines for determining the products customers want and designing the products they want to buy. Examples used to demonstrate the importance of company-wide focus on product include (among others) Ford, Canon, and Toshiba. Using these case studies, the authors demonstrate how organisations can achieve high market performance and improve their current strategies.

Product Leadership: Creating and Launching Superior New Products

Robert G. Cooper
Cambridge, Massachusetts: Perseus, 1999
314pp ISBN: 0738201561
Over a third of new products fail at launch, and many never gain a profitable return. So how do companies like 3M, Merck, and Procter & Gamble continually lead the way with exceptional new products? Cooper reveals the winners' secrets, and offers valuable advice on implementing and overseeing new product processes and strategies, managing product portfolios, determining which products to develop, and fostering ingenuity to outperform the competition.

The Product Manager's Handbook 2nd ed

Linda Gorchels
Maidenhead: McGraw-Hill/NTC, 2000
304pp ISBN: 0658001353
This book focuses on skills acquisition, making it suitable for new product managers or people interested in moving into that line of work. The text is written as an overview and introduction to the skill set necessary for product managers, but segments of the book are also devoted to product development and launch.

Successful Product Development: Speeding from Opportunity to Profit

Milton D. Rosenau, Jr
Chichester: John Wiley, 1999
164pp ISBN: 047131532X
This book sets out the process of product development from beginning to end, starting with the formation of ideas and moving through design and engineering to the finished product. It is intended for all practitioners involved with any aspect of developing new products and services.

WEBSITES
American Productivity and Quality Center
www.apqc.org
This site features articles on training, conferences, case studies, presentations, executive summaries and more. It also makes available several government white papers on product development. The APQC is essentially a group working towards corporate organisational improvement. It sponsors conferences on product development as well as providing resources online.

Experts on New Product Development
www.expertson.com/New_Product_ Development/new_product_ development.html
The resources on which information is available from this site include new product development associations, new product development centres, directories, newsgroups, mailing lists, new product development publications, and new product development reference tools.

Global New Products Database
www.gnpd.com
This site can be used to access a comprehensive database that monitors worldwide product innovation in the consumer packaged-goods market, offering coverage of new product activity for both competitor monitoring and product idea generation.

Product Development and Management Association
www.pdma.org
This site is everyone's first stop when trolling the Internet for information on product development. It features articles, a job bank, conference listings, a discussion board, and more. Of special interest may be the access this site provides to the *PDMA Toolbook of New Product Development*.

ORGANISATIONS
Product Development and Management Association, UK and Ireland
Innovaro, 78 Belsize Park Gardens, London, NW3 4NG

T: +44 (0) 7801 755 054
www.pdma.org.uk
This is the UK and Ireland branch of the PDMA of America, a professional non-profit organisation dedicated to serving people with an interest in new products and services. In addition to providing knowledge and tools intended to improve the effectiveness of new product development and management, it arranges conferences, publications, awards, meetings, and workshops, and sponsors research.

SEE ALSO
Product and Brand Management (p. 537)

Outsourcing

BOOKS AND DIRECTORIES
Inside Outsourcing: The Insider's Guide to Managing Strategic Sourcing
Charles L. Gay, James Essinger
London: Nicholas Brealey, 2000
256pp ISBN: 1857882040
The authors together offer an insider's knowledge of the realities of managing the outsourcing process. The topics they explore are: the decision-making process; the different types of outsourcing (they also include a discussion of insourcing); co-sourcing and partnering; planning; and selecting service providers. They also discuss legal aspects and human resources issues, and present a survey of the outsourcing practices of 500 of the United Kingdom's largest organisations.

Outsourcing in Brief
Mike Johnson
Oxford: Butterworth-Heinemann, 1997
200pp (In Brief Series)
ISBN: 0750628766
This practical guide presents an overview of outsourcing and reviews the pros and cons of the technique. The way to go about outsourcing is explained, and checklists and case studies illustrate specific issues and options.

Outsourcing IT: The Legal Aspects
Rachel Burnett
Aldershot: Gower, 1998
243pp ISBN: 0566076985
This comprehensive guide to outsourcing the information technology function focuses on the need to obtain a properly negotiated formal contract. It discusses the structure of such a contract, and then goes on to cover the provisions that relate to staffing, location, software, costs, management liaison, allowing for change, security, duration, termination, and other matters. It also gives advice on public procurement and choosing a supplier.

WEBSITES
Network Outsourcing Association
www.noa.co.uk
This site provides access to recent articles by members and details of Association events. It also has a members-only section.

Outsourcing Center
www.outsourcing-center.com
This website provides comprehensive information and links regarding outsourcing. Its content includes industry-specific outsourcing information, research, outsourcing processes, and an online

journal. It also provides answers to FAQs, and material on suppliers, legal issues, and jobs.

The Outsourcing Institute
www.outsourcing.com
The Outsourcing Institute is a professional association providing information and networking resources related to outsourcing. Its website offers information on the outsourcing process, including needs assessment and the selection of service providers. It also has information targeted at buyers and sellers of outsourcing services. Registration is required for some information; online membership is free.

The Outsourcing Management Zone
www.theoutsourcerzone.com
This site is aimed at both outsourcing professionals and those new to the concept. It provides numerous articles, a directory, information on outsourcing, and also explains how and why outsourcing can affect your business.

Outsourcing Research Center
www.cio.com/forums/outsourcing
The site provides online access to recent articles and gives details of forthcoming events.

TechWeb Business Technology Network
www.techweb.com
This site focuses on recent news and articles on IT outsourcing, plus links to events.

Virtual Corporations and Outsourcing
www.brint.com
Recent articles on outsourcing can be sourced from this site.

ORGANISATIONS
Network Outsourcing Association
Martyn Hart, Chair
Keswick House, 207 Anerley Road, London, SE20 8ER
T: +44 (0) 20 8778 9449
F: +44 (0) 20 8778 8402
E: admin@noa.co.uk
www.noa.co.uk
The Association is an independent body, formed in the early 1990s, that acts as a forum for the business technology outsourcing community. Its membership is made up of UK and overseas companies with experience in outsourcing, and suppliers and consultants who support the industry.

Packaging

BOOKS AND DIRECTORIES
Fifty Trade Secrets of Great Design Packaging
Stafford Cliff
Gloucester, Massachusetts: Rockport, 1999
224pp ISBN: 1564965996
This international collection of 50 outstanding packaging designs covers a broad selection of products and approaches. Each of the designs is individually profiled, outlining the challenges and problems each designer faced with the particular product. The case studies document the packaging design process and include discussion of new materials and methods of construction.

The Marketer's Guide to Successful Package Design
Herbert M. Meyers, Murray J. Lubliner
Maidenhead: McGraw-Hill/NTC, 1998
320pp ISBN: 0844234389
A guide for product marketers, this book explores the elements of marketing and design that can lead to successful packaging results. The authors' approach to the subject is practical and analytical, including discussions on the research, budgeting, and planning involved in launching a new design.

Packaging Design—Design Brief to Finished Product

Conway Lloyd Morgan, Russell Sellers, eds
Hove: Rotovision, 1997
155pp ISBN: 2880462622
A model design brief is used throughout the text in a structured and systematic way, as the reader is guided through the whole production process from the design brief to the finished article. In addition, the contributors discuss real products and brands and also give useful advice on the briefing, planning, and execution of packaging design.

The Packaging Designer's Book of Patterns 2nd ed

Laszlo Roth, George L. Wybenga
Chichester: John Wiley, 2000
608pp ISBN: 0471385042
This book features over 500 patterns for paper packaging. Folding cartons, trays, tubes, sleeves, wraps, folders, corrugated containers, rigid paper boxes, and point-of-purchase displays are featured and ready for application on 100% recyclable paper products. An interesting history of papermaking is included in the introduction.

Packaging in the Environment

Geoffrey Levy, ed
London: Aspen Publishers, 1992
288pp ISBN: 0751400912
This book appraises the key environmental issues for packaging and how they affect trends and developments within the industry. It discusses and compares the relative environmental merits of different packaging materials and systems, while reviewing the action being taken to address these issues in different parts of the world. It also considers legislative and regulatory developments worldwide.

Packaging: The Facts

Jim McDermott, Anne Emblem
Melton Mowbray: The Institute of Packaging, 2000
131pp ISBN: 0946467048

Although primarily aimed at schools and colleges, this book is also an excellent general introduction for those new to packaging. It covers all aspects, explaining the packaging process in detail and discussing the materials involved from glass to shrink-and-stretch wrapping. It also deals with the economics, marketing, and environmental issues of packaging.

Total Branding by Design: How to Make Your Brand's Packaging More Effective

Paul Southgate
London: Kogan Page, 1994
172pp ISBN: 0749408677
This book is a detailed and practical guide to exploiting the full potential of design as a marketing tool in building and sustaining brands. It illustrates how packaging design can be used to increase a brand's market share and therefore its profitability, using examples to back up its points.

WEBSITES

Environmental Packaging International
www.enviro-pac.com
Sponsored by a consultancy firm specialising in compliance with state and international environmental packaging and product laws, the site provides a list of services, industry news, and links to other sites.

Packaging Business
www.packagingbusiness.com
Sponsored by a private company in the packaging industry, the site offers industry news, discussions, classifieds, job fair information, and links to other sites.

Packaging Digest
www.packagingdigest.com
This site contains articles from current and past issues of *Packaging Digest*, together with other information resources including news and reports of developments in packaging materials, machinery, technology, and market trends from around the world.

Packaging Network
www.packagingnetwork.com

This site is primarily a marketplace that also provides news, access to a library, a discussion forum, trade publications, and a job search. Site visitors may buy, sell, and advertise online. A free e-newsletter is also available.

Packaging Strategies
www.packstrat.com

This site provides a newsletter, articles, news, a product guide, and a calendar of events.

Packaging World
www.packworld.com

This online packaging magazine from the United States has databases of topical articles on machinery, products, companies, design, materials, and regulations, along with information about jobs, events, associations, and schools connected with the packaging industry.

ORGANISATIONS
Institute of Packaging

Sysonby Lodge, Nottingham Road, Melton Mowbray, Leicestershire, LE13 0NU

T: +44 (0) 1664 500055
F: +44 (0) 1664 564164
E: info@iop.co.uk
www.iop.co.uk

The aim of the Institute is to advance public education in, and improve the technology of, packaging in all its aspects, in particular by promoting the education and training of anyone engaged or interested in packaging as an occupation.

The Packaging Federation

Suite 2.9, Vigilant House, 120 Wilton Road, London, SW1V 1JZ
T: +44 (0) 20 7808 7217
F: +44 (0) 20 7808 7218
E: enquiries@packagingfedn.co.uk
www.packagingfedn.co.uk

The Federation is a trade organisation representing all the material streams within the industry. Its aims are to improve significantly the way in which the industry is perceived and to protect the interests of packaging manufacturers through properly managed lobbying and public relations programmes.

Presentation/Speaking

BOOKS AND DIRECTORIES
Business Presentations

Angela Murray
London: Hodder and Stoughton, 1999
176pp (Teach Yourself Series)
ISBN: 0340720522

The author gives an overview of the skills and techniques necessary to make any presentation effective and engaging. She identifies the key stages of the presentation process and offers tips on effective planning, creative thinking, successful delivery, and meaningful evaluation. The book aims to provide both support and guidance for the novice and some fresh ideas for the more experienced presenter.

Effective Presentation: How to Create and Deliver a Winning Presentation

Antony Jay, Ros Jay
Harlow: Prentice Hall, 1999
174pp (Smarter Solutions series)
ISBN: 027364498X

Drawing on their own experience and on tips from experts and trainers in presentation and communication skills, the authors offer a step-by-step guide to planning, designing, and delivering successful presentations. They give advice on scheduling and staging the presentation, choosing appropriate visual aids, and engaging the audience.

Effective Presentation Skills: A Practical Guide for Better Speaking
Steve Mandel
Menlo Park, California: Crisp Publications, 2000
94pp ISBN: 1560525266
This basic overview of presentations offers advice on topics including skill assessment, presentation planning, visual aids, teleconferencing and videoconferencing, the presentation environment, and dealing with hostile questions. It contains an especially useful section on dealing with anxiety and projecting confidence.

Point, Click and Wow!: A Quick Guide to Brilliant Laptop Presentations
2nd ed
Claudyne Wilder, Jennifer Rotondo
Chichester: Jossey-Bass Wiley, 2002
240pp ISBN: 0787956694
Aimed at business people of all levels, this book offers a practical guide to using technology in effective presentations. The authors explore how to balance on-screen activity and human interaction, how to deal with software and hardware issues, and how, when, and where to practise. The book includes checklists and illustrations.

Say It with Presentations: How to Design and Deliver Successful Business Presentations
Gene Zelazny
Maidenhead: McGraw-Hill, 1999
153pp ISBN: 0071354077
Intended as a simple overview of presentations, this book is targeted mainly at beginners but could also offer some tips to experienced presenters. The topics it covers include defining the purpose of the presentation, keeping the audience in mind, designing charts, and using humour. Its main focus is on how to deliver presentations with confidence and conviction.

WEBSITES
Advanced Public Speaking Institute
www.public-speaking.org

This site offers free advice and articles on all aspects of public speaking, including performance and storytelling techniques, how to develop a topic, the use of props and handouts, humour, tricks, gimmicks, and stage fright.

Art of Speaking in Public
www.artofspeaking.com
This site offers a collection of over 60 rapid read tips for powerful public speaking and effective performance in classes, presentations, conferences, seminars, events, and discussions.

PowerPointers
www.powerpointers.com
This site has many articles on making and creating effective presentations. Areas of interest include communicating effectively, building and planning a presentation, and communicating in your specialty.

Presentations.com
www.presentations.com
The online counterpart to *Presentations* magazine, the site offers news, articles, information on upcoming conferences and events, technological information, and resources.

ORGANISATIONS
Association of Speakers' Clubs
152 Aylesbury Road, Hockley Heath, Solihull, West Midlands, B94 6PP
T: +44 (0) 1564 774907
E: info@the-asc.org.uk
www.the-asc.org.uk
The ASC is a non-profit self-help organisation dedicated to improving the art of speaking in public and to promoting, encouraging, and developing proficiency in the spoken word. It is linked to 175 local clubs in eight districts across the United Kingdom.

The Speakers Trust
19 Waterer Rise, Wallington, Surrey, SM6 9DN
T: +44 (0) 20 8669 3003
www.speakerstrust.org.uk

The Trust promotes the work of speakers' clubs across the United Kingdom, with a view to making them better known and understood and increasing their membership. It offers support to existing clubs by organising competitions, sponsoring new members, providing funds, and producing educational materials.

Pricing

BOOKS AND DIRECTORIES
Costing, Pricing and Getting Paid: How to Improve Profitability; How to Get Paid Promptly
Keith Kirkland, Stuart Howard
London: Kogan Page, 1998
189pp (Simple and Practical Business Series)
ISBN: 074942930
This practical workbook for those running small businesses, or for students taking pricing-related qualifications, focuses on the different methods of setting prices, calculating costs, estimating sales volumes, and controlling credit and debt. The text includes interactive exercises, sample documentation, and a CD-ROM.

The Strategy and Tactics of Pricing: A Guide to Profitable Decision Making
3rd ed
Thomas T. Nagle, Reed K. Holden
Harlow: Prentice Hall, 2002
400pp ISBN: 013026248X
This is a complete guide that integrates pricing with overall managerial goals. It utilises mini-case studies to illustrate success stories and examples of pricing failures. The elements of strategic pricing are explained. Other topics included are competition, segmentation of buyers, pricing and marketing mix, the psychology of pricing, and the ethical and legal aspects of pricing. Step-by-step procedures for problem analysis and strategy are provided.

WEBSITES
Professional Pricing Society
www.pricing-advisor.com
Sponsored by a professional society dedicated to pricing management, the site offers articles, discussion groups, workshop information, job postings, publications, consulting services, and survey information. Members have access to additional articles and an archive search.

Strategic Pricing Group
www.strategicpricinggroup.com
Sponsored by a consultancy firm that specialises in strategic pricing, this site provides articles, self-assessment, recommended reading, a calendar of events, and information on educational services and consulting.

SEE ALSO
Marketing Management (p. 523)
Packaging (p. 533)

Product and Brand Management

BOOKS AND DIRECTORIES
The 22 Immutable Laws of Branding
Al Ries, Laura Ries
London: HarperCollins, 2000
160pp ISBN: 0006531296
In this title, the authors argue that branding is the basis of a strong marketing programme. If it is not possible to create a strong brand, then nothing a company does, including advertising campaigns and public relations events, will help. The book looks at both successful brands and those

that have failed, providing coherent explanations of the various factors involved, from product context to buyer psychology.

Brand Warfare: 10 Rules for Building the Killer Brand
David F. D'Alessandro, Michele Owens
Maidenhead: McGraw-Hill, 2001
208pp ISBN: 0071362932
This book considers ways in which companies often mishandle their brands. The authors offer advice, based on their own experience and on company examples such as FedEx, Rdex, and Starbucks, to those wishing to build a successful brand in any market. The book is written in a witty, irrelevant, and intensely practical style.

Building Strong Brands
David A. Aaker
Chichester: Jossey-Bass Wiley, 1994
390pp ISBN: 002900151X
Aaker discusses the varying elements of a brand, and emphasises the need for managers to be aware of the importance of strong brands in today's marketplace. In discussing various large corporations (such as McDonald's and Kodak) Aaker demonstrates the process of managing a hugely successful brand. The author also explores ways of retaining a certain brand while under some pressure to alter it. The book serves as a useful reference tool for anybody involved in brand management.

Differentiate or Die: Survival in Our Era of Killer Competition
Jack Trout, Steve Rivkin
Chichester: John Wiley, 2000
230pp ISBN: 0471357642
This title is a useful guide on how to make your product differ from those of everyone else and lists several ways to achieve this. These include being the first person to do something, being the latest person to do a version of something, and becoming the first choice of a certain type of consumer group.

Product Strategy and Management
Michael Baker, Susan Hart
Harlow: Prentice Hall, 1998
550pp ISBN: 0130653683
This textbook is aimed at students and provides a broad introduction to the concepts and techniques of product strategy and management. It explores the theoretical foundations, new product strategy, product management, and product elimination.

Smart Things to Know about Brands and Branding
John Mariotti
Oxford: Capstone, 1999
240pp (Smart Series)
ISBN: 1841120391
Mariotti's purpose in this book is to give managers advice on creating a brand, understanding brand values, growing a brand, becoming a smart brand manager, measuring success, and championing their organisation's brand.

What Makes Winning Brands Different: The Hidden Method behind the World's Most Successful Brands
Andreas Buchholz, Wolfram Wordemann
Chichester: John Wiley, 2000
238pp ISBN: 0471720259
The authors analyse the results of a research study of over 1,000 winning brands in order to establish a blueprint for brand growth and development. They argue that brands can achieve outstanding growth by adhering to specific laws or 'growth codes', of which they identify 27. Putting these 'codes' into effect is explored through case study and best practice examples.

WEBSITES
Allaboutbranding.com
www.allaboutbranding.com
This site has multiple articles concerned with branding's role in the marketplace and what it takes to create and maintain a brand name. Site features include an 'Analyze Your Brand' test, free e-mail updates, quotes,

definitions of useful terms, and sections that accurately cover the field.

brandchannel.com
www.brandchannel.com
This site, produced by Interbrand, provides for an online exchange about branding. It contains a debate area, features, papers, and details of books, training, and jobs.

BrandingAsia.com
www.brandingasia.com
This site focuses on branding issues in Asia, and includes brand news, tips, case studies, articles, and a discussion board. A free monthly e-mail newsletter is available.

Building Brands—Unlocking Your Potential
www.buildingbrands.com
This site contains both free content, with articles, definitions, and did-you-knows, to premium services, which include training, Web seminars, student mentoring, and executive coaching.

KnowThis.com
www.knowthis.com/other/product.htm
This section of the Marketing Virtual Library contains links to resources for product management, branding, and packaging.

The Management Roundtable
www.managementroundtable.com
This site describes itself as the leading information resource for product development professionals. It includes a subscription area giving access to product development best practice reports.

ORGANISATIONS
Product Development and Management Association, UK and Ireland
Innovaro, 78 Belsize Gardens, London, NW3 4NG
T: + 44 (0) 7801 755 054
www.pdma.org.uk
This is the UK and Ireland branch of the PDMA, a professional non-profit organisation dedicated to serving people with an interest in new products and services. It is a recognised provider of knowledge and tools intended to improve the effectiveness of the development and management of new products and services. It also arranges conferences, publications, awards, meetings, and workshops, and sponsors research.

SEE ALSO
Advertising (p. 491)
Marketing Management (p. 523)
New Product Development (p. 530)

Project Management

BOOKS AND DIRECTORIES

The Accidental Project Manager: Surviving the Transition from Techie to Manager
Patricia Ensworth
Chichester: John Wiley, 2001
272pp ISBN: 047141011X
When projects fail it is often because the person in charge has no idea how to manage projects. This no-nonsense guide provides basic project management information including project planning, the roles of team members, the tools of the trade, and project control metrics. It also supplies templates, checklists, and sample forms for the beginner to use.

A Guide to the Project Management Body of Knowledge: 2000 Edition
Project Management Institute
Newtown Square, Pennsylvania: Project Management Institute, 2001
200pp ISBN: 1880410230
This book is the basic project management reference and the accepted standard for the profession. It details the nine knowledge areas and 39 processes essential to a generic project management model that works in any industry. By establishing a standard, the guide also provides a common language for talking about project management. It is a key resource for those seeking Project Management Professional (PMP) certification.

Project
Ros Jay
Harlow: Prentice Hall, 2000
96pp (Fast Thinking)
ISBN: 0273653113
This book aims to help people cut through the muddle of panic that often sets in during the working day and to become more efficient. It offers helpful advice on what to do, say, and plan for when you have a pressing deadline and an objective to meet.

Project Management for Dummies
Stanley Portny
Chichester: John Wiley, 2000
284pp ISBN: 076455283X
Highly recommended by professional project managers, this book explains what project management is and then goes on to offer advice on how best to do it. It includes information on scheduling, assembling teams, and assessing resources.

The Project Manager's MBA: How to Translate Project Decisions into Business Success
Dennis J. Cohen, Robert J. Graham
Chichester: Jossey-Bass Wiley, 2000
336pp (Jossey-Bass Business and Management Series)
ISBN: 0787952567
This text aims to provide an introduction to the business basics that every project manager needs to understand. These include value creation, accounting and finance strategy, and marketing. These concepts are related to the decisions project managers face every day. The aim is to develop the skills of project managers so that they can meet both their technical and their business objectives.

Project Planning, Scheduling, and Control 3rd ed
James P. Lewis
Maidenhead: McGraw-Hill, 2000
350pp ISBN: 0071360506
This book offers an applications-oriented, non-theoretical understanding of the flexibility required in day-to-day management situations, and provides guidelines that apply to every phase of steering a project to its successful conclusion. This third edition has been updated to include easy-to-follow steps for managing multiple projects, effective risk management strategies, and an innovative blueprint for developing a workable project methodology.

Project Skills
Sam Elbeik, Mark Thomas
Oxford: Butterworth-Heinemann, 1998
200pp (New Skills Portfolio Series)
ISBN: 0750639784
The authors provide a practical and
accessible guide to managing projects of all
sizes and across all industries. Presented as
an action-focused training guide, the book
explains real-world project management
and introduces the key skills and techniques
needed in the six stages of managing a
project.

The Project Workout 2nd ed
Robert Buttrick
Harlow: Financial Times Prentice Hall, 2000
432pp ISBN: 027364436X
A best-selling guide to project management,
this book provides an illustrated approach to
the practical theory behind best practice in
the field. This second edition comes with a
CD-ROM to allow interactive practice.

Successful Project Management in a Week
2nd ed
Mark Brown
London: Hodder and Stoughton, 1998
96pp (Business in a Week Series)
ISBN: 0340705396
The book explains the basic principles of
project management for the benefit of
anyone new to the technique and describes
the practical steps involved in managing a
project. It focuses on understanding the
nature of projects, on setting up,
planning, and controlling projects, and on
the role and personal qualities of a project
manager.

WEBSITES
AllPM.com—The Project Manager's Homepage
www.allpm.com
This free site has optional membership,
but still contains plenty of information for
users even if they don't pay. The site offers
a forum, event calendar, articles and tips,
and a project management template
library.

Association for Project Management
www.apm.org.uk
The site offers visitors details of news,
events, qualifications, services, and
publications in the field of project
management. It also has information on
member benefits and links to related
organisations, and provides short reading
lists.

PMFORUM
www.pmforum.org
This information dissemination and
exchange forum includes a portal to
information, resources, and working groups
associated with project manager
accreditation, certification, education,
research, and standards. It also contains
listings of software, consulting services, and
training resources, plus a calendar of events,
and offers access to the electronic journal
Project Management World Today.

Project Management
www.projectmagazine.com
This website is actually a 'magazine' that's
free to anyone. With meaningful articles,
site of the month, news for the field, and
even letters to the editor, this is an audience-
oriented resource for the project manager.

Project Management Institute
www.pmi.org
The Project Management Institute (PMI)
has over 75,000 members worldwide and is
the leading non-profit professional
association in the area of project
management. The site offers information on
member services, including careers and
awards programmes, a bookshop, links to
other project management organisations,
and information on project management
standards. It also provides opportunities for
organisations to contribute to a corporate
council, and lists PMI seminars.

Project Management Library
**www.mapnp.org/library/plan_dec/
project/project.htm**
Part of the Management Assistance Program
for Nonprofits, this site's resources include a

project management overview, information on team building and group leadership, general resources, and on-line discussion groups.

ORGANISATIONS
Association for Project Management
Thornton House, 150 West Wycombe Road, High Wycombe, Buckinghamshire, HP12 3AE
T: +44 (0) 845 458 1944
F: +44 (0) 1494 528937
E: services@apm.org.uk
www.apm.org.uk

A professional body founded in 1970, the APM aims to be the UK national authority on project management. It promotes project management skills and training, and develops standards and certification for project managers. Services are delivered through joint ventures or through its members. The association is affiliated to the International Project Management Association (IPMA), which has 33 member associations around the world.

SEE ALSO
Project Management (p. 540)

Public Relations

BOOKS AND DIRECTORIES
The Complete Guide to Publicity: Maximize Visibility for Your Product, Service, or Organization
Joe Marconi
Maidenhead: McGraw-Hill/NTC, 1999
239pp ISBN: 0844200913
This book provides an effective guide for any person tasked with public relations, whether for a business or non-profit organisation. The author addresses all aspects of running a successful public relations campaign, including the difference between publicity campaigns and paid advertisement, understanding different media, how to create publicity opportunities, and a detailed procedure for creating a publicity campaign.

Effective Writing Skills for Public Relations 2nd ed
John Foster
London: Kogan Page, 2001
191pp ISBN: 0749436328
This book is a practical guide to writing style for students and PR practitioners. It looks at grammar, developing a house style, headlines and captions, press releases, and speeches and public speaking.

Face the Media: The Complete Guide to Getting Publicity and Handling Media Opportunities 2nd ed
Judith Byrne
Oxford: How To Books, 2002
142pp ISBN: 1857037979
This guide offers advice on how to make contacts in the media and generate and sustain interest in your or your business. Issues covered include: securing an interview; talking to journalists; creating the right impression; improving confidence; developing 'soundbites'; and crisis management.

Free Publicity for Your Business in a Week
Guy Clapperton
London: Hodder & Stoughton, 2002
96pp (In a Week)
ISBN: 0340858273
This book is aimed at cash-strapped small business owners and managers who need to make a splash. It covers a range of issues including how to handle the press, what kind of media to aim for, where to look for free coverage, writing effective press releases, responding to feedback, and crisis management if things do not go to plan or you attract the wrong kind of attention.

Guerrilla PR Wired: Waging a Successful Publicity Campaign Online, Offline, and Everywhere in between
Michael Levine
Maidenhead: McGraw-Hill, 2002
292pp ISBN: 0071382313
This book re-examines the principles of 'Guerrilla PR' (introduced in the author's book *Guerrilla PR*, HarperCollins, 1993), the technique for creating cost-effective publicity, for the age of the World Wide Web. The book explains how the key tenets have changed with developments in technology, and introduces new tactics for conveying online messages. Readers will learn how the pros use the Web for publicity, how to focus on a target to get superior results, and how to avoid all the pitfalls that lie in wait for the Web PR novice. The book also features a wide variety of empirical examples.

Planning and Managing a PR Campaign 2nd ed
Anne Gregory
London: Kogan Page, 2001
190pp ISBN: 0749429917
Gregory presents a step-by-step guide to the stages of a PR campaign, covering all the important aspects, and including case studies and a ten-point action plan.

Public Relations: A Practical Guide to the Basics
Philip Henslowe
London: Kogan Page, 1998
159pp (PR in Practice Series)
ISBN: 0749429372
This is an introduction to the basic principles of public relations. It is an easy-to-read reference guide that provides an overview of the main areas, and is suitable for people who are not PR experts, but who need to do some public relations work.

Public Relations Handbook
Alison Theaker
London: Routledge, 2001
320pp ISBN: 0415213347
A detailed introduction to the theory and practice of public relations is provided by this comprehensive handbook. It looks at all aspects of the subject, including training and entry into the profession, ethical issues, the use of new technology, and contains case studies.

Public Relations Kit for Dummies
Eric Yaverbaum, Robert Bly
New York: Hungry Minds, 2000
346pp ISBN: 0764552775
Part of a series offering concise, practical information on a variety of topics, this book addresses what all business owners and managers need to know about effective public relations. Presented in an easy to understand style, this title offers specific strategies and techniques for public relations, along with information on using new technologies, such as the Internet, in PR campaigns. Also included is a CD-ROM with lists of PR firms and media contacts.

Risk Issues and Crisis Management: A Casebook of Best Practice
Michael Regester, Judy Larkin
London: Institute of Public Relations, 1997
160pp (PR in Practice Series)
ISBN: 0749423935
This book deals with the successful handling of crisis situations so that damage and disruption are minimised. Case studies and models illustrate how complex crises have been handled in practice, both successfully and unsuccessfully.

WEBSITES
Managing Public Relations
www.workz.com/content/292.asp
This website serves as a resource for small business owners. It offers comprehensive information on public relations techniques, including guides for creating effective press releases, where and how to distribute press releases, promoting your business's website, and a directory of PR firms and associations.

PR Navigator
www.prnavigator.com
This website serves as a comprehensive resource on public relations for users ranging from business leaders to students. The resources include access to current

research and industry reports, links to online PR journals and newsletters, directories of public relations agencies, and links to PR associations worldwide.

PR Place
www.prplace.com
This site contains a listing of Internet resources on public relations. The categories it covers include organisations in PR, publications, news sources, and databases.

Public Relations Resources
www.publicrelationsresources.com
The mission of this site is to provide regular informative articles on how to promote events, people, and businesses. It includes free articles, news headlines, and a list of links.

Selling and Salesmanship

BOOKS AND DIRECTORIES

Fast Forward MBA in Selling: Become a Self-motivated Profit Center and Prosper
Joy Baldridge
Chichester: John Wiley, 1999
216pp ISBN: 0471348546
This book is a comprehensive guide to becoming a successful salesperson. It explores a wide range of topics, including setting the standards for success, self-motivation, time management, getting and staying connected, preparation, technology, and successful sales calls.

How to Become a Rainmaker: The Rules for Getting and Keeping Customers and Clients
Jeffrey J. Fox
London: Vermilion, 2001
178pp ISBN: 0091876540
This book is written to assist in identifying, attracting, and keeping customers. It identifies Rainmakers (people who bring revenue into organisations), who may be CEOs, owners, partners, sales representatives, or fundraisers. Jeffrey Fox explains how the reader can become a Rainmaker, enabling him/her to attract and retain more customers and rise above the fiercest competition in any company.

Knock Your Socks Off Selling
Jeffrey Gitomer, Ron Zemke
New York: AMACOM, 1999
150pp ISBN: 0814470300
An overview of sales techniques from basic selling to developing relationships, the book is appropriate for salespeople at every level. Placing an emphasis on making a partnership out of the buyer/seller relationship, the book discusses networking, generating leads, making presentations, and following through.

Sales Management: Concepts and Cases 7th ed
Douglas J. Dalrymple, William L. Cron, Thomas E. DeCarlo
Chichester: John Wiley, 2000
608pp ISBN: 0471388807
This book includes theoretical discussions and case studies covering all aspects of sales management. The topics dealt with in its various sections are: strategic planning and budgeting; personal selling; territory management; estimating potentials and forecasting sales; recruiting and selecting personnel; sales training; leadership; motivating salespeople; compensating salespeople; and evaluating performance.

SPIN Selling
Neil Rackham
Aldershot: Gower Publishing, 1995
271pp ISBN: 0566076896
Practical, easy-to-use and understand information on how to make selling easier for the salesperson is the basis for this excellent book. Based on extensive research, its direct and helpful advice may also be helpful in all other work situations.

The SPIN Selling Fieldbook: Practical Tools, Methods, Exercises and Resources
Neil Rackham
Maidenhead: McGraw-Hill, 1996
208pp ISBN: 0070522359
Full of case studies and practical information, this book shows the reader how to put into practice the help and advice given in *SPIN Selling*.

Successful Sales Management: How to Make Your Team the Best
Grant Stewart
Harlow: Prentice Hall, 1999
185pp (Smarter Solutions Series)
ISBN: 0273644882
This is a practical guide for managers on how to manage the sales function. Its contents cover: the sales manager's job; motivation; management style; standards of performance; planning and control; recruitment and selection; sales meetings; and sales audits.

Successful Selling in a Week 2nd ed
Christine Harvey
London: Hodder and Stoughton, 1998
95pp (Business in a Week Series)
ISBN: 0340705388
This is an introductory guide to both the skills and systems of selling. It covers organisational preparation, gaining product expertise, finding emotional motives, a three-part objection process, prospect action systems, overcoming roadblocks and price objections, and self-motivation.

Tough Calls: Selling Strategies to Win Over Your Most Difficult Customers
Josh Gordon
New York: AMACOM, 1997
214pp ISBN: 0814479251
Focusing on the challenges of difficult customers, the book outlines 20 different 'tough sells' and strategies to counteract them. It provides advice on what to do and what not to do with customers who, for example, are incompetent, do not have buying authority, will not see you, buy elsewhere because of company politics, or like what you say but still don't buy.

The Ultimate Sales Letter: Boost Your Sales with Powerful Sales Letters, Based on Madison Avenue Techniques 2nd ed
Daniel Kennedy
Holbrook, Massachusetts: Adams Media Corporation, 2000
224pp ISBN: 1580622577
This text provides clear examples that assist in writing focused sales letters that target specific customer bases. Tips and features include: creating powerful headlines, improving readability, when to use bullet points, which font to use, and which demographics to target. All this is performed within 28 structured steps, and should interest sales reps, business owners, and advertising people.

WEBSITES
BestOfSales.com
www.bestofsales.com
A list of links to sales resources on the Internet is given on this site, including business-to-business exchanges, books on selling, access to new customer information, and much more.

Just Sell
www.justsell.com
This site comprises a sales and marketing portal with areas covering sales leads, sales jobs, daily sales intelligence, an online store, and a resource for locating sales training.

The Sales Crusader
http://sales-crusader.hypermart.net
This site presents articles on all aspects of selling and salesmanship contributed by its readers, who come from a wide variety of industry backgrounds. In addition to these free articles, it also offers recommended book lists and a discussion forum.

Saleslinks.com
www.saleslinks.com/links
Run by Mentor Associates, this site is aimed at anyone who is engaged in selling for a living. It includes links to a large number of sales resources on the Internet, arranged in categories.

Salesmanship
www.dmoz.org/Business/Marketing/ Salesmanship
Maintained as part of the Open Directory Project, this site contains a large list of other websites, each with a brief description, relating to all aspects of salesmanship.

Sales Rep Central
www.salesrepcentral.com
A portal for sales professionals, the site contains news, articles, a community message board, jobs, sales leads, and travel services.

SalesVault
www.salesvault.com
This site is aimed at professional sales people and provides innovative and up-to-date selling information. It also includes articles, news, and advice.

Selling Power
www.sellingpower.com
The online counterpart to *Selling Power* magazine, the site offers archived issues of the magazine, electronic newsletters on several sales-related topics, a weekly quiz, and books and resources.

ORGANISATIONS
Direct Selling Association
29 Floral Street, London, WC2E 9DP
T: + 44 (0)207 497 1234
F: + 44 (0)207 497 3144
E: ukdsa@globalnet.co.uk
www.dsa.org.uk
The DSA aims to promote the understanding of direct selling as a distribution channel. Its benefits are potentially huge, as the site cites figures which claim that direct selling is worth more than £1.6 billion each year. The DSA's website has four major categories: protecting the consumer, direct selling today, information on the Association, and 'A Business of Your Own', which gives information on how direct selling can be helpful to start-up businesses.

Institute of Professional Sales
Moor Hall, Cookham, Maidenhead, Berkshire, SL6 9QH
T: + 44 (0) 1628 427370
F: + 44 (0) 1628 427369
E: johnmayfield@iops.co.uk
www.iops.co.uk
The Institute shares the same facilities, values, and objectives as the Chartered Institute of Marketing with whom it integrated in September 2003. Its training courses and qualifications are now offered through CIM.

Institute of Sales and Marketing Management
Romeland House, Romeland Hill, St Albans, Hertfordshire, AL3 4ET
T: + 44 (0) 1727 812500
F: + 44 (0) 1727 812525
E: sales@ismm.co.uk
www.ismm.co.uk
Established in 1966, the ISMM is a professional body for salespeople in the United Kingdom. It promotes standards of excellence in the industry and provides

qualifications and training. Its members are individuals at all levels from students to sales directors. The organisation holds a conference in Birmingham every October.

Institute of Sales Promotion

Arena House, 66–68 Pentonville Road, London, N1 9HS
T: +44 (0) 20 7837 5340
F: +44 (0) 20 7837 5326
E: enquiries@isp.org.uk
www.isp.org.uk
The Institute of Sales Promotion was set up in 1979. It offers education, training, legal advice, and networking opportunities.

Sales Research Trust Ltd

751 Portswood Road, Southampton, Hampshire, SO17 3SU
T: +44 (0) 23 8067 7416
F: +44 (0) 23 8067 7416
E: enid@sales-research-trust.org
www.sales-research-trust.org
The Trust is a non-profit body that aims to

provide a focus for collaboration between practitioners and academics for the advancement of education and research in selling and strategic customer account management. It conducts research and disseminates the results through publications.

Society of Sales Management Administrators Ltd

40 Archdale Road, East Dulwich, London, SE22 9HJ
T: +44 (0) 20 8516 0211
F: +44 (0) 20 8274 5103
This professional body was established in 1980. It exists to encourage the study of selling and sales management, marketing principles and practice, retail management, and international trade. It provides professional status for salespeople and accredits educational programmes.

SEE ALSO
Marketing Management (p. 523)

Taxation

BOOKS AND DIRECTORIES
Company Cars
2nd ed
R. Chidell, A. Sampson
Kingston-upon-Thames: Croner CCH, 2002
170pp ISBN: 1841402184
This annual publication explains all the details relating to the taxation of company cars, under the new rules which came into force in April 2002. There are practical examples, calculations, and frequently asked questions.

IR35 : Personal Service Companies
2nd ed
A. Redston
Kingston-upon-Thames: Croner CCH, 2002
600pp ISBN: 1841402087
The IR35 Rules are explained, with guidance on the employment law implications,

avoidance schemes, and the position of workers coming to the United Kingdom. Best practice is recommended and calculations are illustrated. A CD-Rom is included.

Practical Guide to the New Tax Credits
L. Lathwood
London: Lexis Nexis Butterworths Tolley, 2003
35pp ISBN: 14784653
This has been published as Issue 7, May 2003 of the periodical *Tolley's Tax Digest* but is available as a one-off purchase. The rules for the new Tax Credit Scheme, which came into effect in April 2003, are very complex and there is relatively little official guidance. This explains who can claim the credits, how to claim, the qualifying conditions, how the credits are calculated and how they are paid, the rules for enquiries and penalties, and how to appeal.

Preparing Company Accounts 2003/2004

R. Mayes
Kingston-upon-Thames: Croner CCH, 2003
262pp ISBN: 1841403431
An annual publication which provides an understanding of the statutory accounts provisions for small companies, including developments in generally accepted accounting principles (GAAP) and the key elements of the Financial Reporting Standard for Smaller Entities (FRSSE). It includes model accounts, checklists, diagrams and illustrative tables.

Reference Book for the Self-employed and Smaller Business

Kingston-upon-Thames: Croner CCH
ISBN: 185524022X
This is a package which includes a variety of different resources and can also be used online. The main work is a looseleaf volume, updated monthly. There is also a newsletter, a CD-Rom, and a business support helpline. As well as covering taxation, value added tax, and national insurance contributions, the work also deals with employment regulations, health and safety rules, consumer law, company law, and finance.

Simon's Calculating Taxable Trading Profits

K. Walton
London: Lexis Nexis Butterworths Tolley
487pp ISBN: 040695853X
This handbook provides guidance on calculating taxable trading profits, including identifying capital and revenue items, the treatment and valuation of trading stock, computational issues relevant to special classes of business, expenditure on trading assets, and other trading expenditure such as patent royalties and bad debts. Lists are included summarising allowable and non-allowable deductions.

Small Business Adviser's Toolkit: Taxation

M. Truman
Kingston-upon-Thames: Croner CCH
256pp ISBN: 1853559008
Practical advice for owner-managed businesses and SMEs, with guidance on all key transactions in the lifetime of a typical business. Each section has checklists, briefings, specimen letters, and forms.

Small Business Tax Guide

John Whiteley
Oxford: How To Books, 2002
240pp ISBN: 1857037685
A comprehensive guide for the small business person on how to comply with tax laws and pay promptly, but pay less and increase profits.

Tolley's Businesswise: Financial Planning for the Small and Medium-sized Enterprise 2nd ed

P. Lyons
London: Lexis Nexis Butterworths Tolley
ISBN: 0754517853
Designed for small to medium-sized businesses, this work takes the financial assets and liabilities of an enterprise, and describes how they can be made to work in a realistic manner to improve performance in the real world of business. There is an overview of business strategy, business recovery and why businesses do not survive, evaluating a business, and applying for grant assistance.

Tolley's Guide to the Tax Treatment of Specialist Occupations

K. Gordon
London: Lexis Nexis Butterworths Tolley, 2002
267pp ISBN: 075451630X
Many occupations have special tax rules that apply to their particular circumstances. Entertainers and sportspeople, builders and subcontractors, farmers, medical practitioners, ministers of religion, writers and artists, and lorry drivers are some of the occupations covered in this book. The rules covering early retirement ages, payment of National Insurance Contributions and

deductions available to employees in certain occupations are also described.

Tolley's Tax and Accountancy Dictionary
David Collison
London: Lexis Nexis Butterworths Tolley, 2001
286pp ISBN: 0754510093
A reference guide to the specific meanings of terms used in accountancy and taxation.

Tolley's Tax and the Business Car 2003-04
A. Chapman
London: Lexis Nexis Butterworths Tolley, 2003
150pp ISBN: 0754521990
A CD-Rom is included with this book, which explains the rules covering company cars, with planning points and case studies.

Tolley's Tax Data
Butterworths Tolley
London: Lexis Nexis Butterworths Tolley, 2003
116pp ISBN: 0754516997
Issued twice a year, following the Budget and Finance Act, this contains information on tax rates, reliefs, exemptions, interest rates, exchange rates, and benefits.

Tolley's Tax Essentials: Employment Taxes 2003
G. Antczak
London: Lexis Nexis Butterworths Tolley, 2003
250pp ISBN: 0754521850
Issued as a spiral-bound book which opens flat when in use, this deals with P11D, the PAYE system, the penalties for non-compliance, VAT, and the Construction Industry Scheme. Each form of earnings is listed individually in a table, showing how it is taxed, referring to more detailed treatment of the subject elsewhere in the text.

Tolley's Tax Guide 2003-04
A. Homer, R. Burrows
London: Lexis Nexis Butterworths Tolley, 2003
809pp ISBN: 0754521532
This annual publication takes everyday situations in commercial and personal life and explains the relevant taxes which must be taken into consideration in the United Kingdom. It contains worked examples, checklists and tax planning aids, tables of the current tax rates, and a summary of any tax changes within the past year.

Tolley's Tax Office Directory 2003
London, 2003
182pp ISBN: 0754522008
Published twice a year, this vital directory lists all the essential addresses, phone and fax numbers, and e-mail addresses of extensive departments within the Inland Revenue, Customs and Excise, and Contributions Agency.

Tolley's Tax Planning for Family and Owner-managed Companies 2003-04 7th ed
P. Rayney
London: Lexis Nexis Butterworths Tolley, 2003
540pp ISBN: 0754521273
The tax position of the family company, and of the individuals responsible for running it, is outlined. Personal and corporate tax issues are dealt with as they affect the company and both working and non-working shareholders.

Zurich Tax Handbook 2003/2004
Tony Foreman ed
Harlow: Pearson Education, 2003
660pp ISBN: 027367529X
This comprehensive guide to the tax system in the United Kingdom offers practical advice to the individual on managing his or her tax affairs, including self-assessment and completion of the tax return, dealing with the Inland Revenue, stakeholder pensions, and employee share schemes.

WEBSITES
Chartered Institute of Taxation
www.tax.org.uk
This site includes CIOT press releases, technical articles and research papers, and letters of engagement. It also has useful external links to equivalent tax organisations in other countries.

Customs and Excise
www.hmce.gov.uk
This site includes all Customs and Excise notices, forms and information sheets, as well as information on VAT and other taxes and duties and customs allowances.

Inland Revenue
www.inlandrevenue.gov.uk
This site features news and information on tax and national insurance matters in the United Kingdom. It includes all Inland Revenue publications and forms (many of which are downloadable), selected parts of the Inland Revenue Manuals, tax rates, and statistics. There are specific sections for individuals, established businesses, start-up businesses, employers, practitioners, non-UK residents, and charities. Enquiry points and local offices are also listed.

Inland Revenue: Starting Up in Business
www.ir.gov.uk/startingup/index.htm
This section of the main Inland Revenue website sets out to help small business people identify key areas of compliance in the areas of tax and National Insurance. An easy-to-use series of frequently asked questions and links takes users to the areas of most interest to them. The site also highlights other important legal areas that are not within the Revenue's own remit, but which also need to be considered, and provides a helpful series of links.

Institute for Fiscal Studies
www.ifs.org.uk
The site of the Institute of Fiscal Studies details its conferences and publications with the full text of some working papers and articles. It has a useful section giving tax rates going back to 1973.

Tax and Accounting Sites Directory
www.taxsites.com
This site provides an international gateway to country-specific tax and accounting resources on the Web. It has a US bias.

UK Taxation Directory
www.uktax.demon.co.uk
This site is a gateway to UK tax websites which provide material of potential interest to tax professionals and others seeking online information on UK tax matters.

ORGANISATIONS
Association of Taxation Technicians
12 Upper Belgrave Street, London,
SW1X 8BB
T: +44 (0) 20 7235 9381
F: +44 (0) 20 7235 4571
E: info@att.org.uk
www.att.org.uk
Established in 1989, the Association of Taxation Technicians provides a qualification for individuals undertaking tax compliance work, namely the preparation of tax returns for corporate and individual taxpayers.

Chartered Institute of Taxation
12 Upper Belgrave Street, London,
SW1X 8BB
T: +44 (0) 20 7235 9381
F: +44 (0) 20 7235 2562
E: post@ciot.org.uk
www.tax.org.uk
As the senior professional body in the United Kingdom concerned solely with all aspects of taxation, the Chartered Institute of Taxation aims to advance public education in, and promote the study of, the administration and practice of taxation. It has nearly 12,000 members encompassing the professions and many occupations in industry, commerce, the public sector, and the taxation authorities. Membership is acquired by examination and members have the practising title of 'Chartered Tax Adviser'.

Customs and Excise
New King's Beam House, 22 Upper Ground, London, SE1 9PJ
T: +44 (0) 845 010 9000
www.hmce.gov.uk
HM Customs and Excise is responsible for collecting and administering customs and excise duties and VAT. The Department is

also responsible for preventing and detecting the evasion of revenue laws and enforcing import laws. Telephone, fax, and e-mail addresses vary for each office location. To find your nearest office, please refer to the website.

Inland Revenue
Somerset House, Strand, London, WC2R 1LB
T: +44 (0) 20 7438 6420
www.inlandrevenue.gov.uk
The Inland Revenue, which was set up in 1849, administers and collects direct taxes: income tax, corporation tax, capital gains tax, inheritance tax, stamp duty, and petroleum revenue tax. Telephone, fax, and e-mail addresses vary for each office location. To find your nearest office, please refer to the website.

Institute for Fiscal Studies
7 Ridgemount Street, London, WC1E 7AE
T: +44 (0) 20 7291 4800
F: +44 (0) 20 7323 4780
E: mailbox@ifs.org.uk
www.ifs.org.uk
The IFS aims to promote and disseminate the economic implications of tax and fiscal policy in Britain and elsewhere.

Institute of Chartered Accountants in England and Wales
Chartered Accountants' Hall, PO Box 433, Moorgate Place, London, EC2P 2BJ
T: +44 (0) 20 7920 8100
F: +44 (0) 20 7920 8547
E: dsbds@icaew.co.uk
www.icaew.co.uk
This, the largest professional accountancy organisation in Europe with over 120,000 members, is responsible for educating and training chartered accountants and maintaining professional standards.

Institute of Chartered Accountants in Scotland
CA House, 21 Haymarket Yards, Edinburgh, Scotland, EH12 5BH
T: +44 (0) 131 347 0100
F: +44 (0) 131 347 0105
E: enquiries@icas.org.uk
www.icas.org.uk
ICAS is the leading professional accounting body in Scotland, and the oldest professional body of accountants in the world.

SEE ALSO
Accounting (p. 487)
Budgeting (p. 494)

Venture Capital

BOOKS AND DIRECTORIES
2001 Financing Start-ups: How to Raise Money for Emerging Companies
Robert Brown, Alan S. Gutterman
London: Aspen Publishers, 2000
617pp ISBN: 0156071916
This book aims to guide owners and managers of start-ups through the rigours of finding funding, from sourcing initial funds to IPOs.

Business Angels: Securing Start Up Finance
Patrick Coveney, Karl Moore
Chichester: John Wiley, 1998
244pp ISBN: 0471977187
This book takes the would-be entrepreneur through the process of identifying the ideal business angel and securing a deal. It covers reasons for turning to an angel, types of business angels, and the task of creating a business plan. The role of business introduction services is also considered.

Finance for Growing Enterprises
Roger Buckland, Edward Davis, eds
London: Routledge, 1995
288pp (European Financial Institutions and
Markets Series)
ISBN. 0415082331
This book examines the mechanisms by
which businesses with the capacity to grow
acquire the cash to make growth possible. It
draws together contemporary research
studies and covers the issues of market
failure and gaps in funding. The financing
choices facing the growing firm are also
investigated.

Lucius Cary's Guide to Raising Capital for the Smaller Business
Lucius Cary
Oxford: Seed Capital Publishing, 1998
236pp ISBN: 1899540105
This guide underlines the importance of the
business plan as the cornerstone of any
capital-raising project. It also covers finding
the right type of lender, model agreement
letters, and legal issues, and provides a
glossary of terms. Detailed interviews with
three entrepreneurs who have founded
successful businesses are included.

Raising Start-up Finance
Phil Stone
Oxford: How To Books, 2001
93pp (Essentials) ISBN 1857037065
This practical guide covers key steps in
securing finance for your business,
including: preparing your case; what the
banks can offer; alternatives for the
purchase of assets; using business resources
to gain funding; and additional sources of
finance.

The VC Way: Investment Secrets from the Wizards of Venture Capital
Jeffrey Zygmont
Cambridge, Massachusetts: Perseus, 2002
224pp ISBN: 0738203874
This text offers a behind-the-scenes
perspective of the venture capital market,
revealing to investors how to strategise and
invest in successful companies before their
profits are certain. Zygmont also offers the
reader a brief tutorial in creating a portfolio
of holdings that may increase in value, as
Apple and Yahoo did.

Where to Go When the Bank Says No: Alternatives for Financing Your Business
David R. Evanson
Princeton, New Jersey: Bloomberg, 1998
304pp (Bloomberg Small Business Series)
ISBN: 1576600173
Practical advice for small or new businesses
on raising capital is provided here by an
expert in the field. He discusses the pros
and cons of alternative options such as
equity capital, initial public offerings
(IPOs), and venture capital, and gives
guidance on valuing a business and
drawing up business plans and financial
reports. A resources guide with contact
details of organisations in the field is also
included.

WEBSITES
PriceWaterhouseCoopers Moneytree Survey
www.pwcmoneytree.com
This survey, sponsored by the accounting
firm of PriceWaterhouseCoopers, provides a
comprehensive list of venture capital
investing by industry, stage of funding,
geography, and type of financing on a
quarterly basis. The report tracks venture
capital firm investments and the enterprises
receiving capital are listed by region and
industry.

vcapital
www.vcapital.com
This is an exchange site for entrepreneurs,
venture capitalists, and business service
providers, sponsored by Batterson Venture
Partners. It features an Ask the Expert
section with articles giving practical advice
and help.

Venture Economics
www.ventureeconomics.com
News, statistics, product information, and a
glossary of terms are to be found on this site,
provided by a publisher of journals and
research on the venture capital industry
worldwide.

ORGANISATIONS
British Venture Capital Association
3 Clements Inn, London,
WC2A 2AZ
T: +44 (0) 20 7025 2590
E: bvca@bvca.co.uk
www.bvca.co.uk
The BVCA was founded in 1983 and is the representative body for the UK venture capital industry. It promotes private equity and venture capital for the benefit of entrepreneurs, investors, practitioners, and the economy as a whole. Its members are venture capital companies and professional firms involved in advising on venture capital transactions. Its activities include training, workshops, lobbying, and research, and it produces publications.

European Private Equity and Venture Capital Association (EVCA)
Minervastraat 4, 1930 Zaventem, Belgium
T: +32 2 715 00 20
F: +32 2 725 07 04
E: evca@evca.com
www.evca.com
EVCA was founded in 1983 and now has over 850 members. Its aim is to promote and facilitate the development of the European venture capital industry through lobbying and initiatives such as conferences, training, and networking opportunities. The organisation was involved in the creation of EASD (European Association of Security Dealers) and the EASDAQ pan-European capital market.

National Business Angels Network
40–42 Cannon Street, London, EC4N 6JJ
T: +44 (0) 20 7246 0765
E: info@bestmatch.co.uk
www.nban.com
NBAN is a non-profit company sponsored by financial institutions and the Department of Trade and Industry in the United Kingdom. It provides a service linking businesses seeking equity finance with investors seeking opportunities through a network of associates across the country. A monthly bulletin of opportunities is sent to all registered investors. An online service, BestMatch, is also provided to bring together investors and those looking for capital.

SEE ALSO
Entrepreneurs (p. 510)

Index